ROME

ROME

AN EMPIRE'S STORY

SECOND EDITION

GREG WOOLF

OXFORD
UNIVERSITY PRESS

Oxford University Press is a department of the University of Oxford. It furthers
the University's objective of excellence in research, scholarship, and education
by publishing worldwide. Oxford is a registered trade mark of Oxford University
Press in the UK and certain other countries.

Published in the United States of America by Oxford University Press
198 Madison Avenue, New York, NY 10016, United States of America.

Library of Congress Control Number: 2021939906

ISBN 978-0-19-068745-8

DOI: 10.1093/oso/9780190687458.001.0001

1 3 5 7 9 8 6 4 2

Printed by LSC Communications, United States of America

For my Students

Preface

All histories of Rome are histories of empire. Her rise to power, the long peace, and the even longer decline together form the background to every story told about the Romans. My subject, however, is empire itself. How did it grow? What enabled it to resist defeats and capitalize on victories? Why did Rome succeed when its rivals failed? How did empire survive crises, dig itself in, and replace chaotic campaigns of conquest with stability? How did empire come to coordinate the great flows of wealth and populations on which it depended? How did it evolve to face new needs and new threats? Why did it falter, regain its balance, and then shrink under a series of military blows until it was, once again, a city state? What circumstances and technologies made the creation and maintenance of an empire possible, in just this place and at just that time? What institutions, habits, and beliefs suited Rome for the role? And what did the fact of empire do to all the beliefs, habits, and institutions with which the world had been conquered? What part did chance play in its successes and its failures?

The long arc that stretches from a scatter of villages on the River Tiber to a medieval city on the Bosporus Straits dreaming of ancient glory takes a millennium and a half. Telling that story in a single volume is perhaps a crazy endeavour, but it has also been an exhilarating one. Perhaps Roman history has no special claim on us, among the many periods of the past we can think about and that have shaped our world. But as a student I felt the fascination of studying something so vast, an entity that stretched over so much time and space. What could sustain a human enterprise conceived on such a vast scale? How could anything human last so long? Our own world experiences change at an extraordinary rate. Earlier generations, confident of the permanence of their own empires and of the uninterrupted march of progress, were spellbound by Rome's decline and fall. For us it is the longevity of Rome that grasps the imagination. My own fascination has not diminished since my student days. Even now the Roman world still sometimes feels like a vast sandpit in which I can play, or else a huge historical laboratory in which all sorts of long-lived processes and entities can be studied. Roman history is like astronomy in that respect. New experiments cannot be designed and carried out. But a vast mass of distant and ancient phenomena can be observed through tiny packets of residual data, and the forces and cataclysmic events that formed the observable universe can be reconstructed. Like astronomers, ancient historians look for patterns and try to explain them. This book is an attempt to explain those that I have observed.

The Roman Empire invites metaphor. Ancients often used a biological analogy: each empire or state had its youth, its maturity, and its old age. One modern historian has used the metaphor of the vampire bat, seeing the empire as a means through which the Romans sucked the life out of peasants and slaves upon whose labour the empire depended. The Roman Empire does not seem to me much like an organic entity, unless it is an epidemic spreading throughout a host population feeding off the energies of the infected until it burns itself out. Analogies from natural science seem to capture the pattern of empire better. The Roman Empire was like a great tidal wave sweeping up more and more water before dissipating its energy. Or it was an avalanche, starting small, accelerated by the patterns of snow and rock across which it moved, and then slowed again at the base of the slope. Either metaphor captures the sense of a grand pattern that starts small, draws in more matter and more energy, and then dissipates. That pattern—empire—moves through time, and for a while crowds out other patterns, until it dissipates or is overwritten by other great movements. Empire grows, not always smoothly, dominates for a while, and then abates. One former vice-chancellor of St Andrews suggested that I think of this in terms of resonance, the gradual establishment of a pattern of vibration across a vast mass of people and things that eventually loses coherence and breaks down into smaller patterns. That does seem to capture precisely the emergence of an imperial order and its subsequent dissipation. The essence of empire is the assertion of a great pattern at the expense of smaller ones. That pattern is typically less equal and more hierarchical than what went before. New levels of complexity mean some of the rich becoming richer, some of the poor being subjected to harsher discipline, although the social mobility that empire stirs up means there are winners and losers at every level. Materially, the pattern of empire involves regular movements of people and things, great flows of taxes and of commercial goods. Those routines of movement are now reflected by traces of roads and ports, the fossilized skeleton around which the soft matter of the human empire once hung. I have tried to give attention to the hard matter. But one of the joys of Roman history is that we can also hear the voices of so many of those caught up in it. I have attempted to capture and report their perceptions of empire as well.

Writing this book, I have tried to hold in my mind this sense that empire is a movement through historical time, not a fixed set of institutions. By the end of my story, in Byzantium, everything has changed. Romans speak Greek instead of Latin, the capital is now in what was once a conquered province, and barbarians rule in the old city of Rome. It has a new god, new customs, a new sense of its past and its future. A world of cities had become (again) the world ruled by a single city. Istanbul derives ultimately, from the medieval Greek phrase *eis tēn polin*, 'into the city'. Yet it was still Rome.

All the same, some institutions were, for long periods, absolutely central to the long history of empire, and in important ways the world within which Roman power was extended and then contracted was a stable one. I have tried to capture this combination of constant evolution with long-lasting structural stability by alternating chapters that carry the story forward with chapters that allow me to stand back for a moment—out of time as it were—and point out something of enduring significance. Attentive readers will notice, as I have, that this division does not absolutely hold. But every so often historians have to make concessions to their material. Another concession to my material is the list of key dates that precedes each narrative chapter: the Romans' journey was complex as well as long, and as we sit in the passenger seat, the odd road map is occasionally helpful.

Metaphors are one kind of inspiration. Comparison is another. This book is not an exercise in systematic comparative history, measuring Rome against other ancient (or, for that matter, modern) empires. Comparison is an interesting method, but it is fantastically difficult given the gaps in our knowledge of ancient empires and the inconvenience that from one empire to another they are not usually the same gaps. But my argument is informed by reflecting on other empires, sometimes trying to spot a general trend, more often as a way of spotting what is unusual or even unique about the Roman case. Wide reading helps, but I am very conscious how much I have learned from participating in conferences and meetings at which experts in other disciplines have generously shared their knowledge. From many such occasions, I would like to single out a conference organized by Susan Alcock, Terry D'Altroy, Kathy Morrison, and Carla Sinopoli at Las

Mijas in 1997, generously funded by the Wenner-Gren Foundation, which first gave me the idea for this project, and also an entire series of workshops devoted to the comparative study of empires, organized with extraordinary energy by Peter Fibiger Bang, with funding from the European Science Foundation under COST Action A36 'Tributary Empires Compared'.

My understanding also depends, of course, on the research of numerous other historians of Rome. It is impossible to acknowledge all of those whose works have been inspirations or essential guides or both. This book is not a total history of Rome, but an exploration of the theme of empire. All the same, empire is so central to Roman history that I have drawn on a great fund of published works to write it. I have tried in the notes and suggestions for Further Reading to indicate just a few to which I owe a particular debt, and I have tried to indicate recent work above all else, since we have now such good syntheses of past scholarship and since research is moving so fast in this field. Most of this book was written in St Andrews during leave generously funded by the Leverhulme Trust. But parts of it were drafted at UNICAMP, São Paulo, where I was a visiting professor in early 2011 at the invitation of Pedro Paulo Funari. The first draft was completed later that same year at the Max Weber Kolleg of the University of Erfurt, where Jörg Rüpke was (once again) my host.

Many others have contributed to making it possible to write this book. I would like to thank especially my agent Georgina Capel, for encouragement and much more; Stefan Vranka and Matthew Cotton at Oxford University Press for their patience, advice, and enthusiasm; Stefan again and Nate Rosenstein for detailed comments on an earlier draft which has saved me from many errors and made this book much more readable; Emma Barber, Emmanuelle Peri, and Jackie Pritchard at Oxford for their help in the various stages of production; my family for tolerance and reality checks. This is not, of course, my first attempt to explain the larger patterns behind Rome's imperial history. Reading and contemplation are all very well, but every teacher knows that the true test of understanding is whether or not one can explain an idea to someone else. Professional historians usually try out explanations on each other. But we know too much already, and as listeners and critics we are often too charitable. Any aptitude I have acquired in explanation, I owe to successive generations of students in Cambridge and Leicester, Oxford and St Andrews. For this reason, this book is dedicated to them, with thanks.

Preface to Second Edition

Nearly a decade has passed since the first edition of this book.

Much has changed in the world and in Roman history in that time. Some of the original concerns of the book have become even more acute. Imperialism and colonialism remain high on the political agenda, although our debates over them have now moved to questions of decolonizing the curriculum and ensuring that the practice of history promotes racial justice. Also high on the agenda is our relationship with our environment, and ten years of environmental science have only reinforced the urgency of these issues. These were key concerns of the first edition, and remain so in this edition. Roman historians in the meantime have been researching on an ever widening front, from migration studies to the politics of gender, as well as pursuing traditional concerns such as the nature of Roman understandings of their past, the validity of the ways we periodize their history, and the role of the emperor.

The reviewers of the first edition were generous and constructive—for which I am grateful—and I have tried to take their advice when I could. But I have not followed those who suggested major changes of organization or coverage. Other histories of Rome include more detailed narratives, are more (or less) introductory, include more about poetry or less about slavery. It is a good thing that we have many histories of Rome: this one remains fundamentally the same book as the first edition, with (I hope) some improvements.

I have tried to incorporate some of the most exciting new research published since the first edition. Important work has been carried out at either end of Rome's story, on the early Republic and on late antiquity. I have tried to take account of some of this, and in particular I have expanded the treatment of late antiquity in the final chapters. Another area in which this edition differs from its predecessor is in the increased attention given to material culture. For the kinds of questions central to this book the boundaries between history and archaeology are quite porous, and much of the new work I have read in the last few years makes use of both whether to investigate how politics played out in space, how Roman cities functioned and were provisioned, or questions of identity and agency. Eric Wolf famously referred to some of the victims of European expansion in the early modern period as the 'People without History'. Romanists too are now engaged in trying to recover the experiences of those who were silenced in antiquity. For these investigations too the material world is as vital a source of information as the written one.

For the last six years I have been based in London at the Institute of Classical Studies. This has been a joy and a privilege, and I have benefited from easy access to the amazing resources of the Combined Classical library there and from the company of a great community of ancient historians, classicists, and archaeologists scattered among the colleges, institutes, and museums of the capital, and of many visitors. My thanks and appreciation to all of them.

Contents

List of Illustrations

Figures

Picture Boxes

Maps

Notes on Further Reading

The Roman Empire has been the object of serious research for around a century and a half, and imperialism has never been off the agenda. It would be impossible to provide a complete guide to the scholarship on which this book is based, and I have not tried to do so. Each chapter is followed, however, by a few suggestions for further reading. I have recommended only works available in English and have tried to pick the most exciting and most recent works, since new research continues at an astonishing pace. I have also added a few notes to each chapter, some identifying the source of particular quotations or key passages of ancient writers, some acknowledging the source of particular ideas or acknowledging books or articles that were especially helpful when I was writing the chapter. Here too I have concentrated on the most recent work, but I have included a few really crucial items written in other languages. After all, the study of antiquity is an international venture, and the Roman Empire is bigger than any of us. The bibliography at the end of this book gathers together all works cited, but cannot claim to be a comprehensive guide to the subject. Fortunately in the twenty-first century we benefit from a number of very recent and authoritative reference works on all aspects of Roman history.

The best one-volume reference work to all aspects of antiquity is the *Oxford Classical Dictionary* (4th edn, 2011). A digital OCD, edited by Tim Whitmarsh, is being continually updated at https://oxfordre.com/classics/. The best multivolume dictionary is Brill's *New Pauly* (2007), and is also online at https://referenceworks.brillonline.com/browse/brill-s-new-pauly. The *Barrington Atlas of the Greek and Roman World* (2000) is the best guide to the topography of antiquity. Harvard's *Late Antiquity: A Guide to the Post-Classical World* (1999) combines thematic essays with a dictionary

The revised *Cambridge Ancient History* devotes seven volumes to Rome (1989–2005). It remains a magnificent and authoritative account, especially for political and institutional history. The first volume of the *New Cambridge*

Mediaeval History (2005) is also relevant to the end of this story, as are the *Cambridge History of the Byzantine Empire* (2008), the *Cambridge Economic History of the Greco-Roman World* (2007), and the first volume of the *Cambridge History of World Slavery* (2011). The eight-volume *Edinburgh History of Ancient Rome* began appearing in 2012 and is now nearing completion. For those interested in a broad comparative perspective, the *Cambridge World History* is recommended, especially volumes 3 and 4.

KEY DATES IN CHAPTER I

753 BC   Traditional date of the foundation of Rome

509 BC   Traditional date of the expulsion of the kings and the foundation of the *Roman Republic*

264 BC   Pyrrhus invades Italy but fails to break Roman hegemony

216 BC   Battle of Cannae. Rome's worst defeat at the hands of Hannibal

146 BC   Carthage and Corinth sacked by Roman armies

88 BC   Sulla marches on Rome

44 BC   Julius Caesar assassinated on the Ides of March

31 BC   Battle of Actium ends the civil wars of the late Republic. Conventional beginning of the early empire or *Principate*

AD 14   Death of Augustus and accession of Tiberius

AD 117   Death of Trajan marks the greatest extent of the Roman Empire

AD 212   Caracalla extends citizenship to most inhabitants of the empire

AD 235–84   'The Anarchy', a prolonged period of military crisis

AD 284–305   Reign of Diocletian. Conventional beginning of the *Later Roman Empire*

AD 306–37   Reign of Constantine

AD 313   Constantine's Edict of Toleration

AD 361–3   Julian fails to restore the worship of the ancestral gods

AD 378   Battle of Adrianople. Eastern empire's army defeated by Goths

AD 476   Last western emperor deposed by Ostrogoths

AD 527–65   Justinian attempts to reconquer the west

AD 636   Arab armies defeat Roman forces at Yarmuk

AD 711   Arabs cross the Straits of Gibraltar, invading Visigothic Spain

THE WHOLE STORY

Traditions about what happened before the foundation of the city, or while it was being founded, are more suited for poetic fictions than for the trustworthy records of history.

(Livy, *From the Foundation of the City*, Preface)

The story of Rome is a long one. This chapter tells it all—at breakneck speed—hitting just the high spots of the millennium-and-a-half-year story of rise and fall. It is intended as a motorway route planner for the book, or a set of satellite images snapped at long intervals, provided for orientation. If you already know the pattern of the Roman past, feel free to skip ahead. If not, enjoy the ride!

The Kings and the Free Republic

The Romans of the historical period believed that their city had been founded by Romulus at a date that corresponds to our 753 BC. Romulus was the first of seven kings. The earlier kings were honoured as founding fathers, the later ones reviled as tyrants. Eventually, the last of the kings, Tarquin the Proud, was driven out of Rome and a republic was founded. The conventional date for this was 509 BC. After Aeneas and Romulus, this was something like the third foundation of Rome. Its hero was a Brutus. When Julius Caesar made himself dictator for life nearly 500 years later, it was on the base of statues of this first Brutus that graffiti were scrawled, calling on his distant descendant to take up arms and slay the tyrant.

All the surviving accounts of the regal period have this mythic quality. None was written less than three centuries after the supposed foundation of the Republic. Rome in the late sixth century was well below the radar of the Greeks, who would not begin to write even their own history for another century. Yet it is probable enough that Romans did have a monarchy. Many other Mediterranean cities had monarchs in the archaic age, including many of the cities of Etruria just north of Rome. Many of the later institutions of Rome seem best explained as relics of a monarchical state: there was a sacred house in the forum called the *Regia*, the base of the most senior priest the *pontifex maximus*. The official who conducted elections if there was a gap between magistrates was the *interrex*. But few of the details that have been passed down can be trusted. Individual kings were remembered as founders of specific parts of the Roman state. Romulus created the city, populated it, first by declaring it an asylum for criminals and then by organizing the mass kidnapping of Sabine women to provide wives for his followers. Numa, the second king, invented Roman religion. Servius Tullius organized the army, the tribes, and the census, and so on. Stories about the later rulers mostly recall tales told about tyrants across the ancient Mediterranean: they were arrogant rulers and cruel sexual predators, and weak sons followed strong fathers. Charges of this kind were common in the aristocratic republics of the archaic Mediterranean and represent the emergence of new ethics of civil conduct. The Romans also remembered their last kings as foreigners, specifically as Etruscans. Stories about the kings added up to an account of what was central and unique to Rome, at least in the minds of those who told and heard them. Our only real control on these myths is archaeological.

The Republican period lasted nearly five centuries, from the early sixth until the final century BC. It was later remembered as an age of liberty and piety. Those who enjoyed that liberty were the wealthy, especially the aristocratic families which together monopolized political office and religious leadership. The nostalgia of their heirs colours all our history of that period. A few families—the Cornelii Scipiones above all, then later the Caecilii Metelli—were so successful that they effectively dominated the state, rather as the Medici dominated Renaissance Florence. But the source of their wealth was very different. Those who led Rome's conquest of the

Mediterranean world brought back treasure with which to beautify the city, money with which to buy or occupy land, and slaves with whom to farm it. Rome, like most ancient cities, relied on citizen soldiers. At first most of them were peasants who would join campaigns organized for periods of relative quiet in the agricultural year. Many of them did well out of conquest, and those who lived near enough the city had some influence in the political assemblies that elected Rome's leaders and made the greatest decisions, such as whether or not to go to war. But Rome never approached the kind of democracy created in classical Athens, where the wealthy were compelled to conceal their riches and to spend part of them on public projects. At Rome power remained in the hands of the few. Most magistracies lasted for only a year, but former magistrates sat for life in a council, the Senate, which in effect directed government, legislation, state cult, and foreign policy. How the Republican aristocracy remained so dominant is one of the big questions of Roman history. Was it the institution of patronage that pervaded Roman society? Or the religious authority they acquired from their priestly functions? Other cities faced revolutions when disaffected aristocrats roused up the people against their rivals. Roman nobles were as competitive as any aristocracy, but somehow restrained themselves from infighting until the very end of the Republic. When that restraint collapsed, their world fell apart.

The Republic was also the age in which Rome was transformed from an Italian city state to the leading power in the ancient Mediterranean world. The kings must have left Rome relatively powerful. The scale of the walls, the probable size of the population, but most of all the early military successes all suggest Rome was already one of the politically powerful cities of central Italy around the year 500 BC. The history of the first few centuries is hazy, but by the start of the third century BC, Rome's influence extended throughout the Italian peninsula. Colonies dotted strategic points in the Apennines and on the Tyrrhenian Coast, while new roads had opened up communications to the Adriatic. Over the fourth and third centuries Rome fought on all fronts: Gauls to the north, Greeks in the south, a series of Italic peoples in the mountains of the Abruzzi and the arid plains of the Mezzogiorno. In the 270s they attracted the attention of King Pyrrhus of Epirus, who crossed the Adriatic with a large army. Rome was defeated by him in several battles, but survived the war. By the end of the third century, Romans had won two long wars against Phoenician (Punic) Carthage. The first (264–241 BC) was largely a naval war in which Rome captured Sicily

and became master of the Greek and Punic cities on the island as well as
the indigenous Sicilian peoples of the interior. The Second Punic War (218–
201) was fought in Spain and Africa as well as in Italy itself. Hannibal crossed
the Alps in 217 BC and the next year inflicted a terrifying defeat on Rome at
Cannae. But he did not press home his advantage and lingered in southern
Italy until 203, when he had to return to Africa to face Scipio's army.
Hannibal's defeat at Zama the next year marked the end of Carthaginian
power. During the second century BC, Roman armies marched even farther
afield. They took on and defeated the great Macedonian kingdoms of the
east, the heirs of Alexander the Great. Carthage and the ancient Greek city
of Corinth were both razed to the ground in 146 BC. Roman armies defeated Gallic tribes north and south of the Alps, waged war on the Spanish
Meseta, and resisted German invasions. The city grew and grew in size and
was equipped with aqueducts and basilicas and other monuments paid from
the spoils of war. The wealthy became even wealthier; citizen armies spent
longer and longer away from home.

Romans of the later periods imagined that at its height the Republic was
a harmonious system in which the ambitions of the mighty were guided
by the wisdom of the Senate, with the support of a deferential people.
The ruin of the Republic was attributed (in different ways) to the luxury
and arrogance brought by empire. For the early imperial historian Velleius
Paterculus:

The first Scipio paved the way for Roman domination; the second opened the
door to luxury.[1]

Other historians chose other watersheds, but the pattern of virtuous rise
followed by vicious fall was a commonplace. The truth is more complex.
Social conflicts of one sort or another occurred throughout Roman history.
But the urban violence and civil wars that began at the end of the second
century BC were on a new scale. The last century of the free Republic was
at once the period of greatest territorial expansion, the period in which
Roman literary and intellectual culture achieved its classic form, and also
100 years of bloody civil war. Conflicts between Romans and their Italian
allies became conflated with social struggles between the poor (or those
who claimed to represent them) and the rest of the wealthy. Traditional
rivalries between aristocrats were supercharged by the proceeds of imperialism. Politicians recruited first mobs and then armies to fight their corners.

A destructive feedback loop was created between competition at home and aggressive warfare abroad. Generals thought in the short term, with an eye always on opportunities when they returned. They took spectacular risks, attacked Rome's neighbours without the permission of Senate or people, handed over conquered territories to be exploited by their political allies, and gave little thought to the long-term security of Rome. Foreign allies of dubious loyalty were allowed to build huge power bases on the frontiers. Romans were loathed in the provinces. The low point came when Mithridates, the king of Pontus, a former Roman ally whose power had been built up by Rome and whose increasingly aggressive actions had been ignored by a Senate preoccupied with Italian affairs, invaded Roman-controlled western Asia Minor. At Mithridates' command 10,000 Italians were slaughtered in the Greek cities of the province. Rome briefly lost control of all territories east of the Adriatic. This was just another opportunity for Roman generals. Sulla was first given the army, and then deprived of it, but he refused to step down and instead marched his soldiers on Rome. The forum ran with blood, and he got his way, and after organizing Rome as he saw fit, marched east, where he sacked Athens, before returning to fight his way back into Rome. Declaring himself dictator he then 'proscribed' a list of political enemies. Anyone whose name was on the list could be killed without punishment, and their property was forfeit. Sulla was a model for all those generals who came after, including his lieutenant Pompey, his enemy Caesar, and those who came after Caesar, including the future Emperor Augustus. All of these acquired great armies for foreign wars, and ultimately used them to campaign against each other in the provinces, while spending money in Rome on political faction and grand monuments. Conflict came to a stop at the battle of Actium in 31 BC, with the defeat of Mark Antony and Cleopatra by Caesar's heir Octavian, later rebranded as Augustus in a conscious attempt to make civil war (and with it aristocratic liberty and the power of the people) history.

The Early Empire

The long reign of the first emperor, Augustus—he died in AD 14—is the fulcrum of Roman history. Before him there was the Republic; after him only emperors. The 300 years that followed are known as the early empire or (after Augustus' other title of First Citizen, *princeps*) the Principate.

Much of Augustus' way of running Rome was really a continuation of the main themes of Republican history, and this was exactly the way he wanted it to be seen. Once his own position in Rome was secure, and the civil war armies had been largely demobilized, he engaged on campaigns of conquest and civic building on scales that surpassed the achievements of Pompey and Caesar. At his accession, Rome dominated the Mediterranean through a network of provinces and alliances. But civil war and aristocratic rivalry had started many wars beyond the region that remained unresolved. Augustus extended Roman direct rule across half of Europe to the rivers Rhine and Danube, and fixed a boundary and made peace with the Persian Empire. On Julius Caesar's death many building projects had been begun but not yet finished. Augustus completed these and added new ones of his own, turning the Field of Mars into a sort of monumental theme park, and appropriating the Palatine Hill for a complex of imperial residences and temples, the origin of our term 'palace'.

Less ostentatiously, Augustus succeeded in making the Roman state civil-war-proof. The rather shambolic mess of governmental and fiscal expedients imposed by one conquering general after another was drawn into a more regular system of provincial government. Rome now had a dedicated military treasury with which to pay a new standing army. The Roman and Italian aristocracies were given roles in the new order as governors and as military commanders. But the money and the loyalty of the soldiers were kept firmly in Augustus' hands. Augustus, not the people and certainly not the Senate, now decided which aristocrats would occupy which magistracies and which priesthoods. Indeed, all important decisions were now made in the imperial court. The Senate and People of Rome (SPQR) were given greater honours as they lost power. But busts and statues of Augustus were visible everywhere, portraying him as a general, as a priest, and as a god. He and his successors were worshipped in every city and province alongside the ancestral and domestic gods, and by the soldiers in the camps as well.

The real mark of Augustus' success was that he was able to pass on most of his powers to a series of successors. Rome avoided civil war for a hundred years after Actium. Augustus' immediate successors were not all talented: one (Caligula) was assassinated, and another (Nero) committed suicide because he thought he had lost control of the empire. But the system survived, with few modifications. When conflict between generals did break out after the disaster of Nero's reign, it was only because none of Augustus' family survived to provide a new emperor. The war lasted less than two years (AD

69–70) and the victor, Vespasian, engineered a very Augustan restoration. The empire shuddered but was left undamaged. Without any formal establishment of a new constitution or title, the Roman emperor had become effectively the chief officer of the Roman state. Weak and incompetent individuals could not now discredit the system, and there is no sign that anyone wished to do without the emperors. When Caligula was killed in AD 41, the Senate did briefly discuss a return to the Republic, but spent more time thinking about a possible successor. While they debated, the Praetorian Guard found Caligula's uncle Claudius hiding behind a curtain in the palace and made him emperor. From this point on the question was always simply 'Who should be emperor?'

And emperor followed emperor. The Flavian dynasty ruled for most of the late first century AD. Wars of conquest added Britain and parts of south-west Germany to the empire, client kingdoms were swallowed up, and frontiers fortified. A series of imperial forums extended out from the old Republican Capitol to the valley of the Colosseum. The city gradually acquired the trappings of an imperial capital. The assassination in AD 96 of the last Flavian, Domitian, shook the system much less than the death of Nero had. During the second century a series of long-reigning emperors presided over a relatively stable empire. Trajan (98–117) led wars of conquest north of the Danube and into what is now Iraq. His successor Hadrian (117–38) travelled widely around the empire. The emperors became more overtly monarchical and dynastic, especially outside Rome, where they did not need to worry about senatorial sensibilities. An itinerant court emerged, one in which favourites and concubines competed for influence, scholars and poets were entertained, and the prefects of the Praetorian Guard acted as grand viziers. Provincial communities sent streams of ambassadors to track down the emperor wherever he might be. They might have found Hadrian on the banks of the Nile or supervising the construction of the great wall that crossed northern Britain, helping plan his great new temple of Venus opposite the Colosseum, making a speech to soldiers on parade in Africa, or at ease in his vast palace at Tivoli or in his beloved Athens. The empire was ruled from wherever the emperor happened to be.

The early Roman Empire was a world at peace. Warfare was minor in scale, and emperors rarely had difficulty in restricting it to the frontiers. The economy and population grew. The number of Roman citizens increased as provincial aristocrats, former soldiers, and freed slaves were granted citizenship. By an edict of the early third-century Emperor Caracalla (198–217), almost everyone in the empire was enfranchised. Roman law suddenly embraced everyone. The lawyer Ulpian, writing in the aftermath of this most spectacular of imperial benefactions, insisted wills would be valid in any language, Celtic or Syriac, as well as Greek and Latin. Roman ways of life were widely adopted; new technologies of architecture and manufacturing spread in the provinces. The rich in particular decorated their spectacular mansions with imported marbles and donated grand buildings to their native cities. Shared cultures of bathing, of education, of eating emerged in the cities of the empire. Even the poorest spectated at gladiatorial combats, beast hunts, athletic festivals, and other ceremonies, often focused on the imperial house. This period marked the apogee of ancient urbanism. To be sure, there were parts of the empire where nine out of ten people still lived in the countryside. But in central Italy and western Anatolia, in North Africa, and Syria and Egypt, maybe thirty per cent of the population lived in cities or large villages. Most of the monuments of the Roman Empire that impress us so much today when we travel around its former provinces were built in this period. Trajan's conquest of Dacia was the last extension of the empire. Wars continued to be fought through the second century, but generally on the emperors' terms. Emperors and local elites alike seem to have been relatively prosperous, although it is unclear how far this rested on genuine growth and how far on the gathering of property into a smaller and smaller number of hands.

Conditions changed around the turn of the second and third centuries AD. Urban building declined from before 200 in the west and before 250 elsewhere. No new theatres or amphitheatres were built after this point, the number of surviving inscriptions plummets, and temple dedications seem fewer. At least some cities began to shrink in size, again especially in the west. Meanwhile, the wars on the northern frontier seem to have taken more of the emperors' time and resources. Perhaps this began as early as the reign of Marcus Aurelius, when wars against the Marcomanni of the middle Danube raged almost continuously between 166 and 180. Another round of civil war followed the murder in 192 of Marcus' son Commodus. The struggle between provincial generals was a close rerun of what had followed Nero's suicide, and the Severan dynasty that emerged ruled Rome 193–235 in a fairly traditional manner. But the revival of the Persian Empire under the Sassanian dynasty in the early third century put the army (and the treasury) under new pressure. For the next half-century, the empire was subjected to increased warfare on the Danube and the Rhine, suffered raids deep into the empire that resulted in the sack of cities like Athens and Tarragona which had hardly seen a soldier in 300 years, fought off major Persian offensives, and had to deal with secessions that for a while split the empire into three separate territories. Most emperors lasted only a few years, some only a few months, and few died in their beds. Increasingly they were drawn from military backgrounds, and their links with Rome and the Senate became even more attenuated. Military recovery began in the 260s, but the empire was not a unified whole until the end of the century. The long reign of Diocletian, declared emperor in 284 and abdicating in 305, marked the empire's recovery.

The Later Roman Empire

By the early fourth century, the Roman world was a very different place. Cities had in some regions shrunk back to tiny walled circuits built hurriedly out of dismantled monuments. Some of the most recently conquered territories had been abandoned in what is now south-west Germany, Morocco, and Romania. There was still a Senate in Rome, but its members no longer had much role in government or military command. The empire had a new religion, Christianity, and a new capital at Constantinople with its own Senate, its own Seven Hills, and its own imperial palace. The empire had a new currency too, with which to pay much higher taxes than ever before, needed to pay bigger armies and a growing bureaucracy. There was now a college of up to four emperors at any one time, the senior ones titled Augusti, the junior ones Caesars. Each had his own court and each was to concentrate on a different region of the empire, but especially on the northern and eastern frontiers. From now on the emperors had to keep a constant watch on the barbarians and had to manage a difficult relationship with the rival empire of Persia.

The history of Persia in this period parallels that of Rome in many respects. Shapur II, the Persian king of kings (309–79), created a highly centralized empire in which a bureaucracy replaced the quasi-feudal baronies that had often barely acknowledged the authority of the Parthian kings. The Persian Empire too had a state religion, Zoroastrianism. Throughout late antiquity the frontier hardly shifted. Both empires had to deal with religious minorities and powerful priests. Wars were frequent and some cities regularly changed hands within a great border zone that stretched from Armenia in the north through Syria to the Arab world. But there were also periods of relative calm, and traders, missionaries, spies, and envoys moved back and forward between the two brother empires. That situation lasted until the seventh century, when the Arab conquests destroyed the Sassanian Empire and very nearly the Roman one too.

Writing the history of the late empire has always proved difficult. At first the problem was the rival viewpoints of pagans and Christians, after Constantine I (306–37) replaced persecution with toleration and then began to patronize the Church on a grand scale. All his successors were Christians except for one, Julian, who tried to reverse Constantine's reform in his brief reign (361–3). By the end of the century, general toleration had been replaced by attacks on the temples of polytheists, and emperors devoted more and more of their energy to the fight against heresy. Enough influential polytheists survived to blame the new religion for the disasters of the fifth century. Our historical sources are bitterly divided. Then, there is the problem of hindsight. How can we ignore the fact that the loss of Trajan's Dacian provinces was just the first of many losses of territory that saw Britain and northern Gaul slip out of Roman control in the mid-fifth century and the replacement of the last western emperor by a series of barbarian kings before 500?

Nevertheless, the fourth century was in some senses an optimistic era, one that saw a partial recovery of intellectual life, much building (if now of churches and palaces rather than the traditional monuments of the classical city), and in the east some real prosperity. Even when a great group of Ostrogoths was allowed to cross the Danube in 376, Romans could reasonably remember other peoples settled inside the empire as allies. But the defeat of the eastern army by the Goths in 378 at the battle of Adrianople set in motion a set of migrations and diplomatic manoeuvres that led within a century to the total loss of the west. From the early fifth century new groups entered the empire, seeking their own share of territory, settlement as 'guests' of Rome, and perhaps sometimes safety from their own enemies, like the ferocious Huns. Rome itself was sacked twice, first by the Goths in 410 and then again by the Vandals in 455. The last emperor in the west was deposed in 476, although perhaps it did not seem a watershed at the time. By AD 500 the Vandals ruled a kingdom based on Carthage, the Visigoths and Sueves controlled Spain and Gaul, Burgundians and Franks the rest of what is now France, and an Ostrogothic king ruled in the former imperial capital of Milan. The eastern emperors—bankrupt, without an army, and preoccupied with Persia—had to acquiesce. So too did Roman elites, stranded, as it were, behind enemy lines. For a few generations, Roman bishops and intellectuals served the new kings of the west, helping to create societies in which Romans and barbarians divided up roles and their wealth. Archaeological evidence shows quite clearly that trade across the Mediterranean was not severely disrupted, and in some areas urban life and even Latin literature thrived. The rulers of these kingdoms were Christians (if mostly Arian heretics in the eyes of eastern Roman bishops). Most attempted to preserve elements of Roman civilization, even rebuilding Roman monuments and intermarrying with Roman aristocratic families. Most relied on Roman bureaucrats to manage the complex fiscal systems they had inherited, preserving their warbands as an army to defend their acquisitions. Their kings lived in Roman palaces in the major cities of their realms, they issued coinage with Latin legends, devised law codes, and some even watched gladiatorial games.

Then, in the early sixth century, the eastern empire struck back. During Justinian's reign (527–65) his generals snatched Africa from the Vandals and fought a long and damaging war up and down Italy culminating in the end of the Ostrogothic kingdom. Visigothic Spain was invaded. At Constantinople, great building projects were undertaken, a huge codification of Roman civil law was carried out, and administrative reforms put into place. (The complaints of one senior bureaucrat, John the Lydian, show how the 'new' bureaucracy created by Diocletian and Constantine was now regarded by its members as a set of ancient and venerable institutions.) For a generation, a Mediterranean Roman Empire seemed reborn. Then it folded up again. The Lombards invaded Italy, the Franks expanded their power in Gaul, and, except for a foothold around Ravenna, Roman territory was confined to North Africa and Sicily. Meanwhile, the emperors were once again locked into war with Persia. The Persian Emperor Khusrau II swept back over the Syrian frontier once again and this time captured Jerusalem. Persian forces raided north into Anatolia and south-west into Egypt, where Alexandria fell in 619. The emperors could do little to help because the invasion coincided with an invasion from the north-west by the Avars. Constantinople, under siege from both sides, could well have fallen in 626. A new emperor, Heraclius, managed to pay off the Avars, defeat the Persians, and carry war to their own capitals in southern Mesopotamia. Humiliated by defeat, Khusrau was assassinated in 628. Heraclius triumphed in Jerusalem and Constantinople.

And then the world changed. Among the many peoples drawn into the long Romano-Persian conflicts were the tribes of the Arabian peninsula.

In the process they had developed considerable military experience and knowledge of both sides, but it was the religious movement started by the Prophet Muhammad that galvanized them into concerted action. At the battle of Yarmuk in 636, the Roman forces suffered a devastating defeat. By 642 Egypt, Syria, and Palestine were all under Arab rule and would never be recovered. The empire had shrunk to a third of its size, a Balkan state with territory in western Anatolia and some distant western provinces, most of which it would lose as the Arab armies moved westwards across North Africa and up into Spain, and as they mastered the sea. Cut off from the grain of Egypt, the urban population of Constantinople plummeted. The Persians were not so lucky. They too suffered a devastating defeat in 636, at Qadisyya. Their capital, Ctesiphon, was occupied the next year. The last remnant of the army was destroyed in 642 at the battle of Nihavand, and their last emperor perished, on the run, in 651.

Fixing the end of the Roman Empire is not easy. Certainly those emperors who defended Constantinople when the Arabs besieged it in 717 considered themselves Romans. So too did their successors right up until Constantinople finally did succumb, not to Arabs but to Turks, in the fifteenth century. We do not have to agree with them, but any other date we pick is arbitrary. Much of Roman and of Persian civilization did survive the Arab conquest. The cities of Syria flourished under the caliphate, and the tax systems of Khusrau II had an afterlife in Iran, just as Roman ones did in the barbarian kingdoms of the west. Charlemagne the Frank dreamt of becoming Roman emperor, and in 800 his dream came true in a ceremony conducted in Rome by Pope Leo III. Does Byzantium have a special claim to be more of an heir to Rome than either western Christendom or medieval Islam? I am not sure that it does, and so for me, the story of the Roman Empire ends here.

Further Reading

Many excellent narrative accounts of Roman history exist. My shortlist of favourites is the following. Simon Price and Peter Thonemann's *The Birth of Classical Europe* (London, 2010) and Chris Wickham's *The Inheritance of Rome* (London, 2009), respectively the first and second volumes of the Penguin History of Europe, are excellent accounts. Mary Beard's *SPQR: A History of Ancient Rome* (London, 2015) succeeds in the difficult job of combining gripping narrative with thoughtful analysis. Two very good guides to social and economic history for the imperial period are Peter Garnsey and Richard Saller, *The Roman Empire: Economy, Society, Culture* (rev. 2nd edn, London, 2015) and Peter Garnsey and Caroline

Humfress, *The Evolution of the Late Antique World* (Cambridge, 2001). Michael Crawford's *The Roman Republic* (rev. edn, London, 1992) is a model of how Roman history can and should be written, argumentatively and based on every available kind of evidence from archaeology, coins, and inscriptions to contemporary documents and later literature. *The Cambridge Ancient History* in fourteen volumes remains unrivalled for those who want to dig deeper.

EMPIRES OF THE MIND

Then Romulus, proudly clad in the tawny pelt of the she-wolf who nursed him, will ensure the future of the race, will found the martial walls and from his own name call them ROMANS. I have fixed no boundaries to their dominions, no term to their rule, I have given them EMPIRE WITHOUT END. Even harsh Juno, who at present fills land and sea and sky with fear, will in the end think better of them, and at my side will show her favour to the Romans, masters of the world, the people of the toga. This has been decreed.

(Virgil, *Aeneid* 1.275–83)

Empire came to bewitch the Roman imagination. Ours too. Every study of ancient Rome, whether of its love poetry or festivals, its monumental art or the routines of the family, now invokes empire as one—sometimes as *the*—crucial context. But what they understood and we understand by 'empire' is not always the same thing. This chapter explores some of different senses of empire that are entwined at the heart of our stories of Rome.

An Imperial People

Sometimes it feels as if empire was written into Roman DNA. The Romans of the classical period definitely believed something like this. When epic poets or historians imagined the very earliest days of the city's history, they pictured it as already fixed on a course for greatness. The coming of empire was the central theme of the *Aeneid*, a great epic poem composed by Virgil in the court of Augustus.[1] The epigraph of this chapter is taken from Jupiter's prophecy of Rome's future greatness that stands near the start of that epic. If at first it was designed to serve the immediate political needs of the poet and his patron, it had a much more influential afterlife. The *Aeneid* was the starting point of education in Italy and the western provinces for centuries to come. It occupied a place in Roman culture much as the Declaration of Independence and Constitution do in America, or as Shakespeare does in Britain. Constantly quoted and instantly recognizable, lines of the *Aeneid* are even ubiquitous as graffiti across the empire. Most come from the first book of the epic, suggesting most pupils did not get very far. But the children of provincial notables will have read Jupiter's famous lines as they struggled to learn Latin, and in the process learnt what it was to be Roman too.

The *Aeneid* does not tell the story of Augustus' rise to power, or even of Rome's conquest of Italy and the Mediterranean. Instead, the story is set in the heroic age, the period immediately following that of Homer's two great Greek epics, the *Iliad* and the *Odyssey*. It tells how Prince Aeneas led a band of refugees away from the blazing ruin of Troy, after it had been sacked by the Greeks. The first six books follow their wanderings farther and farther west, driven first by fear, then drawn on by destiny into a strange and strangely modern new world. Monsters, hostile natives, and angry gods try to frustrate their journey. Then, there are temptations along the way. No berth is more alluring than Carthage, which the Trojans find under construction and ruled by Dido, the beautiful Phoenician queen and another refugee from the eastern Mediterranean. Of course, Dido and Aeneas fall in love, and, of course, their love is doomed: this is, after all, epic not romance, although it takes Aeneas a while to realize it. For the gods have a plan, and the plan is Rome. Aeneas leads his men, his son, and the sacred cult objects of Troy to the coast of Latium in central Italy. There war, prophecy, and marriage will eventually allow them to settle in the town of Alba Longa. From there, Aeneas' distant descendant—Romulus—will set out to found the city.

Aeneas was the son of a goddess, Venus, worshipped in Rome as Venus Genetrix, Venus our Ancestor. Julius Caesar built a temple to her at the heart of the new forum he paid for from the spoils of the Gallic War. After his assassination, his heir, the future Emperor Augustus, completed the project. The temple was finished not long before the composition of the *Aeneid*.

Both of these monumental works mark stages in the process by which a single authorized version of Roman history was created out of a mass of contradictory traditions. One reason for this was the shift from a Republican form of government to a monarchy. Many traditions were linked to particular families, but now one family dominated the city. Julius Caesar, and so Augustus too, claimed to be direct descendants of Aeneas and Venus. Another reason was that Roman historians had only just begun to construct a reliable chronology of their own past. Scholars of the last generation of the free Republic, including Cicero's friends Varro, Nepos, and Atticus, had worked hard to correlate events in Roman tradition with the timelines established by Greek historians. Their conclusions—although often based on what to us seems like very shaky arguments—were never seriously challenged in antiquity. It was more important that Rome had a genuine and agreed history than that it was the right one. Augustus was equally concerned to fix the past. The historian Livy dryly records how Augustus himself engaged in research in ancient history to establish that no subordinate officer could be accorded the exceptional honour of the *spolia opima* awarded only to a general who killed his opponent in single combat.[2] Less controversially, great bronze tablets were set up recording the *fasti*, the exact sequence of consuls from the start of the Republic to the present day. The consuls were the pair of annual magistrates after whom each year was traditionally named. Caesar and Augustus promoted research into the calendar, and published it.[3]

Fixed by Homer's epic at the end of the heroic age, Aeneas lived far too early to found the city of Rome himself. Greek scholars had calculated that Troy had fallen in 1183 BC, while the date of the foundation of Rome was calculated as 753 BC. That left quite a gap. But Virgil's epic allowed Aeneas several visions of the future—Virgil's present that is—as an imperial age in which, under Augustus' rule, the Romans would rule the world according to the decrees of Jupiter. Most impressive was a descent into the Underworld, where Aeneas' dead father showed him the great Romans of history waiting to be born and gave him hints of their fates. Aeneas also took a trip up the Tiber to visit the future site of the city of Rome, still a pastoral idyll and settled by yet other refugees from the east, Greeks from Arcadia this time, who told him the story of how Hercules had passed by that very spot and defeated the terrifying monster Cacus there. Virgil wove together the many legends of ancient Rome, making out of them a narrative that could only culminate in Augustus.

The foundation of the city of Rome itself was left to one of Aeneas' descendants, Romulus, who with his brother Remus was the son of a princess

Fig. 1. The Prima Porta Augustus displayed in the Braccio Nuovo new wing of Museo Chiaramonti, Vatican Museums, Rome, Italy

of Aeneas' line and also of the god Mars, conveniently giving the Romans a second divine ancestor. When Augustus built his own forum and temple, he dedicated the latter to Mars and set images of Venus, Mars, and Julius Caesar (now a god as well) on the pediment.[4] Livy, who wrote not long after Virgil, opened his history *From the Foundation of the City* with the declaration that if any nation had the right to claim descent from Mars, the god of war, that nation was Rome.[5] Romans found in the myths of early Rome more than simply a justification for their current greatness. The story of how Romulus killed his brother because he dared step over the boundary he had just marked for the new city was understood as a sign that civil war too was written into the Roman psyche. The Rome of Augustus was, after all, in recovery from nearly a century of civil wars. When Virgil describes the Africans rising against Dido after she chose a foreign prince, the Italians attacking the Trojans when Aeneas won the hand of the local princess, or when Livy tells how Romulus supplied his followers with women by kidnapping the wives and daughters of the neighbouring Sabines, we can see how Romans sought an explanation for their own apparently ingrained traditions of violence.[6] That darker investigation runs alongside the repeated retellings of how much it had cost to found the Roman state and fulfil the city's divine destiny. The atrocities of the end of the Republic—with its riots, lynchings, and cold-blooded political murders—must have made it impossible to tell a convincing story of Rome only in terms of successive acts of heroism and piety.

Becoming Imperial

Myths of the deep past accumulated over time. Of course, they were rewritten as Rome's empire grew. If we compare stories like these with the foundation myths of other cities in the ancient Mediterranean, it immediately becomes clear that many of Rome's traditions were not very unusual. A startling number of cities claimed descent from Trojan or Greek refugees.[7] This was presumably because Homer's epics had such great prestige, and because so little else was known about the early first millennium BC. Others claimed to be descended from wandering heroes, Hercules especially, but also Odysseus, Perseus, Antenor, and others. Most Greek colonies claimed divine sanction for their possession of the land, and the dispossession of the previous inhabitants. That sanction might take the form of signs, oracles, or miraculous events. Many paid cult to their founders, as the Romans in fact worshipped Romulus under the name Quirinus. Violent beginnings, battles with indigenous peoples, and marriages between incomers and native women are also standard elements.[8] Even the foundling turned founder has many parallels. Presumably these were the central elements of the first versions of Rome's tales of origin. Only at a later stage can the prophecies have begun to include world dominion and the legends started to explore the darker side of Roman nature.

Unfortunately, we know very little of how Romans thought about themselves before they became an imperial power. The first Latin literature was created as a deliberate project of collective cultural assertion at the end of the third century BC.[9] By that time Rome was without question the major power in the western Mediterranean basin, and it had for generations dominated the Italian peninsula. The first Roman historians, Fabius Pictor writing in Greek and Cato the Elder in Latin, were already setting out to explain how Rome had overtaken Carthage. Fabius Pictor had taken part in the wars against the Gauls of north Italy in the late third century and was one of a delegation of senior senators who visited the oracle at Delphi in Greece seeking advice after Hannibal's great victory at Cannae in 216 BC. Cato (234–149 BC) saw the defeat of Hannibal, and also took part in the first wars against the great kingdoms of the eastern Mediterranean. His book of *Origins* was the product of combing Greek scholarship for information about the prehistory of the peoples of Italy. Most of what he gathered must have been foundation legends similar to that of Rome. Earlier Greek historians of the classical period knew a little about Rome; but not much of what they had to say has survived. Rome seems to spring into history fully formed as an imperial power, spectacularly aggressive, with institutions well developed for surviving occasional defeats and converting military victories into lasting political dominion.[10]

The Romans of this period already had a sense of their history as a rise to greatness. A contemporary of Cato, Quintus Ennius (239–169 BC), wrote an epic poem that was in effect a history of Rome from the beginning until his own day. It was called the *Annales*, and was the basis of education in the late Republic in the same way as the *Aeneid* was under the empire. Cicero adored it, but only fragments now survive. All the same, we have a good sense of Ennius' 'plot'. The first three books told the story of Rome from the fall of Troy through the foundation of the city and the rule of its seven kings until the Republic was created. Then followed twelve books relating Rome's wars against other Italian communities; against the Macedonian king Pyrrhus; against Carthage, culminating in the conquest of Greek cities in Italy and Sicily; and then the first wars in Spain; and those fought in the Balkans during the early second century BC against the great kingdoms of the east. Ennius then added three more books describing the victories of his patron, the general Marcus Fulvius Nobilior, whom he had accompanied on campaign in the northern Balkans in 189–188 BC. On their return Nobilior built a great temple on the Field of Mars, one dedicated to Hercules and the Muses. A prototype of Augustus' *Fasti* was also displayed in it. From the beginning, then, war and poetry went hand in hand. And Roman history *was* the history of Roman imperialism. Roman power was extended, just war by just war, until the entire sequence came to seem to have been sanctioned by the gods of Rome.[11] Their favour could never be taken for granted, but through repeated acts of piety the Roman people retained the divine mandate. Triumph after triumph proclaimed the support of the gods.[12] And while these epics and histories (and dramas too, although few have survived) were composed, the city itself became filled with victory temples, many vowed in battle and funded by the spoils donated by individual generals. The same generals decorated their own homes with trophies.

This, then, gives us a Roman sense of empire. The rule of one people, the people of the toga, over those whom they had defeated in war—a rule sanctioned by the gods of Rome as a mark of their favour for a people who were uniquely pious. Only in the last century of the Republic did Romans develop a means of describing the great political entity they had created.[13] Our term 'empire' derives from the Latin *imperium*. Its fundamental meaning was 'command', and right up until the end of the Republic, this remained its primary sense. As late as Julius Caesar's day the word *imperator* (the origin of our 'emperor') simply meant a general, someone invested with command. Soldiers on a battlefield might chant out the title after a battle as a way to honour their commander. *Imperium* was a temporary power and a personal one, granted him with solemn rituals for the duration of one campaign. Stepping back inside the city, which he had to do if he wanted to celebrate a triumph, meant relinquishing this power. Augustus was the first who never relinquished it. Indeed he was portrayed as a victorious general on the larger-than life statue found at the villa at Prima Porta to which his widow Livia retired after his death (Figure 1). One sense that *imperium* acquired only very late in the process was the total territory controlled by Rome. Augustus' account of his own life, inscribed on pillars before his tomb and disseminated as copies throughout the empire, proclaimed world hegemony and made clear that allied states and defeated enemies were all subject to Rome's command.

The Archetypal Empire

The modern idea of empire has its own history. Yet Rome has a key place in the history of this idea. The Romans created a set of ideas and symbols that exercised a fascination over many subsequent generations. Other empires had touched the Mediterranean world before Rome, most recently those of the Persians and of Alexander. But their repertoire of ceremonials, titles, and images has had less of an afterlife, in part because Romans refused to acknowledge them as their equals and invented their own language of world domination, in part because the Latin vocabulary of empire was the one adopted by later powers. The history of the idea of empire in the west is very largely the history of successive imitations of Rome. Each time Rome was copied, directly or indirectly, the idea of empire was modified. Yet Latin titles and imperial eagles lasted well into the twentieth century. 'Empire' plunges through European and finally world history like a snowball rolling downhill.[14]

The Roman Empire had many imitators and would-be successors. The rulers of the medieval west lived among the ruins of Roman monuments. Roman coins were still to be found in the fields. Roman walls embraced the tiny towns of Europe, and the best roads remained for centuries those the Romans had built, roads that still crossed rivers on stone bridges that early medieval monarchs could not rival. Latin remained the main language of literature, and classical texts were widely read and treated with exaggerated awe. And knowing Rome was inseparable from knowing about its empire. When Frankish kings began to extend their power over other peoples, Rome was the only possible model. At the end of the twelfth century, the French king was nicknamed Philip Augustus, and his main rivals were the German emperor and the Angevin kings of England, who included lesser kings among their vassals. Emperor meant, for much of the Middle Ages, the supreme secular position of leadership. Ordinary kings ranked below him, popes on a par.

Besides, there were still live Roman emperors to admire and rival. They ruled in Constantinople on the Bosporus, the city we know as Istanbul and which had been Byzantium before. These emperors justifiably regarded themselves as Romans, the heirs of Justinian and Constantine at least, as well as of their pagan predecessors. The language of their empire might now be Greek, and its domains had shrunk to the lands around the Aegean Sea, but the palace, the hippodrome, and the libraries of Byzantium, as well as the ceremonial and titulature of the court, proclaimed its authentic Roman imperial style. North and west of Byzantium a great penumbra of peoples were drawn into its cultural sphere. Viking adventurers travelled across the European rivers to Novgorod and then on to the city they called Miklagard, the Great City. One of them carved some runes, still visible today, into the balcony of the great imperial church of Hagia Sophia built by the sixth-century emperor Justinian. Its dome provided the model for Islamic mosques, themselves often built on the site of Roman temples or churches and often employing Roman columns in their construction. After the Fourth Crusade (1202–4) there were Frankish emperors in Byzantium for a while, briefly drawing the western and eastern traditions together. Even when the restored Greek emperors finally lost the city to the Turks in the fifteenth century there was no total rupture. Various princes took the opportunity to declare their own states a 'Third Rome': Moscow is the most famous. For a while there had in any case been a sultanate of Rûm ruling former Byzantine possessions in Asia Minor, and the Ottomans staged grand ceremonies in the hippodrome and worshipped in Hagia Sophia, now a mosque, just like their Christian predecessors. Roman political models had been less influential elsewhere in the Islamic world. Other aspects of Roman civilization periodically fascinated. The cities of Byzantine Syria had a brief period of prosperity after the Arab conquest. During the ninth century the Abbasid caliphs employed some of their Christian subjects to trawl Greek literature and translate whatever was valuable. Many medical texts and some works of philosophy have survived only in Arabic translation.[15]

Empire had lasting resonance, then, as a set of symbols. From our distant vantage point we can watch the baton being passed down, generation to generation. The predominant dynamic seems to have been competition. Charlemagne employed the language of empire to consolidate Frankish hegemony. He and the papacy also found it a helpful tool in keeping the Byzantine emperor at bay. Four centuries later, the author of the *Chanson de Roland* imagined Charlemagne as a great proto-crusader who at God's command would defend Christendom against the *païen* (the pagan). A few of the medieval German emperors took up this challenge. But mostly they employed the title of emperor to express their sense of being at the pinnacle of a worldly hierarchy, overlords of prince-electors, petty kings, and free cities from the Baltic to the Mediterranean. During the three centuries in which the Habsburg family provided Holy Roman Emperors, the imperial style was further elaborated in Spain, Austria, and Germany. The enduring power vested in these symbols is demonstrated by the decision of Napoleon to abolish the Holy Roman Empire and to proclaim the first French empire in 1804. Austria responded by declaring the Austrian Empire the same year. Nineteenth-century France experienced an alternation of republics and empires. The French Second Empire perished after the Franco-Prussian War of 1870; the German Empire was born the next year. The British Queen

Victoria took the title Empress of India in 1876. The nineteenth century saw brief New World empires established in Brazil, Haiti, and Mexico. The Austro-Hungarian Empire lasted until 1918. The Russian tsars lost their empire just a year earlier; their title tsar (derived naturally from Caesar) can be tracked back in Slav languages as far as the rulers of tenth-century Bulgaria, some of Byzantium's most formidable opponents. British monarchs retained the imperial title until 1948. The latest emperor in this tradition was Bokassa, who ruled the Central African Empire between 1976 and 1979.

It is an obvious point to make, perhaps, but these polities had almost nothing in common. Nor do they correspond very well, in any age, to the list of imperial powers we might draw up on other criteria. The British, by most estimates, ruled an empire (or perhaps two) long before Victoria was persuaded to take the title. Spain was clearly an early modern empire, whether or not the ruling Habsburg happened to be emperor. On the other hand, these claims cannot be dismissed entirely as megalomaniac fantasies. What we are observing is the enduring power of Roman models of empire to fascinate, especially at moments of intense competition for precedence. When monarchies vied for prestige, they reached for the eagles, the Latin titles, wreaths, and classicizing architecture. Their value was that they were instantly recognizable. Even Bokassa, as he seized power in the Central African Republic, demonstrated how well he had learned the symbolic language of European colonialism.

The revival of the language of empire in the modern age seems particularly surprising. Rivalry between European monarchies was clearly one factor. Perhaps there were simply not many alternative vocabularies to express the global differentials of power being created. But there were multiple local factors too. Napoleon's empire was not just about dominion abroad: it was also about the working out of the Republican project in post—Revolutionary France. Victoria's assumption of the title Empress of India was not just about rivalry with her German son-in-law Kaiser Wilhelm: it may also have reflected a growing recognition of the national identity of India. The last Mughal (deposed by the British in 1858) had taken the Urdu title *Badishah-e-Hind*, which is often translated as Emperor of India. The Russian monarchs' use of the Slavic term czar or tsar also evoked the guardianship of Orthodox Christianity.

Behind all this we can sense the emergence of a group of nation states that regarded each other as in a league of their own, as great powers. Today, in the first decades of the twenty-first century, only three members of the

G8 and only one of the five permanent members of the UN Security Council are still monarchies of any kind. But for much of the nineteenth century, all the leading nations had hereditary heads of state. The nineteenth century was also the high watermark of European interest in the Classics, and especially in Rome. Perhaps it is not surprising that, by one route or another, so many of these monarchs became emperors, at least for a short while. The language and trappings of empire offered a way to express a sense that they were more than simply kings and queens, and that the nation states over which they reigned were not ordinary nations.

Empire did not lose its charm until the middle of the twentieth century. One by one monarchies were abolished or rendered peripheral. Communist states found Rome a less attractive model than had their predecessors. Fascism was the last major political movement to make use of Roman models. Mussolini's imitation of Rome was the most explicit: as well as using Roman precedent to make a claim to Mediterranean hegemony, his party was named after the *fasces*, the bundle of rods surrounding an axe that was the symbol carried before a Roman magistrate. The *fasces* was a common symbol in British and US imagery in the early twentieth century (see Figure 2). German Fascism too made much use of classical Roman imagery, especially in the architecture of the Third Reich.[16] After the Second World War the Japanese emperor was made to renounce his divinity, European empires were dismantled, and imperialism came to acquire a more and more pejorative sense. The British monarchy quietly put away the title after the end of the British Raj. Classical imagery was in any case less and less effective as the new professional and governing classes had less and less knowledge about Rome. 'Imperialist' became a term of abuse directed against colonial powers by newly independent peoples, and the label was used as a term of condemnation by all sides in the Cold War. Discussions of whether or not the USA is today an empire are rarely sympathetic towards American foreign policy.

The multiple afterlives of the Roman Empire are one reason for the enduring importance of Rome. But they can also obscure our vision of Rome itself. It is worthwhile considering some of the less obvious contrasts between Rome and her nineteenth-century imitators. For one thing, the Roman Empire admitted no equals and recognized no predecessor. There was no notion of a community of nations, no elite club of superpowers; the Romans were a single people over and against the rest. Not all of their subjects and neighbours saw things this way. But empire for Rome was novel and unique. Rome was restoring nothing, and the world empire it created seemed, for a while, without precedent.

Empire as a Category

The last notion of empire that I want to introduce is one the Romans would have found hard to credit. This is the idea that empire is a particular kind of political entity, one that has occurred on several occasions and in several locations in world history. This usage makes the term 'empire' into a timeless socio-historical category, the very opposite of a phenomenon with its own history.

We are all familiar, naturally, with the idea that 'empire' denotes a particular kind of thing. Alongside the Roman Empire we might want to set the British Empire, the New World empires of the Aztecs and Incas, the Persians and the Assyrians in antiquity, the Spaniards in the early modern period, and so on. For everyday purposes, we associate empire with the conquest of other peoples or states, with grand capital cities and rich court ceremonial, with rule over a great swathe of territory, and with a leading place in historical narratives. Empires rise and fall, they dominate their neighbours, they gather exotic treasures from the edges of the earth, and they claim to be at the centre of it. Empire evokes dreams of universal dominion: a Reich that lasts a thousand years, a flag the sun never sets on, a ruler who is a king of kings.[17]

It turns out to be not so easy to develop more rigorous definitions. We can hardly rely on the rulers' preferred description, which usually depended on local rivalries and whether the term would win or lose them support. Besides, what are we to do when we consider places outside those traditions that placed Rome at its root? Most historians would agree that the Incas and the Chinese created empires comparable to those of Europe and the Middle East; yet how are we to decide which Quechua or Mandarin terms have the same semantic range as 'empire' or 'emperors'? The ancients themselves did not always agree on what was or was not an empire. Roman emperors generally treated Persia as a lesser state; yet Persians on occasion addressed them as 'brother emperors'.[18] The historical sociologist finds it especially difficult to distinguish small empires from large states, since most states are built on domination, and since only the tiniest states have no internal peripheries. Did the English ever exercise *imperial* rule over Wales and Ireland or over Scotland? That English governments dominated these regions is without doubt, but the language chosen to describe them was never imperial. Scots were eventually presented as partners in the British Empire. But was not this mere ideology, a device to disguise English hegemony and to claim that the inhabitants of Scotland were in some sense privileged relative to those of other subjected territories? Empires are certainly states, and there are certainly rulers and ruled. But there are also those subjects who join in conquering and ruling, both their own people and others. Scale ought to be a good criterion. But fixing the limit is impossible. The Bronze Age empires of Mesopotamia and the classical Athenian empire were tiny compared to those of Rome, Persia, and north India. Yet it would seem odd either to deny the title 'empire' to them or alternatively to term virtually all the kingdoms of medieval and modern Europe imperial.

What most historians concerned with comparative analysis do is to divide up the term 'empire' into subcategories and to try to compare only like with like.[19] It makes sense, for example, to treat separately the late nineteenth- and early twentieth-century European empires in which nation states enjoyed brief control of distant regions with much weaker economies, largely through their technological superiority. Even within pre-industrial (or, if you prefer, premodern or precapitalist) empires, some comparisons seem hazardous. Can we really compare the maritime empire of early modern Portugal with the chronologically contemporaneous empires of the valley of Mexico whose rulers did not use writing, iron, or pack animals and whose political horizons were so much narrower? Perhaps these definitional questions do not matter too much: small empires are difficult to distinguish from large states precisely because they are, in many respects, very similar. Unless it is important to establish an unambiguous separation of categories (for example, if one were trying to show how some things were always true of empires and never true of anything else), the vagueness of the term is not a problem. Lenin needed clear definitions for his proposition that imperialism was a particular historical stage, but that is not my purpose here.[20]

The empires to which I will most often compare Rome are those that resembled it most closely in scale and technology. That means great states like Achaemenid and Sassanian Persia, the Mauryan Empire of north India, and China after the Qin dynasty. All these were states with productive agricultural economies, generally dependent on Iron Age technology, and had no source of energy beyond human and animal power, firewood, and perhaps watermills. All employed some form of writing or similar record-keeping, and also standardized systems of money, weights, and measures. All were so vast it took weeks to get a message from one side to the other by the fastest communications media of the day, and months for an army to cross. All had elaborate social hierarchies, especially at their courts, and made extensive use of ceremonial and ritual. States of this kind are sometimes called tributary or aristocratic empires. Empires of this kind were typically created when one or more ruling peoples conquered—generally rather rapidly—a number of previously independent subject peoples. Achaemenid Persia was formed from the forced merger of the kingdoms of the Medes, Babylonia, Lydia, and Egypt, all between 550 and 520 BC. Rome became imperial by first swallowing up other Italian states, then defeating Carthage, and finally subjugating the major kingdoms of the eastern Mediterranean. The Qin became imperial by conquering six or seven other kingdoms at the end of the Warring States Period. There are many other examples of this pattern known from around the world. But conquest was only the first stage, and many empires collapsed at the moment expansion stopped: the fate of Alexander the Great's empire is a case in point. Conquest states needed to transform themselves into stable structures of domination. Their rulers came to depend not only on the use and threat of violence, but also on the tacit support of local elites of various kinds. Through their help levies, tithes, taxes, or some combination of these was extracted. Local rulers took a portion, and most of the surplus was put to the task of maintaining order and defending the empire. The residue paid for the extravagant lifestyle of the rulers of the empire. Those rulers also invested heavily in ceremonial and monuments. Most claimed the mandate of heaven, both to reassure themselves and to cow their subjects. Rome was, in all these respects, a fairly typical pre-industrial empire.

What is to be gained from thinking about Rome in these terms? One benefit is that comparison sometimes explains some feature of society that seems odd to us today. That Roman emperors were worshipped as gods seems less strange when we appreciate quite how widespread practices of this kind were in ancient empires.[21] Comparison can also sometimes help us appreciate how unusual one or another feature of the Roman version of early empire was. Citizenship, for example, an inheritance from the city state cultures of the archaic and classical Mediterranean, is a good example of one respect in which the Roman Empire was unusual. Persian shahs and the Chinese sons of heaven had subjects, not fellow citizens. Perhaps a final advantage is that this kind of exercise reminds us of the difference between appropriate and inappropriate comparisons. Many historians today find themselves making comparisons between modern imperialisms and those of the Roman past. The reasons are obvious enough. Our age has rejected the language of empire, arguably without always surrendering much of its power. Rome enters the discussion not because it is a very close analogy, but because it is familiar and because modern empires have made so much use of Roman symbols. Modern empires are unlike Rome: the principal difference is not one of morality (racism versus slavery, anyone?) but of technology. Lenin was right to insist on the ineradicably modern origins of nineteenth- and twentieth-century imperialism. Comparative history gives us a sense of perspective: Rome was not unique, nor was it very like either the British Raj or twenty-first-century superpowers. Rome has its own Romance.

Further Reading

Roman myth-makings about their past and their gradual awakening to an imperial destiny are the subject of Erich Gruen's *Culture and National Identity in Republican Rome* (London, 1992) and Emma Dench's *Romulus' Asylum* (Oxford, 2005). Andrew Erskine's *Troy between Greece and Rome* (Oxford, 2001) is a wonderful study of Rome's discovery of its Trojan origins. A vivid account of Roman myth-making is Peter Wiseman's *Myths of Rome* (Exeter, 2004).

The study of later receptions of Greece and Rome is one of the fastest-growing areas of classical scholarship. For the afterlife of Rome and for Rome as a model of empire, see Catharine Edwards's *Roman Presences* (Cambridge, 1999) and Margaret Malamud's *Ancient Rome and Modern America* (Oxford, 2009). A valuable set of essays is Richard Hingley's *Images of Rome: Perceptions of Ancient Rome in Europe and the United States in the Modern Age* (Portsmouth, RI, 2001).

The best introduction to the comparative history of the premodern world is Patricia Crone's *Preindustrial Societies* (Oxford, 1989). One of the most influential studies of early empires was Jon Kautsky's *The Politics of Aristocratic Empires* (Chapel Hill, NC, 1982). Susan Alcock, Terence D'Altroy, Kathy Morrison, and Carla Sinopoli's *Empires: Perspectives from Archaeology and History* (Cambridge, 2001) faithfully reproduces the exciting conference that gave rise to it. *The Roman Empire in Context: Historical and Comparative Perspectives*, edited by Johann P. Arnason and Kurt Raaflaub (Malden, MA, and Oxford, 2011), compares Rome with other early empires. Two other recent collections on early empires are Peter Fibiger

Bang and Dariusz Kolodziejczyz's *Universal Empire: A Comparative Approach to Imperial Culture and Representation in Eurasian History* (Cambridge, 2012) and *Cosmopolitanism and Empire: Universal Rulers, Local Elites, and Cultural Integration in the Ancient near East and Mediterranean,* edited by Myles Lavan, Richard E. Payne, and John Weisweiler (Cambridge, 2016). For a recent essay in systematic comparative history, see Walter Scheidel, *Rome and China* (Oxford, 2009).

KEY DATES IN CHAPTER III

753–510 BC   The Regal Period of Roman history, as calculated by Varro (But an average reign of over thirty years for each of seven kings of Rome is implausible)

509 BC   Rome's first treaty with Carthage (others followed in 348 and 306) supposedly following rapidly on the foundation of the Republic

496 BC   Traditional date of the battle of Lake Regillus in which Rome defeats the Latin League

494 BC   Traditional date for the first secession of the *plebs*, the beginning of a long struggle for political emancipation conventionally termed the 'Conflict of the Orders'

396 BC   Traditional date of the destruction of Veii by Rome

390 BC   Traditional date of the Gallic sack of Rome

343–290 BC   Rome frequently at war with Samnites of central Italy (later remembered as three Samnite wars)

340–338 BC   War with the Latins ends in the disbanding of the Latin League.

336–323 BC   Reign of Alexander III (the Great) of Macedon

287 BC   The *Lex Hortensia* makes decisions of the plebeians binding on the community as a whole. The conventional end of the Conflict of the Orders.

280–275 BC   Pyrrhus of Epirus campaigns in Italy against Rome and Sicily against Carthage and then returns across the Adriatic

NB Most dates before Pyrrhus' invasion derive from conjectures made by antiquarians in the last century BC. The first serious histories of the west were those written by Timaeus of Sicilian Tauromenium and by Fabius Pictor (of Rome) in the early and later third century BC respectively. Both works are lost, but later writers made some use of them in works written in the second century BC and after.

RULERS OF ITALY

What you see before you, stranger, now mighty Rome, were grassy hills before the days of Trojan Aeneas. Evander's wandering cattle rested where now the Palatine temple to Naval Apollo stands high. These golden temples grew for terracotta gods, content to live in simple houses built without art.

(Propertius, *Elegies* 4.1.1–6)

Almost no Greek writer mentions Rome before 300 BC, and no native historian before 200 BC. By the time these histories were written, Rome was already the dominant power within Italy (Map 1). During the third century BC, the Romans fended off Pyrrhus of Epirus' invasion of southern Italy; fought and won a twenty-three-year-long naval war against Carthage; consolidated their power over the Greek cities of Campania and southern Italy and the peoples of the peninsula's mountainous spine; and began the conquest of the Gallic inhabitants of the regions north of the Apennines and south of the Alps. The final two decades of the century saw Rome survive Hannibal's invasion of Italy and carry war back to Carthage. Victory at Zama in 202 ended Carthaginian regional ambitions forever, even if the city survived another half-century before it was obliterated. Rome at the start of the second century BC enjoyed a dominant position at the geopolitical centre of the inland sea. It was equipped with institutions, ideologies, and

Map 1. The peoples of Italy around 300 BC

experience geared to conquest. From that point on, control of the whole Mediterranean world was only a matter of time.

How the Romans reached that position is more puzzling. Ancient narratives are transparently written in the knowledge of (and often to explain) Rome's imperial destiny. Myths of divine favour and mortal virtue, and tales of the heroic exploits of the ancestors of this or that aristocratic clan, can hardly be the basis for our history. Even those Roman historians who were reasonably sceptical of those stories tended to use the better-known histories of Greek cities as a pattern for their own reconstructions. Their accounts present a Rome at times impossibly primitive, like the pastoral idyll Propertius summons up beneath the golden temples of Augustan Rome, or else relate fantastic tales of palace intrigues worthy of Homeric courts. For all these reasons, a reliable account of early Rome must begin from archaeology.

The City on the Tiber

Perhaps no archaeological site has been the object of such intense scrutiny as the city of Rome.[1] The site has been continually occupied since the Bronze Age. Layered remains of medieval, Renaissance, and later cities make it difficult to reconstruct even the imperial capital of Augustus in detail. That megalopolis, with its great monuments and a population of around a million, was itself the product of centuries of rebuilding. Construction reached a particularly frantic phase during the late Republic. It was already widely reported in Pliny the Elder's day (the early Flavian period) that in 78 BC:

no house in Rome was more beautiful than that of Marcus Lepidus [the consul], but by Hercules within thirty-five years the same house did not rank in the top one hundred mansions.[2]

By the end of the Republic many aristocratic houses and temples were being reconstructed every generation on ever more lavish scales, funded by the proceeds of overseas conquest. Recovering material from the origins of Rome beneath all of this is very difficult, and its interpretation remains highly controversial.[3]

At the beginning of the last millennium BC communities of Iron Age farmers had already established villages on the tops of the low hills that approached the River Tiber where it made a slow curve around the little plain that would become the Field of Mars. Each village had one or more cemeteries. The best known is at Osteria dell'Osa, in use from the ninth to the seventh centuries BC.[4] The organization of the burials and the distribution of the grave goods suggest it was shared by a number of clans, and also that it was used both by families of high status and by their humbler dependants. It is likely that the separate identities of these villages, and of their ruling families, also explain the later location of a number of key temples on each of the hills of Rome. How—and how early—these

Fig. 2. A US Mercury Dime, depicting the Roman *fasces*

communities began to work together as a single polity is obscure: there are far too many gaps in the record.

The story of urbanism in central Italy is interwoven with that of Phoenician and Greek penetration of the western Mediterranean. Phoenicians and Greeks first appeared in the tenth and eighth centuries BC respectively, powered by economic growth at home and exploiting slight but significant technological advantages in navigation and warfare.[5] Indigenous Iron Age societies were everywhere drawn into relationships of one kind or another with the new arrivals.[6] Exploration and trade typically came first; colonial foundations followed in some areas. Eventually, Phoenicians would settle in North Africa, western Sicily, and southern Spain; Greeks in eastern Sicily and southern Italy and eventually Mediterranean France. Bases like Marseilles near the mouth of the Rhône, and Spina at the northern end of the Adriatic, opened up trade routes into central Europe. Phoenicians and Greeks went on to explore the Atlantic coast too, seeking tin from the British Isles and exotic goods such as ivory from West Africa. But at first things were probably much more confused. There is early evidence for both Phoenician and Greek presence in coastal Etruria. It was metals that first drew visitors to central Italy.[7] During the eighth century the Etruscans to the north of Rome and Campanians to the south began to be enriched by trade with the newcomers. Etruscans had already begun to develop complex urban societies and states before easterners arrived; they were well positioned to repel would-be colonists, and enthusiastically traded metal grain for eastern luxuries.[8] Their enthusiasm was so marked that this period of Etruscan culture is often called the Orientalizing period, and for a while many scholars believed that in their case the myths of eastern origins were actually true. Farther south, Campanians and others were less able to resist Greek settlement: a string of new Greek cities were founded in southern Italy, the most northerly being Cumae.

Rome was located between the two, in the region known to ancients as Old Latium. During the ninth and eighth centuries the material culture of this region diverged from that of neighbouring regions and developed a style of its own, but one noted for its relative poverty. There are fewer rich burials than in Etruria, its warrior graves contained many fewer eastern imports, its population probably did increase, but it was scattered in smallish settlements that could not compare either with southern Etruscan centres like Veii, Tarquinii, and Caere or with the Greek cities at Cumae and Naples. At the northern edge of Latium was the cluster of villages at the Tiber crossing.

When did this cluster of villages first come to form the community of the Romans? Recent excavations have uncovered a number of huts and burials and some kind of defensive wall dating to the eighth century, but it is very difficult to be certain what these tantalizing fragments represent. Was Rome already on the road to urbanism? Or still just a scatter of villages? During the sixth century the swampy valley north of the Palatine was drained, creating what would become the forum. The earliest of Rome's great temples, on and around the Capitol, are also sixth-century in date. From the sixth century, too, survive the first traces of massive aristocratic houses, located on the southern edge of the forum. From this point on it seems reasonable to think of Rome as a city with defined districts and some centralized institutions. But the division of space was fairly rudimentary. The early forum perhaps served a whole range of commercial, political, and religious functions, and the Capitoline Hill would for centuries be both a religious sanctuary and a refuge/citadel. But for some purposes at least the inhabitants of Rome seem have come together as a single people.

This emergence of cities through the coming together of clusters of villages was a common process across the archaic Mediterranean world. Athens followed a similar sequence, growing out of hamlets, each with its own cemetery in the area around the acropolis. The first public space of Athens, the *agora*, also served all sorts of functions as late as the sixth century; a more differentiated use of space followed only later. The history of early Corinth is not very different. Southern Etruria also followed this route to urbanism. Veii, just 16 kilometres (10 miles) north of Rome, grew up on a plateau of the soft volcanic rock known as tuff. A cluster of villages, cemeteries, and hilltop sanctuaries gradually coalesced to form what by ancient standards was a massive city. Piecemeal fortifications closed the gaps in natural defences until, in the early fourth century, a six-kilometre-long (about 4 miles) circuit wall was built. Rome's 'Servian' wall circuit (see Picture Box 1), built almost contemporaneously, was 11 kilometres (about 7 miles) long and enclosed over 400 hectares (about 1,000 acres). By the standards of the age this was a huge occupied area, telling us that Rome already stood out among her Italian neighbours, and especially among the Latins, who mostly lived in much smaller settlements. It was also a massive undertaking. One recent estimate is that constructing the wall circuit took nearly seven million days' labour, whether by citizens or slaves or both.[9]

Rome resembled Etruscan cities like Veii more than it did Athens or Corinth. Similarities of culture and technology—and also of geology and climate—had created a regional style of urbanism in central Italy. Perhaps too it made a difference that in the late Bronze Age there had been palaces and states in southern Greece with strong links to Egypt and the Near East, whereas the Italian Bronze Age had been organized on a much smaller and more local scale, more like that of northern Europe in fact. But Tyrrhenian Italy had its own advantages. Then, as now, it was a fertile region thanks to the combination of Atlantic rainfall and volcanic soils. The plateau sites favoured by Bronze and Iron Age farmers were also the product of volcanism, spurs of soft tuff formed from volcanic ash. Hilltop sites were not only preferred for defence: they were also healthier, given the prevalence of malaria in the marshes of the coastal plain. Architecturally too there was a regional style. While archaic Greek cities were building temples and carving sculpture out of the spectacular marbles found around the Aegean Sea, their western counterparts were constructing temples out of tuff and brick, roofing and decorating them with brightly painted terracotta tiles moulded with faces, images, and abstract designs. Even the statues of the gods were ceramic rather than stone. These were the ancient terracotta gods in their simple homes that Propertius contrasted with the marble splendours of his own day.

The most difficult thing to explain is what factors made Rome emerge out of the general poverty of Latial culture to rival the great cities of Etruria. Location probably played an important part. The Tiber is not one of the

Picture Box 1 The 'Servian' Walls of Rome

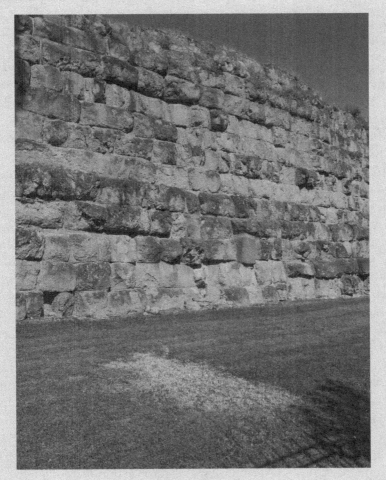

This wall circuit is still visible in many parts of the city including here beside the main railway station, Stazione Termini. Although traditionally known as the Servian Walls, after the third king of Rome, this circuit was in fact constructed much later, around the beginning of the fourth century BC.

The wall circuit was 11 kilometres (7 miles) in length and it enclosed 400 hectares (988 acres). This area included the traditional seven hills of Rome (the Quirinal, Viminal, and Esquiline, which are spurs descending from the east, the Aventine to the south, and between them the Caelian,

Palatine, and Capitol) and also the forum Romanum, the Circus Maximus, and other public spaces. There had been earlier defences around individual hills, but this project shows Rome united as a community. It also represents a huge investment of materials and labour. What survives today is the ashlar masonry, which in some places was at least 10 metres (32 feet) in height. Originally there was also an earth bank behind it, and a ditch in front. Stone for its construction came from quarries inside the city and also from areas around Rome including the territory of the Etruscan city of Veii destroyed by Rome in 396 BC. Probably the stone brought in from a distance was used to provide an impressive facade, with lower-quality stone used inside the structure. Fortified gatehouses were dotted around the circuit. It would have been difficult to approach the wall at any other point as the ditch was more than 30 metres (98 feet) wide and 17 metres (56 feet) deep. The bank behind the wall was even longer. Creating a structure of this size must have been a significant organizational task. It also required a great deal of labour. Some of the stone blocks weighed as much as 850 kilos each. It has been estimated that the circuit would have taken nearly 7 million person days to construct. It is very likely that the work force included forced labour, perhaps a combination of corvée labour by citizens and work required of slaves and perhaps prisoners of war.

There are no contemporary inscriptions associated with these walls and the main historical sources are Dionysius of Halicarnassus and Livy, both writing nearly four hundred years later. The building of the walls was associated by then with the much mythologized Gallic Sack of Rome, dated to 390 BC. Archaeologically, the scale of the project recalls the very large cities of southern Etruria, including Veii, Caere, and Tarquinia, which each covered more than 100 hectares (250 acres) and were protected by a mixture of walls and plateau edges. The construction methods, however, are more similar to those of Greek Syracuse. The mid-Republican wall circuit of Rome, however, was longer and higher than any of these. The scale of the project makes it not only the most significant monument of mid-Republican Rome but also one of the best indicators of just how early Roman power came to dominate the Italian peninsula.

Further Reading

Seth Bernard, *Building Mid-Republican Rome: Labor, Architecture, and the Urban Economy* (New York: Oxford University Press, 2018).

great rivers of the Mediterranean, but in ancient times it offered both a boundary between peoples and a communication route from Rome down to the coast and into the interior. To the north of the river there were the Etruscans, to the south the Latins. The Tiber gave access to the Sabine hills to the east as well as to Umbria in the north. By the imperial period, the Tiber Valley provided timber and building stone for Rome, its tributaries supplied much of the aqueduct system, and its claybeds were exploited for brick production.[10] Rome was located at the intersection of ecological zones, always an advantageous position. Rome is about 25 kilometres (15 miles) from the sea. An outpost was established at the mouth of the Tiber at Ostia as early as the fourth century. Long before this there were coastal saltpans there, and the Salt Road (the *via Salaria*) ran through Rome and over the Apennines to the Adriatic. Rome did not sit in an area with great metal resources like the Colline Metallifere that had attracted Greeks to Northern Etruria. Nor was the countryside as productive of grain or as suitable for vines as that of Campania. But perhaps when the tendrils of exchange networks extended deeper into Italy, the river port of the city on the Tiber seemed a good entry point.

A second advantage was perhaps Rome's location on the margins of the Etruscan world. Sixth-century Rome was in some senses a hybrid, and hybrids have their own vigour. Physically the city resembled the great cities of southern Etruria—Tarquinia, Cerveteri, Orvieto, and Vulci, as well as Veii. Etruscan influence is everywhere in the form of the hard black Etruscan pottery called *bucchero*. But Romans shared a language and some sanctuaries with the Latins, whom they considered as their kin. Archaeologically, the balance seems to have shifted over time. The ninth-century huts and burials of Rome are very similar to those known elsewhere in Latium. Rome did not participate in the growth experienced by Etruria and some other parts of Italy in the eighth century, when the Greeks arrived in search of metals. Yet at some point in the early sixth century Rome began to stand out, and to stand comparison with its Etruscan neighbours to the north.

Etruscan cities had emerged as a cluster of what archaeologists some-times call 'peer polities', a group of states which for a while seem to develop on parallel lines at an accelerated rate as they compete with each other and learn from each other's successful experiments and mistakes.[11] The same idea has been used in the Greek world to explain the rapid diffusion of innovations as varied as law codes, temple building, and tyranny. Etruscan cities had a common history of this kind from their first nucleations in the ninth century to the shared taste for oriental art in the eighth. Peer-polity systems have other effects, however, including a certain amount of institutional inbreeding and a tendency to limit the success of their strongest members. The Greek world in the fourth century offers a good example, with successive leading city states brought down to size by alliances made among the others. The unification of Greece came, in the end, only in the form of conquest by a state that had developed on the geographical margins of the system, the kingdom of Macedon, led first by Philip and then Alexander the Great. Growth at the margins is another common phenomenon. The ancient competition between Egypt, Assyria, Babylonia, and various Syrian and Anatolian states ended in the Iron Age, not when one drew ahead of the rest, but when all were conquered from outside by the Persians. Equally, the first Chinese Empire was created by one of the marginal polities of the Warring States Period, the Qin. Rome would again enjoy the benefits of growth at the margin during the early second century BC, when it took over the Macedonian-led kingdoms to its east, kingdoms that had been engaged for a couple of centuries in expensive and inconclusive competition for influence over the Aegean, southern Turkey, and southern Syria. Perhaps at the start of its history too, Rome's rise was due in part to the fact that it was *not* central to developments in Etruria.

History and Myth

Tradition had a different take on the Latin–Etruscan hybridity of early Rome. The last kings of Rome were remembered as Etruscans, the Tarquins from—inevitably, if suspiciously—the city of Tarquinii. It was they, so legend ran, who had drained the forum with forced labour. The traditional chronology is close enough to the archaeological traces of urban growth in the late sixth century to persuade some that the story preserves elements of fact.[12] The Tarquins, the story goes, had also begun building the great temple of Jupiter on the Capitol, commissioning the master potter Vulca to come from Veii to create a spectacular terracotta cult statue. But they did not survive to see the work finished: the foundation of the temple of Capitoline Jupiter coincided with the birth of the Republic. The founding myth told how native Roman aristocrats had expelled the Etruscan tyrants and set up a constitution in which popular assemblies were sovereign. Those assemblies would elect magistrates—first praetors and then consuls—who would govern in pairs, and for no more than one year at a time, advised by a council of former magistrates, the Senate. The most important decisions—declarations of war and the passing of new laws—remained the prerogative of the entire community. A conventional narrative of liberation from tyranny was thus given an ethnic dimension and linked to the creation of a unique political system. Rome became more Roman by shedding its Etruscan rulers.

The foundation of the temple of Jupiter was a critical reference point for later reflections on the Roman past, just as the temple itself provided a central focus in the ritual year, and for the collective life of the city. At least one late fourth-century scribe dated events from the foundation of the temple. Augustus' *Fasti* began in the same year with the first ever pair of consuls. So the expulsion of the Tarquins marked (for some) the beginning of Roman history.[13] But it is not easy now to construct a narrative of events from that point until the end of the third century BC. Nor was it easy then. Pictor, Cato, Polybius, and their contemporaries looked back from the turn of the third and second centuries, but their vision was limited. There were hardly any written documents. To be sure, there was a mass of traditions: some glorified particular families and individuals; some perhaps presented more or less popular views; some may have been in the form of dramas or songs, linked to particular places, cults, or temples. Sifting contradictory and competing versions and arranging them in time was a formidable task, for which the only tools were guesswork, analogy from Greek history, and imaginative reconstruction. When historians of the late Republic and early Principate set about completing the task, they faced even more formidable difficulties. Polybius had set out to write an account of Rome's conquest of the Mediterranean between 220 and 168 BC; that story began around twenty years before his birth and he had witnessed the later phases, from the vantage point of an honoured hostage, travelling in the train of Scipio Aemilianus. Polybius preceded his account with a shorter summary of events from 264 BC, the start of the First Punic War and the end of Timaeus' *Histories* of the west. When, under Augustus, Dionysius set out to write *Roman Antiquities*, which ended more or less where Polybius began, and when Livy around the same time began his total history of Rome *From the Foundation of the City*, they had to engage in a completely different enterprise, the rationalization of a set of memories organized around powerful social myths.

One set of stories chronicled the rise of Rome as a military superpower. The Etruscans made repeated attempts to recapture Rome, but all of them were foiled. For over a century, Rome and Veii glared at each other across the Tiber—three separate wars and two great truces were remembered—before the Romans sacked the city. Traditionally, this was dated to 396 BC. Meanwhile, Rome fought wars against and in alliance with the Latins, the Hernici, and more distant opponents, the Volsci and the Aequi. The world within which these conflicts took place was tiny—barely 50 kilometres (about 30 miles) across—yet they were remembered on an epic scale. Even more mythologized was the Gallic sack of Rome, conventionally dated to 390 BC.[14] Traditions about this event varied wildly. Did the Gauls sack all or part of the city? Did they keep their ransom or was it recovered? Which Roman heroes were most responsible for survival and recovery? Or was it in fact an Etruscan army from Cerveteri which saw them off? That last version, unsurprisingly, occurs in Greek but not Roman accounts. Yet another set of traditions concerned the series of wars Rome fought against the peoples of the central Apennines.[15] The Samnites were represented as barbarian highlanders. Roman tradition recorded three wars fought between the middle of the fourth century and the start of the third. No doubt these campaigns were in reality less coherent than they seemed in hindsight, and the Samnites were definitely not exactly the savages they were portrayed. In fact, monumental sanctuaries in the Abruzzi like that at Pietrabbondante made greater use of Greek architecture than did those of Rome in the same period.

Much of what was remembered is probably true, especially for the later stages of the Samnite Wars that ended just before Pyrrhus' invasion. Dates were only put to them much later, of course, and many depended on 'synchronism' with events in Greek history. Rome apparently ejected its tyrants around the same date Athens expelled hers; the century-long grudge match with Veii in the fifth century looks suspiciously like the long and contemporaneous rivalry between Athens and Sparta; even the Gallic invasion sets Romans alongside Greeks as victims of temple-pillaging northerners, or else might be paralleled by the Persian sack of Athens. How much massaging was necessary to give Rome a *proper* past? How far were events telescoped or compressed to bring out the correspondences? What was omitted because it was useless to the narrative being created, or even contradicted it?

A second problem is that many stories seem to have clear moral ends. Time and again, individual Romans put the survival of the city ahead of their own interests. Horatius fought off Lars Porsenna's invading army in a series of single combats while the bridge over the Tiber was cut down behind him. Camillus, exiled by Rome, refused to lead an enemy army against his ungrateful homeland. The epic poet Ennius summed up the ideology in the line:

The Roman state depends on its ancient customs and heroes.[16]

Or consider how repeated power struggles between aristocratic patricians and the excluded masses (the *plebs*)—social conflicts of a kind quite common in the archaic Mediterranean—are again and again resolved by compromise and constitutional innovations. Stories of self-sacrifice and affirmations of social solidarity were comforting ideals for an age in which civil conflict was tearing the state apart. But they are hardly reliable history, any more than the stereotypes such as Livy's portrayal of Roman women either as victims of tyranny or inspirations to their menfolk or both. All wars, naturally, were just wars, and the gods were always on Rome's side.

Ways and Means

There are hints that, even at the very beginning of the Republic, Rome was already a powerful state. Polybius described three treaties, each made between Rome and Carthage in the period before the Pyrrhic War.[17] The earliest, written in archaic Latin, was dated to the first year of the free Republic. Its terms seem sufficiently anachronistic by Polybius' day to be genuinely ancient, and he went to some lengths to try to explain them. In the treaty the Romans promise to respect Carthaginian territories in Sicily, Sardinia, and Africa and not to deliberately sail beyond 'the Fair Promontory' (probably Cap Farina just north of Carthage). The Carthaginians on their side promised not to intervene in Latium, either in the cities Rome controlled or in those she did not. Intervention of that kind was a realistic prospect. Three gold tablets from the Etruscan port city of Pyrgi dating to about the same time record dedications in both Etruscan and Punic to the goddess the Carthaginians called Astarte and the Etruscan ruler of Caere, Uni. Other provisions of this treaty provided for trade. Perhaps most significantly of all, Rome treated on behalf of her allies as well as herself. The treaty, in other words, evokes a half-forgotten world of hegemonic politics and spheres of influence, a world in which larger communities dominated their smaller neighbours without absorbing them into formal empires, all at the end of the sixth century BC. We could compare the kind of leadership exercised by Carthage over other Punic cities, some of them named in the second of the three treaties, or Spartan leadership of the Peloponnese in the fifth century, and Athenian control of the islands and coasts of the Aegean only a little later. Marseilles in southern Gaul, Syracuse in Sicily, and Tarentum in southern Italy all acquired regional influence of this kind. The history of the fifth and fourth centuries may be maddeningly obscure, but by the time Pyrrhus crossed the Adriatic in 280 at the invitation of the Tarentines, Rome had joined this small group of leading cities. The big question is how Rome managed to get to this point, given the small scale of her fifth-century wars within Latium and its adjacent districts.

Rome's comparative advantage over its rivals was partly institutional; geopolitics played a part; and so did the level of manpower available at least by the early fourth century when those spectacular walls were built. Romans enjoyed no technological edge over their opponents, not even in the field of warfare. But frequent campaigning meant that Roman citizen armies eventually became more experienced than those of some of their opponents. The Romans were probably not unusually militaristic. The celebrations of warriors in funerary art throughout central Italy, as well as those treaties, make it clear that it was not at all unusual for societies to be warlike. Short wars between neighbouring peoples were, in fact, probably more or less the norm, a competition for booty, prisoners, and prestige. It may be that many of the early wars remembered in Roman tradition consisted of raids and counter-raids of this kind.[18]

The difference came when Romans began to impose on their defeated opponents permanent obligations. During the fourth century Romans began to institutionalize their position as the pre-eminent city of Latium to create a federation of states with Rome at its heart. The innermost circle comprised the Latins, citizens of those communities with whom Romans enjoyed certain reciprocal rights, such as intermarriage and trade. Beyond them were other allies, the *socii*.

Formally, Rome's allies were communities, not individuals, and to begin with most were bound to Rome by permanent and unequal treaties. Imposing a treaty of this kind almost always followed military victory. Greek cities concluded wars with treaties and then reverted to splendid autonomy. Rome had, it was said, agreed to several limited-term truces with Veii, and its treaties with Carthage imply equality between the parties. But the treaties that created allies were signs of permanent subordination. Allied states retained a separate citizenship and a notional internal autonomy—not that Romans did not intervene when they wished—but they had to supply troops when Rome demanded, and they had very limited independence when it came to relations with other states.

Informally, these treaties between communities were underpinned by connections between their ruling families.[19] The warfare remembered and celebrated by later historians was real enough, but many Italian elites saw the advantage of participating in the Roman project. Family connections and patronage cemented these links. When Rome did expand overseas, Italian elite families benefited from a share in the booty and eventually the trade opportunities offered. In return, they had to deliver the manpower of their local subjects to Rome. That mediating role grew harder as the nature of Roman hegemony changed. After the Hannibalic War those communities that were not regarded as having been loyal to Rome were treated harshly. By the early second century BC, Roman rule had become more direct. One of the earliest surviving decrees of the Senate is a bronze tablet recording restrictions issued in 186 BC on the worship of the god Bacchus. The decree applied throughout Italy. Defeated states also often lost land to Rome. Colonies were created in key strategic locations, like tiny Alba Fucens perched up in the Abruzzi to keep an eye on the neighbouring tribes.[20] Other settlers were simply given conquered land to farm in return for paying a rent to the state. Roman control of Italy generated an ever wider distribution of public land and settlers, and an increased sense of the prerogatives of power.

When a Roman army marched out against Samnites or Tarentines, Epirots or Gauls, its general commanded an army composed of citizens and allies.[21] When consuls levied their citizen armies, each allied community was sent orders to provide its own quota of troops. Allied detachments were commanded by their own leaders and brigaded alongside the Roman forces. Those leaders were drawn from the same sort of propertied classes as ruled Rome: Romans tended to support those classes in allied communities, siding with Greek oligarchs against democrats, and Etruscan nobles against their serfs.[22] The ruling classes of Italian cities had much in common with each other, and a community of interest must also have consolidated Roman power. Athens's short-lived empire had foundered in part on the promotion of democracy among its lesser allies, and on strengthening the ideology of citizenship; Roman hegemony, by contrast, always stressed class solidarity among the elites. The seeds of an aristocratic empire had been sown. Rome exacted no regular taxes or any tribute in kind from its allies: they generally received a share of booty from victorious campaigns, and in some colonial foundations some of the Latins even received grants of land. Perhaps Roman rule did not seem entirely oppressive to members of the propertied classes, more like a movement that benefited those drawn into it.

Pyrrhus and History

King Pyrrhus (see Figure 3) had ruled the tiny Balkan kingdom of the Molossians since 306 BC. Macedon had expanded on the margins of the Greek world to produce Alexander, who died in 323 BC master of the Persian Empire and overlord of most of the Greek world. Pyrrhus' kingdom was on the margins of Macedonia, and he spent most of his career trying to imitate his great neighbour and predecessor. Epirus corresponds roughly to what is now north-west Greece. It looks westwards, towards the Adriatic, and beyond it to that part of southern Italy known as Magna Graecia (Greater Greece) because of the wealth accumulated there by the Greek cities founded in the archaic period. The Greeks of southern Italy and Sicily had had their own complex history through the archaic and classical periods, fighting wars between each other and against and alongside Etruscans and Carthaginians. During the fifth century some of the Greek cities immediately south of Rome were captured and taken over by peoples from the Italian interior. Lucanians took control of Poseidonia around 390 and ruled it for just over a century before Rome took control in 273 and made it into the Latin colony of Paestum. Majestic archaic Greek temples, Lucanian tombs, and a model Roman city stand side by side today.

But in the far south of the peninsula, and in Sicily, the larger Greek cities were more successful. If Rome and Carthage were hegemonic powers, then so were Greek Syracuse and Tarentum. It was Tarentum which called in Pyrrhus. This was nothing new for them. They had had an alliance with one of Pyrrhus' predecessors and had tried to get help from Sparta and others in recent years. The novelty was the enemy, Rome, which in 284 had founded a colony on the Adriatic at Sena Gallica. For Rome, this was an extension of their wars in the Apennines: the name of the colony shows they had their eyes on the Gallic tribes of the Marche and the Po Valley. But the Tarentines were right that the Romans had more grandiose ambitions. Two years later they intervened in the affairs of Rhegium, on the toe of Italy,

Fig. 3. A bust of Pyrrhus, King of Epirus, Roman copy after a Greek original, from the Villa of the Papyri, Ercolano (ancient Herculaneum), Campania Region, Italy

and of Tarentum's neighbour Thurii, which led to direct conflict. No one can have been in any doubt that Rome was extending its hegemony in all directions. Tarentum was next.

Pyrrhus' expedition into southern Italy hardly changed the world. He arrived in 281 and inflicted a couple of defeats on the Romans. He might have won the battles, but the cost was so high that it has given us the phrase a 'Pyrrhic victory'. He was then invited to Sicily to fight Carthage on behalf of Greek cities there, which he did with less success. Returning to Italy, he was defeated by a Punic fleet and then fought another, less conclusive battle with a Roman army. Those reverses prompted him to return to Epirus in 275. Pyrrhus was no Alexander. Three years later he was dead, killed in a botched attempt to wrest control of the Greek city of Argos from Macedon. The Romans took Tarentum the same year. The significance of the Pyrrhic War, however, was that it put Rome on the Greek map. From this point on, Rome has proper history. One of the Greeks who wrote an account of Rome's war with Pyrrhus was his contemporary Timaeus, a native of Taormina in Sicily, who spent fifty years in exile in Athens writing the first connected history of the western Mediterranean. That work is lost, but it has left traces in the histories and geographies composed by Greeks and Romans over the following centuries. Roman history was only a minor part of his output. But so little else had been written that it was a vital source even for the first Roman to write history, Fabius Pictor, and both directly and indirectly also for Polybius, the Greek historian who wrote a continuation during his own exile in Rome. Thanks to Timaeus and his continuators it is possible, from the third century on at least, to write detailed political history with secure chronology. Thanks to Pyrrhus, the scale of Roman hegemony was now clear across the Mediterranean. Greek cities began to send embassies to Rome from the early second century. Among them were appeals for military help, as Greek cities and Balkan peoples asked the Romans to cross the Adriatic in the opposite direction to that of Pyrrhus.

Further Reading

Archaeological understanding of the appearance of cities and states in the early last millennium BC is progressing rapidly thanks not only to new evidence but also to advances in the way we understand it. The state of the question is presented in a series of essays edited by Robin Osborne and Barry Cunliffe and entitled *Mediterranean Urbanization 800–600 BC*. On the immediate vicinity of Rome, see Christopher Smith's *Early Rome and Latium* (Oxford, 1996). Excellent introductions to the Etruscans are provided by Graeme Barker and Tom Rasmussen, *The Etruscans* (Oxford, 1998) and Christopher Smith, *The Etruscans: A Very Short Introduction* (Oxford, 2014). Guy Bradley, Elena Isayev, and Corinna Riva's *Ancient Italy* (Exeter, 2007) gives a good sense of the wider Italian world into which Rome expanded. An important new account of how that expansion happened is offered by Nicola Terrenato, *The Early Roman Expansion into Italy* (Cambridge 2019).

Tim Cornell's *The Beginnings of Rome* (London, 1995) is the standard introduction to early Roman history. Mario Torelli's *Studies in the Romanization of Italy* (Edmonton, AB, 1995) gives an excellent sense of how archaeological and historical evidence can be effectively combined in the study of this period.

The earliest stages of Roman imperialism are the subject of William Harris's *War and Imperialism in Republican Rome 327–70 BC* (Oxford, 1979) and of several chapters of John Rich and Graham Shipley's *War and Society in the Roman World* (London, 1993). Jacques Heurgon's *The Rise of Rome to 264 BC* (London, 1973) remains full of interesting insights. Jean-Michel David's *Roman Conquest of Italy* (Oxford, 1996) tells the whole story up to the end of the Republic.

IMPERIAL ECOLOGY

Next comes the earth, that one part of nature that for her many gifts to us
we honour with the name of Mother. She is our realm, as the sky belongs
to the gods. She welcomes us when we are born, nurtures us as we grow,
and when we are adults sustains us always.

(Pliny, *Natural History* 2.154)

From its foundation to the Arab conquests the story of Rome was played
out over a millennium and a half. At first expansion was so slow that few
outside Italy can have noticed it. But by the reign of Augustus the empire was bounded by the Atlantic to the west and the Sahara to the south,
its northern frontier bisected temperate Europe, and its eastern edge was
extended deep into western Asia. There the frontiers more or less rested
until disintegration began at the end of the fourth century, once again slow
at first but eventually collapsing into the Aegean world of seventh-cen-
tury Byzantium. That fifty-generation tale of rise and fall is an epic one in
human terms.

Geologically, however, a millennium and a half is the blink of an eye.
The Roman Empire was a bubble that grew on the surface of the pond and
then burst. During this time the physical environment of the Roman world
hardly changed. New crops and methods of agriculture spread, but they had
only a little impact on the landscapes Rome ruled over. Had Romulus been

transported seven centuries forward at his death (rather than taken up into heaven) he might well have been amazed at what his heirs had achieved, but he would not have been puzzled at how they did it. All this is hard to imagine today, living as we do at the end of two centuries of accelerating technological change, change that is having major impacts on the entire biosphere and moves now at a pace hard to adjust to psychologically even in our own brief lifetimes. This chapter explores the long-term stability of the ancient world and the slow secular changes against which the whole of Rome's imperial story was played out.

The Environment in Classical Antiquity

Let us begin with the visible. The coastline of the Mediterranean 3,000 years ago was hardly different from what it is today. Slight changes can be spotted around the mouths of the larger rivers: the harbour of Ephesus is now around six kilometres (3.7 miles) from the coast, and half of Ostia, the port of Rome, has been washed away. Just off Pozzuoli in the Bay of Naples, a series of luxurious villas lie just a few metres under water. So does the great harbour of Alexandria. But these are marginal changes in highly susceptible locations. Sea levels did begin to rise gradually at the end of antiquity, but the only regions where this had a marked impact were low-lying areas such as the Fenland of eastern England and the areas around the Rhine mouth in the Netherlands, where late antique villages are built on low mounds, *terpen*, for protection against floods. Unsurprisingly, the ancients had no sense of geological time or incremental environmental change. There was almost no ancient science of seismology, and the explanations suggested for earthquakes were underground counterparts of those developed for meteorology.[1] A few writers were so committed to this steady-state idea of the world that they believed marble would, eventually, grow back from where it had been quarried.[2] Their world was eternal; the gods had wandered in the same forests and mountains they knew.

In reality the Mediterranean is shrinking, as the African tectonic plate moves northwards. But this is happening very slowly. Tectonic movement today generates volcanism in Sicily, the Lipari Islands, and Campania, and earthquakes in central Italy, central and southern Greece, and western Turkey. These are the same places that in the ancient Mediterranean world were most susceptible to earthquakes. Poseidon the Earthshaker had a major sanctuary at the Isthmus of Corinth, not far from the epicentre of a terrible earthquake in 1981. The cities of what is now Aegean Turkey received five years' remission of tribute in AD 17 from the Emperor Tiberius to help them rebuild after a devastating earthquake. A series of quakes in central Italy in the middle of the first century AD perhaps inspired Seneca to write the first surviving discussion of them, in the sixth book of his *Natural Questions*. An undersea earthquake in AD 365 triggered a tsunami that devastated cities on Crete and in southern Greece and did damage as far away as Alexandria. As today most quakes were localized and small scale.

The Roman period experienced no cataclysmic volcanic eruptions that can be compared to those of Santorini in the second millennium BC or Krakatoa in the late nineteenth century AD. There are extinct volcanoes in some other parts of the Roman world—north and south of the city of Rome, for example, in central France, and in southern Scotland—but the ancients had no memory of their eruptions. Etna, into which the philosopher Empedocles reputedly threw himself, Vesuvius, which buried Pompeii and Herculaneum, and Santorini are all still active today; they remain the most spectacular volcanoes of the Mediterranean world. There were, however, spectacular volcanic events elsewhere in the world during this period. Because major eruptions have a planet-wide impact on global temperatures and weather systems, it is likely that Mediterranean populations did feel their effects in the form of years of unusual drought or floods and years when crop yields were very low.[3]

Climate history more generally is the subject of much current research. In very broad terms, the ancient Mediterranean climate was similar to the one we know today.[4] We live within the same interglacial period as the Romans, the Holocene, which began around 12,000 years ago with the retreat of the European glaciers and the northward expansion of the Sahara Desert. As the region warmed, there were consequent movements of plant and animal species. Such movements are slow; in botanical terms the Mediterranean can be considered as still in postglacial recovery, and not all its native species of plants are yet well adapted to the current climate. Around 6,000 years ago the Mediterranean basin became significantly warmer, establishing today's pattern of mild wet winters and warm dry summers. 'Mild' means no long freezes which kill many species of tree and plant. 'Dry' means the Mediterranean as a whole was, and remains, an arid environment. There was never sufficient rainfall to support either dense forests or the grasslands on which herds of ruminants such as cattle, horses, and bison depend. Some parts of the Mediterranean world are exposed to droughts severe enough to cause many crops, including wheat, to fail as often as one year in four. Droughts of that kind are not predictable and have knock-on effects on species that depend on susceptible crops. Humans who farm are among such species. Classical civilization was built in the shadow of scarcity and risk.[5]

The Roman Empire originated in the Mediterranean basin. But from the end of the last century BC, it had expanded into adjacent ecological zones. The climate changed most dramatically as one went north or south. This ecological gradient had economic consequences, since many of the central components of the polite culture adopted by local elite members across the empire remained Mediterranean in character. Wine was the alcoholic drink of choice, even where it was easier to produce beer. In the early first century AD some Mediterranean producers grew rich producing wine for export until grape varieties were developed that could survive in the Rhineland and even southern Britain. Olives could not (and still cannot) be cultivated in regions susceptible to frost. Yet olive oil was essential not only for cooking but also as fuel for lamps and for use in Roman bathing, where it was rubbed onto the skin and then scraped off along with any dirt. Olive oil was consequently traded northwards in great quantities.[6] The southern half of the Mediterranean is notably warmer. From the late second century BC, great quantities of grain were being exported from modern-day Tunisia, Sicily, and Egypt to cities in the northern half of the Mediterranean.[7] By the early first century AD olive oil production had also increased in southern Spain and various parts of North Africa.[8] North of the Mediterranean basin, temperate Europe had harsher winters and much more plentiful rainfall. That made it a much better area for raising large domesticates, especially horses and cattle. Rome's European provinces came to supply much of her cavalry. The accumulating evidence of animal bones found on Roman period sites also shows much more beef eaten north of the Alps, with sheep and goat most evident in the assemblages from sites in the more arid south and east of the empire.[9] Studies of faunal material (bones), of seeds and other biofacts, and of container amphorae all also show how the most powerful and privileged members of Roman society—local aristocrats and soldiers for the main part—were able to consume more or less what they liked wherever they were. The main limit on exchange across these sharp ecological contrasts (ecotones) was the cost of transport. Even the journey to north Italy made olive oil so expensive, according to St Augustine, who was born and brought up in North Africa, that it was too expensive to burn lights all night long. Traffic beyond the Mediterranean basin was blocked at several points by mountain ranges. A few cities located at the southern terminals of north–south river valleys or mountain passes grew rich on trade: Aquileia and Aosta in Italy, Arles and Narbonne in southern France still impress visitors with their Roman period monuments.

Yet the climate of Holocene Europe has not been completely stable. To make it more complicated, there are different kinds of instability. Volcanic eruptions can create acute but short-term changes in global temperatures. An explosion in 1815 on Mount Tambora in Indonesia threw so much material into the atmosphere that global temperatures plummeted, which created a 'year without a summer' that led to crop failures in Europe. It seems likely that 'volcanic forcing' explains years of very low rainfall in the regions feeding the Nile in the last centuries BC and that an eruption of the Okmok volcano in Alaska had a devastating effect on world climate in the 40s BC. Terrifying for those who live through them, events like this have not had lasting effects on the climate, at least not in the last twenty thousand years or so.

But alongside these catastrophic effects there have been some longer-term fluctuations in temperature. So, a relatively warm period in the Middle Ages was followed by the Little Ice Age which ran from 1300 to 1800 and was at its coldest at the end of the seventeenth century. Mean temperatures were perhaps a degree or more below those today, but this was enough to make the Thames freeze over on a regular basis. A decade ago there was a growing consensus that there was a Roman Warm Period, one that perhaps raised the mean temperature as much as two degrees above that of today.[10] The proposed peak was around 150 AD, with temperatures dipping until they began to rise again at the start of the Medieval Warm Period, perhaps around 900 AD. There seemed to be a rough correlation between higher global temperatures and the period of the empire's expansion and prosperity, and between a cooler period and the political troubles of late antiquity. Perhaps, it seemed, warmer weather improved agricultural yields and enabled imperial expansion, and perhaps too a deterioration in conditions may have put pressure on the empire and on its neighbours at the end of antiquity.

Further research has made this picture both more precise and more complicated.[11] It makes use of data from lake sediments, from Greenland ice cores, from tree rings, from the movement of glaciers, from the build-up of speleothems in caves and also proxy data for variations in solar activity. It combines all this with archaeobotanical data (especially pollen diagrammes) and historical records. The last are the most problematic, since many changes were too slow to be noticed by ancient observers, and their records lack the quantitative precision we are used to today. There is no longer any doubt that global climate did fluctuate during the long period in which Rome's empire expanded and then contracted. But the thesis of a simple correlation between global temperatures and imperial success now looks too simplistic. For one thing, it was not only temperature that changed, but also the stability of the climate. Two factors that disrupt the earth's climatic regimes are volcanic activity (mentioned already) and unusual solar activity. It seems neither was very severe during the first half of the first millennium AD compared with the centuries that followed. Secondly, warming did happen, but it was more complicated than a simple pattern of rise and fall. Different indicators provide different chronologies of the process. Crucially, the impact of any global change was not the same everywhere. This raises one of the big problems in climate history. The complexity of the world's weather systems means that the impact of global changes varies enormously from one area to another. For example, there were periods in the later Roman Empire when some areas became wetter, and others drier. These changes affected the likelihood of local droughts and patterns of rainfall in the catchment areas of great river systems such as the Nile. Different agricultural systems also fared differently. Farmers dependent on river floods were affected differently from those relying on rainfall. Herders on the steppe might be disrupted from their usual circuits. Some crops were more sensitive than others to temperature changes. Some communities lived closer to the edge than others.

None of this means that we should give up on climate history or on correlating it with political events. The latest surveys do suggest a case can be made that periods of stable warm climate played some part in enabling Roman expansion, and that periods of instability may have caused problems for it. But the relationships between temperature, rainfall, demography, and economics need to be worked out on a regional scale. Easy correlations between the rise and fall of temperatures and of empires are no longer very convincing. Human actions and reactions also need to be factored into environmental change, not just the often catastrophic results of mining and deforestation, but also the more everyday practices of farming and water management which varied from one culture to the next.

A World of Farmers

Unlike many early modern conquerors, the Romans expanded into worlds that were ecologically and economically familiar. Agriculture was an invention of the Holocene, one made independently on at least half a dozen occasions, around the globe. Each invention was based on different combinations of crops—cultigens—that could together supply the carbohydrate needs of humans and some of their protein. Societies that experienced a Neolithic revolution were utterly different from those that had preceded them. Population levels rose, permanent settlements were almost always necessary, and in these growing villages and cities new social discipline was required. As Neolithic societies achieved a new order, so too did Neolithic landscapes. Areas suitable for agriculture were cleared, with hunting restricted to marginal territories. Meat eating began to decline. Populations who lived on high-carbohydrate diets in closer than ever proximity to each other were less healthy than their ancestors. The domestication of successive animals improved the protein supply, but brought more diseases. Our leap down the food chain came at a heavy price, but once population levels had risen, it was in effect irreversible.[12]

The nearest farming revolution to the Mediterranean world was also the earliest on the planet. It began around 7000 BC in the Near East in what is sometimes called the Fertile Crescent. This broad band of territory arcs from Jordan up through Syria and down through modern Iraq to the Persian Gulf, skirting the northern desert of the Arabian Peninsula. Successive innovations had their origins in this region and in its surrounding upland margins, especially in Anatolia. The move from gathering to cultivating wild crops was followed by the domestication of animals first for food and later for hides, wool, milk, and traction. Arable farming moved across Europe at the rate of about 25 kilometres (15 miles) a generation, reaching the Atlantic by 3000 BC. The first farmers used tools of flint or obsidian with handles of wood and bone, and they had no traction animals. Forests were hard to clear with stone axes, and wooden scratch ploughs (*ards*) were most effective on lighter soils. The main crops farmed were husked varieties of wheat, emmer, and einkorn, and in the most arid regions barley. Grains were supplemented in their diets by pulses and some green vegetables. Hunting and fishing made up a tiny proportion of most people's nutrition. Agriculture spread more rapidly in the Mediterranean world than in temperate Europe for two reasons. First, communications were easier across the islands and coastal settlements of the inland sea than through the forests and mountains of Europe. Second, the aridity of the Fertile Crescent meant the ecological distance was less to the dry Mediterranean than to colder and wetter regions. These two factors together explain why population growth, cities, and states came to Mediterranean Europe before they reached the continental interior. But the Mediterranean only had a head start. Once northern populations had mastered the techniques of farming and developed ways to unlock the much greater potential of Europe's deeper soils and more abundant and more dependable rainfall, the Mediterranean would lose its advantage. Today southern Europe is the poorer half of the continent, the recipient of subsidies provided by richer economies of the north. That shift took place in the Middle Ages. Classical antiquity is very largely the history of the period in which the Mediterranean kept ahead of temperate Europe in this respect.

The great story of the Mediterranean Holocene is one of successive movements from east to west.[13] New cultigens, domesticated animals, technologies, and social forms all had their origins south or east of the Mediterranean world, around the Black Sea, in Anatolia, Egypt, and Mesopotamia. Technologies and artistic forms in particular were adapted and put to new uses in the Mediterranean world. Greek statuary is unthinkable without Egypt, but the two could never be confused, and images of sphinxes or heroes fighting lions acquired new resonance in cult and myth. Greek and Roman writers themselves treated the Mediterranean as the normal centre of the world. The farther one went away from it, the stranger were the peoples and plants and animals one encountered. But in reality the Romans' *orbis terrarum* was just one of several peripheries to the continental mass of Eurasia and Africa.[14] The Old World, in ecological and civilizational terms, has always had a common history within which Mediterranean and European history has always been a secondary development.

The reasons are fundamental. Plant and animal species move most easily within the same latitudes, where mean temperatures are broadly similar. Migrations of species—both the recolonization of Europe after the glaciers retreated and the spread of the cultigens and domesticated animal species engineered by the first farmers—took place most easily between similar environments. The expansion of the Sahara accentuated this effect, creating a barrier between the Mediterranean and the rest of Africa. Ecologically, the Mediterranean world is a long corridor leading westwards out of western Asia. The climate becomes significantly wetter farther west owing to the proximity of the Atlantic. Within the Mediterranean this is expressed in the differences in rainfall between the wetter west-facing coasts of Italy, Greece, and Turkey, and their more arid east-facing coasts. The farther west along the corridor a species moved, the greater the contrast with the ecology within which it had originated. It is as if the corridor was on a gradient, sloping upwards, so making westward progress increasingly difficult.

Domesticated animals first appeared in Europe in the third millennium BC and again spread westwards. The origins of domestication were again mostly in the Near East, and the main domesticates were widespread by the start of the last millennium BC. Oxen and horses provided traction. Cattle, sheep, goats, and pigs provided meat. Cattle, sheep, and goats might be milked. Sheep and goats provided wool. All might provide bone and leather, and in sophisticated agricultural regimes manure as well. By the end of the second millennium BC, humans were using one or another variation of this complex of cultigens and domesticates across Europe and the Mediterranean. Geese had been domesticated in ancient Egypt. Chickens, descended from jungle fowl in the Far East, appeared sometime in the middle of the last millennium. (There are no chickens in the *Iliad*, but Socrates' last words were that he owed a cockerel to the god Asclepius.) Camels, domesticated much earlier in the Arabian peninsula, also moved progressively farther west during the last millennium BC. Rabbits were confined to the Iberian peninsula until the turn of the millennium. Small animals like chickens and rabbits might seem insignificant, but they were valuable, as they might be bred fast and fed cheaply. In a world without refrigerators, small animals also posed fewer meat storage problems.

The main technological innovations in agriculture also preceded Rome. Most important was metallurgy, also invented in the east. Gold was easiest to extract, but was nearly useless for making tools. Copper and then bronze working began in the Near East in the middle of the fourth millennium BC. What really made the difference to agriculture was the appearance of abundant iron tools, cheaper to produce and harder-wearing than other metals. Ironworking was almost certainly discovered in north-west Anatolia towards the end of the second millennium BC; from there it spread throughout the Old World, reaching the Yangtzee, southern India, and Scandinavia by the middle of the last millennium BC. Iron agricultural tools were especially important in northern Europe, where they made forest clearance and the cultivation of heavy soils much easier. The growth in the availability of iron tools in the middle of the last millennium BC runs parallel with agricultural and demographic expansion in the European interior. Evidence is provided not only by the great size of late Iron Age hillforts and other settlements, but also by the huge armies that began raiding and invading the Mediterranean world from the fourth century BC. Greeks and Roman were terrified by these invasions, but had no real notion of their causes.

The temperate Europe that Julius Caesar and his successors found when they began serious warfare north of the Alps was already tamed. There were no longer any hunter-gatherer populations. Nor was there any primeval forest. Forests had expanded in the early Holocene, following the retreat of the glaciers, but they had mostly been felled by the first farmers. The woodlands that replaced them were created and managed by human activity. Roman poets wrote of northern Europe as utterly savage, a continent of dense forests full of wild beasts. But Roman generals, and the tax collectors that followed in the early empire, will have appreciated the phenomenal agricultural productivity of European landscapes compared with the arid Mediterranean. Forests and game certainly survived, as they do today, but only on the higher ground between cultivated landscapes. Around the Mediterranean there was already the present-day landscape of *garrigue*, a characteristic type of scrubland rather like chaparral, formed of plants that can tolerate the summer heat, alternating with small cleared plains on which cereals might be grown.

Prehistoric agriculture was not limited to the production of grains: woodlands and wetlands were also exploited; salt, vital for preserving meat and fish, was mined, gathered from coastal salt pans, and traded; large herds of livestock were raised, and short-range transhumance was already practised. The range of animal and plant species cultivated by prehistoric societies might seem relatively small, but the impact of farming on the early Holocene fauna was already phenomenal. The top predators which had expanded out of Ice Age refugia into Europe now diminished in number as their prey and habitats were removed. Lions disappeared from Europe and eventually western Asia, while populations of wolves and bears were fragmented. Greek heroes fought with savage beasts that threatened grain-growing lowlands, monsters like the Nemean Lion and the Calydonian Boar. Those myths reveal a world already imagined in terms of a stark opposition between civilization and the wilderness. And the wilderness was in retreat. Over the Iron Age and Roman centuries, smaller domesticated cattle replaced aurochs in much of temperate Europe, and bison and elk were restricted to the far north. Deer retreated into the remnant forests and resurgent woodlands. Hunting became rarer and less exciting. When the Emperor Trajan wanted to hunt game in Italy, he had to climb to the summits of the Abruzzi. The Roman generals who conquered the east were amazed to find Hellenistic kings had, in imitation of the Persian emperors, created reserves in order to preserve animals worthy of a royal hunt. The Persian word was *paradeisos*, which gives us our term 'paradise'. Wilderness had become a scarce commodity, a luxury that needed to be conserved and cultivated. We can easily imagine this today, just as we can easily imagine the rich rewards that would follow Roman possession of the waking giant of temperate Europe.

Ecology and Empire

Imperial expansion since the fifteenth century has often had dire environmental consequences. One reason is that globalizing movements often connected up regions that had been out of contact for long periods. Most dramatic was the Columbian Exchange of plant and animal species that followed European discovery of the Americas and led to extinctions and the catastrophic merging of disease pools, as well as the transformation of Old World diets with the introduction of coffee and chocolate, potatoes, and cane sugar.[15] Then there have been deliberate modifications of colonial ecosystems in modern times, such as the creation of cotton and coffee plantations in the Americas, the introduction of cattle ranching into parts of North and South America, of sheep farming into Australasia, and the transplantation of maize from the New World into Africa. Cash crops often replaced subsistence agriculture, and the needs of distant imperial markets took priority over those of indigenous populations, who were sometimes dispossessed and sometimes conscripted to labour within new agricultural regimes. Slavery notoriously allowed the wholesale transplantation of human populations. There are some prehistoric precedents. Human expansion at the end of the Pleistocene era into first Australia and later Europe and the Americas seems to have led to the extinction of native megafauna, from 2,000 kilogram (two-tonne) giant wombats and three-metre-tall (about 10 feet) kangaroos to the American lion and giant sloths. The settlement of the Pacific Islands and New Zealand was accomplished only because explorers took pigs, chickens, dogs, and various domesticated crops with them in their canoes.

Roman expansion did not have such dramatic ecological effects. The empire expanded within a region, the inhabitants of which used broadly the same domesticated species as themselves. When areas beyond the Mediterranean were eventually incorporated into the empire, this was usually just the latest phase in long histories of contact. As a result, Romans rarely encountered economies or ecologies very different from their own. The environmental changes that Roman expansion brought were, on the whole, more piecemeal and more subtle than those introduced by European empires.

All this marks an important difference between the ecologies of modern and ancient empires. Roman expansion was facilitated by what the conquerors shared with their new subjects. The first tax levied (on Sicily) was a simple tithe of grain, and when armies campaigned in Spain in the second century or Gaul in the first century BC, their local allies were expected to provide food. African Lepcis Magna paid a great indemnity in olive oil, and the Frisians at the Rhine mouth were taxed in hides. Taxation in kind was always an important part of Roman fiscal systems. Yet even when cash was required, provincials could earn it simply by intensifying the production of crops they already grew, since these were the crops Romans already knew and desired. Monocultures and cash crops never squeezed out pre-existing regimes in the Roman period. We know of no disastrous experiments with new crops. The empire expanded into regions that were already productive, and in most areas did no more than stimulate a modest intensification.

The political unification of the Mediterranean has even been seen as simply the latest—political—phase in a much longer story, one that had begun with the spread of farming out from the Near East. It has been suggested that the limits of Roman expansion were set, in some regions at least, by the limits of this Old World agricultural complex. To be sure, there was no ecological frontier dividing Roman from Persian spheres of influence; indeed, that frontier cut through areas in north Syria that in every possible respect—cultural, religious, linguistic, technological, and ecological—formed a unity. Yet Rome's northern frontier at points reached areas where the returns from this style of agriculture do not seem to have been impressive during the Iron Age. Perhaps Roman conquest reached an ecological limit in northern Britain or the Low Countries.[16] Most of the long European frontier ran through rich agricultural land. Where Roman rule did meet real ecological limits was the Atlantic and the Sahara. The empire had successfully gained control of the southern part of that western corridor leading out of the Near East; threats came to it from north and east.

Roman expansion followed agricultural change, and brought with it few new technologies, species, or diseases; consequently, Roman conquest had no cataclysmic ecological impact. But this does not mean that Romans were not positively interested in promoting intensification or that their activities had no significant environmental consequences. One sign of Roman interest is the care they took to learn from the agricultural regimes they incorporated. The only book the Romans took from the libraries of Carthage after the sack of the city in 146 BC was Mago's twenty-eight-book agricultural treatise, which was then translated into Latin. Generals returning from the east brought back new species of plants, including cherry trees. Roman writers of the early empire were actually very well aware of how recently many nuts and fruit crops had been brought to Italy from the east. More than 40 per cent of the plants named in Columella's first-century AD book *On Agriculture* were Greek in origin. The *Natural History* of his near contemporary Pliny the Elder describes in detail the various trees and other crops found in different parts of the empire, and their nutritional and sometimes medical benefits. Medical texts produce a wealth of information about cultivable species. Pliny was just as interested in the plants and animals of the western Mediterranean and even temperate Europe, but it is obvious from his account that the main direction of movement remained east to west.

Roman entrepreneurs not only brought eastern crops to Italy, but also attempted to transplant various Mediterranean species north of the Alps. Apples, pears, cherries, plums, and walnuts were introduced to northern Europe very early on, as were celery, garlic, asparagus, cabbage, and carrots. Chestnut, probably used for wood rather than primarily as a food source, followed a little later. What these trees and vegetables had in common—and what separated them from cereals—is that they required cultivation in gardens or orchards. Arboriculture involved a range of new specialized skills, such as grafting. It also required much greater inputs of energy and time in return for greater calorific and financial returns per hectare. The northward progress of these crops—like that of the vine—reflects the spread of Mediterranean taste, as well as of agricultural knowledge. Carbonized remains of these crops appear on settlement sites alongside those of others that could not be domesticated north of the Alps, such as figs, chickpeas, pistachios, almonds, pine nuts, and melons. The expansion of arboriculture and gardening was also closely linked to urbanization. Not only is it labour-intensive but it also relies on levels of consumer demand most easily found where populations are densely packed and relatively prosperous. It additionally offers vital supplements to a diet high in carbohydrates, providing sugar, protein, and vitamins. It was urban populations that had the greatest needs of these supplements.[17] It is no accident we know most about it from Roman Egypt and the environs of Rome, the most urbanized parts of the ancient world.

More generally, the spread of arboriculture allows us to observe Romans as enthusiastic adopters of new cultigens. Profit and the desire for a wider range of tastes were no doubt key motivators. But there was a sound ecological logic too. The principal weakness of the earliest agricultural regimes in all parts of the world was the small number of cultigens on which each depended. Dependence on a single crop is enormously risky, and diversification provided a key buffer against crop failure. Hence the early importance of pulses, and the steady growth of the variety of grains cultivated, naked wheats joining emmer and einkorn alongside spelt and barley, and rye, oats, and millet being grown in some regions. The wider range of cereals not only provided better matches for particular local microclimates. Barley was less favoured as a food but could resist drought, millet could be grown over the summer, and chestnuts and other nuts provided a key protein source when crops failed, or fodder for pigs when they did not. The range of cultigens increased over time.

Other ecological niches were subjected to the same process of intensification: wetlands and mountains, woodlands and the pre-desert. Roman construction technology allowed a few innovations here, most notably in the imperial period. Injections of capital are difficult to document, but they must lie behind some agricultural development, such as the construction of massive sheep pens on the plain of the Crau in south-east France, and the development of industrial-scale production of fish sauces. A small amount of irrigation farming was introduced, a spin-off of the aqueducts bringing water from highland areas down to the cities of the plain.[18] Terraces were constructed across seasonal river courses in the Libyan pre-desert to catch floodwater. Drainage of marshes took place across the empire from central Italy to the English Fenland. Hydraulic engineering allowed for advances in fish farming. Establishments dedicated to salting and pickling fish appeared wherever catches were abundant, including on both sides of the straits of Gibraltar, up the Atlantic coasts of Spain and Gaul. The processing, storage, and transportation of agricultural produce were in general improved. Large mills driven by water, animals, and slave labour supplemented hand mills, and large-scale olive presses were constructed.[19] Advances in granary construction and harbour installations went hand in hand with the manufacture of earthenware containers and ships better adapted to the transport of bulky produce. Road infrastructure was improved, perhaps first for military reasons, but others benefited too. Closely allied to this was increased production in the most common urban manufacturing sectors, such as textiles.[20]

A different form of intensification is evident in stock raising. The scale of sheep farming increased in several parts of the empire, including Italy and south-east Gaul, where very large flocks clearly catered to demand from outside the region. There were highly successful efforts made to increase the size of the main meat-producing domesticates; the growth of cattle of various breeds is now well documented from faunal remains in Italy. North of the Alps it occurred so rapidly that it seems almost certain that new breeds were introduced. This reversed a long trend in Europe towards smaller and smaller animals, showing very clearly the impact of new priorities and techniques.

The cumulative impact of these improvements was economically significant. Appreciating them helps us understand how the Roman Empire sustained, in such an unpromising environment as the Mediterranean basin, a ratio of consumers to producers that rose by the early third century from one to ten to three to ten in some regions. City life brought a demand for bread instead of porridge and for a more varied diet. The archaeologically visible result was a proliferation of bakeries and food markets, *macella*, that sold fresh meat, vegetables, and dairy products. Improved communications and the muscle of civic and imperial authorities and of landlords made such a diet possible for a minority. When the cities (and so their aggregate demand) shrank, and when authorities could no longer maintain roads, aqueducts, and the like, rural economies shifted back to a more local scale.

The Roman urban boom did have some negative environmental impacts. All intensification carries a risk of decreasing biodiversity and introducing new strains on ecosystems. Exploring these impacts is a growing field of research. After much debate it is now clear that the urban appetite for both firewood and timber affected some regions severely. Timber supplies in particular came under pressure, especially forests that provided large timbers needed in monumental construction and for shipbuilding. Emperors were already making some efforts to preserve their access to key forests.[21] Mining for metals generated levels of heavy-metal pollution that would not be reached again until the Industrial Revolution. While this did not create general conditions of air pollution on a modern scale, the toxicity of some ancient mining communities is only now coming to light.[22]

Further Reading

The most influential environmentally organized account of antiquity is Peregrine Horden and Nicholas Purcell's *The Corrupting Sea: A Study of Mediterranean History* (Oxford, 2000), which has already prompted many responses, some of which are gathered in William Harris's *Rethinking the Mediterranean* (Oxford, 2005). Equally innovative is Robert Sallares's *The Ecology of the Ancient Greek World* (London, 1991). Conditions on the steppe are discussed in Roger Batty's *Rome and the Nomads* (Oxford, 2007). Brent Shaw's essays on North Africa are collected in *Environment and Society in Roman North Africa* (Aldershot, 1995). No environmentally oriented account of Roman temperate Europe has yet been produced, but there is much of relevance in Chris Wickham's *Framing the Early Middle Ages* (Oxford, 2005). Two very well-written introductions to the prehistoric background are Tim Champion et al., *Prehistoric Europe* (London, 1984) and Graeme Barker's *Prehistoric Farming in Europe* (Cambridge, 1985).

One of the most active areas of research since the first edition of this book has been the question of climate change. Kyle Harper's bold *The Fate of Rome: Climate, Disease and the End of an Empire* (Princeton, NJ, 2017) is a must-read. Some of the new techniques being used are foregrounded in a collection edited by Walter Scheidel entitled *The Science of Roman History. Biology, Climate and the Future of the Past* (Princeton, NJ, 2018). Expect more in the next few years.

The growing realization of quite how precarious conditions could be in parts of the ancient Mediterranean is relatively recent. A pioneering collection of answers to the question of how ancient farmers managed was Paul Halstead and John O'Shea's *Bad Year Economics* (Cambridge, 1989). On the means through which classical civilization was sustained in the face of these stresses the fundamental work is Peter Garnsey's *Famine and Food Supply in the Greco-Roman World* (Cambridge, 1988). I have explored some of the implications of this work in *The Life and Death of Ancient Cities: A Natural History* (Oxford 2020).

The impact of Roman agriculture and especially of mining on the environment is another topic of current debate. A good starting point is the collection edited by Graham Shipley and John Salmon, *Human Landscapes in Classical Antiquity* (London, 1996). William Harris' collection *The Ancient Mediterranean Environment between Science and History* (Leiden 2013) includes new research on deforestation, droughts, and much else.

KEY DATES IN CHAPTER V

272 BC   Rome defeats Tarentum, the major Greek city of southern Italy, just three years after the departure of Pyrrhus

264–241 BC   The First Punic War results in the defeat of Carthage and Rome's first overseas province, Sicily

225 BC   The battle of Telamon marks the defeat of the Gauls of northern Italy. Conquest and colonization of the area resumed after the defeat of Hannibal

218–201 BC   The Second Punic War, during which Hannibal invades Italy and remains there until 203

216 BC   The battle of Cannae, Rome's most serious defeat at the hands of Hannibal

213–211 BC   Siege and capture of Syracuse by Marcellus

202 BC   Battle of Zama. Scipio defeats Hannibal just outside Carthage

197 BC   King Philip V of Macedon defeated at the battle of Cynoscephalae. The next year Flamininus declares the freedom of the Greeks

193–188 BC   War between Rome and Antiochus III of Syria. Antiochus defeated first at Thermopylae and then Magnesia, and in the Treaty of Apamea in 188 renounces all Seleucid claims to Asia Minor

189 BC   Manlius Vulso campaigns against the Galatians in central Anatolia

184 BC   The censorship of Cato the Elder

168 BC   King Perseus of Macedon defeated at the battle of Pydna. Macedonian kingdom dismantled

168 BC   The Seleucid king Antiochus IV is forbidden to invade Egypt by an envoy of the Senate

167–150 BC   Polybius of Megalopolis a hostage in Rome, where he becomes a friend of Scipio Africanus and accompanies him on his campaigns

149–146 BC   Third Punic War culminates in the Roman destruction of Carthage

146 BC   Roman destruction of Corinth

133 BC   The capture of the Celtiberian stronghold of Numantia in Spain

133 BC   Attalus III of Pergamum dies, leaving his kingdom to Rome

MEDITERRANEAN HEGEMONY

What man can be so frivolous and lazy that he does not wonder how it has come about, and under what kind of political regime, that almost the entire civilized world has in less than fifty-three years been brought under the sole rule of Rome? These events are unprecedented.

(Polybius, *Histories* 1.1.5)

The Rivals of Rome

The expansion of Roman influence within Italy, related in Chapter III, had been a slow process. But during the century and a half that followed Pyrrhus' invasion, Roman hegemony mushroomed to cover the entire Mediterranean world (Map 2). That did not mean that second-century BC Rome (yet) ruled a well-ordered tributary state, divided into territorial provinces over which were extended imperial systems of law and taxation administered by a colonial bureaucracy. Roman rule remained, in modern terms, both informal and indirect. Supremacy meant simply that Rome no longer had any rival in the region. And Polybius was correct that the rulers of Rome in the mid-second century BC (many of whom he knew well) felt they could issue orders to whomever they wished. This chapter tells how this was achieved.

Map 2. The Mediterranean and its continental hinterlands, showing major mountain ranges and rivers

Black Sea

Istanbul

Crete

Cyprus

e a n   S e a

Rome's unification of the Mediterranean was the culmination of processes of political growth that characterized the last millennium BC.[1] By the third century, Mediterranean politics was dominated by a small number of great powers. At the western end of the Mediterranean, that meant Rome and—until 201 BC —Carthage. Less powerful cities retained their nominal independence in North Africa, Italy, and southern France. Around them were tribal societies of various kinds and sizes. During the third century the biggest cities had either challenged Rome and lost—as had Syracuse and Tarentum—or else were now subordinate allies, like Marseilles and the major cities of Etruria and Campania. East of the Adriatic, the political map was dominated by the kingdoms formed when Alexander's empire fragmented on his death in 323 BC. The big three were Antigonid Macedon, Seleucid Syria, and Ptolemaic Egypt. Around them were a plethora of smaller states. These included Persian successor kingdoms in Anatolia, breakaway Greek kingdoms in Afghanistan and western Turkey, federal leagues of communities in southern and north-west Greece, and a few independent city states, including Sparta, the naval power Rhodes, and a much diminished Athens. This was the Greek—sometimes called the Hellenistic—world into which Rome would expand. No nation could take on and defeat every single city and tribe, and the Romans did not try. Hegemony only required the defeat of all conceivable rivals. That was the process that Polybius claimed had taken less than fifty-three years, from the outbreak of the Second Punic War, that is, until the defeat of Macedon in 167 BC.

Events unfolded at a breakneck pace.[2] The retreat of Pyrrhus, his death, and the fall of Tarentum in 272 removed all Rome's rivals south of the Apennines. Carthage and Rome had allied against Pyrrhus, but their spheres of influence were now so close it is rather surprising it took them until 264 to fall out. The cause was, unsurprisingly, control of the island of Sicily, which lay between them. The First Punic War, fought mainly in naval engagements around the Tyrrhenian Sea (see Picture Box 2), ended in 241 with Rome controlling most of Sicily as a province and the remainder through an alliance with Syracuse. Shortly afterwards Romans seized control of first Sardinia and then Corsica. The Second Punic War broke out in 218, when spheres of influence in Spain clashed. A new Punic empire had been created there, based on New Carthage (Cartagena) and the rich silver mines in the vicinity. Geopolitical considerations suggest the competition for influence in Iberia was as inevitable as it had been in the case of Sicily. Roman historians preferred to believe the real reasons lay in bitter

Picture Box 2 Naval ram from the battle of the Egadi Islands.

This bronze ram was once fixed to the prow of a warship sunk in a naval battle around the Egadi Islands just to the north-west of Sicily. It is most likely that this battle was one that took place in 241 BC at the end of the First Punic War between Rome and Carthage and that it involved hundreds of warships.

A number of these rams (*rostra*) have been recovered from the seabed since 2004, the first by a fisherman and then others as the result of a systematic underwater survey. Because the battlefield lies under 80 metres (260 feet) of water, the survey used a multibeam echo sounder to map the seabed. Anything unusual was then investigated by a remotely operated vehicle (ROV). Trawling had disturbed the sea floor over much of the area, but where there were rocky outcrops, clusters of artefacts survived intact.

The survey recovered many remains of battle, including helmets, amphorae, and anchors, but no warships. In most instances the wood and rigging of ancient shipping has perished, eaten by marine parasites. Many merchant vessels have been discovered from the remains of their cargoes, usually transport amphorae, but sometimes building stone, and

occasionally metals or statuary. Warships carried no such cargoes but
their rams are very distinctive. A number are known from other locations,
including the beautiful Athlit ram from Israel. Captured rams sometimes
formed part of victory monuments, like the column set up in the forum
to commemorate Gaius Duilius, the first Roman to celebrate a triumph
for a naval victory (also over the Carthaginians). Images of rams are also
part of the victory monument that commemorated Octavian's defeat of
Anthony and Cleopatra at Actium.

Their function in battle was to pierce the hulls of enemy ships, and
much of the skill in naval warfare consisted of manoeuvring a vessel to
catch an enemy side on and then build up enough speed from rowing to
drive the ram in. At the Egades Islands the same technology was used by
both sides. Romans had allegedly copied a captured Carthaginian warship earlier in the war. This is demonstrated by elaborate inscriptions cut
into the rams. Most of the surviving ones are in Latin but at least one is
inscribed in Punic. Ships were often captured and reused by the other
side, so we cannot be sure who was in each vessel when it sank, but it is
clear that the two sides were using similar armaments.

Unlike inscriptions from slingshots, which are often insulting and ob-
scene, the inscriptions on the rams are official, recording the name of the
quaestor or quaestors and the word *probavet* or *probaverunt*. Quaestors were
senatorial magistrates who often had some responsibility for financial
matters and *probatio* means something like 'ratification' or 'approval'. In
the context of state expenditure, it usually refers to the process whereby
a magistrate looked at work carried out for the state by contractors and
then signed off on it as satisfactory. Bronze rams were expensive. Each
one required more than 100 kilos (220 pounds) of high-quality bronze,
and they had to be flawless to avoid shattering on impact. The rams
recovered from the seabed testify not only to the savagery of naval warfare, but also to the existence in the mid-third century BC of the process of putting out work to public contractors (*publicani*) that Polybius
describes nearly a century later.

Further Reading

Jonathan R. Prag, 'Bronze rostra from the Egadi Islands off NW Sicily: The Latin
    Inscriptions', *Journal of Roman Archaeology*, 27 (2014): 33–59.
Sebastiano Tusa and Jeffrey Royal, 'The Landscape of the Naval Battle at the
    Egadi Islands (241 BC)', *Journal of Roman Archaeology*, 25 (2012): 7–48.

resentment of Rome fostered by the Barcid dynasty, of whom Hannibal was the most famous member. The conflict begun in Spain was swiftly carried into Italy by Hannibal's audacious march through southern France and across the Alps. Initial victories at Trasimene (217) and Cannae (216) seemed to bring Rome to the brink of disaster, and Hannibal went on to occupy much of the south, detaching Roman allies. But the long-feared assault on Rome never materialized. During the deadlock Rome made advances in other theatres, especially in Spain and Sicily. After more than a decade in southern Italy, Hannibal was eventually forced to return to North Africa to meet a Roman army outside the walls of Carthage itself. Scipio's victory at Zama in 202 ended the war.

Between the First and Second Punic Wars, while the Barcids had been busy in Spain, the Romans had continued to extend their influence in Italy, especially over the Gallic peoples north of the Apennines.[3] Major victories had been won over Gallic armies at Telamon in 225 and Clastidium in 222. As soon as Carthage was defeated, Roman generals resumed this priority. During the 180s a series of colonies were founded north of the Apennines, anchored on the via Aemilia that remains today the main highway down the Po Valley.[4] Roman magistrates led campaigns against either Gauls or Ligurians almost every year until the start of the Third Macedonian War in 168. There were further campaigns in Liguria in the 150s. By the end of the second century the whole area up to the foothills of the Alps was in effect a Roman province. The defeat of Hannibal allowed Rome to increase its influence elsewhere in Italy too. Exemplary punishments were handed out to former Roman allies who had defected to the Punic cause, and much of their territory was confiscated.[5] New Roman colonies were founded on spear-won territory in southern Italy, some imposed on existing cities, and others on greenfield sites. Syracuse had picked the wrong side in the war: her defeat left Sicily entirely under the rule of the Roman praetors. Spain too was now available for conquest, thanks to the campaigns of Scipio which had swept the Carthaginians out of the peninsula. By 197 there were two provinces, one in the south, where local societies were most urbanized and where there were rich supplies of silver, and another in the north-east, the territory of the Iberians. Up until the end of the 170s there were generally four legions in Spain at any one time. Like the campaigns in north Italy, these wars could usually be put on hold when Rome was occupied elsewhere and started up again when other fronts closed down. Major campaigns restarted in Spain in the 150s and culminated in great

wars against the Celtiberians of the interior that only ended with the capture in 133 of their citadel at Numantia. There were other conflicts around
the Alps in this period too, and two short but ferocious wars in the Rhône
Valley in the mid-120s. Not all these campaigns were of Rome's choosing.
There were colonists and settlers to defend in northern Italy, and Rome
faced attacks from the Lusitanians in Spain and the Arverni in Gaul. Nor
was Rome always fighting flat out: there were decades of intensive warfare
and others when fewer troops were in the field each year.[6] All the same, it is
impossible to avoid the impression that Rome was now geared up to more
or less continuous expansion and that the Roman west was always there
when more lucrative or threatening campaigns were not available.

For Rome's greatest rivals during the second century BC were the rich
monarchies of the eastern Mediterranean. It was the humbling of the great
kingdoms of Antigonid Macedonia, Seleucid Syria, and Ptolemaic Egypt
that Polybius had in mind when he wrote of Rome's takeover of the entire
civilized world. Those kingdoms had squabbled since the death of Alexander
the Great for control of the Greek world and its Balkan, Asian, and African
hinterlands. The defeat of Carthage in 202 left Rome free to join—and
end—this competition.

Two years after Scipio's victory over Hannibal at Zama, Roman armies
crossed the Adriatic to take on Philip V, king of Macedon. The reasons remain a matter of controversy. One provocation was a treaty made between
Philip and Hannibal when the latter was still a threat to Rome. Another
may have been earlier attempts by Philip to expand his interests at Roman
expense in the Adriatic, although this was really a minor part of his wider
ambitions in the Balkans and beyond. A number of Greek states were anxious about Philip, and Rome's status as a world power was now clearer than
ever. Embassies came to Rome from Attalus of Pergamum, from Rhodes,
and from Athens, and Roman ambassadors were sent to other parts of
Greece. But the Romans could certainly have safely ignored these requests
and left Macedon alone had they wished for peace. Clearly they did not.
Or at least a majority did not, since the first time the Roman assembly
was asked to approve war it refused. That decision was rapidly reversed.
What arguments were used to persuade the people to assent? Were they
terrorized with stories of Philip's aggression, reminded of his past hostility
as Hannibal's ally, or just encouraged with the hope of more booty? During
the Hannibalic war Rome had fought a brief war with Macedon. In 211
the Romans had made an alliance with the Aetolians of north-west Greece

agreeing that in any joint actions the Aetolians should keep any territory captured, while Rome would take any slaves and booty. Not much had come of this in practice, but perhaps Macedon was still looked on as a good place to plunder. And perhaps a generation of warfare had actually accustomed Rome to conflict, inspiring a new generation of Roman leaders to seek conflicts in which to distinguish themselves, and a new generation of soldiers to seek their fortune in wars of conquest?

Whatever the reasons, the vote for war was won in 200. The next year a Roman army invaded Macedonia, once again in alliance with the Aetolians. The command passed to Titus Quinctius Flamininus in 199. Hard fighting in the Balkans and tough diplomacy gave him the advantage over Philip and made allies of the Achaean League, to which most of the important cities of southern Greece belonged. Philip rejected terms and Flamininus pushed on to defeat him decisively early in 197 at the battle of Cynoscephalae. Rome's new allies the Achaeans were delighted. But the Aetolians felt they had not received all the rewards they deserved. Macedon was left intact, but compelled to stay out of southern Greece, and a heavy indemnity was imposed, as in fact it had been on Carthage. At the Isthmian Games in 196 Flamininus declared the freedom of the Greeks. The language of his proclamation and its location echoed Alexander's proclamations at Corinth in 337 BC, and also much subsequent Hellenistic diplomacy. Romans had evidently learned the diplomatic manners of the Greek east. Their ambitions were different but they were not about to let any other power replace Macedon. The Seleucid king Antiochus III was warned off, and Flamininus fought another campaign against Nabis, the tyrant of Sparta, before in 194 Roman armies returned home.

Diplomacy did not keep Antiochus at bay. In 192 he crossed into Greece, now in alliance with the Aetolians. The Roman response was immediate. Antiochus was met and defeated at Thermopylae in 191 and retreated to Asia, pursued by the consul Scipio (the brother of Africanus, the conqueror of Carthage), who would take the title Asiaticus after this campaign. Antiochus was defeated at Magnesia, sued for peace, and by the Treaty of Apamea signed in 188 renounced all Seleucid claims of territory in Asia Minor. Like Macedon, the Seleucid kingdom was permitted to survive on condition it paid an indemnity, and, like Macedon, its sphere of influence had been limited. The western Balkans, southern Greece, and Anatolia were now no longer dominated by any of the great powers.

Roman armies campaigned in these regions for a little while. During 189 Fulvius Nobilior fought wars in Ambracia on Macedon's western borders, and Manlius Vulso campaigned against the Galatians of central Anatolia. Both wars were infamously profitable, and Rome swooned before spectacular triumphs and monuments. But when the booty was gone, the Romans left too, abandoning their former allies and defeated enemies to jockey for position in a new world order. From now on, all politics in the eastern Mediterranean was referred to Rome. Embassy after embassy sought the support of the Senate or its envoys in tiny disputes. Rome's allies, like the kingdom of Pergamum, the Achaeans, and (for a while) Rhodes, grew in influence. Yet often Romans seemed uninterested in what they did. Military attention was diverted to wars in north Italy and Spain. Philip himself died in 179 and was succeeded by Perseus, who cautiously began building up alliances with other kings. His ambitions were denounced to the Senate by Eumenes of Pergamum in 172, and the next year Roman soldiers were back in the Balkans. This Third Macedonian War took a little longer to bring to a conclusion, perhaps because Rome's allies seemed not wholeheartedly in support. But in 168 Aemilius Paullus defeated Perseus at Pydna (see Figure 4). The kingdom of Macedon was abolished, its territory divided between four republics. Roman armies sacked city after city; a rumoured 150,000 people were enslaved in Epirus. The king was captured and brought back to march through Rome in the triumphal procession of his victor. Meanwhile the leading members of anti-Roman factions from the cities of Greece were taken into exile in Italy. Polybius was among them.

The same year Antiochus IV tried to restore Seleucid fortunes by invading Egypt. A Roman envoy, Popilius Laenas, met him and his army just outside Alexandria and ordered him back home. Antiochus asked for time to consider his response. Laenas drew the original line in the sand, a circle around the king, and insisted:

Before you step out of that circle give me your reply to bring to the Senate.[7]

Antiochus had no option but to obey. Livy followed up this anecdote of Antiochus with an account of how the Senate had received embassies from the Seleucids and the Ptolemies and ambassadors from the kings of Pergamum and Numidia, bringing congratulations on the defeat of Macedon.

Roman hegemony did not, however, ensure political stability. Greek observers were evidently a little puzzled by Roman objectives east of the Adriatic. Rome's victories in 197, 188, and 168 had each changed the

Fig. 4. The monument at Delphi that commemorated Aemilius Paullus' victory at Pydna

balance of power in the east. Yet, after each campaign, the Roman armies had returned home. Between these wars their diplomacy seemed inconsistent. Even Polybius, who had the best position of all to observe Roman policymaking in action, was caught out, believing a watershed had been reached after the obliteration of Macedon. Beginning with his deportation to Rome in 167 BC, he spent nearly twenty years as a kind of honoured prisoner in Rome, in the process getting to know some of the leading figures of the day, including Cato the Elder and the Scipio brothers. Yet he was not ready for the sequel.

During the aftermath of Pydna, relations between Rome and her allies in the eastern Mediterranean deteriorated rapidly. Rhodes was felt not to have given the support it might have done in the war with Perseus. In 167 it was punished when the Romans declared Delos a free port in a successful attempt to damage Rhodian commercial interests. Next, Pergamum fell temporarily from grace, and its power in Asia Minor was limited. During the 150s and 140s Rome made sporadic diplomatic interventions in conflicts between the cities and kingdoms of Anatolia, and kept an interest in succession disputes in Syria and Egypt. But there were no more military expeditions until 149, when a pretender to the throne of Macedon had some brief success before being defeated by a Roman army supported by Pergamese allies. But Roman attention had been attracted. By now Rhodes and Pergamum were back in favour, but the Achaean League was not. To the horror of Polybius, war broke out between Rome and the Achaeans, and this time Roman victory did not simply result in indemnities and loss of territory. The ancient city of Corinth was sacked, its treasures plundered by Mummius and given to his soldiers and as rewards to allied communities, and the city of Corinth was abolished. This was an atrocity not seen in the Greek world since Alexander the Great had destroyed the city of Thebes as a symbol of what he could do if he wished.

Polybius' world revolved around Greece. But the Romans had a different perspective. The Achaean war was something of a sideshow. During the 150s more Roman eyes had been fixed on the recovery of Carthage. It posed no realistic threat to Rome, even if its offer to pay off its war indemnity early showed its economic recovery. Its political and diplomatic actions were confined to Africa, and seem mostly designed to protect itself from the neighbouring Numidian tribes. But successive Roman embassies returned from Carthage to fuel domestic anxieties. Cato the Elder was among the most influential advocates of striking at Carthage before it could grow any stronger. Eventually the Senate issued an ultimatum requiring the Carthaginians to move their city inland, an impossible demand. The result was a Roman invasion in 149 and the capture of the city in 146. Polybius travelled with Scipio Africanus on the campaign that resulted in the final destruction of Carthage and watched the city burn. Like Corinth, it was simply destroyed, and in the same year. The synchronism provides a vital clue to the Roman perspective.[8] Greeks inhabited a political world centred on the Aegean Sea, a world of old cities surrounded by new kingdoms—and Rome. They were not used to being on the periphery of politics. Yet Romans were just as interested in Carthage as in Corinth.

Mid-Republican Imperialism

Rome's expansionist dynamic looks clear enough to us, but maybe did not seem quite so obvious to the Romans. Did they conceive of Mediterranean hegemony as a goal? If not, they would not have been the only nation to discover their imperial vocation only in retrospect. Romans had, after all, no model of empire to follow. Greek writers of the imperial age sometimes set up Alexander as a kind of rival to Rome. But during the last centuries BC, Alexander was mostly looked back on as a model king and conquering general. When Roman hegemony *was* thought of as a system, it was compared to the hegemonies of other 'tyrant cities', Athens and Sparta above all.

The first attempt to account for the rise of Rome—the first we can read, that is—was that of Polybius. Polybius' answer was based on the superiority of Rome's institutions to those of her rivals, although it also gave roles to chance and geography, and also to the virtue and foolishness of various individuals. Perhaps his investigations helped the Roman ruling class formulate their own ideas about hegemony. Or perhaps they reflect in part ideas they already had. Fragments of Cato the Elder's writings sometimes seem to contain some of the same ideas, for example the notion that Roman institutions and public conduct had worked better in the recent past. But then Roman society was still a very small world, and intellectual society smaller still. Perhaps the clearest sign that the Roman elite agreed that the world was now subject to their power alone was the decision to destroy both Carthage and Corinth. Ancient wars typically ended in treaties. The obliteration of two ancient cities is one indication that Romans had come to think of their hegemony as unlike any other.

Roman expansion in the middle Republic was remorseless. No sooner was one war done than another was started. Republican Rome sometimes had several fronts open at the same time, and two years in a row rarely went by between wars. War touched all levels of society. It was difficult to have a successful political career without also holding one or more military command. Between 10 and 25 per cent of the male population were under arms during any one campaigning season. These figures bear comparison with the level of participation in warfare of the general population of European countries during the First World War. During the worst days of the Hannibalic war, between 218 and 215 BC, one in six adult males died on the battlefield. But when a campaign went well, the booty was spread widely, if unevenly, among the participants. During the conquest of Italy, some citizens would be allocated grants of land and places in new colonies on spear-won territory. The whole population of the city witnessed the triumphal processions that followed each successful campaign. Prisoners and booty were paraded through the streets in a pageant that might last days. Games and feasts were provided and afterwards temples were built to repay the gods for the favour they had shown Romans during combat.[9] Looking back on Rome's rise to power, it is very tempting to look for one single force propelling their martial march through history. Many Romans eventually came to believe in a divine mandate, while their enemies saw them as unusually militaristic. The reality is more complex.

Explanations for Roman expansion tend to stress either internal or external factors. Internal factors include the variety of political and economic pressures that made Romans take opportunities for conflict when they presented themselves. External factors include actual threats (both real and imagined), but also the political configuration of the world into which Rome expanded. To some extent the disagreements between proponents of each approach come down to preferences about how to explain events in general, whether by examining the structure of a system or looking at the agency of individual players. Similar discussions could be had about many large-scale conflicts from the Peloponnesian War to the Cold War, and also about other complex systems such as economic crashes. But in this case it also involves a discussion about how unusual Rome was in the ancient Mediterranean, and here we are hampered by the fact we know much more about the ideologies and social structures of the Romans than those of most of their rivals.

Naturally, internal and external factors interacted, the external environment shaping the evolution of Roman society as it sought ways to outcompete its rivals and in turn the internal dynamics of Roman society impacting on the wider world. Over time, Rome behaved less and less like other states, for example by dropping the conventional diplomatic language with which it first presented itself to the Greeks. The more powerful Rome became, the more it shaped the world it had to deal with. For historians of Roman imperialism this means that the multistate approach works less and less well as Rome separated from the rest of the pack.

Let us begin with internal factors. I have already described how Rome became hooked on annual warfare probably during the fifth century BC. The attraction of booty and prestige is obvious; both could be represented as in the interests of the community as well as of the individuals concerned. But this is not a sufficient explanation for Roman imperialism, since many ancient states were geared to frequent warfare, and very few became hegemonic powers. It was the structure of alliances built up from the fourth century that locked Rome into expansion. The process had its own outward dynamic. It was not simply that the Romans could only exercise their leadership by summoning the allies to fight alongside them: the more peoples were reduced to allied status, the farther away from Rome potential enemies came to be located. There are many parallels for such a process, from the imperial expansions of the ancient Near East to those of the New World empires of the Aztecs and the Incas.[10] Meanwhile Roman institutions, Roman ideology, and even Roman religion were progressively adapted to incremental expansion.[11] I described already how it was institutions—not technology or motivation or resources—that gave Rome its comparative advantage over its earliest enemies. But those institutions—the sequence of triumphs, the aristocratic families tending their ancestors' victory temples, the frequent distributions of booty and especially of land—raised expectations. Once again there is a close parallel with the success of the Qin state in contemporary China, one among a group of rival kingdoms in what is known as the Warring States Period, which had in the fourth century BC developed a powerful set of administrative and agrarian systems, and the ideologies to accompany them that enabled it to mobilize land and population much more effectively than its rivals. Qin expansion too involved drawing on the resources of the conquered and programmes of settlement, and culminated in 221 BC in the creation of the first unified empire.[12] Unlike Rome, however, it then faced no external rivals of equivalent power.

Rome emerged from Italy into a hostile world. Stopping expansion after the defeat of Pyrrhus might have been possible—after all, Augustus would later be able to stop the much bigger juggernaut of late first-century expansion—but only if Italy had been quite remote. The reality was that the western Mediterranean contained several rival powers enmeshed in complex relations with each other.[13] The region was not a priority for the main powers in the east, locked as they were in conflicts with each other. But the war with Pyrrhus and the conflicts with Carthage attracted the attention of Greek cities, the kingdom of Macedon to their north and then of all other major players. By the time Rome and her allies faced no serious competition within Italy, their future rivals were already watching them with apprehension.

The third- and second-century wars with Carthage, Macedon, and Syria were of a different nature from those of any that Rome had fought within Italy. They were larger in scale, were sometimes fought on multiple fronts, and, once started, they were difficult to disengage from until a decisive victory had been won. The Punic Wars threatened Rome with much more than humiliation in the event of defeat. Hannibal was quite successful in detaching some allies from Rome. Signs of the seriousness with which the Senate treated Hannibal's victory at Cannae in 216 included the collection of almost all gold jewellery from Roman matrons, and apparently also the live burial of a Gallic couple and a Greek couple in the Roman forum. The kingdoms of the east were also serious opponents. When Antiochus III invaded Greece in 191, he was making an explicit challenge to Roman hegemony in the Balkans. Like Pyrrhus, he saw himself following in the steps of Alexander, but his resources were vastly greater. His kingdom stretched to the border of modern Pakistan. He had personally defeated rebellions in its eastern provinces and Anatolia, had won back southern Syria and Asia Minor from Egypt, and conquered Armenia and Afghanistan. Rome, in other words, was faced with genuine and major threats in the late third and early second centuries BC.

The result was a transformation of Roman warfare and the way Romans managed their hegemony. For a start, the number of legions levied each year increased significantly, being reduced in the 160s only after the defeats of Carthage, Macedon, and Syria, the completion of the conquest of Italy, and major advances in Spain. Back in the fourth century it had generally been possible to confine warfare to a short summer campaigning season, which allowed generals to revert to being civil magistrates and soldiers to work their farms at other times of the year. That alternation came under increasing pressure as some wars grew in scale and length, and as theatres of war were increasingly located farther and farther from Rome. Rome found herself fighting Carthage by sea in the third century, and the second-century wars in Spain and the Balkans required generals to lead out armies that might not return for years. Magistrates could not always command distant armies along with all their other duties. The Roman elite, innovative as ever, developed new ways of managing warfare. Former magistrates, and sometimes just experienced leaders, were increasingly given commands, and some were extended year after year. Generals operating overseas had to be allowed greater freedom of action too, to decide in effect on war and peace within only fairly broad parameters set by their initial commands.[14]

The armies they commanded were also changing. The core of a Roman army remained its citizen levies until the reign of Augustus, but in terms of equipment, tactics, and support troops it was in constant evolution. City state warfare in the classical Mediterranean had been conducted between bodies of heavy armed spearmen, drawn up in the formation called a *phalanx* and supported by small numbers of missile troops and lightly armed cavalry. Greeks, Romans, Carthaginians, Etruscans, and Campanians all fielded different versions of this kind of army in the fifth and fourth centuries BC.

Armies grew more complex when warfare came to involve populations who fought in other ways, as did the Gauls, Samnites, Thracians, Iberians, Numidians, and so on. Not only did the emergent imperial powers have to be able to deal more flexibly with their opponents: they were increasingly able to draw on conquered or allied populations or else hire mercenaries to supplement heavily armed infantry. Carthaginians and Romans alike relied on a wide range of troop types on the battlefield. The armies fielded by Macedon, Syria, and Egypt were also supported by cavalry, light infantry, and missile troops, in their case supporting a phalanx that employed very long pikes. Between the fourth and second centuries BC, the core of the Roman army was transformed from a phalanx of spearmen to a body of heavily armed troops equipped with javelins and swords. A variety of smaller tactical units were developed, in particular the maniple of around 120 men and the cohort of around 400. The flexibility allowed by these systems and weapons gave Roman armies some advantages over both the phalanx of Greek armies (as happened at Cynoscephalae) and less well-equipped opponents like the Gauls.

Empire's Rewards and the Cost of Empire

Meanwhile the economics of hegemony became more complex. Apart from booty and initial confiscation of land, Rome regularly extracted only levies of manpower from her defeated Italian enemies. Yet the period of overseas expansions ushered in what has aptly been termed an economic revolution.[15] Carthage and the kings could be made to pay indemnities extended over decades to provide the Roman state with a regular income. It has been estimated that in the first half of the second century BC booty and indemnities brought the equivalent of more than 1,000 tons of silver to Rome. Much of this was spent funding grandiose building in the capital.[16] Building works were contracted out by the censors to Roman citizens, who in this way shared in the proceeds of empire. Polybius was struck by the scale of this operation:

The people are subordinated to the Senate and must defer to them both collectively and also as private individuals. For a very great number of public contracts are issued by the censors for the construction and repair of public works all over Italy. It would not be easy to enumerate them all; and there are also contracts for the management of rivers, of ports, of orchards, of mines and land: in short, all those things that are in the power of the Roman state. The general populace is involved in all these affairs, so much so that one might almost say that everyone has an interest in these contracts and projects. For there are some who bid before the censors in the forum to have the contracts for themselves; others go into partnership with them; some stand surety for the sums involved; while yet others pledge their own wealth to the state for them.[17]

From the 180s we begin to hear of great construction projects around the forum, spending on the harbours of Rome, and on roads and colonies. During his censorship Marcus Porcius Cato the Elder commissioned a vast covered hall for indoor meetings, known grandiosely as the Basilica Porcia after the Royal Stoa (the Stoa Basilike given to Athens by the King of Pergamum). It was funded not from booty or private wealth, but from public revenues.

The influx of wealth had transformative effects on almost all aspects of economic activity. Public building projects redistributed state money to private citizens. Coin minted from booty drove an increase in the money supply. The influx of capital triggered processes of land acquisition that would drive social change and political life for the remainder of the Republic. Those who could, not only purchased land but also improved it. Agricultural intensification, urban production, the construction of properties for rental use and a growth in the scale of maritime trade were all made possible by the availability first of cash and then of credit. To begin with, the benefits were widely shared. The final defeat of Macedon in 167 resulted in a permanent exemption for Roman citizens from direct taxation. The destruction of Carthage in 146 was followed almost immediately by the construction of the magnificent aqueduct known as the Aqua Marcia. Less welcome was the effective end to colonial settlement, a practical consequence of the conquest of Italy linked to a less rational reluctance to settle Romans beyond the peninsula. Spending in Rome and the end of colonization helped swell the size of the capital, and so (again) the demand for public works and for slaves. Rome was now locked into a cycle of urban growth as well as one of imperial expansion.

The effects of all this were felt well beyond Italy. Indemnities were extracted from those wealthy powers whose economies had been left intact, but they were spent mostly in Italy. The needs of armies operating in the new overseas territories had to be supplied by other means. The cities of Sicily had paid an annual tithe to Syracuse, and Rome appropriated this. Spanish tribes supplied their occupiers first with grain and then with cash tribute. Roman power over Spain also allowed them to license exploitation of the silver mines around Cartagena (New Carthage), the former Punic capital.[18] These origins of a provincial tax system do not seem to follow a grand plan. It was often left to Roman conquerors and generals to devise systems that worked locally, and these were often based on pre-Roman precedents. Fragments of the fiscal systems of Hiero of Syracuse and of the kings of Pergamum survived long into the imperial taxation systems. Wherever locals did not undertake the relevant collection or exploitation themselves, contracts were once again issued to Roman citizens. The attractions of running an empire through public contracts are obvious: the state did not need to create a colonial administration, what risks there might be were borne by private individuals, and a wide circle benefited from the proceeds of victory. Polybius added that their dependence on the Senate and the censors kept those who wanted contracts subservient. But the downsides to public contracting are only too well known today. Contractors took the short-term view and were prepared to exploit provincial subjects without mercy while they held the contract. The Roman term for contractors, *publicani*, is regularly paired with 'sinners' in the Gospels.

Rome's struggles with other Mediterranean hegemonic powers also changed the politics of warfare. Alongside the increased scale of conflict, there appear voices of restraint. Real differences seem to have emerged both in the Senate and in the assembly about the advisability of particular wars. The war against Philip V of Macedon was almost headed off in the assembly. Cato the Elder had to badger the Senate for years to finish off Carthage. The destruction of Carthage and Corinth clearly appalled some Romans. One reason Rome's eastern allies found it difficult to second-guess Roman policy in their region during the second century was that it genuinely was unpredictable. There was a marked resistance to acquiring territory east of the Adriatic, even after Rome had more or less had to create a province in Macedonia in the 140s. When, in 133, Attalus III of Pergamum died, leaving his kingdom to Rome, the legacy was only accepted when Tiberius Gracchus took it to the popular assembly and promised that the proceeds would be used to fund renewed land distributions within Italy.

Not all the wars of the late third and early second century were conflicts between great powers. Roman armies fought in Spain and north Italy for much of the period, ventured into the Gallic interior, and were drawn into or provoked secondary wars in the Balkans and Asia Minor. Generally, these wars were less controversial, but occasionally senators complained about wars fought with no formal authority against distant peoples; attempts were made to deny triumphs to some of these generals. Generals might well respond that the Senate did not understand the situation on the ground, and some pointed to the proceeds of their victories. Occasionally, commissions of senators were dispatched to regularize post-campaign settlements or to inspect colonies. Embassies visited Rome from all sides. It is a sinister sign that in 149 BC a law court was set up to deal with accusations of corruption by representatives of the Roman state abroad. The leadership of allies under arms had mutated into a different form of imperial rule.

Meanwhile the fabric of the city and civic life were transformed. The city welcomed captured statuary taken from Syracuse in 212 and Corinth in 146. Successful campaigns had often been followed by the construction of what we call 'victory temples' fulfilling battlefield vows made to the gods by Roman commanders. The scale of temple building now increased. The creation of a Latin literature began in the same period, promoted by the Roman elite first of all to enhance dramatic festivals, then to make a statement about Rome's parity with Greek cities. The setting up of statues and monuments, and the staging of hymns and dramas involved all the population and not just the élite. These are accurately described as acts of appropriation, the violent seizure and reuse of objects of cultural value and their repurposing to express a new sense of superiority.[19] Once again, this is something we can easily relate to today.

Comprehending Empire

Looking at Roman expansion in terms of the comparative advantages of its institutions makes good sense to us, as it did to the Greek Polybius. Like him, we are heirs to a style of political analysis that goes back to Aristotle. But it is worth asking how the Romans comprehended this extraordinary story. A rich example is provided by one family that did more than most to lead Rome over these centuries.

The Cornelii were one of the largest of the clans out of which the Republican aristocracy, or rather its inner circle, was comprised. The Cornelii Scipiones made up one section of the clan. The family is well known from historical writing and would be famous even if their rock-cut tomb had not been found beside the Appian Way leading out of Rome and excavated in the late eighteenth century. The tomb contains nine sarcophagi—there would once have been many more—each with an epitaph. As it happens, these fill out parts of the family tree least well known from the narratives of Polybius and Livy. The family was of patrician status, which Romans sometimes understood to mean descendants of the aristocracy of the Regal Period. By the third century patrician families no longer monopolized high political office or the great priesthoods, but they were certainly over-represented in them.

The eldest of those whose epitaphs were found in the tomb, Scipio Barbatus (see Figure 5), was consul in 298 BC, his two sons were consuls in 260 and 258, and one held a rare second consulship in 254. The next generation held consulships in 222, 221, and 218, and their children in 205, 191, 190, and 176. The consul of 205 was the victor of Zama, the battle that had ended the Second Punic War. He took the name Scipio Africanus and held a second consulship in 194. Through his influence, his brother was consul in 190 and led the war against Antiochus, for which he took the title Asiaticus. These continental nicknames accurately express the scale of their reputations, or their egos.

Livy tells the story of how, late in life, Africanus was tried before the people for corruption. On the second day of the trial he was summoned before the tribunes. He approached them where they were seated on the Rostra at one end of the Roman forum, accompanied by a great crowd of his friends and clients. Silence fell, and he addressed them:

On this very day, tribunes of the people and you too my fellow citizens, I fought a battle against Hannibal and the Carthaginians, with good fortune and with success. So, since it seems reasonable that all cases and procedures be suspended for today, I am going at once from here up onto the Capitol to praise Jupiter the Greatest and Best, to Juno, to Minerva and to the other gods who preside on the Capitol and the Citadel. And I will thank them that on this very day, and on other occasions, they gave me the strength and wisdom to do great service to the state. Citizens, those of you who are able, come with me and pray to the gods that you may always have leaders like myself. For from the time when I was seventeen years old right up to my old age you have always given me honours appropriate to men older than myself, and I have always anticipated your honours by my deeds.[20]

The court rose, the story goes, and followed him on a tour of the temples of the city. Maybe it is a fiction, and Africanus seems to have lived his last years in a voluntary exile in Liternum on the Bay of Naples, so perhaps he did not get off scot free. But the anecdote tells us how he was remembered.

Fig. 5. The sarcophagus of Scipio Barbatus, Museo Pio-Clementino, Vatican

The next generation of the Scipiones was not so distinguished, although one was consul as late as 138. But the name was unstoppable. By adopting the son of another great family, the Aemilii Pauli, one of whom had destroyed the Macedonian kingdom in 168, the family recruited Publius Cornelius Scipio Aemilianus. He served as consul in 147 and commanded the force that finally destroyed Carthage once and for all, a second Africanus. As a statesman and a patron of the arts, he was idealized by Cicero as guiding the state during the years before civil war became endemic.

Family traditions are created by remembering, and memory is always selective. The epitaphs in the tomb were particularly susceptible to this process, but for what it is worth the image that emerges is a consistent one.[21] Each of the Scipiones is praised for personal qualities—often beauty as well as virtue—and some, at least, of their offices are listed, but the great field of achievement is war. Barbatus won wars against Etruscans and Samnites and subdued all of Lucania in the south of the peninsula. As well as to the consulship, he was elected censor and held the most prestigious priesthood in Rome, the position of *pontifex maximus*. His son, the consul of 259, also made censor. His victories were naval ones, conquering almost all of Corsica from the Carthaginians. On his return he set up a temple to the goddesses of the storms. His brother triumphed in 253 after capturing the city of Panormus in Sicily. And on and on. The consul of 222 led the conquest of Milan and the Gallic tribe of the Insubres, whose capital it was. His son was selected in 204 as the noblest Roman citizen and so the best suited to welcome the arrival of the Great Mother Goddess from Asia Minor when her cult statue was brought to Rome. He too had his victories over the Gauls. Successive victories were won farther and farther afield, the honours expressed in the same words generation after generation. From our perspective, we see the profound structural changes Rome underwent as it moved from an aggressive Italian city state to the ruler of the Mediterranean. But for the Cornelii Scipiones—and doubtless too for the Fabii Maximi, the Sempronii Gracchi, and all those other great families that rivalled them, married into them, and told the same story of Rome with only slightly different inflections—their family history formed part, a leading part, of a narrative of conquest that lasted for centuries.

Further Reading

William Harris's *War and Imperialism in Republican Rome* (Oxford, 1979) changed the way Roman imperialism is discussed, moving attention from Roman justifications for wars to the internal political, social, and ideological factors driving expansion. These arguments are extended and expanded in his *Roman Power* (Cambridge, 2016). The Roman takeover of the Greek east is chronicled in Erich Gruen's *Hellenistic World and the Coming of Rome* (Berkeley, CA, 1984). Arthur Eckstein's *Mediterranean Anarchy, Interstate War and the Rise of Rome* (Berkeley, CA, 2006) offers an interpretation based on political science and the broader structure of the Hellenistic Mediterranean. Liv Yarrow and Christopher Smith gather responses to this debate in *Imperialism, Cultural Politics and Polybius* (Oxford, 2012). Graham Shipley's *The*

Greek World after Alexander (London, 2000) is a marvellous guide to the world that Rome destroyed. John Richardson discusses Rome's less glamorous, but enormously significant first experiments in imperialism in the west in *Hispaniae* (Cambridge, 1986).

Modern debates over the domestic consequences of Roman overseas expansion begin from Peter Brunt's *Italian Manpower* (Oxford, 1971). The first chapters of Keith Hopkins's *Conquerors and Slaves* (Cambridge, 1978) present a lucid argument relating imperialism to the growth of slavery and the expansion of the city of Rome. But the demography has recently come under renewed scrutiny. Excellent starting points for this debate are Nathan Rosenstein's *Rome at War* (Chapel Hill, NC, 2004) and a collection of papers edited by Luuk de Ligt and Simon Northwood under the title *People, Land and Politics* (Leiden, 2008). Denis Feeney's *Beyond Greek: The Beginnings of Latin Literature* (Cambridge, MA, 2016) provides a brilliant account of the transformation of Roman civic culture in this period.

SLAVERY AND EMPIRE

Aiming to reconcile a population that was scattered and primitive—so quick to take up arms—to a peaceful and leisured existence by providing luxurious amenities, he gave private encouragement and public assistance to them to build temples, market places and urban mansions, praising those who were quick to do so, and criticizing those who were slow. This way a competition for honour took the place of compulsion. He provided the sons of the chiefs with a proper education, and he praised the natural aptitude of the Britons over the hard work of the Gauls, so those who had refused to learn Latin began to acquire oratorical skills. Even our national style of dress became popular; the toga was often to be seen. And little by little they were led towards those things that encourage vice, colonnades, bathing and elegant banquets. In their inexperience they took all this for civilization; in fact it was part of their enslavement.

(Tacitus, *Agricola* 21)

A Patrimonial Empire

Every empire bears the mark of the kind of society that creates it. Nomad empires like that of the Mongols ruled through tribes and clans. The British Empire began as a trading venture, was conquered and governed by members of the aristocracy, and was administered by a colonial bureaucracy

staffed from the professional middle classes.[1] Each of these social groups left
its mark on the empire. Republican Rome was a city state run by its greatest
families. It was also a slave-owning society. It is no surprise that the empire
it created was aristocratic and that it depended for its management on the
family and on slavery.

Family and slavery might seem an odd combination today. But in many
premodern societies the two fitted closely together.[2] Many economic
and governmental functions that are in the modern world organized by
corporations, companies, and bureaucracies of various kinds were in the past
mostly managed by individuals who relied for help on networks of families
and friends, 'kith and kin'. Perhaps the most basic economic activity in antiquity is farming, whether that of tribal cultivators who organized their work
through ideologies of kinship or that of peasant families. Slavery appeared in
both kinds of society as a means of supplementing the workforce. Typically,
it appeared alongside friendship and clientage. Slaves provided labour all the
year round; others might help for particular needs. The aristocratic rulers of
mid-Republican Rome had much more to organize than their family estates. Some owned several farms, others buildings in the city, trading vessels,
potteries, and small shops. No one had enough relatives to staff or manage
all these ventures. Wage labour existed, but it was rarely used, and mostly
for piecework. Military aggression made the growth of slavery possible, and
the more complex society that resulted from expansion generated new roles
that slaves could fill. Roman property owners—and slaves were property,
of course—made use of slavery in every possible capacity. Slaves worked in
the fields and the mines, served at table and in the bedroom, were teachers,
financial managers, and confidants. Romans famously freed many of their
slaves and gave them a limited form of citizenship. The reason was not sentimental: the slaves who were freed were generally the most skilled, and as ex-
slaves or freedmen they remained closely tied to the houses of their former
masters. By the end of the Republic a great part of the city consisted of
grand houses, each of which might include hundreds of slaves, and around
them a penumbra of former slaves still closely tied to their former masters.
Most Roman aristocrats spent only a small part of their lives in public service, as generals or governors or other officials; while on service their family,
friends, and former slaves assisted them. The state owned a few slaves, but—
until the emperors expanded their own family and slave household to form
the kernel of a civil service—the empire was governed patrimonially, that is,
by the kith, kin, and slaves of its leading members.

The family also generated powerful images of authority, images which were easily transferred to other spheres. The ideological focus was the *pater-familias*, the normal head of the household. Roman fathers were imagined to exercise benevolent care and moral leadership as well as authority. Formally, the Roman *paterfamilias* owned all the property of those persons under his authority, a group that included his adult children, the children of his sons, their slaves and ex-slaves. He also exercised a kind of guardianship over his female relatives, and even his married daughters remained under his authority. The *paterfamilias* was magistrate and priest in his own household, representing it to the state and to the gods. He presided over the family cult, might convene a council of his friends to help him decide on family matters, and might turn this into a family court to try members of the household: until Augustus even adultery was a matter for the jurisdiction of the head of the household. Slaves might be subjected to beatings at his command or set free; ex-slaves might in principle be re-enslaved.

Recent research on the Roman family has shown that reality was more complex. For a start, the idea of most adult males being completely under the thumb of an aged *paterfamilias* has to be rejected for all periods of Roman history. In a world where men typically did not marry for the first time until their late twenties and where life expectancy was at premodern levels, many adult Romans will have had no living parents. Those old men who did survive were treated with enormous respect; the situation was closer to that of traditional Japanese and Chinese society than to that of western Europe today. Tales of antique severity were part of a general tendency of Roman writers to evoke a morally stable past when attacking individuals in the present. Yet this myth made the *pater* an excellent figure with which to represent benevolent authority in other contexts. Senators were formally addressed as *patres conscripti*. The title *pater patriae* (father of the fatherland) was given to Cicero, to Caesar, and then to Augustus, after whom it became a standard component of imperial titulature.

Beyond the family extended webs of patronage, that complex of relationships that connected powerful Romans to their freeborn clients of various kinds. Patronage meant exchanges of favours and respect between people of different status or standing.[3] It included the senior senator offering support to a younger one, the landowner helping out a poorer neighbour, and the backing provided by a patron of the arts for poets; it faded out into the social dimensions of the legally enforceable dependence of ex-slaves, tenants, and debtors. The powerful could offer their

social subordinates allowances, loans of capital, or positions as managers
of businesses and the occasional meal. Relationships of this kind were in
principle inheritable, and some lesser families probably did remain in the
orbit of larger ones for a few generations. The returns might be financial or
presented as political support—although it was impolite to mention it—and
urban clients also provided an entourage on formal occasions. With their
grander friends—younger senators on the make, *equestrians*, and members
of municipal aristocracies—the powerful could make connections, and perhaps obtain for them through their brokerage magistracies, priesthoods, social promotions, and the like. Friends also felt an obligation to help the
widows and orphaned children of their connections. Orators offered free
representation in the courts for their greater and lesser friends, and *literati*
read and listened to each other's compositions. For these services, the return was gratitude and the reputation of a man who honoured his social
obligations, his *officia*.

Patronage offered many models and metaphors for imperial rule.
Provincial communities who wished to prosecute governors for corruption needed first to find a senator who would represent them as *patronus*;
some were honoured for the service by Greek cities.[4] Roman generals on
occasion became the protectors of foreign communities, first in Italy and
then overseas.[5] Some bonds endured for a surprisingly long time. When
Cicero was consul in 63 BC, a group of conspirators tried to get the support
of the Gallic Allobroges. They were not persuaded and exposed the plot,
but did so by approaching Cicero through a minor senator named Fabius
Sanga, whose ancestor had originally defeated them in the 120s. The language of patronage could be applied to relations between entire peoples
and the Roman state as a whole. During the late Republic various foreign
peoples and kings were formally hailed as 'friends and allies' of the Roman
people.[6] No one in Rome would have understood this as a relationship
between equals. All the same, the relationship carried a real sense of mutual obligations. When Rome was divided against itself, these relationships
might draw in foreigners. Sallust opens his account of the war against the
Numidian prince Jugurtha with Scipio Aemilanus advising his young ally
to seek the friendship of the Roman people as a whole, not of individual
Romans.[7] The civil wars of the 40s and 30s BC were fought mainly outside
Italy and involved tribes and kings from all around the empire: Cleopatra
in Egypt, Herod in Judaea, Juba of Mauretania were among those trying to
guess future winners in Roman politics. That problem only resolved itself

with the end of political pluralism. The emperor became the ultimate source of all benefits, senatorial patrons increasingly acted as brokers connecting their clients to imperial largesse, and Augustus boasted in his autobiography how distant German tribes had sent envoys seeking his friendship and that of the Roman people.[8]

Slavery and the Roman Economy

Slavery and the family acquired more and more functions as Roman power expanded over the last centuries BC. Nowhere is this clearer than in the management of the public and private proceeds of empire.

Perhaps most original was the development of legal devices to enable these institutions to be used more effectively to manage economic activity.[9] A good example is provided by the *peculium*, an amount of property that an individual might use, despite the fact that the ultimate owner was the head of the household. Families needed all their adult members to be able to operate as effective economic agents: a *peculium* allowed a son to run a farm or to buy and sell goods without constant reference to his father. By allowing some slaves a *peculium*, they could act as commercial agents and farm managers or could run shops or tenements. It became common for some slaves to retain money they earned with the intention of eventually buying their freedom from their owners: the sum would allow the master to replace the slave, and he retained the services of a freedman. Augustus allowed soldiers a *peculium*, a practical measure, given some would spend decades at a great distance from their fathers. From the early second century BC, a law of agency, the *lex institoria*, supplemented these arrangements. Roman property owners were able to appoint free, freed, or even slave agents (*institores*) who could enter into contracts and incur liabilities on their behalf. Something of this kind was vital once some Romans had business interests and estates in several provinces or might be engaged in long-distance trade or contracts to provision distant Roman armies. Yet another example, also from the early second century, is the development of partnerships (*societates*), originally a device to allow heirs to manage an inheritance jointly, but now adapted to allow a number of parties to pool their assets and share the profits and losses of common enterprises. This was especially useful as the potential scale of economic activities increased: the Elder Cato is said to have joined in a partnership of fifty to fund a commercial voyage.[10] The greatest public contracts of the late Republic—the collection of five years of public revenues from the province of Asia is the most famous example—demanded huge financial guarantees. Partnership was vital to enterprises of this sort. Other empires faced similar problems but dealt with them in different ways. Early modern Europe developed the joint-stock company as a means of pooling capital and risk. Rome employed the institutions of the family and slavery, and through law extended their utility.

The economic sphere in which we can best track change is agriculture. It is not clear how early some Romans started to acquire multiple properties up and down the peninsula; for the fourth and third centuries there is much more evidence of colonial and other settlement. Archaeological evidence for villa building and an increased concern with surplus production is scarce in many parts of Italy before the late second century BC. Literary accounts of tranquil rural retreats begin even later. But around 160 BC, Cato the Elder wrote a treatise *On Farming*, which borrowed from earlier Greek manuals on farming, yet was adapted to Roman needs. It includes, for example, lists of the Italian towns in which the best items of various kinds of equipment can be purchased. At its heart is a thoroughly Roman model of slavery. Cato's prescriptions suit a moderate-sized farm practising a mixed agriculture based on the most common Italian crops. It produced a little of everything to supply the needs of the servile workforce, the farm manager, and the owner, but was also designed to produce a surplus for the market.

The market for agricultural produce was a growing one in the second century BC. Powering this was urbanization. The city of Rome probably already had more than 100,000 inhabitants. It was expanding rapidly as a result of the public spending organized by the censors, and perhaps too because colonization had stopped at the end of the 170s. After the destruction of Corinth in 146 BC it had also became the central commercial hub of the western Mediterranean. As the proportion of the population who did not live on the land grew, so did the demand for foodstuffs. Importing from a distance was expensive and risky. Rome would resort to this eventually, as the city approached a million souls in the reign of Augustus. But for now there was a simpler solution. The confiscation of land from disloyal allies after the Hannibalic war had increased the amount of public property, and wars of overseas conquest had enriched some at least of the landowning classes. Some of this wealth they used to purchase farms, some of it to invest in them. Slaves, in the period of overseas expansion, offered a cheap workforce. Capital-intensive agriculture became a way that short-term windfalls of booty could be transformed into ventures that would make money in the long term. That was the logic to which Cato responded. There was, in fact, a widespread and consistent interest in ways of improving the value of farmland. Varro produced a longer treatise on agriculture in the early 30s BC, and by the time Columella and Pliny were writing in the later first century AD, they could evidently draw on a library of agronomical works. At the heart of all of them was slave labour.[11]

Cato wrote for landowners who were planting vineyards, equipping their farms with mills and presses, building storage facilities, and purchasing iron farming equipment and, to use it, slaves. The farm he envisaged was run by a manager with a permanent staff of around twenty slaves, supplemented when needed, as for the vintage, by the casual labour of free peasants or townsfolk.[12] Slaves offered a core workforce that could be worked exceptionally hard, the sick and old could be easily disposed of, no idle mouths need be tolerated, and the workforce could be increased or decreased in size easily enough. Slaves were not subject to military levies. Cato's recommendations have horrified many for the banality of their cruelty. The production of grain and wine were the key market-oriented enterprises. Landowners also exploited non-agricultural resources on their estates, such as clay pits and woodland. Clay pits were vital for making the pottery containers or *amphorae* in which wine and oil were exported and the vats or *dolia* used for storage. The city of Rome was greedy for bricks and tiles. Some properties could supply timber and firewood. Farms close to Rome developed irrigated fruit and vegetable gardening, the raising of fowl, beekeeping, and even the rearing of game of various kinds.[13] Property owners also invested in transport infrastructure, built markets for fresh produce, and rented out shops to their clients along the frontages of their homes. At all stages of this economic growth the propertied classes led the way. No new commercial classes emerged, as the capital came from the social elites and they entrusted the management of these enterprises to their clients, freedmen, and slaves.[14]

Roman landowners needed farm bailiffs, building managers, shopkeepers, and supervisors of small workshops, and trusted representatives to collect rent from urban and rural tenants, to conduct business in distant ports, and to manage the complex bookkeeping on each estate and of the household as a whole. Those who dealt with contracts or had to report or else receive written instructions had to be literate. Landowners depended on numerate individuals to manage what must have been complex flows of cash, to record and chase arrears, and to check the returns on loans. They used slave and ex-slave secretaries, some of whom travelled with them wherever they went, assisting in their official business as well as in their private affairs. Slaves and freedmen provided for all this.[15]

Why slaves? Roman society had no equivalent of the educated but relatively poor urban classes who supplied Victorian entrepreneurs with their waged clerical assistants. The citizen army produced no retired officers with the kind of generalized administrative experience depended on today in many sectors of business and government. Nor did the freeborn have access to anything like the social and commercial institutions that today allow those with talent and energy to develop career paths to positions of increasing responsibility. Slaves, on the other hand, were malleable. Some were highly educated; indeed most Roman education took place within aristocratic households. Owned for long periods, they could be trained and disciplined to suit their masters' needs. Most slaves were completely detached from the societies in which they had grown up, or else they were 'home-bred'. Neither group had any real hope of achieving better conditions except with their owners' support. Besides, slaves were utterly dependent on their masters.[16] The sanctions for disobedience or dishonesty were horrifying. It was in principle illegal to kill a slave, deliberately at least, although who would bring a case against a master? But slaves might be routinely confined, beaten, even tortured, and there were many lesser sanctions. Cato recommended access to slave women be used as an incentive. Some slaves were allowed to start families, but their partners and children could be sold at a master's whim. Slaves might hope for softer jobs and their eventual freedom, but they could be reassigned to hard labour if the master preferred. Was there a connection too between the Romans' increasingly autocratic treatment of their enemies and their habitual command over their slaves? It is difficult to test such a thesis, but when one reads Cato on his slaves, it is difficult to forget him ending every public speech he made at the end of his life with the words *Delenda est Carthago*, 'Carthage must be destroyed.'

Cato's ideal farm would have looked tiny to later generations. Purpose-built villas with slave quarters appear in the last century BC, often equipped with luxurious residential quarters. A great mansion excavated at Settefinestre in Tuscany provides a vivid model. An entire urban mansion, secluded garden included, has been transplanted into the countryside and bolted onto a working farm. When the master was present, he would arrive with servile attendants to look after his every need and desire. Meanwhile, a very different category of slaves worked his vineyards, his fields, his mills, and his potteries. Most agricultural slaves were not made to work in chains—hardly practical in most circumstances—but many were branded or wore collars (see Figure 6). Even worse were the conditions of the slaves who worked in the mines. And Apuleius, in his novel the *Golden Ass*, provides a horrific description of a grain mill where slaves ground grain by turning a horizontally mounted wheel in unbearable heat.

O gods above, what poor subhuman creatures were there, their bodies bruised all with livid marks, their backs scarred from beatings, covered rather than clothed, in rags, some just wearing loincloths to preserve their dignity, all of them so practically naked. Some had been branded on the forehead, some had their hair shaved off and some wore shackles. They looked ghastly, and in fact they could hardly see as their eyes were dimmed with muck and smoke in the foul-smelling darkness of that place.[17]

Meanwhile, the lavish servile households of the super-rich kept growing. Slave teachers and barbers took their place alongside concubines and all kinds of chefs, doormen, dressers, bakers, wet nurses, poetry readers, gardeners, and physical trainers. Literally hundreds of occupational designations are known from the elaborate graves their masters often provided for them. Extraordinarily intricate societies arose within single households, societies marked by subtle hierarchies and minute differentiations of role and title. Slaves were so ubiquitous they often seem invisible. It is easy to forget that a free man or woman of any status was almost never alone and never needed to exert themselves, because there was always another pair of hands to do it for them.

Slaves, Citizens, and Soldiers

Slaves, to begin with, were luxuries. When we can tell—rarely—how much a slave cost, the price in today's terms is about that of a new car. Only the rich needed or could afford such skilled servants to supplement their clients and tenants and dependent relatives. Yet Cato's farm employed less-skilled slaves. How did Rome become a society based on mass slavery? And how did this change relate to Roman imperialism?

Part of this story has been told already. During the second century BC there are many signs that slavery was becoming more and more important

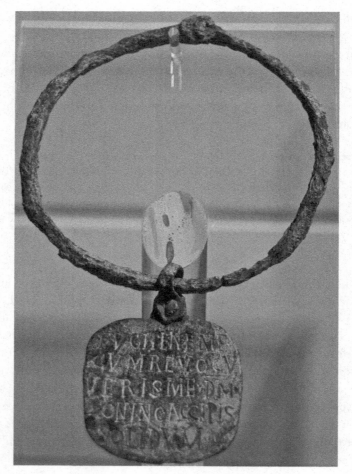

Fig. 6. A slave collar (original in the Museo Nazionale Romano, Terme di Diocleziano in Rome)

in the Roman economy. Cato's description is an early piece of evidence. Anecdotes begin to pile up. At the end of the second century BC, Nicomedes, king of Bithynia, refused to send troops to fight alongside Rome on the grounds that so many of his subjects had been captured by slave traders. Nearer to home there were two major slave rebellions in Sicily in the late second century (135–132 and 104–100 BC), while the Spartacus war of 73 BC took two Roman armies to suppress. If the growth of agricultural slavery can be matched to the development of wine production for export, then the pace of the transformation through the late second and early first centuries BC can be measured by a wide range of archaeological criteria from the number of container amphorae found from each period to the growing number of wrecked cargo vessels that have been located by divers along the Mediterranean coasts.[18]

The growth of Roman slavery was so rapid that it was one of the very few social transformations actually noticed by ancient writers. The geographer Strabo explained how one part of southern Asia Minor, Cilicia, became a major centre for piracy.[19] It began with a local rebellion against the kings of Syria. The rebels then began to raid Syria for slaves, because they discovered the slave market on Delos could handle a turnover of 10,000 slaves a day. The reason, says Strabo, was that after the defeat of Carthage and Corinth in 146 BC the Romans had become rich and started to use great numbers of slaves. Other powers in the area—the city of Rhodes, the kings of Cyprus and of Egypt—were either enemies of Syria or for other reasons did not interfere, and the Romans were not concerned with matters beyond the Taurus. Strabo got it right—more or less—but even he did not appreciate the full combination of factors that had turned the eastern Mediterranean into a playground for pirates and slave traders. Roman expansion was the root cause of most of them. First, it was Rome's wars against the kings that had left the eastern Mediterranean unpoliced. Rome would not even begin to try to suppress piracy until the very end of the second century BC. It remained a menace until Pompey swept the inland sea from end to end in the 60s, and Augustus created the first permanent Roman fleets.[20] Second, Romans had indeed begun to gear their economy to slave labour, but not just because of their wealth and not just after 146 BC. Cheap slaves first become available during Rome's Balkan wars in the first decades of the second century. That notorious agreement made between Romans and their then allies the Aetolians promised the latter any cities and territory captured, so long as Rome could take the movable booty and the population.[21] Prisoners of war were from that point on a major component of booty from most major campaigns.

Not all agricultural slaves were used on villas like those described by Cato. Accounts of the Sicilian Slave Wars also mention slave shepherds on the great farms of the south. But the great demand was to staff the new-style villas, and Roman warfare was not quite regular enough to ensure a steady supply of captives. Many fewer legions were fielded during the 160s, for example, than in the 190s, when Rome faced both Macedon and Syria, or in the years leading to the fall of Corinth and Carthage. This is where Delos came in. When there were no captives available, Rome turned to slave traders, who supplied themselves from piracy and raiding in the chaotic conditions left by Rome's ventures in the eastern Mediterranean.[22] At other times there were fresh consignments of war captives. Traders followed the armies, buying captives from individual soldiers. Others began to exploit new populations in northern Europe. There is some sign that—just as in Africa in the early modern period—some tribes took to raiding their neighbours for slaves whom they could exchange for imported goods, goods that in antiquity included Mediterranean wine. As long as Rome had the appetite for slaves, there would be no end to the trade in one form or another.

Why were Roman landowners so committed to slave labour? The population of Italy was not small; indeed, it had probably never been so high as under Roman rule. Until the early second century most of the agricultural workforce was supplied by peasants, some owning their own land, others tenants on state land or on farms belonging to others, a few working for cash, and probably many families doing a little of all these things. Arguments have raged since antiquity over how far and how fast free peasants were displaced by slaves, and they continue today.[23] Changes certainly took place, and they seem to have unfolded gradually. Peasant freeholders, sharecroppers, and tenants are well attested in the Principate and may even have increased in number to judge from the latest archaeological research.[24] Citizen death rates on campaign were never catastrophic. Regional differences are clearer than ever in the archaeological data. Yet agricultural slavery and intensive agriculture did expand, and many of the soldiers who fought in the armies of the late Republic were landless. One way or another, the ancient link between soldier-citizen and citizen-farmer had been broken.

A Culture of Servility?

Historians have focused on the economic importance of slaves for many reasons. There are those ancient sources which complain about them displacing peasant farmers, there is more recent experience of slaves working on plantations in Brazil, the Caribbean, and the southern states of the US, and there are arguments derived from Marxist thought about slaves in production. But more recently an investigation has begun into other ways that the institution of slavery changed Rome. Slaves are ubiquitous in Latin literature, especially in comic drama and in genres like satire that often engage with question of popular morality. Some of the first surviving works of Latin literature were the comedies composed by Plautus at the end of the third and start of the second centuries BC. Modelled on Greek New Comedy, the plays were not simple translations but dealt with themes and characters familiar from the city of Rome where they were first performed during festivals. Slaves play a major role in many plots, and although part of their function is to show up the foolishness and inexperience of freeborn protagonists, their speeches and complaints offer a vivid and believable account of slave experience, including suffering beatings, separations from family, and other kinds of abuse. The population of Rome in this period, during and after the Hannibalic wars, already included many slaves and ex-slaves, and most of those involved in the production, performance, and enjoyment of these slaves did not come from the Roman élite. Slaves in satire also often challenge the slave owners, and they are used as figures to reflect on Roman notions of humanity and morality, some of them quoting philosophical maxims at their masters.[25]

Slavery also entered into the Roman imagination more widely. Elegaic poets of the last century BC and the first century AD described themselves as enslaved to those they loved. Slavery here stood for complete subjection to the wills and whims of their mistress. A more sinister development was the way Roman aristocrats began to describe their relations to foreign peoples in the language of slave owning or of *patrocinium,* the kind of patronage exercised over former slaves. [26] Emperors would eventually be addressed as *domine.* We usually translated this as 'my lord' but it is also the Latin term for 'master'. Just as British imperialists looked for (and found) analogues of class in the societies they ruled, so Romans often thought about their power over subjects in the same way as they thought about their power over slaves. Even when Nero boasted of freeing an entire province (Achaea), his language reflected an assumption that most provincials were not free, or at least not as free as their Roman masters.

Further Reading

One of the great achievements of the last generation of research has been a realization of the centrality of the family to all aspects of Roman society. Beryl Rawson's collection

The Family in Ancient Rome (London, 1986) is an excellent starting point, including papers by most of the major scholars in the field. Paul Weaver's *Familia Caesaris* (Cambridge, 1972) revealed the use the emperors made of slaves in governing the empire. Rawson and Weaver together edited a follow-up volume entitled *The Roman Family in Italy* (Oxford, 1997). Richard Saller's *Patriarchy, Property and Death in the Roman Family* (Cambridge, 1994) harnessed demography and social science to show the gap between myth and reality when it came to the power of the *paterfamilias*. The best starting points for finding out more about Roman slavery are the first volume of *The Cambridge History of World Slavery* (Cambridge, 2011) edited by Paul Cartledge and Keith Bradley, and Bradley's *Slavery and Society at Rome* (Cambridge, 1994). Although concerned with much more than slavery, Christer Bruun and Jonathan Edmondson's magnificent *Oxford Handbook of Roman Epigraphy* (Oxford, 2014) contains many chapters on the subject.

For the relationship between the growth of a slave society in Rome and Roman imperialism, see the books by Hopkins and Rosenstein noted in the Further Reading for Chapter V. The great debate over the significance of slavery in the Roman economy has been conducted mostly in Italian. Dominic Rathbone's article 'The Slave Mode of Production in Italy', published in the *Journal of Roman Studies* in 1983, provides a sympathetic overview. Ulrike Roth's *Thinking Tools* (London, 2007) offers an important challenge to the orthodoxy. Jean-Jacques Aubert's *Business Managers in Ancient Rome* (Leiden, 1994) shows brilliantly how Romans adapted traditional institutions to cope with the demands of an ever more complex society. Two new works approach slavery through its archaeology: Michele George's edited collection *Roman Slavery and Roman Material Culture* (Toronto, 2013) and Sandra Joshel and Lauren Hackworth Petersen's 2014. *The Material Life of Roman Slaves* (Cambridge, 2014).

KEY DATES IN CHAPTER VII

146 BC   Both Carthage and Corinth sacked by Roman armies

133–129 BC   Rome takes control of the kingdom of Pergamum, creating the province of Asia and making client kings out of the rulers of Bithynia, Pontus, and Cappadocia

133 BC   Tribunate of Tiberius Gracchus marks the beginning of *popularis* politics in Rome

125–122 BC   Roman armies campaign in the Rhône Valley

123 BC   Tribunate of Gaius Gracchus marks an acceleration of urban violence in Rome

120 BC   Mithridates VI succeeds to the throne of Pontus

112–104 BC   War in North Africa against Jugurtha of Numidia

110–101 BC   Wars against the Cimbri and Teutones in Gaul, Spain, and north Italy. Marius holds an unprecedented six consulships in this period

103–100 BC   Tribunates of Saturninus. Pitched battles in Rome, as tension increases between Senate and people, Senate and equestrians, and Marius and the Senate

102 BC   Antonius' campaign against the pirates

91–87 BC   The Social War in Italy. Rome at war with her allies, defeats them, and then grants most Roman citizenship

89 BC   Mithridates invades Asia, orders the killing of around 100,000 Roman and Italian residents, and crosses to Greece where he is welcomed into Athens. All Roman territory east of the Adriatic is now in enemy hands

CRISIS

As Scipio watched the city completely destroyed while the flames consumed it, he is said to have shed tears and lamented openly for his enemies. After reflecting for a while he considered that all cities and peoples and empires pass away, just as all men have their own fates. Troy had suffered this, although once a prosperous city, and the empires of the Assyrians and the Medes, and that of Persia, the greatest empire of its day, and that of Macedon, which had just recently been so famous. Whether or not deliberately, he quoted the following lines of the poet:

> The day will come when Holy Ilium will perish
> And Priam, and his people, will be slain

And I spoke to him—for I was his teacher—and asked him what he meant. Without any dissimulation, he answered that he was thinking of his own country, for which he feared when he reflected on the fate of all mortal things.

(Polybius, *Histories* 39.5)

The destruction of Corinth and Carthage in 146 BC, following hard on the dismantling of the kingdom of Macedon and the humiliation of Syria and Egypt, made the Romans masters of the Mediterranean world. Polybius was right about that. Yet, within fifty years, they temporarily lost control of all their eastern territory, and nearly lost Italy too in a war against their Italian allies that caught them completely unprepared. Romans were also compelled to fight major wars against new enemies emerging from the interiors of Africa and Spain, Gaul and Germany, and to deal with the growing menace of piracy. Even worse, the crisis of the Republican empire coincided with the onset of internal strife that would lead to multiple political murders and civil wars. Rome survived this bloody century, just. But its civil institutions did not. The assemblies and the Senate lost their power, the courts were first politicized and then marginalized, and the army found a permanent place at the heart of Roman politics. This chapter asks how Rome nearly lost the imperial plot forever.

The Last Superpower

Polybius' eyewitness account of Scipio weeping to see Carthage burn is a nice anecdote, but it expresses a sense of Rome's historic destiny, not a genuine consciousness of risk. There is no sign that either Roman generals or Greek historians really understood the volatile condition to which the Mediterranean world had been reduced by the middle of the second century BC. The neglect of the seas that had allowed piracy to flourish was just one symptom of a much wider problem. Throughout the middle Republic, Roman armies had demonstrated their capacity to smash rival power blocks. But almost nothing had been put in their place. Rome was still much more of a conquest state—a society whose ideologies, economies, and political institutions were geared to constant expansion—than a tributary empire with stable fiscal, governmental, and security systems. Conquest states are common enough in world history, but most have been short-lived and failed to institutionalize their power. Rome nearly joined them.

At the time (167 BC) when Polybius declared Rome ruler of the inhabited world, its *directly* administered territory consisted of a scattering of colonies and public lands up and down Italy; the islands of Sicily, Sardinia, and Corsica; and a strip of territory along the Mediterranean coast of Spain. By 146 BC there had been some modest expansion in the Iberian peninsula; otherwise, the only additions were a province replacing the former kingdom of Macedon in the central Balkans, and another cut out of the immediate hinterland of Carthage. Rome's *informal* authority extended beyond these territories, but quite how far no one knew for sure. Even within areas that were certainly under Roman hegemony, such as the allied communities in Italy, the Greek cities of the Aegean world, and the minor kingdoms of western Asia Minor and North Africa, it was unclear precisely what level of control Romans wished to exercise. Perhaps the Romans themselves had not agreed on this question.

That uncertainty was an unfamiliar feature of international relations in the ancient world. Politically pluralist systems, like the world of the classical Greek city states or the mosaic of Macedonian kingdoms that succeeded them, had tended to develop common rules of engagement. Rome's first decades in the eastern Mediterranean were marked by attempts to observe some of the diplomatic protocols developed between Graeco-Macedonian kingdoms.[1] A city state could never deal with kings entirely on an equal footing. Cato the Elder was said to have defined a king as 'a creature that ate flesh'. He put it in Greek, so it might not be misunderstood. Offers of crowns to Roman senators—and reputedly the occasional marriage offer made by a king to an aristocratic Roman woman—did more to raise tensions than to calm them. But Romans learned the slogans and the critical terms of Greek diplomacy, such as the special nuances of terms like *autonomia* (the right to use one's own laws), and they learned Greek.[2] During the early second century, some senators became quite skilled in the complex diplomatic world of the Greeks, just as some Greeks made themselves experts on Roman habits. But progressively, Rome seemed to depart from the rules, or perhaps to revert to her own. For Greeks, a treaty that concluded a war—like the Peace of Apamea signed with Antiochus III of Syria in 188—recognized the independence of the two parties. The Roman presumption that they could still order around their successors— like Antiochus IV en route to conquer Egypt—must have seemed very odd. Romans, perhaps, were simply treating kings the way they treated Italian allies. Cultural misunderstanding only explains so much, however, given how well some Greeks and Romans knew each other. This sort of treatment was humiliating for kings, and perhaps that was the point. But the behaviour that caused the greatest difficulties was probably not intentional. This was the fact that Rome's interventions in the east were inconsistent and unpredictable. A number of allies increased their power by stages with no reaction from Rome, only to find that some final expansion provoked a savage response. Rhodes had been an ally against Philip V and Antiochus III and gained territory and influence after their defeats, but fell spectacularly from grace in 167. Delos's infamous rise was the result of the Romans deliberately deciding to limit Rhodian naval influence by creating a free port in the middle of the Aegean. I have already described how even Polybius, who knew Roman decision-making better than most, was astonished at the treatment meted out to the Achaean League.

One cause of Roman unpredictability was the volatility of domestic politics. A characteristic of all imperial systems is that disputes in the centre of power—the metropole—have disproportionate ramifications in the imperial peripheries.[3] Cities, kings, and tribes around the Mediterranean were now peripheral to Rome. It is too simple to say that the Roman Senate was divided into advocates of expansion and those who opposed it. It seems to have been common ground that the expansion of Roman power, of the rule or majesty of the Roman people, was a good thing. But on specific issues there were disagreements. Some were generated by personal rivalries. The enemies of Fulvius Nobilior and Manlius Vulso claimed that their campaigns against the Ambraciots and the Galatians respectively, both waged in the 180s in the aftermath of the great wars against Macedon and Syria, were opportunistic and unnecessary wars carried out for personal glory and gain. They were probably right. Other disagreements may have been on more fundamental principles. Cato campaigned for years before persuading the Senate that the city of Carthage, already twice defeated and subjected to crippling terms, should be destroyed. Eventually he won, but the obliteration of an ancient city shocked others besides Scipio. There was a particular reluctance to expand the areas under direct rule, perhaps from apprehension of the new costs and responsibilities that might follow annexation. Many of those reluctant were apparently senators on whom those responsibilities might fall, while some of the advocates of expansion were those who hoped to benefit from the public contracts that new provinces tended to generate. Tension began to rise between the senatorial aristocracy and the equestrian order from which many of the richer contractors, the *publicani*, were drawn.

Pressures for expansion were not always internally generated. For a variety of reasons, most to do with their short-term interest, a number of kings made Rome or the Roman people their heirs.[4] When Attalus III of Pergamum died in 133, leaving his royal lands and prerogatives to Rome, many senators did not wish to accept the legacy. But the tribune Tiberius Gracchus, desperate for additional revenue to fund his populist programme of land reform, took the issue to the assembly. As a result, Rome acquired first a rebellion and then a province in western Asia Minor. A decade later Rome acquired permanent responsibilities in southern France after a series of wars to protect her ally Marseilles and the land route to Spain. It is not clear whether a province was set up in 125 or a little later. Republican provinces are easier for us to spot when they were created by absorbing a pre-existing kingdom like that of Syracuse or Pergamum; in the west it is more a matter of noticing that the presence of pro-magistrates and armies had become regular instead of occasional.

Even when Romans did take overseas territory into direct rule, they were very selective in doing so. The kings of Pergamum had made their name defending Greek cities from Galatian attacks, and became powerful when Rome excluded the Seleucid kings of Syria from Asia Minor. Their kingdom included a number of ancient Greek cities grown rich on the wealth of the fertile river valleys that flow west from the Anatolian plateau into the Aegean, and also some much poorer highland marches, their defensive line against aggressors from the Anatolian interior. These border territories Rome had no interest in, and promptly handed them over to the minor kings to which she was allied. The security consequences should have been predictable. Yet similar decisions were taking place at the other end of the Mediterranean. Rome administered directly what had been the rich agricultural hinterland of Carthage. But the rest of Carthage's African empire, the defensive hinterlands, was handed over to the lesser kings of the Numidians and the Moors. The policy, in both spheres, was short-sighted. By the end of the second century, some of Rome's fiercest enemies were to be drawn from the petty monarchs whom she had strengthened in Asia and Africa. The modern parallels are depressingly obvious: Manuel Noriega in Panama, the Taliban in Afghanistan, and Saddam Hussein in Iraq all began their rise to power as allies of the West.

The career of Jugurtha, king of Numidia, provides a case in point. The Numidians were a federation of peoples living south and west of Carthage's territory. On the destruction of Carthage in 146 BC they were not just given territory and booty, but as Roman allies were also expected to provide troops for Roman wars. Jugurtha enters history in 133 BC as the leader of an allied Numidian detachment supporting Scipio Aemilianus' eight-month-long siege of the Celtiberian fortress of Numantia in northern Spain. The Roman historian Sallust tells the story of how, immediately after the victory, Scipio took Jugurtha aside, praised his ability, but then advised him to cultivate the friendship of the Roman people as a whole, not of individual Romans. Jugurtha proceeded to do the opposite. The lack of political consensus in Rome meant that it was always possible for him to find some supporters among the Senate, and as he murdered and intrigued his way into a more and more powerful position at home, he protected himself from the complaints to the Senate by bribing prominent figures. Sallust puts into Jugurtha's mouth the famous description of Rome as 'a city for sale and ready for destruction just as soon as it finds a buyer'.[5]

By 118 Jugurtha had murdered one heir to the throne and was at war with another; in 112 he ignored a senatorially mediated partition of the kingdom and two Roman embassies, killed his brother (massacring a group of Italian merchants in the final siege of Cirta), and survived both a Roman invasion and a summons to Rome. Eventually, Rome could ignore the situation no longer: a half-hearted war was fought by a succession of senatorial generals until the arrival of Gaius Marius. Jugurtha's capture in 107 and execution in 104 marked the end of a very long defiance of Rome.

Others watched and learned. Mithridates V of Pontus was one of those minor kings of Asia Minor whose power grew in the vacuum created by Rome's defeat of Seleucid Syria. Anatolia had been within the sphere of influence of the Seleucid monarchs, even if not always very firmly under their control, until Rome's defeat of Antiochus III first at Thermopylae in Greece and then at Magnesia in what is now western Turkey. The Treaty of Apamea signed in 188 BC effectively excluded the Seleucids from any further involvement in Asia Minor. A series of minor kingdoms grew up, some looking more Macedonian in style, some more Persian, all revolving around Rome. Pontus, which stretched along the southern coast of the Black Sea, formed its own hybrid identity, combining Greek titles with Iranian dynastic names. The king of Pontus too sent troops to help Rome against Carthage. When Attalus III of Pergamum, the most important of the Anatolian kingdoms, left his royal lands and prerogatives to Rome in 133, Pontic troops were among the allies helping Rome claim her inheritance, and the king was rewarded with some of the territory Rome did not want. Like Jugurtha, Mithridates V also exploited Roman friendship to expand his power at the expense of his rivals, in particular the kings of Cappadocia. On his death in 120 BC his son, Mithridates VI (see Figure 7), used this territory as the basis for an empire that included much of the Black Sea coast and more territory in Anatolia. Soon he too was a threat to Rome's interests, ignoring diplomatic warnings and gradually accumulating power. But the Romans were unable to confront him, for by then their hegemony was under threat from other directions.

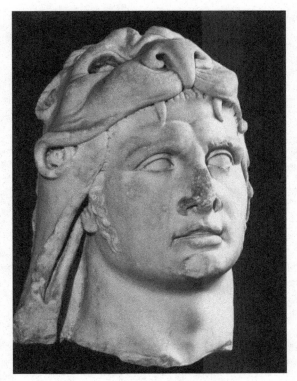

Fig. 7. Mithridates VI Eupator King of Pontus portrayed as Hercules. The Louvre, Paris

The Limitations of Mediterranean Hegemony

Roman hegemony created problems across the Mediterranean (see Map 3). A few historians have imagined a great conspiracy emerging between Mithridates, rebel slaves, and pirates. But the root cause was an imperialism that generated few structures of security to replace those it destroyed, and responded in an inconsistent way to challenges to its authority. This was not the only structural weakness of the Republican empire. Even if the Senate and people had been able to agree on how to exercise their power, had compelled generals on the ground to toe the line, and had conveyed a clear set of expectations to the cities, kings, and peoples under their indirect authority, Roman rule faced another fundamental weakness, this time geographical.

Map 3. The Republican empire around 100 BC

Roman territory at start of last century BC

ANTIOCH
CILICIA
Alexandria
ASIA
Ephesus
Cyrene
MACEDONIA
ILLYRICUM
Syracuse
SICILY
CISALPINE GAUL
Rome
SARDINIA
AFRICA
TRANSALPINE GAUL
Narbonne
CORSICA
Tarragona
HITHER SPAIN
FURTHER SPAIN

0   250   500   750   1000 km
0   250   500 miles

The defeats of Carthage, Macedon, and Syria had won Rome a Mediterranean empire. It was not just that the directly governed territories were easier to reach by sea than by land. This was in fact true; even provinces that were not actually islands were often separated from Italy by territory not under direct control. But a bigger difficulty was that Romans were most interested in controlling landscapes like those of Italy. Republican imperialism, taking direct rule and informal hegemony together, was exercised over a collection of coastal plains and islands. That is unsurprising. Most imperial nations begin by expanding within a single ecological zone. Chinese empires did not really expand into the tropical south until the Middle Ages.[6] European empires fought in the eighteenth century mostly over temperate territories—the so-called Neo-Europes[7]—before eventually trying to control sub-Saharan Africa and east Asia; the various central Asian empires—Persian, Macedonian, and Islamic—expanded east and west rather than north. Empire is rarely ecologically adventurous. Settlers prefer familiar landscapes where familiar crops may grow. Romans were slow to master mountains or forests and treated these landscapes and their inhabitants with distrust.[8]

Unfortunately for Rome, however, the Mediterranean has never been a closed system. The Middle Sea is located at the junction of three continents, the interiors of which have always been closely linked to the coastal fringe.[9] Ecotones between Mediterranean landscapes and continental hinterlands had promoted exchanges of goods, technologies, and peoples since the beginning of the Holocene.[10] In Africa and Asia Minor, in Gaul, Spain, and the Balkans, Rome tried to separate off the upland interiors from the parts she wished to control. That strategy was doomed to failure. Rome never had any chance of staying within her ecological comfort zone. It was not the first Mediterranean city state to underestimate the economic and demographic resources of areas it regarded as barbarous. Greek history is littered with accounts of the terrifying power of groups from the interior, such as Scythians and Thracians and in the end Macedonians. The Arab historian Ibn Khaldun saw a great pattern in Middle Eastern history in which nomads from the margins repeatedly invaded the settled civilizations of the Fertile Crescent, and were then absorbed by them. Chinese history too has been written in terms of a constant struggle for control of its Inner Asian Frontier, the long boundary between the lands of rice-cultivating city dwellers and peoples of the steppe.[11] Both Jugurtha and Mithridates challenged Rome with resources drawn from outside the Mediterranean world. In Jugurtha's case the

Romans had only themselves to blame, since it was they who had tried to restrict him to the Wild West of Numidian territory. From the uplands of the Maghreb he created a powerful army, and based himself in a landscape that Roman armies found hard to deal with. Mithridates made similar use of Anatolia and the Pontic regions, areas that Rome had disdained to rule.

Roman generals were progressively drawn into other continental interiors. The occupation of what is now Andalusia and Mediterranean Spain brought Rome into contact with the much larger tribes of the Meseta, peoples like the Celtiberians, with whom two generations of Romans fought between the 180s and the fall of Numantia in 133 BC. There were no easy frontiers before the Atlantic, and it took until the reign of Augustus to reach it. Possession of the Po Valley involved Romans in campaigns to control the Alpine valleys and Liguria. That, together with alliances left over from the war with Hannibal, brought Roman troops to the mouth of the Rhône and the territory of the Greek city of Marseilles. Minor campaigns escalated during the 120s into conflicts with the much larger tribal confederacies of the Allobroges based in the middle Rhône Valley and the Arverni of the Massif Central. Rome also exercised some sort of hegemony over the Greek cities and Illyrian tribes of the eastern Adriatic. But behind them, and to the north of the new province of Macedonia, were powerful nations like the Dacians and the Bastarnae, and to their east the Thracians.

Rome had little experience to draw on in dealing with threats of this kind. The major tribal confederacies of temperate Europe could marshal armies numbered in the hundreds of thousands, were technologically on a par with Roman troops, and had impressive fortified sites, even if they did not possess an infrastructure of cities and roads.[12] Greek and Roman sources presented northern barbarians as unpredictable savages. But these barbarians were also feared. Romans never forgot the Gallic sack of Rome in 390. Traditions varied about whether all or part of the city had fallen, and who should take the credit for Rome's survival, but treasure was piled up against further Gallic menaces until Julius Caesar's day, and the constitutions of Italian cities long had a clause in them requiring them to provide troops in the event of a *tumultus Gallicus*. Greeks, on the other hand, remembered the events of 279 BC, when a raiding party from the Balkans, identified as Celts or Galatians, had got as far as the sanctuary of Delphi before being driven off, perhaps by the god Apollo himself. Not long after these events three Galatian tribes had crossed over into Asia Minor and set up tribal kingdoms on the plateau, from which Galatian raiding parties held coastal cities to ransom. The reputation of the Attalid dynasty of Pergamum had been founded on their success in containing the Galatian threat. After the defeat of the Seleucids, the Roman general Manlius Vulso marched up onto the plateau and defeated them once again, bringing back great quantities of booty to Rome. But Romans and Greeks alike were well aware that great populations of similar barbarians occupied Europe from the Black Sea to the Atlantic, and further migrations and invasions were possible in the future.

That fear was rekindled in 113, when another horde ran into a Roman army in Noricum in the eastern Alps. Over the next dozen years the horde passed through Switzerland and the Rhône Valley, through central France, down into Spain, and then back again into Italy. En route they defeated a second and a third Roman army in 110 and 105. It was only Marius, the vanquisher of Jugurtha, who finally defeated the two parts of the migration, the Teutones in 102 at Aix-en-Provence, and the Cimbri in 101 at Vercellae in northern Italy. Romans did not feel like rulers of the world now. Eastern kings openly defied their requests for help, watching the growth of Mithridates' power closer at hand. Marius, despite his origins outside the charmed circle of the nobles and his links with the equestrians and populist politicians, was elected to an unprecedented six successive consulships to deal with the emergency.

Solutions and Failures

Romans were no fools, and the failures of their second-century hegemony were clear to them. Their analysis, however, was rather different from ours. We see inadequate infrastructure; an unsustainable preference for occasional booty over a tributary economy; and an unrealistic desire to control familiar landscapes, while ignoring the hinterlands with which they were joined. Knowing what came next we find it difficult to see why Rome did not move more quickly to institutionalize her power. Romans, however, saw a lack of the moral qualities advertised in the tomb of the Scipiones.[13] Both the rise of Jugurtha and the ineffectiveness of the first armies sent to deal with him were laid, by Sallust, at the door of the inner circle of the aristocracy, the nobles. Their susceptibility to bribery and their failures of generalship were signs of moral weakness. It was Marius, a man with no senatorial ancestors, yet possessed of traditional virtues, who had saved the day first against Jugurtha and then against the Germans.

One of Marius' associates, Marcus Antonius, was appointed to a command in 102 against the pirates. By good fortune we have large parts of a law passed around this time designed to improve the government of Rome's directly administered territories in the east.[14] One revolutionary feature was that it required Roman governors and commanders to coordinate their efforts to suppress piracy. It is a sign of a new consciousness of the obligations of empire and of the will of at least some of Rome's leaders to try to design solutions that went beyond telling a general to raise an army and deal with this or that king or people or threat in whatever manner he thought fit. The law was inscribed on stone and set up in a number of Greek cities. That fact too shows some awareness on the part of the drafters that Rome was no longer regarded as the liberating power. They were certainly right about this. A permanent law court had been set up in 123 BC to hear corruption cases brought by provincials against Romans in the provinces, one with more powerful provisions than its predecessor. It had received a good deal of use.

The decision of the assembly to accept the legacy of Attalus III, the passing of this great law, the commands of Marius and of Antonius, all emerged from a new style of politics that appeared in Rome in the late second century. It was created and led by a small group of senators who presented themselves as champions of the people, the *populus Romanus*. All Roman politics was cast in traditional terms, and they too claimed precedents and predecessors. But in reality both the problems they addressed and the solutions they proposed were new, as was in fact the politicized urban crowd to whom this politics was addressed.[15] The most common term for the new leaders was *populares*.

The most prominent members were Tiberius Gracchus and his brother Gaius, tribunes of the people in 133 and 123 respectively, and descendants of a family that had intermarried with the Cornelii Scipiones and played a prominent part in the conquest of Spain. Other leading figures included some men from quite different backgrounds, like Marius, but also others from ancient families. Julius Caesar was later to be associated with this movement. They sought the support of the popular assemblies, as their views could not achieve consensus in the Senate, and their rhetoric spoke of the ancient rights and prerogatives of the people. Their legislation included proposals to distribute public land to poorer citizens, to found new colonies outside Italy, and to provide subsidized (and later free) grain to the population of the city of Rome. Many chose to stand as tribunes of the people, converting what had been a minor political office designed to protect the interests of plebeians into a platform for wide-ranging reform. But they were hardly revolutionaries. Introducing the secret ballot into elections was the limit of their constitutional reform, and they seemed quite content with the structure of assemblies that gave more influence to the propertied classes, and with the senatorial monopoly of magistracies and priesthoods. Nor were their laws limited to matters of immediate concern to the people, let alone the poor of the city of Rome. No issue of Roman politics, from diplomacy and war to state revenues, the law courts, and Rome's deteriorating relations with her Italian allies, was beyond their interests. What united their proposals was a willingness to form radical solutions to the crisis of the empire, and the oratorical skill to persuade the assemblies to back them when the Senate would not.[16]

The programme of the Gracchi and their successors was no more consistent than the policies of earlier generations of senators. The proposal to redistribute public land brought howls of protest from allied communities, many of whose members had quietly, if irregularly, rented it for generations. Yet they also proposed more rights for the Italians. Their improved corruption court put senators at the mercy of Rome's equestrian order, ostensibly to improve the capacity of provincials to get redress against governors. But the organization of Asia handed the provincials over to those same equestrians by allocating them tax-farming contracts in a way that encouraged short-term exploitation from which governors were now afraid to restrain them. Opponents of these proposals found a common thread in the challenge posed to the leadership of the Senate. The law on piracy required magistrates to swear one by one to uphold it. Clauses like this appear in other legislation of the period. The implication was a grave insult to those who felt part of a class with a hereditary right to rule.

Mutual frustration and distrust led to ferocious condemnations and eventually violence. Both Gracchi brothers died in pitched battles in the streets of Rome, effectively between rival mobs of senators reinforced by their clients. Invoking the rights of the people and proposing radical legislation was not original in Rome. Cato too had made political capital out of his allegedly humble origins as a weapon against opponents of most ancient families. But political murder was something new. The deaths of the Gracchi were only the beginning. Marius was, for a while, an active supporter of another radical tribune, Lucius Appuleius Saturninus. Colonization, land distribution, and attacks on the nobles were once again on the agenda, the popular assemblies were again used to circumvent the Senate, and once again it ended in violence. Marius could have summoned his veteran soldiers to save Saturninus, but he refused to do so. This was the last time such restraint would be shown.

Roman orators and historians since Cicero have spent a good deal of time wondering how things had come to this pass. Ancient accounts stress the corrupting effects of wealth and the arrogance brought by empire. Modern writers note the explosive potential of the city of Rome, doubling in size each generation, a good part of the population composed of migrants without secure employment or close links of clientage to the ancient houses. The measures proposed show a keen sense of the scale and range of Rome's problems, and the solutions included genuinely innovative ideas, some borrowed from Greek history and philosophy. Most of all they show how dealing with the structural problems of the city of Rome, the Italian alliance, and the Mediterranean empire was no longer within the competence of the Senate alone. That these radical solutions were first proposed by political *insiders* perhaps tells us something of unrecorded collective failures of nerve and imagination by the ruling classes of Rome in the decades following the destruction of Corinth and Carthage.

Perhaps the most surprising failure was closest to home. By the late second century the role of Rome's Italian allies had become increasingly problematic: they shared in the strains of continual warfare, but received only a fraction of the benefits. When warfare pressed hard on the Roman citizenry, it pressed hard on the allies too. But the allies did not have a chance to vote on declarations of war, and although they usually received a share of the booty, it was not always an equal share. Their commanders took orders from Roman magistrates in the field. The Italians were partners in profiteering from empire, as well as in its acquisition. We find their names on inscriptions set up around the marketplaces of Delos, and in the politics of the great cities of Asia Minor. Overseas, they all spoke Latin and were collectively known, and treated, as Romans. Often the same families can be traced making money overseas and spending it in the towns of central Italy. Italians were energetic members of the trade networks that linked the slaving grounds of the east and north, the breadbaskets of the south, the vineyards of Tuscany and Campania, and the metal sources of Spain and the Alps to Rome.

At the centre of these networks was Rome, and many Italians visited, but their interests were generally excluded from the new politics of the *populares*. At best, this meant they were excluded from some of the rewards of empire:

cheap grain, grand building schemes sponsored by the state, lavish festival games and triumphs, the lucrative opportunities offered by public contracts for which only Roman citizens were eligible, and the growing protection offered by Roman courts. At worst, they might be the collateral damage of Roman politics, as when the Gracchan land redistributions unintentionally dispossessed Italian tenants on state land. Roman rule over Italy also seems to have become more autocratic. Ancient testimony gathers anecdotes about arrogant acts on the part of individual magistrates. These were the grievances of which they were conscious, but there were certainly other causes of tension. The growth on the peninsula of a city of half a million must have had profound effects on other Italian towns, especially drawing manpower to Rome. Colonization initiatives had petered out with the final conquest of the lands north of the Apennines: that removed both a possible source of tension and opportunities for allies who had sometimes been allowed to share in the schemes. The enrichment of the Roman elite and their investment in slave villas had effects that are difficult to map. But in every case the Italians suffered from a lack of representation, which created a need to depend on Roman aristocrats who were willing to patronize them. The *domi nobiles* (men who were aristocrats in their own communities) were forced to behave as clients.

The problem had begun to be noticed by the end of the second century, even by the *populares*. But schemes to offer the Italians various kinds of citizenship or legal redress came to nothing. Expectations were repeatedly raised only to be disappointed when the Senate and/or the people refused to back them. The flashpoint finally came in 91 BC. A tribune named Marcus Livius Drusus had proposed a comprehensive political programme designed to heal the political rifts opened by the proposals and murders of the Gracchi and of Saturninus. The plan was an ambitious one, including bringing 300 equestrians into the Senate to smooth over relations there and a great colonization programme. Some of these elements would re-emerge in Sulla's dictatorship. But it also included granting citizenship to the Italians. Hopes were raised again, and then dashed. The laws he had passed were abolished, and Drusus himself was murdered. This was the final straw. A great alliance appeared almost overnight, one in which the hill peoples of the Apennines, the Marsi, the Samnites, and others, took the lead. Historians disagree about their precise aims—did they want to destroy the Roman state or become a full part of it? Perhaps the allies themselves were divided.[17] Italian voices are now lost: the speeches made at the time were not recorded, and all historical accounts of the Social or Italian War are coloured by a desire for reconciliation and the teleology of the fall of the Republic. But their tactics were well worked out. Italian leaders knew each other well from service together on Roman campaigns and from participating in a social world that centred on the great houses of their Roman friends. A new capital was declared at Corfinium (renamed Italia), in the heart of the Abruzzi mountains. Coins were issued for a new Italian state. Some depicted an Italian bull trampling on a Roman wolf. Rome suddenly found herself struggling for control of the peninsula for the first time since Hannibal's rout.

Politicians of all sides rallied to Rome's cause. Marius, no longer as popular as when he had routed the Cimbri and Teutones, fought alongside his rival Sulla. There were two frantic years of fighting, between 90 and 89, with a couple more years of mopping-up actions. Rome won the battles, but conceded all that had been demanded. By 87 most Italians were Roman citizens. The reasons were straightforward. Rome had been fighting wars she had not chosen for nearly two decades, she had only just escaped a repeat of the Gallic sack, and the domestic political system was imploding. Survival without the Italians was unthinkable. And just to encourage them to do the right thing, yet another threat emerged.

War in Italy offered Mithridates of Pontus an unmissable opportunity. His armies annexed the neighbouring kingdoms of Bithynia and Cappadocia in 89 BC. The deposed kings bribed the Roman ambassador Manius Aquillius to compel Mithridates to restore them. But when Aquillius ordered Bithynia to invade Pontus in punishment, Mithridates invaded the Roman province of Asia, executed Aquillius by pouring molten gold down his throat to punish him for his greed, and instructed the Greek cities to demonstrate their loyalty by killing all their Roman residents. Estimates of the Roman and Italian dead range between 80,000 and 150,000. The Pontic armies swept across the Aegean to Athens; there the anti-Roman faction welcomed them with open arms. Victory was short-lived. Sulla marched east to sack Athens. The peace he made with Mithridates was not a permanent solution, but enough to allow him to return to Rome determined to purge the city of *popularis* politics and of its main exponents. At home and abroad politics had entered a new and bloodier phase.

Further Reading

Robert Morstein-Marx's *From Hegemony to Empire* (Berkeley, CA, 1995) expertly tracks the evolution of Roman rule in the east between the fall of Carthage and the supremacy of Pompey. The opening chapters of the first volume of Stephen Mitchell's *Anatolia* (Oxford,

1993) set this story in a rich geographic frame. Rome's equally tentative search for stable limits of power in the western Mediterranean is the subject of Stephen Dyson's *The Creation of the Roman Frontier* (Princeton, NJ, 1985); one of the many strengths of this work is the inspiration it draws from comparative studies. The implications of seeing the Mediterranean as a region in which continents meet, rather than a world enclosed in itself, are discussed in several contributions to William Harris's *Rethinking the Mediterranean* (Oxford, 2005).

The best single account of the collapse of the Republican system is the title essay in Peter Brunt's *The Fall of the Roman Republic* (Oxford, 1988). Mary Beard and Michael Crawford's *Rome in the Late Republic* (London, 1999) is full of ideas. Anyone seeking a detailed account of the period is referred to volume ix of *The Cambridge Ancient History*, edited by Andrew Lintott, John Crook, and Elizabeth Rawson (Cambridge, 1994). Modern understandings of what the *populares* thought they were doing, at home and in the provinces, have been revolutionized by the publication of a marvellous edition of their epigraphic laws in Michael Crawford's *Roman Statutes* (London, 1996). Andrew Lintott's *Judicial Reform and Land Reform in the Roman Republic* (Cambridge, 1992) contributes to the same debate. Important essays on the role of the people in this period are now helpfully gathered in the first volume of Fergus Millar's collected papers, *Rome, the Greek East and the World* (Chapel Hill, NC, 2002).

VIII

AT HEAVEN'S COMMAND?

The most important respect in which Roman civil society surpasses that of other states seems to me to be how it treats the gods. I think too that the very thing that among other people is viewed unfavourably is, among the Romans, a source of cohesion: I mean their respect of the gods. For it is developed to such an extraordinary extent among them—both in their private affairs and in the common business of the community—that nothing is treated as more important than this. This fact seems astonishing to many people.

(Polybius, *Histories* 6.56.6–8)

A Moral Empire

We are, in many ways, still Greeks when we contemplate the rise of Rome. It is not just that we rely heavily on Greek narrative accounts or even that we share with our Greek witnesses—Polybius and Diodorus, Dionysius and Plutarch, among many others—a sense of ourselves as outsiders looking in on Rome. Even more fundamentally, the way we try to understand how societies work remains firmly based in a tradition of political science that can be traced directly back to classical Greece. When Polybius asked why it was Rome that had conquered the Mediterranean, he found his answer in a unique balance of political and military institutions—a perfect blend of monarchical, aristocratic, and democratic elements—along with the attitudes and habits they inculcated. Religious awe was just one component; he followed the passage quoted above with a good functionalist explanation of its role in stabilizing the social hierarchy. He looked, in other words, for Rome's comparative advantage over its competitors. Another Greek, Aelius Aristides, in a speech of praise addressed to Rome nearly three centuries later, compared Roman success in government with the failures of earlier empires. One key variable he identified was inclusiveness, that Romans were unusually willing to incorporate those they had subjected into the citizen body.[1] Whether or not we agree with these particular arguments, the analytical procedure is familiar.

Romans did not think like this, or not until the Greeks taught them to do so. Even after Rome had grown its own philosophers, they did not supply the most influential explanations of Roman success and failure. To access those we have to investigate the interlinked worlds of moral discourse and religious practice. For from the very earliest records we can access, Roman texts and monuments alike proclaim that Rome had grown great through the virtue of her men and the favour of her gods.

During the Republic, it was common to attribute Roman successes to the virtue of its leaders, and Roman failures to their vices or occasionally to errors they had made in preparatory rituals. One result was a moralizing rhetoric that coloured all surviving speeches, histories, and biographies and many other kinds of literature.[2] Right back in the third century BC, the first of the *elogia* carved on the sarcophagi from the tomb of the Scipiones shows the close connection made between what we would call private moral qualities and public conduct. A rich tradition of invective preserves many more accusations of vice than memorials of virtue. The political reputation of Caesar was damaged by allegations that he had allowed King Nicomedes of Bithynia to have sex with him. Few of Cicero's opponents in the trials in which he made his name escaped attacks of this kind. Virtue and vice were also manifested in the public sphere, where Romans performed as speakers and priests and magistrates and generals. So, Caesar's success in conquering Gaul was proof of his own dynamic virtues. Sallust, writing in the 40s BC, recalled an ancient habit of taking the examples of virtuous men as models for one's own conduct:

For I have often heard that Quintus Maximus, Publius Scipio and the most famous citizens of our state were in the habit of saying that their hearts were set ablaze with the ardent desire for virtue when they looked on the images of our ancestors.[3]

The remark forms part of a justification of history, but he goes on to say how the practice has fallen into decline, and people today only want to outdo their ancestors in wealth rather than virtues. Similar sentiments were expressed by Tacitus; writing nearly two centuries later he made similar comments at the beginning of his account of the exemplary life of Agricola.[4] Even the emperors would find themselves under this moral spotlight, as they did in Suetonius' *Lives of the Caesars* or Juvenal's *Satires*, although condemnation was generally reserved for those who were safely dead. Roman writers in every age lament the decline of traditional morality, but in fact the moral tradition at Rome was extraordinarily long-lived.[5] That did not mean that values were absolutely fixed: even long-lasting terms like *virtus* and *pudicitia* were contested and reworked as the conditions within which individuals lived their lives changed. The shift to autocracy at the start of the Principate limited the ways in which men could exercise the kind of virtue celebrated on the epitaphs of the Scipiones, while women too found their spheres of action remodelled from above.[6] Perhaps vices were more stable: Procopius' *Secret History* offers an unexpurgated account of Justinian's court that would have delighted early imperial readers.

That mode of thought also offered an interpretation of the collective history of the Roman people. Roman prosperity derived from the proper management of relations with Rome's gods and from ethical behaviour; periods of crisis might be understood as signs of a breakdown in those relations and of moral decadence. Rome's gods had issued no detailed code of personal ethics, but their support might be lost either by neglecting their cult or through acts of impiety. Polybius followed his account of Roman piety with the observation that Romans always abided by their oaths. Equally, the gods gave support to the brave and virtuous, concepts the Romans barely distinguished. When disasters struck or when dreadful omens were reported, the Senate might ask a particular college of priests to consult the oracles known as the Sibylline Books, which generally prescribed a major public ritual or the invitation of a new god to Rome. Occasionally, more sinister remedies were employed. Some disasters might be caused by one of the Vestals breaking her vow of virginity. If she was found guilty she would be buried alive.

No crisis was greater than the civil wars that convulsed the state between the murder of the Gracchi and Octavian's victory over Antony and Cleopatra at the battle of Actium. Naturally these wars came to be explained in terms of collective moral failure, perhaps the effects of the corrupting luxury brought by imperial success. The period saw its fair share of contested omens and struggle for the control of religious institutions.[7] Trials of Vestals were held not long after the murder of Gaius Gracchus, and one source reports the Romans even resorted to human sacrifice as well. A sequence of public panics—we might almost call them episodes of religious hysteria—also gave rise to some wider feeling that failures in moral conduct were in some sense the root of the troubles of the late Republic. Livy addressed this in the preface to his great history, itself a product of the crisis, but not completed until the reign of Augustus. He begins by sketching out the narrative arc of how Rome grew from small beginnings to the point where it is now overburdened by its greatness, contrasts its pristine virtue with the terrible contemporary circumstances, and asks the reader to reflect on:

the way of life and customs, and the sort of men and means by which good order at home and empire abroad were won and extended: then as decline sets in, let him reflect on how standards began to slip little by little, then began to slide faster and faster and eventually collapsed until we reach the situation today, where we can bear neither our vices nor the remedies they call for.[8]

Livy's interpretation was not exactly Augustan: the closing phrase is altogether too pessimistic. But the huge investment Augustus put into moral rearmament suggests that ideas of this kind were fairly widespread.[9]

So too does the way reconciliation took place in the years after the battle of Actium brought the civil wars to an end. In 27 BC, the Senate and people of Rome presented Octavian with a great shield on which were listed Courage, Justice, Mercy, and Piety towards the gods and his country. Courage translates *virtus*, the origin of our notion of virtue, but meaning something rather different to Romans. *Virtus* was not a condition but an active force, one connected to manliness, a power that might transform the world. Justice and Mercy were conventional regal qualities. Piety, *pietas*, was the set of dispositions that held Rome's hierarchical society together. It was the signature virtue of Virgil's Aeneas, repeatedly displayed towards the gods and his father. Freedmen and clients owed *pietas* to their former masters and patrons. It includes recognition of duties, as well as respect for persons. Augustus had displayed these qualities, the shield proclaims. Perhaps the senators also hoped he would continue to display them. The battle of Actium was presented as a 'secular miracle':[10] by winning it Octavian had saved the state. The title 'Augustus' was awarded to him around the same time. It was not an office, nor did it already have some established meaning, but its connotations were easily understood as religious. Augustus' virtues had saved the state, and Rome might now return to a golden age.[11] The original shield, itself made of gold, was hung in the Curia Julia in Rome, where the Senate often met. A few years later an issue of denarii, the coin in which soldiers were paid, carried an image of the shield. Other coins bear the image of the civic oak crown, a traditional reward for saving the life of a fellow citizen. That too had been awarded to Augustus. Signs of this kind formed both a rationalization of recent history and a manifesto for the future. Rome, they declared, was back on track.

Religious Imperialism?

If disasters signalled a breakdown in relations with the gods, it followed that success was a sign of divine favour. The general whose battlefield vow was answered paid his dues by building a temple to the god in question (see Picture Box 3). Each triumph culminated in the temple of Jupiter on the Capitoline. As with morality and history, this could be imagined on a larger scale. Romans certainly came to believe the gods supported their wider hegemony. Virgil's *Aeneid* plots the rise of Rome as the fulfilment of a divine plan, the will of Jupiter. How early did Romans begin to suspect they were especially beloved of heaven? There are a few tantalizing hints that already in the third century BC some Romans had begun to feel that the gods— their gods—had some special plan for them, and so that their religious action was not exactly on a par with those of others. In the ruins of the temple of Dionysus on the Greek island of Teos, an inscription was found that records a letter sent by a Roman magistrate in the 190s BC confirming the temple's privileges. It also asserts that the Roman people were the most religious of men.[12]

It is possible that when Polybius remarked on the exceptional piety of the Romans he was reflecting the self-image of the Roman elite. Was the exceptional religiosity of the Romans already a theme of the lost history written by the senator Fabius Pictor, a work to which we owe (indirectly) our most detailed accounts of Rome's earliest major festival, the *Ludi Romani*?[13] Pictor had also been part of a delegation sent by the Senate to the oracle of Delphi after Hannibal's victory at Cannae in 216 BC. Polybius had, naturally, many opportunities for observing the religious life of Rome,

Picture Box 3 Victory temples of the Largo di Torre Argentina

The remains of these four temples are conserved in the Largo di Torre Argentina, a modern square in the historic centre of the city of Rome. Although they are all aligned roughly the same way, facing east, they were not constructed as part of a single programme: Temples A and C were probably constructed in the third century, Temple D in the second, and Temple B (the circular one) in the early first century BC. Dating them is complicated not only by the fact they were excavated very rapidly in 1929, but also because they were repaired and rebuilt many times in antiquity. Together, they are a tiny fraction of the victory or votive temples built over the last four centuries BC. There is another cluster at the church of S. Nicola in Carcere, itself a converted temple. The temples of Portunus and the Round Temple by the Tiber port also survived because they were converted into churches. Many other temples are known from documentary sources.

Many or most of these small temples were set up to fulfil vows made by commanders, often on the battlefield. A general would promise to build a temple to a particular deity if he won a victory. The temples, therefore, (a) commemorate particular successes, (b) signify the piety of the dedicator, and (c) recognize the assistance given by the god. Many gods received these vows, not just familiar gods such as Juno and Jupiter but also gods appropriate to the particular battle. The epitaph of Lucius Cornelius Scipio records that he built a Temple to the Storms (*tempestates*) during a naval battle, and Temple B at Largo di Torre Argentina was dedicated to Good Fortune on This Day (*Fortuna Huiusce Diei*). Permission to build was in the hands of the Senate, but at least some victory temples were looked after and repaired by the families of the original dedicators, so that they served an additional function as signs of the antiquity and piety of particular *gentes*. A few victory temples were associated with the tombs of the family of the dedicator: a Claudian tomb was located near the Temple of Bellona built by Appius Claudius Caecus.

The habit of building victory temples was unusual in the ancient world. Most ancient cities had one or more central temples, like the Temple of Jupiter on the Capitol, and usually a number of others dedicated to particular gods. Victory temples gave Republican Rome a distinctive monumental style, perhaps especially striking to visitors from the Greek world, who were also struck by the lack of other monumental types, such as theatres and (until Cato the Elder built the Basilica Porcia in 184 BC) stoas and porticoes. For citizens of Rome, the effects would have been different. The steady accumulation of these monuments must have contributed to a sense of the support given by the gods for Roman war, and also of the historical successes of Roman armies. Although few had spectacular ceremonies associated with them, they may have acquired particular significance when triumphal processions wound around the city. The built environment may have had as powerful effect on popular attitudes to war and the gods as the speeches of orators which sometimes referred to them.

Further Reading

Amanda Claridge, *Rome: An Oxford Archaeological Guide*. 2nd edn (Oxford: Oxford University Press, 2010).

Eric Orlin, *Temples, Religion and Politics in the Roman Republic* (Leiden: Brill, 1996).

Dan-el Padilla Peralta, *Divine Institutions. Religions and Communit in the Middle Roman Republic* (Princeton, NJ: Princeton University Press, 2020).

Amy Russell, *The Politics of Public Space in Republican Rome* (Cambridge: Cambridge University Press, 2016), 114–20.

and ritual was an important concern for many members of the elite. Many senators held priesthoods, and unlike magistracies these were generally held for life. The most important were regularly signalled in ceremony, and were commemorated long after their death. Caesar, Cicero, and Pliny the Younger all held major priesthoods, and their writings show how important this was to them. Priestly colleges co-opted new members on the death of an incumbent; the numbers were tightly restricted, and it was a convention not to co-opt an immediate relative. Support in winning priesthoods established lasting ties of gratitude. The *populares* briefly introduced elections, but the emperors ended this, making priesthoods another of the gifts they might bestow. Their prestige survived these transformations. Both in ritual performances and in the meetings of the colleges and the Senate itself, senatorial priests devoted an extraordinary amount of time and energy to the precise management of cult and to dealing with prodigies and religious problems, such as how exactly to declare war on a distant enemy or what ceremonies should be used to bring a particular new god into Rome. Religious knowledge at Rome consisted of expertise in ritual, not in theology, and rituals were fundamental to the workings of the state.[14] Assemblies, meetings of the Senate, even battles could not begin until the auguries had been taken, that is, until the approval of the gods had been established, usually by divining from the flight of birds. Once a general had been given his command, his *imperium*, he acquired a whole range of temporary ritual duties and prerogatives. Magistrates too performed sacrifices in the course of their civil duties. The Senate was the ultimate mediator between the Romans and their gods. It has even been suggested that the collective authority of the senatorial aristocracy largely derived from its religious functions.[15] All ancient communities had priests, but perhaps in Rome the correlation between political and religious authority was unusually strong.

Yet if we compare the rituals, beliefs, and religious institutions of Rome with those of their neighbours, the Romans seem in many respects very conventional.[16] Most peoples of the ancient world were polytheists: they believed in a plurality of gods and paid cult to a number of them. A merchant who travelled the Mediterranean around the turn of the millennium would find, in every city he visited, monumental temples, images of the gods, and priests conducting rituals on behalf of the community. The gods were generally treated as powerful social beings—physically close at hand, but of an order of being that transcended the everyday. Rituals were designed to establish their wishes and to win their support. Winning support almost always involved animal sacrifice. Mostly the animals that were sacrificed were drawn from that small range of domesticates on which all these economies depended. Processions, purifications, hymns, prayers, and music might be added to involve more people. Festivals took place, generally on an annual cycle, but also to mark special events, and might involve games or contests of various kinds. Kings and cities were the focus of the grandest cults, but there were also domestic and village cults and even private, personal vows and offerings made to gods. Oracles of various sorts and healing shrines were ubiquitous. All this was true of Greeks and Etruscans, Phoenicians and Samnites, and most of the other peoples of the Mediterranean world.

Each community had its own cults, of course, and there were differences that perhaps mattered enormously to worshippers. A few peculiarities were infamous: the Egyptian gods had the heads of animals; the Jews had only one god; the Druids were rumoured to sacrifice not only animals, but also humans. But these scandals stood out against a background of broad similarity. Many gods were in any case shared among peoples who felt themselves related, so all the Greeks worshipped Athena; and all the western Phoenicians Melqart (originally the great god of Tyre), and so on. The Romans had their own bizarre rituals: Greek scholars like Dionysius and Plutarch, as well as Roman ones, devoted some effort to trying to work out what rituals like the October Horse were all about.[17] Quite probably there was no ancient consensus, and the origins of most Roman rituals are now lost, even if we can sometimes see how they functioned in later ages, to mark time, to draw the community together, and to assert the relative status of those who presided, participated, and only watched.

From at least the archaic period, there had been attempts to find equivalences between the gods of different peoples—Jupiter and Zeus, Hercules and Melqart, Uni and Astarte, and so on. Those connections were made not only by philosophers, antiquarians, historians, and poets, but also by traders, migrants, and envoys who encountered new gods in the communities they visited and wondered how new they were. The bilingual dedications to Astarte/Uni at Pyrgi described in Chapter III show how closer relations between nearby peoples, in this case Phoenicians and Etruscans, might bring their gods into a new relationship. It was common to behave as if a single divine order lurked behind the myriad local cults.

Eventually, some religious leaders made a virtue of this by deliberately asserting syncretisms: the goddess Isis in Apuleius' *Metamorphoses* claims to be known as the Great Mother of the Gods at Pessinus, Cecropian Minerva in Attica, Venus of Paphos on Cyprus, Dictyan Diana to the Cretans, Stygian Prosperina to the Sicilians, Ceres at Eleusis, and also as Juno, Bellona, Hecate, and the goddess of Rhamnous, but really Queen Isis, the form used by the Ethiopians and Egyptians.[18] The Baal of the city of Doliche in Syria spread through the Roman world as Jupiter Optimus Maximus Dolichenus. Philosophers reached even more radical conclusions, for example that none of the traditional gods was correctly imagined or that the gods of the poets were demons, lesser deities created by a greater more perfect god who did not share the passions and social roles of humans. Speculations of this kind played a major part in converting the god of the Jews into the universal deity of the Christians. Most of these developments took place in the early imperial period. But Romans were aware of alien gods and the philosophical debate they inspired from the earliest stages of overseas expansion. Pictor's visit to Delphi was not unusual. Many Roman governors of Macedonia visited the sanctuary of the Great Gods on the island of Samothrace, and during the last century BC many prominent Romans were initiated into the mysteries of Demeter and the Maiden at Eleusis; they included Sulla, Cicero, Antony, and Augustus. The literature of the Republic also shows a familiarity with Greek philosophical speculations on the divine: Ennius produced a Latin version of the work of Euhemerus, who argued that the gods of myth had once been great men, Lucretius followed Epicurus' line that the gods were impossibly remote from the material world, or perhaps did not exist at all, Cicero's philosophical dialogues *On the Nature of the Gods* and *On Divination* bring conventional Roman thought into contact with the major philosophical schools of his day.[19]

Equivalences of this kind ought to have posed real problems for the management of Roman ritual. If the gods of the Egyptians were the same as those of the Romans (Thoth = Hermes = Mercury, for example), then why was it important that Romans follow their own customs when sacrificing? After all, even the name used to address the god mattered enormously in some Roman rituals.[20] Equally, if all the Junones of Latium referred to the same goddess (and also to Astarte of Carthage and Uni of Veii), why was it necessary to persuade the Juno of Veii to come to Rome in 396, Juno Sospita to come from Lanuvium in 338, or to establish cults to Juno Lucina in 375 and Juno Moneta in 344? And what about the idea that a city's gods were in some sense its citizens and might be expected to give it particular support? Propertius imagined the gods of the Romans ranged against those of the Egyptians at Actium, while the armies of Octavian and Cleopatra fought below. How could this be related to the idea of a single cosmos? More fundamentally, were the gods of Rome *the gods*, or only the gods of the Romans? No single answer emerged as authoritative. Right up until late antiquity we can find the same Roman senators worshipping a great number of traditional, alien, and syncretized gods, and also debating the minutiae of correct ritual in the priestly colleges. Romans seem to have managed to maintain a mental reservation between a sense of the extreme particularity of individual *cults* and an openness to all sorts of theological and cosmological speculation, between punctiliousness about ritual practice on the one hand, and an apparent lack of concern about belief on the other.[21]

If the Roman elite of the middle Republic thought themselves especially pious, and if they attributed success in war to the favour of their gods, is it possible to see this as a driving force in Roman imperialism? That case seems more difficult to make, especially when Rome is compared with other peoples. First, the religion of the Romans does not seem unusual compared with that of other Mediterranean peoples. Many Etruscan and Latin cities had priesthoods very like those of Rome, and some rituals associated with war, like those surrounding the priesthood of the *fetiales*, were probably shared by Italian states. Other cities attributed their success to the gods and imagined *their* gods to be on *their* side. The statue of Athena spat blood in fury at Augustus' victory over Actium; the god of the Jews lent support against Babylonian, Seleucid, and Roman imperialists.[22] Nor did Roman religion offer particularly effective means of integrating conquered peoples. Rome's gods always remained those of the city. Arguably, the Roman Empire had no collective ritual system until Caracalla extended the citizenship to all Romans in 212, and the Emperor Decius asked them all in 249 to take part in a *supplicatio*, a collective effort in which all citizens would perform sacrifices to the traditional gods, perhaps in expiation of whatever actions or inactions were held to be the cause of the ongoing military crisis of that period.[23]

Religion has had a more central place in other imperial expansions. It has been suggested that it was the demands of the Aztec gods for sacrifices that powered the expansion of their power in Mexico, and the divine calling of the Merovingian kings that led to the unification of Francia and its conversion into the most dynamic and complex of early medieval states.[24] It is difficult to imagine a plausible account of the Arab conquests that did not give

Islam a key role, or a history of the Crusades that did not stress the capacity of the religious authority of the popes to harness the military energy of medieval Europe. The institutions of the Church were powerful mechanisms for organizing conquered lands and peoples from the Norman conquests in the British Isles and Sicily through the eastward expansion of Europe and the settlement of Outremer right up to the early modern conquest of the Americas. Compared with these phenomena Roman religion seems reactive and inward-looking. Other Roman institutions played a much greater part in promoting and facilitating expansion: patronage and slavery, military alliance, and Roman law are obvious examples. The gods, it seems, were passengers on this journey.

Understanding Empire

What the religious traditions of the Romans did offer, however, were new ways of understanding and coming to terms with their growing power.

Ritual was at the centre of these understandings. There were rituals to mark the departures of generals and their returns; rituals to prepare for battles; the ritual of appealing to a named deity on the battlefield itself; the ritual of hailing a general *imperator* after a victory; the ritual extension of the *pomerium*, the sacred boundary of the city, after Roman territory had been increased; special honours paid to generals who killed their opponents in single combat, and so on.[25] Most famous are the set of rituals drawn together into the triumph.[26] Battlefield vows often promised a deity a temple in return for victory. As mentioned already, the city began to be filled with victory temples, many along the routes triumphal processions followed.[27] Most were rather small. But as the scale of booty increased in the early second century, larger complexes were built, including great temple complexes for Jupiter Stator, Juno Regina and Hercules of the Muses by the Circus Flaminius at the southern end of the Field of Mars. Augustus' temple to Mars the Avenger was the culmination of this tradition.

Another mode of using religion to reflect on expansion was offered by antiquarianism. From the late second century BC some writers had become interested in the history of Rome's many and complex cults. This was not an idle interest in the past, nor was it mostly the work of politically marginal scholars. Many of those authors who can be identified were political insiders, and their interest in Roman religion was concentrated on

questions of authority, on the senior priesthoods, and on the public rituals
of the state. It has recently been characterized as a 'civil theology', an ideologically orientated view of ritual which cohered very well with Romans'
perceptions of their place in the world and of the elite's view of their place
in the state.[28] Almost all of this material is lost, but it was used and sometimes cited by later writers. It made possible the most authoritative of all
accounts of Roman religion, Varro's *Antiquities Human and Divine*, which
even 500 years later was still the target of St Augustine's attack on traditional religion in his *City of God*. This tradition has profoundly shaped later
understandings of Roman religion which have been focused on the public
cults of the city of Rome, sometimes to the exclusion of all other aspects of
ritual and belief.[29] For Romans of the late Republic and early Empire the
history of those cults could be told in terms of the accumulation of more
and more foreign gods and ritual traditions. Varro seems to have thought
there was an original core of authentic Roman religion, perhaps the religion established by Numa, the second king of Rome, and Cicero writes
about the Lupercalia as older than the city itself. But otherwise the cults
of the city had accumulated in historical time. The *haruspices* were believed
to have brought from Etruria their art of divining the will of the gods
from the entrails of sacrificial victims and other portents. The worship of
Apollo and Asclepius had been brought from Greek cities in 433 and 291
respectively. Venus of Eryx came in 217 from Sicily, and Cybele, the Great
Mother of the Gods, had come to Rome from Pessinus in Asia Minor in
204. Cults which were considered as imported were managed by a particular priestly college, the *decemviri*, and many were worshipped according
to what Romans called 'the Greek rite', although it corresponded to no
actual set of Greek rituals.[30] The Augustan scholar Verrius Flaccus thought
that whole series of gods had been brought to Rome through the ritual of
the *evocatio* in which the protective deity of an enemy city was persuaded
to defect to Rome. The history of religion thus became a way of telling
imperial history.

   Antiquarian researches were very speculative, but it really does seem that
Romans of the third century BC were aiming to muster the most powerful cults in the Mediterranean world behind their empire. Each new god
arrived following a crisis, but the cumulative effect was to create an annex
of the public cults devoted to the gods of the wider Mediterranean.[31] So
the 'Greek rite' flags Apollo and the rest as immigrant deities. Cybele (see
Figure 8), when she was brought to Rome from her Anatolian cult centre,

was given a temple on the Palatine and games were set up for her in the Roman festival calendar. But elements of her more exotic rituals were preserved as if to retain a sense that she was a foreigner.[32] Fewer new arrivals are attested after the Hannibalic war, and there were periodic expulsions of new cults that had arrived by private agency rather than through the mediation of the Senate and its priests. The Senate's ferocious response to the cult of Bacchus in 186 was the first of several such reactions. Attempts were made to exclude Bacchus, Isis, the god of the Jews, and the god of the Christians. All entered Rome during the early empire. One way or another, accommodations of new cults and links with foreign sanctuaries accumulated right up until the conversion of Constantine.[33]

Finally, there was the emergence of the idea that Roman rule was divinely ordained.[34] By far the most extravagant productions along these lines date to the reign of Augustus, and this is also the point at which the religions of other communities were systematically oriented towards Rome. Yet an air of the divine had long surrounded Rome, and perhaps the emperors did no more than harness the power of the ritual tradition.[35] Octavian began his career as the son of a god, for Julius Caesar had been deified after his death and had received godlike honours just before it. Greek communities had already given honours of that kind to a number of Roman generals. From the start of the second century BC some Greek cities introduced worship of the goddess Roma at home, or else made dedications on the Capitol. There were also cults of the Roman People and of the Universal Roman Benefactors. Less information survives from the west, but in Spain some of Sertorius' followers believed he received prophecies from an enchanted deer, and in Gaul cults sprang up around Caesar after his death.

It is not surprising, then, that Octavian's success at Actium was marked almost immediately by a victory stela at Philae in Egypt on which his name was inscribed in hieroglyphics within a cartouche, a sign that he was considered a pharaoh, or that offers of godlike honours from the Greek cities of Asia followed soon after. The Shield of Virtue and the title Augustus awarded by the Senate and people of Rome pointed in the same direction. Honours from Italian and provincial communities followed, from client kings like Herod of Judaea and Juba of Mauretania, and from Roman colonies like Tarragona. A copy of the Shield of Virtue made in Italian marble and measuring 1 metre (about 3 feet) across has been found at Arles in southern France, where a colony of veteran soldiers had been recently established. If some were apparently spontaneous, in most cases it looks as

Fig. 8. Bronze statuette of Cybele on a cart drawn by lions, 2nd half of 2nd century AD

if careful negotiation preceded cult so as to establish exactly what would prove acceptable. In a few cases, such as the creation in 12 BC of a great altar at Lyons, where representatives of the Gallic communities met once a year to elect a high priest and hold gladiatorial games in honour of Rome and Augustus, it seems as if an imperial prince took the initiative. There was no single empire-wide cult of the emperors. Each community found its own way to indicate his proximity to heaven.[36]

The creation of emperor worship has seemed a watershed in Roman religion. It seemed so to some aristocratic Roman writers who generally deplored and ridiculed it. The emperors were their relatives, and they were all too aware of their very human failings. Poetry was an easier medium in which to suggest connections between Roman destiny, the will of the gods, and the person of Augustus. How Virgil managed this in his *Aeneid* has already been discussed in Chapter II. Augustan monuments deployed the globe prominently alongside traditional symbols of victory, and thousands of identical portraits of the emperor were produced and placed in every conceivable public and private context. The central public spaces of cities in Italy and the west were transformed by the creation of monumental temples and precincts. Greek inscriptions celebrate unprecedented honours and ceremonial. The personality cult of Augustus evokes inescapable echoes of those of the leaders of totalitarian regimes in the twentieth century: the capacity to mass-produce one man's face in a pre-industrial age is even more impressive.[37]

Many imperial nations have come to understand their rule as divinely ordained and sustained. Our idea of the mandate of heaven is Chinese in origin: the sons of heaven mediated between men and gods, and their position depended on the support of the latter. But almost every empire has claimed cosmic sanction. Achaemenid Persian shahs attributed their success to Ahura Mazda. Alexander came to be believed to be the son of Zeus and received godlike honours. Max Weber termed the idea that the powerful were powerful by heaven's will 'the theodicy of good fortune'. Such beliefs offer reassurance that human society is justly ordered and history meaningful. Like all ideologies, beliefs of this kind comfort rulers as well as make their rule seem less arbitrary to their subjects. If we look at early empires more closely, we find it is very common that the same emperors sought support from different gods in different parts of their realms. The Achaemenids patronized Marduk in Babylon, Apollo in Greek Asia Minor, and the god of the Jews in Jerusalem. Alexander won support from the oracle of Ammon in the Siwah Oasis west of Egypt. The Macedonian Ptolemies who ruled after him in Egypt became pharaohs. What would have been really innovative was a secular concept of empire.

Further Reading

Catharine Edwards's *The Politics of Immorality in Ancient Rome* (Cambridge, 1993) has transformed our understanding of Roman morality, inviting us to see moral discourse not as an expression of a particular group of prejudices, but as a highly politicized set of practices central to competition among the elite. Rebecca Langlands's *Sexual Morality in Ancient Rome* (Cambridge, 2007) explores the key virtue of *pudicitia*.

The best introduction to Roman religion is *Religions of Rome* (Cambridge, 1998), a collaboration between Mary Beard, John North, and Simon Price. Also recommended are Jörg Rüpke's *Religion of the Romans* (Cambridge, 2007), the same author's *From Jupiter to Christ* (Oxford, 2014), and James Rives's *Religion in the Roman Empire* (Malden, MA, 2007). Duncan Macrae's *Legible Religion* (Cambridge, MA, 2016) challenges the way we read Roman writing on their own religious tradition. Mary Beard's *The Roman Triumph* (Cambridge, MA, 2007) explores in vivid detail the complex relationships between war and ritual in Rome and the Roman imagination. Paul Zanker's *Power of Images in the Age of Augustus* (Ann Arbor, MI, 1988) brings out the phenomenal visual impact of imperial rituals in Rome, Italy, and the empire.

Picture Box 4 The 'Altar of Ahenobarbus'

These are among the earliest known bas-reliefs from Rome. They were found together in the historic centre of Rome in the late sixteenth or early seventeenth century but are now divided. The upper sequence is in the Louvre in Paris; the lower is in the Munich Glyptothek. They are nearly 1 metre (3 feet) high and originally formed two sides of a base, which perhaps supported a statue group, a cult statue, or conceivably a trophy. Together, they represent a medium of imperial and public art that has almost completely vanished, that of middle Republican Rome. There have been many attempts to provide a fuller interpretation, including connecting them with the historically attested Temple of Neptune (or the Temple of Mars) and with Gnaeus Domitius Ahenobarbus, a consul of 122 BC. But these are just educated guesses, a reminder of how much we do not know about early Rome. The monuments of the Republican city were constantly being replaced and repaired, and are also now mostly lost beneath the even more spectacular Rome of the emperors.

All the same, these fragments do reveal some things about the Republic city. Marble was a rare material in Rome before the last century BC, and both parts of this monument were imported from the Aegean. They may not have arrived at the same time. It has been suggested that the lower of the two, which shows a mythological procession, a Sea Thiasos, perhaps from the marriage of Poseidon and Amphitrite, was originally brought to Rome and may have decorated another temple before being united with the other reliefs. Its mythological sea monsters could have been thought suitable for commemorating a naval victory. The relief on the other side depicts Roman themes and was probably made in Rome, perhaps by Greek sculptors. On the right is the famous sacrifice of the *suovetaurilia*, in which a bull, a ram, and a boar were sacrificed together. In the centre is an altar, on the left a scene that probably refers to the *census*, a uniquely

Roman ceremony in which the citizen rolls were revised every five years and each citizen assigned to a division in which he fought and voted. It has been suggested it celebrates the censorship of the dedicator.

Together, they represent the Roman fascination both with their most ancient institutions and with Greek myth. Both strands can also be found in Latin literature, but these reliefs show that at least some Roman leaders felt they would be comprehensible to a wider public as well.

Further Reading

Florian Stilp, *Mariage et Suovetaurilia: Étude sur le soi-disant 'Autel de Domitius Ahenobarbus'* (Rome: Giorgio Bretschneider, 2001).

Mario Torelli, *Typology and Structure of Roman Historical Reliefs* (Ann Arbor, MI: University of Michigan Press, 1982).

KEY DATES IN CHAPTER IX

89–85 BC First Mithridatic War, ending in the Treaty of Dardanus. Further wars with Rome follow in 83–81, and again in 73

88 BC Sulla marches on Rome rather than give up the command against Mithridates to Marius, initiates a reign of terror, and then marches east

86 BC Marius and his ally Cinna become consuls after recapturing Rome. Widespread political violence. Death of Marius

84 BC Sulla returns from the east to depose his enemies who have established themselves in his absence, and to make himself dictator. Imposes political reforms on Rome, resigns dictatorship, and dies in 79

73–71 BC Spartacus leads a slave revolt, which engulfs central, southern, and eventually part of north Italy until Crassus defeats him in southern Italy

70 BC The consulship of Pompey and Crassus. The trial of Verres for corruption as governor of Sicily establishes Cicero's reputation

67 BC The *Lex Gabinia* creates a super-command against the pirates. Pompey appointed and clears the Mediterranean of pirates in just three months

66–62 BC Pompey replaces Lucullus in the war against Mithridates, and then campaigns in Armenia, Syria, and Palestine, reorganizing Roman provinces and client kingdoms across the entire region

63 BC Cicero's consulship, the conspiracy of Catiline. Julius Caesar elected *pontifex maximus*

62 BC Pompey returns from the east and lays down his command, but the Senate is slow to ratify his settlements or provide land for his veterans

60 BC Pompey, Crassus, and Caesar form a pact to pool their financial resources and political influence

59 BC Caesar consul. Then campaigns between 58 and 53 in Gaul, with raids into southern Britain and Germany

53 BC Death of Crassus following his defeat by the Parthians in the battle of Carrhae

49–48 BC Civil war between Pompey and Caesar ends with Pompey's defeat at Pharsalus and murder in Egypt. Caesar becomes dictator

44 BC Caesar murdered on Ides of March by a conspiracy of senators led by Brutus

43 BC Mark Antony, Lepidus, and Octavian form a pact and eliminate their political enemies, including Cicero

42 BC Mark Antony and Octavian defeat Brutus and Cassius, 'the Liberators', at the battle of Philippi

31 BC Octavian defeats Antony and Cleopatra, ending civil wars

THE GENERALS

His monument is on the Field of Mars, and inscribed on it an epitaph
which he is said to have composed himself. The substance is that none of
his friends outdid him in kindness, nor any of his enemies did him more
harm than they received in return.

(Plutarch, *Life of Sulla* 38.4)

Deadly Rivals

Sulla's epitaph is a chilling memorial to the horrors of politics at the end of
the Republic. Friendship and enmity were both competitions, and Sulla had
won on both accounts. He died owing no debts of gratitude, and leaving
none of his rivals unpunished. Perhaps this was a traditional aspiration, but
the scale of Sulla's realization of it was truly terrifying (see Figure 9).

Sulla had served under Marius in the war against Jugurtha and had pulled
off a political coup by having the Numidian prince betrayed into his, rather
than into Marius' hands in 107 BC. That compounded a rivalry based on
their opposing political positions. Marius, the new man, was the champion of the people, while aristocratic Sulla was better liked by the nobility.
He continued to distinguish himself as a general in the wars against the
Germans, on an eastern command in Anatolia, and then again in the Social
War against the Italians. Elected consul for 88 BC, he was the obvious man

Fig. 9. Bust of Sulla in the Munich Glyptothek

to be given the command against Mithridates, and so he was. But then civil conflict made another of its lethal intersections with Roman imperialism. A tribune named Sulpicius Rufus passed a law transferring the command to Marius. That was a scandal, but one that was dwarfed by what Sulla did next. Refusing to accept the decision, he marched his soldiers into the city, had Sulpicius killed, and drove Marius into exile. Master of Rome, he compelled the Senate to pass his own legislation, including reassigning the eastern command to him. Sulla then marched east to Macedonia, rapidly put Mithridates' generals on the defensive, and laid siege to Athens. He was as implacable there as in Rome: the Athenian *agora*, its ancient marketplace, was awash with blood. The story goes that Sulla only agreed to stop the massacre because of his love of classical Greek culture, saying that he spared the few for the sake of the many, the living for the sake of the dead. Then he pressed on to Asia to make a shameful peace with Mithridates at Dardanus. The king was granted his lands, recognized as a Roman ally once again, and effectively forgiven his crimes in Asia in return for supporting Sulla. For Sulla was keen to return. In his absence he had been outlawed, and his enemies Cinna and Marius had seized control of the city, waging their own reign of terror. Perhaps fortunately, both were dead before Sulla got back home. His army invaded Italy in 84 and he soon seized the city. There he had himself made dictator and issued a list of his enemies, many of them associated with the *popularis* movement and friends of Marius. Those proscribed on the list could be killed with impunity and lost their property; in a cunning move it was auctioned off at knock-down prices, which thereby implicated the buyers in Sulla's coup. A few of the proscribed were killed; others— including the young Julius Caesar—fled for their lives. Sulla then used his dictatorship to impose his own political solution in a series of laws that in some ways resembled those proposed by Drusus just before the Social War. There would be a larger Senate (by recruiting the most prominent of the equestrians and ending the rift between the two orders engineered by the Gracchi); the tribunes were stripped of most of their powers, which made it much more difficult for *popularis* politicians to use the assemblies to out-flank the Senate (as the Gracchi, Saturninus, and Sulpicius Rufus had done); the Senate would control the courts, which freed governors from the need to kowtow to equestrian juries; and senatorial careers were to be subjected to a stricter discipline, with minimum ages for the senior magistracies. Sulla also distributed land to his soldiers, imposing colonies on many Italian cities: Pompeii was among those chosen, and we can follow in detail the uneasy coexistence of ancient Oscan families and Sullan veterans in the politics of the city over the next few decades. Then Sulla surprised everyone once again, by resigning the dictatorship in 80. The next year he died in retire-ment of natural causes.[1]

Sulla left a grim legacy. It was not so much the constitutional laws which were broken and abolished during the 70s with no power to protect them or the administrative reforms, which were uncontroversial. But the example he set was a terrifying one. Sulla was the first general to attack Rome with a Roman army. Sulla made the dictatorship (originally an emergency measure designed for moments when the city was in peril) into a tool for suspending civil society. Sulla invented proscription. His violence and the feuds it stirred up haunted Rome for a generation. When Pompey won his victories in the east in the 60s, it was widely feared he would return 'like Sulla'. Julius Caesar made himself dictator in the 40s. Octavian and Antony issued their own proscriptions. And politics had become incurably partisan. Perhaps the Gracchi had been idealists, and maybe Drusus had genuinely thought he had a solution to the Italian question. After Sulla, Roman politics got personal.

Sulla was not the first or the last reformer to forget that the act of changing the constitution sets a precedent for future changes, even if it is intended to bring harmony and stability. A number of his innovations were perhaps sensible, such as increasing the number of praetorships to provide enough magistrates and ex-magistrates to govern Rome's growing empire. Others, like increasing the size of the Senate, were pragmatic, especially given all the potential new recruits from the enfranchised Italian cities. But his solution did not tackle the conditions that made his rivalry with Marius possible. Personal rivalry was as old as Rome. The tomb of the Scipiones shows the high value placed on individual achievement as well as on the name of the greatest families.[2] From Cato the Elder to late antiquity we can hear aristocrats singing the praise of great figures of the past while condemning the vices of their rivals. Cicero and Sallust occasionally imagined that before the tribunates of the Gracchi the virtues of individuals like Scipio Aemilianus had been harnessed to the common cause. Livy celebrated mythical acts of heroic self-sacrifice in the early days of the Republic.

But the lethal innovation of the last century BC was the involvement of the army. Marius had very nearly deployed his veterans in support of his *popularis* allies, but in the end it was Sulla who took the first step. The close bonds formed between Marius and Sulla and their veterans were not purely sentimental or even a recognition of the great quantities of booty that might be won in some campaigns. The increased recruitment of citizens without land made them depend on their generals for resettlement. Sulla's army marched against Rome on the first occasion because they wanted eastern booty, and on the second in order to win land. He did not disappoint them. Why would future Roman armies not do the same as they had? None of Sulla's reforms touched this problem. Augustus would solve it by creating a military treasury with hypothecated revenue to pay fixed discharge bonuses to the veterans of what had become a standing army, one bound to the emperors by ritual and ideology as well as self-interest. No solution of that kind was, as far as we know, ever discussed during the Republic. Romans still could not conceive of an alternative to a citizen army commanded by an aristocratic general. Besides, Sulla's own career had established a model of the kind of behaviour he tried to outlaw, one that would be imitated by his lieutenants, including Lucullus, Crassus, and Pompey, and his enemies, especially Caesar. The failure of his constitutional solution within a decade of his death in 79 showed the power of the competitive urges he tried to stem. During the 70s the next generation of generals, most of them Sullan protégés, waged ferocious wars around the Mediterranean. Their opponents were very various. Pompey hunted down Marian survivors first in Africa in 82–81 and then in Spain in 77–71; Crassus waged war on Spartacus' slave rebellion in 72–71; Marcus Antonius and Quintus Caecilius Metellus both took the name Creticus for their campaigns against pirate strongholds on Crete in 71 and 69–67; and Sulla's oldest deputy, Lucullus, won the prized command against Mithridates. Every kind of campaign strengthened the bonds between generals and their armies, which made renewed civil war ever more likely.

Most impressive of all was Pompey. After the long campaigns in Spain against Sertorius, Pompey returned to Italy just in time to join Marcus Crassus in the war against Spartacus, and to steal some of his thunder. By 70 BC, Pompey and Crassus were consuls together in an uneasy alliance. This was the year Cicero drove Verres into exile, with a little help from Pompey, in fact. But it was a great command against the pirates, obtained with the help of Gabinius, that finally enabled Pompey to pull ahead of his competitors. His rapid success led to another bill, supported by Cicero among others, by which command in the war against Mithridates was transferred from Lucullus to Pompey. Pompey rapidly repelled Mithridates (who fled to the Crimea and committed suicide), dismantled his kingdom, and pursued his allies. He then remained in the east, in effect conducting a global reorganization of Roman territories and alliances along the Parthian frontier.

During Pompey's absence Rome was gripped once more by civil conflict. Cicero was consul in 63 and had to deal with a conspiracy that drew on a poisonous cocktail of social discontent and frustrated aristocratic ambition. Its leader, Catiline, enjoyed some real support and sympathy, including that of both Crassus and Caesar who shared his *popularis* politics. Cicero was given a free hand to arrest and execute the conspirators largely because the majority of senators, remembering Sulla's terrifying return from the east in 84, feared the kind of solution Pompey that might impose if it were left up to him. The same year Caesar managed to bribe his way to election as the most senior priest, the *pontifex maximus*.

Pompey finally returned in 62 BC and surprised many by stepping down from his command and dismissing his troops. But when the Senate would not ratify his eastern settlements or help find land for his soldiers, he formed a new alliance with Crassus and Julius Caesar. Historians today know this as the First Triumvirate, but it had no formal legal standing. Backed by the threat of Pompey's veterans, combined with Pompey and Crassus' financial muscle and the influence that Crassus and Caesar had over the people, the three effectively ran Rome for nearly a decade, picking the magistrates, allocating provinces and armies (mostly to themselves), and making debate in the Senate or the assemblies pointless. Their control was precarious and frequently challenged, and their opponents repeatedly tried to pull them apart. At times they sponsored different gangs in the city. For much of the 50s, Rome was a scene of mob warfare and appalling violence. Yet mutual interest kept them together.

What they themselves wanted most were super-commands of the kind Pompey had already enjoyed. After holding the consulship in 59, Caesar (see Figure 10) took the province of Cisalpine Gaul, the area that stretched across the Po Valley and up to the Alps. He was assigned a grand army and team of senatorial deputies, termed legates. The province of Transalpine Gaul was soon added to the command. It seems Caesar had first expected to be marching north-east into the Balkans following rumours of war, but news that the Helvetii were planning to leave their Alpine territory and pass through southern Gaul diverted him west of the Alps. That war began eight years of campaigns that resulted in the conquest of Gaul and invasions of Britain and Germany. The first books of his *Commentaries* go to great lengths to explain why each campaign was justified. It is difficult to believe Roman interests were really threatened, even by the Helvetian migration, but memories of the Cimbri and Teutones were recent, and he was careful to make the connection. An element of mission creep is clear. Caesar's later books spent less time justifying particular conflicts and instead emphasized the unprecedented extensions of the power of the Roman people he had brought about.[3] Roman armies had crossed both the Ocean and the Rhine for the first time, and city after city had fallen to his armies. News of his victories was greeted with public rejoicing in Rome. The campaigns were certainly lucrative, allowing Caesar to pay off the debts accumulated in successive election campaigns and to begin several monumental building

Fig. 10. Bust of Julius Caesar. Altes Museum, Berlin

projects in Rome. The same years saw the complete disappearance of the gold and silver coinages of Gaul.

Caesar's successes only inflamed the ambitions of his allies. By agreement among the three of them, Pompey and Crassus took the consulship for 55 BC. Both then claimed their own great provinces. Pompey was given Spain with the unprecedented permission to govern *in absentia* through legates of his own choosing. Crassus was assigned the province of Syria and a command against the Parthian Empire, with an army to match. The Roman and Parthian empires shared a small border and a much greater zone over which each tried to exercise influence. There is no sign that the Parthians wanted war with Rome; indeed, they had declined to support Mithridates. All the same, they looked a tempting target, and in late 55 BC Crassus headed east with an army based on seven legions. He spent the next year in Syria building up his forces. But not long after crossing the Euphrates in 53 BC, Crassus was defeated at Carrhae. His army was slaughtered and their standards were captured. Crassus himself was tracked down and killed. Avenging Crassus was allegedly one of Caesar's future plans when he was assassinated. Two decades later Mark Antony did mount an invasion, one that was unsuccessful, if not as disastrous as that of Crassus. Parthia took advantage of Roman civil wars to raid the east, but seemed content enough to cease hostilities when Augustus offered peace. Every indication shows that Crassus' campaign was as unnecessary as it was disastrous.

Up until the death of Crassus, the three-headed beast that ruled Rome seemed to be going from strength to strength. Together Caesar, Pompey, and Crassus commanded huge armies. Cicero and his friends were outraged, but the generals' exploits made them popular with the people. Only those senators who did not enjoy their patronage were left out of the loop, and it was easy to see the sour grapes behind the high-minded talk of senatorial liberty.

The Governance of the Empire

Rivalry between individuals was traditional in Roman politics. Roman writers even idealized it, seeing a competition to outdo each other in virtue as one of the driving forces of Roman success. A fragment of a speech of Tiberius Gracchus warns the people of Rome that all those who address them are motivated by self-interest, but his own self-interest is in providing them with the best possible advice. That was a rhetorical flourish, but it reflected an ideology as well. Yet the negative side of competition was all too evident. Civil war was bad enough. But there was also an incoherence built into any system that worked by delegating the power to make major decisions to individuals without imposing on them any discipline beyond the fear of the law courts on their return. During the 50s, even that sanction had disappeared. But perhaps one reason the activities of Caesar, Pompey, and Crassus did not arouse more opposition outside the senatorial elite was that the system they had overthrown was clearly badly broken already.

In Chapter VII I told the story of how, in the generation following Rome's final defeat of Macedon, the Mediterranean world was gripped by successive crises. I explained those crises as a result of the inconsistent treatment given former allies such as Jugurtha and Mithridates, combined with an erratic alternation of long periods of neglect of particular regions and terrifying interventions like the sack of Corinth. Where tax collection had been handed over to public contractors with no interest in justice or the long-term viability of imperial government, all the conditions were ready for rebellion. These problems were structural. The Senate's 'policy' was little more than the sum of the individual opinions of its members. There are signs that some *popularis* politicians thought that the behaviour of governors and generals could be controlled through subjecting them to more independent courts and more detailed legislation. One of Gaius Gracchus' most unpopular acts had been to give control of the corruption courts to the equestrians. His enemies were outraged. Why should they be subject to trial by their social inferiors? And anyway, it meant more people who would have to be paid off. Similar ideas lay behind the great law on the provinces that required Roman pro-magistrates to work together and alongside allies, including the kings of Cyrene, Cyprus, and Egypt. But the failure of *popularis* politics after Sulla—and the absence of institutions able to enforce such laws—meant that that provincial government in the last century BC was no better than it had been in the second.

The enemy of consistency was ambition. Many senators never won more than a single magistracy in their lives. For the rest, a provincial command would come once or maybe twice in a lifetime. With competition at home becoming more intense and more expensive, many governors clearly felt they had to make their year of service pay. The infamous Verres, whose prosecution in 70 BC established Cicero's reputation, allegedly quipped that a governor needed to raise three fortunes in his provinces, the first to pay back the debts he had incurred in getting elected, the second for himself, and the third to bribe the jurors on his return. Then there were the many other groups with vested interests in the provinces, Roman landowners and traders, those who lent money to provincials, and most of all those with public contracts, like the tax farmers. These were well connected, and an ambitious politician dared not offend, in his one year in office, a constituency who could help or hinder him for the rest of his career. Government of the provinces was driven almost entirely by struggles among the wealthy conducted in the short space of a command or a public contract. The

Roman state itself was relatively weak and relatively poor compared with the big players.[4] As a result, consistency, stability, and social justice were always secondary concerns. This tension between powerful grandees and a weak state was not new, but the stakes were so much higher in the last generation of the Republic.

Even Cicero, who tried very hard to govern justly during his single period as a governor in Cilicia in 51–50, found it hard to resist demands from back home. One man wanted help recovering sums he had lent provincials at ruinous rates, another wanted Cicero to find some panthers he could display in Rome, and even Cicero wondered if the risk of suppressing some banditry would be worth it if he could return to celebrate an *ovatio*, a sort of lesser triumph. Others had fewer scruples. Pro-magistrates exercised the power of life and death in their provinces, gave justice to cities and kings, and, when far enough away from Rome, they could behave like little autocrats. Many did. Verres allegedly crucified his enemies in sight of Italy. Another governor, when drunk, ordered an enemy envoy to be executed on the spot to please his lover, who complained that by accompanying him on campaign he was missing the games in Rome. Not all governors were wicked, but none wished to be regulated.

To the other structural deficiencies of the Republican hegemony, then, we can add an inability to operate effectively on any scale larger than could be handled by one man with a moderate-sized army and an oversized ego; and a system of government that more or less promoted corruption. Extortion, whether by governors themselves or conducted by tax farmers and other *publicani* with the governor turning a blind eye, increased the support that provincials gave figures like Mithridates. The reluctance of governors to work together made it difficult to tackle very large-scale problems. There had always been stories of failures of cooperation between consuls, both at home and on the battlefield. But as the empire grew, the problems became more acute.

Piracy is a case in point.[5] The enemy was highly mobile, not confined to one particular sphere of command, and indeed could move rapidly between them. Pro-magistrates commanding in Macedonia and Asia, the free cities of the Aegean, and the kings of western Asia could not work together effectively. The first Roman attempt to deal with piracy was probably the campaign waged by Marcus Antonius (Mark Antony's grandfather) in 102 BC. It seems a Roman fleet was moved into the Aegean, based first in the allied city of Athens; it then campaigned off the southern coast of Asia Minor, supported by other allies, including two Greek cities with small fleets, Rhodes and Byzantium. After victories in Cilicia, Antonius was awarded a triumph. But whatever solution he achieved was merely temporary. The *popularis* law on provincial government was passed just a year or two later, and piracy clearly remained a major priority. A new pro-magistrate is now mentioned in Cilicia, notorious as the 'badlands' of Asia Minor. Yet the problem persisted. Some pirate bands cooperated with Mithridates against Rome in the 80s. Pirates were able to kidnap a young Julius Caesar in the mid-70s. Kidnapping for ransom was a nuisance, but the real risk came from the pirates' capacity to interrupt the supply of grain to the city of Rome. The conquest of Crete in 69 was largely motivated by the desire to shut down other pirate bases. Yet pirates were mobile and had many bases. Food shortages and rising prices in Rome pushed piracy to the top of the political agenda. With hindsight we can see the problem was systemic, the product of the absence of any permanent security system in the region. The Macedonian kingdoms could no longer maintain fleets, and naval powers like Rhodes had been humiliated. No permanent fleets or naval patrols were created until the reign of Augustus.

This was the context for Pompey's first great command. One of the tribunes for 67 BC, Aulus Gabinius, passed a law stating that a single commander be appointed against the pirates, with power to coordinate up to twenty-five legates (deputy commanders) and a fleet that perhaps numbered between 250 and 300 vessels, not counting the contribution of allies. Even more radically, the commander would have authority to raise troops in any Roman territory and would outrank (literally have greater power, *imperium maius*, than) any pro-magistrate in an area extending 80 kilometres (50 miles) inland from the coast. The idea of giving any single magistrate or pro-magistrate the right to command other senators, both his deputies (legates) and other regular pro-magistrates in their own provinces, had no precedent. The command was to be for three years. It was designed for Pompey and, after some manoeuvring, he was given it. In practice, he needed only three months. The Mediterranean was swept end to end, piracy was eliminated, and the captured pirates resettled in provincial communities. Pompey's reputation was extraordinary; hence the award of the other major command, that against Mithridates. But the bigger lesson was also clear. Look at how much could be achieved with a new style of general and a new style of command.

During the 50s the lesson was applied elsewhere. Caesar's command in Gaul included not only a number of legions, but also a number of senatorial deputies. As a result, he could divide his army and organize much more complex operations. He was also able to return periodically to southern Gaul or north Italy, leaving his legions under the command of others. Pompey was allocated another great command in 57 BC —a five-year commission to secure the grain supply of the capital—and like Caesar was allocated senatorial legates. Pompey developed a further variant on this theme in 55 BC, when he obtained permission to rule a vast province (and command its armies) from a distance, again through his legates. Crassus' five-year command in Syria was clearly intended to be on the same scale as Caesar's in Gaul, which was renewed for five years at the same time. Brutus and Cassius were given great commands in the east as part of the settlement after their murder of Caesar in 44. They used their commands and provinces to prepare for war against Octavian and Antony, who in their turn acquired vast commands as a means of dividing the spoils of victory at Philippi (and to help them prepare for the next civil war, against each other).

Romans had no special term for these super-commanders. None was needed, since they were so few in number. But there was clearly some recognition that something new had appeared. Greek cities gave them godlike honours similar to those they had previously lavished on the greatest kings. Among Romans a fascination with Alexander the Great appears. Pompey was said to have worn Alexander's cloak in a triumph; Caesar reputedly wept before a statue of the Macedonian king, because he had achieved so little by the age at which Alexander died; Octavian paid homage at Alexander's huge tomb in the heart of Alexandria. With hindsight, we see the role of emperor emerging from the actions of these individuals. Interestingly, it emerges first in the provinces, where the need for coordination of military power and revenues over great regions was most obvious. Only once it was established there was the controlling power of emperors applied to the bitter division of politics in the capital. The empire, in other words, had saved (and captured) the city.

More concretely the experience of the 70s, 60s, and especially the 50s had created a series of institutional innovations which would provide important precedents for the emperors. First, governors (or their equivalents) could now in effect be appointed, not elected, and in ways that separated the role from that of a civil magistrate. Second, the effectiveness of one commander coordinating operations over geographically vast areas and huge armies had been demonstrated. Cicero's speech *On the Command of Gnaeus Pompey* even provides an explicit statement along these lines, the first draft of an imperial ideology. Third, vast armies were now recruited and commanded, deployed, and resettled in ways over which the Senate and people had effectively no say. Finally, systems of revenue raising had in a rather piecemeal manner begun to be fitted to the needs of the imperial state. These innovations were resented by many, most of all by those senators who were not beneficiaries. Yet they would be imitated and adapted over the years of civil war that followed, and provided inspiration in the years ahead. Caesar as dictator initiated great colonial ventures to settle his veterans, and planned wars against Parthia and Dacia on the same scale as that of Pompey against Mithridates. Antony and Octavian settled their own veterans around the Mediterranean. Whenever there was only one such super-general on the scene—Pompey in the 60s, Caesar in the 40s, and Octavian after Actium—Roman military and political action briefly achieved a new coherence. From the chaos of the Republican empire, Rome had sleepwalked into military autocracy, and it worked.[6]

Civil War

Crassus perished in the aftermath of Carrhae in 53 BC. By 50 BC both Pompey and Caesar were preparing for war. Perhaps the pact between the two great generals was inherently unstable. Their marriage alliance had ended in 52 with the death of Pompey's much younger wife Julia, Caesar's daughter. And then there were the efforts of more than half the Senate fuelling distrust and jealousy. The war was mostly fought in the Balkans. Defeated at Pharsalus in 48, Pompey fled to Egypt, the last great kingdom not to have succumbed to Roman arms. There he was killed in an attempt by those in power to ingratiate themselves with Caesar. Caesar himself spent much of the time between Pharsalus and his own assassination in 44 BC tracking down Pompey's supporters. The provinces were easier to master than the capital. Despite granting amnesties to most of his former enemies and lavishing games and monumental building on the city of Rome, Caesar failed to rally Rome around him. Politics was no more free than it had been in the 50s, and neither Caesar nor anyone else had much idea of how his position could be institutionalized. Many of those involved in the conspiracy that led to his murder on the Ides of March, 44 BC, were former supporters of Pompey, but the initial euphoria waned when it was clear they had no solution for Rome's ills. Besides, the army and Caesar's followers could not forgive the murder.

A phoney peace followed. But within two years civil war had resumed, this time with Caesar's heir Octavian allied with Caesar's deputy Mark Antony against the 'Liberators', Brutus and Cassius. Both men died after their defeat at Philippi in 42 BC. Octavian and Antony nearly came to blows the next year, but in the event a new pact was negotiated and each had their great commands. Neither Octavian in the Balkans nor Antony in a campaign against Persia was very successful, and the balance of power was unchanged. Pompey's last son, Sextus, survived until 36 BC. After that everyone was a Caesarian, and it was only a matter of time before conflict between the two broke out. From 33 BC a propaganda war was in full swing, and in 31 the two sides engaged in north-west Greece at the battle of Actium, a victory for Octavian. Like Pompey before them, Antony and Cleopatra made for Egypt, where both committed suicide in 30 BC. Once again there was only one super-commander in place.

The domestic politics of the last generation of the Republic are documented in great detail by Cicero's correspondence, and also by the works of Sallust and Caesar written in the 40s. Contemporary historians were also aware of the importance of this period, but very little of their accounts survives. It has been a major aim of recent scholarship to try to recover their perspective.[7] Writers of the imperial period, including the biographer Plutarch and the historians Appian and Dio, had access to histories that are now vanished, and they used them to write vivid accounts of what they knew to be the last days of the Republic.

All these accounts focus on the struggle between personalities: Marius versus Sulla; Sulla's dictatorship; the competition between his lieutenants Lucullus, Pompey, and Crassus; the abortive coups of Lepidus and Catiline; the alliance between Pompey, Caesar, and Crassus in the 50s; and finally a series of civil wars, Pompey versus Caesar, Caesar's murderers versus Octavian and Antony, Octavian and Antony versus Pompey's son Sextus, and finally Octavian versus Antony. Told in this way, the history of the provinces often seems peripheral. As it happens, there were some universal historians in the tradition of Polybius, but almost none of their works has survived.[8] Much missed is the historical work of the philosopher Posidonius, which picked up where Polybius left off and narrated events into the 80s BC. Like Polybius, he knew the greatest Romans of the day and had travelled widely within their empire. The fragments of his work show he thought hard about the nature of the Roman Empire.[9] Diodorus' *Library* is the last great work composed before Actium, or the latest that has survived. As far as we can tell, this generation of provincial observers accepted the fact of Roman domination, the creation of which had so astonished Polybius, but they found the Roman world a very precarious one in which to live. So much depended on whether a community picked the right side in a civil war, attracted the patronage of a winner, or found itself caught up in a conflict originating far from home. The same picture emerges from the great inscriptions set up by eastern cities, recording honours given to one or another Roman general in the hope of staying on his good side. Rome's subjects feature in much civil war history mostly in a subordinate role. Northern Greece was the setting for three major civil wars in the 40s and 30s; Asia had to pay for the armies raised by Brutus and Cassius; Egypt was acquired by Octavian almost accidentally, because Cleopatra had picked the wrong ally. A few cities consistently chose well, others badly—Sparta and Aphrodisias were exceptionally fortunate, Athens seemed unable to pick a winner (even after Actium). In addition, Roman civil wars offered opportunities for old enemies to settle scores—within or between cities—and even for foreign powers like Parthia to take advantage. Episodes of peace might bring land confiscations and the imposition of colonists. And when rivalry between Roman generals resulted in grandiose foreign wars deep in temperate Europe or on the Persian frontiers, allies and subjects were dragged along. All this is exactly what we would expect. An empire's provinces genuinely are peripheral; their history is always driven by conflicts in the metropole, as it has been in recent times from Eretria to Cuba.

The fall of the Republic probably was good news for many provincials, if only because the emperors took the long view and in the end preferred to rule in partnership with provincial elites.[10] Certainly the impact of Augustan autocracy is immediately visible in the works that follow that of Diodorus, including Livy's vast history, the *Antiquities* of Dionysius of Halicarnassus, and the *Geography* of Strabo. Peace at the centre made the empire itself more predictable, allowed provincial communities and their leaders to plan for the long term, to invest in strategies of loyalty and collaboration. Tacitus put it pithily in a coda to his account of the origins of the Principate:

The provinces had no objection to the new state of affairs. For they distrusted the empire of the senate and people because of the rivalry of the most powerful men and the greed of the magistrates, against which the laws gave no protection, since they were corrupted by violence, ambition and most of all by bribery.[11]

Conquest Unlimited

The same generation that tore Rome apart in civil wars was also responsible for the most dramatic period of Roman expansion. Vast armies marched out in all directions, on the flimsiest of pretexts. They reached the Atlantic Ocean and the Caspian Sea, plunged deep into temperate Europe, and challenged the greatest empire of the day, Parthian Persia.[12] Great tracts of territory were annexed, the number of provinces increased enormously, and military colonies were scattered around the Mediterranean. There were spectacular defeats too: Crassus' invasion of Parthia in 53 BC ended with 20,000 Romans dead and 10,000 captured. There were catastrophic defeats in Germany too, most dramatically the loss of three entire legions in AD 9 during a three-day-long battle in the Teutoberger Forest near present-day Osnabrück.

Other great campaigns almost happened. The Bastarnae of the northern Balkans defeated the governor of Macedonia, Antonius Hybrida, in 62 BC. Cicero's correspondence from the early 50s shows him apprehensive of Burebista, king of the Dacians in what is now Romania, who spent much of the last century BC creating a great tribal federation of peoples. Aulus Gabinius, who had served under Sulla, Lucullus, and Pompey, was proconsul of Syria between 57 and 54 BC; he used it as a base to impose a new king on Egypt and to intervene in the politics of Judaea. Cyrenaica drifted in and out of Roman influence over the same period. Elaborate arguments were made to justify this or that campaign, but there is no doubt that the main driver was competition between the most powerful men in the state. The collapse of the Senate's authority, the creation of super-commands, and most of all the success of Pompey had altered the rules of the game. And it did not matter if ridiculous risks were taken, since, if one general failed, there would always be another waiting to take his place.

But the gains outweighed the losses. When Sulla died in 79 BC, Rome had just regained the position of dominant power in the Mediterranean world. Roman forces controlled Italy up to the Alps and most, if not quite all, of the coastal plains of the western Mediterranean. East of the Adriatic, she controlled parts of the Balkans and the province of Asia. On the death of Augustus in AD 14, just under a century later, the territorial empire flanked the Atlantic from the mouth of the Rhine to the Straits of Gibraltar, and surrounded the Mediterranean ('Our Sea', as the Romans came to call it) in a ring of provinces and client kingdoms. The Black Sea too was virtually a Roman lake, and Anatolia and the Near East were under Roman control. To the south, the frontier ran along the edge of the Sahara and extended to the southern frontier of Egypt. The eastern limit was fixed by the Euphrates and a line that included most of Anatolia. Its northern boundaries were the Rhine and the Danube. Much of this area was administered through provinces, the rest through client kingdoms which were closely controlled by Rome. The greater part of this vast extension had been acquired during the period when Pompey, Caesar, and finally Octavian/Augustus had led the state.

Further Reading

Many narratives, and quite a few novels, tell the story of the lives of the great figures of the last days of the Republic. It is also a period that emerges vividly from ancient writings. Plutarch's lives of Sulla, Caesar, Pompey, Cicero, Crassus, Lucullus, and other figures offer as lively an introduction to these characters as any modern treatment. Even better, Caesar's *Gallic War* and Cicero's *Letters* offer actual contemporary witness to the events of the 50s. Sallust's *Catiline Conspiracy* offers a view of the great crisis of Cicero's consulship written in the 40s BC, when the end of the Republic was not yet in sight.

An age dominated by great men is naturally a gift to biographers. Arthur Keaveney's *Sulla: The Last Republican* (2nd edn, London, 2005) is both learned and lively. Robin Seager's *Pompey the Great: A Political Biography* (2nd edn, London, 2002) is a classic. Cicero and Caesar have attracted many excellent biographers. For vivid evocation of each figure, I recommend Elizabeth Rawson's *Cicero: A Portrait* (London, 1975) and Adrian Goldsworthy's *Caesar: The Life of a Colossus* (London, 2006).

Many of Ronald Syme's interpretations of Roman politics have been challenged, but his *Roman Revolution* (Oxford, 1939) is a gripping read, and in its way is also an interesting document of its age. Our best witness to the imperialism of the age dominated by Pompey and Caesar is Cicero. His own thoughts and words on empire are lucidly discussed in Catherine Steel's *Cicero, Rhetoric and Empire* (Oxford, 2001). The repeated transformation of political institutions in Rome is a theme of Harriet Flower's *Roman Republics* (Princeton, NJ, 2010), and the emergence of the equestrians as a political force is described in the central chapters of Caillan Davenport's splendid *A History of the Roman Equestrian Order* (Cambridge, 2019).

Most ancient writers present this crisis as a Roman tragedy, but they shared it with the entire Mediterranean world. Liv Yarrow's *Historiography at the End of the Republic* (Oxford, 2006) is a subtle and original exercise in looking in on the Republic's collapse from the edge of empire.

THE ENJOYMENT OF EMPIRE

Since we now rule that race of people among whom civilization did not just arise, but from which it is believed to have spread to all other peoples, we have an obligation to pass on its benefits to them, just as we once received it from their hands. For I am not ashamed to say, all the more so given my life and achievements are proof enough of my energy and seriousness, that whatever I have accomplished I owe to the learning and culture which have been passed down to us in the classics and philosophy of Greece.

(Cicero, *Letter to his Brother Quintus* 1.1.27)

The Last Generation of the Free Republic

The Romans who lived between the dictatorships of Sulla and Caesar inhabited what was, in some ways, a new world. Italy was now a peninsula full of Roman citizens, a privileged and prosperous land surrounded by subject provinces. The imperial reach of the Roman people was expanding faster than ever before. Their city was transformed year after year, marble monuments like the Theatre of Pompey (see Figure 11) rising above the ancient temples built of local stone. The chief beneficiaries of imperial expansion were the Roman aristocracy.[1] They were richer than ever before, and with their wealth they created a life of luxury for themselves.[2]

Fig. 11. The theatre of Pompey

Roman aristocrats returned to Athens soon after Sulla's sack, in search of education and high culture. A shipwreck found a century ago by sponge divers off the island of Antikythera at the southern point of Greece revealed a cargo of extraordinary statues and other treasure en route for Italy. Excavations of the luxurious villas constructed in the last century BC show the probable destinations of such cargoes. Ancestral mansions in the city had been rebuilt on ever more lavish scales since the sixth century, but from the later second century Roman aristocrats had begun to expand their property portfolios. Cicero was far from the richest of senators, but even he owned eight villas. The Roman elite acquired summer retreats in hill towns like Tivoli and Tusculum, and coastal villas within easy reach of the city. The movement to invest the profits of empire in viticulture and other intensive agriculture had led them to acquire great farms in Umbria and Tuscany. By the last century BC some at least, like Settefinestre, were also pleasant residences. Most gorgeous of all were the seafront palazzos along the Bay of Naples.[3] The richest villa owners created retreats perched over the sea, equipped with elegant quarters for leisure, dining rooms for summer and winter use, private baths and fishponds, libraries and gardens adorned with artworks imported from the Greek world. Among the bronzes and marbles there were human treasures too, scholars and craftsmen. Some had come to Rome in chains; others had been attracted by the gifts bestowed on architects and artists, teachers and writers of all kinds, philosophers, poets, critics, and historians among them.[4] Roman moralists remained anxious about luxury, but what counted as luxury was different now. Building a temporary theatre out of imported coloured marbles and then reusing them in your urban house was luxury. Cicero considered that he lived a life of moderation.

This generation was the same one that witnessed the collapse of their civil society. Many of those who owned the grandest villas would perish in civil wars; indeed, some of these rich houses changed hands rapidly when their owners were proscribed. But this same elite—through a mixture of patronage and its own creative activity—presided over the formative period of Roman intellectual culture. And for once we can observe it in vivid detail, partly because of the splendid residences and monuments they built, but also thanks to the survival of the writings of Marcus Tullius Cicero and his contemporaries.

An Imperial Life

Cicero was born in 106 BC into a wealthy Roman family from the town of Arpinum in the Volscian hill country just over 100 kilometres (just over 60 miles) south-east of Rome.[5] Arpinum had been ruled by Rome since the late fourth century, and its inhabitants had been citizens long before the Social War, but this municipal background only made Cicero keener to fit in and conform. His politics were also much more traditional than those of blue-blooded radicals like Julius Caesar and the Gracchi brothers. Educated in Rome, he did his military service like any other young equestrian, travelled and studied in Greece, and began to take on legal cases. Roman orators did not charge fees for representing clients, but, if successful, they won gratitude that might be converted into future support. Besides, legal cases involving the aristocracy in this period were often politicized. Cicero's first cases were chosen to align himself with critics of the dictatorship of Sulla. The tactic paid off, and he was elected as a quaestor for 75 BC. This was a junior magistracy but one that made him a senator for life. Being the first in his family to win an office of this kind meant he was, like Marius before him, a *novus homo*, a new man. This was not uncommon. The

Senate was always open to new blood, even when proscription and civil war had not created vacancies.[6] But being a new man was a position he could exploit throughout his career, representing himself as an underdog when it suited. The quaestorship took him to Sicily for first-hand experience of Roman provincial rule. Many of his early cases involved charges of corruption on the part of governors. Some he defended; others—like Verres—he prosecuted.

Elected praetor in 66 BC, Cicero spoke persuasively in favour of transferring the command against Mithridates to Pompey. By 63 he was consul—a significant achievement—and he had to deal with Catiline's attempted coup. Though he was supported at the time in his decision to execute the alleged conspirators, this came back to haunt him, and he was briefly exiled in 58. The consulship was the high point of his influence. Roman politics in the 50s revolved around the alliance between Pompey, Caesar, and Crassus. Cicero was unwilling to support them and tried (unsuccessfully) to break up their pact. For a while, he was even forced to leave Rome to serve as governor of Cilicia. During the civil war between Pompey and Caesar, he attempted to remain neutral; eventually he chose Pompey's cause. Caesar's forgiveness placed him under obligations that effectively drove him out of public life until after the latter's murder on the Ides of March 44 BC. The bulk of his philosophical writing was carried out in the late 50s, when he had been frozen out of politics, and in the last year of Caesar's dictatorship and the eight months that followed. Cicero was bitterly disappointed that the assassination of Caesar did not restore traditional freedoms as he saw them. Fiercely opposed to Mark Antony, he tried to build up Octavian as a counterweight. But when the two formed an alliance, Cicero was proscribed and was hunted down and killed in December 43 BC. His hands and head were displayed in the forum from the speaker's platform, the Rostra, as a grim warning of the dangers of free speech.

Like all his generation, Cicero pursued his career in the shadow of empire. Empire and the Social War had made the propertied classes of Roman Italy into the elite of an imperial nation.[7] Modern empires typically recruited their administrators from the educated middle classes. Participation in running the empire guaranteed them a better lifestyle, and more status than they could hope to enjoy at home. They approached the business of empire as clerks and bureaucrats, ruling by regulation and memorandum. Many became professional servants of empire, and some never returned home. Rome's empire was different. Aristocrats played the leading role in running it, with the help of their family members, friends, and slaves. The conduct of governors, generals, and procurators was guided by principles of ethics and custom rather than by standing orders and protocol. And their eyes remained fixed on the network of friends and relatives back home; they did not 'go native'.

Cicero conformed to this pattern perfectly. Roman governors might display justice and prudence, energy and competence, but there is little sense that any preferred their foreign postings to life back home. What they hoped to bring home were a good reputation (*fama*), the support and gratitude of Roman traders and prominent tax farmers or other aristocrats, maybe even some support from provincial cities or grandees, and, of course, money. Theft, menaces, and accepting bribes were illegal, but there were other legal, if dubious ways of extracting money from provincials, such as moneylending at ruinous rates of interest. Cicero evidently tried to imitate famous governors like Quintus Mucius Scaevola the Pontifex, proconsul of Asia in 94 BC and author of an exemplary edict laying down the principles of good government. But in the changed conditions of the 50s BC, this resolution brought Cicero only grief.

Cicero experienced the empire from many perspectives.[8] As a junior magistrate with financial responsibility in Sicily, he was alternately admiring of and frustrated by the Greek cities of his province. Later in life he had to experience the necessary compromises of a governor, forced to balance the interests of justice with those of his powerful Roman friends back home. As an advocate, he had occasion to speak passionately on behalf of Roman colonists and allies against corruption, and also to urge jurors not to believe non-Roman testimony over the assurances of governors who were noble and Roman. If his orations *Against Verres* are savage condemnations of the abuse of power, his speeches in defence of the governors Flaccus and Fonteius pander to the grossest ethnic prejudices. Most of the issues that confronted him as a politician also seem (to us) to derive from empire. One set derived from the destabilizing effects of massive influxes of wealth, unevenly distributed between rival politicians and social classes, so fuelling the bribery and debt that lay behind Catiline's coup and the power of Crassus, Pompey, and Caesar. Other political crises were a product of the Republic's failure to maintain security in the Mediterranean.

Cicero did not see things quite this way. In his orations—both in the courts and in the Senate—he repeatedly focused on the personal deficiencies (or merits) of the individuals involved. The interests of the Roman people would be best served if men like Verres were punished as they deserved and men like Pompey were given the power they needed to use their exceptional talent in the public interest. Cicero saw no necessary conflict between the interests of the Roman people and those of their subjects. One passage of his treatise *On Duties* claimed that before Sulla, Roman rule over her allies had been more like *patrocinium* (patronage or protection) than *imperium* (imperial rule);[9] there was no reason why that change could not be reversed. An open letter to his brother Quintus, ostensibly offering advice on his governorship of Asia, admitted the tensions that might arise between subjects and tax farmers, but recommended simply that all parties be urged to behave well.[10] In *On Duties*, Cicero argued that the ethical course was always, in fact, the most expedient one. The problems of the Republican empire derived from moral deficiencies, not fundamental conflicts of interest or systemic failures. They demanded (no more than) a moral solution.

We might make two kinds of objection to this. First, there is a striking lack of analysis of structural problems. Was it not obvious that contracting out the collection of state revenues would lead to short-termism and abuse? Was it not clear that raising very large armies without any provision for their ultimate demobilization would cause problems? The answer to both questions must be yes, if only because these problems were not long afterwards conceived and solved in exactly these terms. Under the Principate, the duty of raising tribute was largely devolved to local authorities. They were perhaps no less rapacious, but did have a long-term interest in the stability of their own regions. From Augustus, soldiers were recruited for fixed terms, were discharged individually rather than by detachment, and a military treasury was established to fund their demobilization. It is impossible to know whether Cicero *could* not see these problems or simply would not.

Second, Cicero's concern for the subjects of empire falls a long way short of an imperial vocation for another reason. It seems clear that Romans of Cicero's day had very little concept of empire in a modern sense.[11] One corollary was that subjects and foreigners were treated in much the same way. Both groups, for example, might send embassies, both might be subject to commands, and neither had a recognized stake in the Roman state or a claim to be consulted by it. Romans ruled well because they owed it to their nature to do so, not in respect of the rights of others. The term *imperium* was not used in a territorial sense until Augustus' reign: until then it meant command and the power to do so.

Cicero is not our only witness to Republican imperialism, even if he is our best one. If we compare him with other writers of the period, it is

possible to see how conventional his views were. Sallust, writing history in
the 40s, also saw the rise of Rome as accompanied by a collapse in morality,
and attributed both war in the periphery and conflict in the centre to the
moral deficiencies of Rome's rulers.[12] Livy, writing a little later, seems to
have told a similar story. Cicero perfectly expresses the ideological stance
of the Roman elite, one that was determined not to see a clash between
their own desires and the interests of the state or between Roman interests
and global justice. This did not mean they could not entertain the idea
that Roman rule was brigandage on a large scale. Sallust fictionalized a
wonderful letter sent by Mithridates to the Parthian emperor, condemning
Roman imperialism:

Do you not know that the Romans have turned their arms in this direction only
after Ocean put a limit to their western advance? From the beginning of time they
have possessed nothing they have not stolen, their home, their wives, their lands,
their empire. Once a group of wanderers without kin or homeland, their city has
been founded as a plague for the entire world. No law, human or divine, can prevent them attacking allies and friends, neighbouring peoples and distant races alike,
poor and rich without distinction. Everything that is not subject to their command
they treat as enemies, and kings most of all.[13]

The deft inversion of Rome's own myths of origin—Romulus' asylum, the
Sabine women, and the Trojan settlement of Italy—and verbal allusions to
Varro and others, reveal this as a pastiche aimed at Roman readers. It seems
they enjoyed these travesties of empire, since Tacitus and imperial satirists
also produced anti-Romes of this kind. Yet a belief in the essential justness
of Roman rule was essential to maintain the divine mandate. What emerges
from all these texts is the first signs of a universalizing ideology. The idea
that Rome was patron of the entire world is one example; the comparisons
with Alexander and the use of geographical imagery to sum up the empire
are another.[14] For Cicero and his peers, this universalism was not simply
a matter of politics. It also formed part of an impulse to shape not just a
Roman, but also a universalizing view of classical culture.

Greek Intellectual Life in Rome

Cicero's generation did not create either Latin literature or the idea of a
distinctive Roman educational canon, but they fixed both in what would

become their classical forms. Like most peoples of the ancient Mediterranean, Romans had lived for centuries in a world where culture meant Greek culture. The first works written in Latin were intended for performance—the plays of Plautus, the hymn of Livius, the speeches of Cato.[15] From the beginning of the second century BC, a few historical and antiquarian works were produced in Latin. Cato led here as well. Yet many Roman authors continued to write in Greek, and philosophy and rhetoric, geography, medicine, and science were accessible only to Greek readers. We have little idea how many Romans were even interested in any of these subjects apart from philosophy before the middle of the second century BC. The creation of a comprehensive and self-sufficient Latin literary culture began in the 60s BC .[16]

The issue was not access to Greek knowledge. There had been Greek cities in central Italy since the archaic age, and the influence of the imports, images, and ideas they brought was in some senses ubiquitous. The ancient cities of the Aegean were also easy to reach. Pictor travelled to Delphi and Cato must have had access to many Greek books when writing his account of Italian *Origins*. The first Latin epic poets were well aware not only of Homer, but also of the many later Greek critical and philosophical commentaries on his work. During Polybius' long exile in Rome and his subsequent voluntary residence there, he had used the library of the kings of Macedon brought back as plunder by Aemilius Paullus after the battle of Pydna. The fact that Paullus brought the library home suggests an interest in Greek scholarship as early as the early second century BC. Probably this interest was not new.[17] By the middle of the second century some Greeks seem to have realized the Roman elite was especially interested in philosophy. Athens sent an embassy to the Senate in 155 comprising the heads of the Stoic, Epicurean, and Peripatetic philosophical schools. Paullus' son, Scipio Aemilianus, was the patron of not only Polybius but also of the Stoic Panaetius of Rhodes. Both scholars spent time with him in Rome and accompanied him on his travels. But the total number of Greek scholars actually resident in Rome remained few until the Mithridatic Wars. Perhaps the same was true of the number of Romans who were genuinely interested in what they had to offer.

Things began to change in the late second century. One sign of a new interest in things Greek is a new interest in the Bay of Naples, where the cities of Cumae and Naples were the closest Greek cities to Rome.[18] Rome had created a cluster of colonies in Campania in the 190s. Anecdotes show some members of the Scipio family already had homes there in the early

second century. Yet the first villas described as really spectacular date to the
start of the last century BC: Marius' Campanian retreat, built in the 90s BC,
is one of the first certain examples. By the 60s and 50s the coastline was
covered in those extraordinary pleasure complexes, images of which survive in Pompeian wall paintings (see Figure 12) and which have left flam-
boyant archaeological traces. The Emperor Augustus spent what were in
effect holidays in the area, reserving for it Greek games, entertainments, and
dress, in contrast to the rather sterner Roman traditionalism he displayed
at home. Tiberius' island retreat on Capri—perhaps because access was so
difficult—attracted various stories of tyrannical cruelty and depravity. The
Bay of Naples became imperial Rome's Greek alter ego.

Fig. 12. One of the fresco wall paintings in the *cubiculum* (bedroom) from the
Villa of P. Fannius Synistor at Boscoreale

Young aristocrats were now regularly sent to be educated in the ancient cities of the Aegean world. Athens was the key destination, but there were also many visitors to Rhodes, which had become a major centre for education in rhetoric and philosophy. Both cities already drew young men from other Greek states. Now young Romans began to join them. Cicero and his brother were both in Athens in 79 BC listening to the lectures of the great Academic philosopher Antiochus of Ascalon, a client of Lucullus. They were in their mid-twenties. They then went on to visit Rhodes and Smyrna. Julius Caesar studied on Rhodes a few years later. Some of these visits seem timed to avoid difficult political situations at home, and some probably also served to remove wealthy young men from the temptations of the city. But they left a lasting impression. Cicero's reminiscences of his youthful discovery of Greece evoke something of the Grand Tour of classical and Renaissance sites in Italy undertaken between the late seventeenth and the early nineteenth centuries by wealthy European males as a final stage in their cultural education.

Summers in Campania and educational trips to Greece cast Rome in a new light. Roman writers of Cicero's age were acutely aware that when they entered a library, almost all the books were in Greek. Most of the best libraries in Rome had once belonged to Hellenistic kings. Cicero and many others used the library set up by Lucullus in his retreat in the hill town of Tusculum.[19] Greek scholars as well as Roman ones made use of his collections. Mudslides from the eruption of Vesuvius in AD 79 buried one elegant Herculaneum mansion, now known as the Villa of the Papyri after a great collection of philosophical works recovered there. The villa probably belonged to Calpurnius Piso, Caesar's father-in-law, who was consul in 58 with Gabinius as a colleague. The long lines of its ornamental pond flanked by bronzes and its lavish marble architecture were reproduced by J. Paul Getty in Malibu in the 1970s and have now been recreated again with loving digital reconstruction.[20] Its library of philosophical works was a relic of the long residence there of the Greek polymath Philodemus of Gadara, who wrote on aesthetics and literary criticism as well as Epicureanism.[21]

Vitruvius' manual *On Architecture* confirms what the Vesuvian villas suggest, that the Roman rich deliberately incorporated in their residences spaces designed to evoke Greek culture, and these were often designated by Greek names: the *oecus* was a Greek dining room, the *peristylum* a Greek garden, the *bibliotheke* the regular term for library. Many of these rooms and terms did not correspond very closely to what archaeology shows actually existed in contemporary eastern Mediterranean cities such as Athens and Ephesus. Romans were not trying to recreate a contemporary Greek world in Italy. Cicero's retreat in Tusculum included two areas he called *gymnasia*, adapting the terms from a characteristic Greek institution dedicated to exercise and the education of elite males. One he named the *Lyceum* after Aristotle's school, the other the *Academy* after Plato's. A series of letters survives in which he asks his friend Atticus to try and obtain suitable Greek statuary to decorate these spaces.[22] No doubt his villa near Puteoli had many Greek spaces too. But there was also the sternly Roman *domus* on the Palatine, and probably the Tusculan villa had more Roman spaces for other aspects of his life. He and his peers were not trying to become Greek so much as to incorporate a carefully selected portion of Greek culture into their own lives.[23]

Cicero's correspondence mentions many other Greek writers who lived for decades in Italy as guests of the Roman aristocracy. They came not only from great eastern centres like Athens and Rhodes and Alexandria, but also from Greek cities in Bithynia and Asia and even Syria. From wherever, in fact, Roman generals had passed by. A few taught, but many were resident scholars, creating for their Roman patrons an air of culture, in the same way as did the laid-out gardens with their covered walks for philosophical discussion among bronzes images of gods, mythological figures, philosophers, and kings. Greeks in Rome accommodated themselves to this selective appropriation of their culture. The prefaces of a number of Greek works composed in this period praise the generosity of their Roman friends. The historian Dionysius of Halicarnassus presented himself as an admirer of the Romans; he regarded the similarities between some Roman and Greek institutions and between the Latin and Greek languages as a sign that Romans were Greek in origin. Gabinius brought Timagenes of Alexandria to Rome as a captive in 55 BC. Freed and honoured, he became for a while the house guest of Augustus himself, but had a reputation as a ferocious critic of Rome. He was reported to have said that the only thing to regret about the many fires suffered by the city was that damaged buildings were always replaced on an even more lavish scale. Eventually he moved on to the home of Asinius Pollio, creator of one of the first public libraries in the capital. Other kidnapped Greeks seem to have adapted more easily. Tyrannio of Amisos, brought back as a captive by Lucullus, was freed and patronized by Pompey. He became a friend and intellectual mentor of Cicero, Caesar, and Atticus and taught grammar and criticism in Rome. Greeks as well as

Romans came to study with him, as they did with the physician Asclepiades of Prusias. Poetry was transformed as well as prose. Parthenius of Nicaea, captured in 73 BC during a war against Mithridates, was feted in Rome and inspired a new generation of Latin poets, including Cornelius Gallus and Catullus. Latin poetics would remain preoccupied with love poetry and mythological themes throughout the reign of Augustus and beyond. Then there were the visitors, some at least celebrity academics on lecture tours. Poseidonius of Apamea and Artemidorus of Ephesus visited Rome and some of the western provinces giving lectures and gathering material for their histories and geographies. The cumulative influence on Roman culture was enormous.

Greek scholars always needed patrons. During the third and second centuries they found them in the royal courts of Alexandria, Pergamum, and Syracuse, but in the first century they came to Rome. A key part was played by the generation of Romans born in the last years of the second century BC. They were the first to make the Bay of Naples their playground—half Las Vegas and half the Left Bank of the Seine—and the first to have travelled in their youth in the Aegean world to study in the ancient cities of Greece. A few even lived there for long periods. Cicero's friend Titus Pomponius lived in Athens for so long he acquired the nickname 'Atticus', and Verres fled Cicero's prosecution to live in exile in Greek Marseilles. Tiberius would spend years on Rhodes during a period when he was out of favour at the court of Augustus. When campaigns in the east, or simply their own wealth, gave them the chance to bring Greek intellectuals to Rome, they grasped the opportunity, just as they filled their boats with Greek bronzes and hunted down copies of rare Greek books. They knew Greek philosophy well enough to identify themselves by school: Cicero the Academic, Cassius the Epicurean, Cato the Stoic, and so on.[24] They dropped Greek quotations and words into their private letters and conversations.[25] But the clearest sign of their engagement with Greek culture is the determination of some of that generation to create a matching intellectual culture in Latin.

New Classics for a New Empire

Cicero, in his introduction to the *Tusculan Disputations*, is quite explicit that his philosophical works formed part of a conscious project to supply a set of Latin classics in each of the major genres invented by Greeks:[26]

Those subjects which deal with the correct way to live—the theory and practice of knowledge—are all part of that body of wisdom that is called philosophy. This I have decided to explain in a work written in the Latin language. Philosophy, to be sure, may be learned from books in Greek, or indeed from Greek scholars themselves. I have always thought that our writers have always proved themselves better than the Greeks, either by finding things out for themselves or by improving what they have borrowed from them. Obviously this applies only to those fields of study we have decided are worthy of our efforts.[27]

The *Tusculan Disputations* form a part of a mass of mainly philosophical writing Cicero produced under the dictatorship of Caesar, when he felt he could neither support nor oppose the man who had enslaved the Republic but spared his own life. Tusculum was the site of Cicero's philosophically themed retreat; there he entertained younger senators who shared his political and cultural interests. Many of the works he produced are dramatized as dialogues, recalling Plato's accounts of Socrates debating with his students, but also presenting the Roman elite at their ethical and cultured best. The *Disputations* is in fact dedicated to the same Brutus whose ethics would have such a bloody outcome. Cicero opens by praising the practical morality of the Romans, relative to that of the Greeks, and goes on to argue that although the Greeks may have preceded Romans in many fields, once Romans took up the same pursuits, they invariably eclipsed them. Discussion of various genres of Roman poetry moves on to oratory. Cicero's own work on oratory is presented as a key stage in the creation of a Roman intellectual universe. Now, he says, he will move on to philosophy.

The preface is tendentious in all sorts of ways, and Cicero's history of Latin scholarship, like Horace's history of Latin literature contained in a letter ostensibly written for Augustus, has sometimes been taken too seriously. But it is perfectly true that this generation seem to have seen themselves as filling in the gaps in Latin writing and Roman knowledge. Cicero was not the only Latin philosopher. Lucretius' great Epicurean epic *On the Nature of Things* was nearly complete when he died in 55 BC. Cornelius Nepos and Atticus were engaged in historical research, trying to establish an absolute chronology for the Roman past, one that would allow key dates in Roman history to be coordinated with world (i.e. Greek) history. Then there were Varro's researches into religious antiquities, Roman institutions, the Latin language, and much else. Nigidius Figulus wrote on grammar, the gods, and science. Nepos wrote biographies of famous Romans. Roman intellectuals seemed sometimes to figure themselves as counterparts of the great figures of classical Greek literature. Cicero presented himself as the new Demosthenes and thought of writing a Roman version of the *Geography* of Eratosthenes.

All this activity is sometimes presented as sign of cultural insecurity, but it might just as well be understood as fantastic ambition. Rome had surpassed the Greeks in warfare, why not in literature too? But when Cicero and his collaborators are read carefully, it is clear they were not trying to create an alternative, parallel, and self-sufficient intellectual universe. They advocated an eclectic biculturalism, a cultivated familiarity with both languages (*utraque lingua* 'in either language' became almost a catchphrase), and when they described the moral and cultural superiority they sought, it was not a *Romanitas* modelled on Hellenism, but *humanitas*, a term that embraces the sense of civilization and common humanity. Roman culture, in other words, had a universalizing mission. Just as Roman houses had Greek and Roman rooms and Roman religion had space for domestic and foreign gods, so the values that the last generation of the Republic proclaimed were bigger than either national culture. That made Roman culture, at least in aspiration, a truly imperial civilization.

Further Reading

A fascinating impression of the curiosity and energy of the Roman elite is conveyed by Elizabeth Rawson's *Intellectual Life in the Late Roman Republic* (London, 1985). Rawson also wrote what remains the best and most rounded biography of Cicero, *Cicero: A Portrait* (London, 1975). Many of the studies she produced while working on these two books are gathered in her collected papers, *Roman Culture and Society* (Oxford, 1991). Ingo Gildenhard's *Paideia Romana* (Cambridge, 2007) offers a careful exploration of Cicero's engagement with the Greeks.

The material setting of Roman Italy is brilliantly evoked in Tim Potter's *Roman Italy* (London, 1987) and the special culture of the Bay of Naples in John H. D'Arms, *The Romans on the Bay of Naples* (Cambridge, MA, 1970). The cultural history of Rome is now the subject of Andrew Wallace-Hadrill's amazingly wide-ranging *Roman Cultural Revolution* (Cambridge, 2008). At its heart is an examination of how Romans constantly referred to Greek and Italian models as they grew into an imperial culture. Emma Dench's *Romulus' Asylum* (Oxford, 2005) explores some of the same terrain, showing the many different routes through which Roman identity was reformulated.

KEY DATES IN CHAPTER XI

EMPERORS

In the beginning the City of Rome was ruled by kings. Lucius Brutus established freedom and the consulship. Dictatorships were taken up from time to time; the power of the decemviri endured for only a couple of years; the consular power of the military tribunes did not last much longer. The tyrannies of Cinna and Sulla were short-lived, the power of Pompey and Crassus quickly passed to Caesar, and the armies of Lepidus and Antony surrendered to Augustus, who took control of the whole state, worn out as it was by civil war, with the title First Citizen [*princeps*].

(Tacitus, *Annales* 1.1)

The Return of Monarchy

Rome had an empire before it had emperors. The first half of this book has told the story of how that came about. One city in competition with others, fighting to control first Italy, then the west, and finally the entire Mediterranean basin and more besides. Or as the Romans themselves most often saw it, one *people* winning leadership (*imperium*, *archē*, *hēgemonia*) over the other peoples of the inhabited world. Romans imagined this as a collective effort: Senate and people, Rome and her allies, the men and the gods of the city working together. Only in the final stages did individual leaders emerge from the pack of Scipiones, Fabii, Metelli, Aemilii Paulli, and the other great families. Sulla, Pompey, and Caesar seem—with hindsight—like intimations of monarchy.[1] Great generals provided a coordination of

Map 4. The Roman empire at its greatest extent in the second century AD

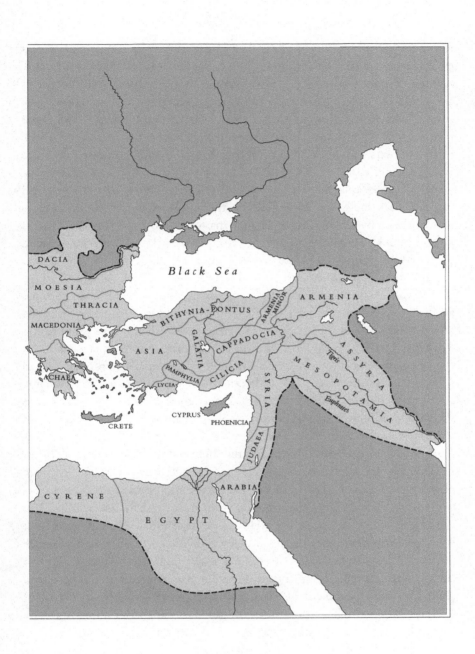

DACIA

MOESIA

THRACIA

MACEDONIA

ACHAEA

CRETE

Black Sea

BITHYNIA-PONTUS

GALATIA

ASIA

PAMPHYLIA

LYCIA

CILICIA

CAPPADOCIA

ARMENIA
MINOR

ARMENIA

ASSYRIA

MESOPOTAMIA

Tigris

Euphrates

SYRIA

CYPRUS

PHOENICIA

JUDAEA

CYRENE

ARABIA

EGYPT

resources and policy that empire badly needed. The emperors did all this even better, and they also imposed peace. The senator and historian Tacitus, writing in the early second century AD (around a century and a half after the battle of Actium), satirically represented Republican government as a brief deviation within a grand narrative of a Roman monarchy. But there is no sign that he or any other senator of his age actually opposed the rule of the Caesars. Emperors had turned out to be a vital component of the Roman Empire.

This chapter tells the story of how the Romans stopped worrying and came to love their new kings, even if they could never bring themselves to call them by that name. That tact mattered most for the Romans of Rome. Greeks were happy to use the word *basileus* (king), Egyptians treated them as pharaohs, provincials everywhere made the family name Caesar and the special title of Augustus, awarded Octavian by the Senate in 27 BC, into synonyms for monarch. The first emperor knew better than to stage an overt revolution; yet over the first three centuries of the empire monarchy comes out of the shadows. Historians still call the early empire the Principate, since the emperors also used the term *princeps*, first citizen. All the same, there is now a consensus that all the essentials of monarchy had been there right from the start: these included an inner circle of favourites, advisers, secretaries, and viziers; palace intrigues, because the palace was where decisions were made; central pooling of information and control of resources; a nexus of patronage centred on the court; and a hereditary principle of succession, even if it was a while before it could be acknowledged.

Like all monarchies, its history is one of struggles for influence at court, of intergenerational conflict, of tangled sexual and political rivalries, of actual and suspected plots. But it is also a history of remarkable stability. If it was largely true that (as one historian has put it) 'Emperors don't die in bed,' it was also true that the murders of many individual emperors seem to have done little to shake the system itself. That is why much of this chapter is concerned with the emerging institution rather than the admittedly colourful characters who occupied the throne. The narrative overlaps with that of Chapter XIII, which will consider the outward face of empire, especially war and diplomacy. That story will be one of two centuries of cautious consolidation and modest advance followed in the third century with a crisis that caught the emperors completely by surprise and from which it took the empire more than a generation to recover. The empire almost collapsed under the combined pressure of invasions from northern Europe and war with a rejuvenated and very aggressive Persian Empire. What survived was, in fact, a new empire. But through all these transformations, the person of the emperor remains at the focus of our gaze, and it is appropriate to begin with the first and greatest.

Augustus

In August 30 BC, Octavian stood almost exactly where his adoptive father Julius Caesar had stood nearly eighteen years before: in Alexandria, contemplating victory amidst the corpses of his enemies. But the Roman world had changed in the decades since Pharsalus. Back in 48, Caesar had lamented the murder of Pompey, swearing he would have spared him. Perhaps he would have done, just as he spared Brutus and Cassius after his victory over Pompey. Nearly two decades later, the new victor was a very different animal. Antony and Cleopatra were both dead, each at their own hands. But it was on Octavian's orders that Caesarion, the boy Cleopatra claimed she had borne to Caesar, was executed. After wrestling with Antony for leadership of the Caesarian party, Octavian would tolerate no other heirs for Caesar. Egypt he took control of too, absorbing the last of the great Macedonian kingdoms into his empire. He would need the treasury of the Ptolemies to settle his and Antony's soldiers. Octavian learned from others' mistakes. He would not rely on terror and legislation to fix the state, as Sulla had done. He would not imitate Pompey's actions in 62 BC by dismissing his legions. He would not forgive, as Caesar had. He would not take the title dictator and sit around in Rome waiting for the assassins' daggers. He meant to rule.

Oceans of ink have been spilled debating the question of how Octavian escaped Caesar's fate. Was he cunning or lucky? He had enemies after Actium, to be sure, and perhaps there were plots too. Did he really face the same challenges? How different was the Rome he returned to rule and the ruling class he converted into his allies? Was Rome now so weary of civil war it would accept any alternative? Had the Senate been cowed by the proscriptions and the civil wars? Had the people really come to accept him as a god who had saved the state?

The problem here is not a lack of evidence: the long reign of Octavian/ Augustus (forty-five years from Actium to his death) is one of the best documented in Roman history. The problem is the success of Octavian

Picture Box 5 Statue of Eumachia from Pompeii

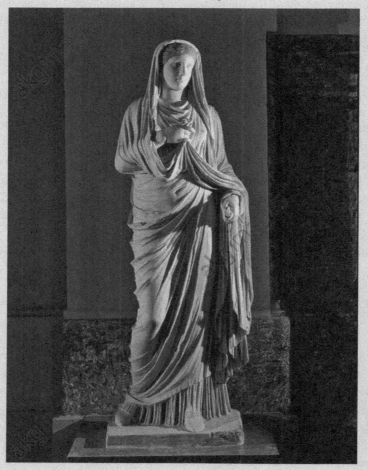

This statue, now in the National Archaeological Museum of Naples, was found in 1820 by workmen clearing rubble from a large building in the centre of Pompeii. That building opened onto the forum, with a grand porch, given the Latinized Greek name *chalcidicum*. Passing through it, you would have entered a large courtyard enclosed by porticos. Behind this were storerooms and a corridor and here too, in a niche, was the statue of the civic benefactor who had built the structure, Eumachia.

The purpose of the building is not known. Perhaps it had several uses, as many porticoes did. A dedicatory inscription proclaims that Eumachia had paid for the building and dedicated it to Augustan Concord and Piety in her name and that of her son. His name shows she had married into one of the wealthiest families in the city. Statues of Aeneas and Romulus in the porch imitated statues from the recently completed Forum of Augustus in Rome. She was also a public priestess. Not a great deal more is known about Eumachia, although there have been many guesses, but she was clearly one of the wealthiest women in Pompeii. Her tomb, outside the Porta Nucera, is the largest of those around the city. The statue to her was set up by the guild of the fullers, an important industry in Pompeii, and it is quite likely that she was their patron.

The statue of Eumachia is completely idealized. No trace of the real woman remains. Its location seems oddly modest, framed in a niche off a back corridor rather than in the centre of the court or in the *chalcidicum*. The originals of Aeneas and Romulus had occupied niches in Rome flanking the great statue of Augustus on a four-horse chariot. Yet her influence in Pompeii was clearly significant. This reflects the curious status of women in Roman cities: barred from voting, jury service, or political office, some were, all the same, independently wealthy. Cities badly needed the financial support of their richest citizens. The priesthood and the honours given to her as a benefactor and patron were public recognitions of her civic-minded behaviour. Others treated in a similar way were rich former slaves, who were also not eligible for high office.

Why did women like Eumachia consent to be so generous to a society that in other respects marginalized them? Unlike future (male) candidates, they did not give in order to win political support. Possibly she and others like her were genuinely public-spirited, or perhaps giving in the name of her son, who might one day stand for election, provided a motive. Whatever the reason, statues and inscriptions like those of Eumachia reveal powerful political and economic actors who are otherwise hardly visible in the formal structure of the Roman city.

Further Reading

Alison E. Cooley and Melvin G. L. Cooley, *Pompeii and Herculaneum: A Sourcebook.* 2nd edn (London: Routledge, 2014), 140–7.

Emily A. Hemelrijk and Greg Woolf, eds., *Women and the Roman City in the Latin West* (Leiden and Boston, MA: Brill, 2013).

and his allies in presenting their version of history as the dominant narrative. Perhaps most striking is the success with which Augustus himself was deliberately placed at the centre of things, so that all successes were his alone, although in reality many others were involved in them. The period was already declared an Augustan epoch in his lifetime. The Augustan Peace was represented as a key turning point, and continuities between Octavian's conduct and that of Caesar, Antony, Pompey and others were obscured.[2]

The approved themes of renewal, moral rearmament, and recovery sponsored by the gods resonate in the poetry created by Propertius, Virgil, and Horace, in the monumental rebuilding of Rome and some major provincial cities, in the elaborate iconographic programmes of the Altar of Peace, of the Fora of Augustus and of Julius Caesar, and of the temples to Mars, Apollo, and other gods the first emperor set about constructing. It was also communicated in performances. It is difficult for us to imagine the experience of watching the great triple triumph of 29 BC celebrating Octavian's victories in the Balkans, in the campaign of Actium, and in Egypt. But the spectators knew this meant the end of civil war. The same applies to the magnificent Saecular Games of 17 BC, ostensibly an ancient festival revived, but used by Augustus as another means to signal the end of one era and the start of the next. Some performances were more subtle. During the 20s BC Octavian gradually rebuilt his image in a series of carefully stage-managed renunciations of his power, each followed by new grants from the Senate. The focal point occurred at two meetings in January 27 BC from which he emerged with the title Augustus, a vast province (essentially that half of the empire that contained armies) granted for ten years, and the right to govern through legates. During 23 BC he finally resigned the last of a series of consulships and received a grant of *imperium maius*, the same kind of command that had allowed Pompey and others to outrank governors in their provinces. In fact, in almost all his titles and powers he was much more the heir of Pompey than of Caesar. The only *popularis* elements were the powers and inviolable status of a tribune. The people had festivals—bread and circuses, in the famous phrase—but the power of the assemblies to actually choose magistracies or pass legislation withered away. Augustus passed his legislation via the Senate, appointed senators to all the major military and political commands, with equestrians taking on the lesser ones, chose some magistrates and reserved the right to veto the appointments of others, and determined the election of the most important priests. Without ever creating a formal constitutional position of emperor, he accumulated, through influence, persuasion, vast wealth, and the threat of overwhelming military force, a determining position in the state. On his death, the whole bundle of powers and almost all the titles were passed on to his successor. Back in the 20s his death was, of course, a long way off, although his frequent illnesses meant no one could count on him not succumbing to one of them. But this gave him a long time to develop the role of emperor. The 20s were about survival, demobilizing armies, touring and securing the provinces, and establishing a delicate cohabitation with the Senate. Keeping physically away from Rome for much of the decade probably helped. A plot in 22 BC caused a momentary crisis, but by 17 BC and the Saecular Games, he was as secure as he ever would be. During the middle part of his reign he initiated great campaigns of conquest. Peace was made with the Parthians in 20 BC, the standards of Crassus were returned, and with the east secure he was able to devote resources to the conquest of Europe. His stepsons Tiberius and Drusus led great armies across the Rhine and up and down the Danube. World conquest was almost certainly devised as a solution to the domestic problem of what did an emperor do. Up until a disastrous defeat in Germany in AD 9 the answer could be, 'The emperor leads Rome in the fulfilment of her historical destiny.' Augustan art and poetry is full of images of world conquest, and the submission of India, Britain, and northern Scythia was confidently predicted. Victory abroad distracted from scandal at home, driven partly by struggles over who would be Augustus' successor. In the end, it was to be Tiberius. No one else was left, alive and untarnished.

Tiberius already shared most of Augustus' formal powers by the time of the latter's death, but he still had to endure his predecessor's final arrangements. A great dynastic mausoleum (recently reopened to visitors) had been built in the Field of Mars not far from the Tiber. Over the years since its completion (in 28 BC) it had accumulated the remains of a number of those who Augustus had once hoped would succeed him, notably his sons-in-law Marcellus and Agrippa, and his grandsons Gaius and Lucius. Only the favoured were admitted: his daughter Julia was forbidden to lie alongside her husbands and sons, his granddaughter was also banned from burial within it, and a final grandson was murdered, allegedly on his orders, as soon as Augustus' death was announced to make sure Tiberius faced no possible rival from within the family. The ruthless Octavian had clearly survived beneath the benevolent figure of Augustus. In this Mausoleum the ashes of Augustus would lie. But first came the send-off.

On the news of Augustus' death the priestesses of Vesta produced his will, which had been left with them for safekeeping.[3] Tiberius and his mother, Augustus' wife Livia, were named as principal heirs of his vast personal property in a ratio of two parts to one. The will also detailed the customary legacies that Roman nobles made to their relatives, friends, and clients. But the scale was now rather different. Augustus included legacies to every single Roman citizen and to every soldier in the Roman army. The will was supplemented by three other documents, codicils. One offered a balance sheet of the entire empire. It detailed where the soldiers were stationed and how many they were in each unit, how much money was in the treasuries, how much tax was owing, and to these lists were added the names of those of Augustus' slaves and ex-slaves who could furnish further details. This is a tacit statement of how far the coordination of the empire had progressed in the ninety years since Gabinius had first proposed that first exceptional command for Pompey against the pirates. It also reveals how Augustus managed the empire through his private household, that is, relying on his own dependants rather than public slaves, senators, or equestrians. No other accounts had ever been offered. But the document was a display of openness, not an invitation to the Senate to take the reins. Augustus' slaves and clients were part of Tiberius' inheritance; he already had *imperium maius* and all the other powers that mattered.

A second codicil included instructions for Augustus' funeral. There would be a grand pageant through the city of Rome, one in which all the orders would participate alongside the members of his family. The funeral procession would make its way to a specially constructed pyre on the Field of Mars. On it was a tower from the top of which an eagle would be released at the moment it was ignited. The eagle would soar to heaven, carrying Augustus' soul with it. He himself would become a god, like Julius Caesar before him.

The third codicil was Augustus' account of his life, not his memoirs or autobiography, but the text for an epigraphic monument. It was to be inscribed on two pillars of bronze outside the mausoleum. They are long gone, but many copies were made and set up all over the empire. The best surviving example is from a temple of the imperial cult at Ankara in central Turkey. The Greek heading reads as follows:

Translated and inscribed below are the deeds and gifts of the god Augustus, the account of which he left in the City of Rome engraved on two bronze tablets.

This precisely describes its contents in thirty-five succinct chapters, which list in exhausting detail the peoples conquered, the monuments built in the city of Rome, and the gifts given to all and sundry. It also offers a highly tendentious account of his role in the civil wars. The Latin original of the title had more nuance. Augustus is described by the term *divus*—deified—rather than the blunt term for god, his achievements are glossed as those by which he made the entire world subject to the will of the Roman people, and his gifts are explained as the sums he expended on behalf of the state and of the people. Saviour, conqueror, benefactor, patron, and a Roman who had outdone all his peers and all his predecessors. It is a longer epitaph than the one Sulla chose for himself, but maybe not so different.

Dynasties

Tiberius' accession in AD 14—long planned for and formidably resourced—went smoothly. This was the first in a number of crucial stages through which the charisma and standing enjoyed by Augustus personally became institutionalized into the role of emperor. Tiberius ruled until AD 37, efficient and cautious, but remote and unpopular. Much of the latter part of his reign he spent away from Rome, ruling the city via his praetorian prefect. There were crises, but he survived them. AD 41 showed the dynasty could survive an assassination, that of Tiberius' successor Caligula. After Caligula's death, the Senate had reportedly discussed a return to Republican government; the debate was still running when the imperial guard installed Claudius on the throne. As far as we know, the issue was never seriously raised again. Nero's suicide in AD 68 left no obvious heirs, and a short civil war followed. It was the first in a century, and it lasted less than two years. Governors in Gaul and Spain had been the first to rebel against Nero, and on his death installed Galba as his successor. But he failed to win over either Rome or the other armies and was murdered on 15 January AD 69, the year remembered as that of four emperors. Otho was backed by the Praetorian Guard, Vitellius by the German legions, and Vespasian by the armies of the Danube and Syria and the prefect of Egypt. But after victory for Vespasian's party, the institutions of empire snapped quickly back into place, and all seemed to continue much as before. It was as if Senate, equites (equestrians), people, army, and provinces all felt a need for one man to hold the centre. A bronze tablet records a senatorial decree passed in December AD 69, and

probably formally approved by the assembly shortly thereafter, which grants
Vespasian a series of privileges, citing powers and rights granted to Augustus,
Tiberius, and Claudius as precedents. By the time it was issued, Vespasian
had no real rivals and the Senate and people no real choice, but it expresses
the will of all sides for a restoration of the status quo before the civil war.

The events of AD 69 show the importance of the person of the emperor as a symbolic centre, as a focus of ritual and cosmological power. For
Vespasian's candidacy was supported by heaven. Josephus, a rebel Jewish
leader in captivity, predicted it; Vespasian waiting at Alexandria performed
healing miracles; the goddess Isis supported his cause. Without an emperor
the Capitol burned and there were rumours of Druidic curses. The world
did seem to be coming apart. German auxiliaries and Gallic rebels dreamt
of founding a new empire on the Rhine. The installation of the new Flavian
dynasty (Vespasian's full name was Titus Flavius Vespasianus) immediately
restored order to the world.

Descent mattered above all else.[4] The title king continued to be avoided
in Rome. But there can have been no doubt from the start that the Roman
Empire was now a family affair. Not only did Augustus advertise himself
as son of the god (of the deified Julius Caesar, that is) but he covered the
city in monuments named after family members and their spouses. The
porticoes of Livia, Octavia, and Julia, the theatre of Marcellus, the baths of
Agrippa joined the Julian and Augustan fora. That monumental idiom was
maintained by his successors. Heirs were designated from his family, and the
coming of age of his grandchildren was celebrated on the grandest scale.
Poets and provincial cities soon got the idea: extravagant honours were
paid to one imperial prince after another. The calendar of a military unit
stationed on the Persian frontier shows many of these festivals were still
being celebrated 200 years later. Consent to the hereditary principle is evident in the support given to otherwise very lacklustre emperors. Claudius,
when raised to the throne by the Praetorians, had only his name and ancestry to recommend him. Many refused to believe Nero dead, and there
were at least three pretenders claiming to be him. When Vespasian won the
support of the eastern and Danubian armies for his bid for the throne, it
is very clear that one major recommendation was that he had two adult
sons, Titus and Domitian, as potential successors. Despite the lack of any
family connection, Vespasian's formal imperial name was Imperator Caesar
Vespasianus Augustus. And in an innovation, the title Caesar was employed
to designate Domitian as his heir.

Imperial women were also deployed to build the reputation of a dynasty. The wives of emperors were public figures, appearing in ceremonial,
honoured by the Senate, people, and army, and often given religious roles.[5]
Augustus married his daughter to a series of potential heirs. Empresses
were also the mothers of potential future emperors. Before her fall from
grace, images of Claudius' beautiful young wife Messalina carrying the
child Britannicus (see Figure 13) advertised the posterity of the dynasty.

Fig. 13. The Empress Messalina and her son Britannicus, AD 45, Roman
sculpture, marble, Louvre

Caligula's sisters feature on his coinage and in portrait sculpture, associated with cardinal virtues.[6] Agrippina the Younger was celebrated as Mother of the Camps. Livia was given honours by the Senate, before and after her death. Imperial women, and even their children, might be given extravagant funerals and consecrated after their deaths as *divae*, the female counterparts of the deified emperors.[7] Provincial cities often had priestesses of the living empress.

Ceremonial only reached so far. The city of Rome was a spectacular stage for dynastic rituals of all kinds. There were not enough triumphs, so new rituals were devised. Princes put on the *toga virilis* (the elite symbols of manhood) in public festivals staged in the monumental fora built by the Caesars. There were games to celebrate the opening of the Colosseum. Festivals were declared to mark imperial anniversaries. The funerals of emperors, often followed by their formal reception as gods, involved all ranks. The games became occasions at which the *princeps* dealt directly with the *plebs*.[8] Versions of these events took place elsewhere, for example when the emperor or his close relatives visited the camps or especially when they visited great cities. The arrival of an emperor, his *adventus* (see Figure 14), became a major imperial ceremony in late antiquity.[9] But the empire was vast, and the emperor could only be in one place at once. In his place images were circulated in all media and imitated for civic monuments in the provinces, for the houses of the wealthy, and on coinage for everyone to use. The efficiency with which imperial messages were received and rebroadcast

Fig. 14. The Roman ceremony of the Adventus depicted on a coin

in the provinces can be seen in coin images and legends. Particular virtues, great acts of conquest, imperial building projects, and benefactions were transmitted out from Rome and amplified around the empire.[10]

The centrality of descent and virtue should not surprise. Aristocratic families had run Rome since the beginning of the Republic. For just as long the Roman elite had claimed a moral authority based on the active power of the virtue. Any other kind of monarchy would have been harder to explain. The Flavian dynasty lasted until AD 96, when Domitian was assassinated. Again the imperial order snapped back into place, without even a civil war this time, and Nerva became emperor. He was not a very successful one, but his adoption of the dynamic general Trajan avoided a less smooth transition. Adopted emperors were particularly prone to having their virtues celebrated. These virtues changed over time. Trajan still advertised his good citizenship, his *civilitas* as well as more monarchic virtues like generosity, *indulgentia*. Another strand of the emperor's virtues was military. Emperors were portrayed in armour on horseback, and on coins trampling defeated barbarians. When they could, they also advertised familial virtues, having themselves portrayed with their wives and above all their children.

None of Nerva, Trajan, Hadrian, or Antoninus Pius had sons and so presented themselves selecting virtuous and capable successors from among their more distant relatives and connections. Nomination was always accompanied by adoption, and if one reads the official names and titles of the emperors, these awkward transitions are obscured. So Trajan ruled as Imperator Caesar Nerva Traianus Augustus, Hadrian as Imperator Caesar Traianus Hadrianus Augustus, and so on. Adoption was in any case a very traditional means by which aristocratic families renewed themselves. Polybius' friend Publius Cornelius Scipio Aemilianus Africanus, who sacked Carthage in 146 and was the victor of Numantia in 133 BC, was, in fact, the natural son of Lucius Aemilius Paullus, the victor of Pydna, but had been adopted in childhood by Scipio Cornelius Africanus to ensure he had an heir. And testamentary adoption was the means by which Octavian (born Gaius Octavius) had become the son of Julius Caesar, in fact his great-uncle. Augustus had formally adopted his stepson Tiberius, and Tiberius adopted his nephew Germanicus. Imperial portraiture was fairly standardized and shows a concern to make Julio-Claudian princes show an exaggerated family resemblance.[11] Adoption expressed continued belief in the importance of families and dynastic succession.

It was no surprise that given Marcus Aurelius did have a son, Commodus, he duly succeeded. His assassination in AD 192 did not result in an orderly replacement. After a couple of false starts, another brief civil war followed between the generals of the major armies. The war was almost a replay of the events of AD 69, with different armies backing their own candidates after the failure of the Senate of Rome and the Praetorians to create a local successor. The victor was Septimius Severus, who founded a dynasty that remained in power until AD 235. Severus' son, now known by his nickname Caracalla, was born Lucius Septimius Bassianus, but eventually ruled as Imperator Caesar Marcus Aurelius Severus Antoninus Pius Augustus. These extravagant displays of continuity not only masked breaks between dynasties, but also asserted the stability of the order despite the frequency of assassinations. Caracalla himself was killed in 217, six years after he had murdered his co-emperor and brother Geta with his own hands. Assassinations only rarely caused civil wars, and these were typically short affairs. However precarious the position of emperor might seem, the institution was very stable and stabilized the empire as a whole.

That stability came to an end in the third decade of the third century. The story of how first of all renewed wars on the northern frontier and then the rise of an aggressive new dynasty in Persia created a military crisis that nearly destroyed the empire will be told in Chapter XIII. The restored empire that re-emerged in the 280s had new military, fiscal, and administrative institutions, a new coinage, and soon a new public religion. But it still had emperors. More than twenty emperors ruled—or tried to do so— between AD 235 and 284. To aristocratic historians some of them seemed almost as brutal and uncouth as the barbarians they spent most of their time fighting. But the emperors of the fourth century busily set about founding their dynasties just as the Severi had done, with fictive adoptions and the use of ancient dynastic names and titles. The dynastic principle actually grew stronger in the centuries that followed. When Theodosius I died in AD 395, his 11-year-old son Honorius, who had already been formally co-emperor for two years, took over the western Roman Empire. Rome had never had a child emperor before. The eastern empire was ruled by his elder brother Arcadius, who was still in his teens. Both emperors struggled to assert themselves against their chief ministers and female relatives. This situation would have been unthinkable in the early empire, but is, in fact, an indication of how deeply entrenched the hereditary principle had become at Rome.

Emperors and Empires

Over the millennium and a half between Augustus' victory and the Turkish capture of Constantinople in 1453 almost every Roman institution disappeared or was utterly transformed. Popular assemblies petered out during the early first century AD. Elections were moved into the Senate by Tiberius, and although we hear of occasional formal acclamations by the people, their political role was over. When the masses gathered to cheer or jeer at emperors, it was in the circus, the theatre, or the amphitheatre. The Senate survived much longer, but it progressively lost its functions: embassies were rarely received in the Senate after the first century AD, and during the second century laws began to take their authority from decisions of the emperor, not from senatorial decrees.[12] During the third century senators lost many of their roles in government. Most of this was accidental rather than planned, consequences of the diminishing time emperors spent in the city of Rome. The restored empire of the fourth century had a separate imperial bureaucracy and multiple imperial courts, one for each member of a college of emperors. Senates existed in Rome and Constantinople, but they had little role in government. The equestrian order, Rome's junior aristocracy, enjoyed a period of prominence in the early empire, supplying junior military commanders, financial officials, and even the governors of a few provinces. During the reign of Gallienus it was reinvented as the foundation of military commands, as senators were quietly distanced from politics. It endured into the fifth century, but by then the order itself had little role to play, while its members chased new honours and ranks.[13] The public priesthoods were swept away by Christianity in the early fifth century. Roman citizenship was extended to provincial aristocrats, to former soldiers, to ex-slaves, and eventually to almost everyone in the early third century. The city of Rome itself became marginalized as the emperors spent less time there. Constantine's new capital on the Bosporus became a rival and then replaced Rome completely when Italy was divided up among barbarian kingdoms.

Yet the emperors survived. Emperors remained central through successive crises and fragmentations, through periods when there were multiple courts, beyond the fall of the west, and also the great losses of territory in the seventh century to Persia and then to the Arabs, and on, beyond the scope of this book, into the Middle Ages. Byzantine emperors preserved many of the court ceremonials of their predecessors, and so did the Frankish emperors who briefly supplanted them in the thirteenth century, the final Greek dynasties, and the first Turkish sultans.[14] Great spectacles took place in the hippodrome of Constantinople before the new Muslim rulers of the city, just as they had before Justinian and Constantine, and in Rome before the Severi, Commodus, Vespasian, and all the other emperors back to Augustus. What made monarchy such a successful component of empire?

It helps to recognize that Rome was not unusual. If we consider other ancient empires, very few lasted for long without monarchy at their centre. The Chinese first emperor of the Qin dynasty (221–206 BC) did not replace a republic, but a series of rival kingdoms that occupied the basins of the Yangtze and Yellow rivers during the Warring States Period. One of the many things that united their populations was a notion of ritual kingship. The kings of the preceding Zhou period played a vital part in managing the ceremonial through which the favour of the gods was maintained. Ancestor cult and lineages were drawn into state worship of heaven. Chinese historiography starts with the annals of Sima Qian, written in the last century BC, more or less at the same time as Varro, Atticus, and Nepos were trying to construct a definitive chronology for Roman history. For Sima Qian, Chinese history began with the legendary yellow emperor, and various other dynasties were identified before the Zhou, who ruled for much of the last millennium BC. The Zhou kings, and then the emperors from the Qin dynasty onwards, set monarchy at the cosmological centre of the Chinese universe. Empire without the sons of heaven was unthinkable.[15]

The Achaemenid Persian emperor too ruled over an empire created from an amalgam of kingdoms, among them those of the Medes and the Persians, the Babylonians and Egyptians and Lydians. The title shahanshah, used in one variant or another by various imperial Persian dynasties until the Iranian Revolution of 1979, means king of kings. Persian monarchs increasingly elaborated a sense of their cosmic role, drawing on a wide variety of religious traditions.[16] The earliest empire in south Asia was that of the Mauryan dynasty (322–185 BC), which in some senses resembled Achaemenid Persia. It was created in the aftermath of Alexander's conquest of Persia, and in north-west India competed with the Seleucids for control of former Persian satrapies. This empire too was created by the conquest of a series of earlier kingdoms. Less is known of the early empires of the Americas, but most of these seem to have had monarchies at their centre. The Incas claimed a cosmological centrality similar to that of the Chinese sons of heaven.

A few general observations occur. First, monarchy was very common not only in early empires, but also in the earlier states out of which many were composed. When kingdoms are united to form an empire, it would be bizarre to expect anything other than a grander kind of monarchy to emerge. The idea that an emperor is to a king what a king is to a subject—the Persian notion of king of kings—is perhaps a fairly obvious one. Hierarchical societies grow by multiplying levels. Second, the emperors very often became the focus of rituals that set them at the cosmological centre of the universe. The details varied. Many ancient emperors were considered gods, the children of gods, or (like the Roman emperors) gods in waiting. Others enjoyed special favour or, like Chinese emperors, were privileged mediators between heaven and earth. Depending on how the local religion was organized, emperors might be priests or might be anointed by them. This personalized aspect of imperial universalism was often presented as traditional, the product of ancient ritual systems being modified to accommodate emperors, but some accommodations were extreme. Cyrus the Persian, Alexander the Great, Asoka the Buddhist monarch of the Mauryan dynasty, the Qin first emperor, and Augustus each have some claim to be a religious innovator. Rome was only unusual in not having been a monarchy from an earlier period and in dispersing religious authority among a broader elite during the Republican period.

But it is not enough to show that most empires ended up with monarchs. The key question is what advantages did monarchy have for an ancient empire relative to other forms of government. One common answer—common since antiquity, in fact[17]—is that monarchy is phenomenally powerful as an organizing force. Accounts of the origins of civilization, from that of Lucretius to the theory of hydraulic despotism pioneered by Karl Wittfogel to explain why the earliest cities and states were so often based on irrigation agriculture, have stressed the importance of monarchs as the chief animators of society.[18] Only monarchy, this theory goes, had the capacity to plan, coordinate, manage, and discipline societies into the collective projects on which they depended. Anthropologists have often seen chiefdoms as necessary precursors to states for similar reasons. State formation is associated with the emergence of legally based authorities, including magistracies; but they often owed their creation to charismatic individuals who had supplanted the traditional authority of elders and lineages. Students of ancient Greece are familiar with the idea that tyranny was in some sense the midwife of political institutions. Cicero argued in favour of Pompey's great commands on the grounds that only under the leadership of such a man could the Roman people solve the formidable problems of empire. This sort of thinking was not confined to the elite. The price of grain collapsed when Pompey took responsibility for it in 57 BC, and in a similar crisis in 22 BC the Roman people tried to get Augustus to take on the role of dictator or consul for life. Romans of all ranks believed in the power of individuals much more than they did in the power of institutions.

A second strand of argument paradoxically finds the utility of ancient monarchy in its weakness. What monarchies do best, it is argued, is act as 'capstones' in complex political structures.[19] Kings balance all the other elements – just as a capstone sits on top of other parts of a structure holding everything in place – but they had little active power or freedom of action. Kings might arbitrate conflicts and take decisions about matters over which it was difficult to achieve consensus. But their capacity to change things or take initiatives was weak. Economically and technologically, ancient states were too feeble to give their chief executives much room for manoeuvre. Emperors were even worse off, since the size of their dominions meant it was very difficult to get reliable information on events happening far away, let alone respond quickly. Emperors were forced to trust the generals, governors, and viceroys on the ground. Even at the centre of power, the rituals of court and the intrigues of courtiers limited the emperors' initiative. The idea of the impotent king at the centre of a vast palace utterly dependent on his slaves, eunuchs, ministers, and courtiers is a romantic one, but it is not completely misleading.

More recently, a third way of looking at the role of emperors has become popular. Emperors and kings, in this idea, are important as symbolic centres, as embodied focuses of ideological power.[20] The person of the emperor, sometimes even his body, represented the empire in a way that abstractions and institutions cannot. The religious dimensions are again obvious, but there are other elements too. As embodied symbols, emperors were more portable than ruling cities or monumental temples. Emperors could travel around their vast domains. Chinese emperors travelled constantly to participate in rituals at particular shrines.[21] Macedonian monarchs often began their reign by visiting their armies and taking personal command of them.[22] Even when the emperor was not physically present, his image and his name might be set up everywhere. Each pharaoh had his own cartouche, a hieroglyphic name enclosed in a lozenge shape, and it appeared on monuments all over the kingdom. Embodied authority offered other potentials for veneration. Imperial birthdays might be celebrated, and the rites of passage of other members of the imperial family. The notion of imperial families could easily be extended into imperial lineages and belief in the distinctiveness of royal blood. Ceremonial easily drifted into taboos on touching, addressing, looking at, or turning one's back on the imperial presence. Some emperors were believed to have the capacity to heal certain illnesses. It was believed medieval Byzantine emperors had to be physically whole, with the result that deposing an emperor was often followed by blinding and castration. Underlying all this was the idea that the emperor's body was something concrete and visible, unlike the empire as a whole.

All these ideas—the emperor as decision-maker, the capstone monarch, and the embodied presence—are helpful when it comes to thinking about the Roman emperor. Roman emperors did indeed resolve conflicts between Senate and people, if only by giving the latter bread and circuses and taking away their power to vote. More significantly, promotion into the various orders, appointment to magistracies and military commands, governorships, and priesthoods were all decided, or at least heavily influenced, by the emperors. Emperors managed the economy of honours and were the ultimate patrons. Emperors were judges and made decisions on diplomatic matters and on the finances of the empire as whole. Even in the first century AD, the Senate was involved in almost none of these decisions.[23]

Equally, there was a sense in which the emperor was often more reactive than proactive, rather as the notion of capstone monarch implies.[24] How far this is true in the case of Rome is a matter of fierce debate. Some historians see emperors as forever on the back foot, responding to requests more than issuing orders, limited by the enormous time it took to communicate with distant provinces and by an imperial budget in which army pay swallowed around three-quarters of the total tax revenue. Other historians point to figures like Trajan, who did initiate major new campaigns in central Europe and a great war with Persia, or Vespasian and his sons, who rebuilt the city of Rome after the dreadful fire of Nero's reign. Romans themselves certainly thought it mattered who was on the throne, and a good deal of effort was expended in trying to remove tyrants. Why bother if they were too weak to matter? Some of this is a question of perspective, of course. Tyranny was most acute at home; maybe from the provinces tyrants and good emperors looked much the same. No one doubts that early empires were slow-moving enterprises, oil tankers rather than speedboats. Perhaps the best answer is that the Roman Empire was never easy to steer, and it was all too easy for weak rulers to allow ritual and routine and their closest courtiers to run the empire. That has certainly been true in other monarchies.[25] But some Roman emperors certainly ruled as well as reigned.

As for the emperor as an embodiment of empire, we find him everywhere. The names and images of the emperors were inserted into public ceremonies all over the Roman world.[26] Annual festivals of the imperial cult conducted by priests wearing images of the emperor on their crowns were just the most prominent version of this. Gods shared their temples with the emperor, allowed his statues to join theirs in processions, and his name was incorporated into prayers and hymns.[27] Emperors' faces were present in many other buildings. The city of Sardis in western Turkey built a vast gymnasium and bathhouse in the centre of the city, a monument to civic culture and civilized values. One room was devoted to portrait busts of the emperors. Coins from all over the empire, both the gold and silver issued by imperial mints and the bronze change occasionally produced in Greek cities, bore images of emperors. Armies too paid cult on the birthday of the emperor, kept his image with their standards, and celebrated the anniversaries of imperial princes. Over time, more and more ceremonial surrounded the imperial presence. By the fourth century it was a special privilege to be allowed to kiss the hem of his purple robe.

Much of this evolved over time. There was no moment when the role of emperor was actually designed; indeed, it lacked a label for a surprising length of time. Octavian drew on ideological support and titulature from all possible sources. *Augustus* had a helpfully vague sense of the divine, *tribunicia potestas* evoked a popular mandate, *princeps senatus* (senior member of the Senate) asserted respect for hierarchies of dignity as well as for the Senate's place in the state, and a cluster of priesthoods and other titles alluding to magisterial power and personal heroism completed the package. Most of this was focused on the city of Rome. Out in the provinces he was king in the Greek world, pharaoh in Egypt, and goodness knows what to Gallic and Spanish tribesmen. The army hailed him as *Imperator*, the title awarded to victorious generals. In return he called them 'fellow soldiers'.[28]

Court and Empire

Historians of the imperial era complained that under the emperors you never knew for sure what was going on. Tacitus and Dio were senators, and they shared the prejudices of their order, but they were not completely wrong.

Empire brought the end of public elections, the end of those meetings of the assembly at which orators competed to persuade the people to go to war or make peace or to accept or reject controversial legislation, the end of *contiones*, those open meetings addressed by magistrates at moments of crisis, the end of political cases in the law courts, and the end of free speech in the Senate. Politics had once taken place largely in the public domain. That space was still there, but it was now for ceremonial. Decision-making took place elsewhere.

Politics had been palatialized. Emperors received information in private and discussed matters of state with their friends and family. Friends might include senators and equestrians. Many emperors had close friendships with individual senators, and many of their relatives were members of one or other of Rome's aristocratic orders. The equestrian commanders of the Praetorian Guard were often very close to the centre of power. Sejanus and Macro were powerbrokers in the Julio-Claudian period, their second-century successors accompanied the emperor on campaigns, acting as effective viziers, and by the fourth century praetorian prefects were the senior figures in the imperial bureaucracy. But this was not the same as formally consulting the Senate or involving them in decision-making.

Besides, there were more sinister influences than the emperor's friends and the praetorian prefects. Aristocrats suspected—with good reason—that some emperors paid more attention to their slaves and ex-slaves than they did to senators. Claudius' attempts to give public honours to imperial freedmen were very unpopular. Later emperors kept their former slaves out of sight, appointing equestrians to be the public heads of departments in which we may suspect freedmen still did most of the work. Imperial women were especially mistrusted. Not only were they believed to exert undue influence over the emperor, but their rivalries were said to divide the imperial house, especially when they were fighting over the succession prospects of their sons and husbands. Rumours abounded, along with all sorts of accusations. Even emperors could feel out of the loop. During one crisis the Emperor Claudius appealed to his most trusted freedmen. 'Am I still emperor?' It was a good question: his empress had divorced him and her new lover was planning to adopt their son.

The location of all this activity is a familiar one. It was the imperial court.[29] All monarchies have courts, and they fulfil vital functions, especially in traditional societies. Courts regulate access to the monarch, ensuring his role as decision-maker is deployed where it matters. Courts offer protection

and services to monarchs. Where there are other powerful institutions—
whether a senate, a church, or a parliament—courts defend the prerogatives
of the monarchy within the state. Courts vary enormously in their nature.
Early medieval kings made do with a warrior band, their family, and household servants. Rituals of entertainment and hospitality were elaborated over
time, and domestic servants, like the chamberlain, came to acquire new
roles in government. The most elaborate courts were those of absolutist
monarchs: at Versailles and similar palaces, ceremonial acted to integrate the
kingdom, employing elaborate etiquette and ritual to create finely nuanced
hierarchies of honour.[30]

The Roman imperial court was a rather shadowy entity in the first century AD. Like the courts of medieval Europe it evolved out of the household,
but in this case out of the slave households of Roman aristocrats. Pompey
and Caesar had depended on trusted ex-slaves and on their clients and
close friends. It is no surprise that the emperors did the same. But to begin
with there were no elaborate ceremonials and indeed no real palace to
stage them in. The Palatine Hill, between the Roman forum and the circus
Maximus, had been an area of aristocratic housing in the late Republic.
Cicero, Crassus, and Antony were among those who had mansions there.
Augustus acquired one of these houses and gradually extended his control of the hill, joining together houses, temples, and open areas to create
what was in effect an imperial compound. More and more buildings were
added by his immediate successors. From the Flavian period on a more
coordinated complex emerged, with great reception areas and decorations
in coloured marble.[31] One probable reason for the initial monumental reti-
cence, in a city now full of spectacular marble temples and places of entertainment, was the lack of a formal description of the position of emperor
in the first century. Augustus was a king everywhere but in Rome, and in
many parts of the empire he was a god as well. Only in the capital did he
have to exercise tact. The palaces of Macedonian kings had been rather
grand structures, with great libraries and also hunting enclosures modelled
on those of Persian emperors. Augustus did have a library on the Palatine
but it was lodged in the temple of Apollo. The wilder entertainments took
place on the Bay of Naples.

Institutionally too, the Roman court was not like that of the Seleucids, the
Antigonids, or the Ptolemies. Roman emperors advertised their *civilitas*—
their sense of civic virtue—yet the gap they really had to watch was not
between ruler and subject, but that between emperor and aristocrat.[32] The

problem was that not much separated the Caesars from other noble families. Macedonian kings had surrounded themselves with companions, young men of noble birth, but their empires contained no real aristocracies apart from the elites of the greater cities. Their courts were places apart. Medieval European kings tried only to marry the daughters of other monarchs, again to separate themselves from their nobility. Yet Roman emperors were members of the Roman nobility, no royal blood ran through their veins, and they were not an anointed lineage. The Senate included their close relatives and—since they never steeled themselves to marry the daughters of Persian emperors—the Senate included their relations by marriage as well. Most emperors had been through a senatorial career of some kind or other, and they knew the prejudices of the senators from the inside. Claudius, interestingly, was an exception. Perhaps this contributed to his giving freedmen public honours, including the right to wear badges of office associated with Republican magistrates. Clearly, there were advantages too in the close relation between emperors and the nobility. Emperors had a wider choice of marriage partners than if they had been restricted to royal princesses. More importantly, ancient institutions like patronage, grand dinners (*cenae*) attended by friends of different status, and the notions of formal friendships and enmities could be adapted to new ends. When an emperor publicly renounced his friendship with a senator, it was the equivalent of a death sentence. Emperors did well too out of the obligation on Romans to leave legacies to their friends. Yet despite this, the city of Rome with all its traditions, including that of the collective authority of the Senate, constrained the court and limited the freedom of the emperors.

And so they left. There was no single moment at which the emperors abandoned the city. Like other aristocrats, they had always maintained residences outside Rome. Tiberius spent the last decade of his reign mostly on Capri and partly on the Bay of Naples. Trajan had a great villa on the coast near modern Civitavecchia, Hadrian built his amazing fantasy residence in Tivoli. From the first decades of Augustus' reign there had also been times when their attention was required elsewhere. Caligula and Claudius spent long periods in the north-west provinces, Nero spent a year and a half in Greece, and Domitian campaigned in Germany. When emperors left Rome, the court went with them. What this meant was that they were accompanied by a vast train of guards and slaves, who included personal attendants of every kind and concubines as well as secretaries, and the heads of the palatine offices.[33] Embassies, if they wanted a decision, had to track down the emperor wherever he was. From the second century AD there are more and more anecdotes concerning formal receptions on the frontier or in great provincial cities. Hadrian notoriously spent a huge proportion of his reign travelling, to Egypt and Africa, to Britain and the northern provinces, to Athens again and again. Marcus felt compelled to spend much of his reign in the Danube provinces, facing the barbarians.

Itinerant monarchy has often been a solution to the problems of communication in large states and early empires. Medieval kings sometimes moved their hungry retainers to wherever the food was rather than try to get provisions to a single capital. Some Chinese emperors toured shrines in an annual cycle. Roman emperors moved to see the world and to get close to the problems that concerned them most at the time. Severus fought campaigns in Persia and Britain even after he was secure on the throne. Since they could govern from anywhere, it mattered little where they were based. True, they could no longer receive foreign visitors in the Senate, or go through the motions of discussing legislation there. But perhaps these were not disadvantages. The city of Rome remained a powerful symbol of empire, even though it played no really essential role in governing the empire.[34] Trajan and Hadrian and Severus and Caracalla all engaged in great building programmes there. Most third- and fourth-century emperors had less time to spare and maybe less money, although that did not prevent them building themselves grand palaces in York and Trier, Sirmium and Split and Constantinople. Most later emperors visited Rome, but it was to look at past glories. Senators worked hard to keep lines of communication open, sent frequent embassies, and even had some of their children enter the imperial bureaucracy. But even as they elaborated the slogan 'Roma Aeterna', they must have known in their hearts that the centre of the empire was no longer the city, but rather wherever the emperor and his court happened to be.

Further Reading

Perhaps no period of Roman history has been subjected to the same scrutiny as the transition from Republic to Empire. The range of approaches and ideas can be sampled in three collections of papers: Fergus Millar and Erich Segal (eds.), *Caesar Augustus* (Oxford, 1984); Kurt Raaflaub and Mark Toher (eds.), *Between Republic and Empire* (Berkeley, 1990) ; and Karl Galinsky's *Cambridge Companion to the Age of Augustus* (Cambridge, 2005). There have been many biographies and assessments of Augustus. The most interesting is his own, the *Res gestae divi Augusti*, which has now been translated and equipped with a marvellous commentary by Alison Cooley (Cambridge, 2009). The bimillennium of his death in AD 14 led to various conferences, some of which have produced collected volumes. Among them are Ingo Gildenhard and others' *Augustus and the Destruction of History: The Politics of the Past in Early Imperial Rome*, Cambridge Classical Journal Supplements (Cambridge, 2019), Kit Morrell and others' *The Alternative Augustan Age* (New York, 2019), and most originally Penelope Goodman's *Afterlives of Augustus* (Cambridge, 2018), which traces his shifting reputation from immediately after his death up to the present day.

Fergus Millar's *Emperor in the Roman World* (London, 1977) set the emperor at the centre of the empire, not as an animating force but as the point at which all other institutions met. It changed fundamentally the way the history of the early empire was written. Brian Campbell's *The Emperor and the Roman Army* (Oxford, 1984) is an essential supplement. How contemporaries understood and described their rulers is the subject of Matthew Roller's brilliant *Constructing Autocracy* (Princeton, NJ, 2001) and also, in a way, of Andrew Wallace-Hadrill's subtle *Suetonius* (London, 1983). Carlos Noreña's thoughtful *Imperial Ideals in the Roman West: Representation, Circulation, Power* (Cambridge, 2011) explores how the images of emperors produced by the centre were adopted all over the empire in a range of media.

Studies of the reigns of individual emperors are too numerous to mention. My favourites include Barbara Levick's *Tiberius the Politician* (London, 1976) and Anthony Birley's *Hadrian: The Restless Emperor* (London, 1997). Miriam Griffin's *Nero: The End of a Dynasty* (London, 1996) is at once the history of a key turning point, the portrait of an exceptional reign, and a study of the culture and politics of the court. It is also a great read.

The different circles around the emperor are surveyed in John Crook's *Consilium principis* (Cambridge, 1955), Paul Weaver's *Familia Caesaris* (Cambridge, 1972), and most recently in Tony Spawforth's *The Court and Court Society in Ancient Monarchies* (Cambridge, 2007), which set Roman palace politics alongside those of Egypt, Persia, Macedon, and Han China. Another collection that deals with some of the same issues is David Cannadine and Simon Price's *Rituals of Royalty* (Cambridge, 1987). Imperial women are not the only subjects of Diana Kleiner and Susan Matheson's two collections entitled *I, Claudia I and II* (Austin, TX, 1996 and 2000), but they gather together a fascinating collection of art historical, historical, and literary studies.

RESOURCING EMPIRE

There were always kingdoms and wars in Gaul right up until you submitted to our laws. Although we have often suffered at your hands, we have, by right of conquest, imposed only this one thing on you, with which we keep the peace. For peace between nations is impossible without soldiers, and there are no soldiers without pay, and no pay unless taxes are paid. Everything else we share with you.

(Tacitus, *Histories* 4.74)

The Political Economy of Tributary Empires

Who paid for empire? Like all imperial rulers, the Romans passed the cost on to their subjects. Romans knew this. Tacitus puts this pithy summary of imperial economics into the mouth of the Roman general Cerealis in a speech aimed at dissuading the Gallic tribes of the Treveri and Lingones from joining the rebellion of AD 69. This was, indeed, the bottom line. By Tacitus' day the army devoured most of what the emperors raised in taxation. Put like this, the resourcing of Roman imperialism seems very simple. Yet the mechanisms employed were phenomenally complex and in constant evolution. Roman history is, in some sense, the story of unending struggles to balance the imperial budget. Perhaps this was true for all imperial states.

A comparative perspective indicates the tight constraints within which Rome had to solve these problems. Early empires were vast redistributive systems. The key resources on which they depended were land and manpower. Metals, timber, and hard stone were also important; correspondence between the Bronze Age kings of the ancient Near East was already often preoccupied with securing these precious resources. But the basis of all ancient economies was agriculture. Every early empire was, in the final analysis, funded from the agricultural surplus. Given that empires were built on inequality and were very large, they also depended on transport infrastructure. Empires typically spent on soldiers, functionaries, and imperial courts, and none of these groups was evenly distributed among the productive landscapes they controlled. There were not many options. Food could be moved to the consumers; the consumers could go to the food; or else monetary systems could be devised which allowed states to pay in cash but required subject populations to sell surplus on the market to earn money to pay taxes, and consumers to use the market to obtain what they needed. Rome eventually used a combination of these, building roads and ports, levying taxes in kind and in cash, providing incentives for traders to bring their cargoes to the imperial capitals, and expecting provincial populations to supply armies and imperial courts on the move.[1]

The Roman solution was, therefore, broadly similar to that employed by other early empires. Great infrastructure projects included the Grand Canal of China, begun in the fifth century BC and nearly 1,600 kilometres (1,000 miles) long by the time of its completion a millennium later; the Persian Royal Road, which ran over more than 2,400 kilometres (1,500 miles) from Sardis to Susa; and the great Inca Road that ran 6,000 kilometres (3,700 miles) along the length of the Andes. Rome was especially fortunate in ruling an empire arranged around an inland sea. Moving the consumers to the food was less practical for empires than for smaller states. Early English kings could move their tiny courts around their little kingdom with relative ease, but empires required more complex systems. As a result, most created imperial monetary systems with which to pay soldiers and state functionaries. Often this involved extending the uses of an earlier coinage, like the copper coins of the Qin kingdom that became the first imperial coinage of China, or Rome's silver denarii, which, in the course of the late Republic, gradually replaced virtually all the other precious metal coinages of the Mediterranean world.[2] Along with imperial coinages there usually went imperial standard measures. The Athenians' conversion of the Delian League into something like an empire was marked when the assembly issued a decree, probably in the mid-420s BC, requiring its allies to use Athenian coins, Athenian weights, and Athenian measures.[3] The Achaemenid Persian Empire issued coinage and demanded some taxes be paid in coin. Hellenistic empires typically made use of standardized monetary systems.[4]

Historians sometimes call this sort of political system a tributary empire.[5] Tributary empires may be contrasted with conquest states, polities with institutions and ideologies geared to constant expansion. The Aztec political order depended on annual war, and it had state rituals that demanded constant supplies of war captives for sacrifice. A run of years without victories would cause political collapse. When conquest states enjoyed a sustained comparative advantage over their neighbours, periods of astonishingly rapid expansion might occur. Typically, this involved not only rewards for the conquerors, but also means by which new members were recruited to their armies. Conquest states moved like tsunamis across political landscapes. The Arab conquest that between 634 and 720 created a caliphate stretching from southern France to the Punjab and the Inca conquest of the Andes in the century after AD 1438 were both movements of this kind. So too was the rapid unification of the Mediterranean that Polybius witnessed. But this kind of forward drive could not be maintained indefinitely. All conquest states were doomed either to sudden collapse (like the empire of Attila the Hun) or else to become institutionalized as tributary empires. Achaemenid Persia provides an excellent example. The empire was created between 559 and 522 by Cyrus and his son Cambyses, who together conquered the kingdoms of the Medes, the Babylonians, and the Egyptians; but their empire nearly collapsed in civil war until Darius I took control, creating a single currency, a tax system, a provincial system, and the Royal Road. Greek and Roman writers, spellbound by the horror of civil war, present the achievement of Augustus mostly in terms of establishing civil peace.[6] But what really saved the empire from collapse was his success in stopping expansion and consolidating it around institutions that could be repurposed to serve the sustainable economics of a tributary empire.

There were only a few fiscal options open to the rulers of tributary empires. Local rulers of various kinds could be recruited to act as agents of empire, tax farmers could be employed or a tax-gathering bureaucracy could be created. Each method had its disadvantages. Depending on local elites meant surrendering some power over the provinces. A detailed comparison has been drawn between Rome's use of local elites and the situation in the Mughal Empire which extracted tax with the help of local zamindars, in the process conceding them significant autonomy.[7] Tax farmers minimized the risks and costs of tax collection, guaranteeing the state a fixed income. But they notoriously had short-term interests and were the least sympathetic to taxpayers. The long-term disadvantages of public–private partnerships are now very familiar to us: private individuals or corporations on limited-term contracts have an interest in short-term profit and much less in promoting the sustainability that the state and its citizens depend on. For tributary empires employing tax farmers, this meant they had to run the risk of revolts and protests stirred up by profiteering. A bureaucracy gave emperors much more control, but it came at a significantly higher cost, one that in the end would have to be recouped from the taxpayers.

The broad path of Rome's own journey through these tangled waters is simply stated. Roman expansion in Italy conforms closely to the ideal type of a conquest state. But as early as the third century BC, elements of more stable revenue extraction appear. Indemnities from defeated powers were replaced over the second century by regular exactions as former Hellenistic kingdoms were absorbed and other territory was won in the west. At first Rome depended on tax farmers: for a state already making the widespread use of public contracts that Polybius observed this was natural. But tax farming was impractical in some regions—notably Spain—and the appalling behaviour of those who held the contract to collect Roman taxes in Asia was widely blamed for the support many Greeks gave Mithridates. Caesar entrusted the collection of land tax in Asia to the local elites of Greek cities in the province, and that system became widespread during the early first century AD except in Italy, which was exempt, and Egypt, where the bureaucracy used by the Ptolemies was preserved, and perhaps some frontier zones where the military acted as different kinds of bureaucrats. The early imperial system remained, however, exceptionally complex, and tax farming continued to be used for many indirect taxes.[8] The Augustan system had most consistency at the very highest level. Further down, there was little desire to tinker with systems that worked well enough, and only a few attempts to make improvements can be documented. All this changed in the crisis of the third century. The empire needed greater revenue at a time when the economy was for one reason or another weaker, and when local aristocracies were under unprecedented pressure. The result was that, as part of the imperial recovery, a new system emerged, with new taxes, a new coinage, and a centralized bureaucracy that lasted into the Byzantine Middle Ages.

Good Times and Bad Times

Fiscal systems can be seen as governmental responses to the economic activities of their subjects. Ideally, they extract as much as possible without harming that activity. As Tiberius is said to have put it, 'I want my sheep shorn, not flayed.' The historical ecology of the Mediterranean basin and its hinterlands has been described already, and its agrarian regimes were essentially stable. Roman rule brought a few new farming techniques and a few new crops into some regions, but there was no revolutionary change. That 'normal' background had some built-in short-term instability, especially in the Mediterranean part of the empire where food crises were not unusual.[9] More generally, the ancient Mediterranean was characterized by highly localized cycles of boom and bust that drove peasant cultivators into strategies of crop diversification, storage, and exchange.[10] Growth, where it took place, was almost entirely the result of intensification. Where landowners had the funds and the desire, we can observe them draining and irrigating; planting vines, olive trees, and gardens that would be more profitable than other crops; experimenting with new varieties of trees; engaged in selective livestock breeding; improving the value of their estates by opening up clay pits and building kilns and olive presses; constructing mills and storage facilities; and improving the transport facilities they used to get their surplus to market. Broadly speaking, the poor feared risk, the rich sought profit, but both pursued their ends by essentially traditional means.

Yet long-term trends did emerge from this activity, trends with which the tributary empire had to deal. Work progresses apace on filling in the details of these trends, and especially on quantifying them.[11] Underwater archaeology has shown how the numbers of shipwrecks rose to a peak in the late Republican period, which suggests this was the period of greatest long-distance trade in the ancient Mediterranean.[12] Over the same period, Italian products, especially wine and ceramic tableware, are found all over the Mediterranean world, and beyond it too. From the early first century AD this evidence diminishes in volume. But there are indications of growth in the provinces, including the production of olive oil for export in North

Picture Box 6 The Hoby Cups

These two silver drinking cups were found in 1920 in a grave at Hoby on the island of Lolland in south-east Denmark. The grave in which they were found was that of a middle-aged man, and it also contained gold rings, a mixing bowl for wine with a wine ladle, a jug, a tray, and two hams. From the contents the grave can be dated to the first century AD. Lolland was well beyond any area visited by Roman armies in the period. But there were Roman naval expeditions to the Baltic, and it is also likely that some German princes made visits to Roman commanders in the field or based in the Rhineland garrisons. The cups are inscribed with the Roman name Silius, and this might refer to a Roman general who campaigned in Germany in the first years of the reign of Tiberius. The most likely route by which they reached Denmark was as a diplomatic gift, either for the man in the grave or for one of his family.

Each cup weighs around 1 kilogram (2.2 lbs) and was produced in the Roman Empire. They are signed Cheirisophos, probably the name of the Greek metalworker who made them. On them are scenes from the Trojan story, one showing scenes from the story of Philoctetes, the other including Priam's visit to Achilles to ask for the return of Hector's body. There are some other pieces of silverwork known from the period with similar designs, but very few have survived from the Roman world because silver is so easily recycled. Only the fact that these examples ended up in a grave preserved them. This is a common phenomenon. Roman period silver plate is mostly known from hoards, and from graves outside the empire.

Educated Romans would have understood the resonances of the myths depicted (including, perhaps, the fact that both depict embassies, which makes these very appropriate diplomatic gifts). The scenes on the cups probably meant less to the chieftain of Hoby or his family. Yet the value placed on these precious Roman artefacts gives some sense of how the Roman Empire was viewed. The other grave goods suggest that ceremonial wine drinking had become important in this society, even though wine would have had to have been imported from the Mediterranean. More generally, they indicate how far Roman goods had an impact beyond the empire. Quite possibly the chief derived some of his status at home from his possession of Mediterranean goods and his ability to obtain more of them. These gifts also reveal an aspect of Romano-Germanic relations rarely recorded in Greek and Latin historical writing, which focused on military conflict. Most of the time, Rome depended on 'friends' beyond the empire to keep the peace and perhaps keep Rome informed. The empire's frontiers were not barriers, but rather broad zones of interaction and exchange. These cups are a rare trace of cross-frontier relationships that served both sides.

Further Reading

C. R. Whittaker, *Frontiers of the Roman Empire: A Social and Economic Study*, Ancient Society and History (Baltimore, MD: Johns Hopkins University Press, 1994).
https://en.natmus.dk/historical-knowledge/denmark/prehistoric-period-until-1050-ad/the-early-iron-age/the-chieftains-grave-from-hoby/, accessed 16 April 2021.

Africa and southern Spain, and the production of wine for local consumption in areas as varied as central France, the environs of Rome, and Egypt. Trade, in other words, boomed first, followed by the capacity to produce the same goods locally.[13] New evidence for increased levels of mining and metal production has come from ice cores drilled through the Greenland ice cap. To judge from the levels of atmospheric lead and copper pollution attested there, the production of metals reached a peak in the early Roman Empire not repeated before the Industrial Revolution.[14]

For the most part, these changes were demand-led. For example, one major stimulus to change was the spread of new styles of consumption across the empire, styles modelled on those of Italian elites. Oil, wine, fish sauces, textiles, bronzes, and ornaments were all in demand among their provincial counterparts. Changes in consumption did not only impact on the circulation of commodities: they also moved the sites of production. Teachers and potters and wall painters found new employment in the provinces. Italian architects, engineers, and craftsmen were already at work on public buildings in the western provinces in the early first century AD.[15] Once these skills had been taught to locals, quarries had been opened up, tile production had begun, and new carpentry techniques and design features were disseminated. We begin to see the transformation of domestic architecture, first in the cities and then in the countryside. Even more sophisticated engineering skills were needed to build aqueducts that powered monumental fountains and bathhouses, signs of new aesthetic and cosmetic sensibilities. All this was expensive, but if some of Rome's subjects were exploited more to pay for it, others might make money satisfying these new tastes.[16]

The greatest change in lifestyle in many parts of the empire was the growth of cities. The number of cities, their density, and the population of the larger centres grew all over the empire. Regions with only villages before Rome—inland Gaul and Spain, central Anatolia, parts of Egypt and the Balkans—experienced the greatest growth. In a few areas, such as the Nile Valley, central Italy, and coastal Asia Minor, the proportion of nonproducers who had to purchase their food crept up to as much as 30 per cent of the population. A large part of this growth was the consequence of the emergence of a small number of enormous cities at the top of the settlement hierarchy. The population of Rome reached around one million, and maybe ten other cities crossed the 100,000 mark. The urban system itself was changing, and in some areas small cities grew smaller as the larger ones swelled in size.[17] But by most estimates, the total urban population of the empire increased to a maximum around AD 200.[18] Add to this the creation of a standing army that fluctuated between a quarter and half a million men, and it is clear where the new demand was coming from.

The Roman Empire promoted these processes accidentally and indirectly. By supporting urbanization and creating a standing army, the empire increased net demand. The models of civilized life that, under Roman rule, spread beyond the Mediterranean basin provided opportunities for merchants, craftsmen, and architects. Roman rule favoured the rich, and to the extent that they became richer, their aggregate purchasing power increased. Standardized currencies and weights and measures, and investment in transport infrastructure—all designed to serve administrative and military ends—also made trade easier. Law, common languages, and peace must have helped. Perhaps taxation played a part as well, stimulating landowners to produce greater surpluses, whether to be supplied in kind to the army or to be sold to pay taxes.[19]

Intensification of this kind, first in Italy and then in the provinces, powered growth from at least the second century BC until some point in the third century AD. But then the process went into reverse. Some cities shrank in size, especially in the north and west. New investment in production seems to have diminished. Certain kinds of long-distance trade in commodities declined in volume. There are many uncertainties. In some cases a decline in trade reflected the growing success of local producers: cycles of production and consumption, in other words, were becoming more localized. Archaeological studies of some commodities, for example ceramic products from North Africa, suggest long-distance trade continued up to and beyond the collapse of the western empire. Africa remained a major exporter of grain, even under the Vandals. Most indicators of economic decline also suggest a more dramatic decline in the north and west of the empire than in its southern and eastern provinces. The local economies of Syria and parts of Asia Minor actually seem to boom in late antiquity. Even less consensus exists about the reasons for the reversal of many of these trends, or indeed about the point at which this reversal began. The peak in shipwrecks is actually in the late Republic, and Italian wine exports reach fewer and fewer regions in bulk from the same period. Could improvements in shipping or increased domestic consumption of wine explain part of this? The urban apogee, however, is around two centuries later.

Once the urban peak was passed, collapsing demand certainly did have a major effect. Many western cities, Rome included, shrank dramatically in population between 200 and 300 AD. The occupied areas of some cities in the north-west provinces were reduced to a quarter of their second-century maximum by the end of the third century. A few cities were even abandoned. Many others must have contained vast areas of crumbling buildings and empty plots in the late empire, and a few huddled around a fortified castle in old monumental centres. Hardly any new urban monuments were constructed after the 230s anywhere. Rome itself dropped to perhaps a third of its size in the same period. All this must have affected the market for foodstuffs and textiles, for ceramics and fuel, and also the construction industry. The rich remained rich, and some became richer: some of the most splendid rural and suburban villas were constructed in the fourth century all over the empire. But their spending alone could not absorb the mass productions that agricultural intensification had aimed at generating.

Many factors have been suggested to explain these changes. It is sometimes suggested that as economies became more and more regional, some parts of the empire had simply opted out of its expensive urbanized civilization. But it is difficult to see the articulation of alternative value systems in the literary texts of the fourth century. Indeed, they are often so nostalgic in tone that they are described as classicizing. The barbarian invasions of the late third century cannot have done this much damage, which is also evident in areas unaffected by those raids such as Britain. Nor had the empire (yet) increased the tax burden to the point where the productive base was under pressure, nor were the wealthy (yet) so wealthy that they had crippled public finances.

Recently explanations in terms of plague and climate change have been revived.[20] Does each age visit its own fears on the fall of the Roman Empire? A terrifying plague certainly did grip the empire in the middle of the second century AD. Vivid descriptions have survived, including one from Galen, the leading physician of the early empire.[21] It looks most likely that the pathogen in question was smallpox, or a close relative of it. It came from the east, brought into the Roman Empire by an army that encountered it while campaigning against the Persians in the 160s AD, and spread rapidly along the militarized areas of the Danube and Rhine eventually reaching Rome, driving refugees (and at one point emperors) before it. But it is difficult to estimate its effect on the long-term operation of the economy. Comparative evidence shows plagues can have a range of effects, some even positive, on economic growth.[22] The question of climate change is even less certain and hinges on very large-scale estimation of fluctuations of mean annual temperature. If there was indeed a slight decrease in temperature around the middle of the first millennium BC, this could have affected agricultural productivity. Then there is the separate issue of whether the climate had become less stable as a result of volcanic eruptions, solar activity, or both. Reconstructions of ancient climate are getting more and more sophisticated, but there are two problems to solve before we can safely move from those reconstructions to an understanding of the history of the ancient economy. As described in Chapter IV, global climatic changes have hugely different impacts locally, because the systems they interact with are so complex. That is true whether we are looking at rainfall patterns, at floods and droughts, or at biological systems. Second, even if we do get to the point where we can be confident about the local environmental history of some well documented regions, such as the Nile Valley or central Italy, we still need to factor in human agency. Not all societies are equally prepared for change, and not all respond equally well. One way to approach this that seems promising is through the idea of resilience. How well were ancient cities and states able to respond to epidemiological or climatic changes? At the moment more is known about how ancient peasants dealt with short–term risk than about how ancient cities provided against it.[23]

However we come to explain it, the evidence for urban shrinkage and a decline in the long–distance transport of commodities in many parts of the empire is unmistakable. The consequences of economic contraction for a tributary empire are clear. Indirect taxes tapped the profits of trade, auctions, and manumissions. If fewer of these took place, the revenue decreased. Direct tax was based on the land, but if land became less profitable, there was a limit to what could be raised. This is, however, clearer to us than it was to them.

Harnessing the Ancient Economy

This picture of the economy that is emerging from the very latest research would have been incomprehensible to the Romans themselves. Their very practical understanding of economic activity did not include the use of predictive or descriptive modelling, they gathered little data from which they could have analysed trends, and ancient science had no concept of the economy as a separate entity. In that sense the emperors were flying blind as they designed and modified their tax systems.

But their solutions to problems were not foolish. When earthquakes devastated the cities of Asia, Tiberius remitted tax income for five years. When Augustus needed more money for the military, he created new taxes. When prices began to soar at the end of the third century, Diocletian tried to fix legal maximums. Historians understood that when new silver mines were opened up, the price of silver would decrease, and also how changes in rules governing interest rates could provoke a shortage of coin (even if they did not have specialized terms for 'supply and demand' or 'liquidity crisis'). It follows that the devices that the emperors employed to tax this vast economy were pragmatic, if also fundamentally reactive and adaptive. Not much effort was put into smoothing out differences between provinces taxed in different ways. Uniformity and consistency were not sought in themselves, and establishing equity between different groups of taxpayers was never a concern. The emperors harvested the economy opportunistically, aiming to take a share of whatever profit was being made. As a result, the early imperial system preserved institutional fossils of every stage of Roman imperialism, and of some earlier ages too.

The political economy of the Roman Republican state before the Punic Wars was almost non-existent. Successful campaigns brought some booty, especially chattel slaves and bullion, most of which was divided between the allies, the citizen soldiers, the general, and the gods. The state had, in any case, few expenses, and did not begin to mint coin regularly until the Pyrrhic War. Most of the monuments built in this period were temples constructed in fulfilment of battlefield vows and paid for out of the general's share of the booty.[24] The Roman census did allocate tax obligations according to wealth, but we know very little of this direct taxation, except that it was abolished forever after the defeat of Macedon in 168 BC. Warfare up and down the peninsula extended Roman control over land and manpower. Conquered manpower it exploited through enslavement and those alliances that required subject states to provide troops to support Roman armies. Captured land became *ager publicus* and was either used to found colonies or rented out to Roman citizens. Those rents (*vectigalia*) became one of the state's first regular and predictable sources of income.[25]

Overseas wars with Carthage and Macedon brought other sources of income. Indemnities were imposed on defeated Carthage in 241 and 201, in both cases spread into a series of annual payments. Macedon and Syria too had to pay massive indemnities after their respective defeats in 196 and 188 BC. During this period great public building works were initiated in Rome.[26] Other public contracts were issued for the provisioning of armies. Only Roman citizens with funds to guarantee them could take public contracts, which were a means of spreading the proceeds of empire among the propertied classes.

The political economy was transformed when Rome began to acquire territory overseas. The first province was Sicily. Carthage had taxed her possessions in the west of the island and perhaps Rome took over their fiscal system after the First Punic War. After the capture of Syracuse in 211 during the Second Punic War, Rome adapted the tax system created by King Hiero. What became known as the Lex Hieronica in effect imposed a tithe on the agricultural produce of most of the Greek cities of the island. Rome allowed a few cities exemption and deprived some others of their land. Using taxation to reward allies and punish enemies became a standard Roman technique. Absorbing this small Hellenistic kingdom probably opened the Romans' eyes to the possibilities of using tax as a means of generating a regular income out of their military supremacy. Certainly, when Tiberius Gracchus successfully urged the takeover of the kingdom of Pergamum in 133, the key motive was to provide an income stream for his own project of land distribution. The Roman people received the income from royal taxes and the royal lands. Tax farmers (*publicani*) made a profit from its collection, and this bought Gracchus political support in Rome.

Tax farming of one kind or another remained important long into the empire for the collection of indirect taxes.[27] An inscription of Nero's day found recently at Ephesus (see Figure 15) shows that the various customs duties created by the kings of Pergamum were still being levied in exactly the same way as they had been more than two centuries after the Roman takeover.[28] Tax farmers remained in charge of collecting internal tariffs long after they had lost the lucrative contracts to collect the land tax in the last years of the Republic. The tariffs levied at the frontiers of the old Pergamene kingdom were probably the model for new internal tariffs, like the 2.5 per cent tax on goods going in and out of the Gallic provinces created in Augustus' reign. To begin with, this was levied by publican companies, then by individual contractors (in both cases under the supervision of equestrian procurators, but the latter were much easier to control), and finally was handed over to state officials in the late second century.[29] That evolution perhaps illustrates a wider trend towards increased central control of taxation, even before economic contraction and the onset of the military crisis in the middle of the third century.

Yet local diversity persisted, wherever local systems worked. The tax systems created in Egypt by the Ptolemies were far more complex than those of Sicily and were administered by a bureaucracy headed by a chief minister in the palace. That system too was simply swallowed up after Actium. The royal *idios logos* was now an equestrian official who reported to the prefect of Alexandria and Egypt rather than to the monarch. Other examples abound. Neither Republican generals nor the emperors seemed to feel much need to impose uniform fiscal systems across their domains, so long as the provinces provided what was needed.

Not all parts of the empire had fiscal systems that could so easily be plugged into that of the empire. It is not clear that private property, in the sense that we or Romans would have understood it, even existed in some

Fig. 15. The tax law of Ephesus (now in Ephesus Museum)

areas of the north and west before the Roman conquest. Caesar mentioned some customs dues levied by Gallic tribes, but most exchange was not monetized. Here the Romans were forced to develop new mechanisms. A partial exception in the west was the former Carthaginian territory in Spain and North Africa acquired by Rome after the Second and Third Punic Wars respectively. The silver mines created around Cartagena by Hannibal were confiscated as state property; they were then exploited by hundreds of small-scale contractors using slave labour. Equally, the tribute in olive oil paid by the cities of Tripolitania to Carthage was diverted to Rome. But in many areas Romans had to improvise, usually driven by the need to feed and pay armies that might be in the field for much longer than one campaign and might have lower expectations of booty. It was during the long campaigns in Spain that the pressure was first felt. Local populations had been required to provide subsistence for the armies since the Punic Wars; irregular levies were also made on allies to pay the troops. At some point during the early second century BC these irregular levies became formalized into regular annual levies of cash and grain.[30]

The reign of Augustus was a period of fiscal reorganization. Even before the military disasters in Germany towards the end of his reign, it was clear that Rome could not keep expanding forever. And the Augustan solution to civil war was expensive. At the centre a military treasury was created in AD 6, funded by a 1 per cent sales tax and a 5 per cent inheritance tax introduced to provide hypothecated income from which veteran discharge bonuses were to be paid. Eventually around 75 per cent of imperial revenue would be spent on the army.[31] So great property assessments were made in many provinces during the 20s BC, renewed in theory at regular intervals thereafter, and permanent tax liabilities were fixed on entire communities. The language used was that of the census, but this was not an exercise in distributing political rights and responsibilities of the kind conducted by Republican censors. Many areas were given a cash assessment; others were instructed to pay taxes in kind. Particularly common were taxes of grain, most likely delivered to nearby military camps. One procurator was based in Trier on the Moselle Valley and coordinated imperial finances across northern France (the province of Belgica) and the Rhineland, where around a third of the imperial army was based in the first century AD. It looks very likely he was responsible for local provisioning from the grain lands of the Paris basin. Some tax assessments were more unusual. The Frisians at the Rhine mouth were assessed in cattle hides; this made perfect sense in terms of the dependence of their local economy on stock raising and also in terms of the military need for leather. Other pragmatic idiosyncrasies existed in other parts of the empire.

Vast tracts of new territory were conquered during Augustus' long reign. Much of it was simply subjected to taxation, with new civic territories created in tribal land rather as Pompey had done in Pontus and tribal leaders given the same governmental responsibilities as the civic elites of Asia and North Africa. A certain amount was expropriated to settle troops. Augustus also retained land for himself, especially former royal lands. Increasingly, the same equestrian procurators who supervised provincial taxation oversaw this imperial property in the provinces. Emperors controlled the greatest quarries, the mines, and much else besides. Some of their vast agricultural holdings had been confiscated from senators, some inherited from their predecessors. At Rome, a scrupulous distinction was maintained between public and imperial finances, but there was no independent oversight of either, and the distinction was most useful because it allowed emperors to pose as personal benefactors.

Augustus did not change the taxation of the empire overnight. The terms 'conquest state' and 'tributary empire' describe ideal types in a sociological sense. From the second century BC, Rome exhibited features of both, but it moved steadily in the direction of a sustainable tributary economy. Booty remained a major objective of campaigning well into Augustus' reign and occasionally beyond. Trajan's great building projects in Rome were funded by his wars in Dacia. But the long-term trend was towards the sustainable income that only taxation could provide.

The early imperial Roman tax system strikes us as unnecessarily complex, and yet it did certain jobs well. Being built up of smaller regional tax systems, it was able to accommodate the major variations in the economic life of Italy and the provinces, including differences in the level of trade, in the nature of land tenure, and even in farming practices. Uniformity matters most either in terms of distributional justice—not a major concern for the emperors—or if it enables centralized bodies to act more efficiently. But little was centralized. However, there were drawbacks. For a start, there was constant uncertainty over which taxes were current. This is useful for historians who rely largely on monumental epigraphic clarifications to reconstruct the system, but it must have wasted much time. Second, there was a tendency in all systems for the weight of taxation to be pressed on the poorest, since exemptions were commonly given to already privileged groups and individuals. Given the vast inequalities of wealth in the empire, the emperors could only really afford to let the rich off lightly when times were good. Lastly, there was little flexibility. Medieval European monarchs could call a parliament to get new taxes, modern governments adjust rates very regularly, but Roman emperors had no way of doing so; indeed, they were vulnerable in tithed areas to poor harvests, and through indirect taxes to decreases in the volume of trade. When times were not good, the fiscal inflexibility of the imperial tax system would catch them out. As the economy went into contraction, things got considerably harder.

Further Reading

The Roman economy has attracted some of the most imaginative work of recent years, and it has also been able to draw on large amounts of new archaeological data of very high quality. Preliminary surveys are Kevin Greene's *Archaeology of the Roman Economy* (London, 1986) and David Mattingly and John Salmon's edited collection entitled *Economies beyond*

Agriculture (London, 2001). The Oxford Roman Economy Project, directed by Alan Bowman and Andrew Wilson, has enormously expanded the range of quantifiable data available for analysis: more than a dozen volumes have appeared since 2009, many dealing with central themes such as agriculture and urbanism, but some considering understudied industries, including fulling, the stone trade and the use of maritime resources. One particularly important new contribution is J. W. Hanson's *An Urban Geography of the Roman World, 100 BC—AD 300* (Oxford, 2016).

There is less consensus than ever about how to describe ancient economies. The most recent global assessment is contained in the *Cambridge Economic History of the Greco-Roman World* (Cambridge, 2007) which makes use of New Institutional Economics. These essays complement the excellent chapters on economic matters and imperial finances in volumes x–xii of the *Cambridge Ancient History*. William Harris has made major contributions to both projects, and the subject more generally: the most important are now collected in his *Rome's Imperial Economy* (Oxford, 2011). Other studies approach human economic activity from the point of view of the natural world. Peregrine Horden and Nicholas Purcell's *The Corrupting Sea* (Oxford, 2000) has inspired reviews, critiques, imitations, and three books of essays. Joseph Manning's *The Open Sea* (Princeton, NJ, 2018) offers an alternative ecological history of the ancient economy.

Christopher Howgego's *Ancient History from Coins* (London, 1995) is not just about Rome or just about the economy, but has fascinating things to say about both, and says them with wonderful clarity. The study of taxation is based above all on papyrological and epigraphic material. Perhaps for that reason, discussion has been mostly technical and mostly published in journals and conference proceedings, although a marvellous recent exception is provided by Michel Cottier et al.'s *The Customs Law of Asia* (Oxford, 2008). The best introductions are Peter Brunt's article 'The Revenues of Rome' originally published in the *Journal of Roman Studies* 1981 and reprinted in his *Roman Imperial Themes* (Oxford, 1990) and Dominic Rathbone's chapter on 'The Imperial Finances' in *Cambridge Ancient History*, volume x. Probably the most influential contribution to this subject was a paper by Keith Hopkins entitled 'Taxes and Trade in the Roman Empire' published in *Journal of Roman Studies* 1980, arguing that the tax system of the early empire actually stimulated the economy. Hopkins returned to this theme on a number of occasions. A number of his papers on the theme have been republished by Christopher Kelly in *Sociological Studies in Ancient History* (Cambridge, 2018).

KEY DATES IN CHAPTER XIII

XIII

WAR

From Caesar Augustus' day to our own time there have been nearly two hundred years. Over that time the Roman people might seem to have grown old and impotent, owing to the laziness of the Caesars, except that under the rule of Trajan it has stirred its limbs and, against everyone's expectation of the old age of empire, it has revived, almost as if it were young once more.

(Florus, *Epitome of Roman History 1*, Preface 8)

The Laziness of the Caesars

The rise of the emperors coincided closely with the effective end of Roman expansion. Contemporaries noticed, and they complained. Tacitus, writing in the early second century, lamented the length of time the conquest of Germany was taking.[1] Florus, writing around the same time, divided Roman history into four ages, each corresponding to one stage of a man's life. Rome's childhood had been under the kings, and its adolescence was the Republican period up until the outbreak of the First Punic War. From then until the reign of Augustus, Rome pacified the entire world: 'This was at once the youth of empire and the robust maturity of Rome.' But in the succeeding period Rome had grown old. The biological analogy no longer seems such a good way to describe imperial history, but the reign of Augustus still seems to mark a rupture.

That break is naturally a simplification. The emperors continued to celebrate their foreign victories on an unparalleled scale. They continued to
fight wars after the death of Augustus, and even conquered a little more
territory. But—leaving to one side a general trend to extend the system
of provinces over regions previously governed by allied kings—there were
only a few areas of genuine expansion. Britain was invaded in Claudius'
reign and conquered (very slowly, and cautiously) over the rest of the
first century AD. In south-west Germany, the frontier was advanced under
Domitian from the Rhine across the Black Forest to the Neckar Valley.
Trajan conquered part of what is now Romania in the early second century
(see Figure 16). He also invaded Mesopotamia, modern-day Syria, and Iraq.
But the scale of these expansions seems feeble compared with the audacious
conquests of the 60s and 50s BC or even those of the heyday of Augustan
expansion between 15 BC and AD 9, when his sons fought their great wars
across Europe. Besides, all the new territories except Britain were rapidly
lost again. Mesopotamia was handed back to the Parthians by Trajan's successor Hadrian. The conquests of Domitian and Trajan in Europe were lost
in the military crisis of the third century AD. Future emperors campaigned

Fig. 16. Trajan's Column showing the triumph of the emperor after the first
campaign against the Dacians

beyond the Danube and the Euphrates, now and again, but the imperial frontiers hardly moved.

Many of the core institutions of the Augustan empire built on the experiments of Caesar, Pompey, and even earlier generations. Alongside developments in taxation we can set the practice of extending the citizenship; a growing dependence on local elites to run their own communities; and the practice of using city states as a basis for government, even in areas where they had never existed before. One way to describe the transformation of the empire at the turn of the millennium is to say that over a long period the Roman state experienced a tension between two divergent tendencies. The first we could label the pursuit for glory, the second the desire for security. A move in one direction made other moves that cohered with it more feasible, and so more likely. The disasters of the mid-second and early first century BC —the Cimbric invasion, the Social and Mithridatic Wars, and the rise of the *populares*—had pushed the state a long way in the direction of security. Hegemony had been converted to empire, and new institutions developed to rule it. By contrast, the accelerating competition between leaders from Sulla to Augustus pushed the empire towards the more risky pursuit of glory. After Actium security always trumped glory.

Perhaps this choice was never made consciously. Roman ideology certainly did not always reflect the new logic of empire. The idea that world conquest was a realistic and laudable aim was repeatedly restated, most influentially in the classroom, where it was encoded in the canon of Latin literature defined in the last century BC. Reading Cicero and Virgil in particular taught young Romans they lived in a martial state. Imperial monuments and imperial ceremonial also reproduced the incidental music of a conquest state, long after it no longer suited the plot of Roman history.[2] But detailed investigation of the military system of the empire—investigations made possible by a wealth of epigraphic data—reveals a set of mutually supporting institutions that were well geared to preserving peace, and that consequently made further conquests difficult and costly. It has even been argued that the emperors made so much noise about conquest to compensate for their reduced willingness to attempt it.[3] Trajan was in some senses a throwback, a proof that an individual emperor need not be trapped by the role. Yet his reign, with its futile and short-lived conquests, is also a demonstration that expansion no longer suited the Roman Empire very well.

Augustus had offered an earlier object lesson when he decided on the conquest of Europe. Some historians have tried to excuse this on the grounds of geographical ignorance: maybe he did think the world was smaller than it was, or had no decent maps? None of this is believable. The diameter of the globe had been estimated two centuries earlier. Geographical works of the day included descriptions of India and mentioned the distant silk people, the Chinese. Africa had been circumnavigated half a millennium before Augustus. Much more likely, Augustus' European front was a tactical error driven by short-term political difficulties. A number of Augustus' challengers in the 20s BC had been commanders of major provinces. Did he dare let someone else achieve victories in the Balkans or south Egypt? Besides, it was still unclear what Augustus' own role in the state would be once he had restored civil peace. Triumphs for his heirs might help their succession plans too. External warfare was evidently still popular in Rome, although it is noticeable that from this point on fewer and fewer Italians fought in the legions. So Augustus fell back on the pursuit of glory when the logic of his situation demanded more efforts to create security. The poetry written in his court advertised future campaigns, promising conquests in Britain and Parthia, India and Scythia, while monumental art offered images of a world already conquered.[4]

But where to start? Persia was a dangerous enemy which had defeated Crassus and humiliated Antony and did not seem to want further conflict. The tribes of northern Europe must have seemed an easy option: Caesar had conquered all Gaul in only eight years with as many legions. Could Britain and Germany offer anything other than easy victories? At first the victories did seem easy, and the armies of Drusus and Tiberius rolled around the Alps, campaigned up to the Danube and across the Rhine as far as the Elbe. But rapid progress was deceptive. Conquered Pannonia rebelled in AD 6, and it took three years to restore order.

Almost immediately a Roman army of three legions was massacred in Germany in AD 9. The Varian disaster—named after the general made to carry the can—was a trauma that echoed through the history and literature of the last years of Augustus' reign. The astrologer Manilius used it as an example of the terrible catastrophes foretold by comets. The actual defeat was a running battle lasting several days. The site was recently located at Kalkriese, near Osnabrück, and has been painstakingly reconstructed. It cost the Roman army nearly 10 per cent of its manpower. All territory east of the Rhine was abandoned. A half-built Roman city has recently been found at Waldgirmes, offering eerie witness to the sudden change of direction. A great new province had been planned, and construction had begun on a network of civil communities just like that created in Gaul after Caesar's conquest and in Pontus by Pompey. Roman accounts, reflecting the official line, blame Varus for behaving as if he was in a conquered province, spending his time giving justice, imposing taxation, and dispersing his troops among native communities. But he was certainly following orders from the emperor. After disaster struck Rome pulled back to the Rhine, Waldgirmes was abandoned, and with it all the territory up to the Elbe. Conquest was never formally renounced, but it was not resumed in Augustus' reign. Another imperial prince, Germanicus, visited the site of the disaster during the next reign, but his campaigns were also—if less dramatically—unsuccessful. The north began to be quietly written off as ungovernable, poor, undesirable. Strabo, writing under the Emperor Tiberius, reported that Britain too would not pay the cost of its occupation.[5] Appian, a second-century historian, went so far as to claim alien nations had begged to be admitted to the empire, but the emperors had turned them down.[6] These were all lies.

For the emperors had much to gain from security, and there were easier routes to glory. Did Augustus ever realize that the real motor for the wars of Pompey and Caesar had been competition? And now there were no rivals. Emperors did not plan for peace, but they learned from their mistakes. The potential rewards offered by military expeditions never justified the risk of failure. Much more could be achieved by diplomacy. And emperors soon found out how to massage the news from the frontier, playing up minor successes, suppressing news of reverses, claiming any victories for themselves, and blaming generals on the ground like Varus when things went badly wrong. The laziness of the Caesars was a very pragmatic response to the absence of rivals.

A World without History?

The choice of security over glory makes for unexciting history. Or so the senators of the imperial age affected to think. Court intrigues and imperial assassinations actually make for rather good drama. The histories written by the senators Tacitus and Dio and the scandalous biographies of the courtier Suetonius and his late imperial successors have inspired their share of racy novels and films. But it is true that it is difficult to find a clear narrative in the political history of the first two centuries AD. Institutionally, culturally, and economically, there were slow changes.[7] The citizen body expanded first gradually and then in the early third century suddenly, when the Universal Edict of Caracalla more or less tripled the number of citizens.[8] As a consequence, Roman law stretched over more and more of the empire's subjects. The greatest cities grew and acquired their complements of monuments. The rich grew richer, building great rural residences and endowing festivals, temples, theatres, and bathhouses in their native cities.[9] Trade flourished across the urban network and between the great ecological divides into which the empire was divided. All these changes were real, but few were visible to contemporaries, and they were not the subject of history as the ancients understood it.

There were gradual changes in the style of imperial rule too. The monarchical nature of the emperors' rule became more overt. As the emperors ruled from their itinerant courts, they seem to have gradually developed a preference for direct over indirect control, and a greater reliance on state officials rather than aristocratic former magistrates. Augustus had travelled widely, but few of his first-century AD successors spent long away from Rome. The expeditions of Trajan and the restless travels of Hadrian were in some senses optional, and Antoninus Pius, who reigned from 138 to 161, spent most of his time in Rome. The situation began to change with Marcus Aurelius, who succeeded him until his death in 180. Marcus and his co-emperor Lucius Verus (161–9), and then his son and successor Commodus, who ruled until his assassination in 192, were all compelled to spend long periods of their reigns on the frontiers. So did all the Severan emperors who ruled Rome between AD 193 and 235. These necessary displacements were accompanied by the emergence of a new and more openly monarchical style. Away from senatorial sensibilities emperors could rule like the kings they had always been.

By the early fourth century there were up to four different courts at any one time, strung out along the northern and eastern frontiers of the empire. Wherever the courts rested for a few years—Trier or Antioch, Sirmium or Ravenna—magnificent palaces were created with great bathhouses, hippodromes, and reception areas. The empire came to be divided into four great prefectures, each headed by a praetorian prefect whose administration extended down into a growing number of provinces. Senators no longer played much part in the administration of the empire, and the Senate itself (or senates after Constantine created a second one in his new capital on the Bosporus) became peripheral to the political system. Ambassadors sought out emperors in the camps; lawmaking had to be by edict rather than senatorial decree; consultation—even for form's sake—was no longer practical. Emperors were away from Rome for years, and then decades. Constantius II, who with his brothers succeeded Constantine in 337, did not visit Rome until AD 357. Before that new order came about, however, the empire had to face a much more serious military emergency, one that in some senses lasted for two entire generations.

The Early Imperial Security System

Historians sometimes write of Rome as having a grand strategy,[10] but there is no real sign that any such thing was ever planned or implemented. The deployment of the legions was accidental, the evolving product of incremental changes made in response to immediate needs. When expansion ended, Augustus' campaigning armies had stopped in their tracks. Troops would be moved for imperial expeditions like Claudius' invasion of Britain, or if they were needed to crush a rebellion or participate in a civil war. Over time, the legions gravitated to the points of stress. Spain was far from the frontiers and relatively peaceful, and as a result the size of its garrison was progressively reduced. On the Danube and in the east, troop numbers increased slightly, but always limited by the salary bill. The emperors knew where the troops were, how many they were, and what they were owed. But there is no sign they made use of this information to plan for anything but the short term.[11]

It is not always clear exactly where the armies were deployed in the early years of Augustus' reign, except that they were kept out of Italy, where only the Praetorian Guard—made loyal through extra pay—were allowed in the capital. But a decade into Tiberius' reign we happen to have a snapshot, from a passage in Tacitus' *Annales*, of the locations of what were now twenty-five legions.[12] They were concentrated overwhelmingly on the northern and eastern frontiers: facing across the Rhine and Danube, that is, and stationed along the long frontier with Parthia and its vassals. Only token forces remained in Spain, Africa, and Egypt. Many other provinces were effectively unarmed. Legions of heavily armed infantry formed the core of the early imperial army. They resembled the Republican armies in terms of their equipment and battlefield tactics. Auxiliary units of cavalry, light infantry, and missile troops supported them, alongside teams of engineers and other specialists. There were naval bases in the Mediterranean, and in time fleets were established on the major rivers. That pattern stayed more or less unchanged until the middle of the third century, although the number of legions increased to thirty-three and some were moved to newly conquered regions like southern Britain and Dacia. The total strength was always very small. At its height the early imperial army numbered fewer than 200,000 legionaries and perhaps as many support troops to protect and control an empire of between 50 and 100 million inhabitants.

Keeping the army small was a financial necessity, given the huge share of the imperial budget it consumed. This meant it had to be highly efficient. The campaigning armies of the late Republic and the reign of Augustus had marched and camped in strength, but a different disposition was needed for their new roles. The logic of the imperial frontiers was all based on establishing a communications advantage over the empire's opponents. Little by little the frontiers became a dense network of bases—some very small—signal stations, barriers, control points, and, most important of all, roads. Hadrian's Wall (see Figure 17) provides an excellent example of the kind of system that developed in the second century, but the ditches and ramparts that so impress us today were among the latest and least vital components of a frontier system. A precious collection of letters from Vindolanda reveals the collection and processing of information on what was happening beyond the frontier; the management of provisioning; the constant redeployments of soldiers along the frontier; and communications back into the province.[13] Signal stations ran down the coasts watching for raids by sea. Groups of scouts operated far north of the wall, and local leaders were cultivated with gifts that Romans called subsidies. A slightly different system of signal stations and forts passed news on barbarian movements up and down the upper German *Limes*, and in the pre-desert of North Africa military installations were different again. Physically, the frontiers developed in a piecemeal way, adapting to local circumstances not a central model, but the guiding logic was the same.

The vast majority of military units were based on the frontiers. Yet soldiers were ubiquitous within the empire. Detachments provided protection for provincial governors and procurators, for messengers and tax collectors, for movements of grain and cash, for the managers of imperial mines and quarries with their workforces of slaves and criminals, and for those trying to rule the larger, more unsettled cities. Centurions in particular acquired a whole range of functions we do not normally associate with the military. They acted as district officers in the northern provinces,

Fig. 17. Hadrian's Wall

could be found on detachment organizing provisioning, and were the most recognizable representatives of Roman government depicted in the New Testament. Particularly trusted soldiers served as *beneficiarii consulares*, effectively aides-de-camp to governors. The early empire had no civil service, and there were some jobs that it was impolitic to entrust to imperial slaves and freedmen.

Imperial propaganda proclaimed that the soldiers protected the provinces. That picture is only half true. The legions were also the emperors' ultimate weapon against both provincial rebellions and aristocratic usurpers.[14] Episodes of resistance and revolt have been a focus of recent research, especially as it has become clearer how Roman public pronouncements played down their significance.[15] It looks now as if there was a constant background of banditry and minor unrest throughout the early empire, mostly very localized and attributed to a mass of different proximate causes. Unrest was more evident in upland areas like Isauria in Asia Minor and close to the frontiers both in Britain, Gaul, and Germany and in the east. Ancient writers recognized this but also often blamed unrest on the unruly and unstable character of their inhabitants. Occasionally, these incidents mushroomed into much larger conflicts, especially when local armies were distracted by civil wars. Revolt seems to have been more common in the generations following conquest, but other factors played a part too. The best-documented revolts, in Judaea, arose from a perfect storm of provocations and opportunities. Revolts failed because the empire could –eventually— concentrate force in the areas effected, but also because provincial elites were rarely wholeheartedly on the side of the rebels. The fact that imperial sources repeatedly played down the significance of particular outbreaks suggests these outbreaks of violence did worry the imperial ruling class. Ideology declared the provinces conquered and peaceful; the reality is that some at least had to be pacified repeatedly. Often this meant moving in troops from other areas, yet another sign that the empire maintained as small a standing army as it felt it could manage with.

The mass demobilization of Roman soldiers at the end of the Triumviral period had been driven by financial and political priorities. Armies were dangerous, unpaid ones doubly so. Now they would be composed of career soldiers who served for twenty or more years, loyal to the emperors, not their commanders.[16] On retirement, the emperors provided each legionary with a substantial bonus, so long as he had proved himself loyal. Commanders, drawn from the senatorial and equestrian orders, came and went. It was the centurions, having risen from the ranks, who provided continuity of command and military expertise. Ceremonial was deployed to bind the soldiers to the imperial family. Army units celebrated imperial birthdays and worshipped the emperors along with the *signa*, their standards. A third-century calendar from the eastern frontier post of Dura lists endless holidays marking the anniversaries of imperial family members, some long dead. Emperors and their sons took care to visit the legions, and even commanded them when it was safe to do so. As for the auxiliaries, they could look forward to grants of citizenship, and many returned home from their long periods of service to transform the societies from which they had been recruited.[17]

Mostly the system worked. Civil wars only broke out in 68 and 196, when entire dynasties had been extinguished. A few rebellious generals discovered to their cost the depth of loyalty the legions felt to the imperial family of the day.[18] That loyalty meant that the legions could also be deployed against provincial rebels. During AD 69 the legions of the Rhineland were deployed first against Vindex, a senator from southern Gaul who had rebelled against Nero, and then against the Batavians of the lower Rhine, who had tried to use the Roman civil war that followed his death as an opportunity to secede. The legions were in principle recruited from Roman citizens, but Italians rarely joined up after Augustus' reign. The main sources of recruits were first the Roman cities of the inner provinces and later the camps themselves. One sign of the success of the emperors' investment in maintaining the loyalty of the troops (and perhaps too of the socialization effects of long service) is that legions almost never made common cause with neighbouring provincial populations. Troops recruited in Gaul and Germany were content to be deployed against British, Gallic, and German rebels, and the army of Numidia to march against African usurpers.[19]

Mostly, however, the soldiers inhabited a world of their own. The larger camps of northern Britain, the Rhineland, the Danube provinces, and Africa eventually came to resemble cities, equipped with monumental walls and gates, stone-built amphitheatres, bathhouses, and shrines. Formally, soldiers could not marry, and camps were organized in barrack blocks arranged in precise parallel lines, but the artefacts and clothes found in them show there were women and children in these communities too, as well as in the informal villages called *canabae* that grew up alongside them. In Syria and Egypt soldiers mostly lived in cities in any case. Documents from Dura show them marrying and buying land and in general assuming the sort of roles in local communities that their relatively good pay and excellent connections could secure them.[20]

The Roman Empire had no grand strategy, but it nevertheless developed a frontier system quite like those of many other tributary empires. The most common point of comparison is China's Inner Asian Frontier, the limit between the areas controlled directly by Chinese officials and a great periphery within which subject nations shaded out into barbarian allies and enemies.[21] China, like Rome, enjoyed some technological advantages over its neighbours, although in some periods there was something of an arms race as China sought to prevent technology transfers to the barbarians.

Map 5. The third-century crisis

China, like Rome, was able to provision and supply its troops from an intensely farmed and taxed hinterland. The Chinese too deployed a mixture of linear barriers and garrisons of regular soldiers with irregular allies, and they too sought an information advantage over their opponents. The information system extended deep into the provinces, to the imperial court or courts. It was not grand strategy that preserved either empire, but the tactical advantages given by information superiority.

Crisis on the Frontiers

The Roman system had, naturally, its weaknesses too. One consequence of depending on an infantry army based at the edge of empire was that it was slow to respond to disasters in the interior or indeed at the other end of the empire. Roman troops were generally successful against provincial rebellions during the first two centuries AD because most rebellions occurred relatively near the frontiers, and the rebels were usually stationary and had no fortifications. Order was generally restored within months. The Jewish War lasted as long as it did in part because the Jews possessed fortresses in the desert. Another problem was that more mobile enemies, once they broke through the frontier, could outrun Roman armies. When the frontiers did collapse, as several did in the third century, and raiding parties penetrated as far as Athens and Ephesus and Tarragona, they found rich cities with no defenders and often no functioning defensive walls.

The gradual social and economic transformations of the first two centuries AD were not confined within the political limits of the empire. The political economy of the empire may be thought of as a vast redistributive system that drew resources from all over the interior and spent them at the frontiers, mostly as army pay. The court was the other main recipient, and this too was increasingly located at the edge rather than the geographical centre of the empire. Perhaps no provincial societies were transformed as utterly as those on the frontiers. The effects can be traced in the spread of new cults, of epigraphy, and of technology, and in the apparent prosperity of areas that had once been marginal. Nor were these effects confined to Roman subjects. The eastern frontier bisected a chain of caravan cities with ancient shared traditions of language, cult, and commerce. Greek and Aramaic and its sister languages were spoken in a great arch that stretched from the Mediterranean to the Persian Gulf. By the late third century there

Picture Box 7 Warehouse at Ostia

This grand brick-built warehouse is named the Horrea Epagathiana et Epaphroditiana. It was constructed in the middle of the second century AD in Ostia, which by then had become part of the extended port complex at the mouth of the Tiber. It looks spectacular, partly because it was excavated and restored in the 1920s and 1930s. But it does give a good indication of the scale of commercial investment.

Ostia originated as a fortress (*castrum*), probably built not long after the mid-Republican 'Servian' Walls discussed in Picture Box 1, but during the second century BC it developed as a port, and most of the grandest monuments visible today are from the period after the construction of the great Trajanic Harbour at nearby Portus, which has itself been the subject of recent archaeological investigation. Warehouses like this one were built by private individuals. The names on the great inscription over the entrance of this one suggests its builders were former slaves, and they incorporated part of the wall of the old *castrum* into the design.

The solid construction did not just provide protection from fire and theft; it also protected the contents from damp and changes in temperature. *Horrea* were originally grain stores, but these probably stored much more valuable goods, since the rooms arranged on two floors around an interior courtyard have elaborate locks. As well as grain, beans, and other dried foodstuffs, these horrea might be used to store spices, textiles, perfumes, papyrus, and manufactured goods. Some excavated horrea had large ceramic vessels known as dolia sunk into the floor to store wine and perhaps also oil. Others had raised floors to keep grain dry and aerated.

Probably rooms in a horreum could be hired for fixed periods. A slightly earlier document from Pompeii shows that the contents of a bay in a horreum in Puteoli (Rome's other main port) could be used as security for a loan, and it is likely that some spaces were used for the safe storage of valuables. The main function of warehouses was to deal with the mismatch between the supply of imports and demand for them. Most maritime cargoes were transported in the sailing season that ran from March until September, but demand in the city of Rome was fairly constant. Releasing goods as soon as they arrived would depress prices and potentially lead to winter shortages. Great cities like Alexandria and Rome and port cities like Puteoli and Caesarea Maritima all had extensive storage facilities to regulate the flow of goods.

The Horrea Epagathiana et Epaphroditiana were an elaborate structure. Apart from the internal provision for storage and security, a row of shops was incorporated on one side of the building. These too were probably let out or managed by slaves or ex-slaves of the builders. The literature produced by and for the elite has little to say about buildings of this sort or the mechanics of business. But unashamedly monumental structures like the Ostian horrea show the care and pride taken by others in Roman commerce.

Further Reading

Simon Keay, ed., *Portus: An Archaeological Survey of the Port of Imperial Rome* (Rome and London: British School at Rome, 2005).

Geoffrey Rickman, *Roman Granaries and Store Buildings* (Cambridge: Cambridge University Press, 1971).

Astrid Van Oyen, *The Socio-Economics of Roman Storage: Agriculture, Trade and Family* (Cambridge: Cambridge University Press, 2020).

were populations of Jews, Christians, and Manichaeans on both sides of the Romano-Persian frontier.

Rome's northern frontier had bisected other peoples with shared prehistoric cultures. The existence of a frontier zone promoted connections. Population densities were low in this region, relative to the Mediterranean world, and there were no cities beyond the Roman provinces. But the agricultural potential was high. Commerce, including slaving, crossed the frontier, and there is archaeological evidence for Roman manufactures in a broad band 50–100 kilometres (around 30–60 miles) wide stretching back from the frontier.[22] There were technology transfers too. The political units and ethnic groups of this zone seem to have been quite unstable. Roman writers sometimes blamed this on differences of temperament and characterized barbarism as a deficiency in the stability of settled, urban societies. Perhaps the larger hegemonies were intrinsically temporary. Yet these populations were not nomadic, and it is possible their political fragmentation was actively managed by Rome, which (like China) gave subsidies to their friends, took hostages, sheltered exiled princes, and generally tried to extend their control well beyond the limit of the provinces. Periodic raids and expeditions by both sides were simply one part of a complex relationship. From early in the first century AD there is also evidence for the recruitment of 'barbarians' to serve in the Roman army, and some rose to high ranks. Romans often found themselves facing enemy armies commanded by former Roman soldiers, like Arminius who had led the massacre of Varus' legions in AD 9. Many even spoke Latin. By the second century, many societies bordering the Roman frontier were locked into a series of interdependent relationships with Roman power. Certainly, the leaders of the groups we hear of in the third century, such as the Alamanni on the upper Rhine and the Goths on the lower Danube, knew the Roman Empire well.[23]

That world began to change in the late second century AD for reasons that are fiercely disputed. One school of thought sees the transformation of barbarian societies as the main cause of the collapse of the frontiers. The long relationship with Rome created better-organized and better-equipped enemies who knew very well the riches the empire had to offer. Eventually Rome lost the arms race, and the frontiers folded. Others see the change originating in Rome's increasing military commitment on the eastern front. As troops were withdrawn from the west to serve first against Persia and then in successive civil wars, the delicate balance on the western frontiers collapsed: Alamanni, Franks, and others walked into provinces that were effectively undefended. Yet others see the origin of the crisis in obscure movements on the distant steppe, where truly nomadic peoples, especially those whom Romans later came to know as the Huns, pressed hard on the settled barbarians of temperate Europe, pushing some populations, like the Goths, south and west onto the Roman frontiers. Large population movements certainly occurred within Europe in some periods and had intruded into Mediterranean world before on several occasions, including the Gallic sacks of Rome and Delphi in the fourth and third centuries BC and the Cimbric wars and the Helvetian migration at the end of the Republic. Climate change has been suggested as another factor destabilizing populations north of the empire. Those historians who believe the Antonine plague triggered a massive and long-lasting demographic crisis see this too as feeding into the collapse of the northern frontiers. Various combinations of all these factors might, naturally, be imagined. The problem is simply that there are too many unknowns, especially when it comes to deciding what (if anything) was changing beyond the Roman frontier. The best we can do is try to describe the sequence and nature of all the discrete events as clearly as possible and then look at possible relationships between them without committing from the start to any single grand theory (see Map 5).

One traditional narrative of the crisis begins in the late second century AD with Marcus Aurelius' wars against the Marcomanni and Sarmatians, wars that kept him occupied for years on the northern frontier. The new provinces he allegedly contemplated creating would have been to the west of the three Dacian provinces founded by Trajan earlier in the century. But unlike Trajan's wars, these did not result from an imperial initiative. The Marcomannic Wars began with a German invasion of Italy in 166 and continued, with only short periods of remission, until 175. A new war drew Marcus back in 177, and he was still campaigning on his death in 180. Commodus abandoned the war rather than finishing it. The frontier evidently held, even while Roman armies were distracted by civil wars in the 190s. Renewed activity on the northern frontier began on the Danube in the 230s with raids on Black Sea vassals of Rome and then on the Roman province of Moesia. Gothic warbands raided Dacia and the Danube provinces in the 240s. Decius, who ruled between 249 and 252, briefly repelled them, but was killed in a counterattack. Goths continued to raid through the 250s. Who were these groups, not yet united into a single force or nation? One possibility is that the Goths originated among populations who had lived on the borders of Trajan's new Dacian provinces, peoples who had recently undergone processes of social transformation of the kind experienced by other German-speaking groups on the Rhine much earlier.[24] Whether wars on the lower Danube led to Roman neglect of points farther west or whether now invisible pressures moved east to west over the century, the security crisis spread.

Rome had never been well equipped to deal with multiple simultaneous threats. It had few means of coordinating information from different parts, and the response times were so slow that even if one area was identified as particularly under-resourced, it might take months to correct this. The consolidation of power and decision-making in the hands of the emperor actually accentuated this problem. Second-century emperors had often dealt with a frontier problem by attending in person. That was not an option when the empire faced multiple threats. On the middle Danube, the Sarmatians raided Noricum, Rhaetia, and Pannonia in the later 250s. At the same time there were raids by the Alamanni across the Rhine into Gaul and down into Spain. During the 260s Tarraco was sacked by the Franks, Athens by the Heruli, and Ephesus by the Goths. The Roman recovery began finally in 268, when Claudius II defeated the Goths at Naissos; thereafter, it was surprisingly fast. Aurelian expelled the Iuthungi from Italy in the early 270s, and Probus repelled the last major invasion of Gaul across the Rhine in 276. As each front was closed down, the others were dealt with more effectively. But it was a close run thing.

The first responses to these linked military emergencies were local. City after city built defensive circuits, sometimes dismantling earlier monuments to create safe zones in the middle of once extensive cities as each in turn felt threatened. The phenomenon of walls built from dismantled monuments was very widespread: a Severan arch was dismantled to build a waterfront wall in London, a new wall bisected the Athenian agora, and one third-century emperor, Aurelian, actually built walls around the centre of the city of Rome. Major structures like amphitheatres and theatres found themselves incorporated into defensive circuits in the centre of cities. This was not the result of a coordinated programme of building. In fact, it shows how in periods of uncertainty local authorities were taking local defence into their own hands, and doing so as quickly and cheaply as possible.

The emperors, by contrast, concentrated on trying to make their armies better able to deal quickly with new threats. The Emperor Gallienus began to develop a more mobile army, one based on cavalry, which could act as a rapid response force. The use of troops of this kind, alongside the legions, became more and more evident in the changed conditions of war on the northern frontier. Constantine too was credited with an enlargement of their role. Meanwhile, at the eastern end of empire Romans and Persians were both developing armies based on heavy cavalry. As fortifications were restored or put in place, there was a revival of siegecraft, important in the

Near East since the Assyrian New Empire and in the classical Greek and Hellenistic world as well. Perhaps without anyone being conscious of it, the idea of pacified provinces surrounded by defences against outsiders had been replaced by local efforts to create safe places and imperial efforts to rapidly encounter raiders wherever they penetrated the empire.

War on Two Fronts

The task of restoring normal relations with the northern peoples was conducted in deadly counterpart with a deterioration of relations on the eastern front. It is common to blame this on the appearance of a new Persian dynasty, the Sassanians, in 226 AD and the aggression of the Emperor Shapur (241–72), who fought several wars against Rome, defeated the Emperor Philip in 240, seized the city of Antioch in 256, and captured and executed the Emperor Valerian in 260. But the Romans bore some responsibility for all this. Again the story can be traced back to the 160s. After Trajan's conquest and Hadrian's withdrawal from his new province of Mesopotamia there had been peace with the Parthians until the joint reign of Marcus and Lucius, when Roman armies once again invaded Persia, without much provocation.[25] Severus did the same a couple of decades later. Roman aggression did a good deal to destabilize the Parthian dynasty, creating an opportunity for the Sassanian takeover. It is difficult to tell for sure now whether Persia exploited Rome's difficulties in the north or vice versa or whether (as seems most likely) the security system of the early Roman Empire was simply incapable of dealing with threats on so many fronts.

What is clear is that the inability of the emperors to defend the great cities and unarmed provinces of the interior of the empire led to a crisis in their legitimacy. One index of failure was that in the period 235–84 more than twenty emperors reigned. The exact number depends on how many rebels are considered as short-lived rulers. A second index of failure was geographical fragmentation. Local rulers, client kings, and army commanders took over responsibility for protecting their immediate localities. When Aurelian came to power in 270, most of Gaul, Spain, and Germany had been ruled from the Rhineland for over a decade, and the monarchs of the caravan city of Palmyra in Syria controlled much of the Near East, including even Alexandria. Usurpations had been attempted in Africa, on the Danube, in Egypt, and in Asia Minor. Successful and unsuccessful usurpers alike were drawn from the military classes, their links to their armies personal and contingent on their continued success. Civil war and failure at the frontiers fed off each other. Only military success could restore legitimacy and reverse the fragmentation of authority. Valerian's son Gallienus (253–68) achieved some external successes. Aurelian (270–5), who had expelled the Iuthungi from Italy, went on to regain control of Egypt (272) and to suppress the secessions led by Palmyra (273) and the emperors of Trier (274). His successors inflicted more defeats on the Germans. Carus finally carried the Persian war into Mesopotamia and captured the Persian capital Ctesiphon. He died on campaign in 283, and his successor Numerian withdrew, but within a year he had been replaced by Diocletian, who ruled until his abdication in 305. During his long reign he too fought on the Danube and against Persia, and had to assert his power in Egypt and against rebels in the west. He left behind a completely reorganized Roman Empire. The period from the end of the Severan dynasty in 235 to the accession of Diocletian in 284 is sometimes known as the Anarchy. Any crisis that lasts for half a century inflicts a huge cost on institutions. Diocletian's empire did indeed need a new coinage, a new taxation system, and a new administration as well as a new military system. Under Constantine it acquired a new capital and a new religion too. But the late Roman Empire was not created in a revolution. Well before Diocletian's reign a new ideal of the emperor had emerged, crowding out the productions of senatorial historians and Greek panegyrists. This emperor was a soldier rather than a fellow citizen, and he was surrounded by spectacular ceremonial and ferocious justice.

For us, looking back with hindsight, the most amazing aspect of this story is not that the crisis occurred, but that the empire survived it at all. The energy of the soldier emperors was clearly one factor, but there were other sources of strength not appreciated at the time. Consider, for example, the commitment of the empire's elite to its continued existence. The 'Gallic emperors' who controlled Gaul, and at times the Spanish and British provinces, between 260 and 274 are a case in point. The main figures, Postumus, Victorinus, and Tetricus I, were all soldiers and all apparently descended from rich local families. Their support was drawn from both local nobles and the army of the Rhine. Their 'empire' originated in a revolt against Gallienus, but its main efforts were directed at survival and the preservation of vested interests. Following the successes of first Claudius II and then Aurelian, provinces, cities, and then even the last of the emperors rejoined the central empire. Throughout the secession, the political propaganda,

known mainly through coinage, was utterly Roman. At the other end of
the empire the fierce resistance put up by Greek cities drew on even older
allegiances. Publius Herennius Dexippus, a historian who organized resistance at Athens, presented his efforts as just the latest episode in a long history
of Athenian resistance to the barbarian. The survival of these allegiances is
impressive testimony to the durability of the identities created in the early
empire. The empire survived because, when it seemed about to come apart,
the ruling classes and many of its subjects *chose* to participate in its rescue.

Further Reading

The evolution of the Roman military machine is surveyed in a number of essays in the
second volume of the *Cambridge History of Greek and Roman Warfare* (Cambridge, 2007) edited
by Philip Sabin, Hans van Wees, and Michael Whitby. Adrian Goldsworthy's *Roman Army at
War* (Oxford, 1996) is a lively account of how it worked in practice. The evolution of a stable
frontier—and its social and economic consequences—is the subject of C. R. Whittaker's
Frontiers of the Roman Empire (Baltimore, MD, 1994). Debate still largely responds to Edward
Luttwak's controversial but stimulating *Grand Strategy of the Roman Empire* (Baltimore, MD,
1976). A good selection of these responses is included in John Rich and Graham Shipley's
collection *War and Society in the Roman World* (London, 1993). Benjamin Isaac's *Limits of
Empire* (Oxford, 1990) discusses the role of Roman armies in controlling the provincial
populations they claimed to protect. Gil Gambash's *Rome and Provincial Resistance* (London
2015) shows what happened when they failed to do so.

The complex history of the third-century crisis is covered in the usual reference works,
but there is a particular good account in David Potter's *The Roman Empire at Bay: AD 180–395*
(Abingdon, 2014). A good sense of what historians are arguing about at the moment is given
by the collection *Crises and the Roman Empire* (Leiden, 2007) edited by Olivier Hekster,
Gerda de Kleijn, and Daniëlle Slootjes.

XIV

IMPERIAL IDENTITIES

Once upon a time kings ruled this city, but they were not fated to have home-grown successors. Outsiders took over their rule, foreigners in fact, for when Numa succeeded Romulus, he came from the Sabine lands— not far away to be sure, but it made him a foreigner in those days. When Tarquin the Elder succeeded Ancus Marcius, well, he was of mixed race, for his father was Demaratus the Corinthian, while his mother was born in Etruscan Tarquinii. She was not a wealthy women, as you might imagine, given she had agreed to such an inferior marriage, and for that reason he was unable to hold office at home. But he migrated to Rome, and here was made king.

(From a speech of Claudius inscribed on bronze, *ILS* 212)

Desperately Seeking the Romans

The Emperor Claudius' speech to the Senate in AD 48 proposed opening up membership of the Senate to the wealthiest and most noble citizens of the provinces of Gaul. Some of his words are preserved on a bronze tablet at Lyons, and Tacitus records the resentment the proposal aroused among senators.[1] Fear that admitting new blood might dilute national identity is all too familiar today. Claudius' appeal to an ancient tradition of inclusiveness maybe did not convince, but then he was an emperor and did not need to. But he was correct that Roman identity was in flux right from the very beginning.

It is impossible to write an account of the Roman Empire without lapsing into writing about the 'Romans', as if it is obvious who should be included in that term. But it is surprisingly difficult to answer the simple question 'Who were the Romans?'

Formal answers exist, of course. If we were to apply strict legal criteria, we would have to focus on Roman citizens.[2] But the nature and composition of that group was repeatedly transformed, as Rome grew from a conventional city state, with its assemblies, taxation, and armies all based on citizenship, into a Mediterranean power composed of different kinds of imperial subjects. En route, we would need to consider the citizens of the middle Republic, concentrated in Rome, but with a penumbra of citizen colonies up and down the peninsula; then Italy after the Social War in which almost all free people were citizens; then the situation in the early empire, when citizenship was acquired by various privileged groups, including provincial aristocrats and auxiliary veterans; and finally the Roman world after Caracalla's Edict, by which citizenship was generalized, which created a world in which most people were citizens and yet the status was strangely still valued.[3] Extensions of the citizenship made a real difference.[4] Caracalla's 'Universal Edict' meant that Roman law, the *ius civile*, suddenly applied to huge sections of the population that had until then had much less engagement with the state, populations who read and spoke neither Latin nor Greek but who could now make wills and contracts with other citizens. The jurist Ulpian spent much of the following years making clear some of the ramification of the edict. Expanding the citizen body also increased those who in some sense were part of the Roman religious community. It paved the way for emperors to require sacrifice and to begin to regulate the religious lives of all their subjects.

It would also be necessary to factor in peculiarities such as the Roman habit of extending citizenship to many former slaves, and also a range of 'half-citizens', most of them termed 'Latins' of one kind or another. That title was extended from its original sense of citizens of other Latin states, first to members of the Latin colonies founded by Rome in Italy in the middle Republican period and filled with a mixture of settlers drawn from Romans and allies; then to citizens of certain provincial communities granted the Latin right in a series of regional grants beginning in Caesar's day; and also to a different category of freedmen who were not fully citizens and were known as Junian Latins (after the *Lex Iunia* which created the status). Other Mediterranean citizenships were drawn into the system.

Within the astonishingly complex society of Roman Egypt, Alexandrine citizens meant not just citizens of the provincial capital but also a status group treated as halfway between other Egyptians and Romans. Multiple citizenships were absolutely normal too, not just in Cicero's sense that he had two homelands—Arpinum and Rome—but also in the sense that many provincial communities had come to allow dual citizenship and had also created half-citizenships of their own, giving resident aliens a range of rights and obligations. Some of these grants were privileges, others devices designed to make sure the ever more mobile propertied classes did not evade local obligations either where they lived or where they were born.[5]

Nor were all citizens equal. There were experiments in the Republican period with creating citizens without the vote. The traditional assemblies were in any case organized in complex ways that gave more weight to the votes of those in higher census categories than to others. Freedmen could vote, but in many cities were not allowed to hold office or become members of the most senior councils. Women of all social statuses faced strict limits on how far they could exercise citizen rights. The wives and daughters of Roman citizens could confer citizenship on their male children, but their political participation was effectively zero, very few had financial autonomy or could make independent use of the law, and their roles in ritual—if often prominent—were always subordinated to the authority of male priests. Many of the things that defined the role of a citizen in Republican Rome—including voting, fighting, sacrificing, being taxed, taking public contracts, and being counted in the census—never applied to women. The crucial point is that Romans did not use citizenship as a way of creating a hard boundary between themselves and aliens. Instead, they used the language of citizenship to express a set of statuses and relationships through which individuals might be involved in the community in different ways, and also to various degrees.

Other ways existed to mark the boundaries. Romans were often contrasted with barbarians, especially in imperial propaganda. A common coin type of the second century depicted a mounted emperor trampling down a cowering barbarian. More elaborate developments of these motifs appear on monuments such as Trajan's Column. Roman literature also displays a rich harvest of xenophobic and racist stereotyping, a legacy presumably of traditions of invective that were so central to Roman oratory.[6] Then again, scholars writing in Latin since Cicero's day differentiated between the writings of the Greeks and those of *nostri*, which literally means 'our people'. Tacitus does this when describing writers who had dealt with Britain before he did, and Pliny the Elder added a list of sources divided into Roman and foreign authorities for each book of his *Natural History*. The arrangement was replicated in Roman libraries, where Greek and Latin books seem, in theory at least, to have been shelved separately. Roman priests also traditionally distinguished a bundle of cults considered of alien origin as needing to be celebrated 'with Greek rituals'; in fact, the rituals were nothing of the kind, but the idea of a difference evidently mattered.[7]

The distinctions between Romans and others probably mattered most *inside* provincial societies. Metal detector users in southern Spain have found a number of fragments of bronze tablets that record constitutions granted local communities by the emperors in the late first century AD.[8] These Latin *municipia* must have been strange worlds, in some ways miniatures of Rome, with councils, collegiate magistracies, priesthoods, gladiatorial *munera*, courts, and so on. One clause of this basic law stipulates that any gaps in its coverage should be dealt with as if the parties were Roman citizens. In fact, almost the only true Roman citizens were the magistrates, those who had been magistrates, and the descendants of those who had been magistrates, plus their ex-slaves, of course.

Citizens were generally the most privileged members of the societies in which they lived. A dramatic scene in the Acts of the Apostles describes how Paul, returning to Jerusalem from his mission in Asia, is caught up by an angry mob, attracting the attention of the Roman soldiers. Addressing them in Greek, he asks permission to defend himself to his fellow Jews, which he does in the vernacular, explaining he is a Jew of Tarsus, educated and brought up in Jerusalem, and he then describes his conversion. His speech rouses the mob to a frenzy, and he is arrested and dragged off by the soldiers to be flogged. At this point (and only then) he reveals to the centurion that he has, in fact, Roman citizenship. The centurion is appalled that he had ordered him to be flogged. There is a nice exchange between the centurion, bitter at having paid for his citizenship, and Paul, who declares he is a citizen by birth. Was this yet another distinction that mattered? The centurion has Paul released at once and handed over to the priestly council of the Sanhedrin, where Paul deftly stirs up a squabble between two priestly factions, the Sadducees and the Pharisees.[9] It does not matter very much how historical these incidents are, because, even if fictionalized, the anecdote reveals interesting assumptions about how identity politics worked in the Roman provinces. Paul is presented as cleverly exploiting his multiple identities as a Jew, as a Roman citizen, as a citizen of Tarsus, as a Pharisee, and as a resident alien within Jerusalem. His ability to speak more than one language clearly helped too.

It is easy to identify other locations in the empire where these fine distinctions mattered. Frontier societies had their own gradations of status.[10] Legionaries were recruited from citizens but auxiliaries from other subject populations, those whom Romans termed *peregrini*, a word that simply meant 'foreigners'. The populations they served among were mostly *peregrini* too, but unlike them the auxiliaries could look forward to citizenship when they were discharged. Hundreds of bronze certificates of these grants, termed *diplomata*, issued to auxiliary veterans have been recovered by archaeologists; they were obviously displayed rather proudly in the homes of former soldiers. During their twenty to twenty-five years of service, soldiers of all kinds naturally formed relationships with local women, but these were not formally marriages, and children born to them would not be citizens. Special dispensations allowed soldiers to make wills, but their wives and children had no automatic rights in respect of them. An auxiliary veteran could make his slave a citizen by freeing him, but any children he had fathered before he was discharged would have to join up themselves if they wanted the same status. Considerations like these mean we can never study 'Roman societies' without including many who were not Romans. Yet if we treat all provincials as 'in some sense' Romans, we obscure distinctions that mattered enormously at the time.

Docile Bodies

Over time, more and more of Rome's subjects were successful in obtaining citizenship. I have already suggested that one reason the Roman world did hold together during the third-century crisis was a sense on the part of enough of Rome's subjects that this was their world. It is also clear that in many ways the lifestyles of provincial populations came to converge, not on a single or uniform imperial culture, but into a world structured by these very Roman differences, differences based on the gradations of education and status and cultural competence that Paul (or rather the author of *Luke–Acts* and his readers) understood so well. Enfranchisement, loyalty, and acculturation are not the same thing, but they were deeply interconnected.

For most parts of the empire, the best evidence for the emergence of Roman habits and attitudes is provided by material culture. Consider Roman baths. Roman bathhouses are very distinctive structures; architects, archaeologists, and cultural historians have studied examples from all over the empire.[11] Greeks too had taken baths; their nakedness had shocked the Elder Cato. But facilities for collective bathing were fairly rudimentary before the last century BC. One reason was technological. Few Greek cities had aqueducts before the Principate, and hydraulic concrete was only developed in Campania just before the turn of the millennium. (Greeks had had to use hip baths, which were a rather subsidiary part of exercise spaces.) Eventually, bath complexes would also exploit new building technologies for covering vast enclosed spaces and would use bricks and tiles to create spaces heated through warmed floors and by circulating air, and in the grandest examples would create glassed solaria. But the spread of bathing was not just a matter of technology. It also stands for the emergence of new social rituals and of a new consensus about cleanliness, health, and beauty. Those ideas can be traced in other ways: the spread of toilet sets, mirrors, and cosmetics, the appearance of standardized hairstyles in statuary, and so on; but let us stick with baths for the moment.

The rich had been the first to develop bathing into a central part of a civilized lifestyle. Unsurprisingly, the first luxurious bathhouses were created in the Bay of Naples in the last century BC, just when so much else of Roman elite culture was being remodelled.[12] Yet even before the end of the Republic, bathing culture was becoming popular in other sectors of society. Public bathhouses, which anyone could pay to use, appeared next. The Stabian Baths in Pompeii (see Figure 18) are one of the earliest known examples. During Augustus' reign, Agrippa incorporated grand baths into his park on the Field of Mars. Even more spectacular complexes, usually called *thermae*, were built in Rome by the emperors Titus and Trajan, Caracalla and Diocletian: they included exercise grounds, swimming pools, saunas, and elaborate displays of the kind of sculpture that Pompey had placed in the porticoes of his theatre. Even today, the surviving shell of Diocletian's baths houses a museum and a couple of churches, while the Baths of Caracalla are the venue for open-air operas and concerts. These imperial benefactions to the capital were the grandest example of a style of civic benefaction known from all the greatest cities of the empire.

Greek cities like Ephesus and Sardis have produced monumental evidence for a variation on this theme, bath complexes combined with

Fig. 18. The Stabian Baths at Pompeii

gymnasia. The gymnasium had in the classical period been the setting for the education and leisure of the better off classes: exercise and discussion took place here in a more public setting than the symposium. But in the new lands conquered by Alexander, where Greeks were usually a privileged (and sometimes embattled) urban minority, the gymnasium had become central to a certain definition of Hellenic culture. Greek education and Greek identity operated in these societies as a culture of exclusion, more than as the marker of a particular ethnic group. Athleticism was central to this identity. Festivals 'equal to the Olympics' were set up by benefactors all over the Greek world, young aristocrats competed in them for prestige rather than cash prizes, professional athletes also emerged, and athleticism became a focus for certain kinds of Greek literature.[13] The civic elites of Roman Egypt were even known as the gymnasial classes, so central were these spaces to that kind of elite culture that looked to Greek models which had, in fact, become widespread only under Rome; they were also, or claimed to be, hereditary and quite separate from the Egyptians among whom they lived. Everywhere, gymnasia became a focus for monumental

architecture, and the gymnasiarch became an important figure in civic society. Long lists of regulations survive from cities all over the Greek world,
showing how gymnasia had come to be thought of as key sites where new
citizens were produced and trained. Bathing fitted easily into this complex
of associations.

Baths were popular everywhere. Soldiers had bathhouses provided for
them in the larger camps, which had come, in any case, to resemble cities.
Some British examples are equipped with indoor exercise grounds in place
of the open *palaestra* common in the Mediterranean. Where hot springs
were discovered, medical establishments were set up. Wealthy landowners
built small bath suites in their rural homes, although they were probably
only in use when the owner was present. Pliny the Younger describes
arriving late at one of his villas and deciding, as an expression of his consideration and lack of pride, to use the baths in the local town rather than
have his own fired up. Bathing had by now become incorporated into aristocratic lifestyles, a social activity that divided the day of work from the evening of leisure. Other adopters included sanctuaries and especially healing
centres, and medical writers have a great deal to say about the advantages
of bathing (only slightly undermined by their lack of understanding of in-
fection). But we are dealing, after all, with ideology. The habits and ideals of
cleanliness had become integral to notions of the self and of civilization that
the empire propagated. No extant texts declare that dirty bodies are barbarian bodies—although trousers and beards receive some mild abuse—but
upwardly mobile provincials could hardly ignore Roman notions of what
constituted civilized standards.

A similar story could be told about food. It would include the spread of
the elaborate manners that surrounded meals; the popularization of wine-
drinking; new styles of cooking, including a preference for bread wheat
over other grains; the creation of new dinner services in ceramic and plate;
the evidence for imports of newly essential ingredients such as olive oil,
pepper, fish sauce, and Mediterranean fruits; and the centrality of the evening meal in Roman society and in Latin literature.[14] The new ways of life
or lifeworlds that had come to be widely shared across the empire had many
other dimensions. There was a new culture of lighting, one made possible
by glass windows in the south and in the north by the spread of lamps and
the olive oil used as fuel; the evening became a new space of time available for work or leisure. New kinds of dress were developed, along with
new notions of posture and etiquettes of gesture. And, of course, there was

the influence of education—never widespread, but no longer restricted to scribes either—and the effects on provincial children of learning Latin and Greek from Cicero and Virgil, Homer and the tragedians, and of learning to speak in public in a particular way.

What we are considering is a change of identity, but it is mostly the kind of identity created by routines and training, an embodied sense of self rather than a set of abstract concepts about 'Romanness'. Those who took to Roman bathing or began to drink wine instead of beer may not have consciously felt this made them more Roman in the way a grant of citizenship did so explicitly. And even those auxiliary *diplomata* displayed in private residences which speak to us of the spread of citizenship might locally have said more about an identity as a veteran, a sign of warrior achievement, even of military virtue.

Material culture in particular is difficult to interpret in a straightforward way.[15] One generation of historians took the use of objects such as red-slip tableware as a sign of some inner transformation. This seems too simplistic now that we are more aware of all the different reasons people make use of new or unfamiliar objects (and in any case, after the first generation, Roman-style tableware was often locally made and completely familiar). There were settings in which objects certainly were displayed to make claims about status and identity: the metal, glass, and ceramic objects buried with the dead are a case in point, and sometimes the objects presented as votives to the gods. But again, when we interpret particular objects as symbolizing or communicating something, we often have to make assumptions about the motives of their owners and the reactions of those who saw them. For some objects, such as the toga, we know quite a lot about their contemporary resonances.[16] For most, we do not.

What we can see, however, is the way that mass-produced Roman objects of all kinds came to populate the physical spaces within which many provincials lived and worked. This included statuettes of metal, stone, and clay; cooking wares and table wares, the latter usually in red-slip and occasionally imprinted with images drawn from the classical visual repertoire; characteristic storage containers, especially amphorae; coins; short texts in Latin on wood, pottery, and rarely stone and metal; a vast range of building material that we find all over the empire, such as tiles, flues, bricks, and paving stones; and metal tools. The list could go on and on. The spread of common artefacts produced in much greater quantities than ever before and with a much greater degree of standardization has aptly been termed the 'Roman

Picture Box 8 Firing list from La Graufesenque

This plate is an example of *terra sigillata*, one of the most widely used tablewares in the Roman world. It was developed in central Italy in the last half of the last century BC and exported around the Mediterranean. Regional productions appeared very rapidly in many provinces. This piece was produced at La Graufesenque in southern France in the first century AD.

Terra sigillata was just the latest in a series of hard shiny tablewares that had been used around the Mediterranean for centuries. It is distinguished from its predecessors by its colour and by various decorative features which draw on technological advances in mould making, in high-temperature kilns, and in the use of a suspension of clay particles to coat the finished product. It also could only be made from particular clays carefully processed before the pots were made. *Terra sigillata* imitates, in a cheaper medium, the gold and silver plate used by the wealthy. Plates, bowls, and cups made of *terra sigillata* were associated with a Mediterranean style of eating and drinking, and they were valued enough to find their way into some graves. In some areas they represent a radical stylistic break with earlier pre-Roman fine wares, and so they have also been associated with conscious attempts to assert either Roman identity or conformity with what Romans regarded as civilized norms.

Another radical difference was the quantities in which it was produced. Each firing of one of the large kilns at La Graufesenque produced tens of thousands of pieces, far more than local or even regional demand could have absorbed. They were widely distributed and sold by specialist merchants around the empire. More than any other medium, apart perhaps from coinage, they impacted visually and in tactile form on the everyday lives of Roman subjects. Manufactures like this have been described as contributing to a new sensorium, a material world that created new sensations in and responses from its users.

The kilns fired far more objects than any one potter or workshop could produce. Tally lists like the one on the plate were one way of trying to keep track of whose manufactures were included in the kiln. Intriguingly, although the style and the kiln design were imported from Italy, the graffiti from the site show a mixture of Latin and Celtic words, sometimes even in the same sentence. This site is one of a number of places where bilingualism and language interference in the Roman provinces are currently being investigated.

Further Reading

Robert Marichal, *Les Graffites de la Graufesenque*, Gallia Supplements (Paris: Éditions CNRS, 1988).

Alex Mullen, *Southern Gaul and the Mediterranean: Multilingualism and Multiple Identities in the Iron Age and Roman Periods* (Cambridge: Cambridge University Press, 2013).

Astrid Van Oyen, *How Things Make History: The Roman Empire and Its terra sigillata Pottery* (Amsterdam: Amsterdam University Press, 2016).

object revolution'. Together, they formed what anthropologists term a 'sensorium', a manufactured world that constantly impinged on the senses. The sensorium made habits and routines visible, reflected them to individuals, and also shaped the way they undertook routine activities. Material culture directed and drilled the sorts of lives people lived, and the ubiquity of these objects created environments that transformed the docile bodies of Rome's subjects more completely than political grants or even education.

These objects, acting en masse, seduced not just populations within the empire who purchased them, but some of those outside it too. Barbarian raiders in the third century had nothing much to offer in replacement of all this, and perhaps were not interested in doing so, while the groups who moved into the empire in the late fourth and fifth centuries were already convinced of the superiority of Roman ways and simply wanted them for themselves. The transformation of everyday life, in other words, was profound, and it had profound effects.

Identities and Empires

Most studies of identity politics in the Roman Empire have concentrated on the largest scale, on identities such as 'Romans' and 'Greeks', and on conscious statements about their attitudes to each other. Great progress has been made in this area in recent years. The enormous range of Greek responses to empire has been explored in particular detail, through studies of explicit statements in literary texts; through discussion of how the opposition between 'Greek' and 'Roman' was constructed through discursive and rhetorical practices; and by playing material culture off against literature.[17] Roman ideals are also clearer now, especially the extent to which the conscious efforts of generation after generation of cultural leaders were focused not on creating an alternative high culture parallel to that of Greece, but rather a universalizing civilization (usually called *humanitas*) in which Greek and Roman both had a part.[18]

Greek and western elites seem now to have a good deal in common, including a shared commitment to rehearsing their differences. Perhaps we should have suspected this, given that many of the Greek writers of the second and third century—including Arrian and Dio—were Roman senators as well as fans of the classical Greek past, while many of their western contemporaries, including Aulus Gellius, Fronto, and the emperors Hadrian and Marcus, were deeply involved in Greek culture and writing. Two educational systems coexisted, and many members of the civic elites were presumably comfortable only in one. Yet most Greek writers must have known and used much more Latin than they ever allowed in their classicizing compositions. The historical researches of the Greek historians of the imperial period are inconceivable without a good knowledge of Latin.

Most telling of all is the broad unity of elite material culture across the Mediterranean world, especially as expressed in their residences, urban and rural alike. No one who comes to elite culture through the elaborate mosaic art of their dining rooms, with its elaborate references to food and myth, astrology and hunting, gladiators and philosophers, or their taste in marble statuary, where gods and monsters and kings and poets jostle for space, or the wall paintings that open up imaginary vistas over cities and landscapes

or make play with stage scenery or portray gardens full of life could imagine for a moment that there were two high cultures rather than one in
the Roman Empire.[19] Many regional variations existed, of course. But the
overwhelming impression is of a single world of the imagination, one accessible through art and literature, whether one was in Sicily or southern
France, Syria or Asia Minor, in North Africa or in Germany.

Identity politics looks very different in discussions of modern imperialisms.
There the focus is not on the emergence of vast imperial identities, but
rather on how imperial regimes have shaped local experiences; on the
emergence of newly self-conscious peoples and nations; on diasporas and
displacements; and on how the experience of migration has impacted on
the lives of countless individuals. Cosmopolitanism, cultural hybridity, and
the persistence of economic and cultural domination after the end of formal
empire are central topics in postcolonial studies. Enormous differences
clearly existed between the long-lasting, but fundamentally weak empires
of antiquity and the short-lived, but phenomenally powerful ones of the last
few hundred years. Ancient imperialisms never effected population transfers
on the scale either of the transport of Africans to the New World as slaves or
of the establishment of populations of south Asian origin in Africa, Europe,
and North America, or of the spread of communities of east Asian origin
around the Pacific, let alone the colonization of much of the world's temperate zones by people of European origin. Modern empires established
vast inequalities of wealth that persist today. Because of their impact on
public health, and because they exported cash cropping and industrializa-
tion into their peripheries, they set in train enormous changes in the global
environment. Cosmopolitanism in the modern world is linked to the creation of huge cities in both the developed and underdeveloped worlds. Any
comparison with antiquity has to bear those differences in mind.[20]

One thing that is clear is an increase in the scale of human mobility
within the Roman world, in part facilitated by peace and better transport
infrastructure, in part generated by the demands of the imperial state and its
richest inhabitants. Long before Rome expanded, both the Mediterranean
world and its continental hinterlands experienced population movements
of various kinds.[21] Nevertheless, Roman imperialism presided over what
was probably unprecedented levels of human mobility in the ancient
Mediterranean world. This has been a major focus of recent research.[22] The
slave trade, the recruitment, redeployment, and resettlement of soldiers, and
the growth of cities all played a part. We should probably imagine net flows

of humans into the core provinces, especially into the most urbanized regions, since ancient cities certainly had higher death rates than birth rates
and relied on immigration to sustain their populations. Roman authorities
also occasionally moved tribal populations across frontiers. Missionaries,
pilgrims, traders, scholars, and craftsmen all travelled back and forth across
the empire, many at least intending to return home.[23] When they did not,
their tombstones provide precious information about their travels, while
a range of techniques for analysing skeletal material provide objective evidence.[24] Alongside this can be set the legal and documentary evidence
for efforts to respond to human mobility and to control it: Greek cities
had already developed regulations for *metoikoi* (resident aliens) and western
ones began to impose financial obligations on wealthy *incolae* (inhabitants
of a community whose formally registered place of origin was elsewhere).[25]
Diasporas of Jews and Syrians and Greeks are reasonably well attested
during the empire.[26] Very often, it is the spread of the worship of particular gods that provides the best evidence for diaspora communities across
the empire.[27] Atargatis, known as Dea Syria, the Syrian goddess, eventually
attracted other worshippers, but it looks as if the founders of her temples
in the Aegean and in Italy were actual migrants. Synagogues are known
throughout the Roman east, and in some parts of the west as well. The fact
that cult centres were established in new locations suggests not only semi-
permanent populations, but also groups who maintained contacts with
fellow immigrants from the same areas. It is important not to exaggerate
this. Most subjects of the empire lived their lives within very small horizons,
the numbers of long-distance travellers were always small, and very few
women moved long distances, except for those who were moved in chains.
Nevertheless, all major Roman cities contained minorities, and where there
is abundant epigraphic evidence, as in the Vesuvian cities, Ostia, and some
North African ports, these communities are often highly visible.

Postcolonial approaches to antiquity are no longer new. Historians lagged
a little behind archaeologists in exploring ways of using these ideas, drawn
from modern critiques of empire, to illuminate experiences of Roman
Empire, but there are now a range of good studies available which together
offer alternative narratives to those based mainly on historical writing and
inscriptions written in Latin and Greek.[28] One common strand is more
caution about observing events and institutions from the point of view of
those who ruled the empire. Stability is a positive thing only for those who
benefit from it, and the same goes for integration, assimilation, and even

pax, which for Romans meant something more muscular and one-sided than the English term 'peace'.[29] Another strand is an interest in using globalization as a means of understanding the very large-scale patterning of the Roman empire.[30] Today, the term refers to the processes by which different parts of the globe have been drawn into closer and closer contact in the post-war period, with the increased volume and speed of trade, travel, and communication in general. It also often describes how local economic, social, and cultural systems are transformed as they become more enmeshed in a world order. There are clear similarities here with the Roman world, as well as differences. A third strand of postcolonial approaches to Rome is a greater appreciation on our part of the creative effects of hybridity, forms, many of them monumental, which draw on multiple traditions as a means of creating and even celebrating identities that are not simply indigenous or imperial.[31] Objects once dismissed as incoherent or incompletely assimilated now seem to tell us more about the complex processes by which all the empire's subjects had to find and express a place in the new order.

There is little sign, however, of any positive value being placed on hybridity or multiculturalism by ancient host societies. Although the rich spent a good deal acquiring exotic foreign raw materials, from Indian Ocean spices to silk, they were not interested in consuming alien cuisine, or dressing in new ways influenced by foreign styles. Jews and Isis worshippers were both hounded out of Rome in the late Republic. The upwardly mobile took care to lose their regional accents. Only Greek orators could make capital out of their exotic origins: Lucian stressed his 'Assyrian' identity, and Favorinus of Arles stated that one of the paradoxes of his life was that although he was a Gaul, he could 'play the Greek'. But what they were stressing was the cultural distance they had travelled. Septimius Severus allegedly would not let his sister come to Rome, even when he was emperor, because he was embarrassed by her African speech.

Being part of an empire also had more subtle effects on the identities claimed by different peoples in the empire. Theorists of globalization today point out that increased connectivity has often had the effect of making a group more conscious of its distinctive location within the whole. It has been suggested that both Greeks and Jews came to formulate their distinctive identities in new ways that responded to the wider imperial world in which they lived.[32] Some aspects of Jewish life, from the use of Greek to a form of worship based on scriptures rather than the rituals of the Temple in Jerusalem, were more portable and so easier to replicate in a

Greek or Roman city. Greek education too was more transferable than rituals based on ancestral shrines. Isis worshippers could use hieroglyphs in their rituals and even imported Nile water, but they could not orient cult on the flooding of the river. Many cults came to resemble each other in their outward-looking faces, while remaining (or even becoming more) distinctive in terms of what worshippers did or knew on the inside. Diasporic populations were not the only ones to find new identities in the empire. Local communities in the east and west developed parallel myth histories peopled with Trojan and Greek founding fathers and a range of similar tropes, the local princess who marries the refugee prince, and the oracle that points to the spot where the city should be founded. This myth-making was an ancient tradition, but it flourished in all parts of the Roman world.[33]

Further Reading

Almost no topic in Roman history has generated as much recent research as the subject of this chapter, although there has been some confusion between attempts to examine the broad social and economic consequences of Roman rule, studies of collective identities as consciously experienced phenomena, as expressed in texts, monuments, and material culture and investigations of the means by which loyalty and solidarity were generated among the emperors' subjects. Those issues are clearly linked, but they are not the same. Emma Dench's *Empire and Political Cultures in the Roman World* (Cambridge, 2018) offers an exciting new exploration of some of this territory.

Studies of the impact of Roman rule vary considerably, especially in how they treat cultural phenomena. Examples include Martin Millett's *Romanization of Britain* (Cambridge, 1990), Nico Roymans's *Tribal Societies in Northern Gaul* (Amsterdam, 1990), Susan Alcock's *Graecia capta* (Cambridge, 1993), David Mattingly's *An Imperial Possession* (London, 2006), Andrew Wallace-Hadrill's *Roman Cultural Revolution* (Cambridge, 2008), and my own *Becoming Roman* (Cambridge, 1998); they offer a selection of approaches, all employing archaeological data, generally in combination with other evidence. So too do two collections, Tom Blagg and Martin Millett's *Early Roman Empire in the West* (Oxford, 2000) and Susan Alcock's *Early Roman Empire in the East* (Oxford, 1997). It would be easy to add to this list.

Conscious expressions of Roman identity are the subject of Emma Dench's *Romulus' Asylum* (Oxford, 2005), while Simon Swain's *Hellenism and Empire* (Oxford, 1996) and Simon Goldhill's *Being Greek under Rome* (Cambridge, 2001) investigate the identity politics of the empire's best-documented subject people. Seth Schwartz's *Imperialism and Jewish Society* (Princeton, NJ, 2001) asks some of the same questions about the second best-known case. Fergus Millar's *Roman Near East* (Cambridge, MA, 1993) opens up a vast field of study, one mostly known from inscriptions written in a bewildering variety of languages. By far the most thoughtful examination so far of how cultural identity, political power, law, and social solidarity were connected during the early empire is Clifford Ando's *Imperial Ideology and Provincial Loyalty in the Roman Empire* (Berkeley, CA, 2000).

Others have asked how particular groups within the empire developed common identities. Three recent collections give an idea of the state of the question: Ton Derks and Nico Roymans's *Ethnic Constructs in Antiquity* (Amsterdam, 2009), Tim Whitmarsh's *Local Knowledge and Microidentities in the Imperial Greek World* (Cambridge, 2010), and Erich Gruen's *Cultural Identities in the Ancient Mediterranean* (Los Angeles, 2011). Migration has been the big new subject of the last decade: Laurens Tacoma's *Moving Romans* (Oxford, 2016) and Elena Isayev's *Migration, Mobility and Place in Ancient Italy* (Cambridge, 2017) are important studies of it, and do not exhaust the topic.

KEY DATES IN CHAPTER XV

RECONSTRUCTION

We may thank the good fortune of our state, as well as the immortal gods, on remembering the wars we have waged successfully. The condition of the world has been placed, tranquil, in the lap of the deepest quiet and peace towards good men. For this reason we have labored and spent our effort lavishly. Now both Roman dignity and majesty desire that the public honor be arranged faithfully and fittingly adorned. We, who by supernatural forces' benevolent support have suppressed the raging depredations of the past by slaughtering the very peoples of the barbarian tribes, will secure the quiet we have established with the reinforcements Justice deserves.

(From the Preface to the *Edict on Maximum Prices*, 301 AD, trans. Kropff)

The Tetrarchs

The extract with which this chapter begins is taken from the long introduction to an even longer edict, one that imposed maximum prices for a long list of commodities. These included the basic foodstuffs (grain, wine, oil, meat, fish) and then went on for nearly forty chapters listing every kind of item of clothing, tools, firewood, timber, animals, slaves, precious metals, and more. These prices were to be fixed throughout the empire and were what we would call an anti-inflation measure. There certainly was price inflation at the end of the third century AD, at least in some parts of the empire, although it is difficult to tell now whether this was a long-term problem or short-term fluctuations, a global trend or local ones, and whether it was caused by diminished production, by increased demand, or by the collapsing value of a debased coinage. Price rises often led to riots in ancient cities and caused other problems for governments that needed to provision armies and palaces. But this edict was the first attempt to solve the problem for the whole empire at once. The preface justifies these measures as a remedy for greed, a greed that impacted most savagely on the poor. The problem was not new, and similar restrictions were imposed in the past. Now, however, things had got so bad that 'the parents of the human race' had decided to intervene. The penalty for breach of any of the regulations they set out would be death.

There is a lot that might be said about this extraordinary document, fragments of which have been found in several cities, mostly in the eastern part of the empire. The problem it sets out to solve is treated entirely in moralizing terms. The solution certainly did not work and was perhaps never even tried in the western part of the empire. It was savagely criticized by the near contemporary Lactantius (although he had other reasons to disapprove of the authors). But this preface, offers a spectacular self-portrait of a new style of imperial monarchy that emerged in the last decades of the third century AD.

The first thing to say is that 'we' is not a royal plural. The edict was issued by four emperors ruling together whose names and titles head the document. The first of these reads as follows:

The Emperor Caesar Gaius Aurelius Valerius Diocletian, dutiful, blessed, unconquered Augustus, chief priest of the Roman state religion, conqueror of the Germans 6 times, conqueror of the Sarmatians 4 times, conqueror of the Persians 2 times, conqueror of the Britons, conqueror of the Carpi, conqueror of the Armenians, conqueror of the Medes, conqueror of the Adiabeni, holding tribunician power for the 18th year, 7 times consul, 18 times acclaimed emperor, Father of our Country, proconsul.

The titles of the co-emperors Maximian, Constantius and Galerius are only a little less grand. Maximian shares all the same titles as Diocletian, including Augustus, Pontifex Maximus, and proconsul. Constantius and Galerius lack these but are both designated *nobilissimus Caesar* (most noble Caesar). The title Caesar had been used for centuries to designate the heir of an Augustus. Most of the elements are very traditional: the priesthoods and magistracies go back to Republican usage, like the title *imperator*, which still had connotations of military distinction. Emperors since Augustus had used numbered annual grants of tribunician power as a kind of regnal year. The emperors also claim traditional virtuous qualities (*pius felix*, meaning 'pious' and 'blest') and achievements (*invictus*, meaning 'undefeated'). The titles seem all the more traditional on the inscriptions since they use abbreviations that had been used for centuries. It was not unusual either for emperors to claim titles from peoples they had defeated, although the number here is unprecedented. But the multiplication of emperors is new. There had been co-emperors before, Lucius and Marcus or Severus and his two sons, but not a group of unrelated individuals presented as a college working together. Universal edicts of this sort are also a sign of a new imperial style. Very few are known from before this period; most early imperial pronouncements take the form of responses (*rescripta*) to petitions sent to them. Now, the emperors speak in unison to all their subjects. The rules are impossibly detailed, and the threatened death penalty also shows a new, more direct style of government. From now on, imperial speech is authoritarian; the penalties threatened are draconian. These are no longer citizen princes. The emperors do still present themselves as public benefactors. They begin with their claim to have restored peace, to have restored Roman dignity and majesty in the face of attacks by barbarian tribes, and to have done this with the help of the gods. Diocletian was in his eighteenth year as emperor when the Edict was issued. Four years later he resigned, and then died in 311.

Collectively the four emperors (but especially Diocletian), claimed to have saved the state and to have done so with the help of the immortal gods. On the military side, that claim was a reasonable one. The third-century military crisis had been a slowly building storm that was most furious in the 250s and 260s AD. For just a few years in the 270s the empire broke up into three parts, with one set of emperors established on the Rhine facing the German threat, another group mostly fighting on the Danube and trying to protect Italy and a new kingdom created by the ruler of Palmyra that was recognized from Asia Minor to Egypt. All presented themselves as Romans. The Gallic and Palmyrene dynasties occasionally recognized the central emperors, but in practice their secessions expressed a lack of faith in distant rulers and a dependence on local help. But the emperors Claudius II, Gallienus, who ruled from 253 to 268, and Aurelian recovered the situation, and fought off the invaders long enough to gain time to defeat their rivals.

In 274 Aurelian held a spectacular triumph in Rome, around which he had built a circuit of walls, much of which still stands today. His prisoners included the last Gallic emperor, Tetricus, and Zenobia, queen of Palmyra. Aurelian was murdered the next year, and six more emperors reigned over the next decade before the succession of Diocletian in 284.

Like many of the emperors and would-be emperors who rose and fell during the third century, Diocletian (Diocles by birth) originated in the Balkans. Nothing certain is known about him until his entry into history as the commander of the bodyguard of the emperor Numerianus, whose father Carus was a praetorian prefect who had rebelled against the emperor Probus in 282. Carus was killed in 283—we do not know how or by whom—and Numerianus ruled for only one year before being murdered in turn by his own praetorian prefect, Aper, but it was Diocles whom the army hailed as Augustus. So far, so conventional. Equally conventional was Diocletian's first campaign, against Carus' other son (and Numerianus' co-emperor) Carinus whom he defeated and killed in 285. For most of the next decade Diocletian fought, first on the eastern frontier, then on the upper Danube, then back in the east, while his ally Maximian, who came from a similar background also in the Balkans, served first as his Caesar and then as his fellow Augustus, mostly on the western frontier.

In 293 Diocletian and Maximian adopted Galerius and Constantius as Caesars. They were from similar backgrounds to their respective Augusti. Collectively, they would be known as the tetrarchy, the rule of four men (see Figure 19). It began with a fanfare of ceremony, two dynasties working together, one named after Jupiter, the other after his son Hercules, each with an Augustus and a more junior Caesar. The plan was that the system would be replicated when each Caesar replaced his Augustus and appointed a new Caesar in turn. That programme did not exactly work out, but throughout the fourth and fifth centuries the empire was, for most of the time, ruled by a group of emperors working together. This reconciled the common belief in the unity of the empire—that all Romans belonged in a single state—with the need to have emperors close by wherever there was a major crisis. The institution of a college of emperors responded directly to the military crisis of the third century. In those terms it was a success. War against northerners and hostilities with Persia continued throughout the fourth century, and there were more civil wars, but for nearly ninety years there was no military disaster and no more secessions.

Fig. 19. Porphyry statue of the Four Tetrarchs at the Basilica di San Marco, St Mark's Square, Venice, Italy

The military crisis changed other things too besides the role of the em-peror. Under the Severan dynasty the majority of provincial governors and legionary commanders were still drawn from the Senate. During the third century this changed. The process began gradually, partly because the number of these posts increased, but also because the emperors were increasingly no longer senators themselves and knew very few of them. Instead, they came to rely on those already serving in the armies, men like themselves. Gallienus is remembered as excluding senators from military positions, Diocletian is said to have done the same for provincial governors. Probably things were more complicated. Diocletian accelerated the process by which the provinces of the early empire were redivided into much smaller ones. The number of military units also multiplied, and they too became smaller, in part as a means of making the army more mobile and flexible. This increased the number of commanders needed. There were new positions to fill in the four imperial courts too. Each emperor was, as a result, able to act more effectively in relation to his subjects. How they did it is recorded in a vast amount of documentation.[1] By the early fourth century there were four praetorian prefects, each heading a large civilian bureaucracy that managed a quarter of the empire.[2] Military and civilian commands had been separated too. Most senior posts were filled by equestrians (although some still went to senators under Constantine) and the more junior ones through recruitment from the municipal aristocracies. The changes introduced by Diocletian and modified by Constantine were unpopular with some members of the traditional elites. But the growing bureaucracy provided many opportunities for educated provincials and even for some barbarian leaders to join in a new ruling class. Once recruited, they were rapidly socialized and created their own traditional ways of doing things, ways they would staunchly defend against further changes in the sixth century.[3] Roman bureaucracy was probably not fantastically efficient. This was not a modern state, patronage remained important, and corruption was endemic.[4] But its internal dynamics had changed.

Some precious documents present us with an image of imperial style in this period. One is the *Notitia Dignitatum*, of which a gloriously illustrated copy made in the sixteenth century survives (see Figure 20). The original was composed at the end of the fourth century, and parts revised, in a complicated manner that is still obscure, through the early fifth century. Each page is devoted to a different office in the hierarchy—praetorian prefects, regional vicars, provincial governors of all kinds—and then the parallel military hierarchy, including armies, forts, and weapons factories. The information contained is exactly what a centralized empire would need, but the fact it was illustrated so expensively and yet would be out of date almost at once suggests it also offered a kind of panorama of power. Each entry is preoccupied with those details that matter most to insiders: precise titles, the orders of precedence and seniority, the number of postal warrants assigned to each official. And the fact it includes western and eastern officials and units in a period in which the empire was effectively divided in two shows

Fig. 20. An image from the late antique *Notitia Dignitatum*

it depicts an order of dignities that was idealized and ideological as much as practical.

The most important decisions were made wherever the emperors happened to be at the time. That was rarely the city of Rome. Imperial courts appeared in Trier, Milan, Ravenna, Serdica, Sirmium, Split,

Thessalonica, Nicomedia, Antioch, and, of course, Constantinople, to name just the most permanent bases. The most spectacular were provided with grand palaces, hippodromes, imperial baths, and all that was needed for the entourage of courtiers and officials to be comfortable and effective. These new architectures were also designed for one more component of the new empire: ceremony.[5] Contemporary accounts notice the sudden increase in court rituals. Ruler and courtiers dressed in extraordinary costumes, as we can see from the mosaics at Ravenna and Istanbul. The arrival of an emperor in a city generated a major festival. At court the favoured few were permitted to kiss the purple robe of the emperor. The Emperor Julian wrote a satire entitled the *Caesars* in which each of his predecessors is caricatured as they arrive for a Saturnalian banquet hosted on Olympus by Romulus. When Diocletian turns up, he makes a grand entrance in a fabulous costume, surrounded by a chorus of the other tetrarchs.[6] The image of the emperor as a fellow citizen who wore simple togas woven by his wife and daughters, was far in the past.[7] Extravagant triumphs were celebrated by (among others) Aurelian, Diocletian, Constantine, Constantius II, and Theodosius I.[8] Anniversary celebrations were held for the tenth, twentieth, and, in Constantine's case, thirtieth anniversaries of an emperor's reign. The cost of all this was considerable. Taxes rose, as did the number of bureaucrats who collected them and distributed the revenue.

Taken together, the tetrarchy, the new ruling elite, the increased use of government by edict, the rise of ceremony, a new coinage, military reforms, and a new tax system can all be seen as parts of a comprehensive and systematic reconstruction of the Roman empire as it emerged from crisis. That view is legitimate and terms like New Empire or Later Roman Empire are convenient labels for historians looking back. The governmental system created around the turn of the third and fourth centuries AD was different from that used in the first three centuries of empire and remained in place, with slight adjustments, until the seventh century. But it looks more like a system with hindsight. This is not how it was experienced or presented at the time. For one thing, the changes arrived piecemeal, some going back to the 260s and others not introduced until the reign of Constantine. Each new change, like the development of a new tax system, had to support earlier ones. A direction of travel became established gradually, beginning with short-term solutions to immediate military and political problems. Some, like relying more on cavalry, were relatively discrete changes. Others, like the creation of hierarchies of officials responsible to praetorian prefects who no longer had any military role, had more consequences. Successful innovations needed to be made sustainable, as when a new system of tax in kind was developed to provision the reorganized army. Some experiments, like the parallel Jovian and Herculean dynasties, were soon abandoned. And there were unexpected and unplanned consequences: senators were now marginal, not because they were deliberately marginalized, but because the political centres of gravity had shifted. Perhaps most political reconfigurations are like this. The Augustan system drew on expedients developed in other circumstances by Marius, Sulla, and Pompey and was not really perfected until the reigns of Tiberius and Claudius. Devising systems of governance is in any case often only possible when leaders have leisure. Leisure was one thing the tetrarchs did not possess. Nor did they present themselves as introducing radical change: in the public pronouncements of the imperial college, all this was presented as a restoration, not a revolution. Rome's dignity and majesty had been restored thanks to the traditional virtues of the emperors and the favour of the ancestral gods. But perhaps the fact the tetrarchs felt they had to assert that so forcefully indicates a sense that there was some persuading to do.

The Collapse of Consensus

The Emperor Diocletian ruled from AD 284 to 305, Constantine I from 306 to 337. They were not the only emperors who reigned during this half-century, and both fought several civil wars. But the length of their reigns combined is a sure sign of increased imperial stability. Another sign is that the frontiers, although never peaceful, held. The military crisis that had nearly resulted in imperial meltdown had been averted.

Yet few of the tetrarchs or their fourth-century successors were remembered in a wholly positive way. There are a number of reasons for this. First of all, there was now a greater divide between those who made history and those who wrote it. Historical writing of the first two and a half centuries AD came largely from the senatorial elite or those in their circles. The soldier emperors came from a different background. A few, like Maximinus Thrax, were portrayed as monstrous and barbaric by writers with senatorial sympathies, even if some were very effective.[9] Many later historians also observed emperors from the perspective of provincial aristocracies for whom emperors were also distant and sometimes threatening figures. Second, it has been difficult for either ancient or modern historians to put out of their minds the military disasters of the late fourth and early fifth centuries. The Roman recovery looks more fragile to us than it did to contemporaries. But the third and most important reason is that all historical writing on this period is coloured by religious conflict.

Ever since Augustus, the emperors had associated themselves with the traditional priesthoods of the city of Rome, repaired and built temples, and tried to harness the emotive power of collective ritual. Severus had organized Saecular Games in AD 204 (as had Augustus, Claudius, and Domitian before him) and the Emperor Philip organized another series in 248 to celebrate the thousand-year anniversary of the city. Aurelian found time in 274 after his victory over Palmyra to found a temple of the Undefeated Sun in Rome and add a senatorial priest of Sol to the College of Pontiffs. The sun god had been closely associated with the person of the emperor on coinage since the early third century. The defeat of Palmyra provided enough booty, and perhaps some imported statuary, to create the magnificent temple.

These activities were all focused on the city of Rome, but Caracalla's Universal Edict had made the entire empire into a potential religious community. Whether he was aware of it or not, this created potential conflicts for those within the empire who were not polytheists. Jews and Christians might pray and sacrifice for the emperors, but not to them or to the traditional gods of the Roman state. This only became a live issue in 250, when the Emperor Decius, in the face of another disaster, required all Roman citizens to perform a *supplicatio* to the gods of Rome and to produce proof they had done so. Some of these 'sacrifice certificates' survive. It is quite likely that this revealed for the first time how many Roman citizens no longer worshipped the gods of Rome.[10] That in turn triggered persecutions of Christians around the empire that continued into the reign of Valerian. By the 250s the Christian communities of major cities like Carthage, Rome, Alexandria, and Antioch were led by bishops who were prominent public figures. Some were arrested, tried, and executed, others exiled. Church property and churches were confiscated. But when Valerian was captured and killed by the Persians in 260, his son Gallienus ended the persecution and ordered the restoration of church property. For a generation there were no further global persecutions. Some Christian communities constructed major churches, and in Rome they began to acquire catacombs. A few cities even seem to have become majority-Christian in this period. It has been estimated that Christians comprised as much as 10 per cent of the population, very unevenly distributed across the empire and perhaps concentrated in the major cities of the Mediterranean world. Tensions continued at a local level and found expression in polemic, but for the moment the emperors stood above this.

For this reason Diocletian's Great Persecution came as a major shock. It seems to have been a systematic attempt to eliminate Christianity, and it traumatized great swathes of the empire between AD 303 and 311.[11] Religious texts were confiscated, churches demolished, and the civil rights of Christians removed. Further edicts ordered the imprisonment of Christian clergy and again commanded they perform sacrifice. Executions and other atrocities are reported from North Africa, Egypt, and Palestine. The experiences in other areas were probably different. The worst of the persecution ended in 305, when the two Augusti stood down, and in 311 Galerius issued an edict of toleration. Constantine's patronage of the church began soon after his victory at the Milvian Bridge in 312, and Maximinus' death in 313 brought a decade of persecution to an end. The exact motivations for Diocletian's revival of anti-Christian measures are unclear. But as the preface to the Price Edict shows, an appeal to the traditional gods expressed a strong sense that imperial unity was reflected in common ritual. A collection of Latin panegyrics performed before various tetrarchs also reflects what we can call their religious ideology, including reference to the Jovian and Herculean dynasties but to other traditional gods as well, and traditional praise of the emperor.[12] Most of these edicts were both a response to popular sentiment (as they understood it) and an attempt to unify Rome under the rule of heaven.

Constantine began by tolerating the new religion and then proceeded rapidly to protect, sponsor, patronize, and eventually seek to regulate and unify it through an ecumenical council held in 325 at Nicaea. By the end of his reign, not only were Christians free to worship, but some could now do so in great churches constructed in Rome, Constantinople, and Jerusalem. The bishops now had easy access to the emperors, and some became powerful figures at court, while others began to dominate their home cities. Even more threatening to polytheists was the first of a long series of prohibitions against sacrifice, repeated with variations and extensions throughout the fourth century.[13] Their temples and priesthoods remained untouched, but their rituals were now under attack.

The effects of the Great Persecution and Constantine's patronage of Christianity were polarizing. All but one of Constantine's successors were

Christians, and Diocletian and Galerius were damned as monsters in texts such as Lactantius' *Deaths of the Persecutors*. Constantine himself was elevated in texts like the biography of him written by Eusebius of Caesarea almost to sainthood. These two perspectives coexisted through much of the fourth and fifth centuries, creating divisions within families and among and between local and imperial ruling classes. These divisions were reflected in all historical writing. The figure of Julian, who renounced Christianity and in his short reign tried to restore some elements of traditional worship, was praised and damned by contemporaries. When the frontiers collapsed again in the late fourth century and when the city of Rome was sacked twice in the fifth century, in 410 by the Goths and in 455 by the Christian Vandals, polytheists like Zosimus (now labelled pagans by their Christian opponents) blamed Rome's humiliation on Constantine's abandonment of the traditional gods.

This polarization has wide implications for our understanding of this period. Before the end of the third century AD there had been a great variety of historical writing in Greek and in Latin: there were local and global histories, total histories of Rome, contemporary histories, and histories that were more like a series of imperial biographies placed end to end. Some historians and biographers stressed the mythological and the marvellous; others were closer to satire and scandal sheets. But they reflected a set of common ideals about the role of the emperor. Those ideals were a blend of Greek ideologies of kingship and Roman notions of good citizenship. Good emperors were just, were successful in battle, deferred to tradition, respected the rights (especially the property rights) of the elite, were modest and merciful, and did not raise new taxes. Their sex lives were dull and unimpeachable. Bad emperors had all the opposite vices: think Caligula, Nero, Domitian, or Commodus.[14] Now one new criterion trumped all the others. How did he stand with the Church? Was he a persecutor or a protector? And then later, was he orthodox or a heretic?

No historian was neutral. Perhaps this is understandable for the generation that lived through the Great Persecution and Constantine's patronage of the Church. Lactantius was an African rhetor summoned by Diocletian to teach at his eastern capital of Nicomedia and then sacked in the persecution of 303. But he moved west and survived to tutor the eldest son of Constantine. His grisly *On the Deaths of the Persecutors* recounted the gruesome punishments God reserved for Diocletian, Galerius, and the others. Eusebius of Caesarea not only produced a biography of Constantine but also a *History of the Church* that was largely composed of pre-existing documents now rearranged by imperial reign to illustrate that canonically bad emperors were (mostly) the enemies of early Christian communities. At least as early as the second century some Christians had claimed that the Roman Empire served a providential function in facilitating the spread of Christ's message. Eusebius and Lactantius each offered new visions of imperial history as a part of God's unfolding plan. Contrasting views can be read in the works of non-Christian writers of the same period. Libanius of Antioch, whose career as an orator and teacher took him to Athens, Constantinople, and Nicomedia, was a great admirer of Julian. Another was Eunapius from Sardis in Asia Minor, whose history of the fourth century is now lost, but whose celebration of pagan intellectuals survived. Both men consciously wrote in a Greek tradition and deplored the decreased support for civic cults, the casual licence given to acts of violence against their temples, and what they saw as the ruinous consequences of abandoning the gods.[15] They had their successors too, including the anti-Christian historians Olympiodorus of Thebes in Egypt and Zosimus, both writing after the disasters of the early fifth century. Yet at the same time, Libanius had Christian pupils and received honours from Christian emperors, and both his work and that of Eunapius were used by Christian historians. The divisions among historians reflect a wider collapse of consensus among the elites of the empire. The empire had to live with these differences well into the fifth century and beyond. They coloured the culture, the politics, and the art of late antiquity.

From our more remote perspective it is easier to see the similarities between Diocletian and Constantine. Both were soldier emperors, similar in many respects to many of their immediate predecessors, but much more successful than them. The pragmatic business of being an emperor—ensuring military security, balancing the budget, surviving court intrigue, and trying to secure the succession—occupied at least as much of their time as did religious disputes. How far the differences in their treatment of Christians were influenced by strongly held personal beliefs is now impossible to say. The policies of both men—persecution, toleration, and promotion alike—were all about imperial unity. Constantine, about whom we know so much more, remains a mysterious figure. Earlier in his career, he made much of connections to Apollo and Sol Invictus. Later, he had plenty of opportunities to play the zealot, especially against heretics, but he resisted most of them. Bishops felt themselves influential at his court—and so some were—but it is difficult to identify any area of policy where Constantine's commitment to Christ did not also serve his vision for the empire.

Fourth-Century Emperors

For most of Diocletian's more than twenty-year-long reign he and his fellow emperors moved back and forth between bases along the northern and eastern frontiers of the empire. The Roman armies were now larger and more mobile, the cities of the east were now fortified bases, and provincial taxation in kind was geared to the needs of the troops. Most wars were fought on the frontier or on foreign territory. Inside the empire, the economy gradually recovered. Some at least of the richest families became very rich, and the empire extracted a larger and larger surplus. Smaller landowners and the peasantries had a less happy experience. The pattern of coups and failed coups which had brought Diocletian to power was largely broken.

The tetrarchy itself began to unravel with the joint abdication of 305. Even before Diocletian's death, probably in 312, the carefully plotted succession plan had had to be varied. Among the changes were the death of Constantius in 306, only a year after his elevation to the rank of Augustus, and the succession of his son Constantine. Relations between the emperors shifted back and forth between collaboration and distrust for a decade, a decade in which Constantine himself campaigned against the Franks. By the end of 312, a new pattern had begun to emerge. Galerius was dead (devoured by worms, if you believe Lactantius, but not before he had formally ended the Great Persecution with an Edict of Toleration); Constantine had won a decisive victory over his rival Maxentius at the battle of the Milvian Bridge, which gave him control of the city of Rome; and he had formed an alliance with Licinius, who was able to eliminate another rival, Maximin Dia, the next year. The alliance with Licinius was a stormy one, but it was not until 325 that Constantine was able to defeat and execute him and rule alone. By then Constantine had celebrated twenty years in power and begun the creation of a great new capital on the site of Byzantium, to be called Constantinople. The final decade of his life was spent largely there, his attention divided between wars on the Danube and the creation of a new college of emperors from his three surviving sons (he had had a fourth, Crispus, executed in 326) and nephews.

The political history of the years that followed looks chaotic. Constantine had already had his wife Fausta and his son Crispus killed. On his death in 337, the empire was left to three surviving sons, Constans, Constantine II, and Constantius II, and a cousin, Dalmatius, who was rapidly disposed of by the brothers. Constantius, who ruled most of the east, allegedly engineered the murder of more of their relatives. Three years later, Constans and Constantine clashed over control of the west, which led to the death of Constantine. The remaining two brothers ruled, each preoccupied with his own geographical sphere, until 350, when Constans was in turn deposed and killed by one of his officers Magnentius. It took Constantius until 353 to defeat Magnentius and become sole Augustus. Before Constantius' death in 361, he had appointed two of his cousins as Caesars. Gallus was stationed in Antioch, while Constantius fought on the northern frontier and was killed on his orders in 354. The following year Gallus' half-brother Julian was made Caesar and sent to northern Gaul to defend the cities against raids from across the Rhine. He had declared himself Augustus and was marching against Constantius when the latter died, leaving Julian a war against Persia to deal with. Julian found time to set in motion his plan to revive traditional cults but perished himself on campaign against the Persians in 363. His death marked the end of official support for polytheism as well as the end of Constantine's dynasty.

Meanwhile, the new normal reasserted itself. The generals on campaign appointed as Julian's successor first Jovian, who died the next year after making peace with Persia, and then Valentinian, both drawn from the military command. Valentinian rapidly appointed his brother Valens co-emperor and assigned him the east. Three years later, in 367, Valentinian's son Gratian, although only 8 years old, was added to the imperial college. On Valentinian's death in 375, Gratian's half-brother was declared Valentinian II. Valens and his nephews remained in power until 376, but they were not unchallenged. Valens easily put down an attempted coup led by Procopius early in his reign, and a coup led by Magnus Maximus in 383 led to Gratian's death and the flight of Valentinian to seek refuge at Constantinople with Theodosius, another military appointee who had taken over on the death of Valens in 376. Theodosius successfully asserted his control over the west, defeating Maximus in 387. Theodosius I ruled until 395, joined before his death by his sons Arcadius and Honorius, raised up in 383 and 393 respectively, the former ruling the east and the latter the west. Valentinian II himself was allowed to remain with a diminished court in Vienne in southern Gaul, but firmly under the control of Theodosius and his general Arbogast. He died there in mysterious circumstances in 392.

Yet below the noisy convulsions on the political surface there was a fundamental continuity of institutions. The organization of the empire with its praetorian prefectures, its separate military and civilian commands, its tax system administered through the greatly increased number of provinces, and the military with their supply system all endured. Alongside these formal institutions new conventions had developed as well, such as that emperors could be made in the field by a consensus of senior military figures and that decisions were made at court by a slightly different inner circle, especially if the emperor was a child. Fundamental to all this was military security. Wars with Persia shifted the frontier back and forth but did not disrupt either power. Threats occasionally appeared from north of the Danube or east of the Rhine, but they were contained, often by barbarian troops and sometimes barbarian generals, but all fighting for Rome.

One vivid illustration of the essential continuity of the work of government is the collection of imperial rulings compiled between 435 and 438 in the reign of Theodosius II. This record of all imperial edicts issued since the start of the reign of Constantine was compiled and then distributed in both halves of the empire.[16] The code illustrates both the strengths and limitations of imperial government. The capacity to plan and execute such a project in such a short time shows how the imperial bureaucracy could be put to work and produce results. Yet the fact that to compile this collection it was necessary to write to provincial governors all over the empire asking for copies of any edicts they had filed away shows an astonishing lack of record-keeping at the centre. The desire to make a complete collection, to order it logically by sixteen themed books, and to remove contradictions and inconsistencies perfectly expresses both the aspiration to rational, universal rule and the gap between that ideal and reality. That it was carried out as late as the 430s shows that, despite the disasters of the generation following Adrianople, the empire and imperial society were definitely one thing and not two in the minds of the emperor and his staff. Starting the record with the reign of Constantine is also a rare testimony to an ancient concept approaching our modern one of a 'later Roman Empire'. Theodosius' great project was identified immediately with imperial monarchy. The clearest sign is not the elaborate ceremony with which the emperor presented a copy to an ambassador of the western Senate attending him in Constantinople or the adulatory acclamations by senators when they received the work, a record of which forms a preface to the work, but the fact that in the centuries to come, whenever barbarian warlords across the former western empire tried to convert themselves into hereditary monarchs with courts and ceremonial of their own, one of the first things they did was to issue their own codes of law.

Behind the Frontiers

The emperors of the fourth century spent most of their reigns with the armies. Support from the troops and their fellow officers had raised many of them to the purple, and some were brought down when they lost it. Some campaigns were fought within the empire, mostly against would-be usurpers like Magnus Maximus, but most were in the northern provinces or on the eastern frontier. Alamanni, Franks, and others threatened Gaul from across the Rhine; north of the Danube were Sarmatians, the provinces of Dacia abandoned by Aurelian, and the Goths across the lower Danube. Tetrarchic bases at Milan, Serdica (modern Sofia, the birthplace of both Aurelian and Galerius), and Sirmium in northern Serbia placed emperors close to the main points from which Italy would be threatened. When affairs with Persia were tense, a base farther east was more useful; hence the cities of Constantinople, Nicomedia, and Nicaea on either side of the Bosporus, and in time of actual warfare Antioch. This long frontier, from York to Alexandria, contained much of the high politics of the fourth century. Church councils and court politics took place there as well as diplomacy and preparations for war.

But this was not the entire empire, and in most of the Mediterranean world conditions were quite different.[17] Most obviously, security had been restored. At the peak of the military crisis, different groups of northerners had raided deep into Gaul and even Iberia, ancient Aegean cities like Athens and Ephesus had been attacked, and even Italy was not immune. The fact that Aurelian took time and expense to build a new massive wall circuit around the city of Rome—the first for six centuries—showed how seriously these threats were taken. Around the empire, there are accounts of local heroes stepping in to defend cities the empire could not save. During the long fourth century, these threats receded again, and civic life flourished.[18] The literature that survives from this period in Latin and especially in Greek provides some vivid glimpses.

The speeches and letters of the orator and teacher Libanius give some sense of how things looked to one member of the traditional civic elites. Libanius was born in 314 and died in 393, so saw the birth of Constantine's Christian empire, got to know Julian, whom he admired, and lived through the disaster of Adrianople in 387 and the establishment of the Theodosian dynasty. But his life, much of which we know through an autobiography composed in his sixtieth year, was mostly lived in the great cities of the eastern Mediterranean. Brought up in Antioch, he went to study in Athens. The emergency defences built across the agora after the city was sacked by the Heruli in 267 AD would have been evident, but the city had recovered as a centre for students from all over the Greek world. He spent the 340s teaching rhetoric at Constantinople and Nicomedia and attracted the patronage of Constantius II but declined an imperially funded post in Athens and instead returned to his native Antioch in 354, mostly teaching but sometimes corresponding with leading figures of the day. Antioch, an old Seleucid capital, was one of the largest cities of the Roman world. It had large Christian and Jewish communities, alongside a sizeable population who worshipped traditional gods, mostly now in a Hellenized form. Libanius' writings illuminate riots, conflicts between the city and various emperors, tensions with the large military garrisons stationed there, and the efforts members of the elite put into maintaining good relations across religious divides. Libanius' pupils included future bishops and fellow polytheists. Some of the same concerns emerge in the writings of the Christian priest John Chrysostom, who preached there from 386–97. Both Libanius and John Chrysostom found themselves at times appealing to emperors on behalf of their fellow citizens, just as the greatest sophists of the second and early third century had done.[19]

Many literary figures writing in Greek looked back not just to the early empire but to classical Greece. Plato was now the central figure for polytheist theologians and philosophers. Many existing genres, such as epigram, thrived. Historians writing in Greek, of whom the most important were Eunapius and Olympiodorus, self-consciously continued a tradition that was nearly a thousand years long. For this reason, they are sometimes termed 'classicizing'.[20] This was not in itself new. Arrian of Nicomedia, who governed Cappadocia in the reign of Hadrian, wrote in the style of Xenophon. Cassius Dio, another Bithynian Greek senator, this time of the Severan period, composed a *Roman History* in which the thought and language of Thucydides is never very far below the surface.[21] So Eunapius imitated and continued Philostratus's biographies of sophists and other intellectuals, now of the fourth century AD. His history, like that of Zosimus in a later age, was a self-conscious alternative to the Christianized versions that were becoming the official narrative.

One change in the social structure of the Greek cities of late antiquity was the emergence of the bishop as a major figure in civic society. During the fourth century bishops were typically elected locally and were very often from the same social and cultural background as those who served on the town councils and held the highest offices in the city. Members of those classes now had a wider range of career paths than had their ancestors or predecessors, who were often compelled by a combination of local pressure and imperial ruling to take on magistracies and priesthoods that were expensive as well as distinguished. Now a small number entered the church, often rising rapidly to the bishopric, and a larger number entered imperial service, so escaping local obligations.[22] Eventually, this had severe consequences for civic finances, but during the fourth century great cities like Antioch, Caesarea, and Alexandria remained major and dynamic centres.

The same was also true in some western centres. The late antique life of North Africa is particularly well known, largely from Christian texts. Among them are the apologetic writings of Tertullian, the letters of Cyprian, bishop of Carthage, and the *Confessions* and letters of Augustine, who was born in 354 and died in 430 AD. Augustine's early career tracks that of his older contemporary Libanius. He was born into the curial classes (if in a much smaller city), and his studies in rhetoric led him into a career in teaching, first in Carthage, where his account of student life compares with Libanius's account of that of Athens, and then via Rome to the imperial court at Milan. Augustine, unlike Libanius, had been born into a Christian family and ended his life as a bishop back in Africa. But en route he offers snapshots of the cultural life of a great city, its public debates, the games, the tensions between local and imperial demands. He was well aware of the high politics of his age, especially during his time in Italy, and lived to see the Vandals invade Africa. Carthage fell to them in 439, just a few years after his death.

Rome itself exemplified all these trends and more. It was no longer the habitual seat of the emperors. Milan was better connected and closer to the frontiers, and perhaps too the imperial court worked better at a slight distance from the seat of ancient religious and political offices. There was

no point at which it ceased being an imperial capital, and the transition
was easier because the vague definition of the powers of early Roman
emperors had never included one particular seat of government. As early
as the reign of Augustus, there had been long periods when ambassadors
and courtiers had to seek out emperors wherever they happened to be.
But up until the Severi, it seemed important for emperors to build in the
city and spend time on the Palatine and with the Senate. Many third-
century emperors never made it to Rome, and after that imperial visits
became major events. Diocletian visited only once, in 303, and when
Constantine defeated Maxentius at the Milvian Bridge just north of the
city, the Senate hurriedly put together a great arch for him, decorated with
elements stripped from existing monuments. He returned only twice in
his long reign. Constantius II visited for the first time in 357; Ammianus
Marcellinus wrote a vivid description of Constantius' visit, twenty years
after his accession. The next imperial visit was that of Theodosius in 389.
Emperors sent money, sponsored the restoration of ancient buildings and
the construction of new churches, but mostly they ruled the city remotely
through a senatorial urban prefect.

One effect of these changes was to open up space for the senatorial
elite to become prominent in the city once again. The correspondence of
Symmachus, who was urban prefect in the 380s, shows something of the
character of this elite, a picture to which archaeology is rapidly adding precision.[23] Some of the families were staggeringly rich, possessing estates all
over the Roman world. Part of this represented a cumulative unification
of the landowning classes of Gaul, Iberia, North Africa, and Italy in particular, since many eastern families were recruited to Constantine's new
senate in Constantinople. The senate still provided governors for many of
these regions. There were still praetors and consuls and all the traditional
priesthoods, the festivals, the games and social rituals. The Latin literature
of the day frequently looked back to Cicero and Livy, Virgil and Caesar,
and Pliny the Younger. Some of this was a minority interest, but oratory
and correspondence referred to a shared past.[24] Their world had contracted;
they no longer provided an aristocracy of service, and the population of
the city of Rome itself was smaller than in the age of Augustus. Politically,
they were more remote from the court than ever, and from time to time
there were breakdowns in relations, although these were generally quickly
mended. And as in other cities, there was now a bishop, the social equal of

aristocrats, if less influential on the wider stage than might be a bishop based in Milan or Constantinople. An elaborate etiquette allowed polytheists and Christians to maintain social ties for much of the time.

Occasional clashes over religion occurred, in Rome as in Antioch and Alexandria. The best-attested is a simmering dispute over the presence of an altar to the goddess Victoria in the Senate House at Rome. Gratian, in 382, had been the first emperor to refuse the title pontifex maximus and followed up by abolishing state support for public ritual, including the salaries paid to the Vestals, and ordering the removal of the altar. Two years later Symmachus appealed to Valentinian for its restoration. An exchange of letters survives including his arguments in favour and the counterarguments of Ambrose, bishop of Milan. The issue divided the Senate, Christian senators siding with Damasus, bishop of Rome, against restoration, the praetorian prefect Vettius Agorius Praetextatus, a polytheist, being presumed to be on the other side. Symmachus was unsuccessful. Less than a decade later, another emperor, Theodosius I, enacted a more hardline edict banning private and public sacrifices of all kinds throughout the empire. The repercussions of the edict issued in February 391 spread over the next few months. In Egypt, it was used by the bishop of Alexandria as a pretext for destroying the temple of Sarapis. In Rome, it combined with the chaos unleashed by the death of Valentinian II to prompt a brief civil war in which the polytheist prae-torian prefect of Italy, Nichomachus Flavianus, and a pretender Eugenius led an army north that was defeated by that of Theodosius on the River Frigidus in 394. These events, however much they passionately engaged contemporaries, represented brief episodes in the history of the western aristocracies and in the replacement of polytheism with various varieties of Christianity. Those social and religious transformations took generations to work through.

For most of the fourth century the elite of Rome, like their counterparts in Alexandria, Antioch, and Carthage, enjoyed a life of relative leisure. The residences of the wealthy, in the city and in their vast rural estates, were spectacular. Below the tip of this social iceberg, the Mediterranean economy flourished, as is clear from the distribution of amphorae and red-slip ceramic, from the archaeology of Ostia and Marseilles and Carthage and Aquileia, and from casual references in many late antique sources.[25] Military threats must have seemed far away, like the emperors whose benefactions and draconian regulations were as unpredictable as the weather.

Further Reading

Tim Barnes's *New Empire of Diocletian and Constantine* (Cambridge, MA, 1982) is the basis for understanding the transformation of Roman government at the end of the third century, and is much more than a companion piece to his *Constantine and Eusebius* (Cambridge, MA, 1981). The institutions of the empire are described in detail in A. H. M. Jones's *Later Roman Empire* (Oxford, 1964): how they worked in practice is the subject of Christopher Kelly's *Ruling the Later Roman Empire* (Cambridge, MA, 2004). John Matthews's *Roman Empire of Ammianus* (London, 1989) offers a vivid picture of the empire before and just after the disasters of Adrianople, one that encompasses politics and society. A particularly useful set of essays is included in Simon Swain and Mark Edwards's *Approaching Late Antiquity* (Oxford, 2004). Among many histories of the period the last two volumes of the Routledge History of the Ancient World, both recently revised, are particularly helpful. They are David Potter's *The Roman Empire at Bay AD 180–395* (Abingdon, 2014) and Averil Cameron's *The Mediterranean World in Late Antiquity AD 395–700* (London, 2012)

Alongside these studies focused on politics and institutions, late antiquity has emerged as a vast field of cultural history. Peter Brown's *World of Late Antiquity* (London, 1971) was in some ways the manifesto for this approach. His own voluminous writings and those of his students and associates have explored with subtlety the rich material offered by Christian writings. His *Augustine of Hippo* (rev. edn, London, 2000) shows just how much can be mined from this seam. Perhaps the best conspectus of late antiquity is offered by *Late Antiquity: A Guide to the Postclassical World*, edited by Glen Bowersock, Peter Brown, and Oleg Grabar (Cambridge, MA, 1999).

A CHRISTIAN EMPIRE

> You asked me to write an answer to the lying distortions spouted by those people who are strangers to the City of God. They are called pagans after the rustic crossroads and villages (*pagi*) they inhabit and foreigners (*gentiles*) because all they know about are earthly matters. They have no interest in things to come; as for the past, they have either forgotten it or are simply ignorant. Nevertheless, they still claim that the present day is unusually beset with disasters for this one reason alone, that men believe in Christ and worship God, while idols receive less and less cult.
>
> (Orosius, *History against the Pagans*, Preface 9)

The Rise of Religions

Once upon a time, the Romans felt they enjoyed the special favour of their gods. Those gods were in a sense their fellow citizens. I described in Chapter VIII how their worship in the public rituals—the *sacra publica*—of Rome was the organizing centre of the religious lives and identities of the Romans. How this cohered with the public cults of the other communities of the empire was never formally specified. But the many polytheistic religious systems of the peoples living around the Mediterranean were broadly similar. Roman rule had made them more alike, and local gods were often represented as the counterparts of Jupiter, Mercury, Mars, Saturn, Juno, and the rest. Most now had temples and statues in human form and received the same kind of prayers, offerings and sacrifices as the gods long worshipped in Italy. Worship of the emperors had now been added in most areas. Across the empire, the wealthy built temples, took on priesthoods, and celebrated festivals: all seemed to prosper.[1]

Abandoning this pact with heaven must have disturbed many polytheists. As the empire's defences began to collapse again at the end of the fourth century, it seemed an act of lunacy. No wonder Rome's fortune was faltering now it had abandoned the gods who promoted her rise. Augustine, writing *The City of God* after the first sack of Rome in 410, felt he had to answer these charges. Roman success owed nothing to the cult of the gods, he argued, since there were disasters even in the period of pagan worship. Religious piety brought rewards in the next world, not this one. Earthly disasters like the sack of Rome were irrelevant. Can Augustine have really thought this? He wrote *The City of God* as bishop of the African city of Hippo Regius, but in his earlier career he had been a professor at Carthage, had then been headhunted by the senatorial prefect of Rome for a more prestigious position there, and then finally went to the western imperial capital at Milan. Only in Milan had God claimed him and brought him back via communities of contemplative scholars to lead the Christians of this small town in North Africa, not so far from the even smaller town where he had been brought up. Even so, he cannot have failed to be shocked by the events of the early fifth century. Africa was far from the collapsing northern frontier, and the world Augustine had been born into, where he had studied and taught, had been thoroughly Roman. The move to Rome had attracted him because of the reputed quietness of the students compared with those of Carthage. At Milan he must have become more aware of the deteriorating situation, but the fall of Rome shocked everyone. The Vandals were already in Spain as he wrote; before his death they would cross the Straits of Gibraltar and begin the short war that would result in their capture of Carthage.

Among the refugees from Spain who fled to Africa was Orosius, who became a pupil of Augustine and in 417 wrote at his suggestion another response, a seven-volume *History against the Pagans*. The preface states that pagans in their ignorance had claimed that there were now more calamities and disasters because men believed in Christ and worshipped God and increasingly neglected the worship of idols. Orosius set out to demonstrate the many disasters of earlier days. The result is an alternative history of the world, six books relating events up to the birth of Christ, the last offering a fascinating narration of Roman history in which acts of imperial tyranny and military disasters are ameliorated by the power of God as the number of Christians in the empire grows.

The gap between traditional beliefs and the new Christian history was just part of a wider shift in world view. Christians not only disagreed with others about the reason for the current crisis; they also disagreed about the relationship of the cosmological with the political and social order of things. Traditionally, ritual action had been mostly performed by and for existing social entities, such as the family, the city, the army unit, or the empire itself. Christian communities, by contrast, were composed of believers who might have little in common except their belief, and who might be separated by that belief from other members of their families, cities, and so on. Nor were Christians alone in this. Manichaeans, Jews, and several other groups had also come to think of their religious identities as something separable from other aspects of their social roles. Augustine expressed this more clearly than most in his distinction between the temporal Earthly City and the City of God, but the idea had become widespread. It is this idea from which has grown our notion of 'religion' as a separate sphere of life. The history of the Roman Empire had intersected with an even grander narrative, the rise of religions.

The emergence of religions—in the sense of bounded entities with their own beliefs, practices, structures of authority and so on—is a relatively recent development in world history.[2] Humans have had ritual much longer, probably as long as there have been humans. Ritual behaviour is one of the few things that genuinely separates us from other animal species. There are other species which make and use tools, have some kind of language, and live in complex societies. Humans alone bury their dead, make art and music and dance, and perform ceremonies together.[3] Our capacity to do so most likely derives from specific modes of cognition that all humans share; it is reflected in our habit of 'ritualizing' everyday objects, places, and especially activities. For most of history ritual has been closely woven into our experience of everyday life, carried out at births and deaths, when crops were sown or harvested, when animals were hunted or killed, at special meals, and on other occasions through the year. City state societies harnessed the power of collective ritual when they were created, marking out common spaces as sanctuaries and temples, and establishing calendars of festivals that brought the community together at regular intervals. Religious authority was usually concentrated in the hands of their rulers. This can be attested from early states around the world, but the societies of the ancient Mediterranean are unusually well documented. It was more or less impossible to separate Athenian or Roman religious identity from their wider senses of belonging. Conversion is more or less meaningless in antiquity, unless as one component of changing one's citizenship.[4] Our modern concept of a religion as an organized body of people, practices, and beliefs, and a sense of exclusive adherence and identity—that one must choose which *one* religion to belong to—only became generalized around the world in the nineteenth century.[5] The Roman period was, in western Eurasia, a key moment in the emergence of entities that would give rise to modern religions.

The separation out of religion as a distinct sphere that occurred during the last centuries BC had many roots. The new differentiated groups that were created with religion at their core drew on various models. Euripides' *Bacchae*, written at the very end of the fifth century BC, told the story of how Pentheus, the king of Thebes, refused to allow his people to worship the god Dionysus, whose ecstatic rites challenged the rational order of the city. The god easily escaped imprisonment and lured Pentheus out onto the mountainside, where he was attacked and dismembered by a party of Dionysus' frenzied women followers led by Pentheus' mother. The play dramatizes the disruptive power of a religious movement that challenged the religious authority of leading members of the city and might divide families and communities down the middle. This Dionysiac cult represents one of several origins of religious pluralism. Rome experienced its own panic about Bacchanales in 186 BC. Rumours circulated, as they later did in the case of Christianity, about strange nocturnal rituals. But it is clear that what really shocked was the lack of respect for social boundaries and the implicit challenge to existing religious authority and social convention.

These specifically religious groups became more widespread in the Hellenistic and early Roman periods.[6] The name Dionysus appears in texts from the Greek Bronze Age, and he had a central role in Athenian public religion signified by the festival of the Greater Dionysia. It was not the god himself, but the form of worship and association represented by Bacchism and its challenge to existing religious authority that shocked. Other groups began as the cults of migrant populations which then attracted worshippers from their host communities. The goddess Isis, originally part of the Bronze Age pantheon of Egypt, underwent various transformations and, in a Hellenized form, became popular around the Mediterranean.[7] So did the Baalim of various Syrian cities, the Great Mother of the Gods from Pessinus in Asia Minor, and the god of the Jews. Populations moved about within the Persian, Hellenistic, and Roman empires for all sorts of reasons; traders, slaves, soldiers, colonists, and missionaries circulated around the urban system, bringing their gods with them.[8] Some were given public cult in some cities, as Thracian Bendis was in Athens and Phrygian Magna Mater in Rome, while others remained marginal.

Another model was provided by the mystery cults that proliferated in this period, many imitating the original Mysteries of Demeter and the Maiden at Eleusis, once the main cult of an independent city but swallowed up into Athenian religion in the archaic age. The key feature here was the creation of a group of initiates, which in the Hellenistic period came to include individuals from far and wide. Sanctuaries like that of the Great Gods on Samothrace attracted pilgrims too.[9] Some more mobile groups, including the worshippers of Cybele and Mithras, developed their own mysteries.[10] Philosophical sects provided yet another model of groups with a single name—Epicureans, Stoics, Cynics—often a charismatic founder, and authoritative texts, a group one could join or leave as one chose. Some Greek and Roman writers thought of Christianity as very similar to these philosophical groups. Around the same time, Jewish writers identified different traditions within Judaism; at least one, the Qumran community known from the Dead Sea Scrolls, looks very much like a religion. As diasporas proliferated in new conditions created by empires, urbanization, and increased long distance travel, there is a common pattern where local traditions that had originated in one specific place and were associated with one particular people were globalized. This process often included a shift of emphasis from a real to a mythologized sacred landscape, an emphasis on texts and lifestyles over particular temples or rituals tied to particular places, a simplification of divine hierarchies, and claims of universal validity. It is possible to see this happening with traditional Roman, Egyptian, and Greek cult. Examples of this move from 'locative' to 'utopian' forms also include the creation of Hellenized versions of Egyptian deities like Isis and Serapis, the growth of rabbinical traditions within Judaism, and, of course, Christianity. Almost all these groups were occasionally targeted in one city or another as new or foreign. Roman authorities turned their fire on Bacchanales, Isis worshippers, Jews, astrologers, and Christians.

Yet religious groups of this kind continued to thrive, and new ones were created by charismatic founders. Mithraism and Manichaeanism both represent religions created from scratch, drawing on symbols, rituals, and divine names from older traditions but brought together into completely new combinations, well suited to the social environments within which they sought recruits. There was some competition for worshippers, or at least for the gifts they might bring. Successful features of one tradition would be imitated and appropriated by another. The ancient Mysteries of Eleusis were copied on Samothrace, by the worshippers of Cybele, Mithras, and other groups; standard Greek anthropomorphic imagery was widely adopted; astrology was incorporated into almost every religious tradition from Judaism and Mithraism to the worship of Egyptian and German deities. Another sign of competition was the effort made to retain the attention of worshippers. Mithraists, in at least some places, were invited to proceed through a series of grades; initiates at Eleusis had to return for a second initiation in a subsequent year; the ritual of the Taurobolium, a bull sacrifice associated with Cybele, had to be repeated every twenty years; and priests at healing sanctuaries and oracles advertised their successes and encouraged return visits.

Perhaps the first claims to a monopoly on truth emerged out of this competitive urge. The idea that a person might focus in a personal way on one god within a polytheist pantheon was an old one, and one exploited by Romans from the Republican period on.[11] Sulla cultivated the idea he was a special favourite of Venus, Augustus claimed the favour of Apollo, Vespasian was assisted in his coup by Isis, and so on. Many gods were hailed in dedicatory inscriptions as the 'Greatest and Best' or the 'Most High'.[12] Giving one deity a special place is sometimes called henotheism. Some Isiac revelatory texts claim Isis is the 'true' name of a goddess also worshipped under other names, including Cybele, Artemis, Venus, and Hecate. It was a further step to claim all other gods were powerless or malevolent demons or did not even exist. The history of Judaism shows a gradual move from polytheism to monotheism, and from disparaging the gods of others to regarding them as not divine or even non existant. Ideas of this kind became a source of conflict in the larger cities, where different groups met, and when those sorts of claims encountered the equally exclusive demands of universal empires.

Early Christianity emerged from within this complex religious environment, in some senses a utopian and universalized version of Judaism, but also borrowing language from philosophical groups and the idea of a *mystērion* from Greek religious traditions. One inheritance from its Jewish roots was the demand that members form an exclusive attachment to Christ, something other initiatory traditions did not demand. The earliest Christian texts emphasise the novelty and uniqueness of the group. Paul had declared that in Christ 'there is neither Jew nor Greek, slave nor free, male nor female'.[13] Texts like this assert the existence of a new social identity based solely on religious membership, one that cuts across the most fundamental social boundaries of antiquity. Christian tradition often presents this as a single moment of revelatory refinement, a parting of the ways with Judaism, a radical change. Reality was more complex. There were Jewish Christians and there were Christians for whom traditional gods were quite real but demonic. There were other traditions emerging from the same background like the Mandaeans of Mesopotamia, whose rituals and texts were formed in the course of a long dialogue with Judaism, Zoroastrianism, Christianity, and later Islam. Christianity was itself appropriated, modified, and incorporated by other new groups like the Manichaeans, whose founder drew on Christian, Zoroastrian, Jewish, and Buddhist traditions. Julian's paganism imitated the organizational structure of Christianity, while rejecting its content for a universal polytheism in which Platonic philosophy, the ancient cults of Rome, and the traditions of Greek Antioch and Jewish Jerusalem would all have a place. Manichaean missionaries were sent to North Africa, India, and ultimately central Asia and China too. Some of these changes were gradual but, in some cases, like the creation of Manichaeism and or Islam, were experienced as moments of revelatory simplification and refinement. This was no longer the world of ethnic polytheisms within which Rome and its rival city states had been formed. Empires had partly brought about the conditions for this reconfiguration of the religious landscape, but this did not mean they found it easy to deal with.

The Rise of Christianity

Modern estimates of the growth of Christianity stress the very small scale of its beginnings. It is difficult to imagine what life was like for the first generation of Christians: they had no Gospels or other Scriptures, most had been born Jews, and many still thought of themselves as bound by Mosaic Law. They numbered in the low thousands and were widely scattered, mostly in the larger cities of the eastern Mediterranean world.[14] Paul's Letters and the account of his travels in Acts give some sense of how these groups kept in touch and maintained some sort of cohesion. Authority, purity, and the relationship with the Jewish tradition were already issues in the first century

AD communities he interacted with around the Aegean world. But there are huge gaps in our knowledge. By late antiquity there were major Christian communities in North Africa and Egypt, but we know virtually nothing of their origins. The emergence of a greater concern with orthodoxy and discipline in later centuries produced highly edited accounts of the early Church. But the story they tell of a single set of teachings communicated and spread by a small corps of Apostles is a pious invention. So are many later accounts of second- and third-century martyrs produced for congregations for whom persecution was receding into the past and who had much to gain from elevating the status of local saints. Christian writers and Jewish leaders, for their own reasons, also came to assert a sharp and early divide between Christianity and Judaism. That divide would be entrenched in the fourth century with the aid of imperial muscle.[15] Constantine's religious legislation differentiated firmly between Jews and Christians, subjecting the former to severe restrictions and distributing privileges to the latter. It is only recently that historians have begun to appreciate how polemical and untrustworthy many early texts (from all sides) are.

Christianity emerges from the shadows during the second century AD.[16] House-based communities and elders gave way over that century to city-wide communities each led by one bishop. Who this would be was often disputed. Ideally, a bishop was both chosen by the community and endorsed by other bishops in the vicinity. There was no organization at a higher level, although bishops of larger cities, like Cyprian of Carthage, often exercised a regional influence. Meanwhile, the number of Christians grew exponentially. Many must have felt themselves surrounded by converts and part of a mushrooming movement. Yet absolute numbers remained small: non-Christian texts hardly remark on the existence of Christians before the year 200. From the later second century, we have the first evidence for Christian communities in North Africa and in Gaul. Most seem to have used Greek, which suggests their closest connections remained with the eastern Mediterranean. Something close to our notion of the New Testament had emerged by this period too, although the inclusion of some books, such as Revelation, remained controversial. A mass of other writing is known too, among them letters, apologetic writing, the first martyr acts, and theological treatises. Latin translations of Christian Scripture began to circulate by the middle of the second century. By the end of the second century many works were directed at heretics, those considered to hold false beliefs, like the Marcionites, who rejected the Jewish scriptures in their entirety. Schismatics were those thought to have had the right beliefs but rejected the authority of the proper authorities. Heresy and schism were, naturally, a matter of perspective.

The rise of episcopal authority was intimately connected with the rise of orthodoxy. The life and work of Irenaeus of Lyons offers an early example. Eusebius, in his *History of the Church* written shortly after Constantine's conversion, states that Irenaeus was a pupil of the martyred Bishop Polycarp of Smyrna, himself believed to be a disciple of the Apostle John. But that kind of genealogy was a conventional way of establishing authority. At some point, Irenaeus appears as a priest in the Greek-speaking Christian community of Lyons, around the time of a local persecution recorded by Eusebius and dated to the reign of Marcus Aurelius. That community sent Irenaeus as an envoy to the Bishop of Rome because of their concerns about the news that Montanus, a priest in central Anatolia, claimed to have received a new prophecy from God. Montanism was just the first heresy Irenaeus set out to refute. As Bishop of Lyons, he wrote copious works in Greek, among them a defence of the canonical status of the four Gospels, and one of the earliest heresiologies, or catalogues of heresies. The immediate inspiration for that work was the arrival in Lyons of a group of Greek merchants spreading the ideas of Valentinus, whose blend of Christian thought and mystical revelation produced an early form of what is now termed Gnosticism. But for Irenaeus the error could be traced all the way back to the magician Simon Magus, who appears in Acts, thus creating a genealogy of error that could be set against the genealogy of orthodox teaching. Hippolytus, the Bishop of Rome, also opposed Valentinianism, using some of Irenaeus' writings to do so. Both the campaign against Montanism and that against the teachings of Valentinus illustrate the interconnectedness of early Christian communities across the Mediterranean. Within that network new ideas circulated rapidly, carried by both missionaries and texts. From late antiquity several large bodies of episcopal letters survive, concerned above all to maintain a united front against schism and heresy. The organization of the Church was generated from below, its institutions and higher-level authorities a creation of those obsessed by unity. Bishops closed ranks around Scripture and opposed the threats to their authority posed by new revelations and charismatic prophets.[17]

Christian communities devoted enormous energy to this activity, but it was largely esoteric. Non-Christians probably knew relatively little about their actual beliefs or concerns, just as many were ignorant about the Jews in their midst. A small number of local persecutions are recorded. Most are known through the writings of Eusebius and his early fourth-century contemporaries, who were keen to gather accounts of the deeds and deaths of martyrs. Roman governors and emperors did not extend to Christians the protection they sometimes gave Jewish communities in similar circumstances. Letters between Pliny while governor of Bithynia-Pontus and Trajan indicate that some kind of ban existed—the origins are obscure—but emperors were not keen to enforce it. Persecution was probably less common than simple unpopularity. Until the early third century, Christians were perhaps a rather introverted group, if a growing one. Few scholars believe more than 10 per cent of the empire's subjects were Christians in Constantine's day, and the figures could easily be even smaller. Very few Christians of high social status are known before the third century AD.

The first general persecution, as discussed in Chapter XV, was that organized by the Emperor Decius in 250 AD. The immediate context was the refusal of some Christian leaders and communities to participate in a great *supplicatio* declared because of the military crisis, and also the unintended consequences of Caracalla's mass enfranchisement.[18] But there are broader contexts to the persecutions led by Decius and Valerian and Diocletian, and also the various edicts of toleration from Gallienus and Galerius to Constantine and Licinius. These tend to be written as episodes in the relations between the emperors and the Christians, and so they were. But they also reflect a wider encounter between the universal empires of late antiquity and the newly emergent world religions.

Diocletian's edict against the Christians in 303 was preceded the year before by a letter to the proconsul of Egypt commanding him to punish the Manichaeans. The stated objections were the novelty of their ideas, their opposition to the traditional gods, and their association with Persia. The teachings of Mani were condemned as superstitions and errors and were also contrasted with the traditional and ancestral cults of the gods. Manichaean missionaries and sacred texts should be burned, and if any Roman of high status had converted, then his property was forfeit, and he would be sent to the mines. It was quite correct that Mani had been born in Persia and spent much of his life there, but by Diocletian's reign Manichaeans were being persecuted in the Persian Empire. They were not alone. The Persian emperor Sapor died in 270, and under his successors the Zoroastrian priesthood gained increased influence at court. The priest Kirdir boasted in a rock-cut inscription that he had promoted the worship of Ahura-Mazda throughout every province of the empire and led attacks on 'Jews, and Buddhists and Brahmins and Aramaic- and Greek-speaking Christians and Baptisers and Manichaeans'.[19] The Baptizers were a Mesopotamian group derived from Jewish Christians opposed to the Apostle Paul, and the community in which Mani had himself grown up. Persecution of non-Zoroastrians persisted in the Persian Empire. During the last years of Constantine's reign some Christians in Persia looked to him as a natural ally against their Sassanian overlords, but his support further alienated them from the Persians.[20]

These events illustrate several things. It is striking how many different religious groups existed in the late third century that no longer fitted into the social frames provided by family, city, and empire. The Roman and Persian emperors seem still to have been thinking (or at least speaking) an older language of religion. They worried about novelty (as had Socrates' accusers) and an attack on traditional gods. They associated religious movements with populations (Jews, Romans, Persians, and so on) and were disturbed by religious practices they regarded as foreign in those terms, just as the worship of Egyptian and Jewish gods had sometimes been viewed in the past. One thing that was new was a shared assumption that each empire should have a primary religious identity, whether polytheist, Christian, or Zoroastrian. Behind this seems to be an anxiety about dissonance between universal empires and universal religions. The Romans of the early empire had never imposed one religion on their subjects. What we term the imperial cult was in fact the product of the insertion of the emperor's name and image into hundreds of local systems. The Achaemenid Persians, in some respects the model for Sapor and his successors, sponsored the worship of Marduk in Babylonia, Yahweh in Jerusalem, and Apollo at Magnesia on the Maeander, as well as Ahura Mazda, the Zoroastrian deity. Perhaps neither Roman nor Persian emperors realized how much the religious world had changed, but it had.

A Christian Emperor

Why was persecution abandoned? If it was popular and created an enhanced sense of loyalty and solidarity within the empire, why stop? Christian apologists claimed that persecution accelerated conversion, because the example set by the martyrs impressed persecutors and (in the arena) audiences too. Yet comparative evidence does suggest the near eradication of Christianity was not an unrealistic aim. Manichaeism was eventually persecuted out of existence in the west by the combined action of Christian Roman emperors and Zoroastrian Persian shahs. Buddhism was more or less extinguished in medieval India, first by monarchs dominated by Brahmin elites, and then by Muslim conquerors. Only fragments of the Christian communities of Roman Syria, Africa, and Spain survived the rule of the Islamic caliphate, despite the fact that overt religious discrimination was, in fact, unusual in its territories. Perhaps Diocletian could not have completely wiped out a group growing so fast, but he might well have been able to marginalize it and reverse the progress it was making in higher-status social groups. Was persecution of Christians a failure in the Roman world because Christians were not sufficiently hated to make a suitable target? Were their enemies insufficiently organized or motivated? Or was persecution simply too expensive to promote in regions where there were no local zealots?

The Great Persecution had a lasting legacy. Church historians emphasized martyrdom, but this was probably rare in many parts of the empire. There is some question how far the persecution was put into effect in the western provinces apart from Africa. The few who had died for their faith and those who had been tortured rather than surrender sacred texts were later idolized, to the irritation of those bishops who had neither died nor been tortured. A schism broke out in North Africa between those Christians who had handed over sacred books and those who were accused of effectively seeking out martyrdom. The death in 311 of Mensurius, the Bishop of Carthage, associated with those who had not taken a stand, triggered a crisis of authority. That culminated in a division between the Donatists (named after their bishop Donatus) and those who followed Mensurius' line. Rival bishops and congregations appeared in many cities, and the division remained until the early fifth century.

Emperors, on the other hand, were all probably motivated by a desire for unity. If persecution could not unite the empire, something else would have to be tried. Edicts of Toleration were issued by Galerius in 311 and by Constantine and Licinius at Milan in 313. Toleration, or at least a cessation of persecution, was not in itself so strange. Something similar had in effect happened between the reigns of Valerian and Diocletian. Much more remarkable was that, around 312, Constantine began to actively patronize the Christians. Almost immediately he began work on a great series of basilicas around the city of Rome: St John Lateran and the original (Old) St Peter's are among them. Most were complete by the mid-320s.

There are various literary references to churches in the third century AD but few, if any, can have been monumental. Christian communities, who initially used all sorts of buildings for worship, many of them private houses, are almost invisible archaeologically before the later second century.[21] In this respect at least, Constantine's patronage was revolutionary for Christians. Other second- and third-century emperors had paid particular attention to specific deities, and some had built them vast temples in the capital. Hadrian built the great temple of Venus and Rome on a platform between the forum Romanum and the Colosseum. Commodus had himself portrayed as Hercules and had the Neronian colossal statue of Sol remodelled as Hercules.[22] Less successful was the attempt by Elagabalus to install the cult of the chief god of Syrian Emesa in Rome. But Aurelian created a vast temple of the Sun with the spoils of his war against the Palmyran secessionists, and Diocletian used Jupiter and Hercules to represent himself and Maximinus, and the parallel adoptive dynasties they were to found. During his rise to power Constantine had been associated in much more conventional ways with Hercules, Apollo, and the Undefeated Sun. The city of Rome in Constantine's day had not been Christianized; rather, the temples of yet another emperor's divine familiar had been added to its crowded sacred landscape.[23] Christ was, however, a different kind of deity, one not recognizable to most Romans in the way that Hercules and Sol were. Nor were his worshippers influential figures whose support was worth seeking. While the tradition of imperial temple building offers one kind of context to understand Constantine's actions, and conversion offered Christians another context, neither seems to offer a complete explanation. The polarization of the source tradition does not help us reconstruct Constantine's designs, but sometimes it feels as if he was deliberately engaged in a complex balancing act.

Constantine did not require his courtiers to convert; yet many did. And there were new, powerful figures around the emperor. Constantine gave a range of legal privileges to Christian bishops, and some had extraordinary access to him; as always in the imperial court, access meant influence. Constantine also lavished on them the most precious resource an emperor possessed, his own time. Almost as soon as he had declared his patronage of Christianity, he was petitioned by members of both factions in the Donatist schism. Petitioning an emperor was a perfectly common procedure, and it is not surprising that Christians made use of it. Yet where many petitions received a short answer or resulted in an instruction to a governor or city council, in this case the emperor did give it his genuinely personal attention. It can only be concluded that at a very early stage Constantine's advisers had impressed on him not just the importance of unity and orthodoxy, but also that neutrality was not an option for the emperor. Was Constantine an innocent drawn into problems, the complexity of which he did not understand? Or a zealot inspired to devote the juridical power of the emperor, as well as his wealth, to the benefit of the Church? Or was he, in fact, a very traditional Roman emperor concerned to win the support of the most powerful gods for the Roman people?

Either way, his inability to orchestrate an immediate reconciliation between the African bishops did not deter him from further efforts to achieve unity. Most ambitious was the summoning of the Council of Nicaea in 324, for which bishops were given permission to use the imperial transport system. Eusebius provides a vivid account. Bishops were summoned from all over the empire and met in the imperial palace, where the emperor addressed them in Latin, his words translated into Greek for the benefit of the majority. The immediate cause was another attempt at reconciliation, but this time not of a schism but of a heresy, Arianism. At the centre of this dispute was an argument over the nature of Christ, how his human and his divine natures were related, and how he stood in relation to God the Father. Constantine's concern seems to have been to achieve unity. His biographer Eusebius claimed that he achieved it: a common account of the nature of Christ was formulated, and a common date for Easter and the Nicaean Creed were agreed. Constantine's own proclamation also has much to say on the wickedness of the Jews. The bishops were also then entertained and involved in the celebration of the twenty-year anniversary of his reign. Unity was not, of course, achieved. The Arian heresy remained a central source of division through the fourth century, when several of Constantine's successors embraced it. Christian missionaries to barbarian peoples also spread Arian ideas, most seriously to Gothic and Vandal groups, so that most of the new kings of the west were divided from the eastern empire and from their own Christian subjects on doctrinal grounds. Yet the long-term prestige Constantine gained from setting himself at the heart of the triumphant Church was enormous. On his death in 337, the position of the Church was unassailable.

Constantine himself had set some limits on the influence of the bishops. The Edict of Milan extended toleration to all religious practice. Jewish 'clergy' benefited from some of the same privileges as Christian clergy, although terrifying punishments were set for those Jews who tried to convert Christians, owned Christian slaves, or circumcised them. Ancient temples were preserved in Byzantium even after it had been refounded as Constantinople in 324. Indeed, some new temples were added, and the foundation of the city had involved astrologers and augurs. Constantine had, however, banned blood sacrifice, along with the consultation of oracles and the setting up of statues to the old gods. These were the central rituals in traditional religion. It is not surprising that none of these bans was universally accepted and that controversy continued over ritual practice until the end of the century. The fact the ban was issued, along with the legal restrictions imposed on Jews, shows Constantine had no great vision of a multifaith imperial society within which each religious community might pursue its own course under the benevolent and even-handed protection of a secular state. Pragmatism seems more likely from a soldier emperor who emerged from civil wars to reign for thirty years (see Figure 21).

Constantine's religious motivations will always be obscure, but the pattern he set for Christian emperors is clearer. Even through the hagiographic filter of Eusebius' *Life*, he emerges as an emperor whose success was in some respects highly traditional. He fought and survived civil wars and palace intrigues. He founded new cities and patronized the Senate and people of Rome. Militarily and fiscally, the empire was left in better shape at the end of his long reign than it was at his accession. The style of rule was literally spectacular: power was enhanced by everyday ceremonial and occasional festivities performed on magnificent stages. The nature of his engagement with Christianity had to cohere with all this. It offered a new field of monumental building and some new kinds of ceremonies. Ideologically, it enabled him to draw implicit analogies between the divine ruler and his own rule. It brought him a new body of supporters. But if it was meant to offer new ideological solidarity, it failed. Christians in the fourth century all seem to have agreed on the importance of a common orthodoxy and common authority. Their ecumenical councils were quite unlike modern ecumenism, which advocates tolerance of differences in belief and ritual and a loose federation of different churches. Yet fourth-century Christianity was riven by schism and heresy. As a result, the Christian empire would be more divided than what had preceded it. To a modern eye, the amount of time Constantine and his successors devoted to questions of heresy and schism seems excessive. How, with the northern frontiers collapsing and relations with Persia so difficult, could they justify the energy and time they spent on the Church? Bishops, of course, had their own priorities, and their influence only grew over time. But emperors were neither fools nor dupes.

Fig. 21. The head of a gigantic statue of Emperor Constantine in the Palazzo dei Conservatori at the Capitoline Museum, Rome

The ideological support offered by Christianity and the rhetorical power of the bishops was potentially of enormous value to the embattled empire, but emperors could not afford to neglect its divisive potential.

The Bishops and the Empire

If Diocletian or Constantine imagined that their engagement with emerging religions would help unify the empire, they would have been disappointed at the results. For one thing, there was no immediate end to religious pluralism. A few communities were probably majority-Christian in the late third century: the city of Orcistus claimed as much in a petition to Constantine in the mid-320s. There are some signs that the imperial court had largely adopted Christianity by the end of the fourth century. But public worship of the traditional gods continued in great centres like Rome, Antioch, and Athens into the fifth century, and polytheism probably survived in remoter regions of the empire into the sixth century.[24] Change was uneven from one area to another. This emerges particularly clearly from recent archaeological work which makes it possible to compare regions in terms of when churches were constructed. There were parts of Greece where monumental churches were not built until the fifth, sixth, or even seventh centuries, others where they appeared in the fourth.[25] It is also the case that well into the fourth century even those who regarded themselves as Christians continued to perform older rituals, while images from classical mythology and classical literature continued to be made for and used by the elite.

Emperors played various roles in these processes. For most of the fourth century emperors continued a broadly Constantinian line of patronizing Christian communities, engaging with Christian leaders, but trying to restrain fresh conflict. Attacks on pagan temples were rare before the end of the fourth century. Julian's short and divisive reign showed there were still some polytheists who hoped for a return to traditional worship, but also that they were not numerous or strong enough to bring this about. There were no further attempts to reinstate imperial support for the old gods. In the dispute over the Altar of Victory in the 380s the polytheists seem to have been asking for toleration alongside Christians. Emperors were usually more reluctant than bishops to allow hostilities to recommence. But they were not always able to resist pressure from powerful bishops. Constantine had attempted to adjudicate between Donatist bishops and their rivals and in convening the Council of Nicaea in 325 had tried to find common ground between Arians and their opponents. The agreed compromise broke down almost immediately. Constantine and Constantius II struggled to broker agreements, tried and exiled bishops, but none of these interventions succeeded in creating unity. Julian's own notion of a unified polytheism was resisted by local polytheists as well as Christians. Meanwhile, successive bishops pressed emperors to take a harder line on sacrifice, on public worship of the old gods, and on holy places.

One way to understand this is in terms of the structural changes brought about in the empire by Constantine's decision to patronize the Christians. The empire was a highly centralized organization, but Christians remained organized at a very local level. There was no agreed-upon church hierarchy, and the list of attendees at various church councils show there was a no definitive list of bishops either. Before Constantine, just a few regional councils or synods are known. One at Elvira in southern Spain, held sometime in the first decade of the fourth century, brought together nineteen bishops from the area and a larger group of priests and laypeople to agree a list of canons on particular offences and the punishments that Christian communities should impose for each. Councils of this kind proliferated in the fourth and fifth centuries, but none had the power to bind all Christians. Bishops of major cities often exercised more influence, both on other bishops and on state authorities. Some at least owed their influence to the power of their sermons and the persuasiveness of their theological discourse. Others relied on individual charisma and their networks of correspondents. Yet others were respected because of the antiquity and wealth of the communities that had elected them. But there was no single church hierarchy with which emperors could deal. There was also a fundamental difference of interest. Emperors wanted support or at least harmony, and they continued to have all the other concerns that their polytheist predecessors had, including military security, the state finances, and maintaining their control over the court and the army. Bishops were typically more interested in issues of truth and purity, and their consequences for community and authority. Emperors lived in the short timescale of politics, generally looking no further ahead than their succession; bishops operated in the theology of eternity. All the factors came together to prevent a harmonious alliance of Church and state, not that those terms would have been recognizable in the fourth century.

This can be illustrated at several scales. In some cities the rise of bishops introduced a new element into the traditional political triangle of the masses, the property-owning curial classes, and the empire or its representatives. The bishops of Rome gradually overtook the traditional aristocracy and their urban prefect as the main sources of support for the people and the stronger link to the emperors. But it was a slow process. Damasus, bishop from 366 to 384, was on good terms with influential members of the senatorial aristocracy while also building a strong relationship with that sector of the population who relied on the church for alms. His monuments and those put up by polytheist senators staked out alternative sacred geographies in the same city. Leo I, bishop from 440 to 461, had much greater influence. An aristocrat himself, he played a major part in organizing disaster relief in the city and was credited with dissuading Attila from invading Italy. He also persuaded Valentinian III to back his claims to jurisdiction over other bishops and used this to oppose those in Spain, Gaul, north Italy, and Africa whom he judged heretics. Leo I also organized ceremonies and processions throughout the year at set places in the city, establishing what was in effect a Christian public cult. Gregory I, bishop from 590 to 604, was the first bishop of Rome to take the old title *pontifex maximus*. He was born into a senatorial family who had prospered through the end of the western empire and (especially) under Gothic rule, remaining powerful in Rome and retaining estates in Italy and Sicily. As bishop, he represented Rome to the emperors in Constantinople (where he had already served as an ambassador for some years), organized famine relief in the city, protected refugees from the invading Lombards, asserted Rome's primacy over western churches, and organized missions. By this point, the bishop was, in effect, the ruler of Rome and its representative to the outside world.

Rome was exceptional, but some of the same broad trends can be found in many other cities, especially those in areas ceded by the emperors to barbarian rulers. During the fifth century bishops across Spain and Gaul came to judge disputes and to deal with the outside world.[26] Increasingly, they were elected from members of the local aristocracy, and increasingly, they had at their disposal greater resources than any other group in the city. Bishops increased their power through charity and discipline, and made use of their religious authority to confront secular rulers in ways no aristocratic sophist of the second or fourth century would have dared.

The best-documented cases all concern those bishops of the largest cities who confronted emperors. Ambrose, bishop of Milan from 374 to 397, is among the most famous. A Christian whose father and patrons had served as praetorian prefects, he was governor of a north Italian province that included the city of Milan, an imperial capital, when he was unexpectedly made bishop. He built his reputation locally by sponsoring the cult of local martyrs and through his sermons, of which Augustine has left a vivid account. He rapidly extended his influence over other north Italian towns and fostered the growth of ceremony and liturgy. He was also adept at negotiating between the various imperial courts of the day. Like many of his contemporaries he tried to encourage emperors to take a firmer line against non-Christians. He dissuaded Gratian from restoring the Altar of Victory to the Senate House in Rome in 384 and Theodosius from rebuilding a synagogue destroyed by a Christian mob in 388. After Theodosius was implicated in the massacre of a mob at Thessalonica in 390, he excommunicated the emperor. His influence is credited with pressing Theodosius to take a more aggressive line against sacrifice.[27]

Athanasius was elected bishop of Alexandria in 328 and died as bishop there in 373.[28] But in the intervening period he had been exiled and restored to power five times. The central issue was his opposition to Arianism, both in Alexandria and at the imperial court, but it was played out in numerous church councils which became major theological events, hundreds of bishops of different allegiances gathering at Tyre in 335, Alexandria in 339, Rome in 340, Antioch in 341, Serdica in 343, Arles in 353, and Milan in 355. It prompted interventions by the emperors Constantine, Constans, Constantius II, Julian, Jovian, and Valens. Athanasius' career, and the long-running arguments over Arianism which he was at the centre of—played out at the tetrarchic capitals around the empire—show how much division Constantine had imported when he gave the bishops a key place in the political structure. Arianism did not reflect existing geographical or social divisions. At its heart was a disagreement about the relationship between Christ and God, and although named after one particular person (Arius), there was no Arian manifesto or creed: accusations of Arianism were made against people who held a variety of views and allegiances. It redivided Roman society at a local level, and the management of the dispute required significant resources and time. The pattern would be repeated over the centuries as different groups were attacked for having the wrong views in the eyes of their accusers. Historians of early Christianity now typically study accusations of heresy rather than accepting the heresiologists' claims about their opponents. Structurally, these conflicts had their roots in a consensus that all Christians should believe the same thing and follow more or less the same rituals. This concern with purity and unity was, in fact, a powerful force for division; imperial attempts to encourage toleration or find compromise formulas like the Nicene Creed were doomed from the start.

From the bishops' point of view, of course, empire was incidental to the large Christian mission. Most church leaders in the fourth and fifth century were drawn from the Latin- or Greek-speaking curial classes, the wealthy elites of the empire's cities. But Christians themselves were now a much broader and more diverse community than the citizen bodies of Greek and Roman cities. Some of Athanasius' writings survive in Coptic, a written form of the indigenous language of Egypt. There were Aramaic-speaking Christians on both sides of the border with Persia and Christian rulers in Armenia and Ethiopia. Monastic communities were growing in Egypt and Syria, providing alternatives to the classical city that even some bishops found attractive. From the fourth century there were also missionaries among the peoples north of the empire. One factor prolonging the Arian controversy was that even when the emperors were no longer being accused of being Arians—in effect from the reign of Theodosius I—the Christianity of Vandals, Goths, and other groups was regarded as Arian. When they established kingdoms in what had been the Roman west, the dispute reignited. By the end the fifth century, disputes over Christian unity took place in a politically divided world.

Further Reading

Tim Barnes's *Constantine and Eusebius* (Cambridge, MA, 1981) is without doubt the best introduction to the complex history of his reign, even if it has not convinced all experts that Constantine was wholly Christian right from the beginning.

The literature on the rise of Christianity is immense. William Harris's collection *The Spread of Christianity* (Leiden, 2005) gathers a fine selection of views without trying to impose one answer. Ramsay MacMullen's *Christianizing the Roman Empire* AD *100–400* (New Haven, 1984) is a clear account, full of insight. Rodney Stark's *Rise of Christianity* (Princeton, NJ, 1996) has been a good provocation for many historians. The first two volumes of the *Cambridge History of Christianity* (Cambridge, 2006, 2007) provide an up-to-date account of every aspect of their subject. Mary Beard, John North, and Simon Price helpfully set Christianity alongside other changes in *Religions of Rome* (Cambridge, 1998). Robin Lane Fox's *Pagans and Christians* (London, 1986) conjures up the atmosphere of this exciting period better than any other book on the subject.

The implications for the empire and imperial society of Constantine's decision have generated some of the most innovative scholarship. Peter Brown's *The Body and Society* (New York, 1988) tracks the emergence of new literatures and practices of asceticism; the accommodation of Christianity and imperial high culture is the subject of Averil Cameron's *Christianity and the Rhetoric of Empire* (Berkeley, CA, 1991); Dominic Janes's highly original *God and Gold in Late Antiquity* (Cambridge, 1998) explores how a religion born in poverty came to terms with fabulous riches; Garth Fowden's *Empire to Commonwealth* (Princeton, NJ, 1993) follows the tensions and interplay between religious and imperial universalisms through to the early Middle Ages. Alan Cameron's *The Last Pagans of Rome* (New York, 2011) is a vivid portrait of the culture, politics, and society of a generation.

KEY DATES IN CHAPTER XVII

EMPERORS AND KINGS

When Polybius of Megalopolis decided to make a record of the most significant events of his own day, he thought it was appropriate to begin by demonstrating, on the basis of the facts, that the Romans did not win a great empire in the six hundred years following the foundation of the city, even though they were regularly at war with their neighbours for all this period. On the contrary, that occurred only after they had captured a part of Italy and then lost it once again after the invasion of Hannibal, the defeat at Cannae, and only after they had actually seen from their walls the enemy threatening. Only then did they begin to be so favoured by fortune that in less than fifty-three years they took control not only of all Italy but all Africa as well. The Iberians of the west submitted to them. Setting out on an even greater project, they crossed the Adriatic, conquered the Greeks, and dissolved the empire of Macedon, capturing alive their king and carrying him off to Rome as a prisoner. Nobody could attribute this success to human might alone. The explanation must lie in the immutable plan of the Fates, the influence of the planets, or the will of God that favours all human enterprises so long as they are just. For these things establish a pattern of causation that leads future events to come out in just such a way that shows just how right they are who believe that human affairs are subject to some kind of Divine Providence. So that when their energy is aroused, they flourish; but when they become displeasing to the gods, their affairs decline to a state like that which now exists. The truth of this proposition will be demonstrated by the events I will now relate.

(Zosimus, *New History* 1.1.1–2)

Disaster

In 364 the Roman Empire seemed in good shape. It had survived Julian's attempt to reverse Constantine's alignment of the empire with Christianity, and also the end of Constantine's dynasty brought about by Julian's death on the Persian front. Two brothers, Valens and Valentinian I, now ruled over the empire. Valentinian took charge of the Praetorian Prefectures of the west and the centre, while Valens had responsibility for the east. Order seemed to have been restored.

In fact, a disaster was about to unfold. In 376 Valens allowed a large party of Goths to cross the Danube. Two years later Romans and Goths came to blows at Adrianople, not far from Constantinople. Valens himself was killed in the battle, and Roman military power in the east was shattered for a generation. Control over the Gothic groups within the empire was never recovered. In 406 a number of tribes including the Vandals and Suebi crossed the Rhine. In 410 a Gothic army led by Alaric moved from the Balkans into Italy and sacked Rome. The Goths occupied tracts of south-west Gaul in 418 and moved south into the Iberian peninsula. The Vandals crossed the straits of Gibraltar in 429 and captured Carthage in 439. Meanwhile Franks, Burgundians, and Huns joined a confusing struggle for northern Gaul. The Vandals sacked Rome in 455. When Odoacer the Goth deposed the last Roman emperor in 476, no one was put in his place. A century after Valens first admitted the Goths, all territory west of the Adriatic was lost to imperial control. The western empire was replaced by a mosaic of kingdoms whose Germanic kings made use of Roman cities, bureaucrats, and economic institutions to rule a series of hybrid states, and struggled, like their imperial predecessors, to reach arrangements with bishops who mostly regarded them as Arian heretics.

Contemporary testimony is in some ways a poor guide to this dramatic downsizing of empire. The defeat at Adrianople did not seem such a watershed to contemporaries. Arguments over Arianism and over the Altar of Victory continued as if nothing else important was happening, and the eastern court was as worried about Persia as about the Gothic tribes in the Balkans. The emperors and their courtiers were understandably often too preoccupied with immediate events to see larger patterns emerging. Besides, each component of the crisis must have seemed familiar. Emperors had been fighting on the northern frontier on and off for more than a century. Raids into the empire were not unprecedented, even if this was a serious

Map 6. The empire in the year 500 AD

one. It had become common to employ barbarians as soldiers and as generals too. There was a tradition that went back to Augustus of occasionally resettling groups of northerners within the empire. It must have dawned gradually, and probably at different times in different places, that the current individual military and political setbacks were cumulative. Zosimus, quoted at the head of this chapter, was writing with hindsight from Constantinople in the first decade of the sixth century. From his perspective, the century following Constantine's conversion marked the reversal of Rome's rise to Mediterranean hegemony in the middle Republic. Yet even in his day there were some who were not yet ready to give up the chances of another Roman recovery.

Rome and the Northerners

The events of the fifth century were definitely confusing for contemporaries. As time went on, the perspectives expressed in those written accounts that have survived become increasingly localized. Knowledge of distant events was reduced in quantity and reliability, and local crises captured the attention of chroniclers, hagiographers, and historians. Alongside this narrowing of horizons, Christian writers already had a different set of priorities and interests from those of their classicizing contemporaries. Christian historians such as Eusebius of Caesarea and his fifth-century successors Socrates and Sozomen wrote within a narrative tradition in which the life of Christ and the struggles against persecutors and heretics were more important than political convulsions and military conflict. An even more serious limitation is the paucity of evidence from north of the imperial frontiers. Nomad societies in particular, rapidly changing location and names and making no use of writing, were difficult to pin down. More must have been known about the settled societies within a few hundred kilometres of the frontier, but it was probably more in the nature of current intelligence than analytical history. Accounts of what the Goths and others were doing before they entered the empire were eventually created, but these were effectively genealogical charters composed for the new ruling families of kingdoms within the former empire. They owe little to accurate memory or oral tradition.[1] The archaeological understanding of what is termed the Roman Iron Age is improving steadily, but it is difficult to infer political change or even population movements from material culture alone.[2]

What we would like to know most is how conditions north of the Danube and east of the Rhine had changed since the crises of the third century described in Chapter XIII. A series of symbiotic relationships had developed for a couple of hundred years between the Roman frontier provinces in the north and the territories beyond them. Trade of different kinds took place. Typically, provincial manufactures went north, and slaves and rare materials like amber went south. There was probably some economic and demographic growth on both sides of the frontier, but population densities outside the empire remained much lower than in the provinces. There were regular diplomatic contacts which extended to Rome trying to impose chieftains favourable to them, and sometimes giving them subsidies, while holding others as honoured hostages within the empire. There were settlements of northerners within the empire, while others served for long periods in the empire's armies before returning home. The frontiers formed a broad interaction zone within which goods, people, and information moved back and forth.[3]

There had definitely been some changes since the end of the military crisis of the third century. A few tribal names occur more frequently than before, others less often. It is difficult to know when this represents movements of people and when it reflects shifts in the balance of power between different lineages and the formation and dissolution of larger federations of tribes. There were definitely some movements, including the evacuation of many Romans out of the area between the upper Rhine and upper Danube known as the *agri decumates* and from Trajan's Dacian provinces when they were abandoned in the 260s and 270s.

During the fourth century there had been some missionary activity north of the Danube, so that many of the peoples who entered the empire were already Christian, if in most cases Arians. One side effect was the spread of literacy in Germanic languages. Another change was that northerners now made up a greater proportion of Roman armies, perhaps as much as a quarter in some cases. More tended to be recruited when a war with Persia was expected. This two-way traffic across the frontier meant that the nearest populations knew the empire well, better in fact than Romans knew the barbarians.[4] For many northerners the empire seemed to offer all sorts of opportunities. This included a number of generals, figures like Arbogast, Stilicho, and Ricimer, who came to play prominent roles in the imperial courts at the end of the fourth century. This was a new development, even if there had been more junior German commanders of particular auxiliary

units in the first century. Yet, despite their exotic names and origins, most
behaved very much like other courtiers with military backgrounds. When
they could, they held traditional Roman offices and titles, and married into
the senatorial aristocracy and sometimes the imperial house. They owed
their power to their positions in the empire, and so worked hard to preserve it. Their positions and titles offered one model for the first generation
of barbarian kings within the former western provinces, such as Odoacer
in Italy and Athaulf in southern France, when they dealt with the eastern
emperors and also their Roman subjects. We may suspect that in relation
to their fellow Germans the same rulers adopted a different set of titles,
rhetorics, and ceremony, but it is the Roman-style artefacts and texts that
survive. When leaders tried to convert their temporary status as war leaders
into hereditary kingship, as many did after they entered the empire, they
typically looked to Roman and biblical models.[5] Some of these changes
seemed to be working in the empire's favour. During the tetrarchy and the
period when the Constantinian dynasty ruled Rome, the main military
threat was always Persia. Conflicts in the north tended to be small-scale and
easier to manage.[6] Outsiders were attracted by Roman wealth, but joining
the empire or receiving subsidies from it was usually a more effective way
to obtain some of it than through raids. Most groups were small-scale in any
case. Any idea that they wished to destroy or conquer the Roman Empire
is not credible.

If these relationships were mainly mutually beneficial, how should we explain the way they unravelled in the century after Valens allowed the Goths
into the empire? The defeat at Adrianople itself was the result of a perfect storm of Roman misfortune.[7] Political instability following the death
of Valens's brother in 375 and tensions with Persia meant that the eastern
empire's resources were overstretched. There were probably tactical errors on
the day too. Maybe more important is that the empire seemed unable either
to deny the Goths entry in 376 or to manage them as effectively as groups of
immigrants had been in the past or to recover from defeat on the battlefield.
All these are signs of fundamental weaknesses in the late fourth-century empire, weaknesses in terms of revenue, manpower, and command.

The importance of one other factor is a matter of dispute. This is the
arrival on the eastern fringes of Europe of a nomadic people named the
Huns.[8] Contemporary reports present them as completely unlike Romans
or Goths, but very much like the nomads described in earlier histories
such as Herodotus's Scythians. Nomad populations had been exploiting

the steppe more or less since the domestication of the horse for riding in the Bronze Age.[9] Most depended on maintaining relations with settled agriculturalists on the edges of the steppe who could provide goods, equipment, and supplies unavailable to a mobile population. Nomad politics were chaotic, and occasionally one or another group established overlordship of others.[10] There were certainly periodic movements within the steppe. Greek and Near Eastern texts mention movements of Cimmerians, Scythians, Saka, Alans, and Huns throughout the last and first millennia BC. The most common names were applied to different peoples, since most nomads looked alike to the settled populations south of the steppe, and it is not always easy to know when different sources are refering to the same group. Nomad populations were never as large as those of their settled neighbours. The ecology of the steppe and a lifestyle based on herding meant that vast areas of steppe were needed to support even modest populations. Nomad invasions did not, as a result, take the form of great waves of people who could displace farmers. The history of the Huns is a history of shifting patterns of hegemony rather than of mass population movements.

Texts written within the Roman empire claim that towards the end of the fourth century this new political grouping on the steppe attacked, conquered, and terrified a series of agricultural populations living to the north and then west of the Black Sea, including a number of Gothic tribes. There are some signs the Persian Empire felt similar pressure on its northern frontier, but as usual it is difficult to know whether the same nomadic populations were involved. Pressure from the Huns was one reason the Goths wished to cross the Danube into the empire, although there were probably pull factors as well, such as the hope of military service and land, and perhaps a calculation that the emperors were more likely to accommodate them now than in other periods. A generation later the Huns established a kingdom on the middle Danube in which Attila ruled over a number of nomadic and settled groups.[11] They extorted annual tributes in gold from the emperors in the east, and then crossed the Rhine to fight in northern Gaul until their defeat near Chalons in 451. A raid on Italy followed the next year, and Attila was about to move east when he died in 453. Like other nomad empires, that of Attila depended on forcing defeated or terrorized populations to acknowledge the hegemony of one people and its ruling family. On his death, the unity of the Hunnic hegemony collapsed. Within a decade the subject peoples reasserted their independence. Small groups of Huns feature in records of the next century or so but were never again a major threat to Rome. The significance of Attila's empire in the 440s and 450s is not at issue. What is uncertain is how far the movements of the 370s were driven by a new and unusually intense pressure from the steppe, and how far it was simply the weaknesses of the empire that meant that population movements of a kind that had existed for centuries now had a more serious result.[12]

Hybrid Kingdoms

Whatever the complex causes that led various Gothic groups to the borders of the empire, Valens was in no position to deny them entry. He was also in no position to control them once they were inside the empire or to set the terms on which they would coexist with provincial populations. Following his death at the battle of Adrianople in 378, his immediate successors actually became more dependent on their former enemies, and on other northerners who followed them. For a generation, bribery, diplomacy, and threats of force were employed by both western and eastern emperors in a series of attempts to contain and deflect the Goths. But the weakness of the empire was now obvious. The Goths eventually headed into Italy, and Rome was sacked in 410.[13] The emperors in Constantinople retrenched to protect the interior provinces, and the western emperors were left to cope not only with Goths moving west from the Roman Balkans but also with other groups crossing the Rhine into Gaul.

Once within the provinces, the northerners come more into focus. They were clearly difficult to control but were not always terrifying. One reason relations deteriorated before Adrianople is that Gothic migrants were treated badly by provincial populations and Roman officers. There is a broad agreement than most northern armies numbered in the tens of thousands. This was locally formidable, but the population of the empire was in the tens of millions. Historians today no longer write of Rome being overwhelmed by barbarian hordes. Some experts, noting how well northern soldiers and leaders became integrated into the military and political institutions of the empire, see the collapse of the west less as a takeover by outsiders than an inside job. The emperors, in this analysis, were unable to control various elites, including the new military leaders at the head of migrant groups, and the senatorial aristocracy who made less and less of a financial and political contribution to the empire.

Most of the new arrivals were not nomads or strangers. They originated in that broad band of peoples who knew Rome well from long acquaintance, populations of farmers who through war and trade were already in some sense part of the periphery of empire. Most of the groups were relatively small in number, occasionally brought into larger, looser federations like the Alamanni or the Goths, often animated by charismatic leaders whose authority increased in times of war or crisis. One influential idea is that the key traditions associated with these groups were, in fact, transmitted and maintained by small ruling groups whose followers fluctuated from one generation to another.[14] Even when some ethnic names, like the Suevi and the Alans, remained in use for centuries, that too might conceal change. Inside the empire these groups underwent rapid transformations. War leaders consolidated their power and hereditary kingship emerged. This was true even where they were settled for a while by Roman authorities under one or another scheme of accommodation.[15] But not all entrant groups had the same experiences. The Vandals, Suevi, and others crossed the Rhine and headed south through Gaul to Spain and thence to Africa. Others stayed nearer the older centres of Roman power.

The Goths themselves were never a unified group, even before they entered the empire. The very weakness and fluidity of their political structure made it hard to negotiate with them. Gothic groups at times controlled areas of the Balkans and the Danube provinces, and areas of north Italy, and one group moved on from Italy to Aquitaine, where they were settled as 'guests' in 418. From there they expanded their power into Spain, driving other groups ahead of them to establish what historians today call the Visigothic kingdom of Spain. That kingdom is more accurately described as the rule of one group of Gothic leaders over migrant peoples, many but not all of them Goths, and over the majority population of the former Roman provinces. That kingdom controlled the Iberian peninsula for most of the sixth and seventh centuries, ruling from a royal court that settled in Toledo. War leaders solidified their position as kings, established a hereditary right like that claimed by Roman emperors, like them issued coinage and laws in Latin, and like them depended on the support of bishops whom they could never quite control as well as their tribal elites. Where they could, they made use of established infrastructure, especially fiscal systems, but this worked better in some areas than others.

This transition from loosely organized warbands with a leadership that was probably elected to relatively stable hybrid kingdoms, which are often

described as Roman successor states, took place in Italy, Gaul, Spain, and
Africa (see Map 6). The Vandals established a similar kingdom in north
Africa ruled from Carthage, the second greatest city of the Roman west.[16]
Even though they waged war against the last western emperors and sacked
Rome for a second time, the culture of Vandal Africa was in many respects
a continuation of that of Roman Africa.[17] For non-Vandal subjects much
remained unchanged, including their religious affiliation, the conditions on
which they worked the land, and even their export markets in the former
empire. Yet the close connections of old families with kin and friends in Italy
were put under pressure, and Christian bishops objected to the Arianism of
their new masters.

Similar dramas were played out, with local variations, in the former
Gallic provinces. A good deal of literature has survived from this region
making it possible to trace the changing experience of at least the ruling
classes up to and beyond the end of Roman rule. Following Aurelian's suppression of the separatist Gallic emperors who had ruled the region from
260 to 275, the tetrarchs had paid more attention to this part of the empire. Trier, on the Moselle, became an imperial capital, and was provided
by Constantine with a great palace and basilica (see Figure 22) and imperial baths which were never finished, ruins of which survive today alongside those of other monuments from the first and second centuries AD.[18]
A series of panegyrical speeches from the tetrarchic period illustrate the
efforts of local aristocrats to draw imperial favour to their cities, and are a
major source for reconstructing tetrarchic ideology and propaganda. From
the fourth-century court at Trier we have the poems of Ausonius, a teacher
of grammar and rhetoric from Bordeaux who served both as a governor
and as tutor to the boy emperor Gratian in the 370s before rising to the
consulship. His poetry describes his relatives and colleagues in Bordeaux,
the landscape of the Moselle Valley, but most of all the life of the educated
classes in the last generation of the western empire. During the fifth century that world changed by stages.[19] New groups infiltrated the empire
in the north, among them the Franks. Fewer military units were perma-
nently stationed in the north. The courts of emperors and then kings were
located farther south. Valentinian II had ruled from Vienne between 388
and 392, the Praetorian Prefecture was moved from Trier to Arles in 407,
and the usurper Constantine III made it his capital in 408. Communities
in northern Gaul were increasingly left to fend for themselves, and in the
early fifth century Roman influence in Britain ended. Meanwhile, in the

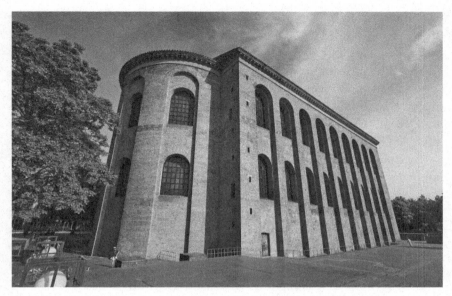

Fig. 22. The basilica, formerly Emperor Constantine's throne room, now a Protestant church, Trier

south-west of Gaul the Visigothic kings ruled from Toulouse and Narbonne before moving their attention south of the Pyrenees. The Alans were briefly settled on the Loire, and the Burgundians on the upper Rhine. The defeat of Attila's Huns in 451 by an alliance between the Roman general Aetius and the Visigothic king Theoderic I seemed to promise some hope of a Roman revival. In Majorian's brief reign as western emperor he not only defeated the Vandals in Italy but also waged war on the Visigoths in south-west France and the Burgundians, but his attack on the Vandal kingdom was a failure, and after his death in 461 there were no further attempts to reassert imperial control in Gaul.

During the second half of the fifth century the barbarian warlords adopting Roman titles became less and less easy to distinguish in terms of their activities from Roman generals behaving like local dynasts.[20] Everywhere, communities sought local protectors as the emperors in Ravenna and Constantinople were less and less able to act beyond the Mediterranean littoral. Many aristocrats in Gaul, Spain, and Africa entered the Church. Some embraced ascetic disciplines; others exercised social authority in their cities as bishops. The letters of Sidonius Apollinaris, who lived through much of the fifth century at Clermont-Ferrand eventually becoming bishop of the Arverni, offer a nuanced picture of the transition from Ausonius' world of educated aristocrats playing sophisticated literary games to a world of churchmen interceding for their people with warrior kings.[21] The growing power of bishops is evident in the Iberian peninsula too, both at the Visigothic court and in cities which for the first time saw major church building within their centres. Not all the propertied classes entered the church. Some at least adopted less literary and more military lifestyles, finding places in the retinues of Germanic kings.

By the middle of the fifth century, the Roman Empire in the west was limited to Italy and parts of southern Gaul. The Gothic sack of Rome in 410 reverberated through the west, but even before that the threat to Roman power had led to the western capital being moved from well-connected Milan to more easily defended Ravenna in 402. Larger and larger numbers of migrants settled in northern Italy under various terms of accommodation, which undermined faith in the emperors. The Ostrogothic kingdom established in 476 was also based in Ravenna. A similar hybrid to Visigothic Spain and Vandal Africa, it depended on a slightly precarious combination of Roman landowning classes, from which bureaucrats and bishops were recruited, and Gothic soldiers ruled by a Gothic king. The first in this dynasty was Theoderic, who as a diplomatic hostage had been educated in Constantinople, and then after a decade or so was a sub-king of a group of Goths in the Roman Danube provinces. Serving and raiding Rome by turns, he was commander of the army of the eastern empire and consul, and then was encouraged by the emperor Zeno to invade Italy with his Gothic followers and depose Odovacer. From 493 until 526 Theoderic ruled as king in Ravenna with the title *patricius* granted by the eastern emperor. He restored the Colosseum. His reign is illuminated by the writings of Cassiodorus, a descendant of Roman bureaucrats, who served Theoderic in a series of completely Roman offices and also wrote—or to be frank invented—a history of the Gothic people in which Theoderic's ancestors took centre stage. Given the background of Theoderic and the mixed group he assembled to run his government, it seems odd to label Ostrogothic Italy a 'barbarian kingdom'.[22]

This first generation of post-Roman kingdoms in the west is well understood precisely because so much governmental infrastructure survived the replacement of the empire by kingdoms that in many ways imitated it.[23] Ostrogoths, Visigoths, Vandals, and Burgundians alike relied on tax systems descended from those established by Diocletian.[24] The invaders had few social institutions of their own that were well suited to governing the kinds of societies and economies they now controlled, and so they had to invent new ones. Kingship in particular was new to them, at least in this form, and their idea of kingship was in many ways modelled on their image of the Roman emperor.[25] They ruled from Roman cities where they created courts that were in many respects quite familiar to the educated Romans who largely populated them. Successive kings issued law codes, just as the Emperor Theodosius did, if on a rather smaller scale. Some of those law codes enshrined the principle of multi-ethnic states, with Romans and others each using their own laws. The kings sustained cities because they and their rulers were vital for the running of the tax system.[26] That situation continued throughout the fifth and sixth centuries until this generation of hybrid kingdoms was replaced by Frankish, Lombard, and Arab conquerors who wished to do things differently. But for a couple of centuries law, coinage, literature, and monuments all show the persistence of Roman elements. Christian letters, sermons, and histories too assert an essential continuity in what mattered most to their authors, the lives of the saints and the triumph of orthodoxy over heresy.

This is not to underplay the scale of change. Observers from Augustine to Zosimus were struck by the reverberations that followed defeat at Adrianople and especially the Gothic sack of the city of Rome. It made a real difference that the collegial unity established in the tetrarchic period had been replaced by a world in which the eastern Mediterranean empire persisted, but the territories west of the Adriatic were ruled by a shifting series of smaller polities. The material culture of Britain, northern Gaul, and Germany shows how rapidly a relatively well integrated economy collapsed in the aftermath of political chaos.[27] But in the areas around the western Mediterranean, something quite Roman persisted for some time.

The Long Fifth Century in the East

Historians have the luxury of being able to focus on one question at a time. Emperors were not so fortunate. The emperors in Constantinople were well aware of the problems of dealing with the Gothic groups admitted into the empire in the last decades of the fourth century, and from a distance observed the loss of Britain, the collapse of the Rhine frontier, and the efforts—sometimes successful, but cumulatively not—of the western emperors and their generals to use one group of migrants against others. But they had other concerns too. Most prominent of these were the ceaseless fight against Christian heresy and the simmering hostility with the Persian Empire. Waiting in the wings too were court politics, control of the army, and the fear of usurpers, perennial issues but ones that were most important when emperors were perceived to be failing.

The most stable element was dynasty. After the death of Valens at Adrianople, the western emperor Gratian appointed as Augustus of the east his experienced general Theodosius. The fact that he ruled until 395 is one indicator of his success, and on the obelisk he set up in the hippodrome of Constantinople five years before, he claimed victories over both the Goths and Persia. In fact, these were the result of treaties signed in 382 and 386, but they did allow Theodosius time and space to assert his authority. After his defeat in 388 of Magnus Maximus, who with an army from Britain had killed Gratian and expelled Valentinian II, Theodosius ruled over the entire empire, the last emperor to do so. Peace with Persia and the Goths also allowed him to devote significant time to working alongside bishops in the west against Arianism, deposing bishops who did not support the Nicene Creed, issuing constitutions, and holding a council to choose a sound bishop for Constantinople. Polytheists too found the emperor less willing than some of his predecessors to protect them. Before his death he presided over the defeat of another usurper, Eugenius, at the battle of the River Frigidus and established his sons Honorius and Arcadius as co-emperors to rule after him. Honorius' reign in the west was not a happy one: low points included the sack of Rome, the marriage of his sister to the Gothic chieftain Athaulf, and a series of usurpers. But the Theodosian dynasty continued in the east through the reigns of Arcadius and his son Theodosius II, who ruled between 401 and 450 AD, and finally through the reign of his sister Pulcheria, the first Roman empress in her own right, ruling with her husband until 453. Politics was a little more chaotic in the second half of the century, with a few emperors lasting just a few months. But Leo I, who ruled from 457 to 474, Zeno, who ruled from 474 to 491, and Anastasius, who ruled from 491 to 518, ensured that at least at the political centre there was some stability. The fact that the empire survived several child emperors in this period and the prominence of some of their female relatives suggest that decision-making was in practice managed for much of the time by a small group and, within the new parameters of action they had accepted for themselves, they did so successfully.[28]

The long reign of Theodosius II is exceptionally well documented by historical accounts, by the Theodosian Code, and by the Acts of various church councils. This has made it a good point from which to examine some of the emerging characteristics of what would soon be the only Roman empire.[29] This was an empire that once again was focused on a single capital, however important Antioch, Alexandria, and Rome might remain. Although there were occasional periods in which junior or co-emperors shared power, there would never again be more than one court, and that was based firmly in Constantinople. Some of the experiments of the tetrarchic period had been swept aside. Structurally and politically, the eastern empire was a simpler place. It was also simpler in religious terms. Polytheism was increasingly marginalized in the east, and the ruling classes were firmly Christian. Linguistically, this was a world that worked in Greek, even if Latin remained a language of government for some time. Its intellectual life was increasingly rooted in Homer and in the Bible, while its political culture was firmly Roman.[30] Economically, the empire was weak for much of the long fifth century. It had lost a good deal of its tax base, and in some periods paid heavy indemnities to northerners and, especially in the time of Attila, to the Huns. But the diminished size of the empire brought some advantages. There were fewer distant provinces where usurpers might raise armies and build factions. Lines of communication were shorter. Those in power in Constantinople could concentrate on a smaller range of priorities: on the Balkans, on relations with Persia, on the city, and on sustaining Catholic Christianity.

This last preoccupation, on which Theodosius II himself spent so much effort, seems strange from the perspective of the comparative study of imperialisms. It is still common to see the religious activities of Theodosius I and Theodosius II represented as attempts to win the support of the bishops or forge an alliance between Church and state as if the pursuit of orthodoxy was a political tactic, a way to sweep away some problems and secure some new backers for non-religious projects that were a higher priority. This is partly a product of our own interest in empire as a secular political institution and on imperialism as a practice of political and economic domination. From the point of view of many bishops, it was empire and the emperor that were instruments, and the highest priority was the defence of proper belief. The Council of Ephesus, held in 431, did assert unity around the Nicene Creed, but it also created disunity by condemning its opponents as heretics, threatening those who did not accept the council's decision with excommunication, and attempting to limit the influence of the bishops of Antioch and Rome. There is no real reason not to think that emperors shared the religious priorities of the bishops. Religious unity may have been a goal in itself rather than a tool with which to remove distractions or muster energy to other aims. The distinction between religious and political viewpoints is another modern perspective, and not a helpful one in this case.

The Theodosian Code, that great compilation of laws already discussed in Chapter XV, was not theological, but it does present a moralizing view of society and of the scope of imperial action. Where earlier emperors had often been happy to leave local legal systems in place, even to some extent after the Edict of Caracalla, Theodosius' project gathered up constitutions issued on numerous occasions and repackaged them as the expression of a consistent and unambiguous ethical position. Like the Acts of Church Councils, the code expresses a universalism that was new in the empire.

A similar convergence of universal religion and universal empire can be detected in Persia with the growing strength of the Zoroastrian priest-hood and decreasing tolerance of religious minorities. There was a good deal of exchange of various kinds across the frontier, and this accounts for some similarities and transfers, but it also seems that these two empires were embarked on parallel paths as each adapted to the changing religious environment.[31] In terms of actual conflict, the long fifth century was less ferocious than the long reign of Shapor I in the third century which had culminated in the capture of Antioch in 252 and the death of Valerian in 260. Energetic campaigns by the tetrarchs, and a period of weakness in Persia had shifted the balance slightly, But the failure of Julian's campaign led to Jovian suing for peace, and Valens' death meant that Theodosius I had to do the same. Theodosius II fought two successful wars in the 420s and 440s. A Persian attack in 502 put the Emperor Anastasius under serious pres-sure. This pattern of alternating peaces and hostilities would continue into the early seventh century, for as long as the Persian Empire lasted.

From our perspective—with hindsight that is—it is easy to see Romano-Persian relations as a stalemate. The geopolitics demanded occasional con-flict but also limited it. Persian armies might raid Syria and Asia Minor but never occupy it for long, and Roman armies could do the same in Mesopotamia. But Rome would always be a Mediterranean empire, and ever since Trajan's invasion the lower Euphrates and Tigris had seemed out of reach. Equally, Persia had its own long northern frontier to worry about and had the same difficulty that the Seleucids and the Achaemenids had

had in keeping control of areas as distant as the former Kushan territory in what is now Afghanistan and the Hindu Kush, the Iranian plateau, and also Babylonia. Over the centuries a group of Syrian cities and fortresses passed back and forth between the two empires, along with influence over the kingdom of Armenia. It sometimes served the interests of an Augustus, a Sapor, a Diocletian or a Khosrow I (who reigned from 531 to 579) to claim the credit either for victory or for peace. From time to time each empire had difficulties with nomadic invaders from the central Asian steppe, and in the seventh century the Arab invasions overwhelmed both. This global perspective is just another instance of hindsight blinding historians to what these conflicts felt like on the ground. Fear, revenge, and greed and the desire for the approval of army and the population seem to have driven hostilities between the brother emperors.

Further Reading

Peter Heather's extraordinary *Emperors and Barbarians. Migration, Development and the Birth of Europe* (London, 2009) is a gripping view of how population movements shaped late antique and early mediaeval history. It is worth reading this alongside Michael Kulikowski's *Imperial Tragedy: From Constantine's Empire to the Destruction of Roman Italy (AD 363–568)* (London, 2019) for whom the causes of the western empire's collapse are largely internal to the empire itself.

The emergence of a new order in the west is regarded very differently from how it was when J. M. Wallace-Hadrill's *The Barbarian West 400–1000* (London, 1952) was written, but it is still an interesting read. For a broader analytical account, it is difficult to beat Chris Wickham's *The Inheritance of Rome: A History of Europe from 400 to 1000* (London, 2009). Julia Smith's *Europe after Rome: A New Cultural History, 500–1000* (Oxford, 2005) offers a brilliantly original view of change in the period that does not begin from politics. The period is also covered by the fourteenth volume of the *Cambridge Ancient History* (Cambridge, 2000) and the first volume of the *Cambridge Mediaeval History* (Cambridge, 2005). Both are invaluable.

Some of the preoccupations of the emperors in the east emerge very clearly from Fergus Millar's *A Greek Roman Empire: Power and Belief under Theodosius II (408–450)* (Berkeley, CA, 2006). The opening chapters of Judith Herrin's *Byzantium: The Surprising Life of a Mediaeval Empire* (London, 2007) present a brilliant portrait of the strange new Rome that was emerging in the east while the west reeled from crisis to crisis.

THE CITY AND THE EMPIRE

Such were the labours accomplished by the Emperor Justinian in connection with the holy places in Byzantium. But to enumerate all the
sacred edifices which he built through the length and breadth of the
whole Roman Empire is a difficult, indeed an altogether impossible task.
So when it becomes necessary for me to mention any city or district by
name, the sanctuaries in that place will be recorded at the proper point.
So the churches, both in the city of Constantinople and in its suburbs,
were built as stated by the Emperor Justinian; but it is not easy to recount
in my narrative each one of the other buildings erected by him. To speak
comprehensively, the majority of the buildings and the most noteworthy
structures of the rest of the city, and particularly of the Palace area, had
been burned and razed to the ground when he undertook to rebuild
them and to restore them all in more beautiful form.

(Procopius *On Buildings*, Book I, chapters 9.17–10.2)

Constantinople in the Age of Justinian

Procopius's *On Buildings* was composed around AD 554. It presents itself as a
supplement to his *History of the Wars* of the Emperor Justinian, who reigned
from 527–65. To say that Procopius' view of Justinian was ambivalent is an
understatement. A third work, *The Secret History*, is the most savage indict-
ment of a reigning emperor to have survived from the ancient world. Some

readers of the *On Buildings* have detected highly coded criticism of Justinian here too. But most obviously it is panegyric. It opens with praise of the emperor for expelling the barbarians, driving out heresy, extending the empire, and revising the law (a reference to the Code of Justinian). *On Buildings* adds to this with a compendious account of Justinian's constructions, first in Constantinople and then throughout the empire. As a builder Justinian mainly engaged in restoration, but this was often carried out on a grander scale than ever before. It begins with the building of the Great Church, Hagia Sophia, constructed to replace one burned down in the deadly Nika riots of 532. Its dome would be the largest in the world until the construction of St Peter's in Rome, which took most of the sixteenth century to build. *On Buildings* goes on to list the other great churches Justinian built for the Mother of God and other saints, new shrines raised to various martyrs, hospices, the many churches visible to visitors arriving in Constantinople by sea, new harbours and market facilities, the Great Palace, and beside it a public square called the Augustaeum and a Senate House and a vast cistern (see Picture Box 9). He built churches in other centres, including a huge church to the Mother of God in Jerusalem, supported on substructures extending out from the top of Mount Zion and famous for its forest of columns. Around the edges of the empire he built walls and other fortifications, but Constantinople was the centrepiece.[1]

The City of Constantinople in the sixth century was an imperial capital in all senses of the term. It is sometimes claimed that neither the empire not its provinces had formal capitals, and this is true if we mean 'capital' in the modern sense of one city formally designated as the centre of government. But in reality there were always centres of various kinds. Constantinople in Justinian's day was the centre of government, because Justinian spent almost no time in his long reign outside the city. The bureaucrats of the empire centred their activities there, amassed their records, and fought each other for influence and resources in a way that strikes modern readers of John Lydus' *On Magistrates* as horribly familiar.[2] Ambassadors from all over the empire and beyond visited too, as well as migrants and refugees.

It was also a symbolic centre for the empire, a space where great ceremonies were performed, including imperial triumphs, the marriages and funerals of members of the imperial house, and a growing mass of religious processions and celebrations that under Justinian were focused on the Roman state. Beside the Church of the Apostles was a mausoleum in which

Picture Box 9 Cistern under Istanbul

This forest of 336 columns supports the roof of the Basilica cistern, the largest of the many underground cisterns that lie beneath the old city of Istanbul. It was around 140 metres (460 feet) long and 70 metres (230 feet) wide, and the columns themselves were 8 metres (26 feet) in height, not counting their bases or capitals. The cistern was constructed early in the reign of Justinian, perhaps on the site of an earlier one. Its name refers to the Stoa Basilica which stood above it, and it was close to Agia Sophia and the Great Palace. Its Turkish name, Yerebatan Saray, means the 'Underground Palace'.

The Greek city of Byzantium was perched on the end of a triangular promontory. When it was expanded, first by Severus, then by Constantine, and again by Theodosius, more and more of the peninsula was included within the wall circuits. But these areas had few sources of water, and the population was growing.

The scarcity of water made Byzantium unusual among ancient cities, especially large ones. Rome had the Tiber, Alexandria the Nile, and Antioch the Orontes. Rome's first aqueducts dated to the end of the fourth century BC. Their number and volume grew in the imperial period, especially with the development of *thermae*, which were greedy for water. Carthage was provided with the 212-kilometre-long (132 miles) Zaghouan aqueduct in the second century AD, around the same time as the Antonine baths were built there. Ancient panegyrics praised cities for being well watered, and spectacular fountains (*nymphaea*) were a feature of the richest cities.

Hadrian provided Byzantium with its first aqueduct. It provided water for the oldest part of the city, which was largely low-lying, around the acropolis. The post-Constantinian growth of the city prompted the construction of a second aqueduct system, completed in the reign of Valens, to bring water from the mountains of Thrace. Beginning on higher ground, it could supply the hills of Constantinople and also fill reservoirs between the walls and the cisterns of the old city. It was expanded in the course of the fifth century. Recent research shows its total length was nearly 600 kilometres (370 miles). This was an enormous undertaking, an indication of the energy emperors could command when they needed to.

The chief value of the cisterns was to store drinking water for the arid summer months. But cisterns also contributed to the security of Constantinople. Aqueducts had developed as a technology of the Roman Peace. If enemy forces controlled the territory around the city, they could cut off the supply. This happened in AD 487, when the emperor Zeno's *magister militum* Theoderic Strabo revolted against him, and again in AD 626 when the Avars besieged the city. The number of major cisterns and reservoirs constructed rose rapidly during the fifth century. Around 200 cisterns of various sizes still survive today. The Basilica cistern itself was probably built in response to a more local threat. During the terrifying Nika riots of 532 the palace had for a while been cut off. A vast cistern would protect Justinian and his successors if they ever again lost control of the city.

Further Reading

James F. Crow, Jonathan Bardill, and Richard Baylis, *The Water Supply of Byzantine Constantinople* (London: Society for the Promotion of Roman Studies, 2008).

Constantine and many of his successors were buried. Nearby was a new one built by Justinian for himself and his successors. Constantinople was a centre of accumulation, a place in which treasures and trophies plundered from all over the empire had been gathered. Most famous were an obelisk from Karnak in Egypt brought there by Theodosius I and the Serpentine Column originally set up in Delphi to mark the victory of the Greeks over the Persians after the battle of Plataea in 479 BC.

Constantinople was also an economic centre. It was by far the biggest city in the empire. Most cities in the ancient Mediterranean world were small, and the largest owed their expansion to imperialism.[3] That was as true of the relics of Hellenistic empires like Alexandria and Antioch—centres that had grown under the Ptolemaic and Seleucid kings—and of Rome and Carthage in the West. Only empires could afford to build megalopoleis and sustain their great populations. The population of Byzantium under Justinian reached perhaps 500,000. That figure included bureaucrats, soldiers, and churchmen but also craftsmen, market gardeners who farmed plots between and beyond the walls, sailors, and members of the eastern Senate and their households. Provisioning this many people required major efforts.[4] Aqueducts brought water to the city from the distant mountains of Thrace; there were vast cisterns, some of which survive today beneath the streets of Istanbul.[5] Grain was brought from Egypt to be distributed to the masses, and the city was a major market. The political, religious, and economic primacy of the city meant the population grew rapidly in the centuries following Constantine's refoundation. The city had many forums and squares, but the crowd met in the Hippodrome built alongside the palace. It was there that the Nika riots broke out from a toxic combination of theological and political differences, protests against taxation, anger over military defeats, and the rivalry of the circus factions of the Blues and the Greens. A week of chaos in January left as many as 30,000 dead and a vast swathe of the city burned down, which provided Justinian with the opportunity for the spectacular rebuilding mentioned by Procopius.

Finally, Constantinople was the major cultural and educational centre of the empire. Philosophy and other disciplines were taught in Athens, Alexandria, and other cities at the start of Justinian's reign, but in 529 new laws prohibited pagans, Manichaeans, Jews, Samaritans, and heretics from teaching, and the philosophical schools of Athens were closed. Constantinople became the central place for the teaching of theology, and its libraries were the main place that classical Greek literature survived until the Renaissance.

Justinian's Constantinople was, in fact, more of an imperial capital than the Roman Empire had had since the second century BC. The centralization of all these functions in one city was in part a response to the shrinking territory of the empire, but not entirely. Justinian sent his generals to wage war in Africa, Spain, and Italy, as well as fighting wars in the Balkans and on the Persian front, and he successfully destroyed the Vandal kingdom in Africa and the Ostrogothic kingdom based in Ravenna. Triumphs for these victories were celebrated in Constantinople, but there were no imperial visits to the west. The centrality of the capital city was a new aspect of imperial style, one that persisted throughout the Byzantine Middle Ages up until its conquest by the Turks in the fifteenth century.

The City of Rome in the Republic and the Early Empire

City states are, by definition, centralized polities. Most were very small, and even those whose territories contained major rural sanctuaries or secondary urban centres took care to bind them into the state and its main city. This was true of Attica, where the Athenians worked hard in the sixth century BC to bind secondary centres to Athens by war and ceremonial. It was true of the Etruscan centres and of archaic Rome as well. Some functions were always reserved to the urban centre. Athenians needed to come to Athens to vote, to serve on juries, and to take part in collective festivals. The first monuments of Athens were temples, and the first public spaces were the agora and the Pnyx, areas reserved for various kinds of economic and political business. A processional way crossed the agora, and a landscaped area on the slopes of the Acropolis was set aside for drama. During the fifth century BC the temples were rebuilt and added to. Gradually a set of public buildings appeared, including covered law courts, a public dining room, and a mint and various other offices. Local supplies of marble and silver helped them do this on a grand scale. During the second half of the fifth century Athenians controversially also spent a portion of the money contributed by their allies to monumentalize the Acropolis, and to build Long Walls to the port of Piraeus that allowed the city to be supplied from the sea.

Early Rome followed a similar path, even though we cannot document it in such detail.[6] The story of its early urbanism was told in Chapter III. The main sanctuaries were in the city, although Roman magistrates did take part in rituals at the temple of Jupiter Latiaris on the Alban Mount, a collective sanctuary for the Latins. Almost all decision-making took place in the centre of the city. Magistrates addressed crowds in the forum, voting took place on the Campus Martius, and the Senate met in various temples. Correlating the growth of Roman power with the changing shape and spaces of the city in the early Republic is difficult because of the lack of archaeological evidence and the unreliability of the historical record. The best that can be said is that the stone from which fifth-century structures were built came from many locations in Latium.[7] The period of military success in the last decades of the fifth century and the start of the fourth does correlate chronologically with an increase in attested building projects. The great majority were small temples, classified today as victory or votive temples, because many were built to fulfil battlefield vows made by Roman commanders. They were then paid for from the commander's share of the spoils of victory. Nearly fifty can be linked to particular campaigns.[8] Temples were vowed for other reasons too, including in times of plague, but cumulatively they must have impressed on the people of Rome, and visitors to the city, quite how successful Roman armies had been. Then, there were the spectacular projects that could only have been achieved with slaves purchased from war spoils or perhaps by prisoners of war themselves. The first of these was the great circuit wall built around the city in the first decades of the fourth century BC, the scale and cost of which has only recently become clear.[9] The first of Rome's great public roads was attributed to Appius Claudius Caecus, censor in 312.[10] He also built the first aqueduct. Rome's second aqueduct was explicitly said to have been built in 296 from the spoils of the Samnite Wars. Most Republican censorial building was funded by the profits of war, since the Roman state had few other sources of revenue in this period. Drainage schemes, public works in the city, even some building in the new colonies founded in central Italy were all paid for by Roman military success. Greek visitors—the only ones whose reactions were recorded—were not always impressed by the appearance of Rome. It lacked marble buildings before the mid-second century and did not have the stone theatres, gymnasia, and other amenities of contemporary Syracuse or Athens. But the size of the city and the scale of building made clear it was an imperial capital.

From the late third century BC the scale of monumental building increased still further. On the southern Campus Martius a series of structures were constructed, including the Circus Flaminius, built by Gaius Flaminius during his censorship in 220, and some spectacular victory temples, including the Temple of Hercules of the Muses built in the 180s from the proceeds of Marcus Fulvius Nobilior's campaigns in Ambracia, the temple of Juno Regina in 179, and that of Jupiter Stator in 131. Cato the Elder, as censor in 184, built the first massive basilica on the Roman forum. The longest of Rome's aqueducts, the Aqua Marcia, was built in the decade following the destruction of Carthage and Corinth, largely funded from the spoils of those campaigns. At some point in the middle of the second century great naval yards, the Navalia, were built on the Tiber just downstream from the city centre. Public infrastructure works like these illustrate how building in the city was shaped by other factors than the ambitions of generals. Censors seem often to have used their control of public contracts as a means of distributing benefits (and paid work) to the city as whole. Entertainment buildings of the Greek kind were not provided, but streets and public spaces were paved and the basilica structure offered spaces for various public gatherings. The shifting nature of Roman politics can be traced in the shifting topography of the city. Public spaces were extended by one kind of politics, and encroached on by others.[11] Porticoes, temples, and public amenities were known by the names of powerful players. The increased scale of ceremonial and political display demanded larger spaces for assembling audiences and also thoroughfares that could accommodate funeral and triumphal processions.[12]

Military campaigns, spoils, indemnities imposed on defeated peoples, grand ceremonies in the city of Rome, and public building were bound together in a tightly formed knot. Plundered artwork, magnificent temples, and parades provided props for orators and material validation of an ideology increasingly geared to conquest. Mid-Republican Rome became a site of accumulation, like imperial capitals before and since.[13] Debates took place about how much and what should be appropriated, which foreign imports glorified Rome, which weakened her. Following the sack of Syracuse in 212, a great mass of Greek statuary was brought to Rome by its conqueror Marcellus. Fabius Maximus ostentatiously left the Tarentines most of their statues when he sacked the city in 209. How the city should be ornamented became a key site of debate where the ethics of empire were debated and rehearsed. Today, its archaeology is the most tangible trace of Republican imperialism.

In many ways these patterns were replicated in the even larger building projects of the last century BC, especially those associated with the campaigns of Pompey, Julius Caesar, and Octavian/Augustus. But in other ways Rome was becoming less of an imperial capital in this period. The extension of warfare around the Mediterranean Basin and the growing scale of commands had increasingly meant that key decisions were made by army commanders rather than referred to the Senate and people in Rome. Manlius Vulso made war on the Galatians in Asia Minor in 187 without prior consultation. Livy's account of these years shows that in formal debates over whether or not to award triumphs, the Senate was increasingly anxious about commanders acting beyond their original instructions in the Balkans, in Iberia and elsewhere. The term 'peripheral imperialism' has been applied to the period, meaning that expansion was being driven by commanders in the field.[14] Leaders like Pompey and Caesar began to receive embassies and to make alliances and wars on their own authority. Ratification of their decisions and settlements became fraught political struggles. While far from Rome, the generals enfranchised allies, made public benefactions, and even issued coinages, behaving in many ways as if they were states themselves.[15] In 56 BC Caesar, Pompey, and Crassus held a summit in Lucca, just north of Pisa, at which commands and magistracies, provinces and armies for the next few years were allocated. It was immediately apparent that in political terms the city of Rome and its institutions were now peripheralized. Meanwhile, they competitively spent money in Rome (often from a distance), Pompey on his theatre, Caesar on the Saepta, Caesar and Augustus on forums and temples, and so on, despite the fact that the popular assemblies and the Senate had less and less political influence.

It would be easy to dismiss this as one feature of the disruptions of the late Republic, and it probably felt that way at the time to many contemporaries. But it turned out that this was not a temporary disruption. Caesar spent much of his dictatorship outside Rome. During the years following his death, much of the empire was governed from wherever Octavian or Anthony happened to be at the time, in the latter's case often Alexandria. Even after his victory at Actium, Augustus spent much of his first decades of sole rule in the provinces. Although most of his immediate successors spent much of their time in or near Rome, the potential for itinerant monarchy was never forgotten. When emperors were elsewhere, which happened more and more from the second century AD, the involvement of the Senate in lawmaking, hearing embassies, and consulting on the government of the empire was greatly reduced.[16] Individual senators retained some responsibilities in the city of Rome. They held all the major priesthoods, and the urban prefect, in effect the emperor's deputy in the city, became more and more important. But a gap had opened up between the traditional institutions of the Roman *res publica* and the new ones of the court, based wherever the emperor happened to be at the time.

Meanwhile, emperors from Augustus on lavished resources on monumental building. Augustus, to begin with, focused on completing the projects of Julius Caesar and on temple building. His *Res Gestae* lists more temples than Procopius' *On Buildings* would churches. In both cases, the accent was on repair and restoration, not on new building. There were also public gardens, circuses, theatres, amphitheatres, a stadium, and more. Many of these were clothed in the kind of luxurious ornament previously reserved for the homes of the richest senators. Pliny the Elder's account of classical art continually breaks away from the chronological narration of artists and their famous works to note where particular artworks were displayed in the city of Rome. By the late first century AD, the city had become a city of galleries, and also of trophies brought from around the world, especially from ancient Greek cities and from Egypt.[17]

Some emperors used building programmes to make political points. For example, Vespasian, after winning the civil war of 69–70 built a Temple of Peace, and he replaced Nero's grand palace with the Flavian Amphitheatre devoted to popular entertainments, the building which we now know as the Colosseum. Along with the triumphal Arch of Titus celebrating the destruction of Jerusalem and a Temple of the Flavian Gens, these monuments conveyed an image of how the new dynasty wanted to be received. Imperial building aspirations pressed architects and builders to develop new forms. After a fire devastated much of the centre in AD 80, the Emperor Domitian took advantage of the rebuilding to create the first purpose-built stadium in Rome for the Greek athletic games he introduced in the city; its outline can be seen in the Piazza Navona. Libraries were set up around the city. The most grandiose were those attached to Trajan's forum. A series of monumental bath complexes, the imperial *thermae* were constructed in the second and third centuries, built on a lavish scale, integrated into the aqueduct system, and provided with statuary and coloured marbles. In the early years of the third century the city itself was compressed into a kind of monument, a vast plan of the city suspended above head height on the interior wall of one of the rooms of the Temple of Peace. The *forma urbis Romae*, as it is sometimes called, was 18 metres (60 feet) across and 13 metres (40 feet) high, and depicted buildings in such detail it remains a key source for the topography of the city. In a gesture of autocratic disdain, the labels were too high and too small to be read, and instead present a visual inventory of the monumental city for all to see and none to comprehend.[18]

One thing lacking from the early imperial city of Rome is administrative buildings beyond those already created in the Republican period for the city itself. This partly reflects the peculiar origins of the imperial monarchy and the extent to which emperors stressed their good citizenship and their kinship with the senatorial elite. Persian and Macedonian monarchs had no qualms about constructing palaces that marked clearly their separation from their subjects. Augustus and his immediate heirs lived in a series of private houses on the Palatine hill overlooking the forum, using temples (and occasionally gardens) as places to meet local and foreign dignitaries. The Palatine was more like an imperial compound than a single palace. Nero did set out to create the Golden House, a purpose-built palace on an exceptional scale. But the disaster of his reign meant later emperors returned to the Palatine. Between AD 81 and 92 Domitian had a great multistorey palace constructed there, equipped with vestibules and courts of various sizes, a great banqueting hall, and a sunken garden, all decorated in coloured marbles brought from all over the Mediterranean. Later emperors made minor modifications. Severus was the first emperor to connect the palace directly to the Circus Maximus, where the crowds might be addressed, a precedent that was followed in the integral connection of the Great Palace of Constantinople and its hippodrome. The palace was both a residence for the members of the extended family of the emperors and a stage for ceremonial, and some emperors at least administered justice there. Less visible, because less architecturally imposing, were areas used by the *familia Caesaris*, including those members of it who managed the finances and logistics of the empire, kept track of correspondence, and presumably maintained some kind of records. There is no sign of dedicated imperial governmental facilities, another indication of the patrimonial nature of early imperial government, and something else that made it easy for emperors to rule from wherever they were. The palace, splendid as it was, was not the administrative hub of the empire, except when the emperor was present, and he had many other residences.

The history of Rome as an economic capital is a little different. A key driver in all periods was the size of the city's population, which over the last century BC grew to around one million, easily the biggest market in the Mediterranean world. This population needed to be provided with food, water, clothing, and fuel, while the growing city needed timber, building stone, and bricks. By the first century BC grain was brought from North Africa, Egypt, Sicily, Sardinia, and other parts of Italy.[19] Oil was shipped from southern Iberia. Timber, building stone, and marble were brought from all over Italy, and in some cases from farther afield. The effects of the city's growth on the agriculture of central Italy were profound.[20] The area immediately around the city, the *suburbium*, became a region of intense cultivation. Market gardening could only be done close to the city (or inside it), because vegetables and eggs went off so quickly. Other areas of central Italy also saw an intensification of farming aimed at producing a surplus for the city. Yet other areas became specialized in the supply of timber, firewood, and particular building stones. Infrastructure was created to make all this possible. Aqueducts continued to be built until the reign of Trajan. The great military roads connecting Rome to other parts of Italy were utilized for commercial purposes. A little could be brought down the Tiber, great food market buildings were constructed from the second century, the docks were improved, and storage facilities were built up and down the Tiber and at Ostia on the coast.[21] During the first century AD harbour facilities were improved at the Tiber mouth. Recent excavations at the great Trajanic complex at Portus have shown quite what a sophisticated system had evolved, with a great basin to shelter seagoing vessels connected by canals and road to the Tiber and to Rome.[22] These facilities were given a monumental aspect too.

Rome was probably already the largest city in the western Mediterranean by the time Carthage was destroyed in 146 BC. Trade networks came to be orientated on Puteoli, Ostia, and the riverine ports of Rome. Once they were created, it is likely that these ports attracted buyers as well as sellers. Empire shaped these exchanges in a range of ways. Tax grain from Sicily and the surpluses of imperially owned estates in Africa represent direct appropriations. The emperors also owned many mines, quarries, and some timber-producing forests. But in all periods there were also commercial shippers who had to be induced to bring commodities to Rome. A Prefect of the Annona had an oversight of the grain supply of the city. Some deals were done with local groups of shippers, and there were tax concessions for those who chose to supply Rome rather than other cities. Direct imperial expenditure in the capital sustained many directly or indirectly. Subsidized and then free grain for a limited number began with the Gracchi in the late second century BC and was continued in various forms through the empire, with oil and other rations being added later.

The building projects commissioned by the censors and then sponsored by generals and emperors brought work. From Augustus' time there were also tens of thousands of persons supported by the state, including the praetorian guards, urban cohorts, *vigiles* (a fire brigade), and freed members of the *familia Caesaris*. On top of this, there were cash distributions to mark key dynastic events. The emperors spent more money on Rome than anywhere else, except on the army.

Early imperial Rome remained a cultural and economic capital, then, but the centre of government was usually elsewhere. There are plenty of modern parallels. Washington DC, Pretoria, Canberra, Brasilia, Ottawa, and even Rome today are not the major economic centres of the countries of which they are the capitals. But there is an important difference. Non-capitals such as New York, Johannesburg, Sydney, São Paulo, Toronto, and Milan owe their modern energy to their international commercial success. Ancient Rome was sustained mainly by imperial favour. Its position was that much less secure as a result.

Alternative Centres

There was no one moment when a decision was made to relocate the court outside Rome. I described in Chapter XI how Tiberius, Trajan, and Hadrian did much of their business from palatial villas on Capri, at Civitavecchia, and Tivoli respectively. Nero had spent a year and a half in Greece, during which time the empire was ruled from wherever he happened to be, and the same must have happened during the brief military expeditions of Caius, Claudius, and Domitian, the longer ones of Trajan, and during Hadrian's travels around the empire. From the middle of the second century, emperors spent more and more of their time near the frontiers and new centres of government were created there. Marcus Aurelius spent some years based at Sirmium and at Carnuntum so as to be close to the Danube frontier. When they travelled, emperors took with them a praetorian prefect, the role of which developed from commander of the guard to a sort of vizier, their secretaries for correspondence in Greek and Latin, and also a staff of imperial freedmen, who acquired increasing governmental responsibilities.[23] The court on the move also included special friends, favourites, relatives, bodyguards, and domestic slaves of all sorts, including cooks, chamberlains, secretaries, concubines, hairdressers, and masseurs.

A few anecdotes suggest that buildings termed *palatia* in Latin and *basileia* in Greek were constructed for emperors anywhere they stopped for long, buildings in which they held audiences and gave justice. The progress of emperors can often be tracked from edicts or letters they issued.[24] Certain cities occur more often than others in the records. The names of Sirmium in modern-day Serbia, Serdica (modern Sofia) in Thrace, and Nicomedia in north-west Turkey occur frequently in letters from the second and third centuries. We can also see imperial courts operating for periods from York, Trier, Vienne, Aquileia, Milan, Thessalonica, Antioch, and Alexandria, and letters were sent from many other cities en route. What these centres had in common was their proximity to military commands and their location on major roads. The Roman Empire is often characterized as a Mediterranean world, and so it was, but many of these emperors spent most of their reigns far from the sea.

Itinerant monarchy depends on the possibility of mobility both for monarchs and for those who needed to find them. One of the many services undertaken for Greek cities by their most prominent citizens was to go on embassies at their own considerable expense. Emperors, wherever they were, received embassies and petitions and responded by letter. Those letters that survive on inscriptions do often concern civic privileges and disputes, but there were also endless reports and queries from governors and military commanders, from the urban prefect in Rome, and also from members of the *familia Caesaris* which never found their way into the epigraphic record. Itinerant monarchy also depends on good supply networks. Probably being based in or close to military camps helped here, since the army already had well-developed logistical systems.

The military crisis of the third century revealed some of the limitations of itinerant monarchy. Diocletian's solution eventually included multiple courts and an increased bureaucracy. Some of the cities that had been the bases for second-century emperors were well suited to house these courts. Trier, Milan, Sirmium, and Nicomedia were the first generation of tetrarchic capitals. New building projects began at once transforming medium-sized Roman cities into imperial capitals. Palaces, basilicas, thermae, and circuses were constructed, and in some cases ceremonial routes were laid out passing through arches or quadriporticoes like the Arch of Galerius in Thessalonica.[25] These stages were provided for grand ceremonies and intimidating audiences. Their populations swelled as a consequence of the imperial presence: figures of around 100,000 have been estimated for Trier,

Milan, and Sirmium at their height. Many were bureaucrats, soldiers, and others supported by imperial funds. Under Constantine, four regional praetorian prefectures were created. This structure persisted even when the locations of the capitals shifted and the number of emperors was reduced below four. Milan lasted until 402, when the Gothic threat forced Honorius to move to Ravenna, better protected by marshes and more easily provisioned by sea. It would become the capital of the Ostrogothic kingdom and then, after Justinian's conquest of Italy, the capital of a Byzantine Exarchate (a province) that survived until the middle of the eighth century. Trier was also abandoned in the early fifth century, around the time of the loss of Britain and the collapse of the Rhine frontier, and the westernmost prefecture was moved to Arles. The city of Trier was conquered by the Franks in AD 459. Sirmium was fought over for much of the fifth century by Goths, Huns, and Romans. Nicomedia, beautified by Diocletian with basilicas, a circus, and royal residences, was supplanted by nearby Constantinople.

Constantinople and Rome

Constantinople at first had much in common with the temporary capitals of the second and third century and the tetrarchic capitals. It was an existing city of medium size, well located on the road network, and unlike most of them it was also well connected by water. It sat on the Sea of Marmara, which opened onto the Black Sea to the north and the Mediterranean to the south. It was close enough to the Danube frontier to keep track of war on that front, and not too far from the territories most often disputed with Persia. The Greek name for the city was Βυζαντιον (Byzantium), and this was what Greek writers such as Procopius continued to call it. Byzantium had withstood a major siege in the Severan civil war and then been rebuilt on an impressive scale, more than doubling its size. It would have made a good tetrarchic base if Nicomedia were not already available about 150 kilometres (90 miles) away on the Asian side of the water. Why Constantine chose this site over Nicomedia is not known. Possibly, it was to avoid the Diocletianic associations, although Constantine had also built in Nicomedia and celebrated the twenty-year anniversary of his reign there as well as in Rome. Perhaps the new city was a memorial of his victory over Licinius at nearby Chrysopolis in 324, rather like Nikopolis created by Augustus to mark his victory at nearby Actium. Perhaps Constantine was attracted by the defensibility of the peninsula on which Byzantium stood and its excellent harbours.

Construction began late in 324, and the 'new' city was inaugurated at a great ceremony in the Hippodrome in 330.[26] Much still remained to be completed, and building works were continuing at the time of Constantine's death seven years later, but the speed with which the new capital was conceived and created is impressive all the same. Constantinople dwarfed the earlier tetrarchic capitals in size. The city was refounded following ancient Roman rituals, and a new wall across the peninsula quadrupled the size of the Severan city. At the eastern point a great palace was built linked to the Hippodrome. Imperial thermae and processional ways were laid out. Great churches were constructed, including the cathedrals of Hagia Irene and Hagia Sophia. There were still some temples to the traditional gods. The city was also full of statues of gods taken from elsewhere, plunder and artworks to some observers, pagan idols to others. The Forum of Constantine and the Hippodrome were particularly ornately decorated. There were various nods to the city of Rome—seven hills, a Temple of Fortuna Romae—but in most respects it was a fresh start. A new street grid was laid out in the new quarters (which never happened in Rome), and the city ringed with harbours and granaries. To populate the new megalopolis, a new population was drafted in, and a second Senate was created. Aqueducts and immense cisterns provided drinking water and supplied the baths of Zeuxippus. Egyptian grain that used to go to Rome was diverted to feed Constantinople. The Church of the Apostles may not have been completed in Constantine's lifetime, but he was buried in the adjacent mausoleum. Tetrarchs had created administrative bases with all the ceremony that late antique governance required, but Constantine had quite deliberately created a new symbolic centre for the empire.

Constantine's plans were grandiose enough, but Constantinople soon expanded beyond his original design. Much of Constantius' reign was spent completing and filling out the original design, providing the city with a full set of institutions and perhaps making it more evidently an imperial capital. Some of this can be observed through the speeches of the orator and teacher Themistius, who was raised to the eastern Senate in 355 and then entrusted by the emperor with increasing its numbers until they were equal to those of the Senate of Rome.[27] The city acquired an Urban Prefect, as Rome had, at some point in the middle of the fourth century. Successive panegyrics delivered by Themistius suggested (or claimed) a role for the

Fig. 23. A 1:250 scale model of Rome in the age of Constantine built by Italo Gismondo between 1933 and 1971 which can be seen in the Museum of Roman Civilization at EUR (Esposizione Universale Roma) in Rome.

eastern Senate in legitimizing the emperor. Meanwhile, the city continued to expand westwards. Yet another massive outer wall circuit (see Figure 24) was built early in the reign of Theodosius II, creating a great eastwards extension within which market gardening, residences, and religious foundations could be protected. The city centre became filled with churches, many of which would be rebuilt on a spectacular scale by Justinian.

Constantinople rose at Rome's expense. Imperial resources were redirected to the new capital. The new senate was partly filled with members of older families invited to come east, incentives for building accommodation drew architects, craftsmen, and capital to Constantinople, and the reduction of state grain made it more difficult for Rome to sustain its population levels. Zosimus was scathing about the waste of resources on the new capital, while Eusebius praised Constantine's religious foundations there.[28] Probably this reflects some controversy around the end of Theodosius II's reign. But at the start of Constantine's reign he certainly did not neglect Rome (see Figure 23). Because imperial building projects always took many years to realize, both cities were still receiving his patronage at the time of his death. Indeed, throughout the fourth century and for a while afterwards, the empire had two symbolic centres, two Romes.[29]

After the defeat of Maxentius in October 312, Constantine behaved very much like other winners of civil wars, especially Augustus, Vespasian, and

Fig. 24. The outermost circuit walls of Constantinople built between 405 and 413 and completed by the praetorian prefect Anthemius, in effect regent for the boy emperor Theodosius II. They were nearly seven kilometres long and linked the Golden Horn and the Sea of Mamara. Often rebuilt, they remained the main defence of the city for over a thousand years.

Severus. Each of these had used building projects in Rome to lay out a programme of sorts for their reigns. The most novel structures initiated by Constantine were a series of great basilical churches around the city. St. John Lateran, begun within a year of his victory and probably completed by 320, was intended as a cathedral for the Christian community of Rome. Throughout the remainder of his reign he and his relatives sponsored a number of other grand churches near the graves of martyrs located in the cemeteries around the city. The churches of St Lawrence outside the walls, of St Agnes, of Saints Marcellinus and Peter the Deacon and Old St Peter's on the Vatican and St Paul outside the walls ringed the city, providing facilities for pilgrims and local Christian communities. There is a debate over how far the location of these churches was directed by the location of the tombs of the martyrs, how far by a sense of tact towards worshippers of the traditional gods whose temples were mostly in the city centre.[30] There were good practical reasons for locating the basilicas where they were; some at least were on imperial ground. How tactful these vast structures were, when they were visible to most entering or leaving the city, is less clear. The construction of Old St Peter's and St Paul's probably began around the same time as work started at Constantinople. Constantine's building in Rome was not limited to churches. He built another set of Thermae, probably quite early in his reign, to rival those of Trajan, Caracalla, and Diocletian. He remodelled the recent basilica of Maxentius on the Forum Romanum and installed a colossal statue of himself in it. There were restorations of the Forum Boarium and the Circus Maximus. Constantine was the last emperor, however, to spend significantly on the city.

The city of Rome remained a major symbolic centre right up to the Ostrogothic kingdom. The later fourth century in particular is exceptionally well documented by Christian writers and members of the senatorial order (the two groups increasingly overlapping, of course) and the culture, society, and politics of the city have been very well explored.[31] The widespread shock at the Gothic sack of the city in 410 is proof enough that Rome still mattered across the empire. But its centrality altered over time. Most obviously, it never again became a political capital or even the capital of an Italian entity before the end of the nineteenth century. The Senate continued to meet, and led by the Urban Prefect continued to run the city as a rather grand town council, and senatorial priestly colleges continued to perform customary rituals until they were forbidden in the late fourth and early fifth centuries. But the decision-making functions were local, and important matters had to be referred to the Praetorian Prefect and the imperial court. All the same, the senatorial aristocracy found they were able, once again, to take possession of their city. During the fourth century they took responsibility for the urban fabric, set up statues of themselves throughout the public spaces, and very occasionally welcomed imperial visitors in style.

Economically, the story is more complex. The families that filled the western senate owned, collectively, a vast amount of land and other assets, especially in the west. During the fourth century some contributed financially to the running of the city and the upkeep of its monuments, and many lived in splendid homes. But over time their wealth came under pressure from two directions. Neither of them, surprisingly enough, was the cash-strapped imperial court. One pressure, difficult to quantify precisely, was the gifts made by these families to religious foundations. The scale of the gifts made by Melania the Younger in the early fifth century scandalized some, although most of the surviving testimony praises her. It is notable, however, that during the fifth century there is less and less sign of money being spent on repairs and restorations of any buildings not connected to the Church. The second area of pressure was the occupation of so much of the west, first by settled barbarian 'guests' and later by the new kingdoms. Alongside these pressures on the wealth of the propertied classes there was the shrinkage of the population of the city, in part no doubt a response to reduced supplies of subsidized grain, in part a sign that commercially Rome was no longer as important a market as before. Yet alongside these changes is the growth of the wealth of the Christian Church, the building activities and growing influence of the bishops of Rome from Damasus in the late fourth century to Leo the Great in the fifth. If the fourth century had been dominated by the dynamics of the relationship between Senate and distant court, then from the fifth century on, the relationship between Pope and aristocracy would begin to shape the public life and public spaces of the city. This political mix was quite different in Constantinople, where Christian ceremony was increasingly bound up with that of emperors, who were mainly physically present in the city, and where the eastern Senate collectively had much less influence. Meanwhile, as Rome shrank in size, Constantine's new capital grew and grew adding new districts and new wall circuits during the fifth century (see Figure 24).

The empire had other centres. One of them was the person of the emperor itself.[32] Those rare imperial ceremonial visits to Rome had such a charge because two centres were for an instant brought into contact. At Constantinople, the emperor and the city coincided more regularly and mostly harmoniously, although the Nika riots illustrate how badly proximity could go wrong. As for other urban centres, the ancient cities of Antioch, Alexandria, and Carthage continued to play their parts in regional exchange systems. The capture of Carthage by the Vandals in 439 did not entirely interrupt this. Despite repeated attempts to recapture the city, the Vandals ruled there until Justinian's general Belisarius reconquered it in 534. Antioch remained a major hub too until the early sixth century, when a devastating earthquake was followed a few years later by a Persian attack which left the city depopulated. Justinian tried to revive it, but with limited success. Alexandria too passed briefly into Persian and then back to Roman hands during the early seventh century. Antioch fell to the Arab invasions in 637, Alexandria in 641, and Carthage in 697. Then there was Jerusalem too, a medium-sized Roman colony since the reign of Hadrian, then the third focus of Constantinian building after Rome and Constantinople. The

Church of the Holy Sepulchre, incorporating another great basilica, was constructed in the last years of Constantine's reign. The site became an early centre for Christian pilgrimage. During the reign of Theodosius II, the Bishop of Jerusalem was recognized as a Patriarch, which gave him equal status to that of the Bishops of Constantinople, Antioch, Alexandria, and (in the eyes of some) Rome. Justinian built two new great churches there, the New Church of the Theotokos (the Mother of God) and the Church of Sion. Jerusalem too was caught up in the wars with Persia of the early seventh century and fell to the Arabs in 638.

The processes which led to Constantinople becoming the unrivalled capital of the Roman world were tortuous ones and were not really the result of any planned centralization. In some ways it makes more sense to think of how the shifting political and military geography and the changing patterns of economic and cultural activity impacted on the urban networks of the empire. The Roman Empire began as a single city state, and it ended the same way, even if it did not contract to the same point from which it had expanded. For most of its history the empire was too large and complex an enterprise to be steered from any single centre.

Further Reading

There are many guides and histories of the ancient city of Rome. The best guidebook in my view is still Amanda Claridge's *Rome: An Oxford Archaeological Guide* (Oxford, 2010). An exceptionally useful collection of essays is Paul Erdkamp's *The Cambridge Companion to Ancient Rome* (Cambridge, 2013). For late antiquity, see John Curran's *Pagan City and Christian Capital: Rome in the Fourth Century* (Oxford, 2000) and Carlos A. R. Machado's *Urban Space and Aristocratic Power in Late Antique Rome AD 270–535* (Oxford, 2019).

Richard Krautheimer's *Three Christian Capitals* (Berkeley, CA, 1983) remains a classic demonstration of how political changes were mirrored in urban topography. Lucy Grig and Gavin Kelly's collection *Two Romes* (Oxford, 2012) discusses some of the contrasts between old and new Rome in the fourth and fifth centuries AD.

KEY DATES IN CHAPTER XIX

XIX

REMAKING THE WORLD

Let the cities return to their former glory, and let nobody prefer the pleasures of the countryside to the monuments of the ancients. Why avoid in peacetime the very places we fought wars to protect? Who finds anything less welcome than the company of the elite? Who does not enjoy conversing with his equals, promenading in the forum, observing the practice of worthy professions, engaging in legal cases in the courts, or playing that game of draughts that Palamedes loved, or visiting the baths with one's fellows, or inviting one another to grand banquets? Yet those who choose to spend all their time in the country with their slaves miss out on all of this.

(Cassiodorus, *Variae* 8.31.8)

How Empires End

Empires do not all have the same fate. Modern studies of collapse and transformation have failed to establish a single theory of imperial decay, offering instead a range of alternative catastrophes.[1] Perhaps this should not surprise. Empires—even early ones—were complicated engines with many parts that might go wrong. The argument of this book has been that it is persistence and survival that need to be explained, not decline and fall. Rome's genius—or good fortune—lay in the ability to recover from crisis after crisis.

Some empires succumb to sudden and unexpected violence from without. The empire of the Incas crumbled before the invasion of Pizarro, and the Achaemenid Persian Empire was swept away by Alexander. The rapidity of their fall often seems to follow as much from the demonstration of the fragility of their rulers' claims to cosmological favour as from any actual losses in manpower and resources that follow the first reverses. Emperors claim so much. When their weakness is exposed, the disappointment is often fatal. Collapses of that sort illustrate how much early empires depended on ideology and symbolism to sustain them.

Other early empires simply fragmented, like the empire of Han China and the Abbasid caliphate. Fragmentation is arguably a risk integral to the structure of tributary empires. Most early empires were, after all, put together when a conqueror accumulated a series of pre-existing kingdoms: Achaemenid Persia and Qin China offer paradigms for this kind of growth. Earlier identities were rarely eroded under the relatively light touch of pre-industrial hegemony and capstone monarchy. Egyptians remembered their pharaohs under Persian, Macedonian, and Roman occupations. Greek writers looked back before Rome and Macedon to the classical age of Athens and Sparta. Even when the issue was not one of ancient traditions, these empires were often composed of separable parts. Tributary empires often simplified their logistics by allowing each region to support its own occupying army and governors. But this made individual regions potentially self-sufficient, and so liable to revolt. Alexander's empire collapsed because it depended on Macedonian armies supplied by local satrapal administrations. Fragmentation usually began at the margins. Action at a distance is a problem for all emperors, and distance was exacerbated by primitive communications. A common response was to create powerful border viceroys, counts palatine, margraves, and the like, with the authority and resources to respond independently to external threats. But when the centre did not hold, these border generals often chose to go it alone. The outer satrapies of the Achaemenid and Seleucid empires were often in revolt. Fragmentation may be temporary, of course. Aurelian reunited the Roman Empire, and Antiochus III did the same for the Seleucid Empire. Chinese imperial history is often presented as an alternation of fragmentation and reintegration.

Yet other empires simply wither away. They lose control of their outer provinces to revolt or conquest, but successfully retrench to their original (or a new) core area. Often their rulers maintained the imperial styles and ceremonies of their grander pasts. Imperial Athens in the fourth century BC,

Map 7. Justinian's reconquest (AD 565)

late Hellenistic Syria and Egypt, the last century of Mughal rule in India all
offer examples. After the Fourth Crusade resulted in the Frankish seizure of
Byzantium in 1204, there remained tiny successor Greek empires in Epirus,
Nicaea, and Trebizond. Historical sociologists have never found it easy to
distinguish large states from small empires. Perhaps it is best to say that some
empires have reverted to ordinary states with extraordinary memories.

During the fifth, sixth, and seventh centuries AD, the Roman Empire
underwent all three of these fates: invasion, fragmentation, and a dramatic
downsizing. The empire was repeatedly invaded. I described in Chapter
XVII how Alemanni, Vandals, Huns, and others followed the Gothic groups
who entered the empire in AD 376. The loss of the western provinces was
not as rapid as the fall of the Incas or the Aztecs. Yet within a hundred years
of the battle of Adrianople, Rome's Mediterranean empire was no more.
Justinian's conquests in Africa, Spain, and Italy seemed to be the beginning
of reunification, but the empire did not survive further invasions during the
sixth and seventh centuries. From the north, the Avars and Slavs invaded
the Balkan provinces, and the Lombards Italy. Periodic Persian raids into
Syria culminated in 540 in the sack of Antioch. Finally, in the early seventh
century, the Arab conquests swept away Byzantine Africa, Egypt, Sicily, and
Syria and went on in the next century to destroy Visigothic Spain.

The empire fragmented too, in the sense that the political unity of the
west came apart in stages, leaving intact for a while Roman tax systems,
Roman cities, and the Latin-speaking elites who ran both.[2] The fact that
taxation was devolved via the praetorian prefectures to the groups of provinces known as dioceses certainly helped make fragmentation feasible. For
some Romans in the west, perhaps only the identity of their rulers seemed
to have changed.[3] Theoderic the Ostrogoth held court in the imperial capital of Ravenna, celebrated games in the Roman Colosseum and Circus,
and patronized the western Senate, even lending some support to efforts to
restore the monuments of the city. The Vandal kingdom also rested on solid
Roman institutional foundations, and the propertied classes and churchmen
derived from them remained part of a Mediterranean community, travelling
back and forth within the boundaries of the former empire.[4] The Roman
senator Cassiodorus had a career at the Gothic court in Ravenna in the
early sixth century first as *quaestor*, then as *magister officiorum*, and finally as
praetorian prefect for Italy.[5] These positions, part of the Ostrogothic inheritance from Rome, were among the most senior in the bureaucracy. Like
senatorial courtiers of the fourth and fifth centuries, he also interrupted his

career for a consulship in Rome. Cassiodorus produced elegant Latin literary works throughout his life alongside the royal letters he was responsible
for drafting. His panegyric of the barbarian king and his (lost) history of the
Goths show how easy it was for educated Romans to accommodate themselves to new circumstances. At the end of his life, he founded a monastery
and turned his attention to religious writing.

It is likely enough that some members of the Roman elite of the west felt
some sort of dissonance between their roles within these kingdoms and the
wider culture and habits they shared. This did not necessarily translate into
political dissidence, although the Justinianic wars did force some to choose
between their loyalties. These identity politics were overlaid, in many places,
by tension between Arian rulers and 'orthodox' Roman subjects. Language,
education, and social function must have continued to create fault lines in
society that external pressures could exacerbate. Many of the first generation of kingdoms in the west—those of the Ostrogoths and Vandals and
Burgundians, for example—were, as I described in Chapter XVII, in effect
hybrid societies; Romans living by one set of laws and performing civil
functions while the barbarian leaders lived by their different customs and
served the military. The exact means by which the barbarian 'guests' were
supported is unclear, and perhaps different modes of accommodation were
developed in different kingdoms.[6] But it is clear that the kings stood at the
head of these societies, tribal leaders and Roman magistrates combined,
issuing laws and distributing favours to all their subjects. The Visigothic
kingdom in Spain preserved elements of this fusion until it was swept away
by the Arab conquests in the early eighth century.

At Constantinople too, some must have taken comfort from the fact that
barbarian kings sometimes claimed to rule as subordinates of the emperor
and put the eastern emperors' heads on their coinage. But in practice, the
emperors had no influence over the succession of kings, or how they ruled.
Mostly, they had enough to worry about defending their territory against
raids from across the Danube or war with Persia. But fragmentation had
been reversed before, and it is not surprising that the eastern emperors did
not immediately give up on the west. Most dramatic of all interventions
were those of Justinian in the middle of the sixth century. Justinian's long
reign (527–65) is exceptionally well documented, most of all by the historical works of Procopius.[7] There is also the *Digest*, a great encyclopedia of
Roman civil law compiled on Justinian's orders. An account of the administration of the empire by one of his praetorian prefects, John the Lydian,

offers a vivid picture of the ideology of the sixth-century empire from a different perspective.[8] Justinian's generals succeeded in recapturing North Africa from the Vandals in 533, gaining control of Sicily and much of Italy from the Ostrogoths by 540, and finally creating a beachhead in Visigothic Spain in 551. But the wars in Italy, which were prolonged until 561, exhausted the empire's finances and made impossible the kind of cohabitation between Romans and Goths created by kings like Theoderic and senators like Cassiodorus. The spectacular mosaics at Ravenna (see Figure 25) celebrate a Justinianic Reconquest, but it was short-lived: in 568 the peninsula was invaded once again, this time by the Lombards.

Finally, the empire collapsed back on itself, and retrenched, not on Rome, of course, but on Byzantium.[9] Retrenchment did not only mean shrinkage: the fundamental economic and administrative structures of the empire were in the process remodelled. Even at the beginning of the eighth century, when everything south of Anatolia was lost and Arab invaders were crossing into Spain, when the Lombards had swept away most of Justinian's

Fig. 25. A mosaic portraying the Emperor Justinian from San Vitale, Ravenna

gains in Italy and much of the Balkans was effectively outside the control of the emperors, Constantinople remained a spectacular city. But it was in some senses now the only real city in a miniature Christian empire stretched around the Aegean Sea. Its complex administrative and legal systems remained characteristically Roman long after Latin had disappeared from everyday use. The language in which they were described and their ideological resonances were fundamentally traditional.[10] The ceremonials and intrigues of the palace were as elaborate as ever.[11] As the power of the Franks grew from the eighth century onwards, Byzantium was the only possible model for imitation, and the city still offered a fascinating spectacle to the descendants of western barbarians as late as the eleventh century, when the crusades brought the societies into yet another relationship. The three heirs of Rome—as western Christendom, Islam, and Byzantium have been aptly called[12]—were the products of fragmentation, invasion, and shrinkage. Each part had its own imperial memories and dreams, but the story of a single Mediterranean empire ends here.

Continuities in the Long Term

The political and military history of the sixth and seventh centuries offers a description of how this happened but not a sufficient explanation. We should not expect this from those who wrote at the time or not long afterwards. Few writers had equally good information about all the parts of the former empire. Universal history was not dead, but competing religious narratives imposed new priorities. Zosimus' *New History* explicitly narrated decline and connected it to the neglect of the traditional gods. He represents a tradition that otherwise survives mainly in fragments. Eusebius and his successors began from the spread of Christianity and progressed from documenting martyrdom to a history of the eradication of heresies. Other historians chronicled particular reigns, as did Procopius for Justinian and Theophylact Simocatta for Maurice. Social, economic, and other trends of any duration were almost invisible from their perspective on the ground. If we are to understand longer-term patterns, we need to form our own arguments about the factors making it easier or more difficult to sustain imperial projects.

During the course of this book, I have drawn attention to a number of factors that made the success of the Roman Empire possible. The

Mediterranean basin offered a corridor within which communication was relatively easy. Goods and ideas moved easily around the empire, and although there were severe limits on the movement of large numbers of people, it was not too difficult to coordinate the activities of regional commands. The Sahara and the Atlantic together provided boundaries that, once reached, did not really need to be defended. The Iron Age civilizations of the Mediterranean world and its hinterlands produced sufficient demographic and agricultural surpluses to support the rise of cities and states, even given the technological limits of antiquity. Climatic conditions, broadly similar to those we experience today, may have contributed to the general prosperity of the early imperial period, making it easier for peasant cultivators to produce the surpluses on which states and empires depended.

Some of this had changed by the seventh century AD.[13] Epidemics of different kinds had moved back and forward between the more densely populated (and so urbanized) portions of the Old World since at least the middle of the last millennium BC. It is likely that this had been happening every so often since the first domestications of animals. Plagues, in the sense of outbreaks of unfamiliar epidemic diseases, figure in the early literature of many parts of the world. But the steady increase of population during the last millennium BC and the first centuries AD, coupled with the growth of urbanism across the empire and in neighbouring regions, and an increase in communications made populations more susceptible across the whole of Eurasia. Mediterranean plagues tended to come from the east, as Chinese ones did from the west. But there were disease corridors leading out of Africa too, and Egypt was connected to Indian Ocean trading systems from the turn of the millennia.[14] Leprosy, moved into the Mediterranean world very slowly and its progress can only be tracked by comparing sources widely separated in time.[15] Literary sources describe terrifying epidemics in the reign of Marcus Aurelius, again in the middle of the third century AD, and then again in the reign of Justinian. From Justinian's reign outbreaks of the plague recur at regular intervals for centuries. It is very difficult, however, to assess the impact of epidemics of this sort on demography, and by extension on the resources of tax and manpower available to the Roman and Persian empires. The nature of some pathogens is still under discussion. Recent forensic work shows the Justinianic plague was caused by *yersinia pestis,* the same bacterium that was responsible for the Black Death. But there is no scientific certainty about the causes of other epidemics, and literary descriptions are rarely precise enough to allow identification. They are also vague about the geographic spread and the mortality. More recent epidemics show how much they vary in which sections of population are most affected: an epidemic that targets the old and the weak will have very different effects from those of one which strikes down those most involved in agricultural labour or war. Even for the Antonine plague, which is relatively well documented, there is real uncertainty as to whether it dealt a long-lasting blow to the population of the empire and its economy or whether its effects (if terrifying to ancient witnesses) were relatively short-lived and limited.

The question of climate change is equally difficult. I discussed in Chapter IV the difficulties in connecting global climatic trends to political changes. Environmental historians of antiquity now mostly prefer to approach these questions at the regional scale. Between the first and fourth centuries AD some regions became drier, others wetter.[16] Sea level rises are recorded in late antiquity in some areas. Tree ring data from other areas has been taken to suggest a slight drop in fertility. The more indicators we use, the more complicated the picture becomes. There is a broad agreement that climate became a little more volatile in late antiquity. Moving from observations like this, however, to explaining events such as the arrival of the Huns or the collapse of Roman frontiers is more or less impossible. The best we can say is that climatically induced changes at local levels prompted local responses. But those responses ranged from settlement relocation, drainage schemes, and shifts in agricultural strategies to migration, changes in local population levels, and occasionally revolts by taxpayers.[17] At the moment, it is probably best to be cautious about relying too heavily on explanations in terms of disease or climate change.[18]

What about the social institutions and customary routines out of which Roman rule had first been constructed and later sustained? I have emphasized the use made of the family, slavery, and the city; the community of interest engineered between local and imperial elites; and the power of ideological productions, including those associated with state cults, to capture the imagination of Rome's other subjects. None of these had remained fossilized over the seven centuries that separated Polybius from Zosimus. But many features of Roman society remained recognizable.

Continuities are most clear at the smallest level of organization, the family and slavery, linked as ever to the primitive conditions of economic production on which the empire rested. Cassiodorus' writings and the legislation of Justinian show us how vital some of these most basic building blocks of empire remained in the sixth century. Roman styles of family life were perhaps more widespread than ever before, disseminated by the spread of citizenship, the moderate extension of education in late antiquity, and the cultural convergence of the empire's elites. Notions of slavery and the family that would have been recognizable to Cicero remained enshrined at the heart of Roman and barbarian law codes alike.[19] Probably the numerical balance between slaves and free had shifted very slightly. But where records are good, as in late antique Egypt, there is no sign of a dramatic change in social structure.[20] Transformation, rather than crisis, is the preferred term among scholars working on these subjects.

Fundamental change is much more evident at what we might term higher levels of organization, where the fates of cities, imperial elites, and imperial government lie. The idea that collapse often occurs through the shedding of the highest levels of social complexity perhaps has some application here.[21] At the highest level, the power and authority of the emperor, there was clearly enormous change as the empire fragmented, for all that it was mystified by traditionalism and ritual.[22] Roman scholars were, to some extent, able to reproduce their accustomed lifestyles in the chaos of Ostrogothic Italy or under the increasingly centralized power of Justinianic Constantinople. Rural lifestyles were least affected. But the picture looks different if we focus attention on that level of imperial society represented by cities, landowning elites, and the fiscal systems through which they had been linked ever since the Roman Empire was transformed from conquest state to tributary empire.

Cities and Their Rulers

The early empire rested on a collusion of interests between the propertied classes of Rome and their counterparts in Italy and the provinces. Many of these elites were already installed within a world of city states, whether of Greek, Punic, Etruscan, or other origin. Others were drawn into that mode of aristocracy and shaped in their image. Across the western and northern provinces, in interior Spain and North Africa and Anatolia, in Syria, and eventually even in Egypt, cities were established on the classical model. Those cities provided the emperors with their most fundamental instrument of government. The local property classes that ruled them kept order and collected taxes, and in return the empire preserved and enhanced their power over other members of their societies.

Today, Roman cities evoke images of temples and basilicas, theatres and bathhouses, grand amphitheatres and enormous circuses, the representative highlights of a monumentality that, with some variations, came to characterize the early Roman Empire wherever it could be afforded.[23] Monuments of this kind represented a commitment—financial and moral—on the part of the rich to a particular urban version of civilization. That civilization included a public style of politics and social life, and a festival culture that alluded to the past, celebrated the present, and was designed to ensure the future.[24] The remains of those monuments are the physical traces of urban societies, the hard fossils from which the ephemeral material of human life and public rhetoric has since withered away.

Sixth-century rulers were as spellbound as we are by these traces of urban civilization. But by their day, they were no more than traces in most parts of the former empire. Almost all the great monuments of provincial cities were built before the middle of the third century AD; even maintaining them was a concern for rulers of all kinds.[25] The letter quoted at the head of this chapter was penned by Cassiodorus for the Gothic king Athalaric, who was keen to encourage the propertied classes to return to their notional urban bases. When Procopius' *On Buildings* is examined closely, we see the emperor's attention was focused almost exclusively on churches and fortifications. When he did found the city of Justiniana Prima at his birthplace in Thrace, it covered around 7 hectares (around 17 acres): early imperial cities often extended well over 100 hectares (just under 250 acres). Already in Italy and much of the west, the propertied classes had moved out to their grand estates hundreds of years before. Urban contraction was most dramatic in the northern provinces, where occupied areas dropped to a third by around AD 300; by the end of the fourth century some were no more than refuges, fortified strongpoints built out of pillaged monuments in the middle of vast deserted towns in which abandoned residential quarters were gradually crumbling where they had not already been turned into gardens and fields.

That vision looks catastrophic to us. But in most areas the process of change was probably a gradual one and the product of choice not necessity. The wealthy had always had homes in both town and country, and over time they spent more time (and money) in the latter than in the former. Public building and the sponsoring of festivals in most cities dried up between AD 200 and 300. Meanwhile, the villas of the fourth century display extravagant elaboration and ornamentation. Wherever the elites were absent from the cities, urban economies shrivelled up without the huge stimulus of their spending and that of their slaves, freedmen, and clients and without the support of their occasional benefactions.

Charting and explaining the collapse of classical urbanism has been a major research priority for archaeologists and for historians of late antiquity.[26] One clear finding is that there were exceptions to this picture, but they are not where we might have expected them. Rome, for example, underwent dramatic population decline. Estimates for the age of Augustus are around one million, by the early fifth century it was about a third of that, and when Justinian's armies recaptured it from the Gothic kings in 536, it was around 80,000. The decline set in far too early to be explained by the Gothic wars or even the fall of the west. On the other hand, a small number of cities show evidence for the building of private housing and extensive trade well into the fifth and sometimes the sixth centuries. Marseilles and Carthage, Ephesus, Alexandria, and Caesarea are particularly well studied; all were, as it happens, port cities.[27] This pattern is superimposed on some broad regional variation that can be (crudely) summarized as follows. Britain, Germany, and northern Gaul experienced earlier and more severe urban contraction than anywhere else, while Syria and western Asia Minor seem to have sustained urban styles of life longest, with clear continuity in Syria into the period of Islamic rule. Spanish cities were transformed during the fourth century, in so far as Christian buildings replacing older monuments is concerned, but there is little third-century construction of public monuments.[28] Many African cities did well into the fourth century and later, but others did not.[29] Urbanism generally did not flourish in the Balkans, but in much of the interior, cities had never been very large. Egypt had no catastrophic decline, but temple building decreased from the third century, sometime before churches begin to appear. Many classical cities had their afterlives, at least as places invested with memories. Many had been built on key sites in communication nodes; centuries of road building and port construction had only emphasized these advantages. Bishoprics were also based on the urban framework of the second century. Many towns survived to the Middle Ages only as wall circuits enclosing churches, and in a few cases the palaces of barbarian kings. Otherwise, the physical cities crumbled or were absorbed. Temples naturally found fewer sponsors after Constantine, and some were physically dismantled, but many became churches. Aqueducts functioned for surprisingly long periods after the end of their construction. Shops, stalls, and markets encroached on the great colonnades and public squares of Syrian cities during the sixth century.[30]

It is still difficult to sum up this picture, let alone explain it in a way that is completely satisfying. But a few trends can be separated out. First, the rich stopped building public monuments and endowing money virtually everywhere before the end of the third century; where new building is attested in the fourth, fifth, and sixth centuries, it generally comprises fortifications, churches, and private mansions. Second, even after elites had transferred their expenditure from public to private, they varied considerably from region to region in how far they chose to live in or near cities. Third, some impoverishment of part of the landowning classes is certain; at least some of this was due to increased burdens imposed by the state, at the same time as more members of local elites were able to escape financial obligations by joining the imperial bureaucracy or indeed the Church.[31] Fourth, civic institutions collapsed, despite efforts made by various emperors to compel local elites to maintain them; their role was taken over by imperial counts and governors, bishops, and groups of first citizens.[32] Fifth, notwithstanding these trends, a small number of port cities seem to have thrived connecting densely farmed landscapes, like those of Egypt, Syria, and North Africa, to distant consumers. Sixth, responsibility for these changes cannot be laid at the door of environmental change or any other external factor. The only plausible culprits are the propertied classes and the empire, and they were certainly not working together.

The State

The highest level of organization was the state itself, including its central and regional administration, its military and its tax-gathering officials, the information systems that kept emperors and their officials abreast of new threats, and the command systems that helped them respond to them. The size and configuration of the imperial state changed many times over the millennium or so of its existence. For much of the time, however, it depended on co-opting the institutions of cities and the energies of their propertied classes. Romans did not exactly choose this course: the Mediterranean urban system long predated Rome's rise to power, and structured the social and political space they expanded into. Even so, cities and civic elites only really became central to the running of the empire in the late Republic, after the shortcomings of other mechanisms—such as unequal alliances, client kings, tax farming, and informal hegemony—had been revealed. Pompey and Caesar had laid the groundwork, and Augustus had generalized the system.

Since then, the empire had experienced a combination of incremental and catastrophic changes. Incremental changes included the gradual expansion of bureaucracy, the development of the court as a governing institution in its own right, and the emergence within the provincial propertied classes of a group of families of exceptional wealth with estates in many provinces and highly diversified business interests. Catastrophic changes included the new monetary and fiscal systems set up by Diocletian and Constantine after the military crisis of the third century. The bureaucracy run by the praetorian prefects and from the early fourth century by the *magister officiorum* (the same position as Cassiodorus had held at the court of Theodoric the Ostrogoth) was much larger than its early imperial counterpart. In effect, these centralizing changes made imperial government much less reliant on those local aristocracies who in the early empire had shouldered the burden of administering provincial communities under very light supervision. Unsurprisingly, the emperors became less and less concerned to require members of the local elites—called *curiales* in the west and *bouleutai* in the east—to carry out their civic obligations if they would prefer to join the imperial service. Squeezed on the one hand by exemptions and on the other by wealth accumulation that reduced the number of families who could be asked to supply magistrates, some cities clearly ran into problems. Yet the fact that other cities seem to have survived and prospered shows this was less of a general threat and more of a possible hazard in the new order. Cities that had many functions and cities well matched to their immediate hinterlands were the most resilient. Those sustained mainly by their role in imperial administration and those dependent on subsidies or provisioning from afar were more at threat. Mostly, cities that did poorly simply shrank, like former tetrarchic capitals that were no longer connected to the lifeblood of the expenditure on the emperors' courts.

Attractive, then, as it might be to see Roman imperialism as a species of macro-parasitism,[33] growing up within classical urban civilization before killing off its host (and so itself), that story is too simple. It does not explain all the variation between the fates of different cities. It also makes no sense of the length of the process by which some (but not all) of the rich fell out of love with city life. An alternative narrative sees those propertied classes as the parasites, using the empire to accumulate wealth and power, and then refusing to pay their dues, with the result that the peasantries became alienated and the emperors ran out of cash to protect the ancient world from the barbarians.[34] Again this is too simplistic. If some elites were indeed efficient at accumulating wealth into a smaller and smaller number of hands, they were not completely immune from the tax system in the fourth century. It is also difficult to show that the peasantries of the empire were generally more disaffected in late antiquity than at other times. Finally, careful reading of the letters of Sidonius, the history of Zosimus, the erudite researches of Cassiodorus, or the passionate apologetics of Augustine and Orosius makes it difficult to reduce the attitudes and motives of the educated and wealthy to such a crude calculation of financial interest.

So if cities were not essential to ancient empires, why should Rome not have reinvented itself as a non-urban empire? The bureaucracy created in the fourth century, combined with the army, could surely raise revenue and secure peace. In a sense, this is what did happen from the seventh century on, in the remnant Byzantine lands left around the Aegean. Constantinople was the only real city left, others were abandoned or became tiny market towns, and the empire was divided into districts called *themata* within which a single official exercised both military and civilian authority, raising locally the resources needed by the troops he commanded.[35] But this system was evidently created in the aftermath of collapse. Using the language of transformation to describe what happened to the Roman Empire between AD 300 and 700 is an evasion. If it is measured in terms of territory, population, influence, and military power, there is no doubt at all about the fact of collapse, or at least dramatic downsizing. Some ancients recognized this, and so should we.

Throughout this story of empire I have emphasized moments of survival. Episodes of expansion are not rare in world history, and many were followed by short-lived periods of hegemony. The exclusive club that Rome joined, however, is that small number of political entities that survived their own expansion and were able to generate new institutions, ideologies, and habits as their circumstances changed. Successful empires are sustained by long-term relationships with other social entities with which they are in some senses symbiotic. The success of the Roman Empire rested on the synergies it engineered between empire and aristocracy, empire and slavery, empire and the city, and empire with various ideals of civilization, Greek, Roman, and Christian, for example. Those synergistic relationships were not immutable. As in biological symbioses, the partners modified each other over time, so that Greek cities became more politically stable, and emperors spent more time listening to speeches made by their ambassadors. What is sometimes called the 'petition and response' model of imperial rule arose, it seems, through trial and error rather than from deliberate planning. The broad alliance between bishops and emperors was also something that emerged after a range of alternative relationships were attempted, changing the nature of the episcopate and the role of the emperor in the process.

Sometimes crises promoted periods of more rapid institutional change. The chaos of the last century BC is an obvious example. The military crisis of the third century is another. Not all the innovations survived. A few ideas, like the idea of multiple emperors, soon outlived their purpose, and some, like imposing maximum prices, were immediate failures. More often the balance shifted subtly in some of the symbiotic relationships on which empire rested. Relations between the empire's many elites and the imperial court fluctuated. The relationship between the classical city and its rulers changed in many regions.[36] For a while classical cities and the elites were more useful to barbarian kings (who lacked governmental infrastructure) than to Byzantine emperors (who were developing more centralized alternatives). Change looks to us like a constant recalibration between the constituent parts of the Roman world. Its capacity to rebalance itself again and again is one measure of the empire's resilience.[37]

Remaking the World

So much for hindsight. From our distant perspective and armed with some knowledge of the historical trajectories followed by other empires, we can discuss and describe the broad pattern of Roman history. But there is a trap here, and that is the historian's desire for a rounded story. We ask, often, for a narrative with a clear progression from start to finish, from rise to decline and fall. It is even tempting to write the history of an institution (as Florus did) in terms borrowed from the lifespan of a single human being, from birth, through growth, mature adulthood, old age and finally death. While a scheme like this might seem quite a good fit to some measures of imperial power, such as the total amount of territory controlled or people ruled, it brings with it some unwelcome baggage. We desire, as readers and writers of history, to achieve closure. There is an eerie satisfaction that the last western emperor was named Romulus, as if events were offering us a kind of ring composition. Gibbon began and ended his *History of the Decline and Fall of the Roman Empire* with a view of the ruins of Rome seen from the Capitol. As we near the end of any book, we have to consciously resist the impulse to wind up the subplots, solve the crime, and bury or marry off any remaining characters.

Contemporaries saw things differently. The inhabitants of the Mediterranean world in the sixth and seventh centuries AD did not consider themselves to be turning out the lights before leaving the building. Within and around the former territories of the empire several groups had a clear focus on the future. Justinian's Byzantium has already been considered. The sixth and seventh centuries are now often viewed as a crucial period of reorientation, shaped naturally by the threats of the day, but also driven by a new sense of purpose.[38] One way to view this is as the aspiration for a new level of cultural coherence. An early indicator is Justinian's closure of the philosophical schools in Athens in 529 AD, just two years after his accession. So is the *Digest of Roman Law*. These centuries are also those in which polytheism seems to have been finally eradicated.[39] Religious uniformity was always a goal rather than an achievement, but great energy was put into promoting what was considered orthodoxy (largely what was agreed by the Council of Chalcedon in 451 AD and its successors). Religion and law were presented as dual pillars of a highly ordered society, one in which Roman imperialism and religious universalism were brought into harmony. At the same time the shrivelling away of municipal elites meant that there was no longer the tension between civic and imperial politics that had characterized much of Roman history. The imperial bureaucracy was a more coherent body, which had rallied around traditional moral and martial values. Internal politics remained liable to faction, both in the palace between rival eunuchs or in the city between circus factions. Yet it was stable in the sense that its institutions were now deeply rooted.

Numerous groups and kingdoms continued to surround Byzantium to the north and west, even after the Roman reconquest of North Africa and parts of Italy and Spain. New entrants appear like the Slavs and Avars in the Balkans and the Lombards in Italy. The major growth story in this period, however, is that of the Franks. Several groups of Franks appear in Roman historical texts in the fourth and fifth century, when they occupied various areas around the northern frontier on the Rhine. As Roman influence in northern Gaul collapsed, they expanded their range southwards. From the early sixth century a dynasty of kings, the Merovingians, succeeded

in unifying the various Frankish groups and building a state that differed
in important ways from those of Goths, Burgundians, and Vandals farther
south. It was less obviously dependent on Roman institutions, especially
on Roman towns and Roman-style taxation. Instead the king relied on a
retinue who led warbands, which were expanded by imposing a levy on
their subjects. Frankish expansion in the sixth century was rapid, absorbing
the Burgundian kingdom in 534 AD and territories in southern Germany
that had never been Roman. Frankish nobles operated from fortified *castra*,
and some of the greater lords were often quite independent of the king.
Yet the Merovingian kingdom, when strong, stretched from the Baltic to
the Pyrenees. A key component of the self-presentation of the monarchy
was as Christian rulers. Their relatively late conversion to Christianity
had the consequence that they were not Arians. Kingship was bolstered
by Old Testament imagery and ceremonial including the annointment of
their kings. The close relationship they built with the Bishop of Rome in
the eighth century would be fundamental to the creation of Carolingian
Francia, the first imperial state in Europe since the collapse of the western
empire.

At the other end of the Mediterranean, the main political growth in
the sixth and seventh centuries was in Arabia. The Arabian peninsula was
flanked to the north and east by the Sassanian Empire and to the north
west by Roman Syria and Palestine. South of Egypt the Axumite kingdom
of Ethiopia was ruled by Christian monarchs. Much of the desert interior
was uninhabited or scarcely populated but there were Arab communities
just west of Mesopotamia, east of Palestine, and especially in western Arabia
and what is now Yemen. Before the seventh century there are few contemporary records, and most naturally focus on how the more northerly
groups were involved in the long conflicts between Rome and Persia.
Long-distance trade routes from the east passed north of Arabia by land
and also south by sea en route to the Red Sea ports. Most traders in the
region were probably involved in local exchanges between settled farmers
and nearby semi-settled populations and between the small towns and
villages of the west, but Mecca at least had wider connections. It was out
of western Arabia that Islam emerged in the early seventh century. The
Prophet was born into one of the more influential tribes in the city of
Mecca. It was there he formulated religious views that set him at odds
with much of the population. His migration (*hijra*) to the town of Yathrib
(later Medina) took place in 622 AD, and in the last ten years of his life he

created an extraordinary community (*ummah*) based on a set of social principles that bound its members closely together. The Koran, which records his revelations, cannot have circulated much before his death. But perhaps a good deal of its content did. What Arabian culture was like before the *hijra* is a matter of current debate. There were certainly Christian strands, probably from Ethiopia and Syria, and Jewish ones, and also older indigenous beliefs, some monotheist or henotheist (focused on one divine entity among many) and some polytheist. The dominant religious grouping in the Sassanian Empire was Zoroastrian, which also came in more and less monotheist forms. There were other religious groups in the wider region, including the Manichaeans and the Mandaeans, drawing from the same broad range of sources. The Prophet shared some emphases with neighbouring peoples. Monotheism was arguably at the centre of some of the main theological debates that consumed both Christians and Zoroastrians; law was central to the ideologies of Romans and Persians as well as of Jews. But the Prophet's particular revelation and the community of the *ummah* were unique. As it began to expand its reach, through warfare first in Arabia and then surrounding lands, it too was focused on the future.

It is striking that each of these sources of innovation had a strong religious component. There had never been any secular states in antiquity, at least not in the modern sense of secular which originated in the Enlightenment. Darius the Mede in his funeral inscription at Behistun declared his dependence on the help given by Ahura Mazda, the first fruits of the tribute paid to Athens by her allies went to Athena, and Romans of different ages had believed in the support of the gods and/or the divinity of the emperor. But religious thought had a different relation to power in late antiquity. It did more than clothe earthly hierarchies with an air of the sacred, or legitimate the actions and status of rulers. In Byzantium, Francia, and the Caliphate faith offered a compelling master narrative of history, a universalizing view of the present state of the world, and clear instructions for how to behave in the future. All these groups appealed to traditional virtues; yet in all cases the use of the past was subordinated to the needs of the present. There was no hesitation in dismissing what was not required, whether it was Greek philosophy or the polytheism of the ancestors. Sassanian Persia had arguably been engaged in similar projects before it was swept away by the Arab invasions. During the sixth century Zoroastrian priests (the *magi*) played a greater and greater role in the judicial system, and different religious communities acquired some legal status. The ceremony and imagery of Sassanian universal monarchy closely parallels that of Byzantine emperors and their courts.[40] Not all visions of the future deliver. But there is an overwhelming sense of new possibilities in these years, and not much sign that contemporaries were looking for closure or felt they were living in the last days.

Further Reading

Michael Maas's *Cambridge Companion to the Age of Justinian* (Cambridge, 2005) surpasses the limits of the genre to present a new portrait of the age. Fundamental to the study of the period are the various works of Procopius of Caesarea. Averil Cameron's *Procopius and the Sixth Century* (London, 1985) is the best introduction. Some of her many important papers on the sixth and seventh centuries are gathered in *Continuity and Change in Sixth-Century Byzantium* (London, 1981) and *Changing Cultures in Early Byzantium* (Aldershot, 1996). For the west, Julia Smith's *Europe after Rome* (Oxford, 2005) presents an original and lucid new synthesis. The first volume of *The New Cambridge History of Islam* edited by Chase F. Robinson (Cambridge 2010) is an invaluable guide to its historiographically complex subject.

The transformation of the ancient urban system has been the focus of much work. Two very useful collections are John Rich's *The City in Late Antiquity* (London, 1992) and Neil Christie and Simon Loseby's *Towns in Transition* (Aldershot, 1996). Wolf Liebeschuetz's *The Decline and Fall of the Roman City* (Oxford, 2001) is the best synthesis. It is worth reading it alongside Chris Wickham's *Framing the Early Middle Ages* (Oxford, 2005). For the city of Rome, see William Harris's collection *The Transformations of* Urbs Roma *in Late Antiquity* (Portsmouth, RI, 1999) and *Early Medieval Rome and the Christian West* (Leiden, 2000) edited by Julia Smith.

THE ROMAN PAST AND
THE ROMAN FUTURE

I shall not perish utterly, for a great part of me will escape death. I will grow, swollen with the praise of future generations, for as long as the priest leads the silent virgin up to the Capitol.

(Horace, *Odes* 3.30.6–9)

The words are those of the poet Horace, composed in the reign of Augustus. As you read them, you surpass his wildest expectations. No pontiffs or vestal virgins are attested after the end of the fourth century AD. The Capitol has been ruined and rebuilt several times since Horace wrote. And yet we do still read Horace's *Odes*. Like so much of Roman culture, he has not perished utterly.

My final chapter is about survival and about how we know so much about the Roman Empire. Accident and chance both play a part in this story, and more recently our own research on which most of this book is based. But there is design as well, and not just Horace's. For the Romans have sent us many messages in bottles, consigned by generation after generation to remote posterity. We cannot take all the credit for the discovery of ancient Rome: the ancient Romans wanted to be found.

Accidents

Few empires lasted as long as that of Rome or made such an impact on those they ruled. I have struggled throughout this book with metaphors, my own and those of others. The Roman Empire has been likened to an epidemic, a machine, a balloon, a vampire bat, and a great resonating vibration, a tsunami and a tide, an organism known only through its fossil body, and a single human life. At times imperial society has seemed like a great dance too, one that drew in more and more dancers, and then was carried on by fewer and fewer until the music was quite different. My last metaphor is an ice age. Tides sweep over beaches and then retreat; fascinating flotsam and jetsam are left behind, but only after a great storm does the beach really look different. But if we consider what the Roman Empire did to tradition and identity, culture and religion, lifestyles and beliefs, we find much more fundamental change. The empire grew like an ice cap, sending glaciers down in all directions. When those glaciers retreated, back to Byzantium rather than Rome, they left entirely new landscapes gouged out and great moraines of boulders around which their new inhabitants had to accommodate themselves. Those peoples were no longer those whom Rome had originally conquered: some were new arrivals, and almost all the rest had forgotten what it was like before the ice.

When we examine the monumental art, the inscriptions, and the written texts that are our main sources for the identities assumed by Rome's provincial subjects, we find that, in most parts of the former empire, all memory of earlier times had been lost. Western peoples, both those the Romans had conquered like the Gauls and the Spaniards and those who had conquered Rome like the Vandals and the Goths had no reliable memories of their pasts before Rome. From early in the empire, many in the western provinces had come to think of themselves as descendants of Trojan refugees and Greek heroes.[1] Ancient place names and the ancestral gods had been forgotten, many of their languages had been lost forever, and the only history they knew was that of Rome. Half a millennium later, Cassiodorus and others helped the new barbarian arrivals create new genealogies, often along the same lines, although now biblical figures jostled with Brutus the Trojan and other legendary figures at the start of their genealogies.[2] Nor was this situation unique to the west. Many of the peoples who inhabited the vast arc of the Roman Near East seem to have preserved almost no earlier memories either.[3] The Jews still had their scriptures, and the history contained in them. Traces of Babylonian and Phoenician and Egyptian historical traditions survived in works written in Greek in the Hellenistic and early Roman periods. Like the western traditions, they had been remodelled to suit Greek norms of memory and tradition.[4] For the most part their identities too had been accommodated to their long subjection to Macedonian and Roman empires. Only the Greek historical tradition, which Roman scholars had long accepted, persisted. Yet even among those writing in Greek, empire had repeatedly reshaped collective identities and the memories they preserved.[5] When one reads historical writing from late antiquity, whether a universal history like that of Zosimus with its nostalgia for the age before Constantine, or the history of John Malalas, the best source on his native Antioch but often hopelessly confused about the wider world, it is striking how their perspectives on the Roman past had changed. The shifting histories of Rome and Christianity had altered everything. It follows that almost everything that has survived, even by accident, preserves traces of a consciousness of empire.

Rome is better documented than most of the other early empires with which I have been comparing it. The explanation includes ecological and economic factors as well as historical and cultural ones. Empires of the tropics, like that of the Vijayanagara emperors of medieval India or the Mayan kingdoms of the Yucatan peninsula, were rapidly swallowed up by vegetation. By contrast the Mediterranean heartland of the Roman Empire is—geophysically at least—a relatively stable environment, one in which stone buildings and tombs can stand for centuries if they are not disturbed by humans. Benign neglect has derived too from the poverty of many Mediterranean lands in the centuries after Rome. Renaissance Italy and early modern Spain notwithstanding, Rome has had few rivals in subsequent centuries. The leading edge of economic power moved in the Middle Ages, north to the lands of the Franks and east to Baghdad. The cities of Spain and Italy and southern France and Greece preserve elements of their Roman street plans not just because more was built there during the Roman period but also because few of them were later subjected to the spectacular rebuilding projects lavished on north European towns in the late Middle Ages and after.

So, Roman city walls and gateways became encrusted with houses that preserved them, sometimes completely concealing them for centuries. The amphitheatre of Roman Arles (see Figure 26) was given towers and made

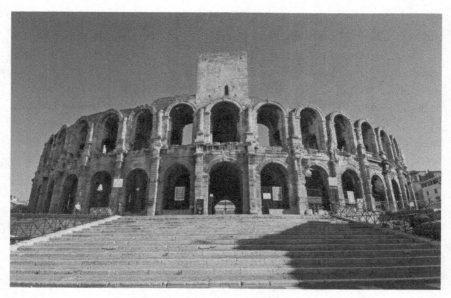

Fig. 26. The amphitheatre at Arles

into a castle, the Porta Nigra of Trier became a church, and the great palace
Diocletian built for himself at Split became a warren of homes and shops,
as it remains today. Sometimes only the shadow of a Roman monument
survives in a maze of medieval streets. It is possible to walk around the
curve of Pompey's great theatre in the *centro storico* of Rome even though
none of the original construction survives above ground; the amphitheatre
of Lucca has left an oval space in the city which was cleared in the 1830s to
create a piazza; the great civic fora and temples of Seville and Lisbon were
replaced first with magnificent mosques, and then after the *reconquista* with
baroque cathedrals. Things were quite different in London and Paris, where
great campaigns of building have obliterated major Roman cities. There
are only a few sites like Silchester where a break in occupation has allowed
something like the whole city plan to be revealed. To be fair, many of the
cities of the peripheral provinces were never as grand as those of the central
provinces, and some were built more of wood and tile than of stone. The
ancient cities of Africa and Syria, many of them, survived even better because they were not major centres after the Arab conquests and were buried
in the sand. All the same, it is still true that the best places to see Roman
monuments today are in the poorer countries of southern Europe, North
Africa, and the Middle East.

Some Roman relics were enveloped not by medieval houses or the desert sands, but by the political designs of Rome's many would-be heirs. I described in Chapter II how successive regimes have made use of Roman symbols of power to develop their own imperial imagery. European history has been characterized by successive 'renaissances' in which groups of scholars or artists self-consciously claimed a new status for their creativity with reference to the Roman past. Carolingian monks, the translators and architects of the caliphate, the clerical scholars of the twelfth century, the artists of the Italian Quattrocento, the first Humanists, the fathers of the Enlightenment, and many others have recuperated various Roman texts, buildings, and artefacts in this way. The relics of empire have been passed on through history like batons in a long relay race.

Finally, there are the objects that lasted simply because of their durability. Early empires were above all great systems of accumulation. By force and the threat of force they drew matter and energy from all over their domains to be consumed and deposited in their capitals. Rome gathered treasure, marbles, and rare beasts from all over the world. The precious metals are long gone, the exotic animals were slaughtered in the arena, but the hard stones remain: brilliant white marble was from Proconnesus in north-west Turkey and Luni in Italy; dark yellow stone from the quarries of African Chemtou; porphyry and rare granites from the eastern deserts of Egypt, and green brescia from the Aegean.[6] The Pantheon and the Baths of Caracalla are genuinely extraordinary even today. The Elder Pliny's *Natural History* includes long accounts of sculpture and bronze statuary. Despite his attempt to order this into a systematic history of art, he is constantly diverted into noting in which temple or portico or garden in Rome a masterpiece may now be seen. For conquest and purchase had assembled the treasures of antiquity—Greek, Egyptian, and other—in the capital.[7] Much has gone, of course, and most bronzes were melted down long before the revival of interest in classical art during the Renaissance. The core of modern collections survived thanks to the energy of Renaissance collectors, who gathered a vast number of marbles which—by various routes—found their way into the royal and later national collections of Europe, there to be supplemented by aggressive acquisitions policies during the eighteenth and nineteenth centuries. Archaeology has added just a few pieces to this body of work, but some are very precious. Our knowledge of ancient bronzes depends substantially on underwater finds, like the Riace Bronzes, two magnificent warriors made in classical Greece but found by a scuba diver off the coast of

Italy in 1972. Current excavations at the cities of Aphrodisias and Sagalassos in Turkey have produced wonderful examples of marble sculpture from the imperial age.

Just a few great buildings were also durable enough to survive as more than traces in the street plans of Italian towns. Rome did not acquire its empire as some modern powers did through major technological advantages over its competitors. But by creating a vast space within which architects and engineers could move about and exchange ideas, and by concentrating wealth in such a way that grand projects could be funded, Rome presided over significant advances in construction techniques. This is evident from technical writing, especially Vitruvius' book *On Architecture*, and also from the study of standing remains.[8] Greek stylistic models remained phenomenally important. But the invention at the end of the last millennium BC of concrete and the increased use and production of bricks and of tiles, along with ever more sophisticated techniques of surveying and design, all combined to make possible buildings on a scale never before seen. Vaults and domes made possible enormous enclosed spaces for basilicas, temples, imperial baths, and palaces. Even today the Pantheon and Hagia Sophia (see Picture Box 10) take our breath away. Aqueducts too consumed vast amounts of energy to build and required amazing engineering skills. A few still functioned into the Middle Ages, and others survived as bridges or simply because they were too well built to crumble and too difficult or remote to dismantle.

Buildings like the Colosseum and the Pont du Gard seem at first sight bound to fascinate.[9] In fact, not all ages have been so entranced by antiquity. The sense that Roman buildings should be preserved whenever possible is relatively recent.[10] Many are now known only through sketches and descriptions made by earlier travellers, architects, and grand tourists. Up until the nineteenth century, when campaigners like Prosper Mérimée in France first began to demand the preservation of ancient monuments as national treasures, it was not unusual for Roman arches or temples to be demolished to make way for projects of modernization. During the twentieth century the struggle moved to trying to secure legal protection for archaeological material that was not visible on the surface. That battle has been largely won in Europe. But there are occasional scandals, and the cost of conserving sites like Herculaneum and Pompeii still gives major concern.

Picture Box 10 Hagia Sophia

Justinian completed Hagia Sophia in AD 537. It is the third church built on the site, the first and second being built by Constantius and Theodosius II in AD 360 and AD 415 respectively. Both of those were basilical churches, on the same general plan as those built by Constantine around Rome. The Justinianic cathedral was a radical departure in its design, which was based around a dome raised on great arches, and in its scale. The enormous construction rose (incredibly) in just five years from the ashes of buildings destroyed in the Nika Riots. It dominated the old city and was the heart of Justinian's rebuilding programme, which also included the square of the Caesars, the *Augusteum*, the new Senate House, and a ceremonial way connecting the church to the Great Palace.

The building was a startling monument from the start. Its exterior was originally clad in bright luminescent marble. Its interiors were decorated with coloured stone, mosaics, and frescoes. Procopius wrote that the roof 'seems not to rest upon solid masonry, but to cover the space with its golden dome suspended from Heaven'. Accounts left by mediaeval visitors from western Europe, from Russia, and from the Arab world show they too were mesmerized by its scale and magnificence, and the same is true today. Its architectural influence first in eastern provinces and later in the Islamic world was profound. It was the central church of Orthodox Christianity for nearly a millennium, aside from the period in the thirteenth century when it was made a Catholic cathedral by the Franks who had seized Constantinople on the Fourth Crusade. After Mehmed II the Conqueror captured the city in 1453, Hagia Sophia became a mosque. In time, much of its interior decor was covered up or removed, and the great dome was surrounded by minarets. The Turkish Republic converted it into a museum in 1935. Now, in 2020, it has become a mosque once more.

Hagia Sophia illustrates the enduring potency of Roman monuments and some of the ways in which subsequent generations have struggled to control their meanings. It is not a unique case. A similar story can be told about the holy places of Jerusalem, in particular the Temple Mount, where the two great Jewish temples were succeeded by a temple to Jupiter Capitolinus, later Jewish and perhaps Christian structures, and then the Al-Aqsa Mosque and the Dome of the Rock. The Parthenon in Athens too has been a temple, a church and a mosque before its ruins became a monument. From Lisbon to Damascus similar histories of use and reuse can be told. There are also stories of acts of symbolic violence, such as the destruction of the great temple of Serapis at Alexandria by Christian monks in AD 391.

Some aspects of the past are easy to forget. Books can be burned or simply allowed to decay, ceremonially banned or abandoned, but large durable material objects need to be accommodated in some way when symbolic orders shift dramatically. The monuments of Roman cities had too much invested in them to be ignored. They had been designed to catch the eye, and it was sometimes difficult to look away or to look past them. The reception of Rome has sometimes been a matter of the selection of themes and their appropriation for new purposes. But in some cases, like that of Hagia Sophia, the objects themselves had an agency that demanded to be dealt with.

Further Reading

Robin Cormack, *Byzantine Art* (Oxford: Oxford University Press, 2000), ch. 2.
Catharine Edwards, ed., *Roman Presences: Receptions of Rome in European Culture, 1789–1945* (Cambridge: Cambridge University Press, 1999).
Judith Herrin, *Byzantium: The Surprising Life of a Medieval Empire* (London: Penguin, 2007), 50–60.

Monuments

Today we use the term 'monument' almost interchangeably with 'remains' But the Latin term *monumentum* had a much more specific meaning. It was a thing deliberately created to commemorate a particular person or event in the past, and it was intended to project that memory into the future.

When a society makes monuments it reveals a lot about collective attitudes to time and the community. We have become much more conscious of all this recently. As I have been revising this book, there have been riots and debates about the removal of statues of Confederate generals in the United States and slave owners in the United Kingdom. At their heart these debates are about what we value from the past and who we want to be in the future. Ancient societies, which also invested effort in making and breaking images, were engaged in essentially the same activity. First of all, building monuments affirms the importance of history. Second, it asserts—however nervously—confidence in posterity, that there will be a future audience or readership. Finally, it imagines a community stretched out in time, those to whom this event or this person mattered, and those to whom it will still matter, both groups connected to the original event. Community, it says, is about continuity. A Roman monument captured, in a moment, that sense of the Roman people, fellow travellers on a common journey from their mythic past to their future destiny. Horace was not talking directly to us, in other words, since we are not part of that community. But we can listen in on the messages Romans sent to their imagined descendants.

Not all societies are so concerned with posterity. One reason we know Rome so well is that monumentality came for a while to be almost a cultural obsession. But things were not always that way. Before the middle of the fourth century BC, Rome was a great power in Italy. Yet very little in the way of monumental architecture was created. Temples are often monuments, of course, but they were also homes for the gods, and their construction seems to have been part of a dialogue in the present between the city's divine and human members. The mid-Republican city seemed unimpressive to many visitors. Writing too had been used for mundane purposes for centuries, but it was hardly ever given a monumental form, whether in great public inscriptions designed to last or in literary works of any kind. Romans were not unusual in this respect by the standards of antiquity. Many societies have been more interested in what has been termed presentism than in tradition. But the decisions not to build great monuments, set up inscriptions, and write great books were choices consciously made: Romans were well aware of the monumental architecture of nearby Greek cities, and perhaps of Greek literature and history as well, and they could certainly have afforded to mimic either. Instead, booty was more often spent on elaborate festivals that spoke to the present, not the future, and although there must have been many traditions about the past, there seems to have been no real concern to develop a common, collective history of Rome.[11]

A new concern with posterity appears at the turn of the fourth and third centuries BC. Appius Claudius Caecus, who was censor in 312 BC, commissioned an aqueduct and a great southern road, known after him as the Aqua Appia and the Via Appia respectively. The inscribed *elogia* of the Scipiones in their elaborate tomb complex constructed at the start of the third century BC explicitly addresses future readers. Who were these imagined readers? The location suggests family members, but when the inscriptions speak of individual Scipiones holding office 'among you', it is difficult not to conjure up the image of the Roman people. During the early second century BC more and more grandiose building projects began to incorporate the names of those who had commissioned them. Cato named the great covered hall he built beside the forum in his censorship the Basilica Porcia, an allusion to the royal (*basilikē*) stoa given to Athens by Attalus, king of Pergamum, and to the gens Porcia, the clan to which Cato belonged. The first aqueduct to approach Rome on a series of great arches was named the Aqua Marcia after the urban praetor Quintus Marcius Rex who built it in 144 BC. Lucius Mummius had his name placed on triumphal monuments in the many communities on which he bestowed a share of the booty plundered from the sack of Corinth. From this point on, the association of public buildings with individuals became absolutely regular. The great generals of the late Republic developed the idiom further. From the middle of the last century BC, a whole new series of monumental types appeared. Theatres, amphitheatres, and circuses are the best known. More than 1,000 were constructed between around 50 BC and AD 250.[12] To this can be added the Saepta Julia, imperial *thermae*, public gardens, libraries, porticoes filled with captured art, and so on. Not all senators were fortunate enough to win booty with which to build victory temples, and only a few held offices like the censorship that allowed them to build with public funds. Besides, it became increasingly difficult to compete over the last century BC, at least as far as public buildings were concerned, once Pompey had set new standards with his great theatre. Tomb building offered a cheaper mode of monumentality. The tombs of the late Republic grew ever more elaborate and varied, including great towers along the Appian Way, and the pyramid built by Cestius now straddling the Aurelianic Walls.

Eventually the emperors drove their competitors out of the city. But the effect was just to move monumental building to the towns of Italy and the provinces.[13] The origins of this movement lay in a growing interest in monumentality that coincides, at least chronologically, with the origins of Roman hegemony and continued up until the crisis of empire. But when we visit Roman ruins today, we are mostly looking at monuments created in a long second century. Over most of the empire this building boom gathered pace over the first century AD, reached a peak around the year 200, and collapsed in the generation that followed.

Plot that pattern on a graph, and it pretty much coincides with the curve made by the rise and fall of Latin epigraphy.[14] Most inscriptions were gravestones. That habit of commemoration originated with the senatorial aristocracy but was taken up by other sectors of society, especially lesser aristocrats and former slaves. The freeborn masses were largely excluded, and so the peasantries of the empire are more or less invisible. Hundreds of thousands of these inscriptions survive from the Roman period, even though we probably have less than 5 per cent of those originally set up. The greatest numbers are found in the city of Rome and surrounding areas, but the habit also spread through the cities of Italy and the provinces and was even taken up by soldiers on the frontier and traders far from home. These too are monuments, deliberate attempts to record human lives for posterity. And they are now a precious source of information on Roman history too, since many record the achievements and ranks of the deceased along with his or her closest relationships, with parents and children, masters and slaves, fellow soldiers and friends. They speak to us of an age when Roman society was at its most energetic, when levels of social mobility were greatest and the urban network of the empire reached its peak. Naturally it is the success stories that are most often commemorated—the slaves given their freedom, the soldiers who won citizenship after long service, the town councillors who collected the set of municipal priesthoods and offices. Their individual pride and anxiety play against a confidence that there will be future readers, that the world in which they had succeeded would continue in roughly the same form as the present.

One final kind of monument can be set alongside tombs and aqueducts, amphitheatres and gravestones, and that is literary texts. Not long after the first monumental tombs appeared, the same Roman aristocracy who built them set out to create a literature in Latin.[15] Like the sarcophagi of the Scipiones, the first works created had clear Greek models. Like them, they were immediately put to new purposes in Rome's very un-Greek social order. Horace's poem, with which I started this chapter, begins by borrowing from the Greek poet Pindar the conceit that a poem is a more effective monument than a physical statue. In practice we do not need to separate monuments and texts too sharply, since Roman monuments were from the start covered in writing, and much poetry was in fact inscribed on stone. The earliest of the sarcophagi in the Tomb of the Scipiones were inscribed with a new verse form developed from Greek models.[16] When Cato created his literary *monumenta*, he was also fixing his name—quite literally—on the vast basilica that flanked the forum. Fulvius Nobilior patronized the epic poet Ennius, as well as building his temple of Hercules of the Muses. These associations only intensified in the early empire, by which point some of the poets and historians are themselves senators or even emperors.

An empire where the elite write poetry is a very unusual thing. All early empires made use of writing, but mostly just for administrative purposes. Many empires contained within them literary groups, monks and court poets, priests and scientists. But few of these were close to the levers of power. Perhaps only the scholar bureaucrats of medieval China come close to the erudite senators and equestrians of imperial Rome, even if in Rome this sort of activity was just one cultural option among many open to the elite.[17] Roman writers sometimes cast Athens as the civilizing counterpart to martial Rome. Yet Athenian festivals in the Roman period were focused on commemorating the military victories of the Persian wars,[18] and Aelius Aristides' speech in honour of Athens flattered it with its imperial past. The Roman Empire, on the other hand, created conditions in which education and literary culture of all kinds flourished. Poets and orators were feted at court, and the emperors endowed positions for teachers of philosophy and rhetoric in many provincial cities. Great libraries were built by emperors in the capital, and by senators and town councillors in other cities. Probably more literary texts were created in the early empire than at any other point in classical antiquity. Most were in Greek, and they covered a huge range of subject matter from medical texts and poems about geometry to erotic epigrams and civic histories. Once again, only a fraction has survived, but through these monuments too we can listen in to the Romans talking to their future selves.

The Futures of Rome

What did the Romans want to tell posterity through their monuments? Many kinds of message can be put in a bottle. Most obvious is the author's desire to preserve his name, not to perish utterly. Imperial monuments were associated with the names of dynasties and individual emperors and their relatives. So the Porticoes of Octavia and Livia, the Forum of Trajan, the Baths of Caracalla made permanent marks on the cityscape of Rome. These were still the monuments that visitors from elsewhere came to see in the fourth century and even later.[19] The great marble plan of the city created in the Severan period is written all over with the names of generations of the Roman powerful. Greek and Latin inscriptions on the wall of gymnasia, theatres, libraries, and other civic buildings commemorated their founders. Even temples, where the names of the gods were most prominent, bore records of those who had paid for their building and successive restorations. Poets often began their works with letters addressed to their patrons. Tombstones listed ranks achieved, priesthoods and magistracies held, the profession, tribe, and age of the deceased, and the names of those left behind who had seen to the burial. All this is completely comprehensible to us now.

All monuments present an ambiguous attitude to the future. The act of creating a monument is an act of faith that there will be future readers; yet the need for one betrays a fear that all will be forgotten. That fear seems reasonable even when we think of the empire at its most secure. What of the period that followed? No agreement yet exists on the reasons for the end of monument building. Did the powerful lose faith in the future or simply run out of the funds needed to communicate with it? Many were certainly impoverished as the imperial economy contracted and as the weight of government pressed harder on those who were not well connected. If the building industry collapsed, perhaps this had knock-on effects for the production even of modest monuments. Yet the rich villas of the fourth century and growing expenditure on churches suggest no simple economic explanation will do.

Besides not all forms of monumentalization did end. It is true that the great mass of tombstones and votive inscriptions through which we know so much about the social life of the early empire peters out. This happens during the third century, at different speeds in different regions and only a little after the end of major building projects in most of the cities of the west. Yet inscriptions continued to be produced in some areas. One group who left a small but rich epigraphic footprint were the senatorial classes of the western empire. Some of their surviving inscriptions show traces of the same fascination with the early empire as does much of the literature they produced and patronized, but this too comprised a message to the future about continuity, about what they valued in their past (even if others no longer did). Religious documents are particularly full of those who have been termed the Last Pagans of Rome. Then there is the great mass of statues produced or reused in late antiquity. The great majority that can be dated were set up in the fourth century, but the statue habit continued during the fifth century and even later.[20] Then there are alternative forms of monumentality promoted by Christian leaders, ranging from the verse memorials of martyrs set up around the city of Rome by Pope Damasus in the late fourth century to the mosaic memorials created in churches for their founders.

A variety of attitudes to antiquity emerged in the literature of the fourth century AD, but no new consensus either about history or the future.[21] Classicizing historians presented themselves as traditionalists, but, of course, they were not. Zosimus gives the game away when he alludes to Polybius' account of Rome's rise and immediately asks who could imagine it was not due to divine favour. The answer, of course, is Polybius, who had offered an explanation based on the comparative advantages of political institutions and the attitudes they inculcated. But the argument had evidently become one about religion. Yet even the Christians did not agree about the past. More than a century before Constantine, Melito, the Bishop of Sardis, had suggested that the birth of Christ at the origin of the Roman Empire showed the Roman world was a providential creation. Orosius tentatively suggested something similar. But this seems to us to deviate from his teacher Augustine's position that the convulsions of the Earthly City had little relevance for citizens of the Heavenly One. Not all Christian futures had Rome in them, nor did all Christian pasts. Gregory of Tours's ten-book *History of the Franks*, composed in the later sixth century, began with the creation of the world and went on to tell the story of Christian Frankish rulers. The western empire fell somewhere in the middle of book 2, but it was not important enough to merit a mention in Gregory's account. For Christians, this flexibility was an advantage. Nothing could catch them out, not the fall of the western empire, the thousand-year succession of Byzantium, or the (to them) terrible events of the Arab conquests.

What about the posterity of Rome today? Looking back down the telescope, we see the worst is now past. Most classical literature ever written was lost between the fifth and eighth centuries AD .[22] When cities contracted, the libraries—public and private—were no longer maintained, and books burnt, rotted, or crumbled away. Many had probably never existed in more than a handful of copies anyway, given the cost of producing multiple versions in an age before print technology. The shift from papyrus scroll to a codex format, essentially that of the modern book, also acted like a filter. What was not transferred onto the new format was lost. For nearly two hundred years in the west almost no copies of any non-Christian text were made. But what survived to the Carolingian Renaissance had a good chance of being gathered by Humanists and preserved until the invention of printing. Almost all classical texts are now available electronically, in the original and in many translations. For the moment those monuments seem safe.

When I wrote the first edition of this book, I suggested that we can also be optimistic about the archaeological heritage. Conservation was firmly established in law, and it is rare now for Roman monuments to be threatened with demolition. Popular interest in the past had saved it, making it an asset for those poorer countries that attract tourists and a symbol of national pride, too. Local activists defended Roman and other antiquities everywhere. This judgement turned out to be parochial and premature. The rise of Daesh in the Near East has led in the last few years to the deliberate destruction of ancient monuments. Local archaeologists did indeed try to defend these, and Khaled Asad, the Director of Antiquities and of the museum in Palmyra, lost his life doing so.[23] Historians ought to know better about predicting the future. The past in more precarious than we (or at least I) had thought.

I have tried in this book to indicate the many areas in which research is transforming our understanding of the Roman Empire. The philologists who established the science of classical antiquity in the nineteenth century have now been joined by archaeologists, art historians, and social scientists of every kind. New answers are being offered to old questions, and new questions are being asked and answered about every aspect of Roman antiquity. Neither the general public nor school and university students have lost that sense of excitement in piecing together a great movement through history that has left so many traces in the world we inhabit today. We are not the posterity that Romans of any age imagined—how could we be?—but in our hands the future of the Roman Empire is an exciting one.

Further Reading

No single book deals with all the issues rounded up in this chapter, but there are several inspiring texts that touch on one aspect or another. The recovery of the past, including that of classical antiquity, is the subject of Alain Schnapp's *Discovery of the Past* (New York, 1997) and of David Lowenthal's *The Past is a Foreign Country* (Cambridge, 1985). Edward Thomas's *Monumentality and the Roman Empire* (Oxford, 2007) is a vivid and learned account of the most tangible of Roman remains. How the Romans saw ancient art is the subject of Jas Elsner's *Roman Eyes* (Princeton, NJ, 2007). Key works on the later reception of Rome are listed under the Further Reading for Chapter II.

Roman memory has been a growth area of study. Alain Gowing's *Empire and Memory* (Cambridge, 2005), Susan Alcock's *Archaeologies of the Greek Past* (Cambridge, 2002), Harriet Flower's *Art of Forgetting* (Chapel Hill, NC, 2006), and Elke Stein-Hölkeskamp, and Karl-Joachim Hölkeskamp (eds.), *Erinnerungsorte der Antike: Die Römische Welt* (Munich, 2006) blazed the trail. James Fenton and Chris Wickham's *Social Memory* (Oxford, 1992) provided inspiration. Some of the newest work has emerged from a wonderful project run by Karl Galinsky: its main publications are Karl Galinsky (ed.), *Memoria Romana: Memory in Rome and Rome in Memory* (Ann Arbor, MI, 2014), Karl Galinsky and Kenneth Lapatin (eds.), *Cultural Memories in the Roman Empire* (Los Angeles, 2015), and Karl Galinsky (ed.), *Memory in Ancient Rome and Early* Christianity (Oxford, 2016). Also notable are Beate Dignas, and R. R. R. Smith (eds.), *Historical and Religious Memory in the Ancient World* (Oxford, 2012), and Kai Sandberg and Christopher Smith (eds.), *Omnium Annalium Monumenta: Historical Writing and Historical Evidence in Republican Rome* (Leiden, 2017).

And for the future, there is now Jonathan J. Price and Katell Berthelot (eds.), *The Future of Rome: Roman, Greek, Jewish and Christian Visions* (Cambridge, 2020).

Notes

CHAPTER I

1. Velleius Paterculus, *Roman History* 2.1.

CHAPTER II

1. Philip Hardie, *Virgil's Aeneid: Cosmos and Imperium* (Oxford: Clarendon Press, 1985).
2. Livy, *From the Foundation of the City* 4.20.
3. Denis Feeney, *Caesar's Calendar: Ancient Time and the Beginnings of History*, Sather Classical Lectures (Berkeley and Los Angeles: University of California Press, 2007).
4. Paul Zanker, *The Power of Images in the Age of Augustus*, Jerome Lectures (Ann Arbor, MI: University of Michigan Press, 1988).
5. Livy, *From the Foundation of the City*, Preface.
6. Emma Dench, *Romulus' Asylum: Roman Identities from the Age of Alexander to the Age of Hadrian* (Oxford: Oxford University Press, 2005); T. Peter Wiseman, *Remus: A Roman Myth* (Cambridge: Cambridge University Press, 1995).
7. Andrew Erskine, *Troy between Greece and Rome: Local Tradition and Imperial Power* (Oxford: Oxford University Press, 2001); Greg Woolf, *Tales of the Barbarians: Ethnography and Empire in the Roman West* (Malden, MA: Blackwell Publishers, 2011).
8. Carol Dougherty, *The Poetics of Colonization: From City to Text in Archaic Greece* (New York: Oxford University Press, 1993).
9. Erich Gruen, *Culture and National Identity in Republican Rome* (London: Duckworth, 1992); Thomas Habinek, *The World of Roman Song: From Ritualized Speech to Social Order* (Baltimore, MA: Johns Hopkins University Press, 2005); Denis Feeney. *Beyond Greek: The Beginnings of Latin Literature* (Cambridge, MA: Harvard University Press, 2016).
10. William Vernon Harris, *War and Imperialism in Republican Rome, 327–70 BC* (Oxford: Clarendon Press, 1979).

11. P. A. Brunt, 'Laus Imperii', in Peter Garnsey and C. R. Whittaker (eds.), *Imperialism in the Ancient World* (Cambridge: Cambridge University Press, 1978; repr. in P. A. Brunt, *Roman Imperial Themes* (Oxford: Oxford University Press, 1990), 288–323).

12. Mary Beard, *The Roman Triumph* (Cambridge, MA: Harvard University Press, 2007).

13. Jean-Louis Ferrary, *Philhellénisme et impérialisme: Aspects idéologiques de la conquête romaine du monde hellénistique, de la Seconde Guerre de Macédoine à la Guerre contre Mithridate*, Bibliothèque des Écoles Françaises d'Athènes et de Rome (Rome: École Française de Rome, 1988); John S. Richardson, *The Language of Empire: Rome and the Idea of Empire from the Third Century BC to the Second Century AD* (Cambridge: Cambridge University Press, 2008).

14. Catharine Edwards (ed.), *Roman Presences: Receptions of Rome in European Culture, 1789–1945* (Cambridge: Cambridge University Press, 1999).

15. Dimitri Gutas, *Greek Thought, Arab Culture: The Graeco-Arabic Translation Movement in Baghdad and Early Abbasid Society (2nd–4th/8th–10th Centuries)* (New York: Routledge, 1998).

16. Alexander Scobie, *Hitler's State Architecture: The Impact of Classical Antiquity*, Monographs on the Fine Arts (University Park, PA: Pennsylvania State University Press, 1990); Luisa Quartermaine, '"Slouching towards Rome": Mussolini's Imperial Vision', in Tim Cornell and Kathryn Lomas (eds.), *Urban Society in Roman Italy*, 203–15 (London: University College London Press, 1995).

17. Peter Fibiger Bang and Dariusz Kolodziejczyz, *Universal Empire. A Comparative Approach to Imperial Culture and Representation in Eurasian History* (Cambridge: Cambridge University Press, 2012); Myles Lavan, Richard E. Payne, and John Weisweiler (eds.), *Cosmopolitanism and Empire. Universal Rulers, Local Elites, and Cultural Integration in the Ancient near East and Mediterranean* (Cambridge: Cambridge University Press, 2016).

18. Matthew P. Canepa, *The Two Eyes of the Earth: Art and Ritual of Kingship between Rome and Sasanian Iran*, The Transformation of the Classical Heritage, vol. xlv, ed. Peter Brown (Berkeley and Los Angeles: University of California Press, 2009).

19. J. H. Kautsky, *The Politics of Aristocratic Empires* (Chapel Hill, NC: University of North Carolina Press, 1982); Shmuel Eisenstadt, *The Political Systems of Empires* (London: Free Press of Glencoe, 1963); Susan E. Alcock et al. (eds.), *Empires: Perspectives from Archaeology and History* (New York: Cambridge University Press, 2001); Ian Morris and Walter Scheidel (eds.), *The Dynamics of Early Empires: State Power from Assyria to Byzantium* (Oxford: Oxford University Press, 2009); Phiroze Vasunia, 'The Comparative Study of Empires', *Journal of Roman Studies*, 101 (2011): 222–37; Peter Fibiger Bang and Christopher A. Bayly (eds.), *Tributary*

Empires in Global History, Cambridge Imperial and Post-Colonial Studies Series (Basingstoke: Palgrave Macmillan, 2011); Peter Fibiger Bang and Christopher A. Bayly (eds.), *Tributary Empires in History: Comparative Perspectives from Antiquity to the Late Medieval: Medieval History Journal*, 2003).

20. V. I. Lenin, *Imperialism, the Highest Stage of Capitalism: A Popular Outline* (Moscow: Co-operative Publishing Society of Foreign Workers in the USSR, 1934).

21. Nicole Brisch (ed.) *Religion and Power: Divine Kingship in the Ancient World and Beyond*, Oriental Institute Seminars (Chicago: Oriental Institute of the University of Chicago, 2008).

CHAPTER III

1. Amanda Claridge, *Rome: An Oxford Archaeological Guide*, 2nd edn (Oxford: Oxford University Press, 2010); Filippo Coarelli, *Rome and Environs: An Archaeological Guide* (Berkeley and Los Angeles: University of California Press, 2007); J. C. N. Coulston and Hazel Dodge (eds.), *Ancient Rome: The Archaeology of the Eternal City*, Oxford University School of Archaeology Monographs (Oxford: Oxford University School of Archaeology, 2000).

2. Pliny, *Natural History* 36.109.

3. Christopher Smith, 'The Beginnings of Urbanization in Rome', in Robin Osborne and Barry Cunliffe (eds.), *Mediterranean Urbanization 800–600 BC*, Proceedings of the British Academy, 91–111 (Oxford: Oxford University Press, 2005).

4. Anna Maria Bietti Sestieri, *The Iron Age Community of Osteria dell'Osa: A Study of Socio-Political Development in Central Tyrrenian Italy*, New Studies in Archaeology (Cambridge: Cambridge University Press, 1993).

5. Maria Eugenia Aubet, *The Phoenicians and the West: Politics, Colonies and Trade*, 2nd edn (Cambridge: Cambridge University Press, 2001); Josephine Quinn, *In Search of the Phoenicians* (Princeton, NJ: Princeton University Press, 2017); Gocha R. Tsetskhladze, *Greek Colonisation: An Account of Greek Colonies and Other Settlements Overseas*, 2 vols., Mnemosyne supplements (Leiden: Brill, 2006); John Boardman, *Greeks Overseas: Their Early Colonies and Trade*, 4th edn (London: Thames and Hudson, 1999).

6. Tamar Hodos, *Local Responses to Colonization in the Iron Age Mediterranean* (Abingdon: Routledge, 2006). I have tried to describe the broad context in part 2 of Greg Woolf, *The Life and Death of Ancient Cities: A Natural History* (Oxford: Oxford University Press, 2020).

7. David Ridgway, *The First Western Greeks* (Cambridge: Cambridge University Press, 1992).

8. Corinna Riva, *The Urbanization of Etruria* (Cambridge: Cambridge University Press, 2010).

9. Bernard, Seth, *Building Mid-Republican Rome: Labor, Architecture, and the Urban Economy* (New York: Oxford University Press, 2018).

10. Filippo Coarelli and Helen Patterson (eds.), *Mercator Placidissimus: The Tiber Valley in Antiquity: New Research in the Upper and Middle River Valley, Rome, 27–28 February 2004*, Quaderni di Eutopia (Rome: Quasar, 2008).

11. Colin Renfrew and John F. Cherry (eds.), *Peer Polity Interaction and Socio-Political Change*, New Directions in Archaeology (Cambridge: Cambridge University Press, 1986).

12. Mauro Cristofani (ed.), *La grande Roma dei Tarquini: Roma, Palazzo delle esposizioni, 12 giugno–30 settembre 1990: Catalogo della mostra* (Rome: 'L'Erma' di Bretschneider, 1990).

13. Nicholas Purcell, 'Becoming Historical: The Roman Case', in David Braund and Christopher Gill (eds.), *Myth, History and Culture in Republican Rome: Studies in Honour of T. P. Wiseman*, 12–40 (Exeter: University of Exeter Press, 2003).

14. Jonathan H. C. Williams, *Beyond the Rubicon: Romans and Gauls in Northern Italy*, Oxford Classical Monographs (Oxford: Oxford University Press, 2001).

15. Emma Dench, *From Barbarians to New Men: Greek, Roman and Modern Perceptions of Peoples of the Central Apennines* (Oxford: Oxford University Press, 1995).

16. Ennius, *Annales* Fragment 156.

17. Polybius, *Histories* 3.22–6.

18. Kurt Raaflaub, 'Born to be Wolves? Origins of Roman Imperialism', in Robert W. Wallace and Edward M. Harris (eds.), *Transitions to Empire: Essays in Greco-Roman History 360–146 B.C. in Honor of E. Badian*, 273–314 (Norman, OK: University of Oklahoma Press, 1996).

19. Nicola Terrenato, *The Early Roman Expansion into Italy: Elite Negotiation and Family Agendas* (Cambridge: Cambridge University Press, 2019).

20. John R. Patterson. 'Colonization and Historiography: The Roman Republic.' in *Greek and Roman Colonization: Origins, Ideologies and Interactions*, edited by Guy Bradley and John-Paul Wilson, 189–212 (Swansea: Classical Press of Wales 2006); Jeromia Pelgrom and Tessa Stek (eds.), *Roman Republican Colonization: New Perspectives from Archaeology and Ancient History*, Papers of the Royal Dutch Institute in Rome, vol. 62 (Rome: Palombi Editori, 2014).

21. Emilio Gabba, *Republican Rome: The Army and the Allies* (Oxford: Blackwell Publishers, 1976).

22. G. E. M. de Ste Croix, *The Class Struggle in the Ancient Greek World: From the Archaic Age to the Arab Conquests* (London: Duckworth, 1981).

CHAPTER IV

1. Harry Hine, 'Seismology and Vulcanology in Antiquity?', in C. J. Tuplin and T. E. Rihll (eds.), *Science and Mathematics in Ancient Greek Culture*, 56–75 (Oxford: Oxford University Press, 2002); Lukas Thommen, *Umweltsgeschichte der Antike* (Munich: Verlag C. H. Beck, 2009).

2. Pliny, *Natural History* 36.125.

3. J. G. Manning, Francis Ludlow, et al. 2017. 'Volcanic Suppression of Nile Summer Flooding Triggers Revolt and Constrains Interstate Conflict in Ancient Egypt'. *Nature Communications*, 8, doi: 10.1038/s41467-017-00957-y; Joseph R McConnell et al., 'Extreme Climate after Massive Eruption of Alaska's Okmok Volcano in 43 BCE and Effects on the Late Roman Republic and Ptolemaic Kingdom', *Proceedings of the National Academy of Sciences*, 117/27 (2020): 15443–9, doi: 10.1073/pnas.2002722117.

4. Robert Sallares, *The Ecology of the Ancient Greek World* (London: Duckworth, 1991), ch. 1.

5. Peter Garnsey, *Famine and Food Supply in the Greco-Roman World: Responses to Risk and Crisis* (Cambridge: Cambridge University Press, 1988), 8–16; Greg Woolf, *The Life and Death of Ancient Cities* (Oxford: Oxford University Press, 2020).

6. André Tchernia, *Le Vin d'Italie romaine: Essai d'histoire économique d'après les amphores*, Bibliothèque des Écoles Françaises d'Athènes et de Rome (Rome: École Française de Rome, 1986); José María Blázquez Martinez and José Remesal Rodriguez (eds.), *Producción y commercio del aceite en la antigüedad: Congreso I* (Madrid: Universidad Complutense, 1980); José María Blázquez Martinez and José Remesal Rodriguez (eds.), *Producción y commercio del aceite en la antigüedad: Congreso II* (Madrid: Universidad Complutense, 1982).

7. Paul Erdkamp, *The Grain Market in the Roman Empire: A Social, Political and Economic Study* (Cambridge: Cambridge University Press, 2005).

8. David Mattingly, 'First Fruit? The Olive in the Roman World', in Graham Shipley and John Salmon (eds.), *Human Landscapes in Classical Antiquity: Environment and Culture*, 213–53 (London: Routledge, 1996).

9. Anthony C. King, 'Diet in the Roman World: A Regional Inter-site Comparison of the Mammal Bones', *Journal of Roman Archaeology*, 12/1 (1999): 168–202.

10. Robert Sallares, 'Ecology', in Walter Scheidel, Ian Morris, and Richard P. Saller (eds.), *The Cambridge Economic History of the Greco-Roman World*, 15–37 (Cambridge: Cambridge University Press, 2007).

11. Michael McCormick et al., 'Climate Change during and after the Roman Empire: Reconstructing the Past from Scientific and Historical Evidence', *Journal of Interdisciplinary History*, 43/2 (2012): 169–220. For one interpretation of this complex data, see Kyle Harper, *The Fate of Rome: Climate, Disease and*

the End of an Empire, Princeton, NJ, and Oxford: Princeton University Press, 2017), with the responses of John F. Haldon and others, 'Plagues, Climate Change, and the End of an Empire: A Response to Kyle Harper's *The Fate of Rome*. Part 1 Climate'. *History Compass* (2018): e12508, doi: 10.1111/hic3.12508, and Kristina Sessa, 'The New Environmental Fall of Rome: A Methodological Consideration', *Journal of Late Antiquity*, 12/1 (2019):211–55.

12. Marshall Sahlins, *Stone Age Economics* (London: Routledge, 1974); William H. McNeill, *Plagues and Peoples* (Garden City, NY: Anchor Press/Doubleday, 1976); Paul A. Colinvaux, *Why Big Fierce Animals Are Rare: An Ecologist's Perspective* (Princeton, NJ: Princeton University Press, 1978). For some other negative consequences of the Neolithic revolution, see James C. Scott, *Against the Grain. A Deep History of the Earliest States* (Newhaven, CT: Yale University Press, 2017).

13. Cyprian Broodbank's *The Making of the Middle Sea: A History of the Mediterranean from the Beginning to the Emergence of the Classical World* (New York and Oxford: Oxford University Press, 2013) offers a vivid account of the transformation of the Mediterranean world in late prehistory. See also A. Bernard Knapp and Peter van Dommelen (eds.), *The Cambridge Prehistory of the Bronze and Iron Age Mediterranean* (New York and Cambridge: Cambridge University Press, 2015).

14. Barry Cunliffe, *Europe between the Oceans: Themes and Variations, 9000 BC–AD 1000* (New Haven, CT: Yale University Press, 2008).

15. Alfred W. Crosby, *Ecological Imperialism: The Biological Expansion of Europe, 900–1900*, Studies in Environment and History (Cambridge: Cambridge University Press, 1986).

16. Richard Reece, 'Romanization: A Point of View', in Tom Blagg and Martin Millett (eds.), *The Early Roman Empire in the West*, 30–4 (Oxford: Oxbow Books, 1990); Nico Roymans (ed.), *From the Sword to the Plough: Three Studies in the Earliest Romanisation of Northern Gaul*, Amsterdam Archaeological Studies (Amsterdam: Amsterdam University Press, 1996).

17. Peter Garnsey, *Food and Society in Classical Antiquity*, Key Themes in Ancient History (Cambridge: Cambridge University Press, 1999); Nicholas Purcell, 'The Way We Used to Eat: Diet, Community, and History at Rome', *American Journal of Philology*, 124/3 (2003): 329–58.

18. Robert Thomas and Andrew Wilson, 'Water Supply for Roman Farms in Latium and South Etruria', *Papers of the British School at Rome*, 62 (1994): 139–96.

19. Andrew Wilson, 'Machines, Power and the Ancient Economy', *Journal of Roman Studies*, 92 (2002): 1–32.

20. David Mattingly and John Salmon (eds.), *Economies beyond Agriculture in the Classical World*, Leicester–Nottingham Studies in Ancient Society (London: Routledge, 2001).

21. William Vernon Harris, 'Defining and Detecting Mediterranean Deforestation, 800 BCE–700 CE', in William Vernon Harris (ed.), *The Ancient Mediterranean Environment between Science and History*, edited by William Vernon Harris, 173–94 (Leiden and Boston, MA: Brill, 2013).

22. On traces of metal pollutants from the Greenland ice cores, a good introduction is de Callataÿ, François, 'The Graeco-Roman Economy in the Super Long Run: Lead, Copper, and Shipwrecks', *Journal of Roman Archaeology*, 18/1 (2005): 361–72. On conditions in ancient mining communities, see David Mattingly, *Imperialism, Power and Identity: Experiencing the Roman Empire*, Miriam S. Balmuth Lectures in Ancient History and Archaeology (Princeton NJ, and Oxford: Princeton University Press, 2011), ch. 7.

CHAPTER V

1. Arthur M. Eckstein, *Mediterranean Anarchy, Interstate War and the Rise of Rome*, Hellenistic Culture and Society (Berkeley and Los Angeles: University of California Press, 2006).

2. Claude Nicolet (ed.), *Rome et la conquête du monde méditerranéen: 264–27 avant J.C.* (Paris: Presses Universitaires de France, 1977).

3. William Vernon Harris, 'Roman Expansion in the West', in A. E. Astin et al. (eds.), *Cambridge Ancient History*, viii: *Rome and the Mediterranean to 133 BC*, 107–62 (Cambridge: Cambridge University Press, 1989); Stephen L. Dyson, *The Creation of the Roman Frontier* (Princeton, NJ: Princeton University Press, 1985).

4. Nicholas Purcell, 'The Creation of Provincial Landscape: The Roman Impact on Cisalpine Gaul', in Tom Blagg and Martin Millett (eds.), *The Early Roman Empire in the West*, 7–29 (Oxford: Oxbow Books, 1990).

5. Saskia T. Roselaar, *Public Land in the Roman Republic: A Social and Economic History of Ager Publicus in Italy, 396–89 BC*, Oxford Studies in Roman Society and Law (Oxford: Oxford University Press, 2010).

6. John Rich, 'Fear, Greed and Glory: The Causes of Roman War-Making in the Middle Republic', in John Rich and Graham Shipley (eds.), *War and Society in the Roman World*, 36–68 (London: Routledge, 1993).

7. Livy, *From the Foundation of the City* 45.12.

8. Nicholas Purcell, 'On the Sacking of Carthage and Corinth', in Doreen Innes, Harry Hine, and Christopher Pelling (eds.), *Ethics and Rhetoric: Classical Essays for Donald Russell on his Seventy-Fifth Birthday*, 133–48 (Oxford: Clarendon Press, 1995).

9. Beard, *The Roman Triumph*.

10. Geoffrey Conrad and Arthur A. Demarest, *Religion and Empire: The Dynamics of Aztec and Inca Expansionism*, New Directions in Archaeology (Cambridge:

Cambridge University Press, 1984); Peter R. Bedford, 'The Neo-Assyrian Empire', in Morris and Scheidel (eds.), *The Dynamics of Ancient Empires*, 30–65.

11. Harris, *War and Imperialism in Republican Rome, 327–70 B.C.*; Karl-Joachim Hölkeskamp, 'Conquest, Competition and Consensus: Roman Expansion in Italy and the Rise of the "Nobilitas"', *Historia: Zeitschrift für Alte Geschichte*, 42/1 (1993): 12–39.

12. Derk Bodde, 'The State and Empire of Ch'in', in Denis Twitchett and Michael Loewe (eds.), *The Cambridge History of China*, i: *The Ch'in and Han Empires, 221 B.C.–A.D. 220*, 21–102 (Cambridge: Cambridge University Press, 1986); R. D. S. Yates, 'Cosmos, Central Authority and Communities in the Early Chinese Empire', in Alcock et al. (eds.), *Empires*, 351–68.

13. Jonathan R.W Prag and Josephine Crawley Quinn (eds.), *The Hellenistic West: Rethinking the Ancient Mediterranean* (Cambridge: Cambridge University Press, 2013). See also Peter van Dommelen and Nicola Terrenato (eds.), *Articulating Local Cultures: Power and Identity under the Expanding Roman Republic*, Supplementary series (Providence, RI: Journal of Roman Archaeology, 2007).

14. Arthur M. Eckstein, *Senate and General: Individual Decision Making and Roman Foreign Relations, 264–194 B.C.* (Berkeley and Los Angeles: University of California Press, 1987); John S. Richardson, *Hispaniae: Spain and the Development of Roman Imperialism* (Cambridge: Cambridge University Press, 1986).

15. Philip Kay, *Rome's Economic Revolution*, Oxford Studies on the Roman Economy (Oxford: Oxford University Press, 2014).

16. Filippo Coarelli, 'Public Building in Rome between the Second Punic War and Sulla', *Papers of the British School at Rome*, 45 (1977): 1–23.

17. Polybius, *Histories* 6.17.

18. John S. Richardson, 'The Spanish Mines and the Development of Provincial Taxation in the Second Century B.C.', *Journal of Roman Studies*, 66 (1976): 139–52.

19. Matthew P. Loar, Carolyn MacDonald, and Dan-el Padilla Peralta (eds.), *Rome, Empire of Plunder: The Dynamics of Cultural Appropriation* (Cambridge: Cambridge University Press, 2018). On the creation of a Latin literature, see Thomas Habinek (ed.), *The Politics of Latin Literature: Writing, Identity and Empire in Ancient Rome* (Cambridge: Cambridge University Press, 1998) and Denis Feeney, *Beyond Greek: The Beginnings of Latin Literature* (Cambridge, MA: Harvard University Press, 2016).

20. Livy, *From the Foundation of the City* 38.51.

21. Harriet I. Flower, *Ancestor Masks and Aristocratic Power in Roman Culture* (Oxford: Clarendon Press, 1996).

CHAPTER VI

1. David Cannadine, *Ornamentalism: How the British Saw Their Empire* (London: Allen Lane, 2001).

2. Orlando Patterson, *Slavery and Social Death: A Comparative Study* (Cambridge, MA: Harvard University Press, 1982).

3. Richard P. Saller, *Personal Patronage under the Early Empire* (Cambridge: Cambridge University Press, 1982); Andrew Wallace-Hadrill (ed.), *Patronage in Ancient Society* (London: Routledge, 1989).

4. Claude Eilers, *Roman Patrons of Greek Cities* (Oxford: Oxford University Press, 2002).

5. Ernst Badian, *Foreign Clientelae (264–70 BC)* (Oxford: Clarendon Press, 1958).

6. David Braund, *Rome and the Friendly King: The Character of the Client Kingship* (London: Croom Helm, 1982).

7. Sallust, *Jugurtha* 8.

8. *The Achievements of the Deified Augustus* 26.4.

9. David Johnston, *Roman Law in Context*, Key Themes in Ancient History (Cambridge: Cambridge University Press, 1999).

10. Plutarch, *Life of Cato the Elder* 21.

11. Andrea Giardina and Aldo Schiavone (eds.), *Società romana e produzione schiavistica* (Rome: Laterza, 1981).

12. Dominic Rathbone, 'The Development of Agriculture in the Ager Cosanus during the Roman Republic: Problems of Evidence and Interpretation', *Journal of Roman Studies*, 71 (1981): 10–23.

13. Nicholas Purcell, 'The Roman Villa and the Landscape of Production', in Tim Cornell and Kathryn Lomas (eds.), *Urban Society in Roman Italy*, 151–79 (London: University College London Press, 1995); Neville Morley, *Metropolis and Hinterland: The City of Rome and the Italian Economy 200 B.C.–A.D. 200* (Cambridge: Cambridge University Press, 1996).

14. Andrew Wallace-Hadrill, 'Elites and Trade in the Roman Town', in John Rich and Andrew Wallace-Hadrill (eds.), *City and Country in the Ancient World*, 241–72 (London: Routledge, 1991).

15. Susan M. Treggiari, *Roman Freedmen during the Late Republic* (Oxford: Clarendon Press, 1969); Henrik Mouritsen, *The Freedman in the Roman World* (Cambridge: Cambridge University Press, 2011).

16. Keith Bradley, *Slaves and Masters in the Roman Empire: A Study in Social Control* (New York: Oxford University Press, 1987).

17. Apuleius, *The Golden Ass* 9.12.

18. Nicholas Purcell, 'Wine and Wealth in Ancient Italy', *Journal of Roman Studies*, 75 (1985): 1–19; Tchernia, *Le Vin d'Italie romaine*; Jean-Paul Morel, 'The

Transformation of Italy 300–133 BC', in Astin et al. (eds.), *Cambridge Ancient History*, viii, 477–516; Jesper Carlsen and Elio Lo Cascio (eds.), *Agricoltura e scambi nell'Italia tardo-repubblicana*, Pragmateiai (Bari: Edipuglia, 2009).

19. Strabo, *Geography* 14.5.4 and 10.5.2.
20. Philip de Souza, *Piracy in the Graeco-Roman World* (Cambridge: Cambridge University Press, 1999).
21. IG IX².1.241.
22. William Vernon Harris, 'Demography, Geography and the Sources of Roman Slaves', *Journal of Roman Studies*, 89 (1999): 62–75.
23. P. A. Brunt, *Italian Manpower 225 B.C.–A.D. 14* (Oxford: Oxford University Press, 1971); Keith Hopkins, *Conquerors and Slaves: Sociological Studies in Roman History I* (Cambridge: Cambridge University Press, 1978); Nathan Stewart Rosenstein, *Rome at War: Farms, Families and Death in the Middle Republic* (Chapel Hill, NC: University of North Carolina Press, 2004); Keith Bradley, 'Slavery in the Roman Republic', in Keith Bradley and Paul Cartledge (eds.), *Cambridge World History of Slavery*, i: *The Ancient Mediterranean World*, 241–64 (Cambridge: Cambridge University Press, 2011).
24. Alessandro Launaro, *Peasants and Slaves: The Rural Population of Roman Italy (200 BC to AD 100)* (Cambridge: Cambridge University Press, 2011).
25. Amy Richlin, *Slave Theater in the Roman Republic: Plautus and Popular Comedy* (Cambridge: Cambridge University Press 2017); William Fitzgerald, *Slavery and the Roman Literary Imagination* (Cambridge: Cambridge University Press, 2000).
26. Myles Lavan, *Slaves to Rome: Paradigms of Empire in Roman Culture* (Cambridge: Cambridge University Press, 2013).

CHAPTER VII

1. Erich Gruen, *The Hellenistic World and the Coming of Rome*, 2 vols. (Berkeley and Los Angeles: University of California Press, 1984).
2. Ferrary, *Philhellénisme et impérialisme*.
3. Elizabeth M. Brumfiel and John W. Fox (eds.), *Factional Competition and Political Development in the New World*, New Directions in Archaeology (Cambridge: Cambridge University Press, 1994).
4. David Braund, 'Royal Wills and Rome', *Papers of the British School at Rome*, 51 (1983): 16–57.
5. Sallust, *Jugurtha* 35.
6. Mark Elvin, *The Pattern of the Chinese Past: A Social and Economic Explanation* (Stanford, CA: Stanford University Press, 1973).
7. Crosby, *Ecological Imperialism*.

8. Brent D Shaw, '"Eaters of Flesh, Drinkers of Milk": The Ancient Mediterranean Ideology of the Pastoral Nomad', *Ancient Society*, 13 (1982): 5–31; Christopher B. Krebs, 'Borealism: Caesar, Seneca, Tacitus and the Roman Discourse about the Germanic North', in Erich Gruen (ed.), *Cultural Identity in the Ancient Mediterranean*, Issues and Debates, 202–21 (Los Angeles: Getty Research Institute, 2011).

9. David Abulafia, 'Mediterraneans', in William Vernon Harris (ed.), *Rethinking the Mediterranean*, 64–93 (Oxford: Oxford University Press, 2005).

10. Cunliffe, *Europe between the Oceans*.

11. Owen Lattimore, *Inner Asian Frontiers of China* (Oxford: Oxford University Press, 1940).

12. John R. Collis, *The European Iron Age* (London: Batsford, 1984); Barry Cunliffe, *Greeks, Romans and Barbarians: Spheres of Interaction* (London: Batsford, 1988).

13. Andrew Lintott, 'Imperial Expansion and Moral Decline in the Roman Republic', *Historia: Zeitschrift für Alte Geschichte*, 21 (1972): 626–38; Barbara Levick, 'Morals, Politics and the Fall of the Roman Republic', *Greece & Rome*, 29 (1982): 53–62.

14. Mark Hassall, Michael H. Crawford, and Joyce Reynolds, 'Rome and the Eastern Provinces at the End of the Second Century BC', *Journal of Roman Studies*, 64 (1974): 195–220.

15. Fergus Millar, 'The Political Character of the Classical Roman Republic, 200–151 B.C.', *Journal of Roman Studies*, 74 (1984): 1–19; Fergus Millar, 'Politics, Persuasion and the People before the Social War (150–90 B.C.)', *Journal of Roman Studies*, 76 (1986): 1–11.

16. A. N. Sherwin-White, 'The Lex Repetundarum and the Political Ideas of Gaius Gracchus', *Journal of Roman Studies*, 72 (1982): 18–31; Andrew Erskine, *The Hellenistic Stoa: Political Thought and Action* (London: Duckworth, 1990). For the broader context of political change during the Republic see Harriet Flower, *Roman Republics* (Princeton, NJ, 2010).

17. P. A. Brunt, 'Italian Aims at the Time of the Social War', *Journal of Roman Studies*, 55 (1965): 90–109; Gabba, *Republican Rome, the Army and the Allies*; Henrik Mouritsen, *Italian Unification: A Study in Ancient and Modern Historiography*, Bulletin of the Institute of Classical Studies Supplements (London: Institute of Classical Studies, 1998).

CHAPTER VIII

1. Aelius Aristides, *Roman Oration* 61.

2. Catharine Edwards, *The Politics of Immorality in Ancient Rome* (Cambridge: Cambridge University Press, 1993).

3. Sallust, *Jugurtha* 4.5.

4. Tacitus, *Agricola* 1.

5. Donald Earl, *The Moral and Political Tradition in Rome*, Aspects of Greek and Roman Life (London: Thames and Hudson, 1967).

6. Rebecca Langlands's *Sexual Morality in Ancient Rome* (Cambridge: Cambridge University Press, 2006) and Matthew B. Roller's *Constructing Autocracy: Aristocrats and Emperors in Julio-Claudian Rome* (Princeton, NJ: Princeton University Press, 2001) track some of the changes. For women's experience of the Augustan age, see Kristina Milnor, *Gender, Domesticity, and the Age of Augustus: Inventing Private Life* (Oxford: Oxford University Press, 2005).

7. Elizabeth Rawson, 'Religion and Politics in the Late Second Century B.C. at Rome', *Phoenix*, 28/2 (1974): 193–212.

8. Livy, *From the Foundation of the City*, Preface.

9. Andrew Wallace-Hadrill, 'Family and Inheritance in the Augustan Marriage-Laws', *Proceedings of the Cambridge Philological Society*, 207 (1981): 58–80; Karl Galinsky, *Augustan Culture* (Princeton, NJ: Princeton University Press, 1996).

10. Zanker, *The Power of Images in the Age of Augustus*.

11. Andrew Wallace-Hadrill, 'The Golden Age and Sin in Augustan Ideology', *Past and Present*, 95 (1982): 19–36.

12. John North, 'Roman Reactions to Empire', *Scripta Classica Israelica*, 12 (1993): 127–38.

13. Dionysius, *Roman Antiquities* 7.70–3.

14. John Scheid, *Quand croire c'est faire: Les Rites sacrificiels des Romains* (Paris: Aubier, 2005); Clifford Ando, *The Matter of the Gods: Religion and the Roman Empire* (Berkeley and Los Angeles: University of California Press, 2008).

15. John North, 'Democratic Politics in Republican Rome', *Past and Present*, 126 (1990): 3–21; Mary Beard and John North (eds.), *Pagan Priests* (London: Duckworth, 1990).

16. Jörg Rüpke, *Pantheon: A New History of Roman Religion* (Princeton: Princeton University Press 2018).

17. Rebecca Preston, 'Roman Questions, Greek Answers: Plutarch and the Construction of Identity', in Simon Goldhill (ed.), *Being Greek under Rome: Cultural Identity, the Second Sophistic and the Development of Empire*, 86–119 (Cambridge: Cambridge University Press, 2001); Mary Beard, 'A Complex of Times: No More Sheep on Romulus' Birthday', *Proceedings of the Cambridge Philological Society*, 33 (1987): 1–15.

18. Apuleius, *Golden Ass* 11.5.

19. Mary Beard, 'Cicero and Divination: The Formation of a Latin Discourse', *Journal of Roman Studies*, 76 (1986): 33–46; David Sedley, *Lucretius and the Transformation of Greek Wisdom* (Cambridge: Cambridge University Press, 1998).

20. Clifford Ando, 'Interpretatio romana', *Classical Philology*, 100 (2005): 41–51.

21. Paul Veyne, *Did the Greeks Believe in Their Myths? An Essay in the Constitutive Imagination*, trans. Paula Wissing (Chicago: University of Chicago Press, 1988); Denis Feeney, *Literature and Religion at Rome: Culture, Contexts and Beliefs*, Latin Literature in Context (Cambridge: Cambridge University Press, 1998).

22. Glen Bowersock, 'The Mechanics of Subversion in the Roman Provinces', in Adalberto Giovannini (ed.), *Oppositions et résistances à l'empire d'Auguste à Trajan*, Entretiens sur l'Antiquité Classique, 291–320 (Geneva: Fondation Hardt, 1987).

23. James B. Rives, 'The Decree of Decius and the Religion of Empire', *Journal of Roman Studies*, 89 (1999): 135–54.

24. Conrad and Demarest, *Religion and Empire*; John Moreland, 'The Carolingian Empire: Rome Reborn?', in Alcock et al. (eds.), *Empires*, 392–418.

25. Jörg Rüpke, *Domi militiae: Die religiöse Konstruktion des Krieges im Rom* (Stuttgart: Steiner, 1990). Now available in English as *Peace and War in Rome: A Religious Construction of Warfare* (Stuttgart: Franz Steiner Verlag, 2019).

26. Beard, *The Roman Triumph*.

27. Eric Orlin, *Temples, Religion and Politics in the Roman Republic*, Mnemosyne Supplements (Leiden: Brill, 1996).

28. Duncan MacRae, *Legible Religion. Books, Gods, and Rituals in Roman Culture* Cambridge, MA: Harvard University Press, 2016.

29. The best defence of this tradition of study is John Scheid, *The Gods, the State, and the Individual: Reflections on Civic Religion in Rome*. Philadelphia, PA: University of Pennsylvania Press, 2016.

30. John Scheid, 'Graeco ritu: A Typically Roman Way of Honouring the Gods', *Harvard Studies in Classical Philology*, 97 Greece in Rome: Influence, Integration, Resistance (1995): 15–21.

31. Eric Orlin, *Foreign Cults in Rome: Creating a Roman Empire*. Oxford and New York: Oxford University Press, 2010; Greg Woolf, 'Foreign Gods in the Age of Cicero', in Claudia Beltrão da Rosa and Federico Santangelo (eds.), *Cicero and Roman Religion: Eight Studies*, 117–33 (Stuttgart: Franz Steiner Verlag, 2020).

32. Mary Beard, 'The Roman and the Foreign: The Cult of the "Great Mother" in Imperial Rome', in Nicholas Thomas and Caroline Humphrey (eds.), *Shamanism, History and the State*, 164–90 (Ann Arbor, MI: University of Michigan Press, 1994).

33. Mary Beard, John North, and Simon Price, *Religions of Rome*, 2 vols. (Cambridge: Cambridge University Press, 1998), i, 313–163; Clifford Ando, 'A Religion for the Empire', in A. J. Boyle and W. J. Dominik (eds.), *Flavian Rome: Culture, Image, Text*, 321–44 (Leiden: Brill, 2003); Alison Cooley, 'Beyond Rome and Latium: Roman Religion in the Age of Augustus', in Celia Schultz and Paul B. Harvey

(eds.), *Religion in Republican Italy*, Yale Classical Studies, 228–52 (Cambridge: Cambridge University Press, 2006).

34. Richard Gordon, 'Religion in the Roman Empire: The Civic Compromise and its Limits', in Beard and North (eds.), *Pagan Priests*, 233–55.

35. Greg Woolf, 'Divinity and Power in Ancient Rome', in Brisch (ed.), *Religion and Power*, 235–55.

36. Simon Price, *Rituals and Power in Roman Asia Minor* (Cambridge: Cambridge University Press, 1984); Ittai Gradel, *Emperor Worship and Roman Religion*, Oxford Classical Monographs (Oxford: Oxford University Press, 2002).

37. Zanker, *The Power of Images in the Age of Augustus*.

CHAPTER IX

1. Arthur Keaveney, *Sulla: The Last Republican*, 2nd edn (London: Routledge, 2005).

2. Flower, *Ancestor Masks and Aristocratic Power in Roman Culture*.

3. Brunt, 'Laus Imperii'; Andrew Riggsby, *War in Words: Caesar in Gaul and Rome* (Austin, TX: University of Texas Press, 2006). On the detail of his campaigns, see Kurt Raaflaub and John T. Ramsey, 'Reconstructing the Chronology of Caesar's Gallic Wars', *Histos* 11 (2017): 1–74.

4. James Tan, *Power and Public Finance at Rome, 264–249 BCE* (New York and Oxford: Oxford University Press, 2017). See also Hans Beck, Martin Jehne, and John Serrati (eds.), *Money and Power in the Roman Republic*, Collection Latomus 355 (Brussels: Éditions Latomus, 2016).

5. De Souza, *Piracy in the Graeco-Roman World*.

6. Michael H. Crawford's 'States Waiting in the Wings. Population Distribution and the End of the Roman Republic', in Luuk de Ligt and Simon Northwood (eds.), *People, Land and Politics: Demographic Developments and the Transformation of Roman Italy 300 BC–AD 14*, 631–43 (Leiden: Brill, 2008) offers a view of this process from the periphery.

7. Erich Gruen, *The Last Generation of the Roman Republic* (Berkeley and Los Angeles: University of California Press, 1974); Liv Mariah Yarrow, *Historiography at the End of the Republic: Provincial Perspectives on Roman Rule* (Oxford: Oxford University Press, 2006).

8. Katherine Clarke, 'Universal Perspectives in Historiography', in Christina Shuttleworth Kraus (ed.), *The Limits of Historiography: Genre and Narrative in Ancient Historical Texts*, Mnemosyne Supplements, 249–79 (Leiden: Brill, 1999).

9. Hermann Strasburger, 'Poseidonios on Problems of the Roman Empire', *Journal of Roman Studies*, 55/1–2 (1965): 40–53; I. G. Kidd, 'Posidonius as Philosopher-Historian', in Miriam Griffin and Jonathan Barnes (eds.), *Philosophia togata*,

i: *Essays on Philosophy and Roman Society*, 38–50 (Oxford: Oxford University Press, 1989).

10. Barbara Levick, 'Popular in the Provinces? À Propos of Tacitus Annales 1.2.2', *Acta classica*, 37 (1994): 49–65.

11. Tacitus, *Annales* 1.2.2.

12. Josef Wiesehöfer (ed.), *Das Partherreich und seine Zeugnisse*, Historia Einzelschriften (Stuttgart: Franz Steiner Verlag, 1998).

CHAPTER X

1. Michael H. Crawford, 'Rome and the Greek World: Economic Relationships', *Economic History Review*, 30/1 (1977): 45–52.

2. The political and social transformation of Italian cities and their élites after the social war is dealt in Edward Bispham's *From Asculum to Actium: The Municipalization of Italy from the Social War to Augustus* (Oxford: Oxford University Press, 2007). The broadening of the Roman elite is the theme of T. P. Wiseman, *New Men in the Roman Senate, 139 B.C.–A.D. 14*. Oxford Classical and Philosophical Monographs (London: Oxford University Press, 1971).

3. John H. D'Arms, *The Romans on the Bay of Naples: A Social and Cultural History of the Villas and Their Owners from 150 B.C. to A.D. 100* (Cambridge, MA: Harvard University Press, 1970); Andrew Wallace-Hadrill, *Houses and Society in Pompeii and Herculaneum* (Princeton, NJ: Princeton University Press, 1994); Eleanor Windsor Leach, *The Social Life of Painting in Ancient Rome and on the Bay of Naples* (Cambridge: Cambridge University Press, 2004). For the villa phenomenon in general, see Annalisa Marzano and Guy P. R. Métraux (eds.), *The Roman Villa in the Mediterranean Basin: Late Republic to Late Antiquity* (Cambridge: Cambridge University Press, 2018).

4. Michael H. Crawford, 'Greek Intellectuals and the Roman Aristocracy in the First Century BC', in Peter Garnsey and C. R. Whittaker (eds.), *Imperialism in the Ancient World*, 193–207 (Cambridge: Cambridge University Press, 1978).

5. Elizabeth Rawson, *Cicero: A Portrait* (London: Allen Lane, 1975).

6. Keith Hopkins, *Death and Renewal: Sociological Studies in Roman History II* (Cambridge: Cambridge University Press, 1983).

7. M. Cébeillac-Gervason (ed.), *Les Bourgeoisies municipales italiennes aux IIe et Ier siècles av. J-C* (Naples: Éditions du CNRS & Bibliothèque de l'Institut Français de Naples, 1981).

8. Catherine Steel, *Cicero, Rhetoric, and Empire* (Oxford: Oxford University Press, 2001).

9. Cicero, *On Duties* 2.27.

10. Cicero, *To His Brother Quintus* 1.1.

11. Richardson, *The Language of Empire*.

12. D. S. Levene, 'Sallust's Jugurtha: An "Historical Fragment"', *Journal of Roman Studies*, 82 (1992): 53–70.

13. Sallust, *Histories* 4.69.17.

14. Claude Nicolet, *Space, Geography and Politics in the Early Roman Empire*, trans. Hélène Leclerc, Jerome Lectures (Ann Arbor, MI: University of Michigan Press, 1991).

15. Gruen, *Culture and National Identity in Republican Rome*; Thomas Habinek (ed.), *The Politics of Latin Literature: Writing, Identity and Empire in Ancient Rome* (Cambridge: Cambridge University Press, 1998). Denis Feeney's *Beyond Greek: The Beginnings of Latin Literature* (Cambridge, MA: Harvard University Press, 2016) has brilliantly rewritten the cultural significance of this moment.

16. Elizabeth Rawson, *Intellectual Life in the Late Roman Republic* (London: Duckworth, 1985); Andrew Wallace-Hadrill, 'Review Article: Greek Knowledge, Roman Power', *Classical Philology*, 83/3 (1988): 224–33; Elaine Fantham, *Roman Literary Culture from Cicero to Apuleius*, Ancient Society and History (Baltimore, MD: Johns Hopkins University Press, 1996).

17. Purcell, 'Becoming Historical'.

18. D'Arms, *The Romans on the Bay of Naples*.

19. T. Keith Dix, 'The Library of Lucullus', *Athenaeum*, 88/2 (2000): 441–64.

20. Mantha Zarmakoupi (ed.), *The Villa of the Papyri at Herculaneum: Archaeology, Reception and Digital Reconstruction* (Berlin: De Gruyter, 2010).

21. Marcello Gigante, *Philodemus in Italy: The Books from Herculaneum*, trans. Dirk Obbink, The Body, in Theory: Histories of Cultural Materialism (Ann Arbor. MI: University of Michigan Press, 1995); David Sider, *The Library of the Villa dei Papiri at Herculaneum* (Los Angeles: Getty, 2005).

22. E. Bartman, 'Sculptural Collecting and Display in the Private Realm', in E. Gazda (ed.), *Roman Art in the Private Sphere: New Perspectives on the Architecture and Decor of the Domus, Villa and Insula*, 71–88 (Ann Arbor, MI: University of Michigan Press, 1991).

23. Andrew Wallace-Hadrill, *Rome's Cultural Revolution* (New York: Cambridge University Press, 2008).

24. David Sedley, 'Philosophical Allegiance in the Greco-Roman World', in Miriam Griffin and Jonathan Barnes (eds.), *Philosophia togata I: Essays on Philosophy and Roman Society*, 97–119 (Oxford: Oxford University Press, 1989).

25. Simon Swain, 'Bilingualism in Cicero? The Evidence of Code-Switching', in J. N. Adams, Mark Janse, and Simon Swain (eds.), *Bilingualism in Ancient Society: Language Contact and the Written Text*, 128–67 (Oxford: Oxford University Press, 2002).

26. Ingo Gildenhard, *Paideia Romana: Cicero's Tusculan Disputations*, Proceedings of the Cambridge Philological Society Supplements, ed. Tim Whitmarsh and James Warren (Cambridge: Cambridge Philological Society, 2007).

27. Cicero, *Tusculan Disputations* 1.1.

CHAPTER XI

1. Elizabeth Rawson, 'Caesar's Heritage: Hellenistic Kings and Their Roman Equals', *Journal of Roman Studies*, 65 (1975): 148–59.

2. The complicity of others was already stressed by Ronald Syme in *The Roman Revolution* (Oxford: Oxford University Press, 1939) but the extent to which we have taken Augustus' centrality for granted has now been exposed in Kit Morrell, Josiah Osgood, and Kathryn Welch (eds.), *The Alternative Augustan Age* (New York: Oxford University Press, 2019).

3. Suetonius, *Life of the Deified Augustus* 101.

4. Olivier Hekster, *Emperors and Ancestors: Roman Rulers and the Constraints of Tradition* (Oxford: Oxford University Press, 2015).

5. Nicholas Purcell, 'Livia and the Womanhood of Rome', *Proceedings of the Cambridge Philological Society*, 32 (1986): 78–105.

6. Susan Wood, 'Messalina, Wife of Claudius: Propaganda Successes and Failures of his Reign', *Journal of Roman Archaeology*, 5 (1992): 219–34; Susan Wood, 'Diva Drusilla Panthea and the Sisters of Caligula', *American Journal of Archaeology*, 99/3 (1995): 457–82.

7. Gwynaeth McIntyre, *A Family of Gods. The Worship of the Imperial Family in the Latin West* (Ann Arbor, MI: University of Michigan Press, 2016).

8. Zvi Yavetz, *Plebs and Princeps* (London: Oxford University Press, 1969).

9. Simon Price, 'From Noble Funerals to Divine Cult: The Consecration of Roman Emperors', in David Cannadine and Simon Price (eds.), *Rituals of Royalty: Power and Ceremonial in Traditional Societies*, 56–105 (Cambridge: Cambridge University Press, 1997).

10. Paul Zanker, *The Power of Images in the Age of Augustus* (Ann Arbor, MI: University of Michigan Press, 1988); Clifford Ando, *Imperial Ideology and Provincial Loyalty in the Roman Empire* (Berkeley, CA: University of California Press, 2000), Carlos Noreña, *Imperial Ideals in the Roman West: Representation, Circulation, Powe* (Cambridge: Cambridge University Press, 2011).

11. R. R. R. Smith, 'The Imperial Reliefs from the Sebasteion at Aphrodisias', *Journal of Roman Studies*, 77 (1987): 88–138.

12. Richard J. A. Talbert, *The Senate of Imperial Rome* (Princeton, NJ: Princeton University Press, 1984).

13. Ségolène Demougin, Hubert Devijver, and Marie-Thérèse Raepsaet-Charlier (eds.), *L'Ordre équestre: Histoire d'une aristocratie (IIe siècle av. J.-C.–IIIe siècle ap. J.-C.)*, Collection de l'École Française de Rome (Rome: École Française de Rome, 1999). For equites and the ordo equester in late antiquity, see Caillan Davenport, *A History of the Roman Equestrian Order* (Cambridge: Cambridge University Press, 2019), chs 11 and 12.

14. Averil Cameron, 'The Construction of Court Ritual: The Byzantine Book of Ceremonies', in David Cannadine and Simon Price (eds.), *Rituals of Royalty: Power and Ceremonial in Traditional Societies*, Past and Present Publications, 106–36 (Cambridge: Cambridge University Press, 1987).

15. Yates, 'Cosmos, Central Authority and Communities in the Early Chinese Empire'; Michael J. Puett, *To Become a God: Cosmology, Sacrifice, and Self-Divinization in Early China*, Harvard-Yenching Institute monograph series. Cambridge, MA: Harvard University Press, 2002).

16. Amélie Kuhrt, 'Usurpation, Conquest and Ceremonial: From Babylon to Persia', in Cannadine and Price (eds.), *Rituals of Royalty*, 20–55; Maria Brosius, 'New out of Old? Court and Court Ceremonies in Achaemenid Persia', in Antony Spawforth (ed.), *The Court and Court Society in Ancient Monarchies*, 17–57 (Cambridge: Cambridge University Press, 2007).

17. Herodotus, *Histories* 3.80–2, Cassius Dio, *Roman History* 52.2–40.

18. Lucretius, *On the Nature of Things* 5.1105–60. Karl August Wittfogel, *Oriental Despotism: A Comparative Study of Total Power* (New York: Yale University Press, 1957).

19. John A. Hall, *Powers and Liberties: The Causes and Consequences of the Rise of the West* (Oxford: Blackwell Publishers, 1985); Patricia Crone, *Pre-Industrial Societies*, New Perspectives on the Past (Oxford: Basil Blackwell, 1989). For a broader discussion of the weakness of ancient states in general, see Clifford Ando and Seth Richardson (eds.), *Ancient States and Infrastructural Power: Europe, Asia, and America*, Empire and After (Philadelphia, PA: University of Pennsylvania Press, 2017).

20. Clifford Geertz, 'Centers, Kings and Charisma: Reflections on the Symbolics of Power', in Joseph Ben-David and Terry Nichols Clarke (eds.), *Culture and Its Creators: Essays in Honor of Edward Shils*, 150–71 (Chicago: University of Chicago Press, 1977); repr., *Local Knowledge: Further Essays in Interpretive Anthropology*, 121–46 (New York: Basic Books, 1983).

21. Jonathan Spence, *Emperor of China: Self Portrait of K'ang-hsi* (London: Cape, 1974).

22. Michel Austin, 'Hellenistic Kings, War and the Economy', *Classical Quarterly*, 36/2 (1986): 450–66.

23. Saller, *Personal Patronage under the Early Empire*; Claude Nicolet, 'Augustus, Government and the Propertied Classes', in Fergus Millar and Erich Segal (eds.), *Caesar Augustus: Seven Aspects*, 129–67 (Oxford: Oxford University Press, 1984).

24. Fergus Millar, *The Emperor in the Roman World* (London: Duckworth, 1977).

25. Norbert Elias, *The Court Society* (Oxford: Blackwell Publishers, 1983).

26. Keith Hopkins, 'Divine Emperors, or the Symbolic Unity of the Roman Empire', in *Conquerors and Slaves: Sociological Studies in Roman History I*, 197–242 (Cambridge: Cambridge University Press, 1978).

27. Price, *Rituals and Power in Roman Asia Minor*.

28. Brian Campbell, *The Emperor and the Roman Army 31 BC–AD 235* (Oxford: Clarendon Press, 1984).

29. Andrew Wallace-Hadrill, 'The Imperial Court', in Alan Bowman, Edward Champlin, and Andrew Lintott (eds.), *Cambridge Ancient History*, X: *The Augustan Empire 43 B.C.–A.D. 69*, 283–308 (Cambridge: Cambridge University Press, 1996); Aloys Winterling, *Aula Caesaris: Studien zur Institutionalisierung des römischen Kaiserhofes in der Zeit von Augustus bis Commodus (31 v. Chr.–192 n. Chr.)* (Munich: R. Oldenburg, 1999); Jeremy Paterson, 'Friends in High Places: The Creation of the Court of the Roman Emperor', in Spawforth (ed.), *The Court and Court Society in Ancient Monarchies*, 121–56.

30. Elias, *The Court Society*; Jeroen Duindam, *Myths of Power: Norbert Elias and the Early Modern European Court* (Amsterdam: Amsterdam University Press, 1994).

31. Paul Zanker, 'Domitian's Palace on the Palatine and the Imperial Image', in Alan Bowman et al. (eds.), *Representations of Empire: Rome and the Mediterranean World*, Proceedings of the British Academy, 105–30 (Oxford: Oxford University Press, 2002).

32. Andrew Wallace-Hadrill, 'Civilis princeps: Between Citizen and King', *Journal of Roman Studies*, 72 (1982): 32–48; Wallace-Hadrill, 'The Imperial Court'.

33. Helmut Halfmann, *Itinera principum: Geschichte und Typologie der Kaiserreisen im Römischen Reich*, Heidelberger althistorische Beiträge und epigraphische Studien (Stuttgart: Franz Steiner Verlag, 1986).

34. Catharine Edwards and Greg Woolf (eds.), *Rome the Cosmopolis* (Cambridge: Cambridge University Press, 2003).

CHAPTER XII

1. Keith Hopkins, 'The Political Economy of the Roman Empire', in Ian Morris and Walter Scheidel (eds.), *The Dynamics of Ancient Empires: State Power from Assyria to Byzantium*, Oxford Studies in Early Empires, 178–204 (New York: Oxford University Press, 2009).

2. Michael H. Crawford, *Coinage and Money under the Roman Republic: Italy and the Mediterranean Economy* (London: Methuen, 1985).

3. Peter Rhodes, 'After the Three-Bar Sigma Controversy: The History of Athenian Imperialism Reassessed', *Classical Quarterly*, 58/2 (2008): 501–6.

4. J. G. Manning, 'Coinage as Code in Ptolemaic Egypt', in William Vernon Harris (ed.), *The Monetary Systems of the Greeks and Romans*, 84–111 (Oxford: Oxford University Press, 2008).

5. Bang and Bayly, *Tributary Empires in History*.

6. Galinsky, *Augustan Culture*.

7. Peter Fibiger Bang, *The Roman Bazaar: A Comparative Study of Trade and Markets in a Tributary Empire*, Cambridge Classical Studies (Cambridge: Cambridge University Press, 2008).

8. P. A. Brunt, 'The Revenues of Rome', *Journal of Roman Studies*, 71 (1981): 161–72; P. A. Brunt, 'Publicans in the Principate', in *Roman Imperial Themes*, 354–432 (Oxford: Oxford University Press, 1990); Michel Cottier et al. (eds.), *The Customs Law of Asia*, Oxford Studies in Ancient Documents (Oxford: Oxford University Press, 2008).

9. Garnsey, *Famine and Food Supply in the Greco-Roman World*.

10. Peregrine Horden and Nicholas Purcell, *The Corrupting Sea: A Study of Mediterranean History* (Oxford: Blackwell Publishers, 2000); Nicholas Purcell, 'The Boundless Sea of Unlikeness? On Defining the Mediterranean', *Mediterranean Historical Review*, 18/2 (2004): 9–29.

11. Alan Bowman and Andrew Wilson (eds.), *Quantifying the Roman Economy: Methods and Problems* (Oxford: Oxford University Press, 2009); Alan Bowman and Andrew Wilson (eds.), *Settlement, Urbanization, and Population* (Oxford: Oxford University Press, 2011); Alan Bowman and Andrew Wilson (eds.), *The Roman Agricultural Economy: Organisation, Investment, and Production* (Oxford: Oxford University Press, 2013); Paul Erdkamp, Koenraad Verboven, and Arjan Zuiderhoek (eds.), *Ownership and Exploitation of Land and Natural Resources in the Roman World* (Oxford: Oxford University Press, 2015); Andrew Wilson, and Alan Bowman (eds.) *Trade, Commerce and the State in the Roman World* (Oxford: Oxford University Press, 2018).

12. Anthony John Parker, *Ancient Shipwrecks of the Mediterranean and the Roman Provinces*, British Archaeological Reports International Series (Oxford: Tempus Reparatum, 1992); Andrew Wilson, 'Approaches to Quantifying Roman Trade', in Bowman and Wilson (eds.), *Quantifying the Roman Economy*, 213–49.

13. Purcell, 'Wine and Wealth in Ancient Italy'; Greg Woolf, 'Imperialism, Empire and the Integration of the Roman Economy', *World Archaeology*, 23/3 (1992): 283–93.

14. Wilson, 'Machines, Power and the Ancient Economy'; François de Callataÿ, 'The Graeco-Roman Economy in the Super Long Run: Lead, Copper, and Shipwrecks', *Journal of Roman Archaeology*, 18/1 (2005): 361–72; Dennis P. Kehoe, 'The Early Roman Empire: Production', in Scheidel, Morris, and Saller (eds.), *Cambridge Economic History of the Greco-Roman World*, 543–69.

15. J. B. Ward-Perkins, 'From Republic to Empire: Reflections on the Early Provincial Architecture of the Roman West', *Journal of Roman Studies*, 60 (1970): 1–19.

16. Greg Woolf, *Becoming Roman: The Origins of Provincial Civilization in Gaul* (Cambridge: Cambridge University Press, 1998), 169–205.

17. Susan E. Alcock, *Graecia capta: The Landscapes of Roman Greece* (Cambridge: Cambridge University Press, 1993).

18. Keith Hopkins, 'Economic Growth and Towns in Classical Antiquity', in Philip Abrams and E. A. Wrigley (eds.), *Towns in Societies: Essays in Economic History and Historical Sociology*, Past and Present Publications, 35–77 (Cambridge: Cambridge University Press, 1978); R. F. J. Jones, 'A False Start? The Roman Urbanisation of Western Europe', *World Archaeology*, 19/1 (1987): 47–58; Greg Woolf, 'The Roman Urbanization of the East', in Susan E. Alcock (ed.), *The Early Roman Empire in the East*, 1–14 (Oxford: Oxbow Books, 1997); J. S. Hanson, *An Urban Geography of the Roman World. 100 BC–AD 300* (Oxford: Archeopress, 2016).

19. Keith Hopkins, 'Rome, Taxes, Rents and Trade', *Kodai*, 6/7 (1995/6): 41–75; R. P. Duncan-Jones, 'Taxes, Trade and Money', in *Structure and Scale in the Roman Economy*, 30–47 (Cambridge: Cambridge University Press, 1990).

20. The fullest account to date is that of Kyle Harper, *The Fate of Rome: Climate, Disease and the End of an Empire* (Princeton, NJ, and Oxford: Princeton University Press, 2017).

21. R. P. Duncan-Jones, 'The Impact of the Antonine Plague', *Journal of Roman Archaeology*, 9 (1996): 108–36. For Galen's evidence see Rebecca Flemming, 'Galen and the Plague', in Caroline Petit (ed.), *Galen's Treatise Περὶ Ἀλυπίας (De indolentia) in Context. A Tale of Resilience*, 219–44 (Leiden and Boston, MA: Brill, 2019).

22. Christer Bruun, 'The Antonine Plague and the "Third-Century Crisis"', in Olivier Hekster, Gerda de Kleijn, and Daniëlle Slootjes (eds.), *Crises and the Roman Empire*, Impact of Empire, 201–17 (Leiden: Brill, 2007); John F. Haldon and others, 'Plagues, Climate Change, and the End of an Empire: A Response to Kyle Harper's *The Fate of Rome*. Part 2 Plagues and a Crisis of Empire'. *History Compass* (2018): e12506, doi: 10.1111/hic3.12506.

23. John F. Haldon. Merle Eisenberg, Lee Mordechai, Adam Izdebski, and Sam White, 'Lessons from the Past, Policies for the Future: Resilience and Sustainability in Past Crises', *Environmental Systems and Decisions*, 40 (2020):

287–97. For a comparison between peasant and civic strategies, see Peter Garnsey, *Famine and Food Supply in the Greco-Roman World: Responses to Risk and Crisis* (Cambridge: Cambridge University Press, 1988) and Thomas W. Gallant, 'Crisis and Response: Risk-Buffering Behavior in Hellenistic Greek Communities', *The Journal of Interdisciplinary History*, 19/3 (1989): 393–413.

24. Orlin, *Temples, Religion and Politics in the Roman Republic*. On building more generally, see Seth Bernard, *Building Mid-Republican Rome: Labor, Architecture, and the Urban Economy* (New York: Oxford University Press, 2018).

25. Roselaar, *Public Land in the Roman Republic*.

26. Coarelli, 'Public Building in Rome between the Second Punic War and Sulla'.

27. Brunt, 'Publicans in the Principate'.

28. Cottier et al., *The Customs Law of Asia*.

29. Jérôme France, *Quadragesima Galliarum: L'Organisation douanière des provinces alpestres, gauloises et germaniques de l'Empire romain, 1er siècle avant J.-C.–3er siècle après J.-C.*, Collections de l'École Française à Rome (Rome: École Française de Rome, 2001).

30. Richardson, 'The Spanish Mines and the Development of Provincial Taxation in the Second Century B.C.'.

31. Dominic Rathbone, 'The Imperial Finances', in Bowman, Champlin, and Lintott (eds.), *Cambridge Ancient History*, x.

CHAPTER XIII

1. Tacitus, *Germany* 37.

2. Rolf Michael Schneider, *Bunte Barbaren: Orientalenstatuen aus farbigem Marmor in der römischen Repräsentationskunst* (Worms: Wernersche Verlagsgesellschaft, 1986); R. R. R. Smith, 'Simulacra gentium: The Ethne from the Sebasteion at Aphrodisias', *Journal of Roman Studies*, 78 (1988): 50–77; M. Sapelli (ed.), *Provinciae fideles: Il fregio del templo di Adriano in Campo Marzio* (Milan: Electa, 1999).

3. Erich Gruen, 'The Expansion of the Empire under Augustus', in Alan Bowman, Edward Champlin, and Andrew Lintott (eds.), *Cambridge Ancient History, x: The Augustan Empire 43 B.C.–A.D. 69*, 147–97 (Cambridge: Cambridge University Press, 1996).

4. Nicolet, *Space, Geography and Politics in the Early Roman Empire*.

5. Strabo, *Geography* 4.5.32.

6. Appian, *Preface*.

7. Peter Garnsey and Richard P. Saller, *The Roman Empire: Economy, Society and Culture*, 2nd rev. edn (London: Bloomsbury, 2015).

8. A. N. Sherwin-White, *The Roman Citizenship*, 2nd edn (Oxford: Clarendon Press, 1973); Peter Garnsey, 'Roman Citizenship and Roman Law in Late

Antiquity', in Simon Swain and Mark Edwards (eds.), *Approaching Late Antiquity: The Transformation from Early to Late Empire*, 133–55 (Oxford: Oxford University Press, 2004). On the impact of the edict of Caracalla, see Myles Lavan, 'The Spread of Roman Citizenship 14–212 CE: Quantification in the Face of High Uncertainty', *Past and Present*, 230/1 (2016): 3–46 and Clifford Ando (ed.), *Citizenship and Empire in Europe 200–1900: The Antonine Constitution after 1800 years* (Stuttgart: Franz Steiner Verlag, 2016).

9. Paul Veyne, *Le Pain et le cirque: Sociologie historique d'un pluralisme politique* (Paris: Seuil, 1976); Arjan Zuiderhoek, *The Politics of Munificence in the Roman Empire: Citizens, Elites and Benefactors in Asia Minor*, Greek Culture in the Roman World (Cambridge: Cambridge University Press, 2009).

10. Edward N. Luttwak, *The Grand Strategy of the Roman Empire: From the First Century AD to the Third* (Baltimore, MD: Johns Hopkins University Press, 1976).

11. Fergus Millar, 'Emperors, Frontiers and Foreign Relations, 31 BC to AD 378', *Britannia*, 13 (1982): 1–23.

12. Tacitus, *Annales* 4.4–5.

13. Alan Bowman, *Life and Letters on the Roman Frontier: Vindolanda and Its People* (London: British Museum Press, 1994).

14. Benjamin Isaac, *The Limits of Empire: The Roman Army in the East* (Oxford: Clarendon Press, 1990).

15. Greg Woolf, 'Provincial Revolts in the Early Roman Empire', in Mladen Popovic (ed.), *The Jewish Revolt against Rome: Interdisciplinary Perspectives*, 27–44 (Leiden and Boston, MA: Brill, 2011); Gil Gambash, *Rome and Provincial Resistance*, Routledge Monographs in Classical Studies (London: Routledge, 2015); Myles Lavan, 'Writing Revolt in the Early Roman Empire', in Justine Firnhaber-Baker and Dirk Schoenaers (eds.), *The Routledge History Handbook of Medieval Revolt*, 19–38 (Abingdon and New York: Routledge, 2017). For Roman revolt patterns in a wider context, see John J. Collins and J.G Manning (eds.), 2016. *Revolt and Resistance in the Ancient Classical World and the Near East: In the Crucible of Empire*, Culture and History of the Ancient Near East (Leiden and New York: Brill, 2016). Stephen L. Dyson 'Native Revolt Patterns in the Roman Empire', in Hildegard Temporini (ed.), *Aufstieg und Niedergang der römischen Welt* II.3, 138–75 (Berlin and New York: De Gruyter, 1975) remains very useful.

16. Campbell, *The Emperor and the Roman Army 31 BC–AD 235*.

17. Ian Haynes, *Blood of the Provinces: The Roman Auxilia and the Making of Provincial Society from Augustus to Diocletian* (Oxford: Oxford University Press, 2013).

18. Egon Flaig, *Den Kaiser herausfordern: Die Usurpation im römischen Reich* (Frankfurt am Main: Campus Verlag, 1992).

19. Brent D. Shaw, 'Soldiers and Society: The Army in Numidia', *Opus*, 2 (1983): 133–9.

20. Ramsay MacMullen, *Soldier and Civilian in the Later Roman Empire* (Cambridge, MA: Harvard University Press, 1963).

21. Lattimore, *Inner Asian Frontier of China*.

22. Jürgen Kunow, *Der römische Import in der Germania libera bis zu den Markomannenkrieg: Studien zu Bronze- und Glasgefässen*, Göttinger Schriften zur Vor- und Frühgeschichte (Neumünster: K. Wachholtz, 1983); L. Hedeager, 'Empire, Frontier and the Barbarian Hinterland: Rome and Northern Europe from A.D. 1–400', in Michael Rowlands, Møgens Trolle Larsen, and Kristian Kristiansen (eds.), *Centre and Periphery in the Ancient World*, 125–40 (Cambridge: Cambridge University Press, 1987); Michael G. Fulford, 'Roman and Barbarian: The Economy of Roman Frontier Systems', in J. C. Barrett (ed.), *Barbarians and Romans in North-West Europe from the Later Republic to Late Antiquity*, International Series, 81–95 (Oxford: British Archaeological Reports, 1989).

23. Michael Kulikowski, *Rome's Gothic Wars from the Third Century to Alaric*, Key Conflicts of Classical Antiquity (New York: Cambridge University Press, 2007); John Drinkwater, *The Alamanni and Rome 213–496 (Caracalla to Clovis)* (Oxford: Oxford University Press, 2007).

24. Kulikowski, *Rome's Gothic Wars from the Third Century to Alaric*.

25. Brian Campbell, 'War and Diplomacy: Rome and Parthia 31 BC–AD 235', in John Rich and Graham Shipley (eds.), *War and Society in the Roman World*, 213–40 (London: Routledge, 1993).

CHAPTER XIV

1. Miriam Griffin, 'Claudius in Tacitus', *Classical Quarterly*, 40/2 (1990): 482–501.

2. Sherwin-White, *The Roman Citizenship*.

3. Garnsey, 'Roman Citizenship and Roman Law in Late Antiquity'.

4. Clifford Ando, *Law, Language and Empire in the Roman Tradition* (Philadelphia, PA: University of Pennsylvania Press, 2011).

5. Fergus Millar, 'Empire and City, Augustus to Julian: Obligations, Excuses and Statuses', *Journal of Roman Studies*, 73 (1983): 76–96.

6. J. P. V. D. Balsdon, *Romans and Aliens* (London: Duckworth, 1979); Benjamin Isaac, *The Invention of Racism in Classical Antiquity* (Princeton, NJ: Princeton University Press, 2004). F. Marco Simón, F. Pina Polo, and J. Remesal Rodríguez (eds.), *Xenofobia y racismo en el mundo antiguo*, Collecio Instrumenta, vol. 64 (Barcelona: Edicions Universitat de Barcelona, 2019).

7. Scheid, 'Graeco ritu'.

8. Julián Gonzáles, 'Lex Irnitana: A New Copy of the Flavian Municipal Law', *Journal of Roman Studies*, 76 (1986): 147–243.

9. Acts 21–2.

10. MacMullen, *Soldier and Civilian in the Later Roman Empire*; Adrian Goldsworthy and Ian Haynes (eds.), *The Roman Army as a Community*, Journal of Roman Archaeology Supplements (Portsmouth, RI: Journal of Roman Archaeology, 1999).

11. Fikret K. Yegul, *Baths and Bathing in the Roman World* (Cambridge, MA: MIT Press, 1992).

12. I. Nielsen, *Thermae et Balnea: The Architecture and Cultural History of Roman Baths*, 2 vols. (Aarhus: Aarhus University Press, 1990).

13. Michael Wörrle, *Stadt und Fest in kaiserzeitlichen Kleinasien: Studien zu einer agonistischen Stiftung aus Oinoanda*, Vestigia (Munich: C. H. Beck, 1988); Onno van Nijf, 'Local Heroes: Athletics, Festivals and Elite Self-Fashioning in the Roman East', in Goldhill (ed.), *Being Greek under Rome*, 309–34; Jason König, *Athletics and Literature in the Roman Empire*, ed. Susan E. Alcock, Jas Elsner, and Simon Goldhill, Greek Culture in the Roman World (Cambridge: Cambridge University Press, 2005); Zahra Newby, *Greek Athletics in the Roman World: Victory and Virtue*, ed. Simon Price, R. R. R. Smith, and Oliver Taplin, Oxford Studies in Ancient Culture and Representation (New York: Oxford University Press, 2005); Fritz Graf, *Roman Festivals in the Greek East: From the Early Empire to the Middle Byzantine Era* (Cambridge: Cambridge University Press, 2015).

14. William J. Slater (ed.), *Dining in a Classical Context* (Ann Arbor, MI: University of Michigan Press, 1991); Emily Gowers, *The Loaded Table: Representations of Food in Roman Literature* (Oxford: Clarendon Press, 1993); Oswyn Murray and Manuela Tecusan (eds.), *In vino veritas* (London: British School at Rome, 1995); Garnsey, *Food and Society in Classical Antiquity*; Purcell, 'The Way We Used to Eat'; Jason König, 'Sympotic Dialogue in the First to Fifth Centuries CE', in Simon Goldhill (ed.), *The End of Dialogue in Antiquity*, 85–113 (Cambridge: Cambridge University Press, 2008).

15. The following discussion draws particularly on Chris Gosden, 'What Do Objects Want?' *Journal of Archaeological Method and Theory*, 12/3 (2005): 193–211; Miguel-John Versluys et al., 'Understanding Objects in Motion: An Archaeological Dialogue on Romanization', *Archaeological Dialogues*, 21/1 (2014): 1–64; Astrid Van Oyen and Martin Pitts (eds.), *Materializing Roman Histories* (Oxford: Oxbow, 2017); and Martin Pitts, *The Roman Object Revolution: Objectscapes and Intra-Cultural Connectivity in Northwest Europe*, Amsterdam Archaeological Studies (Amsterdam: Amsterdam University Press, 2018).

16. Ursula Rothe, *The Toga and Roman Identity* (London: Bloomsbury Academic, 2019).

17. Simon Swain, *Hellenism and Empire: Language, Classicism, and Power in the Greek World, AD 50–250* (Oxford: Clarendon Press, 1996); Tim Whitmarsh, *Greek Literature and the Roman Empire: The Politics of Imitations* (Oxford: Oxford, 2001);

Susan E. Alcock, John F. Cherry, and Jas Elsner (eds.), *Pausanias: Travel and Memory in Roman Greece* (New York: Oxford University Press, 2001).

18. Greg Woolf, 'Becoming Roman, Staying Greek: Culture, Identity and the Civilizing Process in the Roman East', *Proceedings of the Cambridge Philological Society*, 40 (1994): 116–43; Stephen Hinds, *Allusion and Intertext: Dynamics of Appropriation in Roman Poetry*, Latin Literature in Context (Cambridge: Cambridge University Press, 1998); Wallace-Hadrill, *Rome's Cultural Revolution*.

19. John Percival, *The Roman Villa: An Historical Introduction* (London: Batsford, 1976); Roger Ling, *Roman Painting* (Cambridge: Cambridge University Press, 1991); Jas Elsner, *Imperial Rome and Christian Triumph: The Art of the Roman Empire, AD 100–450*, Oxford History of Art (Oxford: Oxford University Press, 1998); Katherine M. Dunbabin, *Mosaics of the Greek and Roman World* (Cambridge: Cambridge University Press, 1999); Leach, *The Social Life of Painting in Ancient Rome and on the Bay of Naples*; Annalisa Marzano and Guy P. R. Métraux (eds.), *The Roman Villa in the Mediterranean Basin: Late Republic to Late Antiquity* (Cambridge: Cambridge University Press, 2018).

20. For attempts to use the concept, see Catharine Edwards and Greg Woolf (eds.), *Rome the Cosmopolis* (Cambridge: Cambridge University Press, 2003); Myles Lavan, Richard E. Payne, and John Weisweiler (eds.), *Cosmopolitanism and Empire: Universal Rulers, Local Elites, and Cultural Integration in the Ancient Near East and Mediterranean* (Cambridge: Cambridge University Press, 2016). Also relevant is Matthew P. Loar, Carolyn MacDonald, and Dan-el Padilla Peralta (eds.), *Rome, Empire of Plunder: The Dynamics of Cultural Appropriation* (Cambridge: Cambridge University Press, 2018).

21. T. C. Champion, 'Mass Migration in Later Prehistoric Europe', in Per Sörbom (ed.), *Transport Technology and Social Change: Papers Delivered at Tekniska Museet Symposium No. 2, Stockholm, 1979*, 33–42 (Stockholm: Tekniska Museet, 1980); Nicholas Purcell, 'Mobility and the Polis', in Oswyn Murray and Simon Price (eds.), *The Greek City from Homer to Alexander*, 29–58 (Oxford: Oxford University Press, 1990).

22. Laurens E. Tacoma, *Moving Romans: Migration to Rome in the Principate* (Oxford: Oxford University Press, 2016); Luuk de Ligt and Laurens E. Tacoma (eds.), *Migration and Mobility in the Early Roman Empire*, vol. 23/7. Leiden: Brill, 2016; Elena Isayev, *Migration, Mobility and Place in Ancient Italy* (Cambridge: Cambridge University Press, 2017); Elio Lo Cascio, Andrea Giardina, and Laurens E. Tacoma (eds.), *The Impact of Mobility and Migration in the Early Roman Empire*, Impact of Empire, vol. 12 (Leiden: Brill, 2017).

23. John F. Matthews, 'Hostages, Philosophers, Pilgrims, and the Diffusion of Ideas in the Late Roman Mediterranean and Near East', in F. M. Clover and R.S.

Humphreys (eds.), *Tradition and Innovation in Late Antiquity*, 29–49 (Madison, WI: University of Wisconsin Press, 1989).

24. David Noy, *Foreigners at Rome: Citizens and Strangers* (London: Duckworth, 2000); Edwards and Woolf, *Rome the Cosmopolis*; Wierschowski, L. *Fremde in Gallien— 'Gallier' in der Fremde: Die epigraphisch bezeugte Mobilität in, von und nach Gallien vom 1. bis 3. Jh. n. Chr. (Texte—Übersetzungen—Kommentare)*, Historia Einzelschriften, Vol. 159. Stuttgart: F. Steiner, 2001); Hella Eckart (ed.), *Roman Diasporas: Archaeological Approaches to Mobility and Diversity in the Roman Empire*, Journal of Roman Archaeology Supplements (Portsmouth, RI: Journal of Roman Archaeology, 2010).

25. Millar, 'Empire and City, Augustus to Julian'; William Broadhead, 'Migration and Transformation in Northern Italy in the 3rd–1st Centuries BC', *Bulletin of the Institute of Classical Studies*, 44 (2000): 145–66; Claudia Moatti (ed.), *La Mobilité des personnes en Méditerranée de l'antiquité à l'époque moderne: Procédures de contrôle et documents d'identification*, Collection de l'École Française de Rome (Rome: École Française de Rome, 2004); Claudia Moatti and Wolfgang Kaiser (eds.), *Gens de passage en Méditerranée de l'antiquité à l'époque moderne: Procédures de contrôle et d'identification*, Collection L'Atelier Méditerranéen (Paris: Maisonneuve & Larose, 2007).

26. Erich Gruen, *Diaspora: Jews among Greeks and Romans* (Cambridge, MA: Harvard University Press, 2002); Christopher P. Jones, 'A Syrian at Lyon', *American Journal of Philology*, 99/3 (1978): 336–53.

27. Ramsay MacMullen, *Paganism in the Roman Empire* (New Haven, CT: Yale University Press, 1981); Anna Collar, *Religious Networks in the Roman Empire: The Spread of New Ideas* (Cambridge: Cambridge University Press, 2013).

28. See, among other studies, David Mattingly (ed.), *Dialogues in Roman Imperialism: Power, Discourse and Discrepant Experience in the Roman Empire*, Journal of Roman Archaeology Supplements (Portsmouth, RI: Journal of Roman Archaeology, 1997); Jane Webster, 'Necessary Comparisons. A Post-Colonial Approach to Religious Syncretism in the Roman Provinces', *World Archaeology*, 28/3 (1997): 324–38; Peter van Dommelen, *On Colonial Grounds: A Comparative Study of Colonialism and Rural Settlement in First Millennium BC West Central Sardinia*, Archaeological Studies Leiden University (Leiden: Faculty of Archaeology, Leiden University, 1998); Jane Webster, 'Creolizing the Roman Provinces', *American Journal of Archaeology*, 105/2 (2001): 209–25; Chris Gosden, *Archaeology and Colonialism: Cultural Contact from 5000 BC to the Present* (Cambridge: Cambridge University Press, 2004); David Mattingly *An Imperial Possession: Britain in the Roman Empire 54 BC –AD 409* (London: Allen Lane, 2006); David Mattingly *Imperialism, Power and Identity: Experiencing the Roman Empire* (Princeton, NJ: Princeton University Press, 2011); Andrew Gardner, 'Thinking

about Roman Imperialism: Postcolonialism, Globalisation and Beyond?' *Britannia*, 44 (2012): 1–25.

29. Hannah Cornwell, *Pax and the Politics of Peace: Republic to Principate* (Oxford: Oxford University Press, 2017).

30. Robert Witcher, 'Globalisation and Roman Imperialism: Perspectives on Identities in Roman Italy', in Edward Herring and Kathryn Lomas (eds.), *The Emergence of State Identities in Italy in the First Millennium B.C.*, 213–25 (London: Accordia Research Institute, 2000); Richard Hingley, *Globalizing Roman Culture: Unity, Diversity and Empire* (London: Routledge, 2005); Rebecca J. Sweetman, 'Roman Knossos: The Nature of a Globalized City', *American Journal of Archaeology*, 111/1 (2007): 61–81; R. Bruce Hitchner, 'Globalization avant la lettre: Globalization and the History of the Roman Empire', *New Global Studies*, 2/2 (2008), doi: 10.2202/1940-0004.1034; Tim Whitmarsh (ed.), *Local Knowledge and Microidentities in the Imperial Greek World* (Cambridge: Cambridge University Press, 2010); Martin Pitts and Miguel John Versluys (eds.), *Globalisation and the Roman World: World History, Connectivity and Material Culture* (New York: Cambridge University Press, 2015).

31. Alicia Jiménez Díez, *Imagines Hibridae. Una aproximación postcolonialista al estudio de las necrópolis de la Bética*, Anejos de Archivo Español de Archeologia (Madrid: Consejo Superior de Investigaciones Científicas, 2008); Miguel John Versluys, *Visual Style and Constructing Identity in the Hellenistic World: Nemrud Dağ and Commagene under Antiochos I* (Cambridge: Cambridge University Press, 2017).

32. Swain, *Hellenism and Empire*; Seth Schwartz, *Imperialism and Jewish Society 200 BCE to 640 CE*, ed. R. Stephen Humphreys, William Chester Jordan, and Peter Schäfer, Jews, Christians and Muslims from the Ancient to the Modern World (Princeton, NJ: Princeton University Press, 2001).

33. Elias Bickermann, 'Origines Gentium', *Classical Philology*, 47 (1952): 65–81; T. Peter Wiseman, 'Domi nobiles and the Roman Cultural Élite', in Cébeillac-Gervason (ed.), *Les Bourgeoisies municipales italiennes aux IIe et Ier siècles av. J.-C.*; Erskine, *Troy between Greece and Rome*; Alan Cameron, *Greek Mythography in the Roman World*, ed. Donald J. Mastronarde, American Philological Association: American Classical Studies (New York: Oxford University Press, 2004); Simon Price, 'Local Mythologies in the Greek East', in Christopher Howgego, Volker Heuchert, and Andrew Burnett (eds.), *Coinage and Identity in the Roman Provinces*, 115–24 (Oxford: Oxford University Press, 2005); Hans-Joachim Gehrke, 'Heroen als Grenzgänger zwischen Griechen und Barbaren', in Erich Gruen (ed.), *Cultural Borrowings and Ethnic Appropriations in Antiquity*, Oriens et Occidens: Studien zu antiken Kulturkontakten und ihren Nachleben, 50–67 (Stuttgart: Franz Steiner Verlag, 2005); Woolf, *Tales of the Barbarians*; Andrew

C. Johnston, *The Sons of Remus: Identity in Roman Gaul and Spain* (Cambridge, MA: Harvard University Press, 2017).

CHAPTER XV

1. Simon Corcoran, *Empire of the Tetrarchs: Imperial Pronouncements and Government, AD 284–324* (Oxford: Clarendon Press, 1996).
2. A. H. M. Jones, *The Later Roman Empire, 284–602*, 2 vols. (Oxford: Blackwell Publishers, 1964).
3. Christopher Kelly, *Ruling the Later Roman Empire* (Cambridge, MA: Belknap Press of Harvard University Press, 2004).
4. Ramsay MacMullen, *Corruption and the Decline of Rome* (New Haven, CT: Yale University Press, 1988).
5. Sabine MacCormack, *Art and Ceremony in Late Antiquity*, Transformation of the Classical Heritage (Berkeley and Los Angeles: University of California Press, 1981).
6. Julian, *Caesars* 315A.
7. Wallace-Hadrill, 'Civilis princeps'.
8. Michael McCormick, *Eternal Victory: Triumphal Rulership in Late Antiquity, Byzantium and the Early Medieval West*, Past and Present Publications (Cambridge: Cambridge University Press, 1986).
9. Garnsey and Humfress, *The Evolution of the Late Antique World*, 9–51.
10. James B. Rives, 'The Decree of Decius and the Religion of Empire', *Journal of Roman Studies*, 89 (1999): 135–54.
11. W. H. C. Frend 'Persecutions: Genesis and Legacy', in Margaret M. Mitchell and Frances M. Young (eds.), *The Cambridge History of Christianity. I Origins to Constantine*, 503–23 (Cambridge: Cambridge University Press, 2006).
12. D. S. Levene, 'God and Man in the Classical Latin Panegyric', *Proceedings of the Cambridge Philological Society*, 43 (1997): 66–103; Roger Rees, *Layers of Loyalty in Latin Panegyric, AD 289–307* (Oxford: Oxford University Press, 2002).
13. The extent of Constantine's own legislation on sacrifice is controversial. T. D. Barnes, 'Constantine's Prohibition of Pagan Sacrifice', *American Journal of Philology*, 105/1: (1984): 69–72; Dorothea Baudy, 'Prohibitions of Religion in Antiquity: Setting the Course of Europe's Religious History', in Clifford Ando and Jörg Rüpke (eds.), *Religion and Law in Classical and Christian Rome*, 100–114. (Stuttgart: Franz Steiner Verlag, 2006); Jas Elsner, 'Sacrifice in Late Roman Art', in Christopher A. Faraone and F. S. Naiden (eds.), *Greek and Roman Animal Sacrifice: Ancient Victims, Modern Observers*, 120–63 (Cambridge: Cambridge University Press, 2012).

14. Matthew B. Roller, *Constructing Autocracy: Aristocrats and Emperors in Julio-Claudian Rome* (Princeton, NJ: Princeton University Press, 2001).

15. Averil Cameron and Stuart G. Hall, *Eusebius' Life of Constantine: Introduction, Translation, and Commentary* (Oxford: Clarendon Press, 1999); Anthony Bowen and Peter Garnsey, *Lactantius' Divine Institutes*, vol. xl, Translated Texts for Historians (Liverpool: Liverpool University Press, 2003); Roger Rees, *Diocletian and the Tetrarchy*, Debates and Documents in Ancient History (Edinburgh: Edinburgh University Press, 2004).

16. Jill Harries and Ian Wood (eds.), *The Theodosian Code: Studies in the Imperial Law of Late Antiquity* (London: Duckworth, 1993); John F. Matthews, *Laying Down the Law: A Study of the Theodosian Code* (New Haven, CT: Yale University Press, 2000). For the context, see Fergus Millar's *A Greek Roman Empire: Power and Belief under Theodosius II (408–450)* (Berkeley and Los Angeles: University of California Press, 2006).

17. For an insightful characterization of the new conditions, see Bryan Ward-Perkins, 'A Most Unusual Empire: Rome in the Fourth Century', in Claudia Rapp and H. A. Drake (eds.), *The City in the Classical and Post-Classical World: Changing Contexts of Power and Identity*, 109–29 (Cambridge: Cambridge University Press, 2014).

18. For a variety of views on late antique urbanism, see J. Rich (ed.), *The City in Late Antiquity* (London: Routledge, 1992); Wolf Liebeschuetz, *The Decline and Fall of the Roman City* (Oxford: Oxford University Press, 2001); Claudia Rapp and H. A. Drake (eds.), *The City in the Classical and Post-Classical World: Changing Contexts of Power and Identity* (Cambridge: Cambridge University Press, 2014).

19. Wolf Liebeschuetz, *Antioch: City and Imperial Administration in the Later Roman Empire* (Oxford: Clarendon Press, 1972); Christine Kondoleon (ed.), *Antioch the Lost Ancient City* (Princeton, NJ: Princeton University Press, 2000); Isabella Sandwell, *Religious Identity in Late Antiquity: Greeks, Jews, and Christians in Antioch*, Greek Culture in the Roman World (Cambridge: Cambridge University Press, 2007).

20. Roger Blockley, *The Fragmentary Classicising Historians of the Later Roman Empire: Eunapius, Olympiodorus, Priscus and Malchus*, 2 vols. (Liverpool: Francis Cairns, 1981–3).

21. Ewan Bowie, 'The Greeks and Their Past in the Second Sophistic', *Past and Present*, 46 (1970): 3–48; Philip A. Stadter, *Arrian of Nicomedia* (Chapel Hill, NC: University of North Carolina Press, 1980); Fergus Millar, *A Study of Cassius Dio* (Oxford: Clarendon Press, 1964); G. J. D. Aalders, 'Cassius Dio and the Greek World', *Mnemosyne*, 39/3–4 (1986): 282–304.

22. Millar, 'Empire and City, Augustus to Julian'.

23. John F. Matthews, *Western Aristocracies and Imperial Court, A.D. 364–425* (Oxford: Clarendon Press, 1975); Michele Salzman, *The Making of a Christian Aristocracy: Social and Religious Change in the Western Roman Empire* (Cambridge, MA: Harvard University Press, 2004); Alan Cameron, *The Last Pagans of Rome* (New York: Oxford University Press, 2011); Carlos A. R. Machado, *Urban Space and Aristocratic Power in Late Antique Rome (AD 270–535)* (Oxford: Oxford University Press, 2019).

24. Graeme Clarke (ed.), *Reading the Past in Late Antiquity* (Rushcutters Bay, NSW: Australian National University Press, 1990); Roger Rees (ed.), *Romane memento: Vergil in the Fourth Century* (London: Duckworth, 2003); Gavin Kelly, *Ammianus Marcellinus: The Allusive Historian* (Cambridge: Cambridge University Press, 2008).

25. S. T. Loseby, 'Marseille: A Late Antique Success Story?', *Journal of Roman Studies*, 82 (1992): 165–85; Claire Sotinel. *Identité civique et christianisme. Aquilée du IIIe au VIe siècle*, Bibliothèque des Écoles françaises d'Athènes et de Rome (Rome: École française de Rome, 2005); Douglas Boin, *Ostia in Late Antiquity* (New York and Cambridge: Cambridge University Press, 2013).

CHAPTER XVI

1. Richard Gordon, 'Religion in the Roman Empire: The Civic Compromise and its Limits', in *Pagan Priests*, edited by Mary Beard and John North, 233–55 (London: Duckworth, 1990).

2. Brent Nongbri, *Before Religion: A History of a Modern Concept* (New Haven, CT, and London: Yale University Press, 2013) drawing on a wider debate in religious studies, for which, see n. 5 below.

3. Steven Mithen and Pascal Boyer, 'Anthropomorphism and the Evolution of Cognition', *Journal of the Royal Anthropological Institute*, 2/4 (1996): 717–21; Stewart E. Guthrie, 'Anthropological Theories of Religion', in Michael Martin (ed.), *The Cambridge Companion to Atheism*, 283–99 (Cambridge: Cambridge University Press, 2007).

4. Arthur Darby Nock, *Conversion: The Old and the New in Religion from Alexander the Great to Augustine of Hippo* (Oxford: Clarendon Press, 1933).

5. Wilfred Cantwell Smith, *The Meaning and End of Religion: A New Approach to the Religious Traditions of Mankind*, Mentor Books (New York: New American Library, 1964); Jonathan Z. Smith, *Drudgery Divine: On the Comparison of Early Christianities and the Religions of Late Antiquity* (Chicago: Chicago University Press, 1990); Talad Asad, *Genealogies of Religion: Discipline and Reasons of Power in Christianity and Islam* (Baltimore, MD: Johns Hopkins University Press, 1993); Tomoko Masuzawa, *The Invention of World Religions: Or, How European*

Universalism was Preserved in the Language of Pluralism (Chicago: Chicago University Press, 2005).

6. John North, 'The Development of Religious Pluralism', in Judith Lieu, John North, and Tessa Rajak (eds.), *The Jews among Pagans and Christians in the Roman Empire*, 174–93 (London: Routledge, 1992); John North, 'Pagan Ritual and Monotheism', in Stephen Mitchell and Peter van Nuffelen (eds.), *One God: Pagan Monotheism in the Roman Empire*, 34–52 (Cambridge: Cambridge University Press, 2010); Julietta Steinhauer, *Religious Associations in the Post-Classical Polis* (Stuttgart: Franz Steiner Verlag, 2014).

7. Greg Woolf, 'Isis and the Evolution of Religions', in Laurent Bricault and Miguel John Versluys (eds.), *Power, Politics, and the Cults of Isis: Proceedings of the Vth International Conference of Isis Studies, Boulogne-sur-Mer, November 27–29, 2008*, 62–92 (Leiden and Boston, MA: Brill, 2014), drawing on Laurent Bricault, 'La Diffusion isiaque. Une Ésquisse', in P. C. Bol, G. Kaminski and C. Maderna (eds.), *Fremdheit–Eigenheit. Ägypten, Griechenland und Rom. Austausch und Verständnis*, 548–56. (Frankfurt am Main: Städel-Jahrbuch, Neue Folge 19, 2004).

8. MacMullen, *Paganism in the Roman Empire*.

9. Jas Elsner and Ian Rutherford (eds.), *Pilgrimage in Graeco-Roman and Early Christian Antiquity: Seeing the Gods* (Oxford: Oxford University Press, 2005).

10. Walter Burkert, *Ancient Mystery Cults*, Carl Newell Jackson Lectures (Cambridge, MA: Harvard University Press, 1987).

11. H. S. Versnel, *Inconsistencies in Greek and Roman Religion 1: Ter unus: Isis, Dionysos, Hermes: Three Studies in Henotheism*, Studies in Greek and Roman Religion (Leiden: Brill, 1990); John North, 'Pagans, Polytheists and the Pendulum', in William Vernon Harris (ed.), *The Spread of Christianity in the First Four Centuries: Essays in Explanation*, Columbia Studies in the Classical Tradition, 125–43 (Leiden: Brill, 2005).

12. Mitchell and van Nuffelen (eds.), *One God*.

13. Paul, *Letter to the Galatians*, 5:28.

14. Wayne A. Meeks, *The First Urban Christians: The Social World of the Apostle Paul* (New Haven, CT: Yale University Press, 1983); Keith Hopkins, 'Christian Number and Its Implications', *Journal of Early Christian Studies*, 6/2 (1998): 185–226; Judith Lieu, *Christian Identity in the Jewish and Graeco-Roman World* (Oxford: Oxford University Press, 2004).

15. Daniel Boyarin, *Border Lines: The Partition of Judaeo-Christianity*, Divinations: Rereading Late Antique Religion (Philadelphia, PA: University of Pennsylvania Press, 2004).

16. James Carleton Paget and Judith Lieu (eds.), *Christianity in the Second Century: Themes and Developments* (Cambridge: Cambridge University Press, 2017).

17. Averil Cameron, 'How to Read Heresiology', *Journal of Medieval and Early Modern Studies*, 33/3 (2003): 471–92.
18. Rives, 'The Decree of Decius and the Religion of Empire'.
19. Translation by Mary Boyce, quoted from David Potter, *The Roman Empire at Bay: AD 180–395*, 2nd edn (Abingdon: Routledge, 2014), 286.
20. T. D. Barnes, 'Constantine and the Christians of Persia', *Journal of Roman Studies*, 75 (1985): 126–36.
21. William R. Caraher, Thomas W. Davis, and David K. Pettegrew (eds.), *The Oxford Handbook to Early Christian Archaeology* (Oxford: Oxford University Press, 2019).
22. Olivier Hekster, *Commodus: An Emperor at the Crossroads*, Dutch Monographs on Ancient History and Archaeology (Amsterdam: J. C. Gieben, 2002).
23. John Curran, *Pagan City and Christian Capital: Rome in the Fourth Century*, Oxford Classical Monographs (Oxford: Clarendon Press, 2000).
24. Glen Bowersock, *Hellenism in Late Antiquity*, Thomas Spenser Jerome Lectures (Cambridge: Cambridge University Press, 1990).
25. Rebecca J. Sweetman, 'The Christianisation of the Peloponnese: The Case for Strategic Change', *Annual of the British School at Athens*, 110 (2015) 285–319.
26. Jill Harries, 'Christianity and the City in Late Antique Gaul', in John Rich (ed.), *The City in Late Antiquity*, 77–98 (London: Routledge, 1992).
27. John F. Matthews, *Western Aristocracies and Imperial Court, A.D. 364–425* (Oxford: Clarendon Press, 1975); Neil McLynn, *Ambrose of Milan: Church and Court in a Christian Capital* (Berkeley, CA: University of California Press, 1994).
28. T. D. Barnes, *Athanasius and Constantius: Theology and Politics in the Constantinian Empire* (Cambridge MA: Harvard University Press, 1993).

CHAPTER XVII

1. Peter Heather, 'Cassiodorus and the Rise of the Amals: Genealogy and the Goths under Hun Domination', *Journal of Roman Studies*, 79 (1989): 103–28.
2. Peter Heather, *Emperors and Barbarians. Migration, Development and the Birth of Europe* (London: Macmillan, 2009).
3. C. R. Whittaker, *Frontiers of the Roman Empire: A Social and Economic Study* (Baltimore, MD: Johns Hopkins University Press, 1994).
4. A. D. Lee, *Information and Frontiers: Roman Foreign Relations in Late Antiquity* (Cambridge: Cambridge University Press, 1993).
5. Peter H. Sawyer and Ian Wood (eds.), *Early Medieval Kingship* (Leeds: School of History, University of Leeds, 1977).
6. Drinkwater, *The Alamanni and Rome 213–496*.

7. On the crisis, see Noel Lenski, *Failure of Empire: Valens and the Roman State in the Fourth Century AD* (Berkeley, CA: University of California Press, 2002).

8. E. A Thompson, *The Huns*, 2nd edn (Oxford: Blackwell, 1996).

9. David W. Anthony, *The Horse, the Wheel and Language: How Bronze Age Riders from the Eurasian Steppes Shaped the Modern World* (Princeton, NJ, and Oxford: Princeton University Press, 2007).

10. Roger Batty, *Rome and the Nomads: The Pontic-Danubian Realm in Antiquity* (Oxford: Oxford University Press, 2007). For the dynamics of nomad empires more widely, see Thomas J. Barfield, 'Shadow Empires: Imperial State-Formation along the Chinese-Nomad Frontier', in Susan E. Alcock, T. D'Altroy, K. D. Morrison, and C. M. Sinopoli (eds.), *Empires: Perspectives from Archaeology and History*, 10–41 (New York and Cambridge: Cambridge University Press, 2001); Nicola Di Cosmo, *Ancient China and Its Enemies. The Rise of Nomadic Power in East Asian History* (Cambridge: Cambridge University Press, 2002).

11. Christopher Kelly, *Attila the Hun: Barbarian Terror and the Fall of the Roman Empire* (London: Bodley Head, 2008).

12. For the Huns as prime movers, see Heather, *Emperors and Barbarians*. For the suggestion that climate change generated these pressures, see Harper, *Fate of Rome*. More sceptical about the impact of the Huns are Michael Kulikowski, *Rome's Gothic Wars from the Third Century to Alaric* (New York: Cambridge University Press, 2007) and Guy Halsall, *Barbarian Migrations and the Roman West 376–568*, Cambridge Medieval Textbooks (Cambridge: Cambridge University Press, 2007).

13. Peter Heather, *Goths and Romans 332–489* (Oxford: Clarendon Press, 1991); Hugh Elton, *Warfare in Roman Europe, AD 350–425* (Oxford: Clarendon Press, 1996). Kulikowski, *Rome's Gothic Wars from the Third Century to Alaric*.

14. Ton Derks, and N. Roymans (eds.), *Ethnic Constructs in Antiquity: The Role of Power and Tradition* (Amsterdam: Amsterdam University Press, 2009); Walter Pohl (ed.), *Kingdoms of the Empire: The Integration of Barbarians in Late Antiquity* (Leiden, New York, and Cologne: Brill, 1997).

15. Walter Goffart, *Barbarians and Romans, A.D. 418–584: The Techniques of Accommodation* (Princeton, NJ: Princeton University Press, 1980).

16. Christian Courtois, *Les Vandales et l'Afrique* (Paris: Arts et Métiers Graphiques, 1955).

17. Jonathan Conant, *Staying Roman: Conquest and Identity in Africa and the Mediterranean, 439–700* (Cambridge: Cambridge University Press, 2012)

18. Edith Mary Wightman, *Roman Trier and the Treveri* (London: Hart-Davis, 1970).

19. John Drinkwater and Hugh Elton (eds.), *Fifth-Century Gaul: A Crisis of Identity* (Cambridge: Cambridge University Press, 1992).

20. Raymond Van Dam, *Leadership and Community in Late Antique Gaul*, Transformation of the Classical Heritage (Berkeley and Los Angeles: University of California Press, 1985).

21. Jill Harries, *Sidonius Apollinaris and the Fall of Rome, AD 407–485* (Oxford: Clarendon Press, 1994).

22. Julia M. H. Smith, *Europe after Rome: A New Cultural History, 500–1000* (Oxford: Oxford University Press, 2005).

23. For this perspective, see Chris Wickham, *The Inheritance of Rome: A History of Europe from 400 to 1000* (London: Allen Lane, 2009).

24. Chris Wickham, 'The Other Transition: From the Ancient World to Feudalism', *Past and Present*, 103 (1984): 3–36.

25. Peter H. Sawyer and Ian Wood (eds.), *Early Medieval Kingship* (Leeds: School of History, University of Leeds, 1977).

26. Wickham, 'The Other Transition'. For the archaeology of these changes, see Simon Esmonde Cleary, *The Roman West, AD 200–500: An Archaeological Study* (Cambridge: Cambridge University Press, 2013).

27. Bryan Ward-Perkins, *The Fall of Rome and the End of Civilization* (Oxford: Oxford University Press, 2005).

28. Kenneth G. Holum, *Theodosian Empresses: Women and Imperial Dominion in Late Antiquity* (Berkeley, CA: University of California Press, 1982).

29. Fergus Millar, *A Greek Roman Empire. Power and Belief under Theodosius II (408–450)* (Berkeley, CA: University of California Press, 2006); Christopher Kelly (ed.), *Theodosius II: Rethinking the Roman Empire in Late Antiquity* (Cambridge: Cambridge University Press, 2013).

30. Anthony Kaldellis, *Hellenism in Byzantium: The Transformations of Greek Identity and the Reception of the Classical Tradition* (Cambridge: Cambridge University Press, 2007).

31. Matthew P. Canepa, *The Two Eyes of the Earth: Art and Ritual of Kingship between Rome and Sasanian Iran* (Berkeley, Los Angeles, and London: University of California Press 2009).

CHAPTER XVIII

1. For a vivid account, see Brian Croke, 'Justinian's Constantinople', in Michael Maas (ed.), *The Cambridge Companion to the Age of Justinian*, 60–86 (New York and Cambridge: Cambridge University Press, 2005).

2. Michael Maas, *John Lydus and the Roman Past: Antiquarianism and Politics in the Age of Justinian* (London: Routledge, 1992); Christopher Kelly, *Ruling the Later Roman Empire* (Cambridge, MA: Belknap Press of Harvard University Press, 2004).

3. Greg Woolf, *The Life and Death of Ancient Cities: A Natural History* (New York and Oxford: Oxford University Press, 2020), ch. 19.

4. Boudewign Sirks, *Food for Rome: The Legal Structure of the Transportation and Processing of Supplies for the Imperial Distributions in Rome and Constantinople* (Amsterdam: J. C. Gieben, 1991).

5. James F. Crow, Jonathan Bardill, and Richard Bayliss, *The Water Supply of Byzantine Constantinople* (London: Society for the Promotion of Roman Studies, 2008).

6. Useful essays on all periods of the city's archaeology are gathered in J. C. N. Coulston, and Hazel Dodge (eds.), *Ancient Rome: The Archaeology of the Eternal City*, Oxford University School of Archaeology Monographs (Oxford: Oxford University School of Archaeology, 2000). For individual buildings, the starting place is Eva Margareta Steinby (ed.), *Lexicon Topographicum Urbis Romae*. 6 vols. (Rome: Edizioni Quazar, 1993–2000).

7. Seth Bernard, *Building Mid-Republican Rome: Labor, Architecture, and the Urban Economy* (New York: Oxford University Press, 2018).

8. Eric Orlin, *Temples, Religion and Politics in the Roman Republic*, Mnemosyne Supplements (Leiden, New York, and Cologne: Brill, 1997).

9. Bernard, *Building Mid-Republican Rome*, ch. 4.

10. Ray Laurence, *The Roads of Roman Italy: Mobility and Cultural Change* (London: Routledge, 1999), ch. 2.

11. Amy Russell, *The Politics of Public Space in Republican Rome* (Cambridge: Cambridge University Press, 2016).

12. On triumphs, see Mary Beard, *The Roman Triumph* (Cambridge MA: Harvard University Press, 2007); Ida Östenberg, *Staging the World: Spoils, Captives and Representations in the Roman Triumphal Procession* (Oxford and New York: Oxford University Press, 2009). One other kinds of processions, see Simon Price, 'From Noble Funerals to Divine Cult: The Consecration of Roman Emperors', in David Cannadine and Simon Price (eds.), *Rituals of Royalty: Power and Ceremonial in Traditional Societies*, 56–105 (Cambridge: Cambridge University Press, 1987); Ida Östenberg, Simon Malmberg, and Jonas Bjørnebye (eds.), *The Moving City: Processions, Passages and Promenades in Ancient Rome*. London and New York: Bloomsbury, 2015).

13. Matthew P. Loar, Carolyn MacDonald, and Dan-el Padilla Peralta (eds.), *Rome, Empire of Plunder: The Dynamics of Cultural Appropriation* (Cambridge: Cambridge University Press, 2018).

14. John S. Richardson, *Hispaniae: Spain and the Development of Roman Imperialism* (Cambridge: Cambridge University Press, 1986).

15. Michael Crawford, 'States Waiting in the Wings: Population Distribution and the End of the Roman Republic', in Luuk de Ligt and Simon Northwood

(eds.), *People, Land and Politics: Demographic Developments and the Transformation of Roman Italy 300 BC–AD 14*, 631–43 (Leiden: Brill, 2008).

16. Richard J. A. Talbert, *The Senate of Imperial Rome* (Princeton, NJ: Princeton University Press, 1984).

17. Catherine Edwards and Greg Woolf (eds.), *Rome the Cosmopolis* (Cambridge: Cambridge University Press, 2003).

18. Jennifer Trimble, 'Visibility and Viewing on the Severan Marble Plan', in Simon Swain, Stephen Harrison, and Jas Elsner (eds.), *Severan Culture*, 368–84 (Cambridge: Cambridge University Press, 2017).

19. Peter Garnsey, *Famine and Food Supply in the Greco-Roman World: Responses to Risk and Crisis* (Cambridge: Cambridge University Press, 1988).

20. Neville Morley, *Metropolis and Hinterland: The City of Rome and the Italian Economy 200 B.C.–A.D.200* (Cambridge: Cambridge University Press, 1996), Tymon de Haas and Gijs Tol (eds.), *Economic Integration of Roman Italy: Rural Communities in a Globalizing World*, Mnemosyne Supplements (Leiden: Brill, 2017).

21. Helen Patterson and Filippo Coarelli (eds.), *Mercator Placidissimus: The Tiber Valley in Antiquity: New Research in the Upper and Middle River Valley, Rome 27–28 February 2004*, Quaderni di Eutopia (Rome: Edizioni Quasar, 2008); Robert Bedon (ed.), 2011. *Macellum, taberna, portus: Les Structures matérielles de l'économie en Gaule romaine et dans les régions voisines* (Limoges: PULIM, 2011); Astrid Van Oyen. *The Socio-Economics of Roman Storage: Agriculture, Trade and Family* (Cambridge: Cambridge University Press, 2020).

22. Simon Keay (ed.), *Rome, Portus and the Mediterranean* (Rome: British School at Rome, 2013).

23. Fergus Millar, *The Emperor in the Roman World (31 BC–AD 337)* (London: Duckworth, 1977), ch. III.

24. Helmut Halfmann, *Itinera Principum: Geschichte und Typologie der Kaiserreisen im Römischen Reich*, Heidelberger althistorische Beiträge und epigraphische Studien (Stuttgart: Franz Steiner Verlag, 1986).

25. Edith Mary Wightman, *Roman Trier and the Treveri* (London: Hart-Davis, 1970); Richard Krautheimer, *Three Christian Capitals: Topography and Politics* (Berkeley, CA: University of California Press, 1983).

26. Gilbert Dagron, *Naissance d'une capitale: Constantinople et ses institutions de 330 à 451* (Paris: Presses Universitaires de France, 1974); Bryan Ward-Perkins, 'Old and New Rome Compared: The Rise of Constantinople', in Lucy Grig and Gavin Kelly (eds.), *Two Romes: Rome and Constantinople in Late Antiquity*, 53–78 (Oxford: Oxford University Press, 2012).

27. John Vanderspoel, *Themistius and the Imperial Court: Oratory, Civic Duty, and Paideia from Constantius to Theodosius* (Ann Arbor, MI: University of Michigan Press, 1995).

28. Zosimus *New History* 2.30–1

29. On the implications, see Lucy Grig and Gavin Kelly (eds.), *Two Romes: Rome and Constantinople in Late Antiquity*, Oxford Studies in Late Antiquity (Oxford: Oxford University Press, 2012).

30. Krautheimer, *Three Christian Capitals*.

31. John F. Matthews. *Western Aristocracies and Imperial Court*, A.D. *364–425* (Oxford: Clarendon Press, 1975); John Curran, *Pagan City and Christian Capital: Rome in the Fourth Century* (Oxford: Clarendon Press, 2000); Michele Renee Salzman, *The Making of a Christian Aristocracy: Social and Religious Change in the Western Roman Empire* (Cambridge, MA: Harvard University Press, 2004); Alan Cameron, *The Last Pagans of Rome* (New York and Oxford: Oxford University Press, 2011); Carlos A. R. Machado, *Urban Space and Aristocratic Power in Late Antique Rome (AD 270–535)* (Oxford: Oxford University Press, 2019).

32. Clifford Ando, *Imperial Ideology and Provincial Loyalty in the Roman Empire* (Berkeley, CA: University of California Press, 2000), ch. 9; Keith Hopkins, 'Divine Emperors, or the Symbolic Unity of the Roman Empire', in *Conquerors and Slaves: Sociological Studies in Roman History I*, 197–242 (Cambridge: Cambridge University Press, 1978); Stéphane Benoist, *Rome, le prince et la cité: Pouvoir impériale et cérémonies publiques (Ier siècle av.–début du IVe siècle apr. J.-C.)* (Paris: Presses Universitaires de France, 2005).

CHAPTER XIX

1. Joseph A. Tainter, *The Collapse of Complex Societies* (Cambridge: Cambridge University Press, 1988); Norman Yoffee and George L. Cowgill (eds.), *The Collapse of Ancient States and Civilizations* (Tucson, AZ: University of Arizona Press, 1988); Mario Liverani, 'The Fall of the Assyrian Empire: Ancient and Modern Interpretations', in Alcock et al. (eds.), *Empires*, 374–91; Jared M. Diamond, *Collapse: How Societies Choose to Fail or Survive* (London: Allen Lane, 2005).

2. Glen Bowersock, 'The Dissolution of the Roman Empire', in Yoffee and Cowgill (eds.), *The Collapse of Ancient States and Civilizations*, 165–75.

3. S. J. B. Barnish, 'Transformation and Survival in the Western Senatorial Aristocracy, c. A.D. 400–700', *Papers of the British School at Rome*, 56 (1988): 120–55; Chris Wickham, *Early Medieval Italy: Central Power and Local Society 400–1000* (London: Macmillan, 1981).

4. Jonathan Conant, *Staying Roman: Conquest and Identity in Africa and the Mediterranean, 439–700* (Cambridge: Cambridge University Press, 2012).

5. James J. O'Donnell, *Cassiodorus* (Berkeley and Los Angeles: University of California Press, 1979).

6. Walter Goffart, *Barbarians and Romans, A.D. 418–584: The Techniques of Accommodation* (Princeton, NJ: Princeton University Press, 1980).

7. Averil Cameron, *Procopius and the Sixth Century* (London: Duckworth, 1985).

8. Michael Maas, *John Lydus and the Roman Past: Antiquarianism and Politics in the Age of Justinian* (London: Routledge, 1992).

9. John F. Haldon, *Byzantium in the Seventh Century: The Transformation of a Culture*, rev. edn (Cambridge: Cambridge University Press, 1997).

10. Anthony Kaldellis, *The Byzantine Republic: People and Power in New Rome* (Cambridge, MA: Harvard University Press, 2015).

11. Cameron, 'The Construction of Court Ritual'.

12. Judith Herrin, *The Formation of Christendom* (Oxford: Blackwell, 1987).

13. Harper *The Fate of Rome,*

14. McNeill, *Plagues and Peoples.*

15. Walter Scheidel, 'Germs for Rome', in Catharine Edwards and Greg Woolf (eds.), *Rome the Cosmopolis*, 158-76 (Cambridge: Cambridge University Press, 2003).

16. Michael, McCormick et al., 'Climate Change during and after the Roman Empire: Reconstructing the Past from Scientific and Historical Evidence', *Journal of Interdisciplinary History*, 43/2 (2012):169–220. On the impact of climate change, see Haldon et al., 'Plagues, Climate Change, and the End of an Empire'.

17. Good examples of locally focused studies include John F. Haldon, et al. 'The Climate and Environment of Byzantine Anatolia: Integrating Science, History and Archaeology', *Journal of Interdisciplinary History*, 35 (2014):113–61; Colin P. Elliott, 'The Antonine Plague, Climate Change and Local Violence in Roman Egypt', *Past & Present*, 231 (2016): 3–31; Manning et al., 'Volcanic suppression of Nile summer flooding triggers revolt and constrains interstate conflict in ancient Egypt'.

18. Kristina Sessa, 'The New Environmental Fall of Rome: A Methodological Consideration', *Journal of Late Antiquity*, 12/1 (2019): 211–55.

19. Kyle Harper, *Slavery in the Late Roman World, AD 275–425* (Cambridge: Cambridge University Press, 2011).

20. Roger Bagnall, *Egypt in Late Antiquity* (Princeton, NJ: Princeton University Press, 1993).

21. Tainter, *The Collapse of Complex Societies.*

22. Gilbert Dagron, *Emperor and Priest: The Imperial Office in Byzantium* (Cambridge: Cambridge University Press, 2003).

23. Edmund Thomas, *Monumentality and the Roman Empire: Architecture in the Antonine Age* (New York: Oxford University Press, 2007).

24. Veyne, *Le Pain et le cirque*; Vivian Nutton, 'The Beneficial Ideology', in Garnsey and Whittaker (eds.), *Imperialism in the Ancient World*, 209–21; Zuiderhoek, *The Politics of Munificence in the Roman Empire.*

25. Bryan Ward-Perkins, *From Classical Antiquity to the Middle Ages: Urban Public Building in Northern and Central Italy AD 300–850*, Oxford Historical Monographs (Oxford: Oxford University Press, 1984). For the western part of the empire, see Esmonde Cleary, *The Roman West, AD 200–500*.

26. Rich (ed.), *The City in Late Antiquity*; Wolf Liebeschuetz, *The Decline and Fall of the Roman City* (Oxford: Oxford University Press, 2001); Kenneth G. Holum, 'The Classical City in the Sixth Century: Survival and Transformation', in Michael Maas (ed.), *The Cambridge Companion to the Age of Justinian*, 87–112 (New York and Cambridge: Cambridge University Press, 2005).

27. Clive Foss, *Ephesus after Antiquity: A Late Antique, Byzantine and Turkish City* (Cambridge: Cambridge University Press, 1979); S. T. Loseby, 'Marseille: A Late Antique Success Story?', *Journal of Roman Studies*, 82 (1992): 165–85; Neil Christie and S. T. Loseby (eds.), *Towns in Transition: Urban Evolution in Late Antiquity and the Early Middle Ages* (Aldershot: Scolar, 1996).

28. Michael Kulikowski, *Late Roman Spain and Its Cities* (Baltimore, MD: Johns Hopkins University Press, 2004).

29. Claude Lepelley, *Les Cités de l'Afrique romaine au bas-empire*, 2 vols. (Paris: Études Augustiniennes, 1979–81).

30. Hugh Kennedy, 'From Polis to Madina: Urban Change in Late Antique and Early Islamic Syria', *Past and Present*, 106/1 (1985): 3–27.

31. Millar, 'Empire and City, Augustus to Julian'.

32. Mark Whittow, 'Ruling the Late Roman and Early Byzantine City: A Continuous History', *Past and Present*, 129 (1990): 3–29.

33. McNeill, *Plagues and Peoples*.

34. De Ste Croix, *The Class Struggle in the Ancient Greek World*.

35. Haldon, *Byzantium in the Seventh Century*.

36. Rapp and Drake (eds.), *The City in the Classical and Post-Classical World*.

37. John F. Haldon, *The Empire That Would Not Die: The Paradox of Eastern Roman Survival 640–740* (Cambridge, MA: Harvard University Press, 2016).

38. Averil Cameron, ed. *Continuity and Change in Sixth-Century Byzantium* (London: Variorum Reprints, 1981); Haldon, *Byzantium in the Seventh Century*.

39. Bowersock, *Hellenism in Late Antiquity*.

40. Canepa, *The Two Eyes of the Earth*.

CHAPTER XX

1. Greg Woolf, 'The Uses of Forgetfulness in Roman Gaul', in Hans-Joachim Gehrke and Astrid Möller (eds.), *Vergangenheit und Lebenswelt: Soziale Kommunikation, Traditionsbildung und historisches Bewußtsein*, ScriptOralia, 361–81 (Tübingen: Gunter Narr Verlag, 1996); Erskine, *Troy between Greece and Rome*; Woolf, *Tales of the Barbarians*.

2. Heather, 'Cassiodorus and the Rise of the Amals'; Ian Wood, 'Defining the Franks: Frankish Origins in Early Mediaeval Historiography', in Simon Forde, Lesley Johnson, and Alan V. Murray (eds.), *Concepts of National Identity in the Middle Ages*, 47–57 (Leeds: Leeds University Press, 1995); Andrew Gillett (ed.), *On Barbarian Identity: Critical Approaches to Ethnicity in the Early Middle Ages*, Studies in the Early Middle Ages (Turnhout: Brepols, 2002).

3. Fergus Millar, *The Roman Near East, 31 BC–AD 337* (Cambridge, MA: Harvard University Press, 1993); Fergus Millar, 'Ethnic Identity in the Roman Near East, 325–450: Language, Religion and Culture', *Mediterranean Archaeology*, 11 (1998): 159–76; Stephen Mitchell and Geoffrey Greatrex (eds.), *Ethnicity and Culture in Late Antiquity* (London: Duckworth and Classical Press of Wales, 2000).

4. Fergus Millar, 'The Phoenician Cities: A Case Study in Hellenization', *Proceedings of the Cambridge Philological Society*, 29 (1983): 54–71; Price, 'Local Mythologies in the Greek East'; John Dillery, 'Greek Historians of the Near East: Clio's "Other" Sons', in John Marincola (ed.), *A Companion to Greek and Roman Historiography*, 221–30 (Malden, MA: Blackwell, 2007); John Dillery, *Clio's Other Sons: Berossus and Manetho, with an Afterword on Demetrius* (Ann Arbor, MI: University of Michigan Press, 2015).

5. Bowie, 'The Greeks and their Past in the Second Sophistic'; Swain, *Hellenism and Empire*; Susan E. Alcock, *Archaeologies of the Greek Past: Landscape, Monuments and Memories* (Cambridge: Cambridge University Press, 2002); Simon Price, 'Memory and Ancient Greece', in Anders Holm Rasmussen and Suzanne William Rasmussen (eds.), *Religion and Society: Rituals, Resources and Identity in the Ancient Graeco-Roman World: The BOMOS Conferences 2002–5*, 167–78 (Rome: Edizioni Quasar, 2008); Christopher P. Jones, 'Ancestry and Identity in the Roman Empire', in Whitmarsh (ed.), *Local Knowledge and Microidentities in the Imperial Greek World*, 111–24.

6. Hazel Dodge and Bryan Ward-Perkins (eds.), *Marble in Antiquity: Collected Papers of J. B. Ward-Perkins* (London: British School at Rome, 1992).

7. Sorcha Carey, *Pliny's Catalogue of Culture: Art and Empire in the Natural History*, Oxford Studies in Ancient Culture and Representation (Oxford: Oxford University Press, 2003); Catharine Edwards, 'Incorporating the Alien: The Art of Conquest', in Edwards and Woolf (eds.), *Rome the Cosmopolis*, 44–70.

8. Sarah Macready and F. H. Thompson (eds.), *Roman Architecture in the Greek World*, Society of Antiquaries of London Occasional Papers (London: Society of Antiquaries, 1987); Thomas, *Monumentality and the Roman Empire*; Serafina Cuomo, *Technology and Culture in Greek and Roman Antiquity*, ed. Paul Cartledge and Peter Garnsey, Key Themes in Ancient History (Cambridge: Cambridge University Press, 2007).

9. Keith Hopkins and Mary Beard, *The Colosseum*, ed. Mary Beard, Wonders of the World (London: Profile Books, 2005); Elke Stein-Hölkeskamp and Karl-Joachim Hölkeskamp (eds.), *Erinnerungsorte der Antike: Die römische Welt* (Munich: C. H. Beck Verlag, 2006).

10. Alain Schnapp, *The Discovery of the Past* (New York: Harry N. Abrams, 1997); Claudia Moatti, *In Search of Ancient Rome*, New Horizons (London: Thames and Hudson, 1993); David Karmon, *The Ruin of the Eternal City: Antiquity and Preservation in Renaissance Rome* (New York: Oxford University Press, 2011).

11. Wiseman, *Remus*; Purcell, 'Becoming Historical'.

12. Jean-Claude Golvin, *L'Amphithéâtre romain: Essai sur la théorisation de sa forme et de ses fonctions*, 2 vols., Publications du Centre Pierre Paris (UA 991) (Paris: De Boccard, 1988).

13. On Italy, see Werner Eck, 'Senatorial Self-Representation: Developments in the Augustan Period', in Millar and Segal (eds.), *Caesar Augustus*, 129–67. For the western provinces see now Ray Laurence, Simon Esmonde Cleary, and Gareth Sears. *The City in the Roman West c. 250 BC–AD 250* (Cambridge: Cambridge University Press, 2011).

14. Ramsay MacMullen, 'The Epigraphic Habit in the Roman Empire', *American Journal of Philology*, 103 (1982): 233–46; Greg Woolf, 'Monumental Writing and the Expansion of Roman Society', *Journal of Roman Studies*, 86 (1996): 22–39.

15. Habinek, *The Politics of Latin Literature*.

16. J. van Sickle, 'The Elogia of the Cornelii Scipiones and the Origins of Epigram at Rome', *American Journal of Philology*, 108 (1987): 41–55.

17. Woolf, 'The City of Letters', in Edwards and Woolf (eds.), Rome the Cosmopolis, 203–21.

18. Antony Spawforth, 'Symbol of Unity? The Persian-Wars Tradition in the Roman Empire', in Simon Hornblower (ed.), *Greek Historiography*, 233–47 (Oxford: Clarendon Press, 1994); Newby, *Greek Athletics in the Roman World*.

19. Catharine Edwards, *Writing Rome: Textual Approaches to the City* (Cambridge: Cambridge University Press, 1996).

20. R. R. R. Smith and Bryan Ward-Perkins (eds.), *The Last Statues of Antiquity* (Oxford: Oxford University Press, 2015).

21. Robert A. Kaster, *Guardians of Language: The Grammarian and Society in Late Antiquity* (Berkeley and Los Angeles: University of California Press, 1988); Clarke, *Reading the Past in Late Antiquity*.

22. Leighton D. Reynolds and Nigel G. Wilson, *Scribes and Scholars: A Guide to the Transmission of Greek and Latin Literature*, 2nd edn (Oxford: Clarendon Press, 1974).

23. J. A. Baird, and Zena Kamash (eds.), *Remembering Roman Syria* (London: Institute of Classical Studies, 2019).

Glossary of Technical Terms

The best place to find full information on Roman institutions is the *Oxford Classical Dictionary* (4th edition, 2012). This glossary is designed to help explain terms used in the text.

adventus The ceremonial entrance of an emperor into a city. The emperor would be welcomed by crowds and speeches, and might hand out gifts to the people. The theme is common on Roman imperial coinages, and the ceremony became especially important in the late empire.

ager publicus Land owned by the state, mostly acquired by conquest and leased out to citizens in return for rents (*vectigalia*).

censor During the Republican period a pair of censors were elected for eighteen months every five years from among the most senior senators. Their duties included reviewing the membership of the Senate and equestrian orders, assigning all citizens to their correct political orders, and issuing contracts for public works. They also came to exercise moral authority. Under the Principate a few emperors took the power of censors or held censorships and in practice assumed many of their functions.

census Originally the headcount of citizens conducted every year by the censors, who also assigned each citizen to an order according to the amount of property he owned. The term later came to be used for periodic assessments of tax liability in the provinces.

centurions The main officers of the legions whose expertise was vital, given that the aristocratic commanders were often relatively inexperienced. Most centurions commanded units of 80–100 men, and during the Republic were selected from the most experienced soldiers. Under the Principate an elaborate hierarchy of ranks and pay developed, and senior centurions were often detached to act as administrators of various kinds.

consul From the early Republic two consuls were elected every year and jointly acted as chief magistrates of the Roman state. Their duties included convening the Senate, presiding at major rituals, leading armies, and holding elections.

curiales Members of the councils of provincial cities of the Roman empire. The Greek equivalent term was *bouleutai*. These groups were in effect local equivalents of the senatorial order in Rome and like them were recruited from the propertied classes.

dictator During times of military emergencies a single dictator was elected in place of the consuls for a limited period only. The term was later appropriated first by Sulla and then by Julius Caesar to provide a traditional name for their control of the state.

equites The richest citizens of the Republic were enrolled in the equestrian order from which senators were elected. Equites are also sometimes termed knights, and at times the term equestrian is used to designate any citizen with the requisite property qualification, whether or not they had been formally enrolled as *equites equo publico*. Augustus created a new senatorial order above the equestrian one, for which the property qualification was higher, and gave both orders specific roles in the government of the empire and the ceremonial of the city.

fasces A bundle of rods surrounding an axe used as a symbol of power and carried before consuls and dictators by their attendants.

hoplite A Greek term for a heavily armed infantryman who fought hand to hand in a close formation termed a phalanx.

imperium The term originally meant a command, both one issued by and one given to a general. Holding *imperium* conferred a range of religious and political powers and obligations, and so it was formally assumed at the start of a campaign and laid down at the end of one. The term was extended to mean the authority of the Roman people, and at the end of the Republic came to be used of the territory subject to the commands of the Romans, from which our sense of territorial empire derives.

legate A legate was a Roman assigned a particular task by the state. Some legates were effectively ambassadors sent to conduct negotiations, some (*legati legionis*) were commanders assigned to legions, and from the last century BC there were also legates assigned to govern parts of very large provinces, such as those awarded to the emperor.

legion From the middle Republic until the late empire, the Roman army was based on units of around 5,000 heavily armed infantrymen, each of which was termed a legion. Typically these units were supported by light infantry, missile troops, cavalry, engineers, and other auxiliaries.

magister officiorum A senior official in the bureaucracy of the late empire and the Ostrogothic kingdom of Italy.

magistrate An official of the Roman state elected by the whole community. The most important magistrates were (in descending order) censors, consuls, praetors, and aediles. A dictator or an interrex (a person appointed solely to hold elections) was a magistrate, but tribunes (elected only by the plebeians) were not.

patricians This inner circle of families within the equestrian order who claimed descent from the aristocracy of the Regal Period. During the Republic they gradually lost control of their monopoly of magistracies but even under the Principate some priesthoods were reserved for patricians. The emperors occasionally created new patricians as an honour and to provide a sufficient number for the various patrician priesthoods.

plebeians All members of the Roman state who were not patricians. Tradition recorded a number of conflicts between patricians and plebeians during the early Republic (known collectively as the Struggle of the Orders) through which the prerogatives of the patricians were reduced and the rights of the plebeians recognized, for example in the institution of the tribunate or in the convention that votes of the plebeians (*plebiscita*) were binding on the entire state.

pontifex maximus The most senior priest of the college of pontiffs and the holder of the most prestigious priesthood in Rome. As well as presiding over the pontiffs, he also supervised a number of other priests, including the priestesses of Vesta.

populares During the last century of the Republic a series of senatorial politicians, of whom the most famous were the Gracchi brothers and Julius Caesar, based their political programme on fighting for the interest of the Roman people. Land distributions, colonial schemes, and subsidized or free grain were distinctive features of their activities, but in practice they became involved in all political debates, often using popular assemblies to outflank their opponents (who adopted the name *optimates*). This conflict contributed to the civil strife of the late Republic.

praetor A magistrate of the Roman state. After the creation of the consulship, the praetors were the more junior magistrates and had a range of judicial, administrative, and military responsibilities. The number of praetors and the diversity of their roles increased as the city and empire expanded.

praetorian prefect An equestrian prefect who was the commander of the praetorian cohorts that formed the main bodyguard of an emperor. From as early as the reign of Tiberius, they came not only to control security in the city (and around the emperor when he was away from it) but also to act as the chief equestrian advisers to the emperor, and effectively as viziers or chief ministers of the imperial court. From the early fourth century AD the empire was divided into praetorian prefectures within which each prefect headed the imperial bureaucracy.

princeps Literally the first (most senior) senator, the title was adopted by Augustus and his successors as a more neutral alternative to *rex* (king), *dictator*, or perpetual consul.

promagistrate Originally Roman armies were commanded by consuls and praetors but after imperial expansion made this impractical, the Senate began to ask former magistrates to take on commands. By the late Republic magistracies seem often to have been regarded as a necessary preliminary to winning a major command, and consuls drew lots for the commands prepared for them. Under the Principate the most senior governors (for example, of Africa, Asia, and Achaea) were proconsuls, and less senior posts went to propraetors, the emperors reserving for themselves one vast province which they governed through legates (*legati Augusti pro praetore*).

provincia Originally the task assigned along with imperium to a magistrate or promagistrate (for example, the war with Antiochus or the command of Sicily), the term eventually acquired the sense of a territorial unit within the empire; hence the modern term 'province'.

publicanus A Roman citizen who had contracted with the state to carry out work, for example provisioning an army, building or repairing a temple or basilica or road, or collecting taxes. The most notorious publicans were the tax farmers, whose brutality and greed in the later Republic became proverbial.

Senate The council of the Roman state, composed mostly of ex-magistrates but topped up every five years by the censors from those with the appropriate census qualification.

spolia opima An exceptional honour granted to generals who had killed their counterparts in single combat. Augustus claimed they had to fight under their own auspices to qualify.

tetrarchy In the aftermath of the military crisis of the third century AD, the empire was for a while ruled by colleges of emperors, originally comprising a pair of senior emperors (termed *Augusti*) and a pair of junior ones (*Caesares*) who were also their designated heirs. The term 'tetrarchy' refers both to this short-lived institution and to the period, while 'tetrarch' refers to one of the four members of the college. Both joint rule and the distinction between *Augusti* and *Caesares* had earlier precedents, but before Diocletian power was always shared between relatives rather than political allies. That was the case once again by the late fourth century AD.

tribune of the people (*tribunus plebis*) An official elected annually to a position created during the Republic to protect the rights of the plebeians against the patricians. Tribunes' persons were sacrosanct, and they had the right to call assemblies and to veto legislation and the acts of magistrates if they thought them against the interests of the plebeians. During the last century of the Republic the post was used first by the Gracchi and other *populares* as a means of passing legislation the Senate might not agree to and later by generals in order to have a veto to protect their interests. The emperors appropriated the sacrosanctity of tribunes as one of their powers, and dated their regnal year by the number of annual grants of tribunicial power they had received.

triumph A ritual which included a great procession into the city and might be awarded to a general who had won a significant victory. The procession was often accompanied by games, banqueting, and extended public holidays. Under the Principate only emperors and their relatives celebrated triumphs.

Bibliography

Aalders, G. J. D. 'Cassius Dio and the Greek World', *Mnemosyne*, 39/3–4 (1986): 282–304.

Abulafia, David. 'Mediterraneans', in *Rethinking the Mediterranean*, edited by William Vernon Harris, 64–93. Oxford: Oxford University Press, 2005.

Alcock, Susan E. *Graecia capta: The Landscapes of Roman Greece.* Cambridge: Cambridge University Press, 1993.

Alcock, Susan E., ed. *The Early Roman Empire in the East.* Oxford: Oxbow Books, 1997.

Alcock, Susan E. *Archaeologies of the Greek Past: Landscape, Monuments and Memories.* Cambridge: Cambridge University Press, 2002.

Alcock, Susan E., John F. Cherry, and Jas Elsner, eds. *Pausanias: Travel and Memory in Roman Greece.* New York: Oxford University Press, 2001.

Alcock, Susan E., T. D'Altroy, K. D. Morrison, and C. M. Sinopoli, eds. *Empires: Perspectives from Archaeology and History.* New York: Cambridge University Press, 2001.

Ando, Clifford. *Imperial Ideology and Provincial Loyalty in the Roman Empire.* Berkeley and Los Angeles: University of California Press, 2000.

Ando, Clifford. 'A Religion for the Empire', in *Flavian Rome: Culture, Image, Text*, edited by A. J. Boyle and W. J. Dominik, 321–44. Leiden: Brill, 2003.

Ando, Clifford. 'Interpretatio romana', *Classical Philology*, 100 (2005): 41–51.

Ando, Clifford. *The Matter of the Gods: Religion and the Roman Empire.* Berkeley and Los Angeles: University of California Press, 2008.

Ando, Clifford. *Law, Language and Empire in the Roman Tradition.* Philadelphia, PA: University of Pennsylvania Press, 2011.

Ando, Clifford, ed. *Citizenship and Empire in Europe 200–1900: The Antonine Constitution after 1800 Years.* Stuttgart: Franz Steiner Verlag, 2016.

Ando, Clifford, and Seth Richardson, eds. *Ancient States and Infrastructural Power: Europe, Asia, and America*, Empire and After. Philadelphia, PA: University of Pennsylvania Press, 2017.

Anthony, David W. *The Horse, the Wheel and Language: How Bronze Age Riders from the Eurasian Steppes Shaped the Modern World.* Princeton, NJ, and Oxford: Princeton University Press, 2007.

Arnason, Johann P., and Kurt Raaflaub, eds. *The Roman Empire in Context: Historical and Comparative Perspectives*. Malden, MA, and Oxford: Wiley-Blackwell, 2011.

Asad, Talad. *Genealogies of Religion: Discipline and Reasons of Power in Christianity and Islam*. Baltimore, MD: Johns Hopkins University Press, 1993.

Aubert, Jean-Jacques. *Business Managers in Ancient Rome: A Social and Economic Study of Institores, 200 B.C.–A.D. 250*, Columbia Studies in the Classical Tradition. Leiden: Brill, 1994.

Aubet, Maria Eugenia. *The Phoenicians and the West: Politics, Colonies and Trade*. 2nd edn. Cambridge: Cambridge University Press, 2001.

Austin, Michel. 'Hellenistic Kings, War and the Economy', *Classical Quarterly*, 36/2 (1986): 450–66.

Badian, Ernst. *Foreign Clientelae (264–70 BC)*. Oxford: Clarendon Press, 1958.

Bagnall, Roger. *Egypt in Late Antiquity*. Princeton, NJ: Princeton University Press, 1993.

Baird, J. A., and Zena Kamash, eds. 2019. *Remembering Roman Syria*, Bulletin of the Institute of Classical Studies, vol. 62/1. London: Institute of Classical Studies.

Balsdon, J. P. V. D. *Romans and Aliens*. London: Duckworth, 1979.

Bang, Peter Fibiger. *The Roman Bazaar: A Comparative Study of Trade and Markets in a Tributary Empire*, Cambridge Classical Studies. Cambridge: Cambridge University Press, 2008.

Bang, Peter Fibiger, and Christopher A. Bayly, eds. *Tributary Empires in History: Comparative Perspectives from Antiquity to the Late Mediaeval. Mediaeval History Journal*, 2003.

Bang, Peter Fibiger, and Christopher A. Bayly, eds. *Tributary Empires in Global History*, Cambridge Imperial and Post-Colonial Studies Series. Basingstoke: Palgrave Macmillan, 2011.

Bang, Peter Fibiger, and Dariusz Kolodziejczyz, eds. *Universal Empire. A Comparative Approach to Imperial Culture and Representation in Eurasian History*. Cambridge: Cambridge University Press, 2012.

Barfield, Thomas J. 'Shadow Empires: Imperial State-Formation along the Chinese-Nomad Frontier', in *Empires: Perspectives from Archaeology and History*, edited by Susan E. Alcock, T. D'Altroy, K. D. Morrison, and C. M. Sinopoli, 10–41. New York and Cambridge: Cambridge University Press, 2001.

Barker, Graeme. *Prehistoric Farming in Europe*, New Directions in Archaeology. Cambridge: Cambridge University Press, 1985.

Barker, Graeme, and Tom Rasmussen. *The Etruscans*, The Peoples of Europe, edited by James Campbell and Barry Cunliffe. 2nd edn. Malden, MA: Blackwell, 1998.

Barnes, T. D. *Constantine and Eusebius*. Cambridge, MA: Harvard University Press, 1981.

Barnes, T. D. *The New Empire of Diocletian and Constantine*. Cambridge, MA: Harvard University Press, 1982.

Barnes, T. D. 'Constantine's Prohibition of Pagan Sacrifice', *American Journal of Philology*, 105/1 (1984): 69–72.

Barnes, T. D. 'Constantine and the Christians of Persia', *Journal of Roman Studies*, 75 (1985): 126–36.

Barnes, T. D. *Athanasius and Constantius: Theology and Politics in the Constantinian Empire*. Cambridge, MA: Harvard University Press, 1993.

Barnish, S. J. B. 'Transformation and Survival in the Western Senatorial Aristocracy, c. A.D. 400–700', *Papers of the British School at Rome*, 56 (1988): 120–55.

Bartman, E. 'Sculptural Collecting and Display in the Private Realm', in *Roman Art in the Private Sphere: New Perspectives on the Architecture and Decor of the Domus, Villa and Insula*, edited by E. Gazda, 71–88. Ann Arbor, MI: University of Michigan Press, 1991.

Batty, Roger. *Rome and the Nomads: The Pontic-Danubian Realm in Antiquity*. Oxford: Oxford University Press, 2007.

Baudy, Dorothea 'Prohibitions of Religion in Antiquity: Setting the Course of Europe's Religious History', in *Religion and Law in Classical and Christian Rome*, edited by Clifford Ando and Jörg Rüpke, 100–114. Stuttgart: Franz Steiner Verlag, 2006.

Beard, Mary. 'Cicero and Divination: The Formation of a Latin Discourse', *Journal of Roman Studies*, 76 (1986): 33–46.

Beard, Mary. 'A Complex of Times: No More Sheep on Romulus' Birthday', *Proceedings of the Cambridge Philological Society*, 33 (1987): 1–15.

Beard, Mary. 'The Roman and the Foreign: The Cult of the "Great Mother" in Imperial Rome', in *Shamanism, History and the State*, edited by Nicholas Thomas and Caroline Humphrey, 164–90. Ann Arbor, MI: University of Michigan Press, 1994.

Beard, Mary. *The Roman Triumph*. Cambridge, MA: Harvard University Press, 2007.

Beard, Mary. *SPQR: A History of Ancient Rome*. London: Profile Books, 2015.

Beard, Mary, and Michael H. Crawford. *Rome in the Late Republic: Problems and Interpretations*. 2nd edn. London: Duckworth, 1999.

Beard, Mary, and John North, eds. *Pagan Priests*. London: Duckworth, 1990.

Beard, Mary, John North, and Simon Price. *Religions of Rome*. 2 vols. Cambridge: Cambridge University Press, 1998.

Beck, Hans, Martin Jehne, and John Serrati, eds. 2016. *Money and Power in the Roman Republic*, Collection Latomus 355. Brussels: Éditions Latomus.

Bedford, Peter R. 'The Neo-Assyrian Empire', in *The Dynamics of Ancient Empires: State Power from Assyria to Byzantium*, edited by Ian Morris and Walter Scheidel, 30–65. New York: Oxford University Press, 2009.

Bedon, Robert, ed. *Macellum, taberna, portus: Les Structures matérielles de l'économie en Gaule romaine et dans les régions voisines*, Caesarodunum, vols. 33–4. Limoges: PULIM, 2011.

Benoist, Stéphane. *Rome, le prince et la cité: Pouvoir impériale et cérémonies publiques (Ier siècle av.–début du IVe siècle apr. J.-C.)*. Paris: Presses Universitaires de France, 2005.

Bernard, Seth. *Building Mid-Republican Rome: Labor, Architecture, and the Urban Economy*. New York: Oxford University Press, 2018.

Bickermann, Elias. 'Origines gentium', *Classical Philology*, 47 (1952): 65–81.

Bietti Sestieri, Anna Maria. *The Iron Age Community of Osteria dell'Osa: A Study of Socio-Political Development in Central Tyrrenian Italy*, New Studies in Archaeology. Cambridge: Cambridge University Press, 1993.

Birley, Anthony R. *Hadrian: The Restless Emperor*. London: Routledge, 1997.

Bispham, Edward. *From Asculum to Actium: The Municipalization of Italy from the Social War to Augustus*. Oxford: Oxford University Press, 2007.

Blagg, Tom, and Martin Millett, eds. *The Early Roman Empire in the West*. Oxford: Oxbow Books, 1990.

Blázquez Martinez, José María, and José Remesal Rodriguez, eds. *Producción y commercio del aceite en la antigüedad: Congresso I*. Madrid: Universidad Complutense, 1980.

Blázquez Martinez, José María, and José Remesal Rodriguez, eds. *Producción y commercio del aceite en la antigüedad: Congresso II*. Madrid: Universidad Complutense, 1982.

Blockley, Roger. *The Fragmentary Classicising Historians of the Later Roman Empire: Eunapius, Olympiodorus, Priscus and Malchus*. 2 vols. Liverpool: Francis Cairns, 1981–3.

Boardman, John. *Greeks Overseas: Their Early Colonies and Trade*. 4th edn. London: Thames and Hudson, 1999.

Bodde, Derk. 'The State and Empire of Ch'in', in *The Cambridge History of China*, i: *The Ch'in and Han Empires, 221 B.C.–A.D. 220*, edited by Denis Twitchett and Michael Loewe, 21–102. Cambridge: Cambridge University Press, 1986.

Boin, Douglas. *Ostia in Late Antiquity*. New York and Cambridge: Cambridge University Press, 2013.

Bowen, Anthony, and Peter Garnsey. *Lactantius' Divine Institutes*, xl, Translated Texts for Historians. Liverpool: Liverpool University Press, 2003.

Bowersock, Glen. 'The Mechanics of Subversion in the Roman Provinces', in *Oppositions et résistances à l'empire d'Auguste à Trajan*, edited by Adalberto Giovannini, 291–320. Geneva: Fondation Hardt, 1987.

Bowersock, Glen. 'The Dissolution of the Roman Empire', in *The Collapse of Ancient States and Civilizations*, edited by Norman Yoffee and George L. Cowgill, 165–75. Tucson, AZ: University of Arizona Press, 1988.

Bowersock, Glen. *Hellenism in Late Antiquity*, Thomas Spenser Jerome Lectures. Cambridge: Cambridge University Press, 1990.

Bowersock, Glen, Peter Brown, and Oleg Grabar, eds. *Late Antiquity: A Guide to the Postclassical World*. Cambridge, MA: Belknap Press of Harvard University Press, 1999.

Bowie, Ewan. 'The Greeks and Their Past in the Second Sophistic', *Past and Present*, 46 (1970): 3–48.

Bowman, Alan. *Life and Letters on the Roman Frontier: Vindolanda and Its People*. London: British Museum Press, 1994.

Bowman, Alan, and Andrew Wilson, eds. *Quantifying the Roman Economy: Methods and Problems*, Oxford Studies on the Roman Economy. Oxford: Oxford University Press, 2009.

Bowman, Alan, and Andrew Wilson, eds. *Settlement, Urbanization, and Population*, Oxford Studies on the Roman Economy. Oxford: Oxford University Press, 2011.

Bowman, Alan, and Andrew Wilson, eds. *The Roman Agricultural Economy: Organisation, Investment, and Production*, Oxford Studies on the Roman Economy. Oxford: Oxford University Press, 2013.

Boyarin, Daniel. *Border Lines: The Partition of Judaeo-Christianity*, Divinations: Rereading Late Antique Religion, edited by Daniel Boyarin, Virginia Burrus, Charlotte Fonrobert, and Robert Gregg. Philadelphia, PA: University of Pennsylvania Press, 2004.

Bradley, Guy, Elena Isayev, and Corinna Riva, eds. *Ancient Italy: Regions without Boundaries*. Exeter: University of Exeter Press, 2007.

Bradley, Keith. *Slaves and Masters in the Roman Empire: A Study in Social Control*. New York: Oxford University Press, 1987.

Bradley, Keith. *Slavery and Society at Rome*, Key Themes in Ancient History, edited by Paul Cartledge and Peter Garnsey. Cambridge: Cambridge University Press, 1994.

Bradley, Keith. 'Slavery in the Roman Republic', in *Cambridge World History of Slavery*, i: *The Ancient Mediterranean World*, edited by Keith Bradley and Paul Cartledge, 241–64. Cambridge: Cambridge University Press, 2011.

Bradley, Keith, and Paul Cartledge, eds. *Cambridge World History of Slavery*, i: *The Ancient Mediterranean World*. Cambridge: Cambridge University Press, 2011.

Braund, David. *Rome and the Friendly King: The Character of the Client Kingship*. London: Croom Helm, 1982.

Braund, David. 'Royal Wills and Rome', *Papers of the British School at Rome*, 51 (1983): 16–57.

Bricault, Laurent. 'La Diffusion isiaque: Une Ésquisse', in *Fremdheit–Eigenheit: Ägypten, Griechenland und Rom: Austausch und Verständnis*, edited by P. C. Bol, G. Kaminski, and C. Maderna, 548–56. Frankfurt am Main: Städel-Jahrbuch, Neue Folge 19, 2004.

Brisch, Nicole, ed. *Religion and Power: Divine Kingship in the Ancient World and Beyond*, Oriental Institute Seminars. Chicago: Oriental Institute of the University of Chicago, 2008.

Broadhead, William. 'Migration and Transformation in Northern Italy in the 3rd–1st Centuries BC', *Bulletin of the Institute of Classical Studies*, 44 (2000): 145–66.

Broodbank, Cyprian. *The Making of the Middle Sea: A History of the Mediterranean from the Beginning to the Emergence of the Classical World*. New York and Oxford: Oxford University Press, 2013.

Brosius, Maria. 'New out of Old? Court and Court Ceremonies in Achaemenid Persia', in *The Court and Court Society in Ancient Monarchies*, edited by Antony Spawforth, 17–57. Cambridge: Cambridge University Press, 2007.

Brown, Peter. *The World of Late Antiquity: From Marcus Aurelius to Muhammad*. London: Thames and Hudson, 1971.

Brown, Peter. *The Body and Society: Men, Women, and Sexual Renunciation in Early Christianity*, Lectures on the History of Religions. New York: Columbia University Press, 1988.

Brown, Peter. *Augustine of Hippo: A Biography*. London: Faber, 2000.

Brumfiel, Elizabeth M., and John W. Fox, eds. *Factional Competition and Political Development in the New World*, New Directions in Archaeology. Cambridge: Cambridge University Press, 1994.

Brunt, P. A. 'Italian Aims at the Time of the Social War', *Journal of Roman Studies*, 55 (1965): 90–109.

Brunt, P. A. *Italian Manpower 225 B.C.–A.D. 14*. Oxford: Oxford University Press, 1971.

Brunt, P. A. 'Laus imperii', in *Imperialism in the Ancient World*, edited by Peter Garnsey and C. R. Whittaker, 159–191. Cambridge: Cambridge University Press, 1978. Repr. P. A. Brunt, *Roman Imperial Themes*. Oxford: Oxford University Press, 1990, 288–323.

Brunt, P. A. 'The Revenues of Rome', *Journal of Roman Studies*, 71 (1981): 161–72.

Brunt, P. A. *The Fall of the Roman Republic, and Related Essays*. Oxford: Clarendon Press, 1988.

Brunt, P. A. 'Publicans in the Principate', in *Roman Imperial Themes*, 354–432. Oxford: Oxford University Press, 1990.

Bruun, Christer. 'The Antonine Plague and the "Third-Century Crisis"', in *Crises and the Roman Empire*, edited by Olivier Hekster, Gerda de Kleijn, and Daniëlle Slootjes, 201–17. Leiden: Brill, 2007.

Bruun, Christer, and Jonathan Edmondson, eds. *The Oxford Handbook of Roman Epigraphy*, New York and Oxford: Oxford University Press, 2014.

Burkert, Walter. *Ancient Mystery Cults*, Carl Newell Jackson Lectures. Cambridge, MA: Harvard University Press, 1987.

Callataÿ, François de. 'The Graeco-Roman Economy in the Super Long Run: Lead, Copper, and Shipwrecks', *Journal of Roman Archaeology*, 18/1 (2005): 361–72.

Cameron, Alan. *Greek Mythography in the Roman World*, American Philological Association: American Classical Studies, edited by Donald J. Mastronarde. New York: Oxford University Press, 2004.

Cameron, Alan. *The Last Pagans of Rome*. New York: Oxford University Press, 2011.

Cameron, Averil, ed. *Continuity and Change in Sixth-Century Byzantium*. London: Variorum Reprints, 1981.

Cameron, Averil. *Procopius and the Sixth Century*. London: Duckworth, 1985.

Cameron, Averil. 'The Construction of Court Ritual: The Byzantine Book of Ceremonies', in *Rituals of Royalty: Power and Ceremonial in Traditional Societies*, edited by David Cannadine and Simon Price, 106–36. Cambridge: Cambridge University Press, 1987.

Cameron, Averil. *Christianity and the Rhetoric of Empire: The Development of Christian Discourse*, Sather Classical Lectures. Berkeley and Los Angeles: University of California Press, 1991.

Cameron, Averil, ed. *Changing Cultures in Early Byzantium*. Aldershot: Variorum Reprints, 1996.

Cameron, Averil. 'How to Read Heresiology', *Journal of Medieval and Early Modern Studies*, 33/3 (2003): 471–92.

Cameron, Averil. *The Mediterranean World in Late Antiquity AD 395-700*. 2nd edn. London: Routledge, 2012.

Cameron, Averil, and Stuart G. Hall. *Eusebius' Life of Constantine: Introduction, Translation, and Commentary*. Oxford: Clarendon Press, 1999.

Campbell, Brian. *The Emperor and the Roman Army 31 BC–AD 235*. Oxford: Clarendon Press, 1984.

Campbell, Brian. 'War and Diplomacy: Rome and Parthia 31 BC–AD 235', in *War and Society in the Roman World*, edited by John Rich and Graham Shipley, 213–40. London: Routledge, 1993.

Canepa, Matthew P. *The Two Eyes of the Earth: Art and Ritual of Kingship between Rome and Sasanian Iran*, edited by Peter Brown, The Transformation of the Classical Heritage, vol. 45. Berkeley and Los Angeles: University of California Press, 2009.

Cannadine, David. *Ornamentalism: How the British Saw Their Empire*. London: Allen Lane, 2001.

Cannadine, David, and Simon Price, eds. *Rituals of Royalty: Power and Ceremonial in Traditional Societies*. Cambridge: Cambridge University Press, 1987.

Caraher, William R., Thomas W. Davis, and David K. Pettegrew, eds. *The Oxford Handbook to Early Christian Archaeology*. Oxford: Oxford University Press, 2019.

Carey, Sorcha. *Pliny's Catalogue of Culture: Art and Empire in the Natural History*, Oxford Studies in Ancient Culture and Representation. Oxford: Oxford University Press, 2003.

Carlsen, Jesper, and Elio Lo Cascio, eds. *Agricoltura e scambi nell'Italia tardo-Repubblicana*, Pragmateiai. Bari: Edipuglia, 2009.

Carleton Paget, James, and Judith Lieu, eds. *Christianity in the Second Century: Themes and Developments*. Cambridge: Cambridge University Press, 2017.

Casiday, Augustine, and Frederick W. Norris, eds. *Cambridge History of Christianity*, ii: *Constantine to c.600*. Cambridge: Cambridge University Press, 2007.

Cébeillac-Gervason, M., ed. *Les Bourgeoisies municipales italiennes aux IIe et Ier siècles av. J-C*. Naples: Éditions du CNRS and Bibliothèque de l'Institut Français de Naples, 1981.

Champion, T. C. 'Mass Migration in Later Prehistoric Europe', in *Transport Technology and Social Change: Papers Delivered at Tekniska Museet Symposium No. 2, Stockholm, 1979*, edited by Per Sörbom, 33–42. Stockholm: Tekniska Museet, 1980.

Champion, Tim, Clive Gamble, Stephen Shennan, and Alasdair Whittle. *Prehistoric Europe*. London: Academic Press, 1984.

Christie, Neil, and S. T. Loseby, eds. *Towns in Transition: Urban Evolution in Late Antiquity and the Early Middle Ages*. Aldershot: Scolar, 1996.

Claridge, Amanda. *Rome: An Oxford Archaeological Guide*. 2nd edn. Oxford: Oxford University Press, 2010.

Clarke, Graeme, ed. *Reading the Past in Late Antiquity*. Rushcutters Bay, NSW: Australian National University Press, 1990.

Clarke, Katherine. 'Universal Perspectives in Historiography', in *The Limits of Historiography: Genre and Narrative in Ancient Historical Texts*, edited by Christina Shuttleworth Kraus, 249–79. Leiden: Brill, 1999.

Coarelli, Filippo. 'Public Building in Rome between the Second Punic War and Sulla', *Papers of the British School at Rome*, 45 (1977): 1–23.

Coarelli, Filippo. *Rome and Environs: An Archaeological Guide*. Berkeley and Los Angeles: University of California Press, 2007.

Coarelli, Filippo, and Helen Patterson, eds. *Mercator placidissimus: The Tiber Valley in Antiquity: New Research in the Upper and Middle River Valley, Rome, 27–28 February 2004*, Quaderni di Eutopia. Rome: Quasar, 2008.

Colinvaux, Paul A. *Why Big Fierce Animals Are Rare: An Ecologist's Perspective*. Princeton, NJ: Princeton University Press, 1978.

Collar, Anna *Religious Networks in the Roman Empire: The Spread of New Ideas*. Cambridge: Cambridge University Press, 2013.

Collins, John J., and J. G Manning, eds. *Revolt and Resistance in the Ancient Classical World and the Near East: In the Crucible of Empire*, Culture and History of the Ancient Near East. Leiden and New York: Brill, 2016.

Collis, John R. *The European Iron Age*. London: Batsford, 1984.

Conant, Jonathan, *Staying Roman: Conquest and Identity in Africa and the Mediterranean, 439–700*, Cambridge Studies in Mediaeval Life and Thought. Cambridge: Cambridge University Press, 2012.

Conrad, Geoffrey, and Arthur A. Demarest. *Religion and Empire: The Dynamics of Aztec and Inca Expansionism*, New Directions in Archaeology. Cambridge: Cambridge University Press, 1984.

Cooley, Alison. 'Beyond Rome and Latium: Roman Religion in the Age of Augustus', in *Religion in Republican Italy*, edited by Celia Schultz and Paul B. Harvey, 228–52. Cambridge: Cambridge University Press, 2006.

Cooley, Alison. *Res gestae divi Augusti: Text, Translation and Commentary*. Cambridge: Cambridge University Press, 2009.

Cooley, Alison, and Melvin G.L. Cooley. *Pompeii and Herculaneum: A Sourcebook*. 2nd edn. London: Routledge, 2014.

Corcoran, Simon. *Empire of the Tetrarchs: Imperial Pronouncements and Government*, AD 284–324. Oxford: Clarendon Press, 1996.

Cormack, Robin. *Byzantine Art*, Oxford History of Art. Oxford: Oxford University Press, 2000.

Cornell, Tim. *The Beginnings of Rome: Italy and Rome from the Bronze Age to the Punic Wars (c.1000–264 BC)*, Routledge History of the Ancient World. London: Routledge, 1995.

Cornwell, Hannah. *Pax and the Politics of Peace: Republic to Principate* Oxford: Oxford University Press, 2017.

Cottier, Michel, Michael H. Crawford, C.V. Crowther, Jean-Louis Ferrary, Barbara Levick, and Michael Wörrle, eds. *The Customs Law of Asia*, Oxford Studies in Ancient Documents, edited by Alan Bowman and Alison Cooley. Oxford: Oxford University Press, 2008.

Coulston, J. C. N., and Hazel Dodge, eds. *Ancient Rome: The Archaeology of the Eternal City*, Oxford University School of Archaeology Monographs. Oxford: Oxford University School of Archaeology, 2000.

Courtois, Christian. *Les Vandales et l'Afrique*. Paris: Arts et Métiers Graphiques, 1955.

Crawford, Michael H. 'Rome and the Greek World: Economic Relationships', *Economic History Review*, 30/1 (1977): 45–52.

Crawford, Michael H. 'Greek Intellectuals and the Roman Aristocracy in the First Century BC', in *Imperialism in the Ancient World*, edited by Peter Garnsey and C. R. Whittaker, 193–207. Cambridge: Cambridge University Press, 1978.

Crawford, Michael H. *Coinage and Money under the Roman Republic: Italy and the Mediterranean Economy*. London: Methuen, 1985.

Crawford, Michael H. *The Roman Republic*. 2nd edn. London: Fontana Press, 1992.

Crawford, Michael H., ed. *Roman Statutes*. 2 vols, Bulletin of the Institute of Classical Studies Supplements. London: Institute of Classical Studies, 1996.

Crawford, Michael H. 'States Waiting in the Wings: Population Distribution and the End of the Roman Republic', in *People, Land and Politics: Demographic*

Developments and the Transformation of Roman Italy 300 BC–AD 14, edited by Luuk de Ligt and Simon Northwood, 631–43. Leiden: Brill, 2008.

Cristofani, Mauro, ed. *La grande Roma dei Tarquini: Roma, Palazzo delle esposizioni, 12 giugno–30 settembre 1990: Catalogo della mostra.* Rome: 'L'Erma' di Bretschneider, 1990.

Croke, Brian. 'Justinian's Constantinople', in *The Cambridge Companion to the Age of Justinian*, edited by Michael Maas, 60–86. New York and Cambridge: Cambridge University Press, 2005.

Crone, Patricia. *Pre-Industrial Societies*, New Perspectives on the Past. Oxford: Basil Blackwell, 1989.

Crook, J. A. *Consilium principis: Imperial Councils and Counsellors from Augustus to Diocletian.* Cambridge: Cambridge University Press, 1955.

Crosby, Alfred W. *Ecological Imperialism: The Biological Expansion of Europe, 900–1900*, Studies in Environment and History. Cambridge: Cambridge University Press, 1986.

Crow, James F., Jonathan Bardill, and Richard Baylis, *The Water Supply of Byzantine Constantinople* London: Society for the Promotion of Roman Studies, 2008.

Cunliffe, Barry. *Greeks, Romans and Barbarians: Spheres of Interaction.* London: Batsford, 1988.

Cunliffe, Barry. *Europe between the Oceans: Themes and Variations, 9000 BC–AD 1000.* New Haven, CT: Yale University Press, 2008.

Cuomo, Serafina. *Technology and Culture in Greek and Roman Antiquity*, edited by Paul Cartledge and Peter Garnsey, Key Themes in Ancient History. Cambridge: Cambridge University Press, 2007.

Curran, John. *Pagan City and Christian Capital: Rome in the Fourth Century*, Oxford Classical Monographs. Oxford: Clarendon Press, 2000.

Dagron, Gilbert, *Naissance d'une capitale: Constantinople et ses institutions de 330 à 451*, Bibliothèque Byzantine, Études 7. Paris: Presses Universitaires de France, 1974.

Dagron, Gilbert. *Emperor and Priest: The Imperial Office in Byzantium.* Cambridge: Cambridge University Press, 2003.

D'Arms, John H. *The Romans on the Bay of Naples: A Social and Cultural History of the Villas and Their Owners from 150 B.C. to A.D. 100.* Cambridge, MA: Harvard University Press, 1970.

Davenport, Caillan. *A History of the Roman Equestrian Order.* Cambridge: Cambridge University Press, 2019.

David, Jean-Michel. *The Roman Conquest of Italy*, The Ancient World, edited by Tim Cornell. Oxford: Blackwell, 1996.

De Haas, Tymon, and Gijs Tol, eds. *Economic Integration of Roman Italy: Rural Communities in a Globalizing World.* Leiden: Brill, 2017.

de Ligt, Luuk, and Simon Northwood, eds. *People, Land and Politics: Demographic Developments and the Transformation of Roman Italy 300 BC–AD 14*, Mnemosyne Supplements. Leiden: Brill, 2008.

de Ligt, Luuk, and Laurens E. Tacoma, eds. *Migration and Mobility in the Early Roman Empire*, vol. 23/7. Leiden: Brill, 2016.

Demougin, Ségolène, Hubert Devijver, and Marie-Thérèse Raepsaet-Charlier, eds. *L'Ordre équestre: Histoire d'une aristocratie (IIe siècle av. J.-C.–IIIe siècle ap. J.-C.)*, Collection de l'École Française de Rome. Rome: École Française de Rome, 1999.

Dench, Emma. *From Barbarians to New Men: Greek, Roman and Modern Perceptions of Peoples of the Central Apennines*. Oxford: Oxford University Press, 1995.

Dench, Emma. *Romulus' Asylum: Roman Identities from the Age of Alexander to the Age of Hadrian*. Oxford: Oxford University Press, 2005.

Dench, Emma. *Empire and Political Cultures in the Roman World*, Cambridge: Cambridge University Press, 2018.

Derks, Ton, and N. Roymans, eds. *Ethnic Constructs in Antiquity: The Role of Power and Tradition*, Amsterdam Archaeological Studies. Amsterdam: Amsterdam University Press, 2009.

de Ste Croix, G. E. M. *The Class Struggle in the Ancient Greek World: From the Archaic Age to the Arab Conquests*. London: Duckworth, 1981.

de Souza, Philip. *Piracy in the Graeco-Roman World*. Cambridge: Cambridge University Press, 1999.

Diamond, Jared M. *Collapse: How Societies Choose to Fail or Survive*. London: Allen Lane, 2005.

Di Cosmo, Nicola. *Ancient China and Its Enemies: The Rise of Nomadic Power in East Asian History*. Cambridge: Cambridge University Press, 2002.

Dignas, Beate, and R. R. R Smith, eds. *Historical and Religious Memory in the Ancient World*. Oxford: Oxford University Press, 2012.

Dillery, John. 'Greek Historians of the Near East: Clio's "Other" Sons', in *A Companion to Greek and Roman Historiography*, edited by John Marincola, 221–30. Malden, MA: Blackwell, 2007.

Dillery, John. *Clio's Other Sons: Berossus and Manetho, with an Afterword on Demetrius*. Ann Arbor, MI: University of Michigan Press, 2015.

Dix, T. Keith. 'The Library of Lucullus', *Athenaeum*, 88/2 (2000): 441–64.

Dodge, Hazel, and Bryan Ward-Perkins, eds. *Marble in Antiquity: Collected Papers of J. B. Ward-Perkins*. London: British School at Rome, 1992.

Dougherty, Carol. *The Poetics of Colonization: From City to Text in Archaic Greece*. New York: Oxford University Press, 1993.

Drinkwater, John. *The Alamanni and Rome 213–496 (Caracalla to Clovis)*. Oxford: Oxford University Press, 2007.

Drinkwater, John, and Hugh Elton, eds. *Fifth-Century Gaul: A Crisis of Identity*. Cambridge: Cambridge University Press, 1992.

Duindam, Jeroen. *Myths of Power: Norbert Elias and the Early Modern European Court*. Amsterdam: Amsterdam University Press, 1994.

Dunbabin, Katherine M. *Mosaics of the Greek and Roman World*. Cambridge: Cambridge University Press, 1999.

Duncan-Jones, R. P. 'Taxes, Trade and Money', in *Structure and Scale in the Roman Economy*, 30–47. Cambridge: Cambridge University Press, 1990.

Duncan-Jones, R. P. 'The Impact of the Antonine Plague', *Journal of Roman Archaeology*, 9 (1996): 108–36.

Dyson, Stephen L. 'Native Revolt Patterns in the Roman Empire', in *Aufstieg und Niedergang der römischen Welt*, II.3 edited by Hildegard Temporini, 138–175. Berlin and New York: De Gruyter, 1975.

Dyson, Stephen L. *The Creation of the Roman Frontier*. Princeton, NJ: Princeton University Press, 1985.

Earl, Donald. *The Moral and Political Tradition in Rome*, Aspects of Greek and Roman Life. London: Thames and Hudson, 1967.

Eck, Werner. 'Senatorial Self-Representation: Developments in the Augustan Period', in *Caesar Augustus: Seven Aspects*, edited by Fergus Millar and Erich Segal, 129–67. Oxford: Oxford University Press, 1984.

Eckart, Hella, ed. *Roman Diasporas: Archaeological Approaches to Mobility and Diversity in the Roman Empire*, Journal of Roman Archaeology Supplements. Portsmouth, RI: Journal of Roman Archaeology, 2010.

Eckstein, Arthur M. *Senate and General: Individual Decision Making and Roman Foreign Relations, 264–194 B.C.* Berkeley and Los Angeles: University of California Press, 1987.

Eckstein, Arthur M. *Mediterranean Anarchy, Interstate War and the Rise of Rome*, Hellenistic Culture and Society. Berkeley and Los Angeles: University of California Press, 2006.

Edwards, Catharine. *The Politics of Immorality in Ancient Rome*. Cambridge: Cambridge University Press, 1993.

Edwards, Catharine. *Writing Rome: Textual Approaches to the City*. Cambridge: Cambridge University Press, 1996.

Edwards, Catharine, ed. *Roman Presences: Receptions of Rome in European Culture, 1789–1945*. Cambridge: Cambridge University Press, 1999.

Edwards, Catharine. 'Incorporating the Alien: The Art of Conquest', in *Rome the Cosmopolis*, edited by Catharine Edwards and Greg Woolf, 44–70. Cambridge: Cambridge University Press, 2003.

Edwards, Catharine, and Greg Woolf, eds. *Rome the Cosmopolis*. Cambridge: Cambridge University Press, 2003.

Eilers, Claude. *Roman Patrons of Greek Cities*. Oxford: Oxford University Press, 2002.

Eisenstadt, Shmuel. *The Political Systems of Empires*. London: Free Press of Glencoe, 1963.

Elias, Norbert. *The Court Society*. Oxford: Blackwell, 1983.

Elliott, Colin P. 'The Antonine Plague, Climate Change and Local Violence in Roman Egypt', *Past & Present*, 231 (2016): 3–31.

Elsner, Jas. *Imperial Rome and Christian Triumph: The Art of the Roman Empire, AD 100–450*, Oxford History of Art. Oxford: Oxford University Press, 1998.

Elsner, Jas. *Roman Eyes: Visuality and Subjectivity in Art and Text*. Princeton, NJ: Princeton University Press, 2007.

Elsner, Jas. 'Sacrifice in Late Roman Art', in *Greek and Roman Animal Sacrifice: Ancient Victims, Modern Observers*, edited by Christopher A. Faraone and F.S. Naiden, 120–63. Cambridge: Cambridge University Press, 2012.

Elsner, Jas, and Ian Rutherford, eds. *Pilgrimage in Graeco-Roman and Early Christian Antiquity: Seeing the Gods*. Oxford: Oxford University Press, 2005.

Elton, Hugh. *Warfare in Roman Europe, AD 350–425*. Oxford: Clarendon Press, 1996.

Elvin, Mark. *The Pattern of the Chinese Past: A Social and Economic Explanation*. Stanford, CA: Stanford University Press, 1973.

Erdkamp, Paul. *The Grain Market in the Roman Empire: A Social, Political and Economic Study*. Cambridge: Cambridge University Press, 2005.

Erdkamp, Paul, ed. *The Cambridge Companion to Ancient Rome*. Cambridge: Cambridge University Press, 2013.

Erdkamp, Paul, Koenraad Verboven, and Arjan Zuiderhoek, eds. *Ownership and Exploitation of Land and Natural Resources in the Roman World*, Oxford Studies on the Roman Economy. Oxford: Oxford University Press, 2015.

Erskine, Andrew. *The Hellenistic Stoa: Political Thought and Action*. London: Duckworth, 1990.

Erskine, Andrew. *Troy between Greece and Rome: Local Tradition and Imperial Power*. Oxford: Oxford University Press, 2001.

Esmonde Cleary, Simon. *The Roman West, AD 200–500: An Archaeological Study* Cambridge: Cambridge University Press, 2013.

Fantham, Elaine. *Roman Literary Culture from Cicero to Apuleius*, Ancient Society and History. Baltimore, MD: Johns Hopkins University Press, 1996.

Feeney, Denis. *Literature and Religion at Rome: Culture, Contexts and Beliefs*, Latin Literature in Context. Cambridge: Cambridge University Press, 1998.

Feeney, Denis. *Caesar's Calendar: Ancient Time and the Beginnings of History*, Sather Classical Lectures. Berkeley and Los Angeles: University of California Press, 2007.

Feeney, Denis. *Beyond Greek: The Beginnings of Latin Literature*. Cambridge, MA: Harvard University Press, 2016.

Fentress, James, and Chris Wickham. *Social Memory*. Oxford: Blackwell, 1992.

Ferrary, Jean-Louis. *Philhellénisme et impérialisme: Aspects idéologiques de la conquête romaine du monde hellénistique, de la Seconde Guerre de Macédoine à la Guerre contre Mithridate*, Bibliothèque des Écoles Françaises d'Athènes et de Rome. Rome: École Française de Rome, 1988.

Fitzgerald, William. *Slavery and the Roman Literary Imagination*. Cambridge: Cambridge University Press, 2000.

Flaig, Egon. *Den Kaiser herausfordern: Die Usurpation im römischen Reich*. Frankfurt am Main: Campus Verlag, 1992.

Flemming, Rebecca. 'Galen and the Plague', in *Galen's Treatise Περὶ Ἀλυπίας (De indolentia) in Context: A Tale of Resilience*, edited by Caroline Petit, 219–244. Leiden and Boston, MA: Brill, 2019.

Flower, Harriet. *Ancestor Masks and Aristocratic Power in Roman Culture*. Oxford: Clarendon Press, 1996.

Flower, Harriet. *The Art of Forgetting: Disgrace and Oblivion in Roman Political Culture*, Studies in the History of Greece and Rome, edited by Robin Osborne, Peter Rhodes, and Richard J. A. Talbert. Chapel Hill, NC: University of North Carolina Press, 2006.

Flower, Harriet. *Roman Republics*. Princeton, NJ: Princeton University Press, 2010.

Foss, Clive. *Ephesus after Antiquity: A Late Antique, Byzantine and Turkish City*. Cambridge: Cambridge University Press, 1979.

Fowden, Garth. *Empire to Commonwealth: Consequences of Monotheism in Late Antiquity*. Princeton, NJ: Princeton University Press, 1993.

France, Jérôme. *Quadragesima Galliarum: L'Organisation douanière des provinces alpestres, gauloises et germaniques de l'Empire romain, 1er siècle avant J.-C.–3er siècle après J.-C.*, Collections de l'École Française à Rome. Rome: École Française de Rome, 2001.

Frederiksen, M. *Campania*. London: British School at Rome, 1984.

Frend, W. H. C. 'Persecutions: Genesis and Legacy', in *The Cambridge History of Christianity*, i: *Origins to Constantine*, edited by Margaret M. Mitchell and Frances M. Young, 503–23. Cambridge: Cambridge University Press, 2006.

Fulford, Michael G. 'Roman and Barbarian: The Economy of Roman Frontier Systems', in *Barbarians and Romans in North-West Europe from the Later Republic to Late Antiquity*, edited by J. C. Barrett, 81–95. Oxford: British Archaeological Reports, 1989.

Gabba, Emilio. *Republican Rome, the Army and the Allies*. Oxford: Blackwell, 1976.

Galinsky, Karl. *Augustan Culture*. Princeton, NJ: Princeton University Press, 1996.

Galinsky, Karl, ed. *The Cambridge Companion to the Age of Augustus*. New York: Cambridge University Press, 2005.

Galinsky, Karl, ed. *Memoria Romana: Memory in Rome and Rome in Memory*, Memoirs of the American Academy in Rome, Supplements. Ann Arbor, MI: University of Michigan Press, 2014.

Galinsky, Karl, ed. *Memory in Ancient Rome and Early Christianity*. Oxford: Oxford University Press, 2016.

Galinsky, Karl, and Kenneth Lapatin, eds. *Cultural Memories in the Roman Empire*. Los Angeles: Getty Publications, 2015.

Gallant, Thomas W. 'Crisis and Response: Risk-Buffering Behavior in Hellenistic Greek Communities', *The Journal of Interdisciplinary History*, 19/3 (1989): 393–413.

Gardner, Andrew. 'Thinking about Roman Imperialism: Postcolonialism, Globalisation and Beyond?', *Britannia*, 44 (2012): 1–25.

Garnsey, Peter. *Famine and Food Supply in the Greco-Roman World: Responses to Risk and Crisis*. Cambridge: Cambridge University Press, 1988.

Garnsey, Peter. *Food and Society in Classical Antiquity*, Key Themes in Ancient History. Cambridge: Cambridge University Press, 1999.

Garnsey, Peter. 'Roman Citizenship and Roman Law in Late Antiquity', in *Approaching Late Antiquity: The Transformation from Early to Late Empire*, edited by Simon Swain and Mark Edwards, 133–55. Oxford: Oxford University Press, 2004.

Garnsey, Peter, and Caroline Humfress. *The Evolution of the Late Antique World*. Cambridge: Orchard Academic, 2001.

Garnsey, Peter, and Richard P. Saller. *The Roman Empire: Economy, Society and Culture*. 2nd rev. edn. London: Bloomsbury, 2015.

Geertz, Clifford. 'Centers, Kings and Charisma: Reflections on the Symbolics of Power', in *Culture and Its Creators: Essays in Honor of Edward Shils*, edited by Joseph Ben-David and Terry Nichols Clarke, 150–71. Chicago: University of Chicago Press, 1977. Repr., *Local Knowledge: Further Essays in Interpretive Anthropology*. New York: Basic Books, 1983, 121–46.

Gehrke, Hans-Joachim. 'Heroen als Grenzgänger zwischen Griechen und Barbaren', in *Cultural Borrowings and Ethnic Appropriations in Antiquity*, edited by Erich Gruen, 50–67. Stuttgart: Franz Steiner Verlag, 2005.

George, Michele, ed. *Roman Slavery and Roman Material Culture*, Toronto: University of Toronto Press, 2013.

Giardina, Andrea, and Aldo Schiavone, eds. *Società romana e produzione schiavistica*. Rome: Laterza, 1981.

Gigante, Marcello. *Philodemus in Italy: The Books from Herculaneum*, translated by Dirk Obbink, The Body, in Theory: Histories of Cultural Materialism. Ann Arbor, MI: University of Michigan Press, 1995.

Gildenhard, Ingo. *Paideia Romana: Cicero's Tusculan Disputations*, Proceedings of the Cambridge Philological Society Supplements, edited by Tim Whitmarsh and James Warren. Cambridge: Cambridge Philological Society, 2007.

Gildenhard, Ingo, Ulrich Gotter, Wolfgang Havener, and Louise Hodgson, eds. *Augustus and the Destruction of History: The Politics of the Past in Early Imperial Rome*, Cambridge Classical Journal Supplements. Cambridge: Cambridge Philological Society, 2019.

Gillett, Andrew, ed. *On Barbarian Identity: Critical Approaches to Ethnicity in the Early Middle Ages*, Studies in the Early Middle Ages. Turnhout: Brepols, 2002.

Goffart, Walter. *Barbarians and Romans, A.D. 418–584: The Techniques of Accommodation.* Princeton, NJ: Princeton University Press, 1980.

Goldhill, Simon, ed. *Being Greek under Rome: Cultural Identity, the Second Sophistic and the Development of Empire.* Cambridge: Cambridge University Press, 2001.

Goldsworthy, Adrian. *The Roman Army at War, 100 B.C.–A.D. 200.* Oxford: Clarendon Press, 1996.

Goldsworthy, Adrian. *Caesar: The Life of a Colossus.* London: Weidenfeld and Nicolson, 2006.

Goldsworthy, Adrian, and Ian Haynes, eds. *The Roman Army as a Community*, Journal of Roman Archaeology Supplements. Portsmouth, RI: Journal of Roman Archaeology, 1999.

Golvin, Jean-Claude. *L'Amphithéâtre romain: Essai sur la théorisation de sa forme et de ses fonctions.* 2 vols., Publications du Centre Pierre Paris (UA 991). Paris: De Boccard, 1988.

Gonzáles, Julián. 'Lex Irnitana: A New Copy of the Flavian Municipal Law', *Journal of Roman Studies*, 76 (1986): 147–243.

Goodman, Penelope, ed. *Afterlives of Augustus, AD 14–2014.* Cambridge: Cambridge University Press, 2018.

Gordon, Richard. 'Religion in the Roman Empire: The Civic Compromise and Its Limits', in *Pagan Priests*, edited by Mary Beard and John North, 233–55. London: Duckworth, 1990.

Gosden, Chris. *Archaeology and Colonialism: Cultural Contact from 5000 BC to the Present*, Topics in Contemporary Archaeology. Cambridge: Cambridge University Press, 2004.

Gosden, Chris. 'What Do Objects Want?', *Journal of Archaeological Method and Theory*, 12/3 (2005): 193–211.

Gowers, Emily. *The Loaded Table: Representations of Food in Roman Literature.* Oxford: Clarendon Press, 1993.

Gowing, Alain M. *Empire and Memory: The Representation of the Roman Republic in Imperial Culture*, Roman Literature and its Contexts, edited by Denis Feeney and Stephen Hinds. Cambridge: Cambridge University Press, 2005.

Gradel, Ittai. *Emperor Worship and Roman Religion*, Oxford Classical Monographs. Oxford: Oxford University Press, 2002.

Graf, Fritz. *Roman Festivals in the Greek East: From the Early Empire to the Middle Byzantine Era.* Cambridge: Cambridge University Press, 2015.

Greene, Kevin. *The Archaeology of the Roman Economy.* London: Batsford, 1986.

Griffin, Miriam. 'Claudius in Tacitus', *Classical Quarterly*, 40/2 (1990): 482–501.

Griffin, Miriam. *Nero: The End of a Dynasty.* 2nd edn. London: Batsford, 1996.

Grig, Lucy, and Gavin Kelly, eds. *Two Romes: Rome and Constantinople in Late Antiquity*, Oxford Studies in Late Antiquity. Oxford: Oxford University Press, 2012.

Gruen, Erich, ed. *The Last Generation of the Roman Republic*. Berkeley and Los Angeles: University of California Press, 1974.

Gruen, Erich. *The Hellenistic World and the Coming of Rome*. 2 vols. Berkeley and Los Angeles: University of California Press, 1984.

Gruen, Erich. *Culture and National Identity in Republican Rome*. London: Duckworth, 1992.

Gruen, Erich. 'The Expansion of the Empire under Augustus', in *The Cambridge Ancient History*, x: *The Augustan Empire 43 B.C.–A.D. 69*, edited by Alan Bowman, Edward Champlin, and Andrew Lintott, 147–97. Cambridge: Cambridge University Press, 1996.

Gruen, Erich. *Diaspora: Jews among Greeks and Romans*. Cambridge, MA: Harvard University Press, 2002.

Gruen, Erich, ed. *Cultural Identity in the Ancient Mediterranean*, Issues and Debates. Los Angeles: Getty Research Institute, 2011.

Gutas, Dimitri. *Greek Thought, Arab Culture: The Graeco-Arabic Translation Movement in Baghdad and Early Abbasid Society (2nd–4th/8th–10th Centuries)*. New York: Routledge, 1998.

Guthrie, Stewart E. 'Anthropological Theories of Religion', in *The Cambridge Companion to Atheism*, edited by Michael Martin, 283–99. Cambridge: Cambridge University Press, 2007.

Habinek, Thomas, ed. *The Politics of Latin Literature: Writing, Identity and Empire in Ancient Rome*. Cambridge: Cambridge University Press, 1998.

Habinek, Thomas. *The World of Roman Song from Ritualised Speech to Social Order*. Baltimore, MD: Johns Hopkins University Press, 2005.

Haldon, John F. *Byzantium in the Seventh Century: The Transformation of a Culture*. Rev. edn. Cambridge: Cambridge University Press, 1997.

Haldon, John F. *The Empire That Would Not Die: The Paradox of Eastern Roman Survival 640–740*. Cambridge, MA: Harvard University Press, 2016.

Haldon, John F. et al. 'The Climate and Environment of Byzantine Anatolia: Integrating Science, History and Archaeology', *Journal of Interdisciplinary History*, 35 (2014): 113–61.

Haldon, John F., Merle Eisenberg, Lee Mordechai, Adam Izdebski, and Sam White. 'Lessons from the Past, Policies for the Future: Resilience and Sustainability in Past Crises', *Environmental Systems and Decisions*, 40 (2020): 287–297.

Haldon, John F., Hugh Elton, Sabine R. Huebner, Adam Izdebski, Lee Mordechai, and Timothy P. Newfield. 'Plagues, Climate Change, and the End of an Empire: A Response to Kyle Harper's *The Fate of Rome*. Part 1 Climate', *History Compass* (2018): e12508.

Haldon, John F., Hugh Elton, Sabine R. Huebner, Adam Izdebski, Lee Mordechai, and Timothy P. Newfield. 'Plagues, Climate Change, and the End of an Empire: A Response to Kyle Harper's *The Fate of Rome*. Part 2 Plagues and a Crisis of Empire', *History Compass* (2018): e12506. doi: 10.1111/hic3.12506.

Haldon, John F., Hugh Elton, Sabine R. Huebner, Adam Izdebski, Lee Mordechai, and Timothy P. Newfield. 'Plagues, Climate Change, and the End of an Empire: A Response to Kyle Harper's *The Fate of Rome*. Part 3 Disease, Agency and Collapse', *History Compass* (2018): e12507. doi: 10.1111/hic3.12507.

Halfmann, Helmut. *Itinera principum: Geschichte und Typologie der Kaiserreisen im Römischen Reich*, Heidelberger althistorische Beiträge und epigraphische Studien. Stuttgart: Franz Steiner Verlag, 1986.

Hall, John A. *Powers and Liberties: The Causes and Consequences of the Rise of the West*. Oxford: Blackwell, 1985.

Halsall, Guy. *Barbarian Migrations and the Roman West 376–568*, Cambridge Medieval Textbooks. Cambridge: Cambridge University Press, 2007.

Halstead, Paul, and John O'Shea, eds. *Bad Year Economics: Cultural Responses to Risk and Uncertainty*, New Directions in Archaeology. Cambridge: Cambridge University Press, 1989.

Hanson, J. W. *An Urban Geography of the Roman World, 100 BC–AD 300*. Oxford: Archeopress, 2016.

Hardie, Philip. *Virgil's Aeneid: Cosmos and Imperium*. Oxford: Clarendon Press, 1985.

Harper, Kyle. *Slavery in the Late Roman World, AD 275–425*. Cambridge: Cambridge University Press, 2011.

Harper, Kyle. *The Fate of Rome: Climate, Disease and the End of an Empire*. Princeton, NJ, and Oxford: Princeton University Press, 2017.

Harries, Jill. *Sidonius Apollinaris and the Fall of Rome, AD 407–485*. Oxford: Clarendon Press, 1994.

Harries, Jill. 'Christianity and the City in Late Antique Gaul', in *The City in Late Antiquity*, edited by John Rich, 77–98. London: Routledge, 1992.

Harries, Jill, and Ian Wood, eds. *The Theodosian Code: Studies in the Imperial Law of Late Antiquity*. London: Duckworth, 1993.

Harris, William Vernon. *War and Imperialism in Republican Rome, 327–70 B.C.* Oxford: Clarendon Press, 1979.

Harris, William Vernon. 'Roman Expansion in the West', in *The Cambridge Ancient History*, viii: *Rome and the Mediterranean to 133 BC*, edited by A. E. Astin, F. Walbank, M. Frederiksen, and R. M. Ogilvie, 107–62. Cambridge: Cambridge University Press, 1989.

Harris, William Vernon. 'Demography, Geography and the Sources of Roman Slaves', *Journal of Roman Studies*, 89 (1999): 62–75.

Harris, William Vernon, ed. *The Transformations of Urbs Roma in Late Antiquity*, Journal of Roman Archaeology Supplements. Portsmouth, RI: Journal of Roman Archaeology, 1999.

Harris, William Vernon, ed. *Rethinking the Mediterranean*. Oxford: Oxford University Press, 2005.

Harris, William Vernon, ed. *The Spread of Christianity in the First Four Centuries: Essays in Explanation*. Leiden: Brill, 2005.

Harris, William Vernon. *The Roman Imperial Economy: Twelve Essays*. Oxford: Oxford University Press, 2011.

Harris, William Vernon, ed. *The Ancient Mediterranean Environment between Science and History*, Leiden and Boston, MA: Brill, 2013.

Harris, William Vernon. 'Defining and Detecting Mediterranean Deforestation, 800 BCE–700 CE', in *The Ancient Mediterranean Environment between Science and History*, edited by William Vernon Harris, 173–94. Leiden and Boston, MA: Brill, 2013.

Harris, William Vernon. *Roman Power: A Thousand Years of Empire*. Cambridge: Cambridge University Press, 2016.

Hassall, Mark, Michael H. Crawford, and Joyce Reynolds. 'Rome and the Eastern Provinces at the End of the Second Century BC', *Journal of Roman Studies*, 64 (1974): 195–220.

Haynes, Ian. *Blood of the Provinces: The Roman Auxilia and the Making of Provincial Society from Augustus to Diocletian*. Oxford: Oxford University Press, 2013.

Heather, Peter. 'Cassiodorus and the Rise of the Amals: Genealogy and the Goths under Hun Domination', *Journal of Roman Studies*, 79 (1989): 103–28.

Heather, Peter. *Goths and Romans 332–489*. Oxford: Clarendon Press, 1991.

Heather, Peter. *Emperors and Barbarians: Migration, Development and the Birth of Europe*. London: Macmillan, 2009.

Hedeager, L. 'Empire, Frontier and the Barbarian Hinterland: Rome and Northern Europe from A.D. 1–400', in *Centre and Periphery in the Ancient World*, edited by Michael Rowlands, Møgens Trolle Larsen, and Kristian Kristiansen, 125–40. Cambridge: Cambridge University Press, 1987.

Hekster, Olivier. *Commodus: An Emperor at the Crossroads*, Dutch Monographs on Ancient History and Archaeology. Amsterdam: J. C. Gieben, 2002.

Hekster, Olivier. *Emperors and Ancestors: Roman Rulers and the Constraints of Tradition*, Oxford Studies in Ancient Culture and Representation. Oxford: Oxford University Press, 2015.

Hekster, Olivier, Gerda de Kleijn, and Daniëlle Slootjes, eds. *Crises and the Roman Empire*, Impact of Empire. Leiden: Brill, 2007.

Hemelrijk, Emily A., and Greg Woolf, eds. *Women and the Roman City in the Latin West*, Mnemosyne, Supplements, History and Archaeology of Classical Antiquity, vol. 360. Leiden and Boston, MA: Brill, 2013.

Herrin, Judith. *The Formation of Christendom*. Oxford: Blackwell, 1987.

Herrin, Judith. *Byzantium: The Surprising Life of a Medieval Empire*. London: Penguin, 2007.

Heurgon, Jacques. *The Rise of Rome to 264 BC*. London: Batsford, 1973.

Hinds, Stephen. *Allusion and Intertext: Dynamics of Appropriation in Roman Poetry*, Latin Literature in Context. Cambridge: Cambridge University Press, 1998.

Hine, Harry. 'Seismology and Vulcanology in Antiquity?', in *Science and Mathematics in Ancient Greek Culture*, edited by C. J. Tuplin and T. E. Rihll, 56–75. Oxford: Oxford University Press, 2002.

Hingley, Richard, ed. *Images of Rome: Perceptions of Ancient Rome in Europe and the United States in the Modern Age*, Journal of Roman Archaeology Supplements, edited by J. H. Humphrey. Portsmouth, RI: Journal of Roman Archaeology, 2001.

Hingley, Richard. *Globalizing Roman Culture: Unity, Diversity and Empire*. London: Routledge, 2005.

Hitchner, R. Bruce. 'Globalization avant la lettre: Globalization and the History of the Roman Empire', *New Global Studies*, 2/2 (2008). doi: 10.2202/1940-0004.1034.

Hodos, Tamar. *Local Responses to Colonization in the Iron Age Mediterranean*. Abingdon: Routledge, 2006.

Hölkeskamp, Karl-Joachim. 'Conquest, Competition and Consensus: Roman Expansion in Italy and the Rise of the "Nobilitas"', *Historia: Zeitschrift für Alte Geschichte*, 42/1 (1993): 12–39.

Holum, Kenneth G. *Theodosian Empresses: Women and Imperial Dominion in Late Antiquity*. Berkeley, CA: University of California Press, 1982.

Holum, Kenneth G. 'The Classical City in the Sixth Century: Survival and Transformation', in *The Cambridge Companion to the Age of Justinian*, edited by Michael Maas, 87–112. New York and Cambridge: Cambridge University Press, 2005.

Hopkins, Keith. *Conquerors and Slaves: Sociological Studies in Roman History I*. Cambridge: Cambridge University Press, 1978.

Hopkins, Keith. 'Divine Emperors, or the Symbolic Unity of the Roman Empire', in *Conquerors and Slaves: Sociological Studies in Roman History I*, 197–242. Cambridge: Cambridge University Press, 1978.

Hopkins, Keith. 'Economic Growth and Towns in Classical Antiquity', in *Towns in Societies: Essays in Economic History and Historical Sociology*, edited by Philip Abrams and E. A. Wrigley, 35–77. Cambridge: Cambridge University Press, 1978.

Hopkins, Keith. 'Taxes and Trade in the Roman Empire, 200 BC–AD 200', *Journal of Roman Studies*, 70 (1980): 101–25.

Hopkins, Keith. *Death and Renewal: Sociological Studies in Roman History II*. Cambridge: Cambridge University Press, 1983.

Hopkins, Keith. 'Rome, Taxes, Rents and Trade', *Kodai*, 6–7 (1995–6): 41–75.

Hopkins, Keith. 'Christian Number and Its Implications', *Journal of Early Christian Studies*, 6/2 (1998): 185–226.

Hopkins, Keith. 'The Political Economy of the Roman Empire', in *The Dynamics of Ancient Empires: State Power from Assyria to Byzantium*, edited by Ian Morris and Walter Scheidel, 178–204. New York: Oxford University Press, 2009.

Hopkins, Keith. *Sociological Studies in Roman History* edited by Christopher Kelly, Cambridge: Cambridge University Press, 2018.

Hopkins, Keith, and Mary Beard. *The Colosseum*, Wonders of the World, edited by Mary Beard. London: Profile Books, 2005.

Horden, Peregrine, and Nicholas Purcell. *The Corrupting Sea: A Study of Mediterranean History*. Oxford: Blackwell, 2000.

Howgego, Christopher. *Ancient History from Coins*. London: Routledge, 1995.

Isaac, Benjamin. *The Limits of Empire: The Roman Army in the East*. Oxford: Clarendon Press, 1990.

Isaac, Benjamin. *The Invention of Racism in Classical Antiquity*. Princeton, NJ: Princeton University Press, 2004.

Isayev, Elena. *Migration, Mobility and Place in Ancient Italy*. Cambridge: Cambridge University Press, 2017.

Janes, Dominic. *God and Gold in Late Antiquity*. Cambridge: Cambridge University Press, 1998.

Jiménez Díez, Alicia. *Imagines Hibridae: Una aproximación postcolonialista al estudio de las necrópolis de la Bética*, Anejos de Archivo Español de Archeologia. Madrid: Consejo Superior de Investigaciones Científicas, 2008.

Johnston, Andrew C. *The Sons of Remus: Identity in Roman Gaul and Spain*. Cambridge, MA: Harvard University Press, 2017.

Johnston, David. *Roman Law in Context*, Key Themes in Ancient History. Cambridge: Cambridge University Press, 1999.

Jones, A. H. M. *The Later Roman Empire, 284–602*. 2 vols. Oxford: Blackwell, 1964.

Jones, Christopher P. 'A Syrian at Lyon', *American Journal of Philology*, 99/3 (1978): 336–53.

Jones, Christopher P. 'Ancestry and Identity in the Roman Empire', in *Local Knowledge and Microidentities in the Imperial Greek World*, edited by Tim Whitmarsh, 111–24. Cambridge: Cambridge University Press, 2010.

Jones, R. F. J. 'A False Start? The Roman Urbanisation of Western Europe', *World Archaeology*, 19/1 (1987): 47–58.

Joshel, Sandra, and Lauren Hackworth Petersen, *The Material Life of Roman Slaves*. Cambridge: Cambridge University Press, 2014.

Kaldellis, Anthony. *Hellenism in Byzantium: The Transformations of Greek Identity and the Reception of the Classical Tradition*, Cambridge: Cambridge University Press, 2007.

Kaldellis, Anthony. *The Byzantine Republic: People and Power in New Rome*. Cambridge, MA: Harvard University Press, 2015.

Karmon, David. *The Ruin of the Eternal City: Antiquity and Preservation in Renaissance Rome*. New York: Oxford University Press, 2011.

Kaster, Robert A. *Guardians of Language: The Grammarian and Society in Late Antiquity*. Berkeley and Los Angeles: University of California Press, 1988.

Kautsky, J. H. *The Politics of Aristocratic Empires*. Chapel Hill, NC: University of North Carolina Press, 1982.

Kay, Philip. *Rome's Economic Revolution*. Oxford: Oxford University Press, 2014.

Keaveney, Arthur. *Sulla: The Last Republican*. 2nd edn. London: Routledge, 2005.

Keay, Simon, ed. *Portus: An Archaeological Survey of the Port of Imperial Rome*, Archaeological Monographs of the British School at Rome. Rome and London: British School at Rome, 2005.

Keay, Simon, ed. *Rome, Portus and the Mediterranean*, Archaeological Monographs of the British School at Rome. Rome: British School at Rome, 2013.

Kehoe, Dennis P. 'The Early Roman Empire: Production', in *The Cambridge Economic History of the Greco-Roman World*, edited by Walter Scheidel, Ian Morris, and Richard P. Saller, 543–69. Cambridge: Cambridge University Press, 2007.

Kelly, Christopher. *Ruling the Later Roman Empire*. Cambridge, MA: Belknap Press of Harvard University Press, 2004.

Kelly, Christopher. *Attila the Hun: Barbarian Terror and the Fall of the Roman Empire*. London: Bodley Head, 2008.

Kelly, Christopher, ed. *Theodosius II: Rethinking the Roman Empire in Late Antiquity*. Cambridge: Cambridge University Press, 2013.

Kelly, Gavin. *Ammianus Marcellinus: The Allusive Historian*. Cambridge: Cambridge University Press, 2008.

Kennedy, Hugh. 'From Polis to Madina: Urban Change in Late Antique and Early Islamic Syria', *Past and Present*, 106/1 (1985): 3–27.

Kidd, I. G. 'Posidonius as Philosopher-Historian', in *Philosophia togata I: Essays on Philosophy and Roman Society*, edited by Miriam Griffin and Jonathan Barnes, 38–50. Oxford: Oxford University Press, 1989.

King, Anthony C. 'Diet in the Roman World: A Regional Inter-Site Comparison of the Mammal Bones', *Journal of Roman Archaeology*, 12/1 (1999): 168–202.

Kleiner, Diana E. E., and Susan B. Matheson, eds. *I Claudia: Women in Ancient Rome*. Austin, TX: University of Texas Press, 1996.

Kleiner, Diana E. E., and Susan B. Matheson, eds. *I Claudia II: Women in Roman Art and Society*. Austin, TX: University of Texas Press, 2000.

Knapp, A. Bernard, and Peter van Dommelen, eds. *The Cambridge Prehistory of the Bronze and Iron Age Mediterranean*. New York and Cambridge: Cambridge University Press, 2015.

Kondoleon, Christine, ed. *Antioch the Lost Ancient City*. Princeton, NJ: Princeton University Press, 2000.

König, Jason. *Athletics and Literature in the Roman Empire*, edited by Susan E. Alcock, Jas Elsner, and Simon Goldhill, Greek Culture in the Roman World. Cambridge: Cambridge University Press, 2005.

König, Jason. 'Sympotic Dialogue in the First to Fifth Centuries CE', in *The End of Dialogue in Antiquity*, edited by Simon Goldhill, 85–113. Cambridge: Cambridge University Press, 2008.

Krautheimer, Richard. 1983. *Three Christian Capitals: Topography and Politics*. Berkeley, CA: University of California Press.

Krebs, Christopher B. 'Borealism: Caesar, Seneca, Tacitus and the Roman Discourse about the Germanic North', in *Cultural Identity in the Ancient Mediterranean*, edited by Erich Gruen, 202–21. Los Angeles: Getty Research Institute, 2011.

Kuhrt, Amélie. 'Usurpation, Conquest and Ceremonial: From Babylon to Persia', in *Rituals of Royalty: Power and Ceremonial in Traditional Societies*, edited by David Cannadine and Simon Price, 20–55. Cambridge: Cambridge University Press, 1987.

Kulikowski, Michael. *Late Roman Spain and Its Cities*. Baltimore, MD: Johns Hopkins University Press, 2004.

Kulikowski, Michael. *Rome's Gothic Wars from the Third Century to Alaric*, New York: Cambridge University Press, 2007.

Kulikowski, Michael. *Imperial Tragedy: From Constantine's Empire to the Destruction of Roman Italy (AD 363–568)*. London: Profile, 2019.

Kunow, Jürgen. *Der römische Import in der Germania libera bis zu den Markomannenkrieg: Studien zu Bronze- und Glasgefässen*, Göttinger Schriften zur Vor- und Frühgeschichte. Neumünster: K. Wachholtz, 1983.

Lane Fox, Robin. *Pagans and Christians in the Mediterranean World from the Second Century A.D. to the Conversion of Constantine*. Harmondsworth: Viking, 1986.

Langlands, Rebecca. *Sexual Morality in Ancient Rome*. Cambridge: Cambridge University Press, 2006.

Lattimore, Owen. *Inner Asian Frontiers of China*. Oxford: Oxford University Press, 1940.

Launaro, Alessandro, *Peasants and Slaves: The Rural Population of Roman Italy (200 BC to AD 100)*. Cambridge: Cambridge University Press, 2011.

Laurence, Ray. *The Roads of Roman Italy: Mobility and Cultural Change*. London: Routledge, 1999.

Laurence, Ray, Simon Esmonde Cleary, and Gareth Sears. *The City in the Roman West c.250 BC–AD 250*. Cambridge: Cambridge University Press, 2011.

Lavan, Myles. *Slaves to Rome: Paradigms of Empire in Roman Culture*. Cambridge: Cambridge University Press, 2013.

Lavan, Myles. 'The Spread of Roman Citizenship 14–212 CE: Quantification in the Face of High Uncertainty', *Past and Present*, 230/1 (2016): 3–46.

Lavan, Myles. 'Writing Revolt in the Early Roman Empire', in *The Routledge History Handbook of Medieval Revolt*, edited by Justine Firnhaber-Baker and Dirk Schoenaers, 19–38. Oxford: Routledge, 2017.

Lavan, Myles, Richard E. Payne, and John Weisweiler, eds. *Cosmopolitanism and Empire: Universal Rulers, Local Elites, and Cultural Integration in the Ancient Near East and Mediterranean*. Cambridge: Cambridge University Press, 2016

Leach, Eleanor Windsor. *The Social Life of Painting in Ancient Rome and on the Bay of Naples*. Cambridge: Cambridge University Press, 2004.

Lee, A. D. *Information and Frontiers: Roman Foreign Relations in Late Antiquity*, Cambridge: Cambridge University Press, 1993.

Lee, A. D. *Warfare in the Roman World*, Cambridge: Cambridge University Press, 2020.

Lenin, V. I. *Imperialism, the Highest Stage of Capitalism: A Popular Outline*. Moscow: Co-operative Publishing Society of Foreign Workers in the USSR, 1934.

Lenski, Noel. *Failure of Empire: Valens and the Roman State in the Fourth Century AD*. Berkeley, CA: University of California Press, 2002.

Lepelley, Claude. *Les Cités de l'Afrique romaine au bas-empire*. 2 vols. Paris: Études Augustiniennes, 1979–81.

Levene, D. S. 'Sallust's Jugurtha: An "Historical Fragment"', *Journal of Roman Studies*, 82 (1992): 53–70.

Levene, D. S. 'God and Man in the Classical Latin Panegyric', *Proceedings of the Cambridge Philological Society*, 43 (1997) 66–103.

Levick, Barbara. *Tiberius the Politician*. London: Thames and Hudson, 1976.

Levick, Barbara. 'Morals, Politics and the Fall of the Roman Republic', *Greece & Rome*, 29 (1982): 53–62.

Levick, Barbara. 'Popular in the Provinces? À Propos of Tacitus Annales 1.2.2', *Acta classica*, 37 (1994): 49–65.

Liebeschuetz, Wolf. *Antioch: City and Imperial Administration in the Later Roman Empire*. Oxford: Clarendon Press, 1972.

Liebeschuetz, Wolf. *The Decline and Fall of the Roman City*. Oxford: Oxford University Press, 2001.

Lieu, Judith. *Christian Identity in the Jewish and Graeco-Roman World*. Oxford: Oxford University Press, 2004.

Ling, Roger. *Roman Painting*. Cambridge: Cambridge University Press, 1991.

Lintott, Andrew. 'Imperial Expansion and Moral Decline in the Roman Republic', *Historia: Zeitschrift für Alte Geschichte*, 21 (1972): 626–38.

Lintott, Andrew. *Judicial Reform and Land Reform in the Roman Republic: A New Edition, with Translation and Commentary, of the Laws from Urbino*. Cambridge: Cambridge University Press, 1992.

Lintott, Andrew, J. A. Crook, and Elizabeth Rawson, eds. *The Cambridge Ancient History*, ix: *The Last Age of the Roman Republic 146–43 BC*. 2nd edn. Cambridge: Cambridge University Press, 1994.

Liverani, Mario. 'The Fall of the Assyrian Empire: Ancient and Modern Interpretations', in *Empires: Perspectives from Archaeology and History*, edited by Susan E. Alcock, T. D'Altroy, K. D. Morrison, and C. M. Sinopoli, 374–91. New York: Cambridge University Press, 2001.

Loar, Matthew P., Carolyn MacDonald, and Dan-el Padilla Peralta, eds. *Rome, Empire of Plunder: The Dynamics of Cultural Appropriation*. Cambridge: Cambridge University Press, 2018.

Lo Cascio, Elio, Andrea Giardina, and Laurens E. Tacoma, eds. *The Impact of Mobility and Migration in the Early Roman Empire*, Impact of Empire, vol. 12. Leiden: Brill, 2017.

Loseby, S. T. 'Marseille: A Late Antique Success Story?', *Journal of Roman Studies*, 82 (1992): 165–85.

Lowenthal, David. *The Past is a Foreign Country*. Cambridge: Cambridge University Press, 1985.

Luttwak, Edward N. *The Grand Strategy of the Roman Empire: From the First Century AD to the Third*. Baltimore, MD: Johns Hopkins University Press, 1976.

Maas, Michael. *John Lydus and the Roman Past: Antiquarianism and Politics in the Age of Justinian*. London: Routledge, 1992.

Maas, Michael, ed. *The Cambridge Companion to the Age of Justinian*. New York and Cambridge: Cambridge University Press, 2005.

McConnell, Joseph R. et al. 'Extreme Climate after Massive Eruption of Alaska's Okmok Volcano in 43 BCE and Effects on the Late Roman Republic and Ptolemaic Kingdom', *Proceedings of the National Academy of Sciences*, 117/27 (2020): 15443–9. doi: 10.1073/pnas.2002722117.

MacCormack, Sabine. *Art and Ceremony in Late Antiquity*, Transformation of the Classical Heritage. Berkeley and Los Angeles: University of California Press, 1981.

McCormick, Michael. *Eternal Victory: Triumphal Rulership in Late Antiquity, Byzantium and the Early Medieval West*, Past and Present Publications. Cambridge: Cambridge University Press, 1986.

McCormick, Michael, and et al. 'Climate Change during and after the Roman Empire: Reconstructing the Past from Scientific and Historical Evidence', *Journal of Interdisciplinary History*, 43/2 (2012): 169–220.

Machado, Carlos A. R. *Urban Space and Aristocratic Power in Late Antique Rome (AD 270–535)*. Oxford: Oxford University Press, 2019.

McIntyre, Gwynaeth. *A Family of Gods: The Worship of the Imperial Family in the Latin West*. Ann Arbor, MI: University of Michigan Press, 2016.

McLynn, Neil. *Ambrose of Milan: Church and Court in a Christian Capital*. Berkeley, CA: University of California Press, 1994.

MacMullen, Ramsay. *Soldier and Civilian in the Later Roman Empire*. Cambridge, MA: Harvard University Press, 1963.

MacMullen, Ramsay. *Paganism in the Roman Empire*. New Haven, CT:Yale University Press, 1981.

MacMullen, Ramsay. 'The Epigraphic Habit in the Roman Empire', *American Journal of Philology*, 103 (1982): 233–46.

MacMullen, Ramsay. *Christianizing the Roman Empire (A.D. 100–400)*. New Haven, CT:Yale University Press, 1984.

MacMullen, Ramsay. *Corruption and the Decline of Rome*. New Haven, CT: Yale University Press, 1988.

McNeill, William H. *Plagues and Peoples*. Garden City, NY: Anchor Press/ Doubleday, 1976.

MacRae, Duncan. *Legible Religion: Books, Gods, and Rituals in Roman Culture* Cambridge, MA: Harvard University Press, 2016.

Macready, Sarah, and F. H. Thompson, eds. *Roman Architecture in the Greek World*, Society of Antiquaries of London Occasional Papers. London: Society of Antiquaries, 1987.

Malamud, Margaret. *Ancient Rome and Modern America*, Classical Receptions. Malden, MA:Wiley-Blackwell, 2009.

Manning, J. G. 'Coinage as Code in Ptolemaic Egypt', in *The Monetary Systems of the Greeks and Romans*, edited by William Vernon Harris, 84–111. Oxford: Oxford University Press, 2008.

Manning, J. G. *The Open Sea:The Economic Life of the Ancient Mediterranean World from the Iron Age to the Rise of Rome*. Princeton, NJ, and Rome: Princeton University Press, 2018.

Manning, J. G., Francis Ludlow, et al. 'Volcanic Suppression of Nile Summer Flooding Triggers Revolt and Constrains Interstate Conflict in Ancient Egypt', *Nature Communications*, 8 (2017). doi: 10.1038/s41467-017-00957-y.

Marco Simón, F., F. Pina Polo, and J. Remesal Rodríguez, eds. *Xenofobia y racismo en el mundo antiguo*, Collecio Instrumenta, vol. 64. Barcelona: Edicions Universitat de Barcelona, 2019.

Marichal, Robert. *Les Graffites de la Graufesenque*, Gallia Supplements. Paris: Éditions CNRS. 1988.

Marzano, Annalisa, and Guy P. R. Métraux, eds. *The Roman Villa in the Mediterranean Basin: Late Republic to Late Antiquity*. Cambridge: Cambridge University Press, 2018.

Masuzawa, Tomoko. *The Invention of World Religions: Or, How European Universalism was Preserved in the Language of Pluralism*. Chicago: Chicago University Press, 2005.

Matthews, John F. *Western Aristocracies and Imperial Court, A.D. 364–425.* Oxford: Clarendon Press, 1975.

Matthews, John F. 'Hostages, Philosophers, Pilgrims, and the Diffusion of Ideas in the Late Roman Mediterranean and Near East', in *Tradition and Innovation in Late Antiquity*, edited by F. M. Clover and R. S. Humphreys, 29–49. Madison, WI: University of Wisconsin Press, 1989.

Matthews, John F. *The Roman Empire of Ammianus.* London: Duckworth, 1989.

Matthews, John F. *Laying Down the Law: A Study of the Theodosian Code.* New Haven, CT: Yale University Press, 2000.

Mattingly, David. 'First Fruit? The Olive in the Roman World', in *Human Landscapes in Classical Antiquity: Environment and Culture*, edited by Graham Shipley and John Salmon, 213–53. London: Routledge, 1996.

Mattingly, David. *Dialogues in Roman Imperialism: Power, Discourse and Discrepant Experience in the Roman Empire*, edited by J. H. Humphrey, Journal of Roman Archaeology Supplements. Portsmouth, RI: Journal of Roman Archaeology, 1997.

Mattingly, David. *An Imperial Possession: Britain in the Roman Empire 54 BC –AD 409.* London: Allen Lane, 2006.

Mattingly, David. *Imperialism, Power and Identity: Experiencing the Roman Empire*, Miriam S. Balmuth Lectures in Ancient History and Archaeology. Princeton, NJ: Princeton University Press, 2011.

Mattingly, David, and John Salmon, eds. *Economies beyond Agriculture in the Classical World*, Leicester–Nottingham Studies in Ancient Society, vol. 9. London: Routledge, 2001.

Meeks, Wayne A. *The First Urban Christians: The Social World of the Apostle Paul.* New Haven, CT: Yale University Press, 1983.

Millar, Fergus. *A Study of Cassius Dio.* Oxford: Clarendon Press, 1964.

Millar, Fergus. *The Emperor in the Roman World (31 BC–AD 337).* London: Duckworth, 1977.

Millar, Fergus. 'Emperors, Frontiers and Foreign Relations, 31 BC to AD 378', *Britannia*, 13 (1982): 1–23.

Millar, Fergus. 'Empire and City, Augustus to Julian: Obligations, Excuses and Statuses', *Journal of Roman Studies*, 73 (1983): 76–96.

Millar, Fergus. 'The Phoenician Cities: A Case Study in Hellenization', *Proceedings of the Cambridge Philological Society*, 29 (1983): 54–71.

Millar, Fergus. 'The Political Character of the Classical Roman Republic, 200–151 B.C', *Journal of Roman Studies*, 74 (1984): 1–19.

Millar, Fergus. 'Politics, Persuasion and the People before the Social War (150–90 B.C.)', *Journal of Roman Studies*, 76 (1986): 1–11.

Millar, Fergus. *The Roman Near East, 31 BC–AD 337.* Cambridge, MA: Harvard University Press, 1993.

Millar, Fergus. 'Ethnic Identity in the Roman Near East, 325–450: Language, Religion and Culture', *Mediterranean Archaeology*, 11 (1998): 159–76.

Millar, Fergus. *Rome, the Greek World and the East*, i: *The Roman Republic and the Augustan Revolution*. Chapel Hill, NC: University of North Carolina Press, 2002.

Millar, Fergus. *A Greek Roman Empire: Power and Belief under Theodosius II (408–450)*, Sather Classical Lectures. Berkeley and Los Angeles: University of California Press, 2006.

Millar, Fergus, and Erich Segal, eds. *Caesar Augustus: Seven Aspects*. Oxford: Oxford University Press, 1984.

Millett, Martin. *The Romanization of Britain: An Archaeological Essay*. Cambridge: Cambridge University Press, 1990.

Milnor, Kristina. *Gender, Domesticity, and the Age of Augustus: Inventing Private Life*. Oxford: Oxford University Press, 2005.

Mitchell, Margaret M., and Frances M. Young, eds. *The Cambridge History of Christianity*, i: *Origins to Constantine*. Cambridge: Cambridge University Press, 2006.

Mitchell, Stephen. *Anatolia: Land, Men and Gods in Asia Minor*, i: *The Celts and the Impact of Roman Rule*. Oxford: Oxford University Press, 1993.

Mitchell, Stephen, and Geoffrey Greatrex, eds. *Ethnicity and Culture in Late Antiquity*. London: Duckworth and Classical Press of Wales, 2000.

Mitchell, Stephen, and Peter van Nuffelen, eds. *One God: Pagan Monotheism in the Roman Empire*. Cambridge: Cambridge University Press, 2010.

Mithen, Steven, and Pascal Boyer. 'Anthropomorphism and the Evolution of Cognition', *Journal of the Royal Anthropological Institute*, 2/4 (1996): 717–21.

Moatti, Claudia. *In Search of Ancient Rome*, New Horizons. London: Thames and Hudson, 1993.

Moatti, Claudia, ed. *La Mobilité des personnes en Méditerranée de l'antiquité à l'époque moderne: Procédures de contrôle et documents d'identification*, Collection de l'École Française de Rome. Rome: École Française de Rome, 2004.

Moatti, Claudia, and Wolfgang Kaiser, eds. *Gens de passage en Méditerranée de l'Antiquité à l'époque moderne: Procédures de contrôle et d'identification*, Collection L'Atelier méditerranéen. Paris: Maisonneuve & Larose, 2007.

Morel, Jean-Paul. 'The Transformation of Italy 300–133 BC', in *The Cambridge Ancient History*, viii: *Rome and the Mediterranean to 133 B.C.*, edited by A. E. Astin, F. W. Walbank, M. W. Frederiksen, and R. M. Ogilvie, 477–516. Cambridge: Cambridge University Press, 1989.

Moreland, John. 'The Carolingian Empire: Rome Reborn?', in *Empires: Perspectives from Archaeology and History*, edited by Susan E. Alcock, T. D'Altroy, K. D. Morrison, and C. M. Sinopoli, 392–418. New York: Cambridge University Press, 2001.

Morley, Neville. *Metropolis and Hinterland: The City of Rome and the Italian Economy 200 B.C. –A.D. 200*. Cambridge: Cambridge University Press, 1996.

Morrell, Kit, Josiah Osgood, and Welch Kathryn, eds. *The Alternative Augustan Age*. New York: Oxford University Press, 2019.

Morris, Ian, and Walter Scheidel, eds. *The Dynamics of Early Empires: State Power from Assyria to Byzantium*. Oxford: Oxford University Press, 2009.

Morstein Kallet-Marx, Robert. *From Hegemony to Empire: The Development of the Roman Imperium in the East from 148 BC to 62 BC*, Hellenistic Culture and Society, edited by Anthony W. Bulloch, Erich Gruen, A. A. Long, and Andrew Stewart, vol. 15. Berkeley and Los Angeles: University of California Press, 1995.

Mouritsen, Henrik. *Italian Unification: A Study in Ancient and Modern Historiography*, Bulletin of the Institute of Classical Studies Supplements. London: Institute of Classical Studies, 1998.

Mouritsen, Henrik. *The Freedman in the Roman World*. Cambridge: Cambridge University Press, 2011.

Mullen, Alex. *Southern Gaul and the Mediterranean: Multilingualism and Multiple Identities in the Iron Age and Roman Periods* Cambridge: Cambridge University Press, 2013.

Murray, Oswyn, and Manuela Tecusan, eds. *In vino veritas*. London: British School at Rome, 1995.

Newby, Zahra. *Greek Athletics in the Roman World: Victory and Virtue*, edited by Simon Price, R. R. R. Smith, and Oliver Taplin, Oxford Studies in Ancient Culture and Representation. New York: Oxford University Press, 2005.

Nicolet, Claude, ed. *Rome et la conquête du monde méditerranéen: 264–27 avant J.C.* Paris: Presses Universitaires de France, 1977.

Nicolet, Claude. 'Augustus, Government and the Propertied Classes', in *Caesar Augustus: Seven Aspects*, edited by Fergus Millar and Erich Segal, 169–88. Oxford: Oxford University Press, 1984.

Nicolet, Claude. *Space, Geography and Politics in the Early Roman Empire*, translated by Hélène Leclerc, Jerome Lectures. Ann Arbor, MI: University of Michigan Press, 1991.

Nielsen, I. *Thermae et Balnea: The Architecture and Cultural History of Roman Baths*. 2 vols. Aarhus: Aarhus University Press, 1990.

Nock, Arthur Darby. *Conversion: The Old and the New in Religion from Alexander the Great to Augustine of Hippo*. Oxford: Clarendon Press, 1933.

Nongbri, Brent. *Before Religion: A History of a Modern Concept*. New Haven, CT, and London: Yale University Press, 2013.

Noreña, Carlos. *Imperial Ideals in the Roman West: Representation, Circulation, Power*. Cambridge: Cambridge University Press, 2011.

North, John. 'Democratic Politics in Republican Rome', *Past and Present*, 126 (1990): 3–21.

North, John. 'The Development of Religious Pluralism', in *The Jews among Pagans and Christians in the Roman Empire*, edited by Judith Lieu, John North, and Tessa Rajak, 174–93. London: Routledge, 1992.

North, John. 'Roman Reactions to Empire', *Scripta classica Israelica*, 12 (1993): 127–38.

North, John. 'Pagans, Polytheists and the Pendulum', in *The Spread of Christianity in the First Four Centuries: Essays in Explanation*, edited by William Vernon Harris, 125–43. Leiden: Brill, 2005.

North, John. 'Pagan Ritual and Monotheism', in *One God: Pagan Monotheism in the Roman Empire*, edited by Stephen Mitchell and Peter van Nuffelen, 34–52. Cambridge: Cambridge University Press, 2010.

Noy, David. *Foreigners at Rome: Citizens and Strangers*. London: Duckworth, 2000.

Nutton, Vivian. 'The Beneficial Ideology', in *Imperialism in the Ancient World*, edited by Peter Garnsey and C. R. Whittaker, 209–21. Cambridge: Cambridge University Press, 1978.

O'Donnell, James J. *Cassiodorus*. Berkeley and Los Angeles: University of California Press, 1979.

Orlin, Eric. *Temples, Religion and Politics in the Roman Republic*, Mnemosyne Supplements. Leiden, New York, and Cologne: Brill, 1997.

Orlin, Eric. *Foreign Cults in Rome: Creating a Roman Empire*. Oxford and New York: Oxford University Press, 2010.

Osborne, Robin, and Barry Cunliffe, eds. *Mediterranean Urbanization 800–600 BC*, Proceedings of the British Academy. Oxford: Oxford University Press, 2005.

Östenberg, Ida. *Staging the World: Spoils, Captives and Representations in the Roman Triumphal Procession*, Oxford Studies in Ancient Culture and Representation. Oxford and New York: Oxford University Press, 2019.

Östenberg, Ida, Simon Malmberg, and Jonas Bjørnebye, eds. *The Moving City: Processions, Passages and Promenades in Ancient Rome*. London and New York: Bloomsbury, 2015.

Padilla Peralta, Dan-el. *Divine Institutions. Religions and communit in the middle Roman Republic*. Princeton NJ: Princeton University Press, 2020.

Parker, Anthony John. *Ancient Shipwrecks of the Mediterranean and the Roman Provinces*, British Archaeological Reports International Series. Oxford: Tempus Reparatum, 1992.

Paterson, Jeremy. 'Friends in High Places: The Creation of the Court of the Roman Emperor', in *The Court and Court Society in Ancient Monarchies*, edited by Antony Spawforth, 121–56. Cambridge: Cambridge University Press, 2007.

Patterson, Helen, and Filippo Coarelli, eds. *Mercator Placidissimus: The Tiber Valley in Antiquity: New Research in the Upper and Middle River Valley, Rome 27–28 February 2004*, Quaderni di Eutopia. Rome: Edizioni Quasar, 2008.

Patterson, John R. 'Colonization and Historiography. The Roman Republic', in *Greek and Roman Colonization: Origins, Ideologies and Interactions*, edited by Guy Bradley and John-Paul Wilson, 189–212. Swansea: Classical Press of Wales, 2006.

Patterson, Orlando. *Slavery and Social Death: A Comparative Study*. Cambridge, MA: Harvard University Press, 1982.

Pelgrom, Jeromia, and Tessa Stek, eds. *Roman Republican Colonization: New Perspectives from Archaeology and Ancient History*, Papers of the Royal Dutch Institute in Rome, vol. 62. Rome: Palombi Editori, 2014.

Percival, John. *The Roman Villa: An Historical Introduction*. London: Batsford, 1976.

Pitts, Martin. *The Roman Object Revolution: Objectscapes and Intra-Cultural Connectivity in Northwest Europe*, Amsterdam Archaeological Studies. Amsterdam: Amsterdam University Press, 2018.

Pitts, Martin, and Miguel John Versluys, eds. *Globalisation and the Roman World: World History, Connectivity and Material Culture*. New York: Cambridge University Press, 2015.

Pohl, Walter, ed. *Kingdoms of the Empire: The Integration of Barbarians in Late Antiquity*, Leiden, New York, and Cologne: Brill, 1997.

Potter, David. *The Roman Empire at Bay: AD 180–395*. 2nd edn. Abingdon: Routledge, 2014.

Potter, Tim. *Roman Italy*. London: British Museum Press, 1987.

Prag, Jonathan R. W. 'Bronze rostra from the Egadi Islands off NW Sicily: The Latin Inscriptions', *Journal of Roman Archaeology*, 27 (2014): 33–59.

Prag, Jonathan R. W., and Josephine Crawley Quinn, eds. *The Hellenistic West: Rethinking the Ancient Mediterranean*. Cambridge: Cambridge University Press, 2013.

Preston, Rebecca. 'Roman Questions, Greek Answers: Plutarch and the Construction of Identity', in *Being Greek under Rome: Cultural Identity, the Second Sophistic and the Development of Empire*, edited by Simon Goldhill, 86–119. Cambridge: Cambridge University Press, 2001.

Price, Jonathan J., and Katell Berthelot, eds. *The Future of Rome: Roman, Greek, Jewish and Christian Visions*. Cambridge: Cambridge University Press, 2020.

Price, Simon. *Rituals and Power in Roman Asia Minor*. Cambridge: Cambridge University Press, 1984.

Price, Simon. 'From Noble Funerals to Divine Cult: The Consecration of Roman Emperors', in *Rituals of Royalty: Power and Ceremonial in Traditional Societies*, edited by David Cannadine and Simon Price, 56–105. Cambridge: Cambridge University Press, 1987.

Price, Simon. 'Local Mythologies in the Greek East', in *Coinage and Identity in the Roman Provinces*, edited by Christopher Howgego, Volker Heuchert, and Andrew Burnett, 115–24. Oxford: Oxford University Press, 2005.

Price, Simon. 'Memory and Ancient Greece', in *Religion and Society: Rituals, Resources and Identity in the Ancient Graeco-Roman World: The BOMOS Conferences 2002–5*, edited by Anders Holm Rasmussen and Suzanne William Rasmussen, 167–78. Rome: Edizioni Quasar, 2008.

Price, Simon, and Peter Thonemann. *The Birth of Classical Europe: A History from Troy to Augustine*, Penguin History of Europe. London: Allen Lane, 2010.

Puett, Michael J. *To Become a God: Cosmology, Sacrifice, and Self-Divinization in Early China*, Harvard-Yenching Institute Monograph Series. Cambridge, MA: Harvard University Press, 2002.

Purcell, Nicholas. 'Wine and Wealth in Ancient Italy', *Journal of Roman Studies*, 75 (1985): 1–19.

Purcell, Nicholas. 'Livia and the Womanhood of Rome', *Proceedings of the Cambridge Philological Society*, 32 (1986): 78–105.

Purcell, Nicholas. 'The Creation of Provincial Landscape: The Roman Impact on Cisalpine Gaul', in *The Early Roman Empire in the West*, edited by Tom Blagg and M. Millett, 7–29. Oxford: Oxbow Books, 1990.

Purcell, Nicholas. 'Mobility and the Polis', in *The Greek City from Homer to Alexander*, edited by Oswyn Murray and Simon Price, 29–58. Oxford: Oxford University Press, 1990.

Purcell, Nicholas. 'On the Sacking of Carthage and Corinth', in *Ethics and Rhetoric: Classical Essays for Donald Russell on his Seventy-Fifth Birthday*, edited by Doreen Innes, Harry Hine, and Christopher Pelling, 133–48. Oxford: Clarendon Press, 1995.

Purcell, Nicholas. 'The Roman Villa and the Landscape of Production', in *Urban Society in Roman Italy*, edited by Tim Cornell and Kathryn Lomas, 151–79. London: University College London Press, 1995.

Purcell, Nicholas. 'Becoming Historical: The Roman Case', in *Myth, History and Culture in Republican Rome: Studies in Honour of T. P. Wiseman*, edited by David Braund and Christopher Gill, 12–40. Exeter: University of Exeter Press, 2003.

Purcell, Nicholas. 'The Way We Used to Eat: Diet, Community, and History at Rome', *American Journal of Philology*, 124/3 (2003): 329–58.

Purcell, Nicholas. 'The Boundless Sea of Unlikeness? On Defining the Mediterranean', *Mediterranean Historical Review*, 18/2 (2004): 9–29.

Quartermaine, Luisa. '"Slouching towards Rome": Mussolini's Imperial Vision', in *Urban Society in Roman Italy*, edited by Tim Cornell and Kathryn Lomas, 203–15. London: University College London Press, 1995.

Quinn, Josephine. *In Search of the Phoenicians*. Princeton, NJ: Princeton University Press, 2017.

Raaflaub, Kurt. 'Born to be Wolves? Origins of Roman Imperialism', in *Transitions to Empire: Essays in Greco-Roman History 360–146 B.C. in Honor of E. Badian*, edited by Robert W. Wallace and Edward M. Harris, 273–314. Norman, OK: University of Oklahoma Press, 1996.

Raaflaub, Kurt, and John T. Ramsey. 'Reconstructing the Chronology of Caesar's Gallic Wars', *Histos*, 11 (2017):1–74.

Raaflaub, Kurt, and Mark Toher, eds. *Between Republic and Empire: Interpretations of Augustus and His Principate*. Berkeley and Los Angeles: University of California Press, 1990.

Rapp, Claudia, and H. A. Drake, eds. *The City in the Classical and Post-Classical World: Changing Contexts of Power and Identity*. Cambridge: Cambridge University Press, 2014.

Rathbone, Dominic. 'The Development of Agriculture in the Ager Cosanus during the Roman Republic: Problems of Evidence and Interpretation', *Journal of Roman Studies*, 71 (1981): 10–23.

Rathbone, Dominic. 'The Slave Mode of Production in Italy', *Journal of Roman Studies*, 73 (1983): 160–8.

Rathbone, Dominic. 'The Imperial Finances', in *The Cambridge Ancient History*, x: *The Augustan Empire 43 B.C.–A.D. 69*, edited by Alan Bowman, Edward Champlin, and Andrew Lintott, 309–23. Cambridge: Cambridge University Press, 1996.

Rawson, Beryl, ed. *The Family in Ancient Rome: New Perspectives*. London: Routledge, 1986.

Rawson, Beryl, and P. R. C. Weaver, eds. *The Roman Family in Italy: Status, Sentiment and Space*. Oxford: Oxford University Press, 1997.

Rawson, Elizabeth. 'Religion and Politics in the Late Second Century B.C. at Rome', *Phoenix*, 28/2 (1974): 193–212.

Rawson, Elizabeth. 'Caesar's Heritage: Hellenistic Kings and Their Roman Equals', *Journal of Roman Studies*, 65 (1975): 148–59.

Rawson, Elizabeth. *Cicero: A Portrait*. London: Allen Lane, 1975.

Rawson, Elizabeth. *Intellectual Life in the Late Roman Republic*. London: Duckworth, 1985.

Rawson, Elizabeth, ed. *Roman Culture and Society: Collected Papers*. Oxford: Clarendon Press, 1991.

Reece, Richard. 'Romanization, a Point of View', in *The Early Roman Empire in the West*, edited by Tom Blagg and Martin Millett, 30–4. Oxford: Oxbow Books, 1990.

Rees, Roger. *Layers of Loyalty in Latin Panegyric, AD 289–307*. Oxford: Oxford University Press, 2002.

Rees, Roger, ed. *Romane memento: Vergil in the Fourth Century*. London: Duckworth, 2003.

Rees, Roger. *Diocletian and the Tetrarchy*, Debates and Documents in Ancient History. Edinburgh: Edinburgh University Press, 2004.

Renfrew, Colin, and John F. Cherry, eds. *Peer Polity Interaction and Socio-Political Change*, New Directions in Archaeology. Cambridge: Cambridge University Press, 1986.

Reynolds, Leighton D., and Nigel G. Wilson. *Scribes and Scholars: A Guide to the Transmission of Greek and Latin Literature.* 2nd edn. Oxford: Clarendon Press, 1974.

Rhodes, Peter. 'After the Three-Bar Sigma Controversy: The History of Athenian Imperialism Reassessed', *Classical Quarterly*, 58/2 (2008): 501–6.

Rich, John, ed. *The City in Late Antiquity*, Leicester–Nottingham Studies in Ancient Society, vol. 3. London: Routledge, 1992.

Rich, John. 'Fear, Greed and Glory: The Causes of Roman War-Making in the Middle Republic', in *War and Society in the Roman World*, edited by John Rich and Graham Shipley, 36–68. London: Routledge, 1993.

Rich, John, and Graham Shipley, eds. *War and Society in the Roman World*, Nottingham–Leicester Studies in Ancient Society. London: Routledge, 1993.

Richardson, John S. 'The Spanish Mines and the Development of Provincial Taxation in the Second Century B.C', *Journal of Roman Studies*, 66 (1976): 139–52.

Richardson, John S. *Hispaniae: Spain and the Development of Roman Imperialism.* Cambridge: Cambridge University Press, 1986.

Richardson, John S. *The Language of Empire: Rome and the Idea of Empire from the Third Century BC to the Second Century AD.* Cambridge: Cambridge University Press, 2008.

Richlin, Amy. *Slave Theater in the Roman Republic: Plautus and Popular Comedy.* Cambridge: Cambridge University Press, 2017.

Rickman, Geoffrey. *Roman Granaries and Store Buildings.* Cambridge: Cambridge University Press, 1971

Ridgway, David. *The First Western Greeks.* Cambridge: Cambridge University Press, 1992.

Riggsby, Andrew. *War in Words: Caesar in Gaul and Rome.* Austin, TX: University of Texas Press, 2006.

Riva, Corinna. *The Urbanization of Etruria.* Cambridge: Cambridge University Press, 2010.

Rives, James B. 'The Decree of Decius and the Religion of Empire', *Journal of Roman Studies*, 89 (1999): 135–54.

Rives, James B. *Religion in the Roman Empire.* Malden, MA: Blackwell, 2007.

Robinson, Chase F., ed. *The New Cambridge History of Islam*, i: *The Formation of the Islamic World Sixth to Eleventh Centuries.* Cambridge: Cambridge University Press, 2010.

Roller, Matthew B. *Constructing Autocracy: Aristocrats and Emperors in Julio-Claudian Rome.* Princeton, NJ: Princeton University Press, 2001.

Roselaar, Saskia T. *Public Land in the Roman Republic: A Social and Economic History of Ager Publicus in Italy, 396–89 BC*, Oxford Studies in Roman Society and Law. Oxford: Oxford University Press, 2010.

Rosenstein, Nathan Stewart. *Rome at War: Farms, Families and Death in the Middle Republic*. Chapel Hill, NC: University of North Carolina Press, 2004.

Roth, Ulrike. *Thinking Tools: Agricultural Slavery between Evidence and Models*, edited by Mike Edwards, Bulletin of the Institute of Classical Studies Supplements. London: Institute of Classical Studies, 2007.

Rothe, Ursula. *The Toga and Roman Identity*. London: Bloomsbury Academic, 2019.

Roymans, Nico. *Tribal Societies in Northern Gaul: An Anthropological Perspective*, Cingula. Amsterdam: Universiteit van Amsterdam, Albert Egges van Giffen Instituut voor Prae- en Protohistorie, 1990.

Roymans, Nico, ed. *From the Sword to the Plough: Three Studies in the Earliest Romanisation of Northern Gaul*, Amsterdam Archaeological Studies. Amsterdam: Amsterdam University Press, 1996.

Rüpke, Jörg. *Domi militiae: Die religiöse Konstruktion des Krieges im Rom*. Stuttgart: Steiner, 1990.

Rüpke, Jörg. *Religion of the Romans*. Cambridge: Polity Press, 2007.

Rüpke, Jörg. *From Jupiter to Christ: On the History of Religion in the Roman Imperial Period*. Oxford: Oxford University Press, 2014.

Rüpke, Jörg. *Pantheon: A New History of Roman Religion*. Princeton, NJ: Princeton University Press, 2018.

Rüpke, Jörg. *Peace and War in Rome: A Religious Construction of Warfare*. Stuttgart: Franz Steiner Verlag, 2019.

Russell, Amy. *The Politics of Public Space in Republican Rome*. Cambridge: Cambridge University Press, 2016.

Sabin, Philip, Hans van Wees, and Michael Whitby, eds. *The Cambridge History of Greek and Roman Warfare*. Cambridge: Cambridge University Press, 2007.

Sahlins, Marshall. *Stone Age Economics*. London: Routledge, 1974.

Sallares, Robert. *The Ecology of the Ancient Greek World*. London: Duckworth, 1991.

Sallares, Robert. 'Ecology', in *The Cambridge Economic History of the Greco-Roman World*, edited by Walter Scheidel, Ian Morris, and Richard P. Saller, 15–37. Cambridge: Cambridge University Press, 2007.

Saller, Richard P. *Personal Patronage under the Early Empire*. Cambridge: Cambridge University Press, 1982.

Saller, Richard P. *Patriarchy, Property and Death in the Roman Family*, Cambridge Studies in Population Economy and Society in Past Time. Cambridge: Cambridge University Press, 1994.

Salzman, Michele Renee. *The Making of a Christian Aristocracy: Social and Religious Change in the Western Roman Empire*. Cambridge, MA: Harvard University Press, 2004.

Sandberg, Kai, and Christopher Smith, eds. *Omnium Annalium Monumenta: Historical Writing and Historical Evidence in Republican Rome*. Leiden: Brill, 2017.

Sandwell, Isabella. *Religious Identity in Late Antiquity: Greeks, Jews, and Christians in Antioch*, Greek Culture in the Roman World. Cambridge: Cambridge University Press, 2007.

Sapelli, M., ed. *Provinciae fideles: Il fregio del templo di Adriano in Campo Marzio*. Milan: Electa, 1999.

Sawyer, Peter H., and Ian Wood, eds. *Early Medieval Kingship*. Leeds: School of History, University of Leeds, 1977.

Scheid, John. 'Graeco ritu: A Typically Roman Way of Honouring the Gods', *Harvard Studies in Classical Philology*, 97 Greece in Rome: Influence, Integration, Resistance (1995): 15–21.

Scheid, John. *Quand croire c'est faire: Les Rites sacrificiels des Romains*. Paris: Aubier, 2005.

Scheid, John. *The Gods, the State, and the Individual: Reflections on Civic Religion in Rome*. Philadelphia, PA: University of Pennsylvania Press, 2016.

Scheidel, Walter. 'Germs for Rome', in *Rome the Cosmopolis*, edited by Catharine Edwards and Greg Woolf, 158–76. Cambridge: Cambridge University Press, 2003.

Scheidel, Walter, ed. *Rome and China: Comparative Perspectives on Ancient World Empires*, Oxford Studies in Early Empires. Oxford: Oxford University Press, 2009.

Scheidel, Walter, ed. *The Science of Roman History. Biology, Climate, and the Future of the Past*. Princeton, NJ, and Oxford: Princeton University Press, 2018.

Scheidel, Walter, and Sitta von Reden, eds. *The Ancient Economy*, Edinburgh Readings on the Ancient World. Edinburgh: Edinburgh University Press, 2002.

Schnapp, Alain. *The Discovery of the Past*. New York: Harry N. Abrams, 1997.

Schneider, Rolf Michael. *Bunte Barbaren: Orientalenstatuen aus farbigem Marmor in der römischen Repräsentationskunst*. Worms: Wernersche Verlagsgesellschaft, 1986.

Schwartz, Seth. *Imperialism and Jewish Society 200 BCE to 640 CE*, edited by R. Stephen Humphreys, William Chester Jordan, and Peter Schäfer, Jews, Christians and Muslims from the Ancient to the Modern World. Princeton, NJ: Princeton University Press, 2001.

Scobie, Alexander. *Hitler's State Architecture: The Impact of Classical Antiquity*, Monographs on the Fine Arts. University Park, PA: Pennsylvania State University Press, 1990.

Scott, James C. *Against the Grain: A Deep History of the Earliest States*. New Haven, CT: Yale University Press, 2017

Seager, Robin. *Pompey the Great: A Political Biography*. 2nd edn. Oxford: Blackwell, 2002.

Sedley, David. 'Philosophical Allegiance in the Greco-Roman World', in *Philosophia togata I: Essays on Philosophy and Roman Society*, edited by Miriam Griffin and Jonathan Barnes, 97–119. Oxford: Oxford University Press, 1989.

Sedley, David. *Lucretius and the Transformation of Greek Wisdom*. Cambridge: Cambridge University Press, 1998.

Sessa, Kristina. 'The New Environmental Fall of Rome: A Methodological Consideration', *Journal of Late Antiquity*, 12/1 (2019): 211–255.

Shaw, Brent D. '"Eaters of Flesh, Drinkers of Milk": The Ancient Mediterranean Ideology of the Pastoral Nomad', *Ancient Society*, 13 (1982): 5–31.

Shaw, Brent D. 'Soldiers and Society: The Army in Numidia', *Opus*, 2 (1983): 133–9.

Shaw, Brent D. *Environment and Society in Roman North Africa: Studies in History and Archaeology*, Variorum Reprints. Aldershot: Variorum, 1995.

Sherwin-White, A. N. *The Roman Citizenship*. 2nd edn. Oxford: Clarendon Press, 1973.

Sherwin-White, A. N. 'The Lex Repetundarum and the Political Ideas of Gaius Gracchus', *Journal of Roman Studies*, 72 (1982): 18–31.

Shipley, Graham. *The Greek World after Alexander, 323–30 B.C.* London: Routledge, 2000.

Shipley, Graham, and John Salmon, eds. *Human Landscapes in Classical Antiquity: Environment and Culture*, Leicester–Nottingham Studies in Ancient Society, vol. 6. London: Routledge, 1996.

Sider, David. *The Library of the Villa dei Papiri at Herculaneum*. Los Angeles: Getty, 2005.

Sirks, Boudewign. *Food for Rome: The Legal Structure of the Transportation and Processing of Supplies for the Imperial Distributions in Rome and Constantinople*. Amsterdam: J. C. Gieben, 1991.

Slater, William J., ed. *Dining in a Classical Context*. Ann Arbor, MI: University of Michigan Press, 1991.

Smith, Christopher. *Early Rome and Latium: Economy and Society c.1000–500 BC*, Oxford Classical Monographs. Oxford: Oxford University Press, 1996.

Smith, Christopher. 'The Beginnings of Urbanization in Rome', in *Mediterranean Urbanization 800–600 BC*, edited by Robin Osborne and Barry Cunliffe, 91–111. Oxford: Oxford University Press, 2005.

Smith, Christopher. *The Etruscans: A Very Short Introduction*. Oxford and New York: Oxford University Press, 2014.

Smith, Jonathan Z. *Drudgery Divine: On the Comparison of Early Christianities and the Religions of Late Antiquity*. Chicago: Chicago University Press, 1990.

Smith, Julia M. H., ed. *Early Medieval Rome and the Christian West: Essays in Honour of Donald A. Bullough*, The Medieval Mediterranean. Leiden: Brill, 2000.

Smith, Julia M. H. *Europe after Rome: A New Cultural History, 500–1000*. Oxford: Oxford University Press, 2005.

Smith, R. R. R. 'The Imperial Reliefs from the Sebasteion at Aphrodisias', *Journal of Roman Studies*, 77 (1987): 88–138.

Smith, R. R. R. 'Simulacra gentium: The Ethne from the Sebasteion at Aphrodisias', *Journal of Roman Studies*, 78 (1988): 50–77.

Smith, R. R. R., and Bryan Ward-Perkins, eds. *The Last Statues of Antiquity*. Oxford: Oxford University Press, 2015.

Smith, Wilfred Cantwell. *The Meaning and End of Religion: A New Approach to the Religious Traditions of Mankind*, Mentor Books. New York: New American Library, 1964.

Sotinel, Claire. *Identité civique et christianisme: Aquilée du IIIe au VIe siècle*, Bibliothèque des Écoles françaises d'Athènes et de Rome. Rome: École française de Rome, 2005.

Spawforth, Antony. 'Symbol of Unity? The Persian-Wars Tradition in the Roman Empire', in *Greek Historiography*, edited by Simon Hornblower, 233–47. Oxford: Clarendon Press, 1994.

Spawforth, Antony. ed. *The Court and Court Society in Ancient Monarchies*. New York: Cambridge University Press, 2007.

Spence, Jonathan. *Emperor of China: Self Portrait of K'ang-hsi*. London: Cape, 1974.

Stadter, Philip A. *Arrian of Nicomedia*. Chapel Hill, NC: University of North Carolina Press, 1980.

Steel, Catherine. *Cicero, Rhetoric, and Empire*. Oxford: Oxford University Press, 2001.

Steinby, Eva Margareta, ed. *Lexicon Topographicum Urbis Romae*. 6 vols. Rome: Edizioni Quazar, 1993–2000.

Steinhauer, Julietta. *Religious Associations in the Post-Classical Polis*, Potsdamer altertumswissenschaftliche Beiträge. Stuttgart: Franz Steiner Verlag, 2014.

Stein-Hölkeskamp, Elke, and Karl-Joachim Hölkeskamp, eds. *Erinnerungsorte der Antike: Die römische Welt*. Munich: C. H. Beck Verlag, 2006.

Stilp, Florian. *Mariage et Suovetaurilia: Étude sur le soi-disant 'Autel de Domitius Ahenobarbus'*. Rome: Giorgio Bretschneider, 2001.

Strasburger, Hermann. 'Poseidonios on Problems of the Roman Empire', *Journal of Roman Studies*, 55/1–2 (1965): 40–53.

Swain, Simon. *Hellenism and Empire: Language, Classicism, and Power in the Greek World, AD 50–250*. Oxford: Clarendon Press, 1996.

Swain, Simon. 'Bilingualism in Cicero? The Evidence of Code-Switching', in *Bilingualism in Ancient Society: Language Contact and the Written Text*, edited by J. N. Adams, Mark Janse, and Simon Swain, 128–67. Oxford: Oxford University Press, 2002.

Swain, Simon, and Mark Edwards, eds. *Approaching Late Antiquity: The Transformation from Early to Late Empire*. Oxford: Oxford University Press, 2004.

Sweetman, Rebecca J. 'Roman Knossos: The Nature of a Globalized City', *American Journal of Archaeology*, 111/1 (2007): 61–81.

Sweetman, Rebecca J. 'The Christianisation of the Peloponnese: The Case for Strategic Change', *Annual of the British School at Athens*, 110 (2015) 285–319.

Syme, Ronald. *The Roman Revolution*. Oxford: Oxford University Press, 1939.

Tacoma, Laurens E. *Moving Romans: Migration to Rome in the Principate*. Oxford: Oxford University Press, 2016.

Tainter, Joseph A. *The Collapse of Complex Societies*. Cambridge: Cambridge University Press, 1988.

Talbert, Richard J. A. *The Senate of Imperial Rome*. Princeton, NJ: Princeton University Press, 1984.

Tan, James. 2017. *Power and Public Finance at Rome, 264-49 BCE*. New York and Oxford: Oxford University Press.

Tchernia, André. *Le Vin d'Italie romaine: Essai d'histoire économique d'après les amphores*, Bibliothèque des Écoles Françaises d'Athènes et de Rome. Rome: École Française de Rome, 1986.

Terrenato, Nicola. *The Early Roman Expansion into Italy: Elite Negotiation and Family Agendas*. Cambridge: Cambridge University Press, 2019

Thomas, Edmund. *Monumentality and the Roman Empire: Architecture in the Antonine Age*. New York: Oxford University Press, 2007.

Thomas, Robert, and Andrew Wilson. 'Water Supply for Roman Farms in Latium and South Etruria', *Papers of the British School at Rome*, 62 (1994): 139–96.

Thommen, Lukas. *An Environmental History of Ancient Greece and Rome*, Cambridge, Cambridge University Press, 2009.

Thompson, E. A. *The Huns*. 2nd edn. Oxford: Blackwell, 1996.

Torelli, Mario. *Typology and Structure of Roman Historical Reliefs*, Ann Arbor, MI: University of Michigan Press, 1982.

Torelli, Mario. *Studies in the Romanization of Italy*. Edmonton, AB: University of Alberta Press, 1995.

Treggiari, Susan M. *Roman Freedmen during the Late Republic*. Oxford: Clarendon Press, 1969.

Trimble, Jennifer. 'Visibility and Viewing on the Severan Marble Plan', in *Severan Culture*, edited by Simon Swain, Stephen Harrison, and Jas Elsner, 368–84. Cambridge: Cambridge University Press, 2007.

Tsetskhladze, Gocha R. *Greek Colonisation: An Account of Greek Colonies and Other Settlements Overseas*. 2 vols., Mnemosyne supplements. Leiden: Brill, 2006.

Tusa, Sebastiano, and Jeffrey Royal, 'The Landscape of the Naval Battle at the Egadi Islands (241 BC)', *Journal of Roman Archaeology*, 25 (2012): 7–48.

Van Dam, Raymond. *Leadership and Community in Late Antique Gaul*, Transformation of the Classical Heritage. Berkeley and Los Angeles: University of California Press, 1985.

Vanderspoel, John. *Themistius and the Imperial Court: Oratory, Civic Duty, and Paideia from Constantius to Theodosius*. Ann Arbor, MI: University of Michigan Press, 1995.

van Dommelen, Peter. *On Colonial Grounds: A Comparative Study of Colonialism and Rural Settlement in First Millennium BC West Central Sardinia*. Archaeological Studies Leiden University. Leiden: Faculty of Archaeology, Leiden University, 1998.

van Dommelen, Peter, and Nicola Terrenato, eds. *Articulating Local Cultures: Power and Identity under the Expanding Roman Republic*. Providence, RI: Journal of Roman Archaeology, 2007.

van Nijf, Onno. 'Local Heroes: Athletics, Festivals and Elite Self-Fashioning in the Roman East', in *Being Greek under Rome: Cultural Identity, the Second Sophistic and the Development of Empire*, edited by Simon Goldhill, 309–34. Cambridge: Cambridge University Press, 2001.

Van Oyen, Astrid. *How Things Make History: The Roman Empire and Its terra sigillata Pottery*, Amsterdam Archaeological Studies. Amsterdam: Amsterdam University Press, 2016.

Van Oyen, Astrid. *The Socio-Economics of Roman Storage: Agriculture, Trade and Family*. Cambridge: Cambridge University Press, 2020.

Van Oyen, Astrid, and Martin Pitts, eds. *Materializing Roman Histories*. Oxford: Oxbow, 2017.

van Sickle, J. 'The Elogia of the Cornelii Scipiones and the Origins of Epigram at Rome', *American Journal of Philology*, 108 (1987): 41–55.

Vasunia, Phiroze. 'The Comparative Study of Empires', *Journal of Roman Studies*, 101 (2011): 222–37.

Versluys, Miguel John. *Visual Style and Constructing Identity in the Hellenistic World: Nemrud Dağ and Commagene under Antiochos I*. Cambridge: Cambridge University Press, 2017.

Versluys, Miguel John, Richard Hingley, Tamar Hodos, Tesse D. Stek, Peter van Dommelen, and Greg Woolf. 'Understanding Objects in Motion: An Archaeological Dialogue on Romanization', *Archaeological Dialogues*, 21/1 (2014): 1–64.

Versnel, H. S. *Inconsistencies in Greek and Roman Religion 1: Ter unus: Isis, Dionysos, Hermes: Three Studies in Henotheism*, Studies in Greek and Roman Religion. Leiden: Brill, 1990.

Veyne, Paul. *Le Pain et le cirque: Sociologie historique d'un pluralisme politique*. Paris: Seuil, 1976.

Veyne, Paul. *Did the Greeks Believe in Their Myths? An Essay in the Constitutive Imagination*, translated by Paula Wissing. Chicago: University of Chicago Press, 1988.

Wallace-Hadrill, Andrew. 'Family and Inheritance in the Augustan Marriage-Laws', *Proceedings of the Cambridge Philological Society*, 207 (1981): 58–80.

Wallace-Hadrill, Andrew. 'Civilis princeps: Between Citizen and King', *Journal of Roman Studies*, 72 (1982): 32–48.

Wallace-Hadrill, Andrew. 'The Golden Age and Sin in Augustan Ideology', *Past and Present*, 95 (1982): 19–36.

Wallace-Hadrill, Andrew. *Suetonius: The Scholar and His Caesars*, Classical Life and Letters. London: Duckworth, 1983.

Wallace-Hadrill, Andrew. 'Review Article: Greek Knowledge, Roman Power', *Classical Philology*, 83/3 (1988): 224–33.

Wallace-Hadrill, Andrew, ed. *Patronage in Ancient Society*. London: Routledge, 1989.

Wallace-Hadrill, Andrew. 'Elites and Trade in the Roman Town', in *City and Country in the Ancient World*, edited by John Rich and Andrew Wallace-Hadrill, 241–72. London: Routledge, 1991.

Wallace-Hadrill, Andrew. *Houses and Society in Pompeii and Herculaneum*. Princeton, NJ: Princeton University Press, 1994.

Wallace-Hadrill, Andrew. 'The Imperial Court', in *The Cambridge Ancient History*, x: *The Augustan Empire 43 B.C.–A.D. 69*, edited by Alan Bowman, Edward Champlin, and Andrew Lintott, 283–308. Cambridge: Cambridge University Press, 1996.

Wallace-Hadrill, Andrew. *Rome's Cultural Revolution*. New York: Cambridge University Press, 2008.

Wallace-Hadrill, J. M. *The Barbarian West 400–1000*. London: Hutchinson University Library, 1952.

Ward-Perkins, Bryan. *From Classical Antiquity to the Middle Ages: Urban Public Building in Northern and Central Italy AD 300–850*, Oxford Historical Monographs. Oxford: Oxford University Press, 1984.

Ward-Perkins, Bryan. *The Fall of Rome and the End of Civilization*. Oxford: Oxford University Press, 2005.

Ward-Perkins, Bryan. 'Old and New Rome Compared: The Rise of Constantinople', in *Two Romes: Rome and Constantinople in Late Antiquity*, edited by Lucy Grig and Gavin Kelly, 53–78. Oxford: Oxford University Press, 2012.

Ward-Perkins, Bryan. 'A Most Unusual Empire: Rome in the Fourth Century', in *The City in the Classical and Post-Classical World: Changing Contexts of Power and Identity*, edited by Claudia Rapp and H. A. Drake, 109–29. Cambridge: Cambridge University Press, 2014.

Ward-Perkins, J. B. 'From Republic to Empire: Reflections on the Early Provincial Architecture of the Roman West', *Journal of Roman Studies*, 60 (1970): 1–19.

Weaver, P. R. C. *Familia Caesaris: A Social Study of the Emperor's Freedmen and Slaves*. Cambridge: Cambridge University Press, 1972.

Webster, Jane. 'Necessary Comparisons: A Post-Colonial Approach to Religious Syncretism in the Roman Provinces', *World Archaeology*, 28/3 (1997): 324–38.

Webster, Jane. 'Creolizing the Roman Provinces', *American Journal of Archaeology*, 105/2 (2001): 209–25.

Whitmarsh, Tim. *Greek Literature and the Roman Empire: The Politics of Imitations*. Oxford: Oxford University Press, 2001.

Whitmarsh, Tim, ed. *Local Knowledge and Microidentities in the Imperial Greek World*, Greek Culture in the Roman World. Cambridge: Cambridge University Press, 2010.

Whittaker, C. R. *Frontiers of the Roman Empire: A Social and Economic Study*, Ancient Society and History. Baltimore, MD: Johns Hopkins University Press, 1994.

Whittow, Mark. 'Ruling the Late Roman and Early Byzantine City: A Continuous History', *Past and Present*, 129 (1990): 3–29.

Wickham, Chris. *Early Medieval Italy: Central Power and Local Society 400–1000* London: Macmillan, 1981.

Wickham, Chris. 'The Other Transition: From the Ancient World to Feudalism', *Past and Present*, 103 (1984): 3–36.

Wickham, Chris. *Framing the Early Middle Ages: Europe and the Mediterranean, 400–800*. Oxford: Oxford University Press, 2005.

Wickham, Chris. *The Inheritance of Rome: A History of Europe from 400 to 1000*, Penguin History of Europe. London: Allen Lane, 2009.

Wierschowski, L. *Fremde in Gallien—'Gallier' in der Fremde: Die epigraphisch bezeugte Mobilität in, von und nach Gallien vom 1. bis 3. Jh. n. Chr. (Texte—Übersetzungen—Kommentare)*, Historia Einzelschriften, vol. 159. Stuttgart: F. Steiner, 2001.

Wiesehöfer, Josef, ed. *Das Partherreich und seine Zeugnisse*, Historia Einzelschriften. Stuttgart: Franz Steiner Verlag, 1998.

Wightman, Edith Mary. *Roman Trier and the Treveri*. London: Hart-Davis, 1970.

Williams, Jonathan H. C. *Beyond the Rubicon: Romans and Gauls in Northern Italy*, Oxford Classical Monographs. Oxford: Oxford University Press, 2001.

Wilson, Andrew. 'Machines, Power and the Ancient Economy', *Journal of Roman Studies*, 92 (2002): 1–32.

Wilson, Andrew. 'Approaches to Quantifying Roman Trade', in *Quantifying the Roman Economy: Methods and Problems*, edited by Alan Bowman and Andrew Wilson, 213–49. Oxford: Oxford University Press, 2009.

Wilson, Andrew, and Alan Bowman, eds. *Trade, Commerce and the State in the Roman World*, Oxford Studies on the Roman Economy. Oxford: Oxford University Press, 2018.

Winterling, Aloys. *Aula Caesaris: Studien zur Institutionalisierung des römischen Kaiserhofes in der Zeit von Augustus bis Commodus (31 v. Chr.–192 n. Chr.)*. Munich: R. Oldenburg, 1999.

Wiseman, T. Peter. *New Men in the Roman Senate, 139 B.C.–A.D. 14*. Oxford Classical and Philosophical Monographs. London: Oxford University Press, 1971.

Wiseman, T. Peter. 'Domi nobiles and the Roman Cultural Élite', in *Les Bourgeoisies municipales italiennes aux IIe et Ier siècles av. J.-C.*, edited by M. Cébeillac-Gervason, 299–307. Naples: Éditions du CNRS and Bibliothèque de l'Institut Français de Naples, 1981.

Wiseman, T. Peter. *Remus: A Roman Myth*. Cambridge: Cambridge University Press, 1995.

Wiseman, T. Peter. *The Myths of Rome*. Exeter: University of Exeter Press, 2004.

Witcher, Robert. 'Globalisation and Roman Imperialism: Perspectives on Identities in Roman Italy', in *The Emergence of State Identities in Italy in the First Millennium B.C.*, edited by Edward Herring and Kathryn Lomas, 213–25. London: Accordia Research Institute, 2000.

Wittfogel, Karl August. *Oriental Despotism: A Comparative Study of Total Power*. New York: Yale University Press, 1957.

Wood, Ian. 'Defining the Franks: Frankish Origins in Early Mediaeval Historiography', in *Concepts of National Identity in the Middle Ages*, edited by Simon Forde, Lesley Johnson, and Alan V. Murray, 47–57. Leeds: Leeds University Press, 1995.

Wood, Susan. 'Messalina, Wife of Claudius: Propaganda Successes and Failures of his Reign', *Journal of Roman Archaeology*, 5 (1992): 219–34.

Wood, Susan. 'Diva Drusilla Panthea and the Sisters of Caligula', *American Journal of Archaeology*, 99/3 (1995): 457–82.

Woolf, Greg. 'Imperialism, Empire and the Integration of the Roman Economy', *World Archaeology*, 23/3 (1992): 283–93.

Woolf, Greg. 'Becoming Roman, Staying Greek: Culture, Identity and the Civilizing Process in the Roman East', *Proceedings of the Cambridge Philological Society*, 40 (1994): 116–43.

Woolf, Greg. 'Monumental Writing and the Expansion of Roman Society', *Journal of Roman Studies*, 86 (1996): 22–39.

Woolf, Greg. 'The Uses of Forgetfulness in Roman Gaul', in *Vergangenheit und Lebenswelt: Soziale Kommunikation, Traditionsbildung und historisches Bewußtsein*, edited by Hans-Joachim Gehrke and Astrid Möller, 361–81. Tübingen: Gunter Narr Verlag, 1996.

Woolf, Greg. 'The Roman Urbanization of the East', in *The Early Roman Empire in the East*, edited by Susan E. Alcock, 1–14. Oxford: Oxbow Books, 1997.

Woolf, Greg. *Becoming Roman: The Origins of Provincial Civilization in Gaul*. Cambridge: Cambridge University Press, 1998.

Woolf, Greg. 'The City of Letters', in *Rome the Cosmopolis*, edited by Catharine Edwards and Greg Woolf, 203–21. Cambridge: Cambridge University Press, 2003.

Woolf, Greg. 'Divinity and Power in Ancient Rome', in *Religion and Power: Divine Kingship in the Ancient World and Beyond*, edited by Nicole Brisch, 235–55. Chicago: Oriental Institute of the University of Chicago, 2008.

Woolf, Greg. 'Provincial Revolts in the Early Roman Empire', in *The Jewish Revolt against Rome: Interdisciplinary Perspectives*, edited by Mladen Popovic, 27–44. Leiden and Boston, MA: Brill, 2011.

Woolf, Greg. *Tales of the Barbarians: Ethnography and Empire in the Roman West.* Malden, MA: Blackwell, 2011.

Woolf, Greg. 'Isis and the Evolution of Religions', in *Power, Politics, and the Cults of Isis: Proceedings of the Vth International Conference of Isis Studies, Boulogne-sur-Mer, November 27–29, 2008*, edited by Laurent Bricault and Miguel John Versluys, 62–92. Leiden and Boston, MA: Brill, 2014.

Woolf, Greg. 'Foreign Gods in the Age of Cicero', in *Cicero and Roman Religion: Eight Studies*, edited by Claudia Beltrão da Rosa and Federico Santangelo, 117–33. Stuttgart: Franz Steiner Verlag, 2020.

Woolf, Greg. *The Life and Death of Ancient Cities: A Natural History.* Oxford: Oxford University Press, 2020.

Wörrle, Michael. *Stadt und Fest in kaiserzeitlichen Kleinasien: Studien zu einer agonistischen Stiftung aus Oinoanda*, Vestigia. Munich: C. H. Beck, 1988.

Yarrow, Liv Mariah. *Historiography at the End of the Republic: Provincial Perspectives on Roman Rule.* Oxford: Oxford University Press, 2006.

Yates, R. D. S. 'Cosmos, Central Authority and Communities in the Early Chinese Empire', in *Empires: Perspectives from Archaeology and History*, edited by Susan E. Alcock, T. D'Altroy, K. D. Morrison, and C. M. Sinopoli, 351–68. New York: Cambridge University Press, 2001.

Yavetz, Zvi. *Plebs and Princeps.* London: Oxford University Press, 1969.

Yegul, Fikret K. *Baths and Bathing in the Roman World.* Cambridge, MA: MIT Press, 1992.

Yoffee, Norman, and George L. Cowgill, eds. *The Collapse of Ancient States and Civilizations.* Tucson, AZ: University of Arizona Press, 1988.

Zanker, Paul. *The Power of Images in the Age of Augustus*, Jerome Lectures. Ann Arbor, MI: University of Michigan Press, 1988.

Zanker, Paul. 'Domitian's Palace on the Palatine and the Imperial Image', in *Representations of Empire: Rome and the Mediterranean World*, edited by Alan Bowman, Hannah Cotton, Martin Goodman, and Simon Price, 105–30. Oxford: Oxford University Press, 2002.

Zarmakoupi, Mantha, ed. *The Villa of the Papyri at Herculaneum: Archaeology, Reception and Digital Reconstruction.* Berlin: De Gruyter, 2010.

Zuiderhoek, Arjan. *The Politics of Munificence in the Roman Empire: Citizens, Elites and Benefactors in Asia Minor*, Greek Culture in the Roman World. Cambridge: Cambridge University Press, 2009.

Photographic Acknowledgements

Index